GREAT BRITAIN
& THE
COMMON MARKET
1957-69

GREAT BRITAIN

& THE

COMMON MARKET

1957-69

Edited by William J. Swift, Ph.D.
Department of Economics
Pace College (New York, N. Y.)

FACTS ON FILE, INC.   NEW YORK

GREAT BRITAIN
& THE
COMMON MARKET
1957-69

Library of Congress Catalog Card Number: 72-124554

ISBN 0-87196-181-4

9   8   7   6   5   4   3   2   1

PRINTED IN THE UNITED STATES OF AMERICA

CONTENTS

i

ii

INTRODUCTION

ANY COMPREHENSIVE STUDY of the relations between Great Britain and the European Economic Community (EEC) should follow 3 parallel lines to be complete. The British economic picture must be presented so that Britain's policy decisions and actions can be understood; the developments in both the EEC as a body and in the EEC member nations must be described so that the EEC's "side" of the British-EEC conflict is in proper perspective, and then the actual British-EEC interplay can be narrated with the first 2 sets of developments forming the background. This is the pattern followed for the most part in this book. Thus, this volume contains somewhat more than just the British-EEC confrontation, but this additional material is important in understanding these British-EEC developments.

International Economic Cooperation

Examples of international economic cooperation involving continental Europe can be found in pre-Christian times. Rome and Carthage signed a treaty establishing trading territories as early as 508-7 BC and again in 348 BC. The 19th-century German *Zollverein* was a form of "common market" in a loose sense. The establishment in 1930 of the Bank for International Settlements (BIS) is a more modern (and the longest-lasting) example of European economic cooperation. The BIS was originally formed to facilitate the German World War I reparation payments and has continued to exist, most presently as a major agency in centralizing European financial stability.

The International Monetary Fund (IMF) and the International Bank for Reconstruction & Development (IBRD, or World Bank) were established at the Bretton Woods (New Hampshire) conference, held July 1944 under the leadership of British economist John Maynard (Lord) Keynes, who died in 1946 before the impact of these 2 groups had been realized. The IMF has functioned as a short-run lending agency for monetary exchange and balance-of-payments difficulties while the IBRD has provided longer-term loans (or, more recently, underwritten such loans) for, at first, post-war reconstruction and more recently economic development. These 2 agencies came into formal existence in 1946 and had 115 members throughout the non-Communist world as of Dec. 1969.

A worldwide conference was held in Havana between Nov. 1947 and Mar. 1948 to form an International Trade Organization (ITO). Pending ratification of the ITO by the participating governments, an interim structure, the General Agreement on Tariffs & Trade (GATT), was established. The U.S. Senate never ratified the ITO Convention, and that group, without American participation, never came into formal existence. GATT has survived as the only worldwide body espousing the principle of reduced trade barriers as its *raison d'etre*. (U.S. participation in GATT was justified on the basis of the 1934 Reciprocal Trade Act, as amended, and was never submitted to the Senate for ratification.) Most non-Communist countries are GATT members.

3 temporary, *ad-hoc* bodies were formed in Western Europe immediately after the end of World War II. These bodies, the Emergency Economic Commission for Europe, the European Coal Organization and the European Central Inland Transport Organization, all formed in 1945, were replaced in 1947 by the UN's Economic Commission for Europe (ECE). The ECE, under the jurisdiction of the UN Relief & Rehabilitation Agency (UNRRA), was established after the severe winter of 1946-7, when Europe suffered a $7 billion balance-of-payments deficit, 70% to the U.S.

On June 5, 1947, U.S. State Secy. George C. Marshall, speaking at Harvard University, proposed massive financial aid for war-torn and Communist-threatened Western Europe. His proposal, put into effect as the European Recovery Program (ERP), or the Marshall Plan, provided $12 billion over a 3 1/2-year period to 16 recipient nations.

To facilitate the Marshall Plan, an Economic Cooperation Administration was established in Europe in 1948. The Commission of Europe in Economic Cooperation had already been formed and had held its first meeting in July 1947. These 2 bodies merged and became the Organization for European Economic Cooperation (OEEC), effective Apr. 16, 1948, under Secy. Gen. Robert Marjolin of France. (Marjolin later became vice president of the EEC commission.) The OEEC ultimately branched out into other areas, including the standardization of electrical grids, appliances, and other matters. The OEEC was considered by Britain to be the proper vehicle for European economic integration, and it had a prominent role in the formation of the European Free Trade Association (EFTA) after 6 continental OEEC members formed the EEC in 1957. In 1960, the OEEC changed its name, becoming the OECD (Organization for Economic Cooperation & Development) and adding the U.S. and Canada (and later Japan and Finland) as full members. 1969 membership totaled 22 nations: Austria, Belgium, Britain, Canada, Denmark, Finland, France, Greece, Iceland, Ireland, Italy, Japan, Luxembourg, the Netherlands, Norway, Portugal, Spain, Sweden, Switzerland, Turkey, the U.S. and West Germany. Yugoslavia has limited status with the OECD, and Australia is a member of the Development Assistance Committee only.

Several other attempts were made in the immediate postwar era to integrate economic (and political) activity, but few prospered.

The Brussels Treaty of Western Union was signed in 1948 by Britain, France, Belgium, the Netherlands and Luxembourg. This was to be a 5-year economic and military cooperative arrangement, but with the formation of NATO in 1949, this group disintegrated as such and became the nucleus of the Western European Union.

The Benelux Convention, signed Sept. 5, 1944 by the exile governments of Belgium, Luxembourg and the Netherlands, provided for economic cooperation among these 3 small states. This pact expanded the 1921 BLEU (Belgium-Luxembourg Economic Union), which had established common currencies, economic policies and external tariffs and had eliminated tariffs between the 2 nations. Although modified by EEC, this (BLEU) pact is still in force.

2 unsuccessful trade groups were "Francita," an Italian proposal of July 12, 1947 for a Franco-Italian customs union, and "Fritalux" (or "Finebel"), an Italian proposal to add the Benelux states to "Francita." Neither group got beyond the discussion stage.

The International Committee of the Movements for Europe (the "European Movement") was organized in Dec. 1947. Britain participated in its meetings, and this group formed the Council of Europe May 5, 1949. Membership included Britain, France, the Benelux nations, Italy, Norway, Sweden, Denmark and Ireland.

On Sept. 9, 1950, Robert Schuman of France proposed a multinational coal and steel community open to members of the Council of Europe. 6 nations—France, West Germany, Italy and the Benelux countries—responded quickly. The treaty they signed Apr. 18, 1951 created the European Coal & Steel Community (ECSC). Britain declined to participate. The treaty was ratified during the summer of 1952, and the ECSC held its first formal meeting Aug. 10, 1952. Schuman, Jean Monnet and West Germany's Walter Hallstein were the 3 acknowledged leaders behind the formation of this group, which served as a basis for the European Economic Community, or Common Market.

As European currency convertibility increased in the late 1940s, a body was needed to facilitate the rising multi-national currency clearing needs and to handle special problems. This body was created in Sept. 1950 under the auspices of the OEEC and was designated the European Payments Union (EPU). The EPU worked closely with and through the BIS. EPU membership encompassed all West European countries except Finland and Spain. This body gradually dwindled in significance and was replaced in 1958 by the European Monetary Agreement as full currency convertibility was achieved.

Wide World

*The Countries forming the European Economic Community (Common Market)
are shown in black; those of the European Free Trade Association are indicated
by cross-hatching.*

A significant, although eventually unsuccessful, proposal, made by French Premier Rene Pleven in Dec. 1950, was to form a European Defense Commission. This proposal, supported by U.S. State Secy. Dean Acheson, envisioned a multi-national military organization consisting of France, Germany, Italy and the Benelux nations. Britain, under Prime Min. Anthony Eden, rejected an invitation to participate. It has been suggested that the EDC was motivated by the 1950 outbreak of war in Korea and fears of further European involvement. (The EDC had been characterized as a "military ECSC.") The EDC was ratified by West Germany and the Benelux nations. Italy, in political turmoil at the time, waited for French action. French governmental changes had occurred in the interim, with Pierre Mendes-France replacing Pleven as premier. Although Mendes-France supported the EDC, the French National Assembly rejected French membership Aug. 30, 1954, and the EDC was never actually formed. The European Political Commission (EPC), a political twin of the EDC, died with the EDC.

The *Conceil Europeen pour la recherche nucleaire* (CERN, or European Nuclear Research Council) was organized in 1952. Its members were Austria, Belgium, Britain, Denmark, Greece, Italy, the Netherlands, Norway, Spain, Sweden, Switzerland and West Germany. Poland, Turkey and Yugoslavia were observers. Although it continued to exist after 1958, CERN lost much of its significance as Euratom was developed.

The 6 members of the ill-fated EDC joined with Britain (under Prime Min. Anthony Eden's encouragement) to form the Western European Union (WEU) in 1955. Preliminary meetings prior to the WEU's actual formation were held in London in Oct. 1954 and in Paris in Nov. 1954. The U.S. and Canada were observers. The WEU also traced its origin to the 1948 Brussels Treaty of Western Union, which had given way to NATO. The WEU has served as a forum for discussion and a vehicle for cultural cooperation among the 7 active members. It has been a vital link for Britain to the EEC, and in 1969 it was a major instrument used by Britain in making its desires to join the EEC known and in eliciting support from EEC members.

In Feb. 1955 Edgar Faure replaced Pierre Mendes-France as French premier. French support for European cooperation had increased following the low point of Aug. 1954, when the National Assembly had vetoed EDC membership. Realizing this change, the ECSC Dec. 2, 1954 had proposed a widening of its own scope, and a conference was scheduled for Messina, Sicily June 1-2, 1955. Invitations were issued to the 6 ECSC members and to Britain, which declined to attend. Under the leadership of Jean Monnet, this "Messina Conference" established a committee headed by Paul-Henri Spaak of Belgium; the Spaak committee's report, submitted in Venice May 29, 1956, became the nucleus of EEC. Spaak was assisted in this project by Prof. Walter Hallstein. Participants in the May 1956 Venice meeting drafted the EEC (and

Euratom) treaties, and the OEEC accepted this proposed structure July 19, 1956. The treaties were formalized Mar. 25, 1957 as the Treaty of Rome, and EEC came into formal being Jan. 1, 1958.

The degree of EEC success in achieving its desired goals can be judged from the following table, reprinted from *World Business* (Oct. 1969, courtesy of Chase Manhattan Bank, N.A.):

PROGRESS TOWARD CREATING A COMMON MARKET

Establishing a Common Market

Goals	Achievements
Abolition of internal customs duties and creation of a common external tariff applied to nonmember imports by the end of the transition period (Dec. 31, 1969).	All customs duties on trade in industrial goods within the Community were abolished July 1, 1968, and the tariffs on goods imported from nonmembers were fully harmonized on the same date.
Elimination of quantitative restrictions and other non-tariff barriers to trade within the community by the end of the transition period.	All quantitative restrictions on trade in industrial goods among the 6 were removed July 1, 1968. Other non-tariff barriers still remain, but are scheduled for elimination by end-1972.
Adoption of a common commercial policy involving harmonizing national export assistance programs and establishing common trade agreements with 3d countries.	Little progress has been made on standardizing national policies of export assistance; member countries still maintain bilateral trade agreements with 3d countries.
Creation of a common agricultural policy providing for free trade within the community and unified marketing and pricing for farm goods, both internally and in external trade, by end-1969.	Common policies have been established for most products, but the 6 must still agree on final agricultural financing arrangements. Also, recent currency moves by France and West Germany have interfered with common price arrangements, at least temporarily.
Harmonization of indirect taxation in order to eliminate export subsidies and border taxes on imports by Dec. 31, 1969.	Four of the members, excluding Italy and Belgium, will have adopted the value-added tax system by year-end; unification of rates has not begun.

Unifying the Economies of the 6

Abolition of restrictions on the movement of workers and on the right to establish a business anywhere in the community, by the end of the transition period.

Elimination of restrictions on capital movements "so far as may be necessary to ensure the proper functioning of the Common Market."

Adoption by end-1969 of common policies for transportation services, which will eliminate discrimination in rates and harmonize conditions of competition.

Establishment of common rules preventing practices which distort or restrain competition, whether by private businesses or member governments.

Coordination of economic and monetary policies through consultations and collaboration of member governments.

Adoption of measures to harmonize national energy policies with regard to sources of supply and pricing, and coordination of science and technology policies.

Creation of a common industrial policy, including elimination of obstacles to cross-frontier mergers and adoption of a uniform company law.

Free movement of workers is close to achievement, and EEC nationals can establish businesses in many sectors without legal restrictions, but some national health and safety regulations discriminate against foreign companies.

Considerable liberalization has been achieved for direct investment among member states, and although other types of capital movements are still controlled, members are working on such matters as harmonizing taxes on security issues.

The community has harmonized some technical regulations, but the 6 must still solve many problems. Therefore, it has been decided that the common policy will be completed in 3 stages ending sometime after 1973.

The definition of unfair business practices has been clarified in a body of case law, but further work is needed to eliminate discrimination arising from national public procurement policies and national aid programs.

The 6 have established a number of consultative committees, but policy making is still a national prerogative. However, members are working on a plan to improve coordination before end-1969.

The community is currently working on a long-term program to establish common policies for energy, but this might prove difficult because differences in natural resources lead to divergent national policies. Science and technology are still under study.

The 6 have agreed to work for a common patent convention, but otherwise progress has been slow because of the wide variety of issues involved and because of opposition to the idea of a single EEC company law.

The British Economy

The upheavals and the political changes brought about in World War I created an economic condition that lasted for decades in Britain. The decade of the '20s was one in which Britain, trying to stay on the gold standard, maintained the convertibility of the pound into gold but lost gold reserves in the process. Unemployment remained a serious problem, averaging 11.4% for the decade, as export sales lagged behind imports. The impact of the worldwide Depression of the '30s forced

Britain to abandon the gold standard. Britain announced Sept. 19, 1931 that, effective Sept. 21, it would stop exchanging pounds for gold at the established rate of $4.86 in gold per pound. The pound, allowed to fluctuate freely, fell to the $3.50 level and then, with the London gold market closed between Sept. 1939 and Mar. 1954, the pound gradually rose in value to $4.03.

Worldwide trade suffered during the '30s, and British commerce was no exception. World War II forced Britain into an all-out economic effort and caused a diminution in resources, greatly increased foreign indebtedness and shifts in colonial relations on which Britain had depended heavily for many foreign trade transactions.

Britain emerged from World War II with an economy that was unable to meet the demands facing it. Britain needed foreign exchange, primarily dollars, and had little to offer in exchange. The result was a devaluation of the pound Sept. 18, 1949, from $4.03 to $2.80, a move that Britain hoped would stimulate sales to the dollar area and generate dollar reserves. This devaluation was unavoidable, even with Marshall Plan aid and a $4.4 billion U.S. loan (of which $650 million was earmarked to settle Lend-Lease indebtedness).

The devaluation and dollar loans were successful, although the concomitant domestic austerity was painful to Britain. Britain had balance-of-payments deficits of £295 million in 1946 and £442 million in 1947 but then surpluses—£7 million in 1948, £38 million in 1949 and £297 million in 1950, the highest surplus of the decade ending 1957. Dollar (and gold) reserves, which had fallen £87 million in 1946, rose £216 million in 1947, £69 million in 1948 and £18 million in 1949. For the 1947-57 period, reserves rose in 8 of the 11 years; the net gain over this period was £465 million. The balance of payments showed a surplus in 8 of the 11 years, a net gain of £535 million.

Domestic improvement was slower. Using 1958 as a base year of 100, industrial production rose from 73 in 1948 to 101 in 1957, employment rose from 93 to 101, but the cost of living rose from 65 to 97 and import prices from 75 to 108. Unemployment in 1947 was 1.8% of the labor force and averaged 1.3% for the decade 1947-57.

England's growth lagged behind continental Europe's and behind that of the 6 EEC nations. For the period 1950-61, British real GNP (GNP adjusted for price changes) grew at a less than 3% annual rate while the 6 EEC nations' real GNP grew at a combined rate of 8%; per capita income rose 26% in Britain but 61% in the 6 EEC nations. Britain was recovering slowly but was falling behind its European neighbors.

Britain & The EEC

An apocryphal incident illustrates the problem of Britain's relationship to continental Europe. Supposedly a bad storm was experienced in the English Channel, and British newspapers were headlined: "Blizzard in Channel. Continent Is Isolated." Is Britain part of Europe or not? This is the question that Britain had to answer in the '50s, and the answer changed. The answer was "no" in the early part of the decade. Britain participated in the OEEC but not in any subsequent continental organizations. Britain declined to attend the Messina Conference and instead worked within the OEEC towards the formation of a loose "free trade area" that would allow it to maintain its ties to the Commonwealth and to the U.S. Europe, having no such strong ties, moved strongly towards economic integration, which, given European geography and resource distribution, appeared to be a logical step.

British isolation was furthered by a Franco-British dispute over the Suez crisis of 1956. Coming at a time when Britain had to decide whether or not to "join" Europe, the conflict widened rather than narrowed the gulf between Britain and the continent.

The EEC, as it was structured, was a form of customs union: a group of nations working for the elimination of tariff barriers among themselves and (unlike usual customs unions) the establishment of identical tariffs with non-member nations. Britain also favored tariff reductions, but Britain saw the OEEC as the vehicle to accomplish this goal. Furthermore, Britain did not favor the objective of a common external tariff. In mid-March 1957, Peter Thorneycroft, then president of the Board of Trade, led a committee to investigate the feasibility of forming another trade group within the framework of the entire OEEC. Participants in an OEEC ministerial meeting chaired by Britain's Reginald Maudling voted Oct. 16-17, 1957 to establish such a "free trade area" consisting of OEEC members. France, under Premier Maurice Faure, rejected this idea. Britain shifted emphasis then to an OEEC free trade area excluding the EEC 6. Meetings continued, in Geneva in Dec. 1958 and in Oslo in Feb. 1959. Finally, in the summer of 1959, at a meeting outside Stockholm, negotiators drafted an agreement to create a European Free Trade Association (EFTA) consisting of 7 non-EEC OEEC members (Britain, Norway, Sweden, Denmark, Portugal, Austria and Switzerland) but not including the 4 least developed OEEC economies of Iceland, Ireland, Greece (which eventually associated with the EEC) and Turkey.

The British stand changed in 1961 after Britain became more aware of the limitations of the EFTA and the advantages of the EEC structure. Prime Min. Harold Macmillan announced this reversal of policy July 31, 1961, when he told Parliament of Britain's plans to apply for EEC membership. Negotiations took place during 1961 and 1962 but ended Jan. 14, 1963 when French Pres. Charles de Gaulle announced at a press conference that he would not accept Britain. Since acceptance of a new EEC member required unanimous agreement by the old members, this decision vetoed Britain's application. De Gaulle May 11, 1967 vetoed a 2d British EEC application. Britain's 3d application, informally proposed in 1969, was pending as 1969 ended.

This book is, basically, a journalistic account of Britain's confrontation with the EEC and of the diplomatic, political and economic events that surrounded and illustrated this confrontation. As in all INTERIM HISTORY books, great pains were taken to present all pertinent material—much of it quite controversial—without bias. Interpretation has been kept to the minimum; where injected, it has been used to clarify confusing or obscure developments rather than to argue a point of view. The material in this book comes largely from the voluminous records of FACTS ON FILE, but supplementary data have been added from press and government and other official sources.

Ray Osrin in the Cleveland Plain Dealer

"The Common Market, Jeeves."

Glossary of Acronyms

Listed below are definitions of acronyms used in this book:
AFP—Agence France Presse (French press agency)
ASP—American selling price
BIS—Bank for International Settlements
CBI—Confederation of British Industry
CDU—Christian Democratic Union (West German political party)
CSU—Christian Social Union (West German political party)
DM—Deutschemark(s)
EAGGF—European Agricultural Guidance & Guarantee Fund
ECSC—European Coal & Steel Community
EDF—European Development Fund
EEC—European Economic Community (Common Market)
EFTA—European Free Trade Association
Euratom—European Atomic Energy Community
FDP—Free Democratic Party (West German political party)
FRB—Federal Reserve Board (also Bank), U.S.
GAB—General Arrangements to Borrow
GATT—General Agreement on Tariffs & Trade
GNP—gross national product
IMF—International Monetary Fund
MP—member of Parliament
NATO—North Atlantic Treaty Organization
NDP—National Democratic Party (West German political party)
OECD—Organization for Economic Cooperation & Development
OEEC—Organization for European Economic Cooperation
PCF—French Communist Party
PSU—United Socialist Party (French)
SPD—Social Democratic Party (West German political party)
TUC—Trades Union Congress (British labor federation)
TV—television
UK—United Kingdom of Great Britain & Northern Ireland
UN—United Nations
UNCTAD—UN Conference on Trade & Development
U.S.—United States of America
USSR—Union of Soviet Socialist Republics (Soviet Union)
WEU—Western European Union

1957

1957 was a formative year for continental Europe and Great Britain. The European Economic Community (EEC, or the Common Market) and the European Community of Atomic Energy (Euratom) were created as a result of the success of the European Coal & Steel Community (ECSC). Great Britain, under the leadership of its new prime minister, Harold Macmillan, chose to remain outside these organizations; but,by the end of the year, discussions regarding the relationship between the EEC and Great Britain were in progress. While the British economy and the pound remained fairly stable during 1957, in part because of American assistance, the French franc was devalued by the end of the summer, and tightened domestic policies were instituted by the de Gaulle government.

BRITAIN'S SITUATION

Macmillan Succeeds Eden as Prime Minister

Sir Anthony Eden, 59, British prime minister since Apr. 6, 1955, resigned the office Jan. 9 on the ground that ill health left him "unable to do my full duty." Harold Macmillan (who became 63 Feb. 10), Eden's chancellor of the exchequer, was designated as the new prime minister and first lord of the Treasury by Queen Elizabeth II Jan. 10.

Eden's plea of ill health was supported by a bulletin his doctors issued Jan. 9 saying that he had suffered "a recurrence of abdominal symptoms" that caused concern in view of an operation he underwent in 1953. The British press generally ascribed his resignation to the failure of his policy of force in the Suez Canal dispute. Widespread British and foreign opposition to his moves on Suez were said to have depressed Eden.

Macmillan was commissioned as Eden's successor in preference to Richard Austen Butler, 54, after the queen had consulted with ex-Prime Min. Winston S. Churchill, 82, and the Marquess of Salisbury, 63, lord president of the Council and Conservative Party leader in the House of Lords. Butler, lord privy seal and House of Commons Conservative leader who had acted as cabinet head during Eden's recent vacation in Jamaica, was rated as an opponent of Eden's Suez policy, which Macmillan had supported. London political reports indicated that Conservative MPs who favored drastic action on Suez would not accept Butler as prime minister but that Macmillan was acceptable to Butler's following.

U.S. officials indicated Jan. 9-10 that they expected improvement in Anglo-U.S. governmental relations after Macmillan took over from Eden. Pres. Dwight D. Eisenhower Jan. 9 expressed anxiety over the illness of Eden, then exchanged messages expressing hope for enduring British-American friendship with Macmillan Jan. 15.

West German Chancellor Konrad Adenauer sent Eden a message of thanks Jan. 10 for Eden's "strong aid" in bringing about West Germany's freedom as a member of the European Defense Community in 1954. Bonn officials informally praised Macmillan as a strong advocate of measures for European unity.

Moscow broadcasts Jan. 10 said Eden was ousted because his Suez action had cost Britain its "70 years of influence in the Middle East, from which it is being squeezed out by the U.S." Moscow criticized Macmillan as a wealthy ally of the British Conservatives' "extreme right wing."

Macmillan announced Feb. 2 that, due to "many preoccupations," he would not carry out plans made by Eden before his resignation for the British prime minister to visit Moscow in May.

Financial Developments

The British Treasury reported Feb. 4 that its gold and dollar reserves had declined by $49 million during January to $2.084 billion. The exchange rate for the pound in New York Jan. 1 was $2.78625; it had fluctuated between $2.81156 and $2.78125 during 1956.

Pres. Eisenhower submitted to Congress Mar. 6 a U.S.-British agreement negotiated by Treasury Secy. George M. Humphrey under which an $81,600,000 interest payment from Britain, due since Dec. 1956, could be postponed. Britain would be allowed to postpone up to 7 annual principal-and-interest installments on its 1945 $3.75 billion loan when economic conditions made this necessary. Britain had made its scheduled $46,400,000 payment of principal for 1956 but had put the interest in escrow pending negotiations on its plea for leniency in view of difficulties stemming from the Suez crisis. Congressional action authorizing this arrangement was completed by 218-167 House vote Apr. 10, and Mr. Eisenhower signed the measure Apr. 20.

Canadian Finance Min. Walter Harris announced Mar. 6 that Canada had received the 1956 $15,500,000 principal payment on its 1946 $1.25 billion loan to Britain and had waived the $22,200,000 interest for the year. He said Canada was prepared to waive principal and interest in the future provided payments to the U.S. were deferred.

British Chancellor of the Exchequer Peter Thorneycroft told the House of Commons Feb. 26 that the U.S. Export-Import Bank had agreed to lend Britain $500 million at 4.5% interest to finance dollar imports. Britain would draw upon the credit as necessary and post as security part of the British government's $750 million worth of U.S. dollar securities.

A shipment of 2,343 silver bars weighing 74 pounds each arrived in New York aboard the liner *Queen Elizabeth* Apr. 2 as Britain's final installment in repaying an 88 million-ounce loan of silver under the U.S. Lend-Lease program in 1943-5. The British had to melt tons of coins— replacing them with copper and nickel coins—to repay the debt. The British Information Service said the silver had been worth $62,480,000 when borrowed but had increased in value to $79,040,000 when returned.

The British budget for fiscal 1957-8, presented in the House of Commons Apr. 9 by Chancellor of the Exchequer Thorneycroft, proposed tax reductions estimated at £98 million ($274 million), primarily in individual and business tax relief for Britons earning £2,000 ($5,600) or more annually. Thorneycroft said the tax reductions, 1/4 to middle class Britons, 1/4 to aid export businesses, 1/4 to lower indirect taxation and 1/4 for general tax easement, would reach £130 million ($364 million) in another year. Laborites attacked the budget Apr. 9 as designed for "the man at the top." British Treasury officials said Apr. 9 that it would lower the British tax burden from 31% of the gross national product in 1951-2 to 25% in 1957-8.

Following the devaluation of the French franc and subsequent pressures on both the pound and the German mark, Thorneycroft Sept. 19 announced an increase of British bank rates from 5% to 7%, the highest level since 1920. Ordering the increased interest rate in an effort to strengthen the pound, Thorneycroft had asked banks to hold future lending to no more than the current year's levels. He asserted that increased government expenditures, including those planned for investment and for the expansion of nationalized industries, would be held to current levels for 2 years. The increased rate was expected to attract money to the London market, restrict lending and discourage borrowing for speculative transactions.

Gold and dollar reserves, continuing to fall, declined by Sept. 30 to $1.85 billion, the lowest level since June 1952. The September loss of $292 million was largely attributed to speculation against the pound. In the period following the bank rate increase, however, reserves actually rose by approximately $3 million and reversed a $295 million loss earlier in the month.

The British government Oct. 30 drew $250 million of the $500 million credit that had been established with the U.S. Export-Import Bank during the Suez Canal crisis. The withdrawal brought British gold and dollar reserves by the end of October to $2.093 billion, an increase of $243 million.

Chancellor of the Exchequer Peter Thorneycroft announced Dec. 17 that Britain would defer interest and capital payments of $143.2 million due the U.S. and $39.2 million due Canada in December. The payments, delayed under agreements permitting Britain to defer 7 annual reimbursements on U.S. loans totalling $4,020,800,000 and Canadian loans of $1,150,800,000, were to be made on the completion of regular annual installments in the year 2000.

The British government announced Jan. 3 1958 that British gold and dollar reserves had reached $2.273 billion at the end of 1957. This was an increase of $140 million during the year despite a Sept. 1957 drop to a 5-year low of $1.85 billion. The reserves, however, included a $250 million credit from the U.S. Export-Import Bank and took into account the deferral of $182,400,000 in payments on U.S. and Canadian loans.

The Board of Trade reported Jan. 13 1958 that British exports had reached a record £3.326 billion ($9,312,800,000) during 1957, an increase of £154 million ($431,200,000) over 1956. 1957 imports were listed at £4.079 billion ($11,421,200,000), a 5% increase, and re-exports at £133 million ($372,400,000), a 9% decrease. The report listed Britain's 1957 trade gap as £620 million ($1.736 billion), £52 million ($145,600,000) more than in 1955.

In contrast with these figures, the annual Treasury survey, issued Apr. 1, 1958 by Chancellor of the Exchequer Heathcoat Amory, listed Britain's 1957 balance-of-payments surplus at £237 million ($663 million), a decrease of £29 million ($81 million) from the 1956 surplus.

Bank Rate Scandal

A 3-man government tribunal headed by Lord Justice Sir Hubert Parker Dec. 2 opened an investigation of charges that British financial interests had used for private profit "leaked" information on the Sept. 19 bank rate change. Sir John Braithwaite, London Stock Exchange chairman, denied foreknowledge of the rate shift Dec. 4, but William J. Keswick, director of the Bank of England and of Jardine Matheson & Co. of Hong Kong, which had sold £1 million worth of government securities Sept. 18, conceded Dec. 6 that a possible rate rise had been discussed in a personal letter Sept. 3 from Humphrey Mynors, Bank of England deputy governor. Lord Kindersley, Bank of England director, confirmed Dec. 11 that he had been informed of the planned rate increase Sept. 16 by Cameron F. Cobbold, Bank of England governor. Kindersley denied, however, that he had discussed the change with any but Bank of England directors or had used the information as head of Lazard Bros. & Co., British Match Corp. and the Royal Exchange Assurance Co. (Lazard Bros. had sold £1,450,000 worth of government securities Sept. 17-18, British Match £300,000 worth Sept. 16 and Royal Exchange £1,412,349 Sept. 18.) ∙

Chancellor of the Exchequer Thorneycroft, appearing Dec. 20 at the final session of the inquiry, denied that he had informed newsmen or Conservative leaders of the increase.

EUROPEAN COMMUNITY AFFAIRS

Common Market & Euratom Created

Representatives of France, West Germany, Italy, Netherlands, Belgium and Luxembourg, meeting in Paris Feb. 19-20, approved provisions for the creation of a European Common Market (the European Economic Community) and an atomic energy pool (Euratom, the European Community of Atomic Energy). The agreement provided for the gradual abolition of tariffs among the 6 states over a period of 12 to 17 years. The treaties under which the EEC and Euratom actually came into being were negotiated later in Rome, where they were signed Mar. 25. The agreement, later implemented in the Treaty of Rome, envisaged the creation of a Common Market comprising Europe and its dependent territories with a unified tariff to be imposed on non-European imports to the area.

A communique issued Feb. 20 said that the 6 nations had agreed to grant Euratom "the property rights in special fissile materials" to be put at the agency's disposal. It said that the 6 nations, already joined in the European Coal & Steel Community (ECSC) and West European Union (WEU), would "pursue their efforts for an increasingly close . . . integration of which the Euratom and Common Market treaties constitute a decisive step."

The agreement supported French proposals for the creation of a Eurafrican economic entity. The 6 states called for the establishment, during a 5-year trial period, of an "association of the overseas territories with the Common Market." They emphasized the "important investment effort which they are willing to undertake" and reportedly set these tentative contributions to an overseas investment fund: France—$200 million; West Germany—$200 million; Netherlands—$70 million; Belgium—$70 million; Italy—$5 million; Luxembourg—$1.25 million. Tentative allotments from the fund: France—$512 million; Netherlands—$35 million; Belgium—$30 million; Italy—$5 million. (West Germany and Luxembourg had no overseas territories.)

Present at the Feb. 19-20 Paris meetings: French Premier Guy Mollet and Foreign Min. Christian Pineau; West German Chancellor Konrad Adenauer and Foreign Min. Heinrich von Brentano; Belgian Premier Achille van Acker and Foreign Min. Paul-Henri Spaak; Italian Premier Antonio Segni and Foreign Min. Gaetano Martino; Luxembourg Premier Joseph Bech; Netherlands Premier Willem Drees and Foreign Min. Joseph M. A. H. Luns.

The Paris agreements followed intensive negotiations by the 6 states' foreign ministers in Brussels Jan. 28-Feb. 4 and in Paris Feb. 18. Dutch objections to Common Market treaty provisions had been overcome in talks in The Hague Feb. 2 between Belgian Foreign Min. Spaak and Dutch Foreign Min. Luns. West German support for the overseas investment program, reportedly essential for full French participation in the Common Market, was assured during the Feb. 18 Paris talks. The French National Assembly had approved negotiations toward a common market treaty by a vote of 322-77 Jan. 22 despite opposition voiced in the Assembly Jan. 18-19 by ex-Premiers Pierre Mendes-France, Antoine Pinay, Paul Reynaud, Edgar Faure and Joseph Laniel.

The finance ministers of 17 West European nations of the Organization for European Economic Cooperation (OEEC) agreed Feb. 14 in Paris to open negotiations on the creation of a West European free trade zone to be linked with the projected 6-nation Common Market. British notes to the Western European Union (WEU) states, disclosed Jan. 30, asked for talks in London to study the possibility of integrating all European economic, political and defense organizations under one central authority. The U.S. State Department said Jan. 16 that the U.S. would welcome the proposed European Common Market and free trade zone as adding to the "cohesion of Western Europe within an expanding Atlantic community."

Plans for the creation of Euratom had been approved unanimously Jan. 9 by the European Consultative Assembly in Strasbourg.

A Soviet statement issued through the Tass news agency Mar. 16 attacked plans for the European Common Market and atomic energy community as "endangering the people of Europe." The Soviet statement was generally regarded in the West as an attempt to delay the signing of the Common Market and Euratom treaties. The Soviet declaration said that enactment of the European trade and atomic accords would: bring European economies, particularly that of France, under the domination of "large American and West German monopolies"; subordinate West Germany to NATO and further complicate the problem of German reunification; "supply West German revanchists with nuclear weapons" and place Euratom under the control of the U.S., its principal supplier of fissionable materials. The USSR proposed "all-European cooperation in the sphere of the peaceful uses of atomic energy" through East-West talks on the establishment of joint atomic research and the construction of "establishments for the generation of atomic energy for industrial, scientific and technical purposes." It also urged (a) the development of hydroelectric stations and an oil and power supply system to overcome "tension in the fuel supply of many European countries," and (b) "mutual economic and financial assistance" and trade agreements among all European nations.

(British, Greek, Yugoslav and Asian delegates to the International Chamber of Commerce's 16th congress in Naples, Italy May 7 criticized provisions of the Common Market treaty that, they charged, would raise European tariff barriers and hamper the flow of agricultural commodities.)

The formal signing of the 2 treaties to create the EEC and Euratom took place in Rome Mar. 25. The treaties were of unlimited duration and subject to ratification by the parliaments of the 6 states; they were signed by West German Chancellor Adenauer, French Foreign Min. Pineau, Italian Premier Segni, Belgian Foreign Min. Spaak, Netherlands Foreign Min. Joseph Luns and Luxembourg Premier Bech.

The 2 treaties provided for the creation of these institutions: a Legislative Assembly to coordinate policies and preside over the Common Market and atomic pool; a Council of Ministers to represent member governments; a Commission to oversee the application of the treaties; a Court of Justice to mediate disputes; an Advisory Economic & Social Committee to represent all economic interests in the 6 states. The Assembly and Court of Justice would also be applied by the 6 nations to the European Coal & Steel Community. The treaties called for the initial election of the 142-member Assembly by national parliaments, but the Assembly thus elected would plan for eventual elections through Europe-wide universal direct suffrage. The 6-member appointed Council of Ministers would have principal executive powers over the Common

Market and atom pool. The Commission would be responsible to the Assembly.

Among other provisions of the 2 treaties:

Common market—Customs duties and taxes equivalent to duties would be abolished in trade among the 6 countries during a 12-year transitional period to be divided into 3 4-year stages. A common tariff on goods imported from outside the 6-nation area would be established and quantitative import restrictions abolished, also within 12 years. Provisions were made for gradual adjustment to free trade in goods entailing national economic problems and for eventual arbitration of disputes over adherence to the free-trade agreement. Free movement of workers within the common market area also was to be achieved within 12 years.

Overseas territories of member states were to be "associated" with the Common Market through the reduction of tariffs (except for necessary protective tariffs). A 5-year common investment fund of $581,250,000 was set up, with France and West Germany contributing $200 million each, Belgium and the Netherlands $70 million each, Italy $40 million, Luxembourg $1,250,000. French overseas territories were to receive $511,250,000 from the fund, Belgian territories $30 million, Dutch territories $35 million, Italian territories $5 million.

A European investment bank was created to finance the economic development of the 6 member countries, with France and West Germany contributing $300 million each, Italy $240 million, Belgium $86.5 million, Netherlands $71.5 million, Luxembourg $2 million.

Atomic pool—The agency was to be the central institution for facilitating research, security measures, investment in facilities and the supply of atomic materials for developing peaceful nuclear power to benefit the 6 nations.

The signing of the Treaty of Rome followed the visit of Belgian Foreign Min. Spaak to London Jan. 15 to discuss the question of British association with the EEC. The Macmillan government Feb. 7 published a White Paper explaining that Britain would not join, in part, at least, because of Commonwealth interests. If it joined, Britain could not grant to Commonwealth members tariff concessions as favorable as those to EEC members. Britain, on the other hand, favored the creation of a "free trade area" that would allow for common tariff reductions among members while granting individual members independence on tariff policies with non-members. In particular, this would free Britain from allegedly discriminatory agricultural price burdens resulting from the loss of Commonwealth preference. Britain's position was repeated by Chancellor of the Exchequer Peter Thorneycroft in Paris at the Feb. 12-13 ministerial meeting of the Organization for European Economic Cooperation (OEEC). At this meeting, Spaak opposed the British position and urged the immediate signing of the Common Market treaty.

Britain's Commonwealth ties were reaffirmed in Bermuda Mar. 25-26 when Macmillan met with Canadian Prime Min. Louis St. Laurent, External Affairs State Secy. Lester B. Pearson and Trade & Commerce Min. C. D. Howe. The Anglo-Canadian talks centered on Canada's UN role in solving the British-Egyptian dispute over Suez and on Commonwealth trade and foreign policies. A communique issued in Bermuda Mar. 26 reaffirmed "the close and continuous cooperation" between Canada and Britain.

Major ratifications of the treaties took place not long after they were signed. The French National Assembly voted by 342-239 July 9 to ratify the 2 treaties; prior to the ratification vote, the Assembly July 9 had approved the Common Market pact by 342-234 and the Euratom treaty by 334-240. The West German Bundestag (lower house) had approved ratification of the 2 pacts July 5; 400 of the Bundestag's 497 deputies approved the treaties in a show-of-hands vote. The Bundestag resolution made formal West German ratification dependent on the completion of parliamentary approval of the pacts by the other signatories. The West German Bundesrat (upper house) had voted preliminary approval of the 2 treaties May 3, and voted unanimously July 19 to complete West German ratification of the treaties. In addition, the 2 pacts were ratified by Italy 311 to 144 (with 54 abstentions) July 30, by the Netherlands 114 to 12 Oct. 4 and by Belgium 174 to 2 (2 abstentions) Nov. 19. Virtually all opposing votes were from Communist representatives.

U.S. Cooperation

U.S. cooperation with coordinated European activity was demonstrated by European Coal & Steel Community (ECSC) success in borrowing money from the U.S. public Apr. 9. This first public borrowing in the U.S. consisted of an offering of $25 million of 5.5% secured bonds (dated Apr. 1, 1957, due Apr. 1, 1975) and $10 million of 5% secured serial notes maturing in 1960, 1961 and 1962. The offering was made through an investment syndicate headed by Kuhn, Loeb & Co., First Boston Corp. and Lazard Freres & Co. Previous outstanding ECSC obligations: $100 million borrowed from the Export-Import Bank in 1954 on 3.875% secured notes due in 1979; $17 million borrowed on secured notes from Belgian, German, Luxembourg and Saar banks; about $12 million on secured 4.25% notes sold publicly on the Swiss market in 1956. The money was for loans to steel and coal enterprises in the ECSC area.

This bond issue was sold after the U.S. Feb. 8 had pledged support to plans for the establishment of a West European atomic power network that would produce 3 million kilowatt hours of electricity by 1963 and 15 million kilowatt hours by 1967. A communique issued Feb. 8 following talks among the U.S. State Department and Atomic Energy Commission and a 3-man Euratom committee termed the project "feasible" and said that the U.S. would "enter into comprehensive and practical engagements" with Euratom. Plans for the proposed $240 million Euratom power network, known as the European Plant for the Extraction of Uranium Isotopes, had been approved in Brussels Jan. 27 by representatives of France, West Germany, Italy, Belgium, Netherlands and Luxembourg. Attending the talks in Washington Feb. 3-8 were: Louis Armand, French State Railway director-general; Franz

Etzel, West German vice president of the ECSC High Authority; Francesco Giordani, Italian National Research Council president. More detailed plans were disclosed May 7 in a report issued by Euratom's "Committee of 3." The report, prepared by Armand, Etzel and Giordani, urged action to order power reactors by 1958 to insure operation of the first European atom power stations by 1963. The committee said that the program, to be developed in cooperation with the U.S., Britain and Canada, would cost $4 billion more than a comparable conventional power program. It warned that Europe currently imported 23% of its energy needs, mostly in Mid-East oil, but would be forced to import 33% of its power by 1967 without rapid nuclear energy development.

(A. V. Zakharov, Soviet delegate to the UN Economic Commission for Europe, had said May 3 that the USSR was ready to join the West in building an East-West European atomic power grid. Zakharov proposed, as an initial step, the exchange of research information between the Soviet bloc's United Institute for Nuclear Research and the 12-nation Organization for Nuclear Research in West Europe. Zakharov denounced the 6-nation Euratom and EEC pacts as intended to increase East-West tensions. The EEC/Euratom states Apr. 29 had rejected previous Soviet charges that the 2 pacts were aggressive in nature.)

Britain & Other Nations

Britain's attitude toward the European Common Market apparently was made plain when Prime Min. Macmillan and Foreign Secy. Selwyn Lloyd met with French Premier Mollet and Foreign Min. Pineau in Paris Mar. 9 for talks on NATO and European trade. Macmillan said Mar. 10 that, although "the reorganization of our forces in Germany" had caused concern in France, the continued presence of British units in NATO was "a pledge that Great Britain has given to Europe and will continue to give." Macmillan, presumably alluding to Britain's reluctance to associate itself with a European trade zone that included the former French colonies, conceded that "the Common Market and the free trade zone will not be established without difficulties."

Contrasting feelings were expressed by Queen Elizabeth II, on her Apr. 8-11 visit to Paris, when she said: "Mutual trust between our 2 countries was fostered and developed during the reigns of my grandfather and my father, until it has become today the firmest link holding together 2 nations of the Old World which can still play a role in the future as inspiring as in the past."

Macmillan visited German Chancellor Konrad Adenauer at Bonn May 7-9, and the West Germans agreed to support British proposals for the creation of a free trade zone in association with the 6-nation EEC.

Macmillan and ex-Prime Min. Sir Winston Churchill, in addresses to a "Britain in Europe" meeting organized by the UK Council of the European Movement, joined in urging July 9 that Britain establish strong economic ties with a united Europe. Churchill said: "My message today to Europe is the same as it was 10 years ago—unite!" Macmillan, defending British proposals for a 17-nation OEEC (Organization for European Economic Cooperation) free-trade zone for industrial goods, warned, however, that "there is real danger that, in trying to create unity in Europe [by forming an exclusive Common Market], new divisions may follow."

British officials at the Commonwealth Prime Ministers Conference in London assured Commonwealth nations July 3 that Britain would continue to protect the Commonwealth trade pattern while moving toward closer economic integration with Europe. Commonwealth officials had stressed July 3 their objections to any integration plans that would end their favored customs and import quota position on the British market. The Commonwealth conference ended July 5 with a communique that called for (a) strengthening of the UN, described as now having "certain deficiencies and weaknesses," and (b) continuing talks on the European Common Market and free-trade-zone proposals.

Macmillan asked Paymaster Gen. Reginald Maudling Aug. 7 to represent Great Britain in talks with continental European nations regarding the formation of a "free trade area." Maudling, who had become paymaster general when Macmillan organized his government in Jan., would relieve Chancellor of the Exchequer Peter Thorneycroft of some responsibilities he had held in representing Britain in such talks.

"Free trade area" discussions had been started by the OEEC Ministerial Council's action of Feb. 3 and Mar. 8 under Thorneycroft. This action closely paralleled the 6-nation (France, West Germany, Italy, Belgium, Luxembourg, and the Netherlands) discussions that culminated in the Treaty of Rome.

The finance and economic affairs ministers of 17 West European nations met Oct. 16-17 in Paris as the OEEC Council and declared Oct. 17 their readiness to join in a Europe-wide free trade zone, principally for industrial goods. The proposed zone would link the 6-nation EEC with the 11 other OEEC states (Austria, Britain, Denmark, Greece, Iceland, Ireland, Norway, Portugal, Sweden, Switzerland, Turkey). The 17 states Oct. 17 named a committee to begin negotiations immediately on the proposed zone.

Thorneycroft, OEEC Council chairman, said at the meeting Oct. 17 that "we have decided there shall be one" Europe. The 17 nations in the OEEC zone would abolish all tariffs and trade barriers against each other but would retain individual barriers against non-European goods. Those of the 17 in the EEC would remove their common tariff against OEEC area goods but maintain tariffs against all outside states. Maudling had told the OEEC ministers Oct. 16 that Britain would not abandon agricultural tariffs aimed at preferential treatment for Commonwealth farm products. (British insistence on limitations of the OEEC trade zone had been criticized Sept. 16 by the National Council of French Employers.)

(Economists from 17 OEEC states had met in Paris Mar. 18 and formed 3 working committees to plan for the creation of a European free trade zone to be linked to the 6-nation Common Market and include Britain.)

Thorneycroft had proposed Sept. 28, at a meeting in Ottawa of British Commonwealth finance ministers, that Britain and Canada form a free trade zone to link the sterling and dollar blocks. Canadian sources had discredited the proposal Sept. 29 as "politically and economically impossible" because of the danger to Canadian light industry from British goods. The meeting had been held in Canada at Prime Min. John G. Diefenbaker's request to discuss his proposals for a transfer of 15% ($600 million worth) of Canadian trade from the U.S. to Britain.

British and other delegates to the 10th annual meeting in Geneva of members of the General Agreement on Tariffs & Trade (GATT) warned Oct. 28-29 that the Common Market would create discrimination in world commerce and could harm agricultural and underdeveloped economies. Sir David Eccles, British Board of Trade president, demanded Oct. 28 that undeveloped areas be given "concrete assurances that their trade will not be penalized" by a preferential trade system under the plan. Eccles warned that proposals for associating overseas territories with the Common Market would require approval by the 37-nation GATT.

Officials of Norway, Denmark, Sweden and Finland in Stockholm Oct. 20 disclosed plans to establish a customs union and common investment plan. Prepared by the Committee for Scandinavian Economic Cooperation, the proposal called for duty-free trade in 80% of the 4 countries' commerce, the abolition of quota restrictions in Scandinavian trade and the creation of a "Scandinavian investment" fund with a minimum capitalization of $300 million. The trade zone would become effective immediately on its ratification by all 4 governments. Its members would negotiate as a unit within the OEEC zone.

Members of the 6-nation European Coal & Steel Community (ECSC) Assembly, meeting in Rome Nov. 5-9, adopted a resolution reassuring Britain and Scandinavian, American and Asian nations that, if necessary, the European Common Market treaty would be amended to avoid protectionism and "emphasize the open character of the market."

French Foreign Affairs Undersecy. Maurice Faure, speaking at the Nov. 14 session of an OEEC Committee of Ministers meeting on a proposed 17-nation OEEC free trade zone in industrial goods, demanded delays to permit the prior establishment and functioning of the 6-nation EEC. He expressed French opposition to British terms for joining the OEEC zone.

OEEC financial reports issued Nov. 11 in Paris had warned that the current economic imbalance between France and West Germany could affect Europe's current prosperity. The OEEC warned that France's adverse foreign trade balance, estimated at $1.2 billion for 1957, could prevent effective French participation on the Common Market plan. It chided West Germany for undervaluation of its currency, which, it said, had brought a mark shortage among West Germany's debtor states.

Prime Min. Macmillan and Pres. Eisenhower had met in Bermuda Mar. 21-24 for talks aimed at mending damage to the Anglo-U.S. alliance caused by differences over policy in the Middle East. A joint communique, issued in Bermuda Mar. 24 by Mr. Eisenhower and Macmillan, reaffirmed Anglo-U.S. "responsibility to seek to coordinate their foreign policies in the interests of peace with justice." It said that the 2 leaders had discussed and reached agreement on: (a) "the importance of closer association of [Britain] with Europe" and (b) benefits of the European "Common Market and the free trade area, provided they do not lead to a high tariff bloc." U.S. State Secy. John Foster Dulles, British Foreign Secy. Selwyn Lloyd, and U.S. Amb.-to-NATO Walter F. George also met in Bermuda Mar. 22 to discuss NATO, European union and the Common Market plan. Lloyd presented British proposals for a European General Assembly to coordinate the functions of current supra-national European organizations and control NATO's political activities. Lloyd reportedly urged Dulles to study the association of the U.S. with Britain's "grand design" for a future European parliament.

Macmillan and Eisenhower met again in Washington Oct. 23-25. Their "declaration of common purpose," issued Oct. 25, stated that collective security must be bolstered by "cooperative economic action," especially toward the European free trade zone and Common Market and the "less developed countries."

A similar communique emerged from the meeting in Paris Dec. 16-19 of the heads of all NATO governments (except Portugal). This communique reaffirmed "the desirability of a closer economic association between the countries of Western Europe." It pledged "encouragement to the successful development of the European Economic Community and of a European [OEEC] free trade zone in which full account would be taken of the interests of the less developed member countries." Western leaders attending the NATO Council meetings, held in the Palais de Chaillot, Paris: *U.S.*—Pres. Eisenhower, State Secy. Dulles; *Britain*—Prime Min. Macmillan, Foreign Secy. Lloyd; *France*—Premier Felix Gaillard, Foreign Min. Christian Pineau; *West Germany*—Chancellor Konrad Adenauer, Foreign Min. Heinrich von Brentano; *Canada*—Prime Min. John Diefenbaker, External Affairs Secy. Sidney Smith; *Italy*—Premier Adone Zoli, Foreign Min. Giuseppe Pella; *Belgium*—Premier Achille Van Acker, Foreign Min. Victor Larock;

Netherlands—Premier Willem Drees, Foreign Min. Joseph Luns; *Luxembourg*—Premier-Foreign Min. Joseph Bech; *Denmark*—Premier Hans C. Hansen, Defense Min. Paul Hansen; *Norway*—Premier Einar H. Gerhardsen, Foreign Min. Halvard Lange; *Iceland*—Premier Hermann Jonassen, Foreign Min. Gudmunder Gudmundsson; *Portugal*—Presidency Min. Marcelo Gaetano, Foreign Min. Paulo Cunha; *Turkey*—Premier Adnan Menderes, Foreign Min. Fatin Rustu Zorlu.

French Devaluation & Other Monetary Developments

The French economy and the strength of the franc showed signs of weakness by early summer of 1957, and steps were taken, by the government and international institutions, to bolster the French position. Eventually, France devalued the franc.

In one of the earlier moves to shore up the economy and franc, the National Assembly, in a 251-10 confidence vote June 24 for the government of Premier Maurice Bourges-Maunoury, approved a financial program providing for (a) 150 billion francs ($428.6 million) in increased taxes (largely on gasoline, sending the price from 83¢ to $1 a gallon), and (b) 250 billion francs ($714 million) in enforced government economies. The Assembly then voted 304-221 June 26 to let the government borrow from the Bank of France 100 billion francs ($285 million) in gold for payments on the foreign trade deficit and 350 billion francs ($1 billion) for short-term government expenditures. The French government June 14 withdrew from the International Monetary Fund (IMF) $42.5 million, the balance of a $262.5 million IMF special credit. The Organization for European Economic Cooperation (OEEC) made available to France June 15, 2 weeks earlier than planned, a $200 million credit to bolster the French account in the European Payments Union. (The EPU reported May 31 that the French deficit had reached $332 million.) Finance Min. Felix Gaillard, acting June 17 to halt a $100-$150 million average monthly increase in the French foreign trade deficit, restored quotas on imports from West European and dollar-zone countries.

The French government informed the OEEC July 13 that it had been forced to suspend free trade with the 16 other OEEC members in an effort to stem the growing French foreign trade deficit. The government reported that a new financial program voted in an effort to stabilize the economy would levy 4,673 billion francs ($13.5 billion) in taxes during 1957, accounting for at least 23.6% of France's estimated 19,800 billion-franc national income.

Premier Bourges-Maunoury met Aug. 6 with Finance Min. Gaillard and other cabinet members in final efforts to reduce the fiscal 1958 budget by 10% (600 billion francs, or $1.714 billion) and thus avert a financial crisis caused by gold reserve losses, growing inflation and foreign payments deficits. Bourges-Maunoury acted after the franc (official rate: 350 to the U.S. dollar) fell Aug. 5 to a free-market rate of 436-445 francs to $1, the lowest point since 1952. Gaillard warned Aug. 5 that unless the budget were cut 10%, further reforms would be "useless" and he would resign. Wilfred Baumgartner, Bank of France governor, in his annual report to Pres. Rene Coty, warned Aug. 5 that France had overdrawn on "the enrichment that the future had promised it." French government price indices rose to 150 Aug. 2, passing the 149.1 level at which a 5.5% rise in the French minimum wage became automatic. The European Payments Union reported Aug. 4 that France's July EPU deficit had been $132.5 million, the highest level in 1957.

Finally, the franc's value was revised officially to 424 instead of 350 to the U.S. dollar for foreign tourists and traders. This move, announced by Finance Min. Gaillard Aug. 10, was taken to reduce France's foreign exchange deficit. He also (1) imposed a 20% tax on all imports except the 40% deemed vital to the French economy (a 15% tax had been in effect on many unessential imports since April), and (2) authorized a 20% franc premium for all legal foreign currency conversions by firms directing 50% or more of their output into export markets (in most cases replacing tax rebates and a complicated system of subsidies).

The Bank of France tightened credit restrictions Aug. 12 by raising the commercial discount rate from 4% to 5%. The government Aug. 13 ordered the reinforcement of its price inspection system and fixed 1957 wheat prices at 10% below the 1956 levels of $9.57 per 200 pounds. (The National Collective Bargaining Board Aug. 13 approved a new 175-item price index to determine future movement of France's sliding-scale minimum wage. All international travel fares paid in francs were increased 20% Aug. 13-14.) Finance Ministry officials reported Aug. 16 that foreign currency reserves had increased by $3 million during the first 3 days of devaluation.

The Paris free market value of the French franc fell to 447 to the U.S. dollar Aug. 19 despite controls imposed following the devaluation.

British and German reaction to the franc's devaluation was prompt and definitive. The British Treasury declared Aug. 19 that the government would not devalue the pound sterling or change its official exchange rates of $2.78 (buying) and $2.82 (selling) despite "pressure from the backwash of the devaluation of the French franc."

German government spokesmen said Aug. 20 that the West German Deutschemark, valued at 23.8¢ U.S., would not be revalued upward despite a "flight" to the mark from British and French currencies following the devaluation of the franc.

These positions were reinforced when British, West German and International Monetary Fund (IMF) leaders Sept. 24 barred any change in current values and exchange rates between the pound and mark.

British Chancellor of the Exchequer Peter Thorneycroft emphasized to IMF delegates that "the question of exchange rates must now be regarded as settled and will not be reopened." The parity rate of the pound "stays at $2.80," he said. Thorneycroft said Britain soon would draw a $500 million U.S. Export-Import Bank standby credit, presumably to deter speculation on the pound.

Hans Karl von Mangold-Reiboldt, managing board chairman of the European Payments Union, declared that the West German government would not "contemplate a change in the dollar value of the Deutschemark." IMF Managing Director Per Jacobsson said the "growing knowledge" that there would be no change in mark or pound should "in itself have a calming effect on the movement of funds."

The West German Federal Bank (Bundesbank) Sept. 19 reduced its rediscount rate from 4.5% to 4%. This was the 3d cut since May 1956, when it had reached a 6-year high of 5.5%. The Bundesbank's action was described as indicating confidence that the West German economy was free from inflationary pressures. It followed the accumulation of surplus capital due to the currency flight from the British pound and French franc.

1958

The European Economic Community (EEC) and European Community of Atomic Energy (Euratom) came into existence in 1958. Britain's decision to remain outside these bodies was bolstered by economic developments both domestically and on the Continent. While the British economy stabilized, France continued to face tightened domestic policies and falling reserves. Greater currency convertibility throughout Western Europe was achieved late in the year, following the election of Charles de Gaulle as French president and the devaluation of the French franc. French and British disagreements on the British relationship to the EEC widened during the year and were reinforced by the de Gaulle election.

BRITISH DEVELOPMENTS

Macmillan Government Criticized

Chancellor of the Exchequer Peter Thorneycroft resigned Jan. 6 in protest against plans to allow 1958-9 budget increases totalling £50 million ($140 million). Thorneycroft told Prime Min. Harold Macmillan that he was "not prepared to approve" budget estimates that might affect the "stability of the pound" and the "stabilization of prices." He said the government must "accept the same measures of financial discipline as it seeks to impose on others." Agriculture Min. Derick Heathcoat Amory was named Jan. 6 to succeed Thorneycroft.

The 1957 charges of an alleged "leak" of information regarding bank rate changes culminated Jan. 21 in the exoneration of Conservative politicians and financiers and Bank of England officials. Laborites had charged that they had "leaked" information of the impending interest rate shift of Sept. 19, 1957 and had used the warning for personal profit. The accused officials were cleared by a 3-man tribunal headed by Sir Hubert Lister Parker, the Lord Justice of Appeal. The tribunal's report, made public Jan. 21 by Home Secy. Richard A. Butler, cleared Deputy Chairman Oliver Poole of the Conservative Party and Directors Lord Kindersley and William J. Keswick of the Bank of England. The tribunal urged, however, that Parliament consider (a) ex-Chancellor of the Exchequer Thorneycroft's alleged disclosure to newsmen Sept. 18, 1957 of then-secret investment and credit measures, and (b) the "difficult and embarrassing" position of Bank of England directors having access to secret financial information and being connected with companies dependent on such information.

Criticism continued, but the Macmillan government was able to withstand it. The House of Commons Jan. 23 rejected, by a 324-262 vote, a Labor Party censure amendment charging Macmillan's cabinet with failure to "secure expanding production, full employment and a stable pound."

The British Economy

Labor Min. Iain MacLeod reported to Parliament Feb. 24 that British unemployment had risen to 423,000 by Feb. 17. MacLeod said that the increase—28,000 in the month ended Feb. 17 and 60,000 in the previous month—appeared to be "real," not seasonal.

The British Trades Union Congress Executive Feb. 26 condemned as "partisan" the report of a government-named Council on Productivity. The council, headed by Lord Cohen, had endorsed government anti-inflation policies and had predicted a "somewhat further" rise in British unemployment due to increased productivity.

A £5.75 billion ($16.1 billion) fiscal 1958-9 budget presented to Parliament Apr. 15 by Chancellor of the Exchequer Derick Heathcoat Amory contained only minor changes in British tax and fiscal policies. Envisaging tax income at £5.44 billion ($15.232 billion), the budget cut purchase taxes from 60% to 30% on some home appliances (a £41 million total reduction), revised current taxes of 30% on distributed profits and 3% on undistributed profits to 10% on all profits, and raised income tax exemptions from £400 ($1,120) to £440 ($1,232) for persons over 65 and from £250 ($700) to £275 ($770) for unmarried persons. All of these acts were expansionary in nature, designed to stimulate economic activity. An additional move designed to stimulate employment was taken when all government restrictions on installment buying were ended by the Board of Trade Oct. 29.

Amory estimated that Britain would have an operating surplus of £364 million ($1,017,200,000) in fiscal 1958-9. He defended the budget by noting the British uncertainty due to the current U.S. recession. Laborite leader Hugh Gaitskell attacked the budget Apr. 15 for its failure to end what he termed the "virtual stagnation" of British industry. A Labor motion to revise the changed company tax provisions was defeated in the House of Commons Apr. 15 by a vote of 300-224.

A reduction from 7% to 6% in the Bank of England's discount rate had been authorized by the government Mar. 20. Treasury officials said the 7% bank rate had been intended only as a "crash measure" to bolster the pound against speculation. They said other anti-inflation measures would remain in effect. A further reduction from 6% to 5.5% in the discount rate was authorized May 22. The interest reduction, considered an indication of confidence in British anti-inflation policies, would lower interest rates charged by discount houses and commercial banks. Prime Min. Macmillan said at a Conservative Party meeting May 22 that although credit restrictions would remain, Britain was "within sight" of winning its anti-inflation battle. The bank rate was cut June 19 from 5.5% to 5% and Aug. 14 from 5% to 4.5%.

Britain's national debt increased by £225 million ($630 million) to £27,232,047,068 ($76,249,731,780) in the fiscal year ended Mar. 31, the Treasury reported Nov. 17.

The British balance of payments showed increasing strength. A Treasury White Paper published Oct. 13 reported that Britain had achieved its first visible trade surplus since 1900 during January-June 1958. The 6-month report listed a total surplus of £334 million ($935.2 million), a visible surplus of £137 million ($383.6 million).

Gold and dollar reserves gained every month until December. The increase of $144 million in April boosted reserves to $2.194 billion, the highest level since Nov. 1, 1954. A 7-year high was reached in October, when reserves rose by $54 million to $3.174 billion. The 1958 peak was reached with the November gain of $41 million to $3.215 billion. This was offset by a December loss of $146 million, which lowered total reserves to $3.069 billion at the year's end for a year's gain of $665 million.

The December loss was caused, in part, by the Dec. 31 payment of loan obligations to the U.S. and Canada. This was the first time since 1955 that both principal and interest had been paid. The payments amounted to $141 million to the U.S. and $42 million (U.S.) to Canada, the latter including the final payment of $7.5 million of an interest-free 1942 loan.

A £426 million ($1.193 billion) British trade deficit during 1958, the lowest trade deficit since 1950, had been reported Jan. 13, 1959 by the British Board of Trade. The report, based on accounting methods differing from those of the Treasury, listed imports of £3.782 billion ($10.589 billion) and exports of £3.208 billion ($8.982 billion) in 1958. It showed decreases of 3.5% in imports and 7% in exports during 1958.

The Treasury's 1959 economic survey, presented to Parliament Apr. 1, 1959 by Chancellor of the Exchequer Derick Heathcoat Amory, reported that Britain's balance of payments surplus had reached a record £455 million ($1.274 billion) during 1958.

The British economy showed clear signs of gains during 1958. Final figures for Britain's gross national product, announced Oct. 3, 1959 by the government, showed a rise to a record £20.13 billion ($56.364 billion). Total personal income rose to £18.928 billion (weekly paid employes' wages £7.7 billion, monthly paid wages £4.32 billion), and savings decreased slightly to £1.341 billion.

EUROPEAN ECONOMIC INTEGRATION

European Economic Community Organizes

The 2 treaties establishing the European Economic Community (Common Market) and European Community of Atomic Energy (Euratom) went into effect Jan. 1. Foreign ministers of the 6 nations involved (Christian Pineau of France, Heinrich von Brentano of West Germany, Giuseppe Pella of Italy, Victor Larock of Belgium, Joseph Bech of Luxembourg and State Secy. E. H. van der Beugel, substituting for Joseph Luns of the Netherlands) met in Paris Jan. 5-7 to organize the administration of the 2 agencies. They failed to reach agreement on a proposed West European economic capital, to be used by the 2 pools and the European Coal & Steel Community, but they announced Jan. 7 their appointment of the following directing commissions for the 2 groups:

Common Market—Foreign Affairs State Secy. Walter Hallstein of West Germany (commission president); P. Malvestiti and G. Petrilli of Italy; Robert Marjolin and R. Lemiegnan of France, M. Rasquin of Luxembourg; Jean Rey of Belgium; S. L. Mansholt of West Germany.

Euratom—Louis Armand, French National Railway chief (commission president); E. Medi of Italy, Paul de Groote of Belgium; Heinz Krekeler of West Germany; Emmanuel M. J. A. Sassen of the Netherlands.

In a reorganization of the parallel European Coal & Steel Community (ECSC), the 6 nations Jan. 7 named Paul Finet, Belgian trade union leader, to succeed Rene Mayer of France as president of the ECSC High Authority. Dirk Spierenburg of Holland was named Authority first vice president to replace Franz Etzel, West German finance minister. Franz Bluecher was appointed to fill the West German vacancy on the Authority.

Pietro Campilli of Italy was named Jan. 7 as president of the European Investment Bank to be set up under the Common Market with $1 billion capital.

The EEC, as established by the Treaty of Rome, would be a form of customs union, involving the prohibition of tariffs (import or export), duties, quotas and other quantitative restrictions on trade among the 6 member nations and the establishment of common tariffs on imports from non-members. These goals would be accomplished over a 12-year transition period starting Jan. 1, 1958. Special agreements and concessions could be negotiated in the area of agricultural products, insofar as these might become necessary. In addition, the right of complete mobility (and the right of settlement) of labor and capital among the members would become effective over the 12-year transition period.

Member nations would maintain complete economic independence (on such matters as currency and monetary policy, balance of payments and foreign exchange affairs) although all would be expected to act in ways beneficial to the common interest of the EEC.

Overseas territories of Belgium, France, Italy and the Netherlands would be considered as associated within the EEC.

Organs of the EEC, designed along lines similar to those of the European Atomic Energy Community, would include: (a) a Parliamentary (legislative) Assembly of 142 elected members, which would be shared with Euratom and the ECSC, (b) a Council of Ministers, with one representative from each member country, (c) a Commission of 9 members jointly appointed by all and (d) a Court of Justice of 7 members jointly appointed.

Members of the EEC Executive Commission held their first formal session in Brussels Jan. 16 and voted to meet alternately in Brussels and Luxembourg until a decision had been reached on a permanent headquarters site for the 6-nation Common Market.

The EEC Council of Ministers met Jan. 25 for the first time. Belgian Foreign Min. Victor Larock was elected president of the EEC Council and Belgian Economic Affairs Min. Roger Motz president of the Council of Euratom.

The EEC Commission met in Luxembourg Jan. 31 for the first time, and the Euratom Commission met in Brussels Feb. 24.

The Ministerial Councils of the EEC and Euratom Feb. 25 announced their decisions to (1) name a 6-man commission to designate a "European capital" as the seat of all European organizations, (2) name a 20-man scientific and technical committee for liaison between the Common Market and Euratom organizations and (3) approve a statute governing the work of a committee empowered to "review" monetary and financial situations of the 6 member states.

The European Coal & Steel Community (ECSC) Assembly met Feb. 28 in Strasbourg for a final session prior to its absorption into the European Parliamentary (legislative) Assembly, formed to replace the European Consultative Assembly and to control Euratom, the Common Market and ECSC.

W. Walton Butterworth, 54, U.S. ambassador to the ECSC since Mar. 1956, was named Feb. 28 as U.S. ambassador to the Common Market and Euratom. Sir William Meiklereid, head of the British delegation to the ECSC, was appointed May 22 by the Macmillan government as British representative to the EEC and Euratom. French Deputy Foreign Min. Maurice Faure had been named Jan. 24 as permanent chief of the French delegation to the EEC, Euratom and ECSC.

142 representatives of France, West Germany, Italy, Belgium, the Netherlands and Luxembourg met in Strasbourg Mar. 19-21 for the initial session of the European Parliamentary Assembly. The Assembly chose French ex-Premier Robert Schumann by acclamation Mar. 19 as its first president. It voted unanimously Mar. 21 to divide representation at future sessions among Europewide groupings of Christian Democratic, Socialist and Liberal (conservative) political tendencies.

An agreement signed Nov. 8 by the U.S. and Euratom provided for joint action to establish a nuclear power network in Europe and to share the knowledge resulting from the program. The accord, signed in Brussels by U.S. Rep.-to-Euratom Butterworth and AEC Chairman John A. McCone for the U.S. and Euratom Commissioners Enrico Medi of Italy, Heinz Krekeler of West Germany, Emmanuel M. J. A. Sassen of the Netherlands and Paul de Groote of Belgium, resulted from discussions started in May. It pledged: (1) a $135 million U.S. loan and a 20-year supply of enriched uranium fuel for the construction of a Euratom network of 6 to 8 reactors capable of producing one million kilowatts; (2) a jointly financed $100 million U.S.-Euratom research program to use the power stations to perfect low-cost nuclear power production.

Representatives of Britain and Euratom met in London June 18-19 and in Brussels July 14-15 to discuss cooperation in the development of atomic energy for peaceful purposes.

Britain Stresses Free Trade Area Concept

British Chancellor of the Exchequer Derick Heathcoat Amory, interviewed by the Paris financial paper *Les Echos,* denied Feb. 28 that Britain would enjoy free trade zone advantages in European nations excluded from similar benefits in Commonwealth markets. He warned that Common Market members must accept association with Britain, Switzerland and the Scandinavian trade zone to prevent "an economic division of Europe" and the "consequences that might follow in the political field."

Pres. Francois Peugeot of the French Federation of Mechanical Industries expressed strong opposition Mar. 23 to British plans for a 17-nation West European free trade zone in industrial goods on the ground that it would endanger French industry by "uncontrolled competition" simultaneously with readjustments necessitated by EEC plans.

West German Chancellor Konrad Adenauer visited London Apr. 16-18 for talks with Prime Min. Macmillan. Adenauer, accompanied by Heinrich von Brentano and Economics Min. Ludwig Erhardt, reached general agreement with British leaders on British proposals for a 17-nation European free trade zone in industrial goods as well as on issues of military significance in Western Europe. (Adenauer, who dined with Queen Elizabeth and Prince Philip Apr. 16, was the first German leader to be entertained by a British sovereign since before World War I.)

The Macmillan government June 24 announced the formation of a committee of British businessmen and union leaders under Sir David Kelly, former ambassador to Argentina, Turkey and the USSR, "to undertake or sponsor organized research on European economic integration." Prime Min. Macmillan and Foreign Min. Selwyn Lloyd flew to Paris June 29 for talks with French Premier de Gaulle and Foreign Min. Maurice Couve de Murville. De Gaulle reportedly expressed unqualified support for the 6-nation European economic and atomic pools but refused to make a commitment on British proposals for a 17-nation European free trade zone in industrial goods.

A memo submitted Oct. 20 by France and the 5 other Common Market nations had proposed the establishment of a free trade zone by Jan. 1, 1959 to conform with the first tariff cuts scheduled by the EEC treaty. It proposed free-trade-zone institutions that would parallel the Common Market's organization, among them a directing council that would be required to reach decisions unanimously. It proposed that free-trade-zone nations agree to (a) fix limits on national tariffs to conform to EEC standards, (b) fix compensatory taxes on goods not subjected to recommended tariffs, (c) coordinate commercial policies toward nations outside the 17-nation zone to prevent low-tariff imports by any member country from upsetting competition among producers within the area, (d) "harmonize" social and labor conditions and legislation where they affected prices and competition. Basic and overtime pay rates would correspond with 1956 French levels or France would be permitted to take "measures of safeguards" provided by the Common-Market treaty.

Talks on the establishment of a 17-nation European free trade zone were suspended indefinitely Nov. 17 by British Paymaster Gen. Reginald Maudling, chairman of the Organization for European Economic Cooperation's free trade zone negotiating committee.

The suspension, which ended negotiations held in Paris Oct. 23-28 and Nov. 13-14, followed an open rift between France and Britain as leaders of the Common Market and non-Common Market groups, respectively. It came after French Information Min. Jacques Soustelle Nov. 14 rejected British plans for extending tariff cuts and increased import quotas among the 6 EEC nations to the 11 other OEEC countries. Soustelle had labelled the free trade zone plan impossible. He urged some other form of "association" among the OEEC nations to prevent a European trade war when Common-Market tariff cuts went into effect in 1959. (An OEEC ministerial committee on establishing a 17-nation free trade zone had ended a 2-day meeting in Paris Jan. 16 after failing to reach agreement on British plans to subject agricultural trade within the zone to strict controls.)

Observers reported that the split was due to British fears that France sought to use the 6-nation Common Market to extend the French protectionist system to EEC tariffs and quotas and thus discriminate against non-EEC nations. France was said to view British proposals for a 17-nation trade zone, members of which would fix their own tariffs, as an attempt to undermine the 6-nation Common Market, protect Britain's exports to Europe and maintain the preferential tariffs it accorded Commonwealth nations. France had urged the 17 nations to agree to fixed tariffs as part of a "common commercial policy" against all outside nations.

A French cabinet statement issued Oct. 29 had declared France's intention to implement the Common Market treaty Jan. 1, 1959 but had reserved a decision on the free-trade-zone plan. The West German government publicly criticized France Nov. 3 for demanding "intolerable" protectionist conditions for its entry into the 17-nation free trade zone. A statement issued in Oslo by 4 Nordic Council nations—Sweden, Denmark, Norway and Iceland (Finland, the 5th Nordic Council member, abstained as a non-member of OEEC)—warned Nov. 13 that a failure to create a free trade zone could bring "far-reaching" European economic warfare.

The 17-nation OEEC met in Paris Dec. 15 in an effort to avert a threatened European trade war between the British-led and French-led factions when the EEC went into effect Jan. 1, 1959. The meeting failed to resolve differences between EEC and non-EEC nations, but it won OEEC agreement to study British and French compromise plans. The meeting had been called to discuss the final report of the OEEC's British-led "Maudling committee" on the creation of a 17-nation free trade zone to prevent the erection of tariff and trade barriers between EEC nations and other European states. The British plan, presented by

Paymaster Gen. Maudling, was rejected by French Foreign Min. Couve de Murville on the ground that EEC commitments had priority over French free trade pledges formerly made in the OEEC. France made clear that it considered major EEC tariff and trade benefits applicable only to EEC states and that the creation of the 6-nation Common Market would necessarily bring discrimination against non-members. Britain warned that the establishment of an exclusive EEC trade area that would impose special tariffs and import quotas on British and other non-EEC goods would divide Europe economically and politically. France was generally supported by other EEC nations, but West German Economics Min. Ludwig Erhard warned France that Europe was "in danger" unless it agreed to ease trade barriers against non-EEC states and compromise with Britain.

(French Premier de Gaulle and West German Chancellor Adenauer had met in Bad Kreuznach, West Germany Nov. 26 and had agreed to oppose the British free trade zone proposal in favor of a looser "multilateral association" of the 6 EEC nations with Britain and other OEEC countries. A de Gaulle-Adenauer communique expressed West German support for French views that the proposed free trade zone would permit non-EEC goods to compete within the EEC without committing the non-member states to adopt EEC provisions for the abolition of trade restrictions and customs barriers.)

A solution of the British-French trade rift was considered to be possible on the basis of these 2 proposals:

(a) An EEC Ministerial Council announcement Dec. 3 that the 10% tariff cut scheduled among the EEC nations Jan. 1 would be extended to all 37 nations of the General Agreement on Tariffs & Trade (GATT). The EEC Ministerial Council said that EEC nations would extend to the 11 other OEEC nations 1/2 of the planned 20% increase in import quotas to be given EEC goods Jan. 1 and would negotiate additional quota increases with outside states on a reciprocal basis.

(b) A British offer, presented to the OEEC Dec. 15 by Sir David Eccles, Board of Trade president, to open British markets to EEC goods in return for increased EEC quotas on British goods. The plan would raise British import quotas to 3% of the national production of any item imported from an EEC nation. The EEC states had agreed to raise import quotas among themselves up to 3% of national production of a specific item in the exporting country.

Benelux Union Strengthened

The premiers and foreign ministers of Belgium, Netherlands and Luxembourg, in the Hague Feb. 3, signed treaties establishing a Benelux Economic Union—already partially operative through prior agreements among the 3 countries. The 50-year Economic Union treaty formalized the abolition of tariffs and restrictions on 97% of Benelux trade. It provided for: (1) free movement of Benelux citizens, goods, services and capital; (2) coordination of national economic, social and financial policies; (3) unification of trade policies to form a Benelux trading unit.

FRENCH SITUATION

France Fights Money & Price Battle

French Premier Felix Gaillard's cabinet won a 253-233 National Assembly vote of confidence Jan. 16 on plans to save 7 billion francs ($16.6 million) on the 1958 budget by paying veterans' pensions in a lump sum at the end of 1958 and delaying war prisoners' payments until 1959. Gaillard demanded the confidence vote to support economic planner Jean Monnet, who had left for the U.S. Jan. 11 to seek (a) the release of $262 million in French credits remaining with the International Monetary Fund, and (b) a delay in the repayment of $110 million worth of postwar loans from the U.S. Export-Import Bank.

The cost of living in the Paris area had risen 10% the past 6 months, France's National Statistical Institute reported Jan. 18.

The French and U.S. governments, the International Monetary Fund (IMF) and the European Payments Union (EPU) announced Jan. 30 in Washington agreements granting France a total of $655,250,000 in aid, of which $525 million was to be made available during 1958. The agreement, negotiated by Jean Monnet of France, U.S. Deputy State Undersecy. (for economic affairs) C. Douglas Dillon and Managing Director Per Jacobsson of the IMF, provided for:

(a) From the U.S.—postponement for up to 5 years of $48 million in annual principal and interest payments on U.S. Export-Import Bank loans to France; delays of up to 3 years of $30 million in installments due each year from France on postwar Lend-Lease settlements; permission for France to purchase with francs $43 million worth of U.S. surplus cotton and $45 million worth of military supplies.

(b) From the IMF—a $131,250,000 standby credit available for French government withdrawals during the next year (to bring French IMF withdrawals to $393,750,000, or 75% of France's original IMF quota).

(c) From the EPU—a special $250 million credit for the settlement of France's monthly European trade deficits.

Finance Min. Pierre Pflimlin reported Apr. 3 that France's balance of payments, favorable during January and February, had a $62 million deficit in March—$57 million to the European Payments Union area, $5 million to the dollar zone.

In a June 27 nationwide radio-TV speech, Premier Charles de Gaulle reported that $234 million, $82 million of it in hoarded gold, had been subscribed to the new national gold loan in a "brilliant indication" of national confidence in his regime. Warning that France was at "the last moment" for the successful launching of an economic redressment, he appealed for the stabilization of current state and private expenditures, wages, prices and profits.

De Gaulle Elected French President

Gen. Charles de Gaulle was elected Dec. 21 to a 7-year term as the first president of France's 5th Republic. He was to relinquish the premiership and succeed Rene Coty as president Jan. 8, 1959.

Final returns Dec. 22 for the indirect presidential election gave de Gaulle 62,395 (78.5%) of 79,414 ballots cast by a special roll of grand electors in France and the French Community. Georges Marrane, Communist, received 10,354 votes and Prof. Albert Chatelet, candidate of the liberal Union of Democratic Forces, 6,722. De Gaulle was supported overwhelmingly in overseas territories of the French Community.

MONETARY DEVELOPMENTS

Franc Devalued

De Gaulle's cabinet announced a 17.55% devaluation of the franc Dec. 27 and made it freely convertible if held by traders or persons resident outside the franc zone. French financial exchanges were closed Dec. 26 to prevent speculation against the franc on news of the devaluation. Currency and exchange controls were maintained on business conducted among Frenchmen or other residents of France and former French areas of North Africa.

(The Moroccan and Tunisian governments refused to follow France into devaluation despite their membership in the franc zone. The Moroccan franc was unpegged from the French franc Dec. 29, and the Tunisian dinar was unpegged Dec. 30. Both currencies were revalued at the rate of 1,000 to 1,175 French francs.)

The de Gaulle cabinet also ordered the abolition of quota restrictions and licensing controls on 90% of France's imports from other European countries. It reversed earlier announcements that France would not be able to keep OEEC commitments to free 75% of its imports (at 1948 levels) from controls by Dec. 18. Controls and quotas on the remaining 10% of France's European imports would be lifted for goods entering from the 5 other EEC states after Jan. 1, 1959. The French government removed import quotas from more than 50% of its imports from the U.S. and Canada Dec. 31. Only 14% of France's U.S. and Canadian imports had been freed from quota restrictions under the Dec. 18 OEEC deadline for relaxing controls.

The exchange value of the franc was fixed in gold at the rate of 493.7 to the U.S. dollar instead of the 420-$1 rate in effect since Aug. 1957. Plans were announced Dec. 27 for the gradual replacement of the current franc with a "heavy franc" valued at 100 old francs. This move, to be accomplished in 1959, would align the franc with more stable European currencies, such as the West German Deutschemark and Swiss franc, having valuations of approximately 20 U.S. cents. It would be divided into 100 centimes, each centime equalling one franc in current use.

De Gaulle appealed to the French people Dec. 28 to accept a "great sacrifice" to aid French efforts "in the great national enterprise of financial and economic recovery." De Gaulle told a nationwide radio-TV audience that France's devaluation of the franc and abolition of protective trade controls would "place the nation on a basis of truth and severity." He predicted that France would "find itself hard-pressed for some time. But the rehabilitation we are aiming at is such that it can make it all worth while." De Gaulle said that taxes would be increased on corporations, persons with high incomes and luxury items. He urged able-bodied war veterans "to renounce their pensions" to aid French recovery. He pledged, however, that low-paid workers, aged pensioners and the unemployed would receive increased aid.

Finance Min. Antoine Pinay disclosed Dec. 29 that the 1959 French budget deficit would be kept within $1.36 billion by the withdrawal of $543 million in subsidies for nationalized industries and the imposition of $626 million in new taxes. The budget, announced Dec. 27, provided for expenditures of $14.6 billion, an increase of $1.1 billion over 1958. Pinay made clear that France's economic reforms would not permit wage rises for any but lowest-paid workers, who were pledged a 4% increase in Feb. 1959. The wage and price policies of the new economic program were attacked bitterly Dec. 29 by the Communist-led General Confederation of Labor, the Socialist Force Ouvriere and the Catholic French Confederation of Christian Workers.

Currency Convertibility Increased

Britain and 9 West European nations Dec. 27 announced plans to restore full external convertibility to their currencies for the first time since World War II. The currency reforms resulted in the abolition of nearly all European exchange controls and were considered to mark a victory for liberal economic policies advocated by Britain and West Germany.

The European financial reform, made effective Dec. 29, was planned in 10 days of joint talks in Paris. It was worked out after Britain and France had split over proposals for a 17-nation European free trade zone to parãllel the 6-nation EEC. It was accompanied by French action to devalue the franc and end quotas on most of France's European imports.

The 10 nations (Britain, France, West Germany, Belgium, Luxembourg, Italy, the Netherlands, Sweden, Norway, Switzerland) abolished the European Payments Union (EPU) and replaced it with the European Monetary Agreement (EMA)—set up by the Organization for European Economic Cooperation (OEEC) in Aug. 1955 but never put into operation. The EPU, created in 1950 to settle European trade balances, provided for 75% payment and 25% automatic credit for the settlement of trade debts. The EMA required payment in full but would (1) permit bilateral trade balancing and (2) create a European Fund with capital of $600 million to provide short-term credit for nations with unfavorable trade balances.

The resumption of free exchange in Europe was welcomed by the U.S. State Department Dec. 27 as "further evidence of the strengthened economic position of Western Europe." It was accompanied by these financial developments in France, Britain and West Germany: The British Treasury announced Dec. 27 that, as "part of a coordinated European move," pounds held by non-residents of the sterling area would be freely convertible into other currencies, including dollars, effective Dec. 29. Strict currency and financial controls remained in effect for British subjects and all other residents of the sterling area (the Commonwealth nations, British-protected Persian Gulf states, Burma, Jordan, Iceland, Iraq, Libya, Ireland). The measure freed British pounds from controls for the first time since 1947, when an attempt to restore sterling convertibility had been ended after 5 weeks due to the drain on British gold and dollar reserves.

The restoration of the pound's convertibility ended differing exchange rates in effect for transferable account sterling (used in commercial transactions outside the sterling and dollar areas) and official sterling (used for business between the dollar and sterling areas). Both types of pounds were merged into a single sterling for "external accounts" convertible at official rates ($2.78-$2.82 to the pound), effective Dec. 29.

West German Deutschemarks (DM) held by foreign businessmen and traders were made freely convertible Dec. 29 into dollars or other currencies at the official rate of 4.17-4.23 DM to the U.S. dollar. The West German Central Bank had announced Dec. 28 that a $60 million credit had been made available to the Bank of France to bolster the franc during its devaluation and appearance as a convertible currency.

1959

Forces dividing Britain from the EEC gained strength slowly but steadily during 1959. The British economy continued to show improvement while French balance-of-payments and domestic austerity problems persisted. By the end of the year, the groundwork had been laid for the establishment of the European Free Trade Association (EFTA), keyed to Britain, as a rival to the European Economic Community (EEC). North American interest in the growing EEC-EFTA rivalry increased as U.S. and Canadian cooperation with and participation in the Organization for European Economic Cooperation (OEEC) increased.

BRITISH ECONOMIC DEVELOPMENTS

International Finance

The British Treasury announced Feb. 3 that British monetary reserves had risen by £15 million in January to a level of £1.111 billion. The Treasury said Feb. 16 that it had been unnecessary to draw on the $250 million available to it from the Export-Import Bank since Feb. 1957. The announcement attributed this favorable situation to "the strengthening in the international position of the pound sterling which has taken place since the line of credit was established in 1957 and later renewed in 1958."

The repayment of $200 million of $561 million drawn from the International Monetary Fund (IMF) in Dec. 1956 was announced Mar. 19 by Chancellor of the Exchequer Heathcoat Amory. Heathcoat Amory announced May 15 that Britain would meet its new $1.95 billion quota in the IMF for May. He said that Britain would pay $162.5 million in gold into IMF accounts and accept $487.5 million worth of interest-free IMF notes.

A $250 million U.S. Export - Import Bank loan due Apr. 1965 was repaid by Britain Oct. 29 with $5.5 million in accrued interest. Heathcoat Amory told Parliament the repayment had been made "in view of the more favorable external financial position of the [UK]." The loan was part of a $500 million U.S. credit negotiated by Britain during the 1956-7 Suez crisis, when it expected to have to make substantial dollar purchases of U.S. oil to offset the loss of Middle Eastern petroleum. Britain retained the right to draw on the unused portion of the credit if future events required it.

The Treasury announced Oct. 2 that British gold and convertible currency reserves had risen by £13 million ($36,400,000) in September to £1.173 billion ($3.284 billion), the highest level since 1951. The situation, however, changed by the end of the year. British gold and foreign currency reserves dropped by £85 million ($238 million) in Dec. 1959 to £977 million ($2.735 billion) at the end of 1959, the Treasury reported Jan. 5, 1960. Net reserve loss during 1959: £119 million ($333,200,000). Total gold and dollar reserves declined from £1.096 billion Jan. 1, 1959 to £997 million Dec. 31. This decline was due in large part to the £58 million ($162.5 million) gold payment to the IMF in May, a £91 million repayment of dollars (plus $5.5 million in interest) to the U.S. Export-Import Bank in late October and a £66 million repayment of dollars Dec. 31 to the U.S. and Canada on past loans.

During 1959 British exports reached a record $9,312,800,000, an increase of 5% over 1958 and 1% over 1957, the previous peak year, according to Board of Trade statistics. Imports during 1959 totaled $11,180,400,000.

One dim spot on the record was unemployment, which remained above 2%. Labor Min. Ian MacLeod reported Feb. 10 that unemployment had risen during January to 620,000, or 2.8% of the working population. The total included 115,000 unemployed (5.4% of the labor force) in Scotland and 45,700 (9%) in Northern Ireland.

1960 Budget

A £5.233 billion ($14.624 billion) fiscal 1960 budget presented to Parliament Apr. 7 by Chancellor of the Exchequer Heathcoat Amory contained tax reductions and other concessions expected to total $1 billion. Revenues were estimated at £5.325 billion ($14.91 billion), leaving an estimated surplus of £102 million ($285.6 million). Defense expenditures were budgeted at £1,514,135,000 ($4,239,578,000), an increase of £49 million, and National Health Services at £534 million ($1.495 billion), an increase of £34.4 million. Heavy expected deficits in the nationalized industries' and ministry budgets, however, were expected to result in an overall budget deficit of £721 million ($2.019 billion).

The new budget, designed to encourage economic expansion, provided substantial reductions in income taxes (9d to 7s 9d on the pound for standard rates, 7d on lower rates) and in purchase taxes (from 60%, 30% and 15% on various categories of goods to 50%, 25% and 12.5% on the same goods). The reductions were expected to lower income tax revenues by £192 million ($537 million) and purchase tax revenues by £59 million ($165.2 million) for the remainder of 1959. The budget also provided £71 million ($198 million) for the first annual repayment of "postwar credit" taxes collected with income tax during World War II on the promise of repayment after the war.

A White Paper on national income and expenditures reported Mar. 31, 1960, that Britain's gross national product had risen by £682 million ($1.9 billion) during 1959 to £20.831 billion ($58.327 billion). Personal income rose by 4.5% in 1959 to £19.723 billion ($55.224 billion), with nearly 1/4 of the increase going into personal savings. Increases in personal expenditures during 1959 ranged from 3% for food and 4% for housing and clothing to 17% for durable goods.

Trade & Travel Restrictions Eased

Quota restrictions on imports from the dollar area were ordered eased or abolished May 28 by the British Board of Trade. The restrictions, to be ended in stages June 8 and Jan. 1, 1960, had been applied principally to consumer imports from the U.S. and Canada. The relaxation would permit more equal competition between imports from the dollar area and Western Europe but would retain current tariffs on all such goods. American Amb.-to-Britain John Hay Whitney told the

Manchester City Council May 29 that the British measure would "strengthen the hands" of those American leaders who were "pressing for an even more liberal U.S. trade policy."

Chancellor of the Exchequer Amory announced Nov. 3 that licensing and quota restrictions on imports from most countries, including the U.S., would be eased or abolished. Details of the program, presented to Parliament Nov. 4 by Board of Trade Chairman Reginald Maudling, provided for abolition Nov. 9 of the entire system of import controls imposed in Britain since 1939. Only 25 items, mostly textiles, dyes, foodstuffs, coal, arms, aircraft and radioactive substances, remained subject to control. The vast majority of imports from all nations except Japan, the Soviet bloc and Communist China were freed from restriction. Imports of U.S. cars, industrial products, textiles and other dollar-zone goods were freed from control.

The £100 ($280) annual limit on foreign currency used for travel and purchases abroad by Britons had been lifted by the Treasury Oct. 19 (effective Nov. 1). This restriction had been imposed Oct. 1, 1945 at £100 per year, reduced gradually to the level of zero Sept. 1947, then raised slowly to £100 by June 1957. New regulations permitted travellers to buy up to £250 ($700) worth of foreign currency from local banks, additional sums from the Bank of England.

Elections

The Labor Party pledged Oct. 1 that if it were voted into power in the general elections Oct. 8, it would abolish purchase taxes on clothes, furniture and other household goods. The Laborite promise was denounced the same day, by Prime Min. Macmillan and by Frank Byers, Liberal Party campaign chairman, as an election bribe. And the Conservatives increased their majority at Labor's expense when the elections took place.

In the elections, 27,862,708 (79%) of an estimated electorate of 34 million voted. The Conservatives gained 28 former Labor seats and one Liberal seat and lost 6 seats. Labor gained 5 seats but lost 28. Liberals won one seat and lost one but nearly doubled their popular vote total from the 722,395 of 1955. Most Liberal gains appeared to be at Labor expense. Macmillan, in a radio-TV address, appealed to Britons Oct. 9 to mend their "fundamental unity" and support his efforts to bring about a lessening of East-West tensions. He said the election results had shown that "the class war is obsolete" as a deciding factor in British politics. Macmillan was reelected by his Bromley constituency with a plurality of 15,452, the greatest of his career.

Hugh Gaitskell, Labor Party leader, said the election results were neither a "landslide" for the Conservatives nor a "disaster" for Labor but a "setback" caused by a shift to the Conservatives of only 3 of every 200 votes cast in the 1955 election.

In his post-election shifts in the cabinet, Macmillan appointed ex-Paymaster Gen. Reginald Maudling to replace Sir David Eccles as Board of Trade chairman.

EUROPEAN ECONOMIC INTEGRATION

EEC & Euratom Come into Being

The 6-nation European Economic Community and Atomic Energy Community treaties became effective Jan. 1. The pacts were designed to weld West Germany, France, Italy, Belgium, Luxembourg and the Netherlands into a single trade unit with a commonly operated nuclear power system.

Economic measures put into effect by the 6 nations Jan. 1 under the Common Market treaty: (1) a 10% reduction in tariffs on goods from all Common Market countries, Organization for European Economic Cooperation (OEEC) members and General Agreement on Tariffs & Trade (GATT) signatories; (2) a mutual increase of 20% in import quotas on Common Market goods, with minimal quotas to be set at 3% of national production of any item in the importing country; (3) a 20% increase in import quotas on industrial goods from OEEC nations; (4) a 10% tariff reduction and 20% quota increase on Common Market agricultural products with importing nations permitted to fix minimum prices to prevent dumping.

The establishment of Common Market provisions followed the Dec. 29, 1958 abolition of external currency controls by the 6 Common Market countries and Britain, Norway, Sweden and Switzerland. It also came after the failure of efforts to end a threatened trade rift between members of the Common Market and the 17-nation OEEC.

The EEC Ministerial Council, meeting in Strasbourg, announced Nov. 24 that import quota liberalizations planned for EEC states Jan. 1, 1960 would be extended to other Western nations. All import quotas were to be enlarged by at least 10%, most by 20%, and a few, on products virtually barred, by 1/3 to levels equal to at least 4% of domestic production of each item in the importing country. The council reached no decision on proposals for extension to non-EEC nations of tariff cuts due July 1, 1960 or on French suggestions made Nov. 16 for doubling the 10% 1960 tariff reductions.

A $29,540,000 budget for EEC and Euratom expenditures in 1959 had been approved May 6 by the Ministerial Council at a meeting in Brussels. Approximately $20 million was for EEC operations, the remainder for Euratom.

The EEC Council voted Nov. 24 to reelect for 2-year terms EEC Pres. Walter Hallstein (West Germany) and Pres. Etienne Hirsch (France) of Euratom. (Hallstein, Hirsch and Pres. Paul Finet of the European Coal & Steel Community [ECSC] High Authority had met with Pres. Eisenhower June 10 during a 3-day visit to the U.S. They had conferred with then-Acting State Secy. C. Douglas Dillon June 9 on proposals for establishing a joint EEC-Euratom-ECSC embassy in Washington.)

Britain & the European Communities

The British government and Euratom in London Feb. 4 signed an agreement on cooperation in the development of peaceful use of atomic energy. Under this pact, research and technical information would be exchanged, licensing would be increased, and nuclear fuels would be shared and processed jointly. Britain and 5 other OEEC members outside the EEC (Austria, Denmark, Norway, Sweden and Switzerland) agreed with Euratom Feb. 12 to develop jointly an experimental reactor in England at Winfrith Heath (Dorset).

West German Chancellor Konrad Adenauer conferred in London and at Chequers with Prime Min. Harold Macmillan Nov. 17-19, and West German Foreign Min. von Brentano met with British Foreign Secy. Selwyn Lloyd Nov. 18-19. At a London news conference Nov. 19, Adenauer announced that agreement had been reached for the establishment of a "working group" to carry out liaison between the projected European free trade association and the EEC and to insure against "economic warfare in Europe."

Lloyd had met with French Pres. de Gaulle, Premier Rene Debre and Foreign Min. Couve de Murville Nov. 11-12 and had achieved accords on (1) British recognition of the importance of the EEC as a guarantee of West German integration within a European system and (2) French pledges to work for lowered Common Market trade barriers to minimize European discrimination against goods of Britain and other non-member states as well as on issues of European defense.

Further British-EEC cooperation was disclosed Nov. 30 with the announcement of British Aviation Min. Duncan Sandys of a British-EEC agreement on high altitude (20,000 feet and higher) air traffic controls.

European Free Trade Association (EFTA) Organized

The apparent cooperation and progress between Great Britain and the EEC seemed ruptured by Britain's action in joining in the organization of a trade group rivalling the EEC. A convention establishing a European Free Trade Association (EFTA) was initialled in Stockholm Nov. 20 by ministers of Britain, Austria, Denmark, Norway, Portugal, Sweden and Switzerland.

A communique issued by the EFTA founders at the end of their Nov. 19-20 meeting expressed hopes that the 7-nation accord would be temporary and "a step toward an agreement" to extend the trade association to the 11 other OEEC (Organization for European Economic Cooperation) states. It called on the 6 EEC nations to agree to renew free-trade-zone negotiations within the OEEC. It welcomed a Finnish request for talks on associate EFTA membership although such talks would be delayed until the signing of the 1960 Soviet-Finnish trade pact.

Finland had previously expressed interest in the EFTA but pressures from the Soviet Union—as expressed in an article in the July 19 *Pravda*—were sufficient to cause Finland not to act positively at that time.

Major EFTA pact provisions:

Tariffs—A 20% reduction of tariffs on industrial goods traded among EFTA states was to take place July 1, 1960. (Agricultural products were the subject of a convention annex containing special provisions for the enlargement of farm trade to benefit EFTA member states whose economies depended on such exports.) 8 further reductions of 10% each were to achieve elimination of such tariffs by Jan. 1970. No common EFTA tariff was to be applied to goods from non-member states, which would remain subject to tariffs fixed individually by each EFTA state. No discriminatory increase of tariffs on goods from nonmembers was planned.

Quotas—Quantitative restrictions on imports from EFTA states were to be reduced progressively to insure the ending of quotas by Jan. 1970. Quotas for reasonable imports from each member state were to be fixed by each member by July 1, 1960 and were to be increased by at least 20% each year until such curbs disappeared.

Enforcement—A council in which each member state exercised one vote was established to oversee enforcement of the convention and carry on negotiations with the EEC, OEEC, General Agreement on Tariffs & Trade (GATT) and other economic groups. The council was to decide all EFTA disputes and insure that competitive benefits of tariffs and quota reductions were not nullified by hidden restrictive measures.

Negotiations to form EFTA had begun after the collapse of British-led efforts to create a European free trade zone for industrial goods that would include all 18 member states of the Organization for European Economic Cooperation, including the 6 EEC nations. (The original British plan for a 17-nation European free trade zone had been put forward before Spain became the 18th OEEC state.)

The Macmillan government, in a White Paper issued Jan. 30, had summarized the British position and stressed Britain's concern with Commonwealth preferences as they affected imports and Britain's right to determine appropriate tariffs thereon. At the Brussels meeting Mar. 16, the EEC rejected this paper and (Mar. 18) issued its reply, the Hallstein Report, in which the incompatibility between the two groups was made clear.

The 7 nations which were to become the EFTA met Mar. 17-18 in Saltsjoebaden, Sweden, a resort near Stockholm, and began negotiations on their own trade area association. The remaining 4 OEEC nations (Greece, Iceland, Ireland, and Turkey), considered economically less developed, did not participate actively.

The decision to negotiate an EFTA convention was made July 19-21 in Saltsjoebaden. At an earlier conference, "outer 7" economic experts, meeting June 1-13 in Saltsjoebaden, had indorsed the EFTA program as feasible. The plan had been accepted by Premiers H. C. Hansen of Denmark, Einar Gerhardsen of Norway and Tage Erlander of Sweden in a meeting July 11-12 in Kungalv, Sweden.

(The Nordic Council—Sweden, Norway, Denmark, Finland, Iceland—at a meeting Nov. 1-7 in Stockholm, agreed to abandon plans for a Scandinavian common market in favor of participation in the EFTA.)

British Prime Min. Macmillan, in a London address Nov. 16, asserted that Britain's economic policies were aimed toward creating a "closer economic association in all Europe." Warning of the dangers of economic warfare among rival Western European trading blocs, Macmillan insisted, however, that Britain had taken "the most practical step" open to it by leading in forming the EFTA.

The EFTA grouped 7 nations with 90 million inhabitants in a trade association less rigid in scope than the EEC, with a population of 170 million. Unlike the EEC, the EFTA envisaged no steps toward political integration of member states, a major reason for British refusal to participate in the EEC. Although the EFTA nations had only 1/2 the population of the EEC states, their combined national incomes were 2/3 and their combined imports and exports 3/4 of the combined totals for the 6 EEC nations.

Reaction to this meeting was swift. The EEC Council, meeting in Strasbourg Nov. 24, announced that a "contact committee" would be created to begin negotiations with the rival EFTA on preventing a permanent economic division of Western Europe. The agreement to seek EEC-EFTA negotiations reportedly was the work of Netherlands Foreign Min. Joseph M. A. H. Luns, who had met with British Foreign Secy. Lloyd in London Nov. 20 to discuss plans for mutual extension of EEC and EFTA tariff cuts to both groups. Ministerial rank economic officials of 35 GATT nations, meeting in Tokyo Oct. 27-29, supported U.S. demands for trade liberalization and pledged "rapid progress . . . in the elimination of all quantitative restrictions on imports by countries no longer experiencing balance-of-payments difficulties." A GATT ministerial communique also urged Oct. 29: (1) expediting of plans for 1960-1 tariff reductions, (2) elimination of agricultural subsidies and import quotas and (3) steps to prevent the use of EEC and EFTA membership for trade discrimination against other nations.

4-Power Summit Conference

Recognition of the significance of EFTA in the overall picture of European economic development was taken at the Paris meeting of Pres. Eisenhower, Prime Min. Macmillan, Pres. de Gaulle and Chancellor Adenauer. A separate communique on economic matters, issued Dec. 21 by the 4 Western leaders, announced that representatives of the U.S., Canada and some member states of the EEC and EFTA would meet in Paris Jan. 13, 1960 for "informal" talks on Western trade relations and coordinated Western aid to less-developed nations. The communique said:

"The heads of state and government have discussed the important changes that have taken place in the international economic situation. Recognizing the great economic progress of Western Europe, they have agreed that virtually all of the industrialized part of the free world is now in a position to devote its energies in increased measure to new and important tasks of cooperative endeavor with the object of: (1) furthering the development of the less developed countries; and (2) pursuing trade policies directed to the sound use of economic resources and the maintenance of harmonious international relations, thus contributing to growth and stability in the world economy and to a general improvement in the standard of living.

"In their view, these cooperative principles should also govern the discussions on commercial problems arising from the existence of European economic regional organizations, which are or will be constituted within the framework of GATT, such as the European Economic Community and the European Free Trade Association. Their relations both with other countries and with each other should be discussed in this spirit.

"The heads of state and government, recognizing that the method of furthering these principles requires intensive study, have agreed to call an informal meeting to be held in Paris in the near future. They suggest that the members and participants of the executive committee of the OEEC and the governments whose nationals are members of the Steering Board for Trade of the OEEC should be represented at this meeting.

"It is proposed that an objective of such a group should be to consider the need for and methods of continuing consultations dealing with the above-mentioned problems."

The economic talks, to be held by the 12 nations represented on the Executive Committee of the Organization for European Economic Cooperation (OEEC), would constitute the first direct U.S. and Canadian participation in European trade negotiations.

FRENCH SITUATION

Economic Picture Worsens

Price decrees issued under plans for the new French austerity budget raised railway fares Jan. 5, postage Jan. 6 and prices of tobacco, meat, gasoline, gas and electricity Jan. 15. Most increases ranged from 15% to 20%. The Federal Union of Association of War Veterans & Victims, a 2.5 million-member group, protested publicly in Paris Jan. 11 against budget provisions ending token $1.20-to-$25 annual pensions for able-bodied veterans under 65.

Paris dispatches reported Apr. 12 that French foreign credits exceeded debts for the first time in 10 years. French credits were reported to total $1.4 billion ($590 million of it in gold held by the Bank of France, the rest in French holdings in the Exchange Stabilization Fund). But the Finance Ministry disclosed May 29 that France's foreign debt currently totalled $3 billion. Leading French creditors were the International Monetary Fund (IMF) ($266 million due in 1960), the defunct European Payments Union (EPU) ($233 million due in 1959-60), the U.S. government ($30 million due in 1959-60) and the U.S. Export-Import Bank ($143 million in 1960). Officials said that France would repay $267 million in foreign debts in 1959 and $559 million in 1960.

The de Gaulle government faced the problem of restoring confidence in the economy in the face of the disquieting reports.

Finance Min. Antoine Pinay told the National Assembly June 23 that the French economy had showed "incontestable signs of recovery" under the economic program begun by de Gaulle but that continued austerity and wage stability were needed to repay pressing foreign debts and to avoid "compromis[ing] everything irreparably."

Territorial Community Established

Premiers of 7 French West African states agreed June 6 to form a customs union that would end trade barriers, result in a sharing of customs revenues among Senegal, French Sudan, Ivory Coast, Mauritania, Niger, Volta and Dahomey. The proposal, advanced by Ivory Coast Premier Felix Houphouet-Boigny, had been opposed by Pres. Sekou Toure of Guinea. The first French Community Senate was installed by de Gaulle July 15 in Paris. The inauguration of the Senate, composed of 155 members from metropolitan France and 129 from the 12 French African republics, French overseas departments and territories and Algeria and the Sahara, completed the formation of the basic institutions of the French Community. The new Senate, limited to a consultative role, could be summoned and recessed only by the president.

The Senate voted July 17 to elect as its president Gaston Monnerville, 61, French Guiana Negro and French Senate president since 1947.

Import Quotas Eased

French Quota restrictions were ended Nov. 5 on a wide variety of goods imported from the U.S., Canada and OEEC countries. Products freed from quantity import restrictions included tools, textiles, photographic equipment, agricultural machinery, commercial refrigerators and clothing. The measure eliminated more than 1/4 of the 800 products subject to import limitations but did not lower French customs duties, levied at up to 60% of the value of goods affected. It was ordered under a European trade liberalization program formulated by the OEEC in 1958 but delayed in the case of France due to the French foreign trade deficit.

Finance Min. Antoine Pinay, presenting a $13 billion 1960 French budget to the National Assembly Nov. 6, pledged that France would end all special restrictions on U. S. trade in "the shortest possible time" and all quota limitations on European and U.S. imports within 2 years. Pinay asserted that French gold and dollar reserves had grown from $600 million in 1957 to $1.911 billion Oct. 31, due, in part, to a favorable trade balance. He said the increased liberalization of trade would be "the best of stimulants and... most effective of disciplines" for the French economy.

1960

In 1960 the principal developments concerned with European economic integration centered around the formal emergence of EFTA (European Free Trade Association) as a rival to the EEC (European Economic Community), the reaction of the EEC to this new group, and the growing involvment of the U.S. in this confrontation. Early signs of growing instability in the British economy resulted in several changes in governmental economic policy. The French economy, under the austerity program instituted by the de Gaulle government, seemed to be stabilizing.

BRITISH ECONOMIC DEVELOPMENTS

Domestic Economic Policy

The British bank rate was increased from 4% to 5% Jan. 21 in what the Treasury described as a precautionary move against inflationary tendencies. The bank rate, charged by the central Bank of England on money borrowed from it by member banks, had been 4% since Nov. 1958.

The Bank of England ended its market support of British government bonds Feb. 24 in an effort to discourage huge sales of the bonds by commercial banks to permit increased credit advances.

A "standstill" budget for fiscal 1961 was presented to Parliament Apr. 4 by Chancellor of the Exchequer Derick Heathcoat Amory. The new budget, described by Amory as designed to reduce spending and to exert a "moderating influence on the rate of [Britain's economic] expansion," estimated expenditures at £5.676 billion ($15,893 billion), revenues at £5.958 billion ($16.682 billion) and the deficit at £331 million ($926,800,000). It provided for increases in corporate profits taxes (from 10% to 12.5%) and tobacco taxes and only one major tax decrease (through raised tax allowances for dependent relatives).

Heathcoat Amory told Parliament that fiscal 1960 expenditures had totalled £5.244 billion ($14,683 billion) and revenues £5.63 billion ($15.764 billion). The apparent surplus of £386 million ($1.09 billion) in the operating budget was transformed into a £314 million ($879,200,000) deficit by loans to nationalized industries and local governments.

Credit was tightened further when measures to restrict British installment buying (hire-purchase) and bank credit were invoked Apr. 28 by Heathcoat Amory to halt an inflationary trend and reverse the foreign trade deficit. The restrictions, first to be imposed since British credit and bank curbs were ended in July and October 1958, included (a) requirements of 10% and 20% down payments and a complete payment within 2 years for automobiles, appliances and other goods previously available on unrestricted installment terms, and (b) the forced deposit with the Bank of England of amounts equal to 1% of the gross deposits held by London clearing banks and 1/2% of the gross deposits held by Scottish clearing banks. Affected banks, required to make the special deposits by June 15, held gross deposits totalling over £7 billion ($19.6 billion).

British consumer credit was reported to have risen by Mar. 1 to £889 million ($2.489 billion), an increase of £293 million ($820,400,000) over Mar. 1, 1959. Bank loans were said to have risen by £99,200,000 ($277,600,000) from Mar. 15 to Apr. 15 and by more than $3 billion to a total of more than $9 billion since July 1958. The foreign trade gap totalled $165,700,000 in February and $200.5 million in March.

The British bank rate was again raised—from 5% to 6%—and the special deposits required by the Bank of England from London and Scottish clearing banks were doubled June 23. Amory, defending the move against attacks by Laborite economic spokesman Harold Wilson, said the economy was "in a very healthy state" and would be maintained so by the regulations. The increase was only temporary; the rate was reduced to 5.5% Oct. 27 and to 5% Dec. 8. The latter decrease was described as an attempt to slow the influx of dollar capital to Britain by narrowing the difference between U.S. interest rates and the higher British rates.

Gold & the Balance of Payments

U. S. gold stocks had been falling for more than a year, and the decline brought about more international financial instability. American gold reserves, down to less than $19 billion for the first time since May 15, 1940, declined to $18,990,202,349.91 Sept. 7. U. S. gold reserves had dropped by more than $1 billion in 1959 and by $466 million since the end of 1959. Subsequently, heavy demand for British gold by private buyers and investors, including many Swiss bankers, caused the price of gold on the London free market to rise sharply (for the first time since it reopened in Mar. 1954) to $35.255 an ounce Oct. 17 and a peak of $40.60 Oct. 20. Toronto, Zurich, Paris and Frankfurt free market prices rose comparably.

The U. S. Treasury Department announced Oct. 20 that, despite the European price rise, it would continue to sell gold to foreign governments and central banks for "legitimate monetary purposes" at its base price of $35 an ounce (plus handling costs of 8.75¢), which had been in effect since Jan. 1934. It denied European rumors of a U.S. intent to devalue the U.S. dollar. Following the announcement, London's gold prices dropped to $36.40 an ounce Oct. 21, rose to about $38 Oct. 24 and closed at $35.71 Oct. 27. The U.S. Treasury Department warned international speculators Oct. 27 that it might underwrite British government attempts to prevent future gold price increases.

This increase in gold demand was reflected in British balance of payments and gold and dollar reserve figures. Reserves continued their 1959 downward trend in Jan. when they fell by £18 million ($50,400,000), to £959 million ($2,685,200,000), the Treasury reported Feb. 2. £12 million of the decline was due to payments on IMF and EPU debts. This trend continued during the year. The Treasury announced Sept. 23 that Britain had suffered a foreign payments deficit estimated at £9 million ($25,200,000) during 1960's 2d quarter. This compared with a surplus of £44 million ($123,200,000) in the first quarter and £96 million ($268 million) in the 2d quarter of 1959. Britain's trade deficit for October totalled $306,880,000, the highest monthly deficit in 1960, the Board of Trade reported Nov. 14.

BRITAIN, THE EEC & EFTA

European Free Trade Association (EFTA) Established

A convention (the Treaty of Stockholm) establishing the European Free Trade Association (EFTA) was signed by cabinet ministers of Austria, Britain, Denmark, Norway, Portugal, Sweden and Switzerland in ceremonies held in each nation's capital Dec. 29, 1959-Jan. 4. The pact, forming a trade association among the "outer 7" European countries not members of the 6-nation European Economic Community (France, West Germany, Italy, Belgium, Netherlands, Luxembourg), was to become effective on Parliamentary ratification by member states. Initial tariff reductions among EFTA states were to take effect July 1.

The ratification of the Treaty of Stockholm was completed within the first 4 months of the year. Denmark ratified the treaty by a 98-6 vote (with 32 abstentions, primarily Communist) Mar. 1; Great Britain acted Mar. 22, Norway (one opposing Communist vote) Mar. 22, Switzerland (3 opposing Communist votes) Mar. 23, Austria (one opposing right-wing vote) Mar. 23, Sweden (only Communist opposition) Mar. 30 and Portugal (unanimously) Apr. 22. The deposit of all ratification instruments in Stockholm May 3 marked the formal creation of the EFTA.

(Attached to the EFTA convention was a protocol applying the EFTA convention to Liechtenstein so long as that nation remained in a customs union with Switzerland and so long as Switzerland remained in the EFTA. Switzerland would represent Liechtenstein in EFTA affairs.)

The first EFTA Ministerial Council meeting was held in Lisbon May 19-20. At this meeting the Council urged cooperation between the EFTA and EEC to "make it possible to settle, in the common interest, the economic problems" of the separate European trade groups. The 2d meeting was held in Berne Oct. 11-12, and the Council reviewed the developments in trade liberalization.

Western Powers Form OECD

In January, 20 Atlantic nations took steps resulting in the creation of a new economic grouping. A 13-nation Special Economic Committee consisting of the U.S., Canada and 11 West European nations agreed at a Paris meeting Jan. 12-13 to improve Western economic cooperation and aid to underdeveloped nations by:

(1) Appointing a committee of 3 or 4 "wise men" to study and report in April on how the Organization for European Economic Cooperation (OEEC) could be improved or replaced to cope with enlarged trade and aid requirements. The U.S. and Canada would assume full membership with the current 18 OEEC members in the resulting body.

(2) Having trade problems created by the division of Western Europe into 2 trade groups (the EEC and EFTA) considered at a Paris meeting to be opened Jan. 14 by the 18 OEEC nations, the U.S. and Canada in consultation with the Common Market commission and the secretary general of the General Agreement on Tariffs & Trade.

(3) Organizing a committee of 8 "creditor" or "capital-exporting" nations to consult and coordinate with countries anywhere in the world on extending aid to underdeveloped nations. Committee members: the U. S., Canada, Britain, West Germany, France, Italy, Belgium and Portugal.

The proposals for revamping the OEEC and for the "wise men" and aid committees had been recommended to the Special Economic Committee by U.S. State Undersecy. C. Douglas Dillon Jan. 12. The Jan. 12-13 meeting was held under the chairmanship of Dutch Foreign Min. Joseph M. A. H. Luns (elected Jan. 12) and was attended by representatives of the U.S. and Canada and of these OEEC nations: Britain, Denmark, Sweden, Switzerland, Portugal, France, West Germany, Italy, Holland, Belgium and Greece.

The U.S., Canada and 18 OEEC states then agreed Jan. 14 to begin work on creating a new 20-nation trade group of Atlantic nations. Proposals for the new trade bloc had been drawn up at a meeting of the 13-nation Special Economic Committee in Paris Jan. 13-14 and were accepted by the 20 countries later Jan. 14 in an OEEC Council of Ministers session. The new organization, to be a transformed OEEC with full U.S. and Canadian participation, would coordinate Atlantic nations' economic aid programs and would be known as the Organization for Economic Cooperation & Development (OECD). It would link the rival 6 Common Market and outer 7 EFTA nations. It would create additional economic ties between North America and Europe and prevent discrimination against dollar trade by the European groups. Full membership of the OECD consisted of the 6 EEC members (Belgium, France, the Netherlands, Luxembourg, Italy and West Germany), the 7 EFTA members (Austria, Britain, Denmark, Norway, Portugal, Sweden and Switzerland), the 5 other OEEC members (Greece, Iceland, Ireland, Turkey and Spain), Canada and the U.S.

Macmillan & de Gaulle Confer, U.S. Consulted

British Prime Min. Macmillan flew to Paris Mar. 12 for 2 days of private talks with French Pres. de Gaulle at de Gaulle's Presidential estate in Rambouillet, near Paris. The meetings centered on the scheduled East-West summit conference and on British-French trade rivalry. Macmillan, who was accompanied by his wife, returned to London Mar. 13.

Macmillan flew to the U.S. Mar. 26, accompanied by Asst. Foreign Office Undersecy. Con D. W. O'Neill, Cabinet Secy. Sir Norman Brook and Sir William Penney of the British Atomic Energy Authority. He met Mar. 28 with U.S. State Secy. Christian Herter and State Undersecy. Dillon at the State Department to discuss the U.S.' position in the EEC-EFTA situation Mar. 28 before flying to Camp David later that day in Pres. Eisenhower's helicopter. Herter, Dillon, Brook, O'Neill, and British Amb.-to-U.S. Sir Harold Caccia were major participants in the Camp David talks. Macmillan flew back to London Mar. 30 after warning Pres. Eisenhower, Herter and Dillon that tariff barriers soon to be erected by the EEC and EFTA risked dividing Western Europe politically as well as economically.

Washington sources reported Mar. 30 that Macmillan had strongly criticized the U.S.' support of the EEC against the British-led EFTA. He was said to have recalled Britain's traditional role in opposing the European hegemony of Napoleon and Hitler and to have implied that Britain would act again to prevent Europe's economic integration and domination by France and West Germany. Macmillan was said to have referred to the alleged danger of a revival of German Nazism and to have threatened to reduce the British contribution to the NATO garrison in West Germany unless the EEC agreed to lower tariffs for non-member, as well as member, states. Macmillan's reported remarks were denied by the British Foreign Office, which said that he had only stressed "the vital British interest in the fundamental unity of Europe and emphasized the dangers of a grave economic split reaching proportions which would inevitably threaten the political unity of Europe, too." Macmillan, in Parliament Apr. 1, denied charges by ex-Chancellor of the Exchequer Peter Thornycroft that there had been a "calculated leak" of his U.S. conversations as a warning to the EEC nations.

De Gaulle flew to London Apr. 5 for a 3-day state visit at the invitation of Queen Elizabeth II. This was his first visit to Britain since his return to France June 14, 1944 with the Allied armies.

At the state banquet for de Gaulle Apr. 5, Queen Elizabeth said: "Geography in the past has made this country rather aloof from the mainland of Europe. Although we are part of Europe, we have perhaps regarded the Channel which separates us from the Continent 'as a moat defensive to a house.' But times have changed. The moat is no longer so effective a physical barrier. We must still, however, beware that it is not a psychological obstacle to real understanding between France and Britain, between Britain and the other countries of Western Europe. The need for unity is great, the time is ripe, and if there is the will, as I believe there is, we can achieve much. And I do not think of Europe alone. We are both joined to Canada and the United States by ties of history, culture and language, as well as of sentiment. Therefore, in strengthening our unity, we strengthen also the links between Europe and America."

In replying, de Gaulle alluded to the potential trade rift between the British-led EFTA and the French-West German EEC. He said:

"Doubtless, certain differences may result from the largely continental character of France's economy and from the nature of yours, which is based essentially on overseas exchanges. But, on the whole, we feel ourselves closely linked by an equal awareness of our duties as powerful and vigorous nations, by a common experience of our world, of its anxieties and its hopes, by a similar attachment to civic liberty and political democracy, and finally to the spiritual, moral, and social values of our civilization. Thus it is, side by side, with the same allies, with the same preoccupations and the same intentions, that France and Great Britain intend to deal with the arduous problems which confront the world. To work for the great and necessary relaxation of international tension, to seek the means of bringing about the limitation and control of armaments, to restore the peace and balance of Europe, to help the parallel development of the Commonwealth and of the Community, to promote the well-being and progress of the peoples which have not yet overcome poverty, but also to prepare ourselves, in the area covered by the Atlantic Alliance and in other areas of the globe, for the grave contingencies which one day might arise—in all this we are together and we are in agreement."

In a May 31 TV address in France, however, de Gaulle asserted that within the framework of proposed East-West cooperation, France intended to remain "ready to defend herself." He said: "She shall remain an integral part of the Atlantic alliance"; "she too must acquire a nuclear armament"; "she must be sole mistress of her resources and her territory"; but France also would work "to build Western Europe into a political, economic, cultural and human group, organized for action, progress and defense," foreseeing "the probable evolution of [a] political regime" and a "European entente from the Atlantic to the Urals."

Limited cooperation between Britain and the EEC was indicated by the signing in Brussels Dec. 12 of a convention for unified air traffic control. This convention emerged from a drafting meeting of the concerned parties in Rome June 9-10.

Western European Talks

Proposals to create mechanisms to give political direction to the NATO alliance and the EEC and to prevent a threatened European trade split between the EEC and EFTA were discussed at meetings held by West German Chancellor Adenauer and de Gaulle near Paris July 29-30 and by Adenauer and Prime Min. Macmillan in Bonn Aug. 10-11.

The de Gaulle-Adenauer conference, paralleled by talks held by Foreign Mins. Couve de Murville and von Brentano and Defense Mins. Pierre Messmer and Franz Josef Strauss, was held at de Gaulle's presidential estate in Rambouillet. The de Gaulle-Adenauer talks took place in secret, and no final communique was issued, but French and West German spokesmen reported July 30 that agreement had been reached on the broad outline of an EEC political secretariat, or "European cabinet," to coordinate policies of the EEC nations. The meetings were said to have partially resolved West German fears that the proposed West European cabinet would be used by France to further de Gaulle's demands for a 3-power NATO political directorate (the U.S., Britain, France) that would exclude West Germany.

Bonn spokesmen said Aug. 2 that the de Gaulle-Adenauer accords contained specific measures to reform NATO's structure and to create a "bridge" between the EEC and EFTA. It had been reported in Bonn July 27 that Adenauer, angered by what he considered recent slights to West Germany by French leaders, had decided to cancel the Rambouillet talks, but had been forced to reverse himself by a French denial of the reports.

The Adenauer-Macmillan talks, considered a major step toward ending a British-West German rift, were said Aug. 11 to have produced agreement on ways to restore European economic unity despite the EEC-EFTA rivalry. In a statement issued for both leaders, Bonn spokesman Felix von Eckardt said that the undisclosed Adenauer-Macmillan trade unity plan would be submitted to EEC and EFTA member states and then presented to the 20-nation OECD. Adenauer and Macmillan were said to have discussed the French-West German plans for NATO and EEC political coordination, but Macmillan reportedly held that existing West European institutions gave ample scope for policy integration. He said in London, on returning, that, with reference to the EEC and the EFTA, he and Adenauer had "agreed that the unity of Europe is an absolutely essential condition of success.... What we have to do is to bring them together. We did not find the answer in a few hours' discussion..., but we have decided to exchange ideas in full loyalty, each of us to our own partners."

This cooperative atmosphere did not last long. The unity of the NATO nations was threatened in September and October by renewed demands of de Gaulle for a reshaping of the alliance into a political and military association that would preserve its member states' "national character." Addressing French cabinet members and 650 newsmen at a Paris news conference Sept. 5, de Gaulle said: European cooperation and unity must be based on the "reality" of the nation-state: It was "true that it has been possible to institute certain organisms [the EEC, ECSC, Euratom] more or less extra- or supra-national; these organisms have their technical value but have not and cannot have authority and... political efficacy." Effective European cooperation in the political, economic, cultural and defense domains must be guided by "an organized, regular concert of the responsible governments." "It involves the periodic deliberation of an assembly which would be formed by the delegates of the national parliaments, and... it must involve... a solemn European referendum so as to give to this launching of Europe the... popular approval and invention which is indispensable to it."

Adenauer, meeting with French Premier Rene Debre in Bonn Oct. 7-8, rejected de Gaulle's proposals for revision of NATO. Debre, who had gone to Bonn to seek Adenauer's views on de Gaulle's July proposal on a West European political confederation to supplement NATO, was told by Adenauer that West Germany would not accept de Gaulle's demands (1) that NATO be transformed into an alliance of national military forces, and (2) that the 6 EEC countries create a defense committee for coordination of their military policies.

The annual advisory conference of NATO opened in Paris Nov. 21. The reply to the de Gaulle position was presented Nov. 26 in the final resolution, which (in part) called for direct negotiations between the EEC and EFTA nations on increased economic and political integration of Western Europe.

1961

Britain formally applied for EEC membership in 1961. British economic conditions had worsened slowly during the year, while France stemmed an economic downturn that had started in 1960. West Germany and the Netherlands raised the values of their currencies in an attempt to reverse an inflow of monetary reserves. The EEC expanded to include Greece in "associate" status; EFTA took similar action in accepting Finland and Greenland as "associates." By the end of the year, no decision had been reached on the British membership application.

THE EEC & EFTA

Tariffs Cut

The 6 EEC nations, carrying out an accelerated program for the Common Market's internal tariff reduction, cut tariffs 10% on industrial imports from member states and 5% on imports of certain agricultural products. Both reductions were effective Jan. 1. This brought to 30% the total of EEC internal tariff cuts since Jan. 1, 1958. Simultaneous adjustments in EEC nations' tariffs on imports from non-member states reduced by 30% the difference between any specific tariff varying more than 15% above or below an agreed EEC average tariff on the specific import.

The EEC tariff cut was matched by the decision of the EFTA Ministerial Council, meeting in Geneva Feb. 14-16, to advance the 2d scheduled tariff cut from Jan. 1, 1962 to July 1, 1961. This became the 3d coordinated 10% tariff cut by EFTA members, including the original cut at the formation of the group. Effective July 1, maximum possible tariffs to be levied by EFTA members were set at 70% of the Jan. 1, 1957 level (except for Portugal, subject to special considerations under the EFTA Convention).

A proposal for a unified Europewide farm economy, placed before EEC governments June 13, called for the abolition by July 1, 1962 of all tariffs, import quotas and price supports for farm products. These controls would be replaced by a "variable levy" applied to farm products entering each EEC country to raise or lower the import price to conform with domestic prices. The variable levy would be reduced among EEC countries and ended within 6 years but would remain on all farm imports from non-EEC countries. French Agriculture Min. Henri Rochereau had announced June 6 that France would halt all EEC tariff reductions after 1961 unless the Common Market adopted a Europewide farm policy. The French and Dutch farm economies produced at the cheapest prices in Europe and would gain the most from such a policy.

The EEC & EFTA Add Associate Members

The Danish government announced June 2 that Greenland was becoming an associate member of EFTA effective July 1. Finland became an associate member June 26 after lengthier negotiations. The Finnish-EFTA agreement had been signed in Helsinki Mar. 27 after Finland granted the Soviet Union most-favored-nation consideration which placed tariffs on Soviet imports into Finland at EFTA levels. The agreement had been scheduled to come into effect July 1 but was delayed pending the initial Finnish reduction of tariffs (of 30% on most items) and import quotas.

An agreement signed June 9 established associate EEC membership for Greece, subject to ratification by the EEC Parliamentary
Assembly and by the parliaments of the 6 EEC members and of Greece.

EEC 'Summit' & Other Meetings

The heads of government and foreign ministers of the 6 EEC
nations (France, West Germany, Italy, Belgium, Netherlands and
Luxembourg) met in Paris Feb. 10-11 to discuss French proposals for a
confederation that would coordinate the 6 countries' economic and
political policies without subordinating their sovereignties to a new
supra-national institution. The 6 nations failed to reach agreement on
the French plan. A communique issued Feb. 11 disclosed, however, that
a commission had been set up to recommend procedures for periodic
EEC political consultation and that a 2d European "summit" meeting
would be held May 19 to consider the recommendations. The communique said the 6 states had studied the organization of a "closer political
cooperation" intended to "lay the basis of a union that will develop
progressively." It said that the envisaged union, while "limited for the
moment" to the EEC states, "could be further extended in the future."
It stressed EEC hopes for the development of "exchanges with other
European countries, in particular with . . . Britain."

The *N.Y. Times* reported Feb. 13 that Britain had informed the 6
countries of Prime Min. Macmillan's readiness to participate in the Paris
discussions but that the offer had been rejected on the ground that it
would not be feasible for Macmillan to take part in the political talks
and be barred from the economic discussions dealing with EEC matters.

It had been reported Feb. 10-11 that France's confederation proposal had met with opposition, particularly from the Netherlands, on the
ground that the de Gaulle plan for establishing a permanent secretariat
to supervise confederal decisions would not lead to genuine political integration based on the EEC and other supra-national European institutions. It also was feared by the Netherlands and West Germany that the
French plan was intended to weld Europe into an economic and military
bloc that would exclude Britain and other EFTA states and would
follow a "3d-force" policy independent of the U.S. This view was expressed again at The Hague Feb. 22 in a speech by Netherlands Foreign
Min. Joseph M. A. H. Luns. Luns stressed strengthening rather than
severing ties between the EEC and the EFTA.

The Paris meeting was attended by French Pres. Charles de
Gaulle, West German Chancellor Konrad Adenauer, Italian Premier
Amintore Fanfani, Belgian Premier Gaston Eyskens, Netherlands
Premier Jan E. de Quay and Luxembourg Premier Pierre Werner.
Adenauer and de Gaulle had conferred privately Feb. 9 before the Paris
meeting. De Gaulle was said to have sought, unsuccessfully, to end
Adenauer's opposition to any plan that would "freeze" the 6 EEC
nations into an exclusive power bloc closed to Britain.

West Germany had disclosed Jan. 13 that it had reassured France that attacks on the EEC made by Economics Min. Ludwig Erhard did not represent West German policy. Erhard had charged that the EEC, by its creation of an exclusive trade area, had divided Europe economically and was driving Britain away from integration with Europe. Erhard later accused EEC Pres. Walter Hallstein of deliberately hampering efforts to integrate the EEC and EFTA zones. The Bonn disavowal reportedly was ordered personally by Adenauer.

Adenauer and West German Foreign Min. Heinrich von Brentano conferred with Macmillan privately Feb. 22-23. Included in the talks, reportedly on the relationship between the EEC and EFTA, were Chancellor of the Exchequer Selwyn Lloyd, Foreign Secy. Lord Home and Edward Heath, Lord Privy Seal (in charge of European affairs).

Meetings continued as de Gaulle visited Bonn May 20 to confer with Adenauer. This trip followed Adenauer's 3-day visit to Washington Apr. 11-13 for the German leader's first meeting with U.S. Pres. Kennedy since the latter's election. Adenauer, accompanied by von Brentano, also met with U.S. State Secy. Dean Rusk Apr. 12. In a joint communique issued Apr. 13, Adenauer and Kennedy pledged to advance the growth of the OECD (Organization for Economic Cooperation & Development) and EEC and to study the international-payments imbalance problem.

Adenauer and de Gaulle met again Dec. 9 in Paris, where discussions were held on European political and economic unification. Their joint communique stated that "these discussions led to the conclusions that complete unity of views exists" on these issues.

The EEC's Ministerial Council recessed a series of meetings Dec. 30 without agreeing on a system of free trade in EEC farm products or on passage of the Common Market treaty to its "2d stage," under which the EEC countries were to move toward a full customs union and economic integration. The Council agreed, however, to meet treaty obligations for decisions on both questions before Dec. 31 by remaining in continuous session and legally extending the Dec. 30 session into 1962.

Under the Treaty of Rome, which had established the EEC in 1957, the date Dec. 31, 1961 had been fixed as the deadline for completing the "first stage" of the EEC's goals. The treaty provided that the transition from the first to the 2d stages could be delayed for up to 3 years, but all 6 EEC nations feared that the treaty would be weakened by a postponement. During the treaty's first stage, all decisions required unanimous agreement; with the 2d stage, the EEC powers would agree to accept majority decisions.

Ex-French Interior Min. Pierre Chatenet had been elected president of the European Atomic Energy Community (Euratom) by the foreign ministers of the 6 Euratom nations at a meeting in Brussels Dec. 20. He was to succeed Etienne Hirsch, also of France, on the expiration of the latter's term Jan. 10, 1962.

The EEC Council of Ministers Dec. 20 announced the reappointment to the EEC Commission of the following members (terms were for the period Jan. 10, 1962 to Jan. 9, 1966, except as noted): *President—* Walter Hallstein (Germany), 2 years. *Vice presidents—*Dr. Sicco Leendert Mansholt (Netherlands), Robert Ernest Marjolin (France) and Giuseppe Caron (Italy), 2 years each. *Members—*Jean Rey (Belgium), Hans von der Groeben (Germany), Lambert Schaus (Luxembourg), Lionello Levi-Sandri (Italy) and Henri Rochereau (France).

FINANCIAL DEVELOPMENTS & ECONOMIC GROWTH

Gold Price Stabilized

The price of gold fell below $35.25 an ounce on the London market Feb. 2 for the first time since Oct. 1960. The price drop, which discouraged speculation, was considered to have ended, at least temporarily, the outflow of U.S.-held gold reserves to the London market ($326 million worth in January). The price drop was attributed to a reported decision by the U.S. Treasury and Bank of England to force down gold prices and to Pres. John F. Kennedy's pledge, in his State-of-the-Union message, to defend the value of the dollar.

German & Dutch Currency Revaluations

Upward currency revaluations of 4.75% were carried out by West Germany Mar. 4 and by the Netherlands Mar. 6. The revaluations were intended to ease European pressure against the U.S. dollar and to reduce West Germany's persistent balance-of-payments surplus.

The West German action, which revalued the Deutschemark from 4.2 to 4 to the U.S. dollar, was put into effect by West German banks Mar. 4. The mark revaluation was undertaken primarily to (a) ease domestic inflation, (b) end the foreign-payments imbalance in West Germany's favor and (c) curtail the growth of Bonn's foreign currency reserves ($6.603 billion Feb. 23). Its immediate effects would be to cheapen West Germany's imports, raise West German export prices and cause a withdrawal of capital and speculative funds from the mark to other currencies, including the U.S. dollar.

The Netherlands revaluation, taken primarily to maintain stability of Netherlands-West German trade and payments and to end the underpricing of Dutch goods abroad, raised the guilder's value from 3.8 to 3.6 to the U.S. dollar.

West Germany's official announcement of its revaluation was made at a Bonn press conference held Mar. 5 by Finance Min. Franz Etzel, Economics Min. Ludwig Erhard and Pres. Karl Blessing of the West German Central Bank. All 3 insisted that the revaluation had not been urged by the U.S. but had been ordered to halt West Germany's current inflation and to defend the mark's value.

The Bonn Central Bank had relaxed reserve requirements Mar. 2 to release an estimated $100 million to the West German capital market and reduce the continued demand for foreign capital.

Britain Draws From IMF

Britain Aug. 8 drew from the International Monetary Fund (IMF) $1.5 billion, the largest amount in IMF's history. In addition the IMF authorized Britain to draw $500 million more over the next year. The withdrawal was made to cover Britain's international debts and bolster the pound sterling. Britain currently had withdrawal rights to $2.4 billion—125% of its IMF payments quota. The withdrawals consisted of $450 million in U.S. dollars, $270 million in West German marks, $270 million in French francs, $120 million in Italian lire, $120 million in Dutch guilders, $90 million in Belgian francs, $75 million in Japanese yen and $30 million in Swedish kroner.

The pound rose above parity in relation to the U.S. dollar Aug. 4 for the first time since Feb. 15. The rise followed both the IMF announcement Aug. 6 that Britain was to draw from the IMF and Britain's July 31 decision to apply for membership in the Common Market.

European Economic Growth

EEC Vice Pres. Robert Marjolin reported to the European Parliamentary Assembly in Strasbourg Jan. 19 that the 6 nations' industrial production had risen 12% and their total gross national products 7% during 1960. (An EEC Commission report had estimated the industrial production increase at 8% in 1960, compared with 14% in 1959.)

The 18 nations of Western Europe were "now enjoying the highest standard of living in all their history" and "stand on the threshold of a period of still further growth that by 1970 will give them an estimated population of 320 million and a combined gross national product of $342 billion, an increase of 55% over 1955." This estimate and prediction were made in *Europe's Needs & Resources,* a 1,198-page study published Oct. 30 by the 20th Century Fund in New York. The 5-year study was directed by Dr. J. Frederic Dewhurst, who reported that: Western Europe's rate of economic progress since 1950 "has been better than anything the United States has achieved as far back as our records go"; nationalization in Western Europe was "in abeyance, having advanced little since the war"; "socialism is dying because capitalism has delivered the goods the Socialists promised"; there had been a virtual revolution in consumer attitudes as mass production, organization and installment-plan buying brought autos, refrigerators, TV sets and foreign travel within the financial reach of the average man; "perhaps just as important is the assurance provided by the welfare state."

BRITAIN APPLIES TO THE EEC

Events Preceding British Application

Months of talks and consultations with EEC and EFTA members, as well as with nations belonging to neither body, preceded Britain's announcement July 31 that it would apply for EEC membership.

Prime Min. Macmillan and Pres. de Gaulle had met Jan. 28-29 for private and informal political discussions at de Gaulle's Presidential estate in Rambouillet, near Paris. Their meetings, held in strict secrecy, were joined Jan. 29 by French Premier Michel Debré and Foreign Min. Maurice Couve de Murville and were said to have centered, *inter alia,* on Europe's threatened economic division.

The EFTA Ministerial Council, meeting in Geneva Feb. 14-16, asserted that "EFTA's wish is to take part, with the EEC, in the creation of a single European market which might comprise over 300 million people." The EFTA offered to cooperate with the EEC on finding "the solution of the problems resulting from the existence of 2 economic groups in Europe."

West German Chancellor Adenauer conferred with Macmillan in London Feb. 22-23 on the Western-payments imbalance and on renewed efforts to end the threatened economic division of Western Europe between the EEC and the British-led EFTA. The London *Times* reported Feb. 24 that Adenauer and Macmillan had agreed on further discussions within the Western European Union on proposals for linking Britain and other EFTA nations with the EEC. Adenauer was said to have expressed support for rapid British membership in the EEC to make possible direct British participation in projected negotiations on EEC political integration. The 2 leaders also announced that Chancellor of the Exchequer Selwyn Lloyd would visit Bonn for talks on the Western-payments imbalance and possible West German measures to ameliorate Britain's continuing payments deficit.

Proposals for the coordination of tariffs on nonfarm imports by Britain and the EEC nations were presented at a Paris meeting of WEU foreign ministers Feb. 27 by Edward Heath, Britain's Lord Privy

Seal. The proposals, favoring the establishment of a vast European industrial trade area, were viewed as a major step toward ending the regional tariff barriers created by the rival EEC and EFTA trade blocs. Heath told the 6 Common Market nations that if they could agree to Britain's retention of preferential tariffs on agricultural imports and on trade with the Commonwealth countries, Britain would "consider a system based on a common or harmonized tariff on raw materials and manufactured goods imported from countries other than the 7 [EFTA states] or the Commonwealth." Heath made it clear that Britain was prepared to extend its cooperation with EEC nations to the political sphere; he asserted that establishment of a common British-EEC tariff system inevitably would require the creation of common institutions. He indicated that Britain would be willing to give up certain of its Commonwealth trade advantages in the interests of a British-EEC tariff system.

Macmillan visited the U.S. and Canada in early April. Speaking Apr. 7 in Cambridge, Mass. at the Massachusetts Institute of Technology, he called for vigorous new efforts to insure the free world's economic expansion. This could be achieved, he said, only through (a) an expansion of free trade to as wide an area of the world as possible; (b) coordinated Western efforts to aid development of less-favored nations; (c) enlargement of Western credit and financial liquidity to deal with temporary payment imbalances; (d) European economic integration to end a rift that had become political and eventually would harm the West's "military coherence and strength." He said: "For us in Europe the urgent need is that of bringing together the 6 and the 8 [EFTA and Finland]"; Britain "must and can do this without detriment to our domestic interests or to our Commonwealth association and without injury to any other nation or group of nations." The *N.Y. Times* reported from Washington Apr. 12 that Macmillan had informed Pres. Kennedy that Britain was studying proposals for its association with the European economic and political integration movement led by the 6 EEC nations. Mr. Kennedy was said to have told Macmillan that the U.S. would support such a step as a major advance toward Western unity.

The EFTA Ministerial Council met in London June 27-28 and again discussed the problems of cooperation with the EEC. An additional meeting was held in Geneva July 28. In a communique, "the Geneva Declaration," issued July 31, the Council reported that both Britain and Denmark were applying for EEC membership. The communique stated that all EFTA members would, "examine with the EEC the ways and means by which all members of EFTA could take part together in a single market embracing some 300 million people." The Council met again in Geneva Nov. 20-21 and discussed the status of the British and Danish applications to the EEC. Austrian, Swedish, and Swiss representatives announced their governments' desires to affiliate with the EEC.

These meetings were held after the EFTA Consultative Committee, established at the EFTA Ministerial Council meeting held in Berne in 1960, had met in London May 9-10 and had also discussed the problems of the economic division of Europe.

Anticipation of Britain's formal membership application increased in the late spring. Writing in the *St. Louis Post Dispatch* June 25, John Bourne of the London *Financial Times* said: "The odds that Britain will take a definite step toward joining the 6 European countries in their Common Market before the summer is out are about 3 to 2 in favor."

In preparation for the British application, the heads of government of the 6 Common Market states met in Bonn July 18 and agreed on establishing a system of regular political consultation and cooperation. The 6 leaders—French Pres. de Gaulle, West German Chancellor Adenauer and Premiers Amintore Fanfani of Italy, Theo Lefevre of Belgium, Jan E. de Quay of the Netherlands and Pierre Werner of Luxembourg—issued a declaration in which they announced their decision to "give form and body to the will of political unity" expressed in the organization of the EEC, the European Coal & Steel Community (ECSC) and Euratom. The declaration said that the 6 had agreed to "organize their cooperation and assure its regularity" and to meet regularly to "coordinate policy . . . to further Europe's political unity and thus strengthen the Atlantic alliance." It disclosed that a working group had been designated to study "ways and means of giving a statutory character to the unity of their peoples." Referring to the EFTA movement toward membership in the EEC and Britain's expected request for special membership conditions, the declaration said: "It is the wish that other European countries may enter the European union, providing they are ready in all fields to assume the same responsibilities and obligations as the present member nations."

It was reported from Bonn July 18 that the agreement had been reached after the Netherlands had dropped its demand for the formation of a supranational European political community that would include Britain. The Netherlands had opposed the French plan for extending political consultation to defense matters and forming a permanent secretariat to prepare periodic EEC summit meetings—all within a framework that would, the Dutch held, permanently exclude Britain and the other EFTA nations. The French proposals were modified and the defense and secretariat plans were dropped to secure Dutch agreement to the main proposal for political consultation. The Dutch were said to have believed that British membership in EEC and its eventual political institutions would prevent French-West German domination of EEC's smaller member states.

Britain Announces Decision to Apply to EEC

Britain's formal decision to apply for EEC membership was announced by Macmillan in Parliament July 31. The decision was viewed as a major step toward ending Britain's isolation from the movement of economic and political integration begun by the Common Market states. It was followed by the announcement that the 6 other EFTA nations would also seek some form of association with the Common Market.

Macmillan told Parliament July 31 that British membership in the EEC would entail fundamental changes in Britain's domestic economy and economic relations with the Commonwealth and other nations. He asserted, however, that Britain and the Commonwealth nations would benefit immeasurably from an association with "a community comprising ... the countries of free Europe" and having the potential of "a very rapidly expanding economy supplying, as eventually it would, a single market approaching 300 million people." Macmillan said: Future relations among the nations of the Commonwealth, the Common Market and the rest of Europe were "matters of capital importance in the life of our country ... of all the countries of the free world"; this was a political as well as an economic issue. "Although the Treaty of Rome is concerned with economic matters, it has an important political objective, namely, to promote unity and stability in Europe." "I believe it is both our duty and our interest to contribute towards that strength by securing the closest possible unity within Europe. At the same time, if a closer relationship between the UK and the countries of the EEC were to disrupt the long-standing and historic ties between the UK and the other nations of the Commonwealth, the loss would be greater than the gain."

Macmillan made it clear that Britain would require special conditions for its EEC membership "to meet the special needs" of the Commonwealth and the EFTA countries. He warned that if the Common Market states refused to recognize these needs and the negotiations failed, "quite a lot of things will happen and quite major changes may have to be made in the foreign policy and commitments of Great Britain."

Macmillan said that Britain would make formal application for Common Market membership in order to initiate negotiations for entry to the EEC under Article 237 of the Rome Treaty*. He pledged, however, that "no agreement will be entered into until it has been approved by the House after full consultation with other Commonwealth countries."

* Article 237: "Any European state may apply to become a member of the Community. It shall address its application to the Council which, after obtaining the opinion of the Commission, shall act by means of a unanimous vote. The conditions of admission and the amendments to this Treaty necessitated thereby shall be the subject of an agreement between the member-states and the applicant state. Such agreement shall be submitted to all the contracting states for ratification in accordance with their respective constitutional rules."

Macmillan's address was interrupted by jeers from rightist members of his own Conservative Party, among them Anthony Fell, who said Macmillan was a "national disaster" and charged that Macmillan had betrayed the interests of 650 million Commonwealth subjects and should resign. The opposition Labor Party was divided on the question.

Britain's decision to seek Common Market membership was generally attributed to the weakening of its economic and trade position since World War II, especially when compared with the 6 EEC nations. Britain was suffering a diminished but still major balance-of-trade deficit. British industry's rate of increase in labor productivity had averaged approximately 1.7% annually, compared with an average of 3.5% for the EEC states; Britain's exports had increased by only 8% since 1957, compared with rates ranging from 23% to 44% for the EEC states. Britain's share of world exports of manufactured goods had fallen from 20% in 1955 to 16% in 1960.

The 6 EEC nations welcomed the British decision Aug. 1 as one of the highest importance for the political and economic future of Europe. The EEC foreign ministers, meeting with British Lord Privy Seal Edward Heath at a Paris session of the Council of the Western European Union, pledged in a communique to conduct the British-EEC negotiations "in a spirit of reciprocal goodwill." They said the EEC nations "had always hoped that ... states who were ready to assume the same obligations in all fields would adhere to the European Community." Heath said at the meeting that Britain also would seek membership in Euratom and the European Coal & Steel Community.

The Council of the EFTA had met in Geneva July 31 and approved Britain's decision to seek EEC membership as "an opportunity to find an appropriate solution for all EFTA countries and thus to promote the solidarity and cohesion of Europe." The British decision had been coordinated with the other EFTA nations at a meeting of the EFTA Ministerial Council in London June 27-28. The communique issued at the end of the London meeting did not disclose that Britain would seek Common Market membership, but it affirmed that the 7 EFTA states had agreed to "coordinate their actions and ... remain united" in any negotiations with the EEC.

Following the British announcement, a similar declaration was issued July 31 by the Danish government. Norwegian Trade Min. Arne Skaug disclosed the same day that Norway also would seek negotiations on EEC membership. The Austrian government said July 31 that it was ready to negotiate with the EEC to seek a form of association compatible with its neutral status.

The U.S. State Department July 31 issued a statement expressing "close and sympathetic interest" in the British decision to join EEC. U.S. support of the British-led movement for affiliation with the Common Market was reiterated by Pres. Kennedy Aug. 10 at a Washington news conference.

Britain's decision to seek Common Market membership was supported Aug. 3 by a 313-5 vote in the House of Commons and by a motion approved without vote by the House of Lords. The Commons vote, after a 2-day debate, was on a Conservative motion supporting the Macmillan government's decision and offering assurances that Commonwealth nations' interests would be safeguarded. The 5 opposing Commons votes were cast by Anthony Fell, a right-wing Conservative, and by 4 independent (leftist) Laborites. A Labor Party motion expressing "regret" that Britain would begin the EEC negotiations in "a position of grave economic weakness" was defeated by votes of 318-209 in the House of Commons and 86-17 in the House of Lords.

Britain's application for membership was submitted to the EEC Council in Brussels Aug. 10. The application was a necessary preliminary to the opening of negotiations on the special conditions posed by Britain for its membership in the 6-nation group. The application did not commit Britain to EEC membership if the conditions were not met. It was signed by Prime Min. Macmillan and addressed to West German Economy Min. Erhard, current president of the EEC Ministerial Council.

Denmark's application for EEC membership was submitted in Brussels later the same day. The Danish government's decision to seek membership had been supported by the Folketing (parliament) Aug. 4 by 152-11 vote. The formal statement of Denmark's intention to join EEC was presented to the EEC Ministerial Council in Brussels Oct. 26.

Irish Prime Min. Sean Lemass had announced Aug. 1 in Dublin that Ireland also would apply for membership in the Common Market. Ireland was not a member of EFTA or the Commonwealth, but its currency was tied to the British pound and its economy was dependent on British purchase of more than 90% of Irish farm exports.

In addition, Austria, Switzerland, and Sweden—Europe's 3 neutrals—proposed Dec. 15 the opening of negotiations on their association with the EEC. The 3 countries, members of EFTA, made the proposal in notes to EEC Pres. Ludwig Erhard.

A British delegation led by Lord Privy Seal Edward Heath met with representatives of the 6 EEC countries in Brussels Nov. 22-25 to negotiate on conditions for British membership. It was reported that Britain had been informed by the EEC that it would have to adopt the Common Market's external tariff system against all "outsider" nations, including Commonwealth nations. Britain, however, was offered these palliatives: a reduction or delay of duties on imports of certain Commonwealth goods; exemptions permitting continued duty-free import of some Commonwealth items.

Commonwealth Objections

Commonwealth objections to British EEC membership had been made clear at the 7th Commonwealth Parliamentary Conference, convened in London Sept. 25 by Queen Elizabeth II. Countering the protests, State Secy. for Commonwealth Relations Duncan Sandys said at the conference Sept. 26 that "if we are faced with the necessity of choosing between the Commonwealth and Europe, we should unquestionably choose the Commonwealth." Nevertheless, nearly every speaker at the conference Sept. 26-27 attacked the British move as a direct danger to the future of the Commonwealth. Macmillan told the delegates Sept. 29 that Britain had been forced to decide to join the EEC to prevent it and the Commonwealth from declining in the face of "the massive groupings of the modern world." Canada emerged as leader of the campaign to halt Britain's entry into the EEC or to impose rigid conditions to safeguard Commonwealth trade.

Commonwealth objections had been voiced for some months prior to Macmillan's July 31 announcement of Britain's intention to apply to the Common Market.

Britain's negotiations with the 6 EEC nations had been largely completed by the end of May, and Macmillan announced in Parliament June 13 that he would send 3 emissaries—Duncan Sandys, Aviation Min. Peter Thorneycroft and Labor Min. John Hare to consult with the Commonwealth countries on the projected British move.

The Commonwealth countries' economies had become increasingly interdependent through a system of preferential trade under which their goods, especially agricultural products, circulated freely among member states. According to the July 30 *N.Y. Herald Tribune,* 57% of New Zealand's exports, 25.5% of Australia's, 17.1% of Canada's and 27.3% of India's were to Britain. Britain, in turn, provided 72% of New Zealand's imports, 51% of Australia's and comparable amounts to other Commonwealth countries. Britain's EEC entry presumably would provide a huge, eventually duty-free European market for British industrial goods. But, unless a special exemption were granted Britain, membership would force British adoption of high EEC tariffs on agricultural imports and give more costly and protected European farm products preference over Commonwealth farm exports to Britain. It was for this reason that Macmillan pledged that he would require special agreements for the protection of Commonwealth trade before agreeing to Britain's joining the EEC.

Britain's plans to join the Common Market were opposed by the major Commonwealth countries despite the assurances of protection given their governments by Sandys, Thorneycroft and Hare. Australia's objections were detailed in a communique, issued in Canberra July 11, in which Britain was warned against joining the EEC "at the cost of division within the Commonwealth or elsewhere in the free world." A New Zealand communique issued in Wellington July 6 made it clear that "New Zealand's economy is highly dependent on the sale of foodstuffs" in Britain and expressed doubt that satisfactory alternate markets could be found. Similar views were expressed in communiques issued by Pakistan in Rawalpindi July 11, India in New Delhi July 14 and Canada in Ottawa the same day. The Ottawa statement stressed "the grave concern of the Canadian government about the... political and economic effects which British membership in the European Economic Community would have on Canada and on the Commonwealth as a whole."

British White Paper on Joining EEC

The formal position of the British government was presented in a White Paper published Nov. 29. The document consisted of a lengthy statement made by Edward Heath in his secret negotiations with the EEC's representatives Oct. 10. An outline of this paper had been presented to the press Oct. 11, and reports that the entire draft had "leaked out" followed shortly. Highlights of Heath's statement to the EEC group:

On the Treaty of Rome—"H.M. government are ready to subscribe fully to the aims which you have set yourselves. In particular, we accept without qualification the objectives laid down in Articles 2 and 3 of the Treaty of Rome, including the elimination of internal tariffs, a common customs tariff, a common commercial policy, and a common agricultural policy. We are ready to accept, and to play our full part in, the institutions established under Article 4 and other articles of the Treaty.

"Now I turn to a central feature of the EEC—the common external tariff. We see no need to ask you for a renegotiation, item by item, of the existing common external tariff of the Community. We assume that some adjustments are a necessary consequence of the admission of a new member. It seems to us that, if the common external tariff of the enlarged Community is to be broadly acceptable to GATT and to 3d countries, it cannot remain precisely at the level of the existing one. At the same time, we recognize that the negotiation of the present common external tariff was a long and difficult process and that you might not wish to begin detailed negotiations all over again. We are, moreover, anxious that the process of adjustment should raise the minimum of practical problems. We think it important, in this and in other fields, to simplify the task before us.

"We are therefore ready—and I think this simple solution may be agreeable to all of you—to accept the structure of the present EEC tariff as the basis of the common tariff of the enlarged Community. In these circumstances we think that the necessary lowering of tariff levels might be achieved by making a linear cut in the common tariff as it stands today. We would suggest that this might be of the order of 20%, a figure which the Community has considered in another context. No doubt both you and we would wish to single out some items for special treatment. I can assure you that our own list will not be long."

On the Commonwealth—"We believe that you share our view of the value of the Commonwealth, not only to the UK but also to yourselves and to the whole free world. The Commonwealth is an association of peoples stretching into every continent and comprising many races. It is a great force in the world for the promotion of ideals and purposes which are widely shared in Europe. Its origins are based in history, in the fact that the members of the Commonwealth were a part of the British Empire, and much of its strength lies in the perpetuation of the links that were then formed. I should be misleading you if I failed to say how deeply the British people feel about this association. That, I am sure, is a sentiment which the members of the Community will fully understand.

"Commonwealth trade is one of the strongest elements in maintaining the Commonwealth association. It would be a tragedy if our entry into the Community forced other members of the Commonwealth to change their whole pattern of trade and consequently, perhaps, their political orientation. I do not think that such a development would be in your interest any more than in ours. Nor, looking at it from the point of view of a potential member of the Community, would any of us wish the Community to be met with the hostility which would flow from a large group of countries strung across the world if they were to feel that their interests had suffered at our hands.

"The economies of most Commonwealth countries have been built up on the basis of supplying the British market, which has traditionally imported their produce duty-free and often on preferential terms. In the last few decades the majority of them have sought to enlarge both the variety of their production and the range of their markets. But the British market is still of great importance to the economies of most Commonwealth countries.

"I am sure that you will understand that Britain could not join the EEC under conditions in which this trade connexion was cut, with grave loss and even ruin for some of the Commonwealth countries. For our remaining dependent territories we have a special and direct responsibility."

On agriculture—"I turn to the question of UK agriculture. Here, let me say at once, we started from common ground. The agricultural objectives of the Treaty of Rome are in line with the objectives of our own agricultural policy. We, like you, are fully committed to the maintenance of a stable, efficient, and prosperous agriculture. The Treaty of Rome aims at increasing agricultural productivity, a fair standard of living for the agricultural population, stable markets, regular supplies, and reasonable prices and supplies to consumers. These objectives command our wholehearted support. Moreover, we are prepared to take the major step of participating with you in a common agricultural policy and in developing a common organization of agricultural markets. We fully accept that the Common Market must extend to agriculture and trade in agricultural products.

"This, however, poses big problems for us. Our system of support, except for horticultural produce, relies mainly on Exchequer payments to ensure the maintenance of a satisfactory standard of living for our farmers. Our tariffs on foodstuffs are low, and a large proportion of our supplies, particularly those from the Commonwealth, enter our market free of duty. We make very little use of import restrictions. Broadly speaking, we buy our food at world free market prices. Our people are therefore accustomed to low prices for food. Their tastes are related to a traditional pattern of food supplies.

"At the same time our farmers have guaranteed prices for all their principal products. These guarantees are provided by means of Exchequer payments which make up the difference between the average price realized by farmers on the market and the guaranteed price determined by the government. In addition, we make direct farming grants designed to encourage improved farming methods and to raise the general efficiency of the industry. The level of the guaranteed prices and of the direct farming grants is settled annually by the government after consultation with the producers' representatives. We have legislation which sets definite limits to the amount of the reductions which may be made from one year to the next both in the general level of support and in the guaranteed prices for individual commodities. The UK government have pledged themselves to make no change in the statutory limits during the lifetime of the present Parliament, which can continue until Oct. 1964."

Domestic British Anti-Inflation Action

Faced with the interrelated problems of curtailing domestic inflation and stimulating exports, the Macmillan government found it necessary to increase its austerity measures.

The budget for fiscal 1961-2, presented to Parliament Apr. 17 by Chancellor of the Exchequer Selwyn Lloyd, estimated revenues at £6.44 billion ($18.032 billion), expenditures at £6.002 billion ($16,805,600,000) and the deficit at £137 million ($383,600,000). Major proposals in the budget called for: (a) Easing individual income taxes by increasing the income level on which a surtax was to be charged from £2,000 ($5,600) to £4,000 ($11,200) and by changing the method of determining the taxable earned income (effective Jan. 1, 1963). (The revenue loss was to be offset by a 2.5% increase in the profits tax, starting with profits earned beginning Apr. 1, 1961.) (b) Increasing the cost of automobile licenses from £12 10 shillings ($35) to £15 ($42). (c) A 10% tax on TV commercials. (d) Increasing the tax on fuel oil, gas oil and kerosene by 2 pence (2.33¢).

The budget called for the adoption of 2 anti-inflationary "regulatory powers" to be used when needed. One would permit the increase or decrease of purchase (sales) taxes and customs and excise duties by up to 10%; the other would authorize an employers' payroll tax of up to 4 shillings (56¢) a week on every employe.

Lloyd reported that 1960-1 revenue had totaled £5.934 billion ($16,615,200,000) and operating expenditures £5.787 billion ($16,203,600,000); there had been an operating surplus of £147 million ($411,600,000). Lloyd called British exports in 1960 "disappointing" and the balance of payments "very unsatisfactory."

A new round of austerity measures, proposed by the Macmillan government, was approved in the House of Commons July 27 by 346-238 vote after a 2-day debate. It had met heavy Labor and Liberal opposition. The measures, which had been introduced July 25 by Chancellor of the Exchequer Lloyd, included proposals to increase the 5% bank rate to 7% and to increase sales taxes and excise duties by 10% and thereby raise prices of tobacco, alcoholic spirits, beer, tea, sugar, coffee and other consumer goods.

Lloyd said: Britain faced a "critical external situation"; "this was the 3d consecutive year in which our overall balance of payments has been in deficit"; Britain's 1960 payments deficit was £350 million ($980 million), and its gold reserves had fallen by £164 million ($460 million) during 1961's first 6 months. (Reserves fell by another £113 million [$319,200,000] during July to £875 million [$2.45 billion], the lowest level since the post-Suez crisis of 1957.) Lloyd said that Britain would try to limit its overseas defense and foreign aid expenditures during fiscal 1961-2 to £400 million ($1.12 billion). He said he would cut domestic government operating costs by £175 million ($490 million) and reduce loans to nationalized industries by £125 million ($350 million). Banks were asked to restrict as much as possible loans for personal consumption, installment buying and speculative building so as to channel funds to finance exports and "productive" industry.

Lloyd said that British wage increases had outstripped industrial growth—that too much money was chasing too few goods. He urged a "pause" in wage increases; this plea was rejected by the British Trades Union Congress Sept. 6 at its convention in Portsmouth.

A Labor motion condemning the Macmillan government's economic policies had been defeated July 18 by a 329-243 Commons vote. Macmillan said he could not "remember a time when the people were better housed . . . clothed and had more employment."

Reginald Maudling was removed from the office of Board of Trade president and appointed colonial secretary Oct. 9 by Macmillan. Frederick J. Erroll became the new Board of Trade president.

British-French Cooperation

Great Britain and France announced in Paris Nov. 22 that agreement had been reached on the joint construction of a supersonic aircraft. Work would start in 1962. The prototype was to be completed in 1965, and delivery was scheduled for 1968.

British and French electrical systems were linked Dec. 8 with the inauguration of the cross-Channel transmission cable. The system was designed to enable the 2 nations to share power during periods of peak loads, approximately 8:30 a.m. in France and 5:00 p.m. in Britain.

1962

During the negotiations of 1962, previously flexible positions became fixed. Britain's prospects for membership in the EEC, which looked favorable at the close of 1961, dimmed considerably. The French position, presented by Pres. de Gaulle, had moved toward the establishment of France as the principal power of the EEC, a position that would be endangered by the admission of Britain. The de Gaulle interpretation of Europe and the EEC precluded a fully integrated community; rather, he saw the EEC more as a loosely confederated customs union. Britain, having bargained away certain tariff privileges in negotiations with the EEC, received strong protests from Commonwealth members over its Common Market membership prospects. These protests were augmented by Labor Party objections to the Macmillan policies in general. Other EFTA members found it necessary to follow Britain's leadership and apply for membership in the EEC, realizing that without Britain, the EFTA would be economically ineffective.

BRITISH ECONOMIC DEVELOPMENTS

Domestic

The budget for fiscal 1963, presented to Parliament Apr. 9 by Chancellor of the Exchequer Selwyn Lloyd, estimated revenues at £6.797 billion ($19.032 billion) and expenditures at £6.364 billion ($17.819 billion). A £211 million ($590,800,000) deficit was anticipated, however, as a result of expected capital outlays—largely loans to local authorities and expenditures of nationalized industries. Defense expenditures were estimated at £1.721 billion ($4.819 billion).

Major proposals of the budget called for: (a) A "speculative gains" tax, largely on securities sold within 6 months of acquisition and on land and property sold within 3 years of purchase; gains were to be taxed as ordinary income for individuals, but companies were to be subject to income and profit taxes. (b) A 15% tax on candy, soft drinks and ice cream and increased levies on furniture and clothing. (c) A sales tax reduction from 55% to 45% on cars, TV sets, appliances and cosmetics. (d) Abolition of an employers' payroll tax, which was adopted in 1961 but never put into effect. (e) Abolition of a special tax on owners of private dwellings that they occupied. (f) An increase in income tax exemptions for persons under 65 from £300 ($840) to £400 ($1,120) and an exemption increase for a married couple over 65 from £440 ($1,232) to £480 ($1,344).

This rearrangement of the tax structure was expected to deprive the government of about £8.5 million ($23.8 million) in annual revenue from direct taxes. Revenues from indirect levies were expected to remain the same.

Labor Party leader Hugh Gaitskell, calling the budget a "no-change budget," charged Apr. 9 that the proposed tax redistribution would impose a heavier burden on lower income groups. He contended that the budget provided insufficient inducement for economic expansion.

The requirement that London clearing banks and Scottish banks keep "special deposits" of almost £80 million ($224 million), introduced July 1961, was abolished May 31, according to an announcement from the Bank of England. The bank stated that "this decision will permit only a slight relaxation in bank lending policy," and it urged that lending institutions pay particular regard to exports while remaining strict on (domestic) speculative ventures.

Hire-purchase (installment sales) controls were relaxed June 4 under rules made public by Frederick J. Erroll, president of the Board of Trade. Minimum down-payment requirements on consumer durables were reduced from 20% to 10% except for automobiles. Erroll noted that the decline in hire-purchase indebtedness made it "possible to allow these modest relaxations to take place." Total installment indebtedness had fallen from £910 million in January to £883 million at the end of April, the lowest level since Feb. 1960. The highest interim level had been £927 million in July 1961.

International Finance

Britain's international payments deficit dropped from $882 million in 1960 to $173,600,000 in 1961, according to a government White Paper made public Mar. 28. Britain's 1961 trade deficit totaled $378 million, compared to $1,094,800,000 in 1960. Reflecting confidence in the growing stability of the pound, the London gold price had dropped Feb. 19 to $35.09625, its lowest level since July 1961.

The Federal Reserve Bank of N.Y. and the British Treasury announced May 31 the exchange with (sale to) the Bank of England of $50 million in dollars for almost £18 million in pounds. The New York bank acted on behalf of the Federal Reserve System in making the 3-month agreement. The British Treasury also announced May 31 that Britain had repaid an additional £25 million ($70 million) of the £535 million it had borrowed from the International Monetary Fund (IMF) Aug. 8, 1961. Total repayment by May 31 amounted to £275 million ($770 million), with an additional £229 million ($641 million) still outstanding. Total British stand-by credit with the IMF amounted to £454 million ($1.217 billion) after this £25 million repayment. The repayment was made in Deutschmarks ($25 million), U.S. dollars ($20 million), Canadian dollars ($20 million) and Swedish kroner ($5 million). Taking the U.S. Federal Reserve Board's dollar sale and the repayment to the IMF into consideration, total British gold and dollar reserves rose by £26 million in May.

The $50 million exchange with the U.S. was reversed in August, as arranged, and an additional £10 million was paid in debts to former European Payments Union members in August. This caused British reserves to fall by £24 million to a level of £1.017 billion Aug. 31. (Adjustments in the U.S. and EPU transactions improved British reserves by £4 million.)

EUROPEAN COMMUNITY

EEC Political Integration Debated

The wishes and philosophies of French Pres. Charles de Gaulle became more pronounced in shaping EEC (European Economic Community) policies during 1962 and led at times to dissent within both the EEC and the French republic. De Gaulle's philosophy was stated clearly in a Feb. 5 radio and TV address on the issue of the Algerian problem.

He said, in part: France "must help to build Western Europe into an organized union of states. . . . No doubt because we are now displaying a determination, building up a force and unfolding a policy that is our own, this . . . run[s] counter to the network of former conventions that assigned us the role of a so-called 'integrated' nation, . . . a back-seat power." French policies "will have to be accepted."

De Gaulle's views on the future political organization of Europe were further clarified at a presidential press conference held May 15. The French president's stand had aroused opposition from the supporters of eventual fullscale European political integration and had caused an unsuccessful political revolt within the French cabinet and National Assembly. De Gaulle specifically rejected any movement toward creating supranational European political institutions. He instead proposed a periodic consultation among European leaders to coordinate their nations' separate policies. Major points of his statement to newsmen:

●"To organize ourselves politically, let us begin at the beginning. Let us organize our cooperation, let our heads of state or government meet periodically to examine our problems together and to take decisions . . . which will be those of Europe. Let us set up a political commission, a defense commission and a cultural commission, just as we already have an economic commission."

●"These opponents [of the French proposals] tell us: You want to make a Europe of the fatherlands; we want to make a supranational Europe—as if a formula were enough to mix together these powerfully established entities which are called peoples and states."

●"I have already said, and I repeat, that at the present time there is not and cannot be any other possible Europe than a Europe of states ["*l'Europe des états*"], apart, of course, from myths, fictions, parades."

De Gaulle especially chided those of his critics who opposed his European consultation plan and at the same time opposed further discussion of the continent's political future until Britain had joined the EEC. He said: "Everybody knows that England, in her capacity as a great state and as a nation faithful to herself, will never agree to dissolve herself into some utopian construction." De Gaulle's phrase "a Europe of the fatherlands" ("*l'Europe des patries*") had gained widespread currency in European press and political circles, particularly among those who criticized his proposals as a reversion to the 19th Century concept of a concert of great European powers. De Gaulle stressed his view that the only "hope of uniting Europe in the political and defense fields" depended on the growing "solidarity between France and Germany." He reiterated French acceptance of the West German stand that "in the present international situation...it is vain to wish for a satisfactory settlement of the German problem." He conceded that "France cannot object to her ally, America, resuming on her own behalf talks [on Berlin] with Moscow which by euphemism are called soundings," but he insisted that "the status of Berlin...should not be changed." France, he declared, would "not be inclined to accept a measure which would submit Western forces in Berlin, ours in particular, to controls other than those fixed by the victors."

5 cabinet ministers, all members of the Roman Catholic Popular Republican Movement (MRP), resigned from the Pompidou government May 16 in protest against de Gaulle's European policies. The resigning ministers were: Pierre Pflimlin (state minister for cooperation with African states), Maurice Schumann (regional planning minister), Robert Buron (public works minister), Paul Bacon (labor minister) and Joseph Fontanet (public health minister). The dissent continued into the summer, when Premier Georges Pompidou called July 12 for a vote of confidence on a finance bill before the National Assembly. This demand was countered by a motion of censure supported by a coalition of Socialist, MRP, Independent and *Entente Democratique* representatives. In the debate, which opened July 16, Socialist leader Guy Mollet said: "We have always said that political authority must form the roof of the economic edifice. We have never believed that a federal [European] constitution would be possible from the first hour. Today, following a French initiative, there is talk of a political union. No proposal will hold our attention unless 2 essential conditions are fulfilled—the existing communities must be unified and strengthened, not threatened; and it must be expressly stated that, after the inevitable period of cooperation, a revision of the engagements undertaken by the [member] states will permit the adaptation to the political sphere of the method which has permitted economic unification." The censure motion was defeated July 17, receiving only 206 votes (an absolute majority of 241 was required for it to pass).

The issue of political integration among the EEC member nations came under careful re-examination during the first half of the year. The 6 EEC states had begun negotiations in July 1961 on the eventual establishment of a European political system. On the basis of an agreement reached at a Feb. 1961 Bonn "summit meeting" of leaders of the 6 states, a committee (known as the Fouchet committee, after its chairman, Christian Fouchet of France) had been charged with preparing a draft treaty for a European political union compatible with the European institutions already existing in the economic and military fields. The Fouchet committee was divided from its inception between those countries (mainly France, with increasing West German support) favoring institutions limited to facilitating the development of common policies by consultation among the sovereign European states, and those (chiefly Belgium and the Netherlands) favoring the development of genuinely supranational European institutions providing for majority rule and representation of the peoples involved.

An initial French draft embodying de Gaulle's consultative proposals had been presented to the committee in 1961, but it had been amended to include these minimal demands made by the other 5 powers: (1) assurances that existing European institutions would be preserved, with economic matters remaining in the hands of the EEC and defense matters under NATO (it was feared that de Gaulle hoped to block further development of the EEC toward majority rule and intended to make European consultation on defense matters the basis for creation of a French-led European bloc within NATO); (2) broadening of the scope of the current European Assembly to give it decision-making powers; (3) creation of a European secretariat and secretary general with functions similar to those of the same UN bodies; (4) revision of the treaty within 3 years to make European political decisions subject to acceptance by some form of qualified majority among member states, rather than the rule by unanimity and veto powers demanded by de Gaulle.

A new French draft was submitted to the 5 other states in Paris Jan. 18. It was reported to have been rejected as an attempt to withdraw the 1961 concessions and make it impossible for the projected European political community to evolve into supranationality. The new French draft reportedly eliminated all safeguards for the EEC and other existing institutions, provided for formation of a European defense bloc within NATO and again limited the projected union to a coordinating body subject to unanimous rule and the veto of any member government. It ignored the other states' demands for eventual provision of a popularly-elected European Assembly, which ultimately would serve as the "seed" of a European government.

The new French draft aroused strong opposition from the 5 other European states, particularly from West Germany, which had tended toward a neutral position in the 1961 negotiations. The European reaction was strengthened by a restatement of French views made by de Gaulle in his Feb. 5 address. De Gaulle, reiterating France's intentions to build a national nuclear striking force and to resist further inroads on French sovereignty by NATO or other international institutions, said that "no doubt ... this ... runs counter to the network of former conventions that assigned us the role of a so-called 'integrated' nation, ... a back-seat power," but France's policies "will have to be accepted" by the rest of the world.

The stalemate over European political unity was discussed by de Gaulle and Chancellor Konrad Adenauer Feb. 15 in Baden-Baden, West Germany. A joint communique issued by the 2 leaders after their talks said they had "agreed that in view of the existing danger to the free world, the work on this [European] organization would be continued and accelerated." It was reported that Adenauer had prevailed on de Gaulle to break the European political deadlock by withdrawing the most objectionable features of the new French draft. Paris dispatches reported, however, that de Gaulle had returned to France convinced that he had won Adenauer's support for his proposal for political consultation among the sovereign European states. This was evidenced in part by the statement in their joint communique that the 2 leaders had "reaffirmed the decision taken July 18, 1961, in common with the heads of government of Belgium, Italy, Luxembourg and the Netherlands, to organize the political unity of Europe." Despite the reports, the Adenauer-de Gaulle meeting did not result in any substantial alteration of the conflict within the Fouchet committee. (Adenauer, in an address Jan. 17 to the West German Bundestag, had declared that "we want to create a European political union." Referring to the growing role of the EEC, he had said: "In a united European economy the governing bodies must be constantly deciding upon national and common political problems—and that is not possible without political unity.")

It was reported from Bonn Apr. 10-11 that an agreement had been reached on terms for revitalizing the European political negotiations. The accord was credited to the intervention of Italian Premier Amintore Fanfani, who had conferred with de Gaulle in Turin Apr. 4 and with Adenauer near Milan Apr. 7. (Turin dispatches Apr. 4 had reported de Gaulle's failure to win Italian support for his proposed "Europe of the fatherlands.") Under the reported agreement, Italy, France and West Germany were to present a new version of a European political draft that would: (a) specifically bar activities in the defense field that would conflict with NATO; (b) permit the governing council of heads of the 6 governments to discuss economic matters but bar them from actions conflicting with or limiting the powers of the EEC; (c) leave open the question of whether the treaty would be revised to provide for greater supranationality.

Britain's readiness to join in the European political negotiations and to adhere to any agreement they might produce was stated Apr. 10 by Lord Privy Seal Edward Heath at a London meeting of the Western European Union's Ministerial Council. A Foreign Office summary of Heath's statement to the 6 foreign ministers of the other WEU countries said: "Mr. Heath ... expressed to the Council the view that the time was now coming when the United Kingdom, as an impending member of the [European Economic] Community, might profitably join with the 6 in working out future political arrangements." London sources reported Apr. 11 that the British government favored a confederal European political system—an association of sovereign states, as envisaged by France—rather than a federal one with member states surrendering part of their sovereignty to a central authority. Bonn dispatches reported Apr. 15 that the French and West German governments had rebuffed as premature the suggested British participation in the political negotiations. But Belgium and the Netherlands were said to have intensified their demands that Britain quickly be brought into the negotiations; the 2 smaller states were said to feel that Britain could be an effective counterweight to the feared domination of a European political system by France and West Germany.

The foreign ministers of the 6 EEC states met in Paris Apr. 17 to examine the compromise political draft submitted by Italy, France and West Germany. The meeting, which had been expected to produce agreement on submitting the compromise draft to a later European "summit" meeting, ended in disagreement when Foreign Mins. Paul-Henri Spaak of Belgium and Joseph M. A. H. Luns of the Netherlands made clear that their governments would refuse even to consider signing a European political treaty until Britain had been granted membership in EEC and had become a participant in the negotiations. A French Foreign Ministry statement said that "it has been impossible to agree on the principle of a European political union" because of the position taken by "2 countries." (Spaak was considered to be one of the leaders of the campaign for supranational European institutions. In an address Jan. 25 at a New York meeting of the Belgian Chamber of Commerce in the U.S., he had warned that European governments could not expect to enjoy the benefits of political unity without surrendering at least some national sovereignty. Referring to the French insistence on retaining national veto powers in the projected European political system, Spaak said: "I cannot conceive of a normally and efficiently functioning Europe unless all parties accept the rule of the majority." Commenting on the failure of the Apr. 17 Paris meeting, Spaak told newsmen in Brussels Apr. 19: It was absolutely necessary that Britain be made a part of the projected European union "to provide equilibrium among the states of the continent and to be a link with America"; Italy and Luxembourg had joined Belgium and the Netherlands in their readiness to accept "a rather weak union to begin with, provided that after 3 years it be strengthened by a directly elected parliament and by adoption of majority rule in place of the rule of unanimity" in the governing European institutions; France had rejected these terms. Spaak, commenting May 16 in Strasbourg on de Gaulle's May 15 declaration opposing a supranational Europe, termed the French view "a step backward" having "no bearing on reality.")

A growing French-West German agreement to force acceptance of de Gaulle's European plans and to prevent Britain's rapid entry into the EEC and the political negotiations was reported in May. West German sources reported May 9 that Chancellor Adenauer had said at a closed meeting of the Berlin Senate May 7 that he now opposed full British participation in EEC and would favor some form of associate EEC membership that would keep Britain outside the projected European political union. (These reports persisted despite a formal denial of their truth May 10 by Bonn press spokesman Felix von Eckardt.) Adenauer's reported shift in position was attributed to the increasing French-West

German political entente and to his dissatisfaction with the continued readiness of the Macmillan and Kennedy governments to negotiate an interim Berlin settlement with the USSR.

A proposal that France, West Germany and Italy begin concrete steps toward a European political union, with or without the participation of the 3 other EEC states, was advanced by Adenauer June 3 in Dortmund, at the annual congress of the Christian Democratic Union. Adenauer warned that the major European powers could not permit the movement toward union to remain stalled indefinitely by the Belgian-Dutch opposition to a consultative confederation and to any agreement reached without British participation. (The *N.Y. Times* reported May 17 that Richard Nikolaus Coudenhove-Kalergi, an Austrian count considered a founder of the Pan-European movement of the 1920s, had recently sent memos proposing such action to the French, West German and Italian governments.)

Adenauer's proposal was rejected by Dutch Foreign Min. Luns June 14 as an attempt to split the European states and as an implied threat to the success of the EEC. It was criticized June 15 by West German Foreign Min. Gerhard Schroeder, who warned that "in the current state of European affairs, nothing is less needed than European experiments on a minor scale."

Adenauer visited France July 2-8 in the first major tour of the country made by a German head of government since World War II. Adenauer's visit was planned to demonstrate the success of his efforts toward a French-West German reconciliation and the integration of West Germany within the new European community. It also apparently was intended by the French to advance de Gaulle's plans to make the growing Bonn-Paris political alliance the foundation stone of a revived and more powerful Europe. De Gaulle said July 3 at a state banquet at the Elysee Palace: "The union of Europe is a fundamental objective for both France and Germany. The great wonder of our times is that our 2 countries, having renounced any domination of the other, have discovered their common duty and recognized the senselessness of their old struggles. . . . They recognize that their union will make possible a European organization—political, economic, cultural, defensive—embracing, in addition to themselves, Italy, the Netherlands, Belgium and Luxembourg; a union which we hope will extend to others, above all Great Britain; a union which will bring great strength to the 'free world' and to the Atlantic Alliance, which will make a major contribution to the progress of the under-developed regions and which can open up future perspectives of equilibrium and cooperation for the whole continent." A joint communique issued July 5 disclosed that de Gaulle and Adenauer had agreed on the need "to bring the discussions on the creation of a [European] political federation . . . to a conclusion as soon as possible, in agreement with their partners." It expressed "the hope that . . . negotiations . . . will allow the problems arising from Great

Britain's request for entry into the European community to be solved in the spirit of strengthening the reconstruction of Europe." According to Gaston Coblentz, writing July 6 in the *N.Y. Herald Tribune,* the de Gaulle-Adenauer talks resulted in agreement on the following procedure and timetable for further progress toward European unity: (1) completion of negotiations for British membership in EEC in 1962; (2) convocation of a European "summit meeting" to fix terms for political federation of the 6 EEC nations despite Dutch-Belgian opposition to such negotiations without the participation of Britain; (3) amendment of the EEC Treaty of Rome by July 1963 to permit British membership; (4) ratification of a revised Rome Treaty after July 1963; (5) consolidation of political federation during 1963; (6) British membership in EEC on or after Jan. 1, 1964; (7) Britain's simultaneous inclusion in the European political system by then under way.

De Gaulle paid a 6-day state visit to West Germany Sept. 4-9. His trip, intended to cement publicly the growing Franco-German reconciliation and the 2 nations' political alliance in Europe, was viewed as an unqualified success. Speaking at a state dinner in Bruehl Castle, the French ambassador's country residence near Bonn, de Gaulle reaffirmed his hopes for Franco-German construction of a European community in which Britain apparently would be limited to a secondary role. De Gaulle declared that there must exist "on the old continent a pillar of power and prosperity of the same order as that which the United States constitutes in the new world." Referring to British negotiations for admission to the EEC, he said: "Without doubt certain...prejudices inside the community, joining themselves with certain influences on the outside, have, momentarily, been able to keep the conclusion in suspense. But France and Germany, which are in agreement on the principles and the methods of this vital construction, have every reason...to reinforce their own solidarity without delay."

The only purely political talks held by de Gaulle during his visit were carried out with Adenauer Sept. 5. Spokesmen said that the 2 had reached broad agreement on close French-West German political cooperation in Europe. Acknowledging Belgian and Dutch resistance to their proposal for establishing a 6-nation European confederation that in effect would exclude Britain, they agreed to postpone indefinitely a summit meeting of EEC leaders originally planned for September. A call for "organic cooperation" between the French and West German armed forces was issued by de Gaulle in Hamburg Sept. 7 in an address to the West German War College. De Gaulle declared that such cooperation was necessary to face the continuing Soviet threat and to provide a military basis for "the union of our 2 countries." In what was presumed to be an allusion to France's expectation of nuclear-military leadership in Europe, he said: "France and Germany will all the better assure themselves of the means of power if they join their possibilities. This would be all the more true if their European neighbors associated their resources to ours."

A joint communique issued Sept. 7 in Bonn said in part: "As regards European policy, note was taken of the current negotiations on the application of Great Britain to join the European Communities, negotiations already mentioned in the Franco-German communique issued in Paris on July 6. Examination of the problems relating to political cooperation allowed the French and German sides to recall the interest which is shown in this question and to express the hope that negotiations can be concluded with the least possible delay. France and Germany remain convinced that their future is linked with the progressive development of a united Europe." De Gaulle flew back to Paris Sept. 9. A communique issued by the French and West German governments on his departure sought to reassure other European nations that the 2 leaders' European plans did not exclude them; it said France and West Germany would "promote with their partners European unification for which the foundation stone has been laid."

EEC Admits Associate Members

In 1962 the European Common Market completed negotiations for differing forms of EEC association with Greece, 18 newly-independent African countries and 2 Dutch colonies.

17 months of negotiation—June 14, 1960 through Nov. 14, 1961— were necessary to complete arrangements for the Netherlands Antilles and Surinam (Dutch Guiana) to achieve associate status within the EEC. The EEC Council of Ministers Feb. 2 approved the convention implementing the terms of the agreement.

The agreement granting Greece associate membership in the EEC entered into force Nov. 1; ratification of the accord, which had been concluded in Athens July 9, 1961, had been completed with an exchange of documents in Brussels Aug. 24, 1962. The Greek agreement, negotiated with special attention to Greece's semi-industrial stage of development, provided for: (a) a goal of gradual abolition of customs barriers with the EEC countries over a 12-year period; (b) tariff increases ("infant industry tariffs"), even on EEC imports, to protect new industries for a period of up to 9 years; (c) extension of the tariff reduction period to 22 years in certain other cases; (d) duty-free entry for up to 10% of normal Greek imports from non-EEC countries; (e) no fixed arrangements for coal, steel, iron and scrap metal imports, which would be regulated by agreements with the European Coal & Steel Community; (f) EEC agreement not to change the common tariffs on tobacco, raisins, resin and turpentine without Greek assent; (g) European Investment Bank loans for Greek projects up to a total of $125 million in 1962-6.

The agreement for the association of 18 African states with the EEC was signed in Paris Dec. 20 but was to become effective only after ratification in 1963. The agreement, a 5-year convention, replaced the expiring association accords that had been negotiated for the 18 in 1957, when they had been dependents of France and Belgium. The new convention granted the African nations free entry to the EEC for their tropical products, principally coffee and cocoa, while the same imports from Latin American countries were to be subjected to EEC tariffs. The EEC nations were to enjoy preferential entry to the 18 African nations, which, however, were to be permitted to protect new industries. The high commodity prices formerly maintained for most of the 18 by France were to be reduced to world levels gradually in 5 years. The convention promised the 18 $730 million in aid within the next 5 years; $500 million of the total was to be allocated to investments and technical cooperation projects. Negotiations on the EEC-African agreement had been concluded in Brussels Oct. 24. The 18 African states: Cameroun, Central African Republic, Chad, the former Belgian Congo, the former French Congo, Dahomey, Gabon, Ivory Coast, Madagascar, Mali, Mauretania, Niger, Ruanda, Senegal, Somalia, Togo, Upper Volta and Burundi.

EEC Tariff Developments

Customs duties within the EEC were cut an additional 10% Jan. 1, making a total cut of 40% in tariffs on industrialized goods within the EEC since its formation. Agricultural tariffs were cut a total of 30% to 35% with the lastest reduction.

The EEC Council of Ministers reached unanimous agreement Jan. 14 on a common agricultural policy for the Common Market. The first major trade provision of the EEC's common agricultural system—the replacement of most import quotas, tariffs and controls on farm products by a single variable import levy—went into effect in the 6 countries July 30. Negotiations to achieve this step had been completed in Brussels June 20. All import and price regulations on grains, poultry, eggs and pork entering the EEC or passing among the EEC states were abolished and replaced by the levy, designed to bring farm imports to the market prices currently prevailing in each EEC importing country. Most controls on fruits and vegetables also were removed, although these were not to be subject to import levies, and tariffs were to be retained on them. The levy initially was imposed in a way to give a slight price advantage to farm imports of EEC origin, but the levy was to be abolished among the EEC nations within 7 years and was to be retained against farm imports from outside nations. Rice, beef and dairy products were to be brought under the levy system within a year.

The EEC completed tariff cuts averaging 20% with the U.S. Mar. 7 under terms of GATT (General Agreement on Tariffs & Trade). An agreement to cut tariffs between the EEC and the United Kingdom by 20% was reached May 16, according to an announcement by Frederick Erroll, president of Britain's Board of Trade. In keeping with GATT principles, Anglo-American tariff cuts were to be negotiated as well.

Tariffs on industrial and other nonfarm trade among the EEC countries were reduced by an additional 10% July 1, bringing the total of such reductions to 50% of the tariffs in effect Jan. 1, 1959, when the first internal EEC tariff cuts were instituted. The July 1 reduction had been ordered under an accelerated tariff-cutting program approved May 15 by the EEC Ministerial Council. The program provided for a reduction of internal EEC tariffs to the 40% level for industrial and nonfarm products by July 1, 1963 and for the attainment of the 2d of 3 stages in the construction of a common EEC external tariff by the same date, 2-1/2 years ahead of the schedule fixed by the Rome Treaty.

The EEC Executive Commission announced Oct. 29 that it planned to work toward completing the 6-nation customs union 3 years earlier than envisaged by the Treaty of Rome—by Jan. 1, 1967 rather than Jan. 1, 1970. A commission memo issued in Brussels outlined plans for the attainment of the EEC treaty's objectives—complete elimination of tariffs among the 6 countries—by 1967, subject to the continued existence of favorable European economic and political conditions. The memo stressed that the EEC's future development would seek to assure (a) potential expansion of the customs union, (b) an effective partnership with the U.S., (c) greater aid to underdeveloped countries and (d) liberal trade policies toward non-member nations. The commission's envisaged action program was to include concrete steps to match Europe's political integration to the attainment of the customs union and to supplement the union with a common European monetary policy and, eventually, an EEC monetary union. Among specific measures mentioned by the memo: reduction of internal EEC tariffs by 80% of the 1957 levels Dec. 31, 1965, prior to complete abolition of internal tariffs Jan. 1, 1967; application of a common EEC external tariff by member states by that same date; abolition of all passport and administrative trade control among EEC states by Jan. 1, 1967; harmonizing of European tax and budgetary systems by 1970; early completion of a highway network linking major European cities and capitals; specific foreign aid quotas for each EEC state, possibly on the basis of a percentage of each nation's budget; common wage and income policies, with a possibility of industrywide collective bargaining throughout the 6 nations; a common economic plan to indicate possible growth targets.

Pres. Walter Hallstein of the EEC Commission warned U.S. business leaders in New York Dec. 5 that the European customs union offered them greater trading opportunities but only at the price of reciprocal access to the U.S. market and sharpened competition between the 2 areas. Hallstein, addressing the NAM's (National Association of Manufacturers) 67th annual meeting, said: "For the first time in history, American businessmen will be dealing with a market comparable to their own, allowing them to apply the methods of production and distribution . . . which they have developed to supply their own market." But "there is no opening of foreign markets without reciprocity. The

[U.S.] Trade Expansion Act is...the...logical answer to what we have built up. Sharper competition is the natural consequence." This warning was repeated by Hallstein in 2 further addresses delivered during his visit to the U.S. Speaking in Lincoln, Neb. Dec. 6, Hallstein advised U.S. farmers not to expect greatly expanded sales in the EEC; he asserted that the solution for the U.S.' farm surplus problem was not to be found in bargaining between the U.S. and Western Europe, but rather in a "worldwide multilateral trading system." Addressing an audience in Omaha Dec. 7, Hallstein said: Such a system would have to "take up the basic questions of supply and demand and prices...international stockage policy and...the needs of the hungry"; the U.S. should prepare for "friendly but fruitful combat" with the EEC; "the Marshall Plan was a common crusade, whereas the [Atlantic] partnership at heart is a kind of competition; the 2 partners are to grow stronger by vying with each other."

U.S. protests against what it considered unreasonable EEC discrimination against American farm products had been rejected by EEC leaders Nov. 22 at a special meeting in Paris of the Organization for Economic Cooperation & Development (OECD). The protests had been presented to EEC Commission Vice Pres. Sicco Mansholt in Brussels Nov. 16 by U.S. Agriculture Secy. Orville L. Freeman. Meeting with newsmen after his session with Mansholt, Freeman had accused the EEC of "unreasonable and arbitrary protectionist action" against key U.S. farm exports, particularly poultry and grain. Freeman added that the U.S. did "not like any part of the Common Market's new variable levy system for controlling imports of grains and poultry." "We are not going to stand by and lightly allow our historical market to be taken away." He noted that the U.S.' new Trade Expansion Act authorized the President to take retaliatory action against any nation or trade group that "arbitrarily" restricted U.S. exports.

The EEC rejection of Freeman's criticism was delivered by French Agriculture Min. Edgard Pisani Nov. 22 at the Paris meeting. Pisani declared that while the EEC was prepared to negotiate on the U.S. protests, it would not retreat from its agreed agricultural system or adopt policies contrary to the system's intent. Answering Freeman's charge that the EEC levy system threatened the "traditional currents of trade" in farm products, Pisani said that the U.S. already had altered such currents by its export of surpluses to Africa, traditionally a European market. The EEC, he said, could not make its tariff policies dependent on their impact on a multiplicity of 3d parties.

A call for a world conference in 1963 on reduction of international trade barriers had been issued by U.S. Pres. John F. Kennedy Oct. 19 in an exchange of letters with Canadian Prime Min. John G. Diefenbaker. Mr. Kennedy, replying to Diefenbaker's suggestions of such a meeting, urged that they "join forces" to press for a ministerial tariff reduction meeting of all GATT nations in Feb.-Mar. 1963. Diefenbaker's suggestion had been made in connection with Canada's search for new trade alternatives if the British market was closed to it by Britain's membership in the EEC. Pres. Kennedy and EEC Commission Pres. Hallstein had conferred at the White House Apr. 12 and had issued a joint communique declaring that an Atlantic partnership must be built by the U.S. and a "strong closely knit European entity." The communique expressed both sides' resolution to negotiate settlement of their trade differences, but it recorded Mr. Kennedy's concern at the threatened loss of European markets for U.S. agricultural exports.

The EEC had raised its common external tariff against U.S. polysterene and polyethylene and synthetic cloth and paints Aug. 1 in retaliation for the raising of U.S. duties June 17 on imports of wool carpets and sheet glass, largely exported by Belgium. The European tariff decision was adopted by the EEC Ministerial Council June 4 after the U.S. had refused to cancel the carpet and glass tariff increases but instead had offered to negotiate reductions of duties on a variety of other items. Pres. Kennedy had ordered the U.S. tariff increases Mar. 19; the EEC had protested the increases formally Apr. 3 and had invoked GATT provisions requiring the U.S. to confer on the tariff changes before imposing them. The ensuing negotiations failed to resolve the dispute, which involved the EEC's export of an estimated $35 million worth of carpets and glass annually. The value of the U.S. exports retaliated against by the Europeans was approximately the same.

(The EEC Commission had reported June 25 that during 1961 trade among the 6 nations had increased by $12 billion, 16% over the amount recorded in 1960. EEC states' trade with outside countries increased during 1961 by $20 billion, 5% over 1960 totals.)

The European Assembly, meeting in Strasbourg, had voted Mar. 27 to elect ex-Italian Foreign Min. Gaetano Martino to replace Hans Furler of West Germany as Assembly president. The Assembly voted Mar. 30 to change its official title to European Parliament.

Euratom

Ex-French Interior Min. Pierre Chatenet assumed the Euratom presidency Jan. 10. He replaced Etienne Hirsch of France, who had held this position since Feb. 2, 1959. France, authorized under Euratom rules to nominate the Euratom president, had not supported Hirsch for another term. It was reported that this decision resulted from Hirsch's failure to support the French opposition to any supranational structure for Euratom.

The Euratom Ministerial Council signed a 20-year agreement June 9 in Brasília for Euratom's cooperation with Brazil in the development of nuclear energy for peaceful purposes. A similar Euratom agreement had been approved with Argentina but was not yet signed.

BRITAIN, THE EEC & EFTA

EFTA Internal Developments

EFTA Ministerial Council meetings were held in Geneva Mar. 2, in Copenhagen June 21-22 and in Oslo Oct. 22. All 3 meetings dealt primarily with pending applications of EFTA members for admission to the EEC as well as with EFTA tariff changes in the light of EEC actions.

At the Copenhagen meeting it was decided to accelerate the proposed schedule of tariff cuts. Tariffs between most of the 7 member states of the European Free Trade Association were reduced by 10% Oct. 31 to 50% of the levels prevailing in 1960, when the first EFTA tariff cuts went into effect. The new reductions were instituted Oct. 31 by Britain, Denmark, Portugal, Sweden and Switzerland; they were imposed by Austria Dec. 31 and were to be put into effect by Norway by Apr. 30, 1963. The cuts to 50% originally had been scheduled to take effect Jan. 1, 1965, but at the meeting in Copenhagen, the EFTA Ministerial Council ordered immediate steps to institute them. EFTA Secy. Gen. Frank E. Figures told newsmen in Copenhagen June 22 that the reductions had been accelerated to bring EFTA tariff rates "in step with the EEC."

The previous internal EFTA tariff reduction—by 10% to 60% of the 1960 level—had been put into effect Mar. 1 by Britain, Denmark, Portugal, Sweden and Switzerland. Austria carried out these reductions July 1, and Norway on Sept. 1. The reduction to 60% originally had been scheduled for July 1, 1963. (Finland, an associate member of EFTA, reduced its tariffs on goods from the EFTA nations by 10% Aug. 1 to 60% of the level prevailing when its association began.)

(A Scandinavian cooperation pact was signed in Helsinki Mar. 23 by the 5 members of the Nordic Council, 4 of which were also EFTA members—Finland, Sweden, Denmark, Norway and Iceland. The pact, which was sent to signatories for ratification, called for preservation and expansion of the past Nordic cooperation in the economic, legal, cultural, labor, social and transport fields.)

Britain Seeks EEC Membership

Prime Min. Harold Macmillan and his government fought unsuccessfully for British admission to the EEC on 4 separate fronts during 1962: (1) Macmillan travelled widely during the year in an effort to obtain worldwide support for his government's stand; (2) he had to overcome internal (Parliamentary) opposition to his plans; (3) he faced substantial criticism from members of the Commonwealth, and (4) he was engaged in the actual negotiation sessions on the European continent. By the end of the year he had not achieved his goal of British membership in the EEC despite minor successes in certain areas.

Macmillan met with West German Chancellor Konrad Adenauer Jan. 8 in Bonn, and Macmillan and Adenauer met Jan. 9 with British Foreign Secy. Lord Home and West German Foreign Min. Gerhard Schroeder. In a Jan. 9 communique, they expressed agreement that Britain and West Germany would work toward "the creation of a wider European community," which would include Britain.

The problems raised by the British-EEC talks were discussed by Macmillan and Italian Premier Amintore Fanfani Jan. 17 during a Fanfani visit to London. The meeting was attended by Home and by Italian Foreign Min. Antonio Segni. The London *Times* reported that the Italian leaders had assured Macmillan of their support for Britain's early entry into the EEC and for its participation in any future European political association. Fanfani reportedly told Macmillan, however, that it was up to Britain to make clear the concessions it required for settling the Commonwealth question.

Fullscale British-Common Market negotiations were resumed in Brussels Feb. 22 by Lord Privy Seal Edward Heath, the minister responsible for Britain's negotiations, and the EEC Ministerial Council. Heath, accompanied by Agriculture Min. Christopher Soames, formally asked the EEC Council to consider giving Britain a 4-year exemption from Common Market agricultrual policies to enable it to gradually accustom British consumers and farmers and Britain's traditional suppliers—the Commonwealth nations—to the new farm trade and price patterns. Soames explained the difficulties that Britain faced in conforming to EEC farm policies; he noted that the EEC nations themselves had taken 4 years to formulate and begin applying their agricultural system. The EEC ministers, led by French Foreign Min. Maurice Couve de Murville, generally expressed opposition to the British request. Couve de Murville asserted that the EEC's agricultural policy had been achieved only with great difficulty and that Britain, if it joined the Common Market, would have to adhere to the timetable under which a common EEC farm production and trade pattern would be fully established by 1970. Ignoring Heath's plea that Commonwealth nations be given "comparable outlets" in Europe if they lost the British market, he insisted that only "limited" palliatives were available for the Commonwealth problem.

Effective negotiations were suspended during March and April while EEC officials worked to analyze their position on the basis of agricultural regulations adopted by the Common Market in January. Addressing the American Newspaper Publishers Association in New York Apr. 26, Macmillan conceded that Britain had "hesitated" in its negotiations for EEC membership but asserted that it hoped for rapid progress in the talks. He added: "It is quite true that we first sought to achieve a form of unity which would not raise quite so many difficult technical problems regarding our economic ties with the Commonwealth. Our present negotiations in Brussels are directed towards a plan by which Britain may be able to do her double duty, as both a Commonwealth and a European country."

Macmillan met with U.S. Pres. Kennedy Apr. 27-29, seeking the American leader's support of the British objectives. A joint communique issued Apr. 29 expressed hope "for success of the current British-EEC negotiations, consonant with the interests of the Commonwealth and other European nations."

West German opposition to full British participation in the Common Market and proposed European political institutions was reported May 9 to have been voiced by Chancellor Adenauer during a visit to West Berlin. Adenauer, meeting privately with political associates in the city, was said to have advocated that Britain be limited by the EEC to a form of associate membership that would keep it outside the European political association sought by France and West Germany. To critics of his views, Adenauer reportedly replied: "Politics is not made from ideals, but from national interests; Britain's interests are different from those of Europe." British government spokesmen made it clear May 10 that Britain would associate itself with Europe only on a basis of full membership in the EEC and European political organization.

Heath and the EEC Council of Ministers resumed their talks in Brussels May 11-12. The meeting was devoted to an examination of proposals advanced by Britain for solving the Commonwealth problem. The British plans included: (1) A phased application of Common Market external tariffs to manufactured goods from the advanced Commonwealth nations. (Currently permitted free entry into Britain, these goods would be made subject to 30% of the EEC tariff in each category beginning in 1965, and the full tariffs were to be applied within 7 years.) (2) Abandonment of the British tariff exemptions currently accorded "temperate foodstuffs" (wheat, dairy products and meat) from the Commonwealth in return for arrangements assuring a comparable market in Western Europe for these same items. Britain urged a positive response to U.S. proposals for worldwide negotiations on reducing tariffs on industrial and agricultural goods.

The meeting ended with an announcement that agreement would be reached by July on the "broad outline" of a Commonwealth trade settlement, but it was reported from Paris May 14 that France again had blocked any real progress in the negotiations. The French were said to have insisted that Britain must choose between the Commonwealth and Europe and that if it chose Europe it must adhere to all major provisions of the Rome Treaty establishing the EEC. Heath told the House of Commons May 16 that the Macmillan government considered its commitment to secure safeguards for the Commonwealth nations "essential."

The first substantive progress in the British-Common Market negotiations was achieved by Heath and the EEC Council of Ministers at a Brussels meeting held May 29-30. It was announced May 29 that the 2 sides had reached agreement on the tariffs to be applied to imports of manufactured goods from the economically advanced Commonwealth nations. Britain would impose a levy equivalent to 30% of the EEC's common external tariff the day it joined the Common Market, would increase it to 60% at the beginning of 1967 and would conform to the full EEC tariff on these goods by the beginning of 1970. The Common Market nations would declare their readiness to participate in talks on worldwide negotiations for reducing tariffs on the goods concerned. (Britain's imports of manufactured goods from the advanced Commonwealth nations—Australia, Canada, and New Zealand—currently totaled $300 million yearly.) Britain May 30 submitted its proposals for safeguarding textile and other manufactured exports from the less advanced Commonwealth nations—India, Pakistan and Ceylon. It suggested that these imports be subjected to a levy equivalent to 30% of the EEC common external tariff when Britain entered the Common Market and that the levy be frozen or dropped if it was found to have affected the 3 nations' trade. Heath also announced May 30 that Britain would accept without major revision all nontrade provisions of the Rome Treaty. These primarily applied to such matters as movement of labor and capital, transportation, social security and anti-trust regulation.

Macmillan flew to France June 2 for 2 days of private talks with de Gaulle on the EEC problem. The 2 leaders, meeting at de Gaulle's Chateau de Champs, near Paris, were joined later by French Premier Georges Pompidou and Foreign Min. Maurice Couve de Murville. French sources reported that the talks had reduced the mistrust that had grown between Britain and France during the Common Market negotiations. In a communique, issued before Macmillan's departure June 3, the 2 leaders affirmed that a "community of interests" existed between France and Britain and would guide their future negotiations. But despite the reports of strengthened Anglo-French amity, the British and French governments later expressed disagreement over the positions taken by de Gaulle and Macmillan in their discussions. French spokesmen reported June 3 that Macmillan had given the impression that he was determined to bring Britain into the EEC without reservations and without special "attachments." British spokesmen rejected the French view June 5 and told newsmen that Macmillan had emphasized his determination to negotiate a settlement that would fulfill Britain's pledges to the Commonwealth. Macmillan told Parliament June 5 that de Gaulle, during their talks, had recognized the "enormous importance" of the Commonwealth and of Britain's obligations to it.

(The British spokesmen also strongly denied the truth of French reports that Macmillan had implied Britain's assent to de Gaulle's plans for a French nuclear striking force. They stressed that Anglo-U.S.

nuclear cooperation within NATO remained the cornerstone of British strategic policy. The French reports had described Macmillan as cognizant of the fact that Britain's entry into the EEC would lead it to a close involvement in the political and military affairs of Europe, to the detriment of its nuclear relationship with the U.S.)

The domestic British political opposition to the negotiations, at first an expression of extreme Tory nationalism and of leftist fears of association with a conservative, Catholic Europe, were swelled by more moderate groups as a result of French-West German resistance to the British approach. Harold Wilson, Laborite spokesman on foreign affairs, warned June 8 that "if a choice has to be made between Europe and the Commonwealth, there can be no doubt where our duty and loyalty lie." Laborite opponents of the talks claimed the support of 100 MPs of their party despite party leader Hugh Gaitskell's refusal to take a public stand on the issue. 40 Conservative Party backbenchers petitioned the Macmillan government July 31 not to abandon the Commonwealth or the members of the EFTA for Common Market membership. A campaign to still growing British political opposition to the European negotiations had been launched by Macmillan and Heath in radio-TV addresses June 20. Both men appealed for popular backing for the negotiations. Heath conceded that EEC membership might cost Britain some measure of sovereignty, but he asserted that it would not compel basic changes in Britain's way of life and would create economic opportunities that would be "best for Britain, for our Commonwealth, for Europe, and for the Western world."

Heath met with the EEC Ministerial Council again June 27-30 to discuss detailed arrangements to safeguard the Commonwealth nations' exports of temperate foodstuffs. Although this was the major problem confronting the negotiators, British sources complained that the EEC ministers failed to produce a promised statement of possible concessions on Commonwealth food exports. The 2 sides agreed, however, on the need for Common Market participation in worldwide negotiations on food and commodity trade. Heath reported that "some common ground" had been discovered for a solution that would assure the Commonwealth future European outlets "comparable" to the British market it probably would lose.

A French demand for the convening of worldwide talks on agricultural trade before British entry into the EEC was issued June 29 by Agriculture Min. Edgard Pisani. The statement warned that without a sweeping reorganization of world trade in farm products, the Commonwealth problem probably could not be solved in a way that would permit Britain to join the Common Market.

The EEC countries had proposed June 20 that if Britain joined the market, the enlarged community sign comprehensive bilateral agreements with India, Pakistan and Ceylon by 1966 to safeguard their trade in commodities and cheap manufactures. The proposal, made at a

Brussels session of a British-EEC negotiating subcommittee, was presented as necessary to avert the collapse of these countries' development programs.

Macmillan and Lord Home had met with U.S. State Secy. Dean Rusk in London June 24-25 to discuss U.S. proposals for a European nuclear force. The *N.Y. Times* reported from London June 24 that it had been agreed no action would be taken on the military question of a European nuclear deterrent until a final accord had been reached on the political and economic question of Britain's entry into the EEC. The British were said to have pressed Rusk for U.S. support in their efforts to win concessions to ameliorate the impact on Commonwealth trade of Britain's admission to the Common Market.

A declaration issued June 26 by the Action Committee for the United States of Europe, an influential European grouping of political and labor leaders from the 6 EEC countries, called for the admission of Britain to the EEC and for negotiations toward a European political union that ultimately would be given supranational institutions. The declaration said that Britain and the EEC countries would be capable of exerting a major influence on world affairs only if they were bound by such a union. It asserted that the envisaged union would be able to build a "partnership between equals" with the U.S. and thus contribute to world stability and peace.

Pres. Kennedy provided support to the British cause in his July 4th speech in Philadelphia when he said: "I will say here and now, on this Day of Independence, that the United States will be ready for a declaration of interdependence, that we will be prepared to discuss with a United Europe the ways and means of forming a concrete Atlantic partnership... between the new union now emerging in Europe and the old American union founded here 175 years ago. All this will not be completed in a year, but let the world know it is our goal." Mr. Kennedy indicated that the partnership he envisaged was one of content rather than form. He did not speak of formal political institutions to bind together the 2 communities but only of practical policies to carry out their common aims: "We believe that a united Europe will be capable of playing a greater role in the common defense, of responding more generously to the needs of poorer nations, of joining with the United States and others in lowering trade barriers, resolving problems of commerce and commodities and currency and developing coordinated policies in all economic, political and diplomatic areas. We see in such a Europe a partner with whom we can deal on a basis of full equality in all the great and burdensome tasks of building and defending a community of free nations.... The first order of business is for our European friends to go forward in forming the more perfect union which will some day make this partnership possible." (The president's address was lauded in statements issued July 4 by the EEC Executive Commission and by the West German and Italian governments. British spokesmen unofficially announced their government's support.)

Pres. Kennedy emphasized at his news conference July 5 that his address was a call for further development of existing Atlantic relationships as Western Europe began to weld itself into "one great institution." He expressed no support for the idea of a U.S.-European political union; he said such matters would have to await further European unification before "precise implementation." He made it clear that he considered Britain's rapid entry into the European Economic Community a necessary prerequisite for Atlantic partnership. He stressed that the proposed association should not be "a rich man's club while the rest of the world gets poorer."

Britain's applications for membership in the European Coal & Steel Community (ECSC) and European Atomic Energy Community (Euratom) had been presented to the ECSC Mar. 2 and to Euratom Mar. 5. Negotiations on the terms of British membership were opened by Edward Heath with the ministerial councils of Euratom July 3 and of the ECSC July 17. Heath informed Euratom that Britain was prepared to participate fully in the atomic "pool" but that the British nuclear armaments program would have to remain outside the agreement and under national control. He told the ECSC that Britain would accept the organization's statute but would require negotiations on demands for alignment of its steel pricing system (steel prices were uniform throughout Britain but varied in Europe according to a schedule based on the user's distance from the mill) and transport policies (British railways negotiated special rates for heavy freight movers whereas European railways used uniform rate schedules). Both "pools" welcomed the British applications but made it clear that approval depended on British entry into the EEC.

Heath and the EEC ministers July 21 announced their agreement on terms for the alignment of British agriculture with the Common Market farm system. Britain agreed to accept the EEC pattern of price supports and other farm measures; in return the EEC was to adopt a form of annual review of farm income similar to that used by Britain to fix the direct subsidies paid to its farmers. An attempt to write a final settlement of the Commonwealth farm trade problem and to fix an agreed timetable for the remaining negotiations was begun by Heath and the EEC Ministerial Council in Brussels July 24. The effort ended in deadlock Aug. 5 despite repeated declarations during 9 days of negotiations (July 24-27, Aug. 1-5) that an accord was imminent.

The setback in the negotiations for British-EEC economic ties was linked closely to a continuing controversy over the form and extent of Europe's proposed political organization and over whether Britain would or should be a full participant in a future European political association. Belgian Foreign Min. Paul-Henri Spaak, considered the leader of the Belgian-Dutch-Luxembourg opposition to the de Gaulle-Adenauer plan for a system of European consultation without Britain, had begun a series of meetings in July to find a formula for the reopening of the political negotiations. Spaak conferred with Netherlands Foreign Min. Joseph M. A. H. Luns July 24, with French Foreign Min. Couve de Murville July 25 and with West German Chancellor Adenauer and Foreign Min. Gerhard Schroeder July 26. Press reports published after these meetings said an agreement had been reached on a Belgian-Dutch proposal to open negotiations on a European political commission that would be—contrary to French demands—"largely independent" of the member governments. Belgium and the Netherlands were said to have accepted the French-West German view that the negotiations should proceed before agreement was reached on British entry to the EEC. They were said, however, to be pressing still for an accord that would include Britain and provide, eventually, for some kind of supra-national European institutions.

The negotiations produced an agreement July 26 that if no suitable worldwide solution had been found for the farm trade problem by 1970, the EEC countries, by then presumably including Britain, would open direct talks on "suitable arrangements" with the Commonwealth and other interested nations. The July 26 accord was based on the tacit agreement that Britain's preferential trade arrangements with the Commonwealth would have been completely liquidated by 1970 and that other transitional arrangements would be granted to Commonwealth farm trade in the interim. But the key question of Britain's traditional Commonwealth ties became the major issue before the negotiators July 27 as they discussed proposals for price levels to be established for grain, meat and other Commonwealth farm exports expected to be most affected by British membership in EEC. The dispute reportedly led Pres. Walter Hallstein of the EEC Executive Commission to warn Heath that Britain would have to place the Common Market nations ahead of the Commonwealth if it seriously intended to continue the membership talks. The first phase of the negotiations recessed for 4 days after failure to effect a compromise between the British and EEC pricing plans. Britain had urged the EEC to agree to pricing mechanisms and levels that would discourage European farmers from maximum production of the "temperate foodstuffs" that the Commonwealth would hope to sell in Europe. The EEC had responded with a promise to maintain "reasonable" prices that would assure European farmers adequate living standards without undue damage to Commonwealth exports. Britain rejected the proposals as vague and insufficient.

Lord Home, British foreign secretary, warned the British House of Lords Aug. 1 that if Britain failed to join the Common Market it would be isolated from Europe's growing power and would become "an off-shore island" with a weakened position in the world. He declared that "Commonwealth countries themselves have got to do some very hard thinking in terms of . . . realities. It seems to me that their own expansion is directly concerned with the expansion of Britain." "I do not believe the Commonwealth is a sufficient answer to Britain's needs in the next

50 years," he said. "Nor are we a sufficient answer to the Commonwealth's needs in the next 50 years if we stand alone."

Negotiations were resumed in Brussels Aug. 1. They were started with an EEC ultimatum to Heath to present within 30 minutes a written draft of the Commonwealth food trade safeguards expected by Britain. Effective talks were delayed for a day after Heath replied he could not give even a verbal reply without 24 hours' preparation. The EEC agreed Aug. 2 to offer Britain's major colonies and former colonies in Africa, the Caribbean and Latin America—but not Australia, New Zealand, Canada, India, Pakistan or Ceylon—associate membership in the Common Market. The EEC countries also agreed Aug. 2 to permit tariff-exempt imports into Europe of Indian and Ceylonese tea, the largest single item exported to Britain by India and Ceylon. They agreed Aug. 3 to a comprehensive program, including special tariff exemptions and "comprehensive agreements" by 1965 (primarily for cheap textiles and manufactured goods) to assure that India, Ceylon and Pakistan would not suffer a loss of foreign markets if Britain joined the EEC.

The crucial negotiating session was begun Aug. 4 with apparent agreement on most of the outstanding problems related to Commonwealth trade. It ended in deadlock later the same day after France introduced a complex EEC financial dispute and demanded its settlement on terms advantageous to itself as a condition to accepting a British-EEC accord.

The proposed Commonwealth trade settlement was worked out in a negotiating session that lasted nearly 22 hours Aug. 3-4. It represented what the EEC nations said were their ultimate terms for a compromise; it was accepted in principle by Britain despite a fear that it did not assure the Commonwealth the trade safeguards it was pledged to obtain. The proposed settlement called for: (1) Negotiations beginning in 1963 on worldwide commodity and farm export agreements that would give the Commonwealth new export opportunities; (2) a "reasonable" EEC farm price policy that would assure a reasonable level of continued farm imports into the expanded community; (3) assurances against the discriminatory revival of quotas on farm imports (abolished under the Common Market); (4) a phased reduction of Commonwealth preferentials in the British market and the elimination of these differentials by 1970; (5) EEC pledges to negotiate bilateral trade arrangements with outside countries, particularly of the Commonwealth, if no worldwide commodity agreement was possible. The proposal also pledged special EEC arrangements, particularly with respect to tea and cheap textiles, with India, Pakistan and Ceylon.

The negotiators were said to have been near agreement on the basis of the EEC proposal when the French delegation introduced its demand for final settlement of the disposition of variable levies to be imposed on farm imports to the Common Market. (Under a previous accord, never made final, the EEC countries had agreed to use the proceeds of these levies to finance the Community's over-all farm program, primarily to the benefit of France and Italy.) The French demand made it impossible for the negotiators to reach an agreement on the Commonwealth problem, and the meeting was recessed until October.

Despite what was described as the angered view of many delegates that France had sabotaged the meeting deliberately, Heath told newsmen Aug. 5 that the talks had resulted in "a broad measure of agreement" on the terms for Britain's membership in the Common Market. British spokesmen stressed that the talks had resulted in an agreement sufficient to permit the Macmillan government to defend its views at a scheduled Commonwealth prime ministers meeting in London. Heath's formal report on the Brussels negotiations, issued Aug. 7, said that an accord had been near "but the French delegation took the view that it was not possible for it to give its agreement to arrangements for temperate agricultural products from the Commonwealth until further consideration had been given to the question of . . . financial regulation." French Foreign Ministry spokesmen disputed the Heath report Aug. 8 and charged that the talks had been broken off when Heath decided to "reserve his position" on the 5-point proposal dealing with Commonwealth farm exports.

With the 2-month recess in formal negotiations in effect on the Continent, Macmillan's attention turned to rising domestic opposition to the concessions required of Britain for EEC membership. Virtually unanimously, Britain's farm, business and labor organizations had come out against the Common Market negotiations or had urged delays in the talks:

●The English and Welsh section of the National Farmers Union, acting with the concurrence of the Scottish and Ulster sections, had denounced the proposed merger Aug. 23 as a threat to British agriculture. It urged instead that negotiations begin on a new world farm trade agreement within an expanded Organization for Economic Cooperation & Development (OECD).

●The Trades Union Congress (TUC), meeting in Blackpool at its annual conference, voted Sept. 6 to adopt a motion deferring a public statement on the EEC negotiations until the course of the talks was clarified. Delegates voted down a motion submitted by 6 of the TUC's most powerful unions calling for total opposition to the negotiations. Despite the TUC's decision, it was reported by the *N.Y. Times* Oct. 1, that every major British union with the exception of the National Union of Railwaymen had agreed to support the Labor Party's opposition to the negotiations.

●The National Association of British Manufacturers called Sept. 16 for a delay in the final decision on joining the EEC. It said: "The future of Britain will be profoundly affected by the decision to join or not to join. . . . It is obviously wise to spend adequate time . . . in negotiating terms which are acceptable to us as well as to other members of the

Commonwealth." Britain, it said, should join only "when we are quite clear as to the terms and then only if they are satisfactory."

Macmillan's drive for public support began Sept. 20 with a radio-TV report to Britain on the London meeting of Commonwealth prime ministers, which had been held Sept. 10-19. Macmillan, hailing Britain's "great decision" to seek EEC membership, noted 2 prime economic factors for the move: (1) British industry could not expand or withstand world competition from European industry unless it had equal access to the huge EEC market; (2) "none of the conditions exist which would allow a common Commonwealth market because these are countries with totally different backgrounds, different races, different stages of development, scattered all over the world." He added that the decision had been made for political as well as economic reasons: "Politically, because we wanted to strengthen the new unity in Europe. Also, because we knew that if we were not in Europe our influence would begin to decline, and with the decline we should lose our influence in the world outside." Asserting that the Commonwealth talks had been frank, Macmillan said: "We have been able, in this way, to make them understand our reasons why we need to join the Common Market and why it will be, in the long run, better both for us and for them."

The Liberal Party's annual conference, meeting Sept. 20 in Llandudno, Wales, overwhelmingly approved the negotiations for British membership in the Common Market. It expressed dissatisfaction with the Macmillan government's position in the talks with the EEC powers and the Commonwealth nations, but it called on the government to "press its negotiations for membership to a successful conclusion."

Labor Party leader Hugh Gaitskell abandoned his uncommitted position on the EEC negotiations Sept. 21. Gaitskell warned that British entry into the Common Market under the terms currently discussed "means the end of Britain as an independent nation." In a nationwide radio-TV address rebutting Macmillan's Sept. 20 speech, Gaitskell declared that if Britain pursued EEC membership under these conditions: "We become no more than Texas or California in the United States. It means the end of 1,000 years of history and the end of the Commonwealth." Gaitskell emphasized that EEC membership would be a benefit if adequate trade safeguards were offered for the Commonwealth nations. "But," he added, "if they refuse that, I can only suspect that we are not going to get decent agreements at all. And if that is the case, I would say it [the EEC] is the wrong club for Britain to join."

Gaitskell presented the case against EEC membership to the Labor Party Oct. 3 at the party's 61st annual conference, held in Brighton. In his address he reiterated his earlier warning against Britain's becoming a "province of Europe": Modern Europe had produced a great civilization, but it also had produced Hitler and Mussolini and political forces still judged reactionary by British standards; Britons "are not prepared to accept supranationalism" if this meant acquiescence in vital decisions made by a projected European parliament without reference to Britain's interest.

The Labor Party conference Oct. 3 approved Gaitskell's position by adopting a policy statement, submitted by the party's National Executive Committee, that said: Britain's entry into the EEC should be subject to (1) strong safeguards for "our friends and partners in the Commonwealth"; (2) fulfillment of Britain's promises to the members of the EFTA; (3) safeguards for British agriculture; (4) "the right to plan our economy"; (5) the right to maintain an independent foreign policy.

The Conservative Party joined the Liberals in supporting the Macmillan stand against the position of the Labor Party and the TUC. The Conservatives' annual party conference in Llandudno, Wales Oct. 11 gave only 50 votes (4,500 voting delegates attending) to a rightist motion that would have declared the party's opposition to further negotiations on EEC membership. A party motion approving the Macmillan government's handling of the current negotiations was adopted by the conference later Oct. 11. Macmillan, addressing the Llandudno meeting Oct. 13, called on Britain to fulfill a new role as a nation with "a double influence" in both European and world affairs. He declared that "British influence would be important and could be decisive" in leading the Common Market powers to assume worldwide responsibilities and that Britain's new European position would mean that its value to the Commonwealth "will be greatly enhanced." He pledged Britain to work within the EEC for a united Europe and a stable world without sacrificing the sovereignty "of the crown, the government and the people of these islands."

Labor Party leader Hugh Gaitskell, in a speech Oct. 13 at a party rally in Cambridge, repeated his objections to the proposed British-EEC merger. He charged that the Macmillan government was insisting that Britain join Europe because this new grouping was to become the 3d great world power. "But," he declared, "to equal the United States and Russia, Europe must become a single political unit. When we are told we have to go into the Common Market because we must be inside this great new European power, this really does mean that we must accept the disappearance of Britain as an independent power."

2 new rounds of ministerial-level talks on conditions for Britain's proposed entry into the EEC were held in Brussels Oct. 25-27 and Nov. 15-19. They ended with the 2 sides still deadlocked on most of the major problems resulting from the British application for membership.

In the 2 months that had elapsed since the Aug. 5 recess, discussions had been carried on and opinions expressed in less formal ways. West German Chancellor Konrad Adenauer's opposition to early British participation in the European political talks was presented publicly in a TV interview broadcast Aug. 28 in West Berlin. Adenauer, charging that Macmillan had shown reluctance to take a full part in a European political association, said it was clear that Britain's involvement in the

Common Market and its participation in European politics were 2
separate issues and should be negotiated separately. Adenauer expressed
doubt as to the truth of the position expressed by Macmillan, in a personal message delivered July 21, that Britain was prepared to participate
fully both in an economic and a political union. Adenauer's statements
aroused strong criticism from London and from members of his own
cabinet; Foreign Min. Gerhard Schroeder told newsmen Aug. 29 that he
favored Britain's entry into Europe. The British Foreign Office Aug. 29
made public portions of the letter in which Macmillan had promised that
Britain would "join wholeheartedly" in the movement for European
political integration.

Foreign Mins. Paul-Henri Spaak of Belgium and Joseph M. A. H.
Luns of the Netherlands conferred in Brussels Sept. 10 and said that in
view of the positions taken by Adenauer and de Gaulle during the
French leader's visit to Germany Sept. 4-9, no European political accord
was in sight. Spaak reiterated that he and Luns were in favor of early
British admission to the EEC and that, "having made that step, Britain
ought to participate in political Europe." British Lord Privy Seal
Edward Heath conferred with Spaak, Luns, and Luxembourg Foreign
Min. Eugene Schaus near London Sept. 19-22 in what was reported to
be an effort to rally support against France's apparently growing
opposition to British EEC membership. He then went to Europe for
talks with West German Foreign Min. Gerhard Schroeder in Bonn Sept.
25, Premier Amintore Fanfani in Rome Sept. 28 and Chancellor Konrad
Adenauer in Cadenabbia, Italy Oct. 1. But no effective opposition to the
"hard" French position was reported. Finally, Heath met with the EEC
ministers in Brussels Oct. 8 to inform them of the results of the recent
Commonwealth conference in London and to fix a timetable for further
negotiations. The Oct. 8 session was the first ministerial-level meeting to
be held by the 2 sides since August.

The renewed Brussels negotiations Oct. 25-7 were planned to advance negotiations on these unresolved questions: (1) the harmonizing of
Britain's system of farm subsidies with the agricultural system adopted
by the EEC; (2) the trade problems faced by India, Pakistan and Ceylon,
the Commonwealth's less-developed members, if British entry into the
Common Market deprived them of the British market; (3) British requests for EEC tariff exemptions for certain key Commonwealth goods
and raw materials that currently enjoyed duty-free entry to Britain
under the system of Commonwealth trade preferences. The opening
session was devoted largely to talks among the 6 EEC nations on their
response to Britain's request for time in which to abolish its subsidy
system gradually and gear Britain's agriculture to the EEC farm
system, scheduled for full application by 1970. The EEC nations announced Oct. 26 that they had rejected the British request and that if
Britain joined the Common Market, it would be expected to apply the
European farm system immediately. Britain had asked for an 8-year

"transition period" during which its farmers would be brought gradually under the EEC agricultural system. The EEC nations contended that such a delay would wreck their delicate farm agreement.

(The major differences between the 2 systems: Within the Common Market, as in the U.S., farm prices and production were to be regulated by state purchases of surpluses and controls over agricultural imports, the latter particularly by making them subject to a variable levy [duty] to bring import prices to the prices prevailing in EEC countries; in Britain, farm products were imported virtually without controls, and British farmers' incomes were assured by cash subsidies when home market prices were driven down by the imports to world price levels deemed unprofitable in view of the British farmers' costs.)

The Brussels negotiators failed Oct. 27 to produce any agreement on requests for continued free access to the British market for Indian, Pakistani and Ceylonese goods or for Britain's demand that certain Commonwealth raw materials be granted "nil-tariff" concessions. The Indian-Pakistani-Ceylonese trade largely involved textiles, tea, hides and jute. The "nil-tariff" concessions were asked by Britain to assure its imports of aluminum, paper and other key raw materials, mainly imported from Canada. The EEC nations offered minor concessions on some of these items, but none were considered acceptable by the British. Britain especially had urged that Indian, Pakistani and Ceylonese imports to Britain be permitted to continue exempt from the common EEC tariffs until the Common Market carried out its pledge of special tariff negotiations with the 3 countries. The EEC offered only a temporary reduction of 15%-30% in tariffs on the 3 countries' major exports, pending the promised special tariff negotiations. Edward Heath, lord privy seal and chief British negotiator, said Oct. 27 that the EEC counter-offers would be studied, but he expressed doubt that they were acceptable in their current form.

The Nov. 15-17 Brussels meeting was devoted largely to the problem of the EEC tariff rates to be applied to Ghana, Nigeria, Tanganyika, Uganda, Kenya and the other current and former British territories of Africa that had, for political reasons, rejected proposals for some form of association with the EEC. It was announced following the Nov. 15 session that an agreement had been reached under which (a) British African countries would remain eligible for associate Common Market membership should they reverse their current position, and (b) Britain would be permitted to apply EEC tariffs to their major exports (cocoa, coffee and other commodities) gradually, with the full tariffs coming into effect by 1970. The Nov. 15 and 16 sessions produced agreements to reduce EEC tariffs on kangaroo meat, mutton and lamb, all relatively minor items currently enjoying duty-free entry to Britain from Australia and New Zealand. Some progress was reported on the question of canned salmon and dried foodstuffs, with EEC tariffs to be applied to these items, largely exported by Australia and Canada, gradually by 1970. No agreement was reached on the tariffs to be applied to aluminum, lead, newsprint and other major raw materials currently imported by Britain from Canada. No attempt was made at the Nov. 15-17 meeting to settle the British-EEC farm problem.

The British government's campaign for domestic political support of its negotiations for Common Market membership was spurred personally by Prime Min. Macmillan following the Commonwealth meeting in September. Macmillan's campaign was viewed as essential in view of the apparently growing British opposition to an association with EEC and an eventual European political federation at the expense of Britain's traditional ties with the Commonwealth nations. This opposition extended to Parliament, where warnings against the course of the British-EEC negotiations had been voiced Nov. 8 by the Earl of Avon and Earl Attlee (former Prime Min. Sir Anthony Eden and Sir Clement Attlee) and the Marquess of Salisbury. Avon warned that if Britain joined the EEC under the terms being negotiated, it would face "a major upheaval" in its pricing and manufacturing. He declared that the current negotiations led inevitably toward a European federation—"a most unsound doctrine"—with countries whose history was "varied" and unlike that of Britain, which had a tradition of "self-government by a free people." Attlee declared that he was "against entry" primarily because it would associate Britain closely with countries whose attachment to parliamentary democracy was dubious. "Germany has had hardly any experience in it, Italy has had very little, and France tends to swing between a dictatorship and—more or less—anarchy." Attlee said that French Pres. de Gaulle was "a very good European provided Europe is run by France," and for that reason he did not want Britain in the European association.

Despite these attacks on Macmillan's policy, the Conservative majority in Parliament upheld the government against opposition Laborite motions demanding a stronger defense of Britain's interests in the EEC negotiations. The Laborite motions were defeated Nov. 8 by 319-221 vote in the House of Commons and by 62-23 in the House of Lords. Conservative motions approving the Macmillan cabinet's handling of the negotiations were approved in both houses without formal vote.

Macmillan's stand was supported somewhat indirectly Dec. 5 by U.S. ex-State Secy. Dean Acheson. Speaking at the 14th annual student conference on U.S. affairs, held at the U.S. Military Academy in West Point, N.Y., Acheson criticized Britain's past efforts to remain an independent world power; his remarks aroused strong protests in Britain. Acheson said:

"Great Britain has lost an empire and has not yet found a role. The attempt to play a separate power role—that is, a role apart from Europe, a role based on being the head of a 'Commonwealth' which has no political structure, or unity, or strength and enjoys a fragile and precarious economic relationship by means of the sterling area and preferences in the British market—this role is about played out. Great Britain, attempting to work alone and to be a broker between the United States and Russia, has seemed to conduct policy as weak as its military power. HMG [her majesty's government] is now attempting—wisely, in my opinion—to reenter Europe. . . . At the moment a decisive turning point lies before modern Europe, posed by the application of the British government to join the Common Market. If this application succeeds, another step forward of vast importance will have been taken. While Western Europe and Britain are pondering and negotiating this momentous decision, the United States should be clarifying its policy on the next steps to take with our European allies. These involve proposals on which this country must take the lead. To take the lead, it must know what it wishes to propose. One proposal should be to devise, agree upon, and carry out a plan for the defense of Europe. A plan itself and the ancillary steps for providing the means to put it into effect' should be part of the proposal. A 2d proposal would deal with economic and fiscal matters—with the reduction of trade barriers, generalized for the benefit of the whole free world, and with the coordination of economic and fiscal policies essential for the expanding production which alone can provide that environment in which free nations can exist and flourish. If wisely formulated and favorably received, the proposals would put us on the verge of another great advance in the development of the Atlantic Community and would require political agreements and political institutions of a most far-reaching nature."

British officials reacted Dec. 6 with what the London *Times* described as "anguish" at the Acheson remarks. London newspapers generally headlined Acheson's address as an attack on the British people and their national traditions; it evoked a spate of anti-U.S. remarks by British politicians. The major public response to Acheson was made personally by Prime Min. Macmillan Dec. 7 in a letter written to Viscount Chandos, president of the Institute of Directors and a former cabinet minister. Macmillan declared that Acheson's logic applied equally to the U.S. and showed that "the doctrine of interdependence must be applied in the world today if peace and prosperity are to be assured." He added, however: "Insofar as he appeared to denigrate the resolution and the will of Britain and the British people, Mr. Acheson has fallen into an error which has been made by quite a lot of people in the course of the last 400 years." Despite U.S. officials' assurances Dec. 6 that Acheson spoke as a private citizen, not as a member of the Kennedy Administration, the speech and the British reaction to it were generally believed to have aggravated the U.S.–British controversy that broke out Dec. 7 with the news that the U.S. intended to halt development of the Skybolt missile, key weapon in Britain's nuclear defense plans.

The last 2 rounds of negotiations in 1962 on Britain's application for membership in the European Economic Community were held in Brussels Dec. 10-11 and 19-20. The talks failed to produce substantive settlement of any of the disputes blocking an agreement. The 2 sides, however, agreed to consult in committee on one of the major barriers to an accord—alignment of the differing British and EEC systems of agricultural protectionism, pricing and subsidies. The failure of the 2 sessions to result in an easing of the British-EEC deadlock was attributed in part to the position publicly adopted by the 6 EEC powers Dec. 5 at a ministerial meeting in Brussels. The 6—France, West Germany, Italy, Belgium, the Netherlands and Luxembourg—agreed at their Dec. 5 meeting to offer Britain the following concessions, all deemed minor by the British: (a) a limited delay in application of the full EEC farm system to Britain (to permit the Macmillan government to honor its pledge that this would not occur during the current Parliament, expiring in Oct. 1964); (b) the right to grant consumer subsidies to offset expected rises in British food prices and to grant cash subsidies to pork and egg producers to offset expected rises in grain prices during a transition period ending in 1969. The EEC powers made it clear, however, that they expected Britain otherwise to apply fully the European farm system immediately on joining the EEC and similarly to apply EEC external tariffs immediately against all outside nations, including those of the Commonwealth and of the EFTA.

(Reacting to the EEC position, made known in a statement issued in Brussels Dec. 5, Foreign Office spokesmen declared in London Dec. 6 that Britain would honor its tariff and trade commitments to the other 6 members of the EFTA. Other unidentified British officials warned the same day that if Britain's application to the EEC was rebuffed, all British military commitments in Western Europe would be reviewed. These officials said that Britain could not afford to maintain 51,000 troops in West Germany if the Bonn government erected high tariffs against British exports to that country.)

The agreement to begin consultation on the British-EEC agricultural dispute was reached at the Dec. 10-11 negotiating session held by Edward Heath and the EEC ministers. A special committee made up of the agriculture ministers of the 7 countries, headed by Sicco Mansholt, Dutch member of the EEC Commission, was ordered formed to examine in detail the expected effects on Britain's agriculture and economy of (a) the immediate application of EEC rules demanded by the European powers and (b) the gradual application of these rules sought by Britain.

(47 prominent backbench members of Prime Min. Macmillan's Conservative Party presented in Parliament Dec. 13 a motion commending the Macmillan government's firm stand in the Brussels talks and urging that this firmness be extended to "proposals made by the 6 affecting sovereignty, the Commonwealth, and EFTA" even if this meant abandonment of the EEC application in favor of "a major Commonweath initiative.")

The Dec. 19-20 Brussels meeting was devoted to continuing the general British-EEC negotiations and to an interim report given Dec. 20 by the special agricultural committee. Although no precise indications of progress were given by the negotiators, Heath reported Dec. 20 that "a large area of Commonwealth matters has been agreed" and both sides hoped for further agreement early in 1963.

Negotiations for British entry into the EEC were the central subject of 2 days of talks held Dec. 15-16 by French Pres. de Gaulle and British Prime Min. Macmillan. Macmillan had flown to France Dec. 14. He conferred privately with de Gaulle beginning Dec. 15 at the latter's

Presidential estate in Rambouillet. A communique issued by the 2 leaders Dec. 16, after their private discussions had ended, conceded that "difficulties... have been encountered" in the British-EEC negotiations. Reports from Paris made it clear, as well, that Macmillan had not won the support he sought from de Gaulle for Britain's effort to join the EEC. It was reported widely that Macmillan had appealed to de Gaulle on grounds of political friendship to relax the rigid French conditions for British membership in EEC and to make it possible for Britain to fulfill its promise to secure trade safeguards for the Commonwealth nations.

In a New Year's eve TV address to the French people, de Gaulle said that: one of France's primary aims was a European union; "this concerns the economic, [foreign] policy, defense and cultural union of Western Europe... establishing a balance with the United States and in this way reinforcing the alliance of the 'free world.' A union ready in the future to welcome an England which can... join it definitely and without reservation."

The Commonwealth

A significant difference between the EEC and EFTA existed in terms of the tariff policies towards non-members. EEC policy dictated that members maintain a common tariff level while EFTA policy allowed individual member nations to determine their own duties on imports from non-members. This was the issue of primary concern to Commonwealth members. It was the feeling within the Commonwealth that should Britain become a Common Market member, past preferential tariff concessions would be lost; to many members, especially those less developed economically, this would create extraordinary economic hardships.

Commonwealth members, therefore, followed 2 general policies during 1962: (a) they sought support and assistance from independent nations, especially the U.S., and (b) they expressed their feelings as strongly as possible at the Commonwealth Conference Sept. 10-19 in London.

Edward Heath, Britain's lord privy seal and in charge of its negotiations for British membership in the EEC, had gone to Canada and the U.S. in January to clarify the issues raised by his Common Market talks. Heath conferred Jan. 3-4 with Canadian Prime Min. John G. Diefenbaker and Finance Min. Donald Fleming and pledged, in a statement at the end of their talks, that Britain would safeguard "the essential trade interests of Canada and the other Commonwealth countries" in its EEC negotiations. Diefenbaker, considered the leader of Commonwealth opposition to British EEC membership, reiterated Jan. 4 his demand that the matter be brought before a conference of Commonwealth prime ministers.

The 7th annual meeting of the U.S.-Canadian Committee on Trade & Economic Affairs, held in Ottawa Jan. 12-13, was devoted to problems caused by the U.S. and British negotiations with the EEC. The meeting reaffirmed both countries' support for freer trade, but it failed to produce agreement on a reported U.S. plan for coordinated U.S.-Canadian tariff-cutting action. Canada was said to oppose such action until the outcome of British-EEC negotiations on the Commonwealth preference systems.

Macmillan visited Canada in April in an attempt to reassure Diefenbaker about Britain's defense of Commonwealth interests in the EEC negotiations. The 2 leaders conferred Apr. 30-May 1 and then issued a communique in which neither indicated he had altered his government's policy. The Macmillan-Diefenbaker meeting was one of a series of similar talks held by Macmillan in May with Commonwealth leaders visiting London. Deputy Prime Min. John Ross Marshall of New Zealand declared at a London news conference May 21 that Britain thus far had failed to win adequate access to the British-EEC market for Commonwealth products; this access "must be secured," he said, if the Commonwealth nations' economies were to survive. Australian Prime Min. Robert Gordon Menzies, in Britain for talks with Macmillan, said in a nationwide radio-TV address June 4 that Australia would be forced to protect "her own interests" if Britain accepted EEC membership at the expense of Commonwealth trade. He warned that Australia, Canada and New Zealand could never accept a preliminary British-EEC accord (negotiated in May) or an end to all Commonwealth trade preferences by 1970.

Archbishop Makarios III, president of Cyprus, conferred with Pres. Kennedy in Washington June 5-6. "American interest in the development program of Cyprus ... and in assisting its implementation" was expressed by Mr. Kennedy in a joint communique issued June 6. The assurance of U.S. aid was reiterated in an exchange of messages June 17 prior to Makarios departure from the U.S. During a visit to New York, Makarios, at a news conference at the UN June 8, expressed doubt that "any safeguards will be found that are satisfactory to the Commonwealth members" if Britain joined the European Common Market.

Prime Min. Robert Gordon Menzies of Australia conferred in Washington June 18-20 with Pres. Kennedy and Administration officials on their countries' potential trade problems if Britain should enter the EEC. A joint communique issued June 20 said the 2 leaders were "encouraged to believe that satisfactory solutions will be found to these problems." Agreement was also reached for the U.S. and Australia to hold technical talks on their trade problems. New Zealand Deputy Prime Min. John Ross Marshall had conferred with Pres. Kennedy June 16 on the similar trade problem facing his country.

Immediately prior to the Sept. 10-19 Commonwealth conference, Commonwealth Labor Party leaders met Sept. 8-9 and issued a statement, declaring: "If Britain were to enter the Common Market on the basis of what has so far been agreed [in the Brussels negotiations], great damage would inevitably be done to many countries in the Commonwealth and therefore to the unity of the Commonwealth itself.... We fully understand the case advanced for Britain's entry into the Common Market. We also recognize that the final decision on this matter is for the British Parliament and the British people alone. Nevertheless, we recall the pledge of the British prime minister on Aug. 2, 1961 that he would not ask Parliament to support entry into Europe if it would injure Britain's relations with, and influence in, the Commonwealth.... The essence of our objection is that while there appears to be a firm commitment to end Commonwealth preferences not later than 1970, and to give European exports a preference in Britain against the Commonwealth, no precise agreements which offer compensating advantages to Commonwealth countries have been reached. We do not believe that Britain should enter the Common Market unless and until the present vague promises and assurances have been converted into precise agreements."

British Labor Party leader Hugh Gaitskell concluded: "We have always recognized that, while the economic arguments are evenly balanced, there are important political considerations which can be said to favor entry. But we have also insisted that we could not go in until certain conditions were fulfilled.... If the government propose to go into the Common Market on terms which the Labor Party regard as wholly unacceptable..., then undoubtedly in my view we should ask for a general election."

Leaders of the 16 Commonwealth nations and of Britain's 8 major colonial territories met in Marlborough House in London Sept. 10-19 for the Commonwealth conference, which was devoted largely to the question of Britain's negotiations for membership in the European Economic Community. While Britain believed it must enter the EEC or face exclusion from Europe and inevitable economic decline, the Commonwealth nations feared the end of the trade and other ties based on their association with Britain. The conferees were unable to produce an agreed solution to the problem. They acknowledged, in a final communique issued Sept. 19, that the decision was Britain's alone, but they expressed hope that the growing British involvement in Europe would not bring the dissolution of the Commonwealth association.

The 16 Commonwealth powers were represented as follows: United Kingdom—Prime Min. Harold Macmillan; Canada—Prime Min. John G. Diefenbaker; Australia—Prime Min. Robert G. Menzies; New Zealand—Prime Min. Keith J. Holyoake; India—Prime Min. Jawaharlal Nehru; Pakistan—Pres. Mohammed Ayub Khan; Ceylon—Sen. S. P. C. Fernando, justice minister (the prime minister, Mrs. Sirimavo Bandaranaike was detained by domestic economic affairs); Malaya—

Deputy Prime Min. Tun Abdul Razak (Prime Min. Tengku Abdul Rahman was unable to travel due to illness); Cyprus—Pres. (Archbishop) Makarios; Ghana—Finance and Trade Min. F. K. D. Goka (Pres. Kwame Nkrumah was occupied with a domestic political crisis and unable to leave); Nigeria—Prime Min. Sir Abubakar Tafawa Balewa; Sierra Leone—Prime Min. Sir Milton Margai; Tanganyika—Prime Min. Rashidi M. Kawawa; Jamaica—Prime Min. Sir Alexander Bustamante; Trinidad & Tobago—Prime Min. Eric Williams; Rhodesia & Nyasaland Federation—Prime Min. Sir Roy Welensky. These 8 dependent territories also sent representatives: Uganda—Prime Min. Milton Obote; Singapore—Prime Min. Lee Kuan Yew; British Guiana—Premier Cheddi Jagan; Kenya—Finance Min. J. Gichuru; Malta—Prime Min. Borg Olivier; West Indies Federation—Barbados Premier E. W. Barrow; Mauritius—Chief Min. S. Ramgoolam; Hong Kong—Financial Secy. J. J. Cowperthwaite.

Prime Min. Macmillan opened the conference Sept. 10 with an address in which he declared that Britain's entry into the EEC would have a radical effect on world trade patterns and present new economic opportunities both for Europe and the Commonwealth. The major points he made (reported to newsmen after the closed session had ended): Britain and Western Europe together would constitute a unit rivaling the U.S. and USSR in population and economic power; their association would effect a basic reshaping of world trade and provide a new capital and export market with rich developmental and trade opportunities for friendly nations; Britain was not being forced to choose between the Commonwealth and Europe; on the contrary, it would be of greater service to its Commonwealth associates when it had won access to European industry and markets. Macmillan's address was followed by one in which Edward Heath, cabinet minister responsible for Britain's negotiations with the EEC, gave a summary of the Brussels negotiations to date.

Commonwealth leaders replied to Macmillan Sept. 11 with a series of addresses in which they attacked Britain's plans for EEC membership, refused to approve the British-European negotiations but said they would not formally oppose them. The attack on the British position was led by the prime ministers of the 3 "old dominions"—John Diefenbaker of Canada, Robert G. Menzies of Australia and Keith J. Holyoake of New Zealand. All 3 asserted that the trade guarantees sought by Britain to protect their Commonwealth-linked economies were insufficient and that Britain's entry into the EEC would mark the end of the current Commonwealth relationship. Diefenbaker warned that Britain's action might drive Canada into the "magnet" of the U.S. economy. He called for a multi-national conference of EEC, EFTA and Commonwealth members together with the U.S., Japan and "other like-minded nations" to work out worldwide tariff cuts. "This should prepare the way for the prospective non-discriminatory tariff negotiations on a most-favored-

nation basis," he said. Menzies said he could not possibly "pro-
nounce... benediction" on Britain's position; Holyoake asserted that
long-range guarantees were not valued "by a man faced with the cer-
tainty of a short-term disaster."

Speaking for the less-developed Commonwealth nations, Pres.
Mohammed Ayub Khan of Pakistan declared that the safeguards
proposed by Britain were inadequate and that the EEC had "summarily
turned down" Pakistan's requests for continued Commonwealth trade
preferences. He reportedly charged the EEC trade bloc with moving in
the direction of "a powerful international cartel" that would profit by
exploitation of the under-developed countries. He warned: "If this would
happen, it would amount to re-establishing imperialism of the worst
kind, the consequences of which would be nothing short of disastrous."

Indian Prime Min. Jawaharlal Nehru questioned the effects on
world stability and peace of the formation of a new and powerful bloc of
Western nations. He said the Commonwealth could not survive without
"radical changes" in Britain's terms for EEC membership. Similar
assessments were made by Ghanaian Finance & Trade Min. F. K. D.
Goka, Ceylonese Justice Min. S. P. C. Fernando, and Prime Min. Sir
Milton Margai of Sierra Leone. Only Margai said his government
might be willing to change its opposition to the British position.

Lessened opposition to Britain's stand was expressed by representatives of the smaller Commonwealth countries in speeches Sept. 12.
Prime Ministers Sir Abubakar Tafawa Balewa of Nigeria and Rashidi
M. Kawawa of Tanganyika said they feared economic dislocation and
could not join other African states in associate EEC membership, but
they said they would not oppose Britain's negotiations. Prime Min. Eric
E. Williams of Trinidad & Tobago, Pres. (Archbishop) Makarios of
Cyprus and Acting Prime Min. Tun Abdul Razak of Malaya said their
governments foresaw some positive advantages to Britain's membership
in EEC and had no objections. Prime Min. Sir Alexander Bustamente of
Jamaica said his government had not yet adopted a position on the
matter, but he expressed regret that the EEC had become "a surgeon's
knife thrust into the body of the Commonwealth, cutting off one
member from another, dividing one friend from another."

Prime Min. Sir Roy Welensky of the Federation of Rhodesia &
Nyasaland was the sole speaker to support Britain's position. Welensky,
an observer at the conference, said the federation would accept associate
membership with the EEC if Britain joined the European group.

The conference broke up into small study groups Sept. 13 for
detailed discussion of the British proposals. These groups completed
their work by Sept. 16. London informants said that most of the
Commonwealth nations had accepted the British position as fixed and
had used the discussions to present suggestions for improving the
Commonwealth's trade arrangements with Britain and the EEC.

Pakistani Pres. Ayub Khan disclosed Sept. 14 that he had suggested a meeting among leaders of the Commonwealth and the EEC countries ("the 6 and the 16") to discuss extension of the trade bloc to non-European countries. Ayub Khan flew to Paris Sept. 15 to discuss his proposal with Pres. de Gaulle, but he failed to win the approval of either France or Britain for the idea. Prior to departing for Paris, Ayub Khan said: "As I see it, the Common Market is the germ of something bigger emerging in the world. The United Nations has ceased to be the effective organ the world wanted it to be. Would it not be better to take this opportunity to enlarge the scope of the Common Market, not necessarily politically, but in the economic field? This is a crucial moment in human history. Something greater and grander can emerge if there is foresight."

Several other Commonwealth leaders also went to Paris for talks with French Pres. de Gaulle, considered the principal opponent of British membership in EEC, during and following the London talks. Prime Mins. Holyoake of New Zealand and Nehru of India met with de Gaulle Sept. 21 and 22, respectively. Holyoake and Nehru told newsmen they had stressed in their talks with de Gaulle the Commonwealth nations' need for special arrangements to protect their traditional market in Britain and to prevent severe damage to their economies. Ayub Khan accompanied Canadian Prime Min. Diefenbaker, another leading opponent of British association with the EEC, to Canada and New York Sept. 20 for further discussion of the problem. Ayub Khan said at a New York news conference Sept. 21 that it was too late for Britain to solve the problem by simultaneous efforts to join Europe and to increase Commonwealth trade. (Diefenbaker said at a news conference Sept. 21 that $423 million of the $909 million worth of Canadian exports to Britain in 1961 were of goods enjoying free entry to Britain under Commonwealth trade preferences that would be ended by British membership in the EEC.)

The Commonwealth Conference concluded its discussion of the British-EEC question Sept. 17 and passed on to other Commonwealth problems. Macmillan ended the trade debate with an address in which he again asserted that Britain's membership in the EEC could be achieved without harm either to the Commonwealth association or to member states' economies. He again pledged that Britain would defend the association's interests when it resumed full-scale negotiations with the EEC. The conference was scheduled to end Sept. 18 but was extended for one day when conferees were unable to agree immediately on a final statement of their conflicting views.

A final communique approved and made public Sept. 19 welcomed the "strenuous efforts" by Britain to protect the Commonwealth's interests in its negotiations with the EEC. It said: "The primary object of this meeting was ... to review the progress made in the negotiations in Brussels about the conditions on which Britain might join the

European Economic Community, and to examine the nature and prospects of safeguards for the trade of other Commonwealth countries. The greater part of the meeting has been devoted to the discussion of this complex question. Although this discussion disclosed many differences of viewpoint and many uncertainties, all the exchanges have been conducted in the frank and friendly atmosphere which characterizes Commonwealth meetings. This has reaffirmed the common determination to strengthen the links between the countries of the Commonwealth." The communique acknowledged that Britain's reasons for seeking EEC membership were pressing, but it made clear that the negotiations were a matter for Britain alone and that the other Commonwealth nations could neither approve nor disapprove them. It noted Macmillan's view that "Britain's accession to the [European Economic] Community on satisfactory terms would have the result of strengthening the position of Britain, of the Commonwealth and of Europe," but it explicitly stated the "special concern" of the other Commonwealth nations for terms that would safeguard their traditional association. It expressed the hope that "these general objectives would be shared by the members of the European Economic Community."

Macmillan summarized the Conference developments in a broadcast Sept. 20. He analyzed the postwar changes within the Commonwealth, presented the thoughts and the gist of the objections to British EEC membership raised by Commonwealth representatives, and concluded: "So we want to preserve and strengthen the Commonwealth. We want also to play our part in Europe. Many of us, especially those who are young in heart or in years, are impatient of the old disputes; intolerant of obsolete conceptions; anxious that our country should take its part, and if possible a leading part, in all these new and hopeful movements. All over Western Europe people are looking to Britain to join them in this work of peace and progress. And given the right terms of entry, I am sure this is the right way ahead for us."

Other EFTA Members Seek EEC Affiliation

By the end of 1962, all 7 EFTA member nations in addition to 3 other nations—Ireland, Spain, and Turkey—had applied for some form of EEC affiliation. The British application had been announced Aug. 10, 1961, and negotiations had opened Nov. 8, 1961. The Danish decision was announced Aug. 10, 1961, and negotiations began Nov. 30, 1961.

Ireland's application, for full membership, announced Aug. 1, 1961, was submitted to the EEC Council in Brussels Jan. 18 by Prime Min. Sean Lemass. The application expressed Ireland's readiness to accept all provisions of the Treaty of Rome but requested a gradual application of tariff changes to prevent a dislocation of Irish industry and commodity markets. Lemass expressed hope that action could be taken on Ireland's application at the same time as Britain's request for EEC membership.

He made it clear that although Ireland had preserved its technical neutrality by shunning affiliation with NATO, it was prepared to assume all non-military obligations as a member of Europe.

Sweden and Austria, both EFTA members, submitted applications for associate EEC membership in Brussels July 28 after announcing their desires Dec. 15, 1961. Both nations stressed their desire to participate fully in Europe's economic integration without compromising their status as neutrals in the East-West power struggle. Both applications stated that the 2 countries could agree to abide by all major provisions of the Rome Treaty without endangering their neutrality. The exceptions that they requested included the right to conclude individual trade treaties with nations outside the EEC—presumably those of the Soviet bloc. (Austrian Chancellor Alfons Gorbach visited the USSR for a week beginning June 28 to confer with Khrushchev and presumably to reassure Russia that Austria intended no alteration of its neutral position by the EEC application.)

The Swiss application, announced Dec. 15, 1961, was presented Sept. 24. It requested associate EEC membership for Switzerland, also an EFTA member, on nearly identical terms to those sought by Sweden and Austria. It cited its traditional neutrality as the chief barrier to full membership.

Norway, another EFTA nation, applied for full EEC membership May 2. The Norwegian application asked for special arrangements, however, to protect Norwegian coastal fishing waters and to permit continued subsidization of the country's relatively inefficient system of small farms. The Norwegian parliament had approved the application for EEC membership Apr. 23 by 113-27 vote and negotiations opened in October.

Portugal applied for an undefined form of EEC association June 4.

Spain had applied for associate membership Feb. 9 with the stated goal of becoming a full member of EEC when its economy was prepared for integration with those of the other European nations. Spanish Information Min. Manuel Fraga Iribarne said in Madrid Nov. 6 that Spain considered its application a serious commitment to European unity, both economically and politically.

Turkey had expressed an interest in associate membership in the EEC July 31, 1959 but took no further action. The Turkish application was presented again Feb. 5 by Foreign Min. Selim Sarper; the EEC Commission ordered negotiations reopened July 25.

Negotiations were begun in Brussels Nov. 26 on Israeli requests for a trade and tariff agreement with the 6 EEC nations. Israel sought special arrangements for relaxation of EEC tariffs on 150 items that it exported to Europe.

The coordinated applications of all EFTA members to the EEC were discussed at the Dec. 4-5 Oslo meeting of the EFTA Consultative Committee. The British Foreign Office announced Dec. 6 that a voluntary agreement of EFTA members to liquidate EFTA could overrule the stipulation in the EFTA Convention that a member give 12 months' notice of intention to withdraw. Lord Privy Seal Edward Heath had said in Parliament Nov. 7-8, in debate on British-EEC negotiations and the state of all EFTA members: "Our obligations are, first, to maintain full consultation with each of the EFTA countries. That has been done to the utmost. I know of no criticism from them about this, and they have kept us fully informed. Secondly, each EFTA country should be given an opportunity in negotiation of satisfying its own legitimate requirements. Thirdly, the arrangements, when made, should come into operation at the same time. These are the obligations to which we all adhere."

Anglo-French Cooperation on the Concorde

Despite the debates and disagreements between France and Britain on Britain's EEC membership application, cooperation continued on the development of a supersonic aircraft, the Concorde. British Aviation Min. Peter Thornycroft and French Transport Min. Robert Buron announced Mar. 26 that agreement had been reached on developmental principles and that both the British Aircraft Corp. and Sud-Aviation would participate. The 2 companies announced their agreement to participate in November.

The formal agreement between France and Britain was signed Nov. 29 in London by new British Aviation Min. Julian Amery and French Amb.-to-Britain Geoffroy de Courcel. The aircraft, scheduled for delivery in 1970, would cost £160 million, of which Britain would pay between £75 and £80 million.

1963

Early in 1963 French Pres. Charles de Gaulle vetoed Britain's application for membership in the European Economic Community. Other EEC members opposed the de Gaulle stand at various times during the year but remained loyal to the EEC concept. A Franco-German treaty was signed and ratified; it established a power axis in which German pressures favoring Britain served to modify but not completely offset the French stand. The solid nature of the EEC was tested during these internal debates, and, as the year ended, the EEC had become a more divided body. 2 major leaders were replaced as Sir Alec Douglas Home succeeded Harold Macmillan as British prime minister and Ludwig Erhard replaced Konrad Adenauer as West German chancellor.

FRANCE VETOES BRITAIN'S EEC APPLICATION

Britain's 1-1/2-year effort to join the European Economic Community seemed doomed Jan. 29. The British-European negotiations, under way in Brussels since Oct. 1960, collapsed when France exercised its veto right to force the negotiators to suspend their talks and, in effect, reject the British application. Moreover, it was apparent by the end of 1963 that the French veto had ended indefinitely the attempt to associate Britain fully with the movement toward the economic and political integration of Western Europe. The French action was viewed widely as a step in Pres. Charles de Gaulle's plan to create a French-led European Community freed of dependence on U.S. military and economic power and able to act as a new great power serving solely European interests. Opposed by the U.S., Britain and the 5 other Common Market member states, the French veto of Britain's membership application was believed to have provoked a major crisis in the postwar relations of the European and Atlantic nations.

The collapse in January of the British-EEC negotiations led to bitter recrimination against de Gaulle, who first had demanded rapid and total British conformity to Common Market practices and then brusquely had ordered French representatives to veto the British application. Despite the efforts of other EEC nations to obtain a reopening of the negotiations for British membership, France blocked such negotiations for the remainder of the year. France ultimately was forced to accept a renewal of periodic contacts with Britain within the framework of the Western European Union, but this was in no sense a reopening of the British bid for EEC membership.

De Gaulle's January Press Conference

Great Britain's attempt to "join Europe"—through negotiations for EEC membership—was rejected by de Gaulle Jan. 14. De Gaulle said at his 8th news conference since his return to power in 1958 that Britain was not a European nation and could not become one unless it submitted to profound changes in its "nature" and "traditions." He warned that Britain's membership could weaken or destroy the Common Market and other existing or planned European institutions.

The French president was asked: "Can you explicitly define France's position concerning the entry of Britain in the Common Market and the political evolution of Europe?" De Gaulle's reply:

". . . When we talk about economic matters, and even more when we are dealing with them, it is essential for what is said and what is done to conform to reality, for otherwise we end up in deadlocks and sometimes even ruined. Concerning this very important question . . ., it is the facts which must be considered first. Sentiments, as favorable as they might be and as they are, cannot be put forward in opposition to the real factors of the problem. What are these factors? The Treaty of Rome was concluded between 6 continental states, states which are, in short, economically of the same nature. Whether in terms of their industrial or agricultural production, of their foreign trade, of their commercial customs and clients, or of their living and working conditions, there are many more similarities than differences between them. Moreover, they are adjacent, they interpenetrate, they are extensions of each other through their communications. The very fact of grouping them and linking them together in such a way that what they produce, buy, sell and consume they produce, buy, sell and consume by preference within their own grouping thus conforms to reality.... [Moreover] from the standpoint of their economic development, their social progress and their technological capability they are, in short, in stride with each other and they are moving forward at more or less the same pace. Furthermore, it happens that there exists between them no kind of political grievance, no border disputes, no rivalry for domination or power.

"To the contrary, there is a feeling of solidarity between them, firstly owing to the awareness they have of together possessing an important part of the origins of our civilization, and also with regard to their security, because they are continental countries and they are confronted by the same single threat from one end of their territorial grouping to the other. Finally, they have a feeling of solidarity because not one of them is linked on the outside by any special political or military agreement.

"Thus it has been psychologically and materially possible to organize an economic community of the 6. Moreover, this was not without difficulty. When the Treaty of Rome was signed in 1957, it was after long discussions, and once concluded, so that something could be accomplished, it was necessary for us French to straighten ourselves out in the economic, financial and monetary domain. And this was done in 1959. From that time on, the Community was workable in principle, but it was then necessary to implement the Treaty. Now this Treaty, which was quite specific and complete on the subject of industry, was not at all specific and complete on the subject of agriculture. And yet, it was essential for our country that this be settled. For it is indeed quite obvious that agriculture is an essential element of our national activity as a whole. We cannot conceive of a Common Market in which French agriculture would not find outlets commensurate with its production, and we agree, moreover, that, among the 6, we are the country for which this necessity is the most imperative. That is why,... when consideration was being given to implementing the 2d stage of the Treaty, in other words, to a practical beginning of application, we were led to set the entry of agriculture into the Common Market as a formal condition. This was finally accepted by our partners, but very complex and difficult arrangements were needed. And some of these arrangements are still being worked out.

"I will note in passing that, in this vast undertaking, all the decisions taken were taken by the governments, for nowhere else is there any authority or responsibility. But I should say that, in order to prepare and clarify matters, the Brussels Commission [whose task was to develop an EEC agricultural policy] worked in a highly objective and pertinent fashion.

"Then Great Britain applied for membership in the Common Market. It did so after refusing earlier to participate in the community that was being built, and after then having created a free trade area with 6 other states, and finally—I can say this, the negotiations conducted for so long on this subject can be recalled—after having put some presure on the 6 in order to prevent the application of the Common Market from really getting started. Britain thus in its turn requested membership, but on its own conditions. This undoubtedly raises for each of the 6 states and for England problems of a very great dimension.

"England is, in effect, insular, maritime, linked through its trade, markets and food supply to very diverse and often very distant countries. Its activities are essentially industrial and commercial, and only slightly agricultural. It has, throughout its work, very marked and original customs and traditions. In short, the nature, structure and economic context of England differ profoundly from those of the other states of the continent.

"What is to be done so that Britain, such as it lives, such as it produces and such as it trades, be incorporated into the Common Market such as it has been conceived and such as it functions? For example, the means by which the people of Great Britain nourish themselves is in fact by importing foodstuffs purchased at low prices in the 2 Americas or in the former dominions, while still granting large subsidies to British farmers. This means is obviously incompatible with the system the 6 have quite naturally set up for themselves.

"The system of the 6 consists of making a pool of the agricultural products of the entire Community, of strictly determining their prices, of forbidding subsidizing, of organizing their consumption between all the members and of making it obligatory for each of these members to pay to the Community any savings they might make by having foodstuffs brought in from outside instead of consuming those offered by the Common Market. Once again, what is to be done to make Britain, such as it is, enter that system?

"One was sometimes led to believe that our British friends, in applying for membership in the Common Market, agreed to change their own ways even to the point of applying all the conditions accepted and practiced by the 6, but the question is to know if Great Britain can at present place itself, with the continent and like it, within a tariff that is truly common, give up all preference with regard to the Commonwealth, cease to claim that its agriculture be privileged and, even more, consider as null and void the commitments it has made with the countries that are part of its free trade area. That question is the one at issue. One cannot say that it has now been resolved. Will it be so one day? Obviously Britain alone can answer that.

"The question is raised all the more since, following Britain, other states, which are linked to her through the free trade area, would or will want to enter the Common Market. It must be agreed that the entry first of Great Britain and then that of those other states will completely change the series of adjustments, agreements, compensations and regulations already established between the 6, because all these states, like Britain, have very important traits of their own. We would then have to envisage the construction of another Common Market. But the 11-member, then 13-member and then perhaps 18-member Common Market that would be built would, without any doubt, hardly resemble the one that 6 have built.

"Moreover, this Community, growing in that way, would be confronted with all the problems of its economic relations with a crowd of other states, and first of all with the United States. It is foreseeable that the cohesion of all its members, who would be very numerous and very diverse, would not hold for long and that in the end there would appear a colossal Atlantic Community under American dependence and leadership which would soon completely swallow up the European Community. This is an assumption that can be perfectly justified in the eyes of some, but it is not at all what France wanted to do and what France is doing, which is a strictly European construction.

"Then, it is possible that Britain would one day come round to transforming itself enough to belong to the European Community without restriction and without reservation and placing it ahead of anything else, and in that case the 6 would open the door to it, and France would place no obstacle in its path, although obviously the mere membership of Britain in the Community would completely change its nature and its volume.

"It is possible, too, that England might not yet be so disposed, and this is certainly what seems to emanate from the long, long Brussels conversations. But if that is the case, there is nothing dramatic about it. First, whatever decision England takes in this matter, there is no reason, as far as we are concerned, for the relations we have with her to be changed. The consideration and the respect which are due to this great country, this great people, will not thereby be in the slightest impaired. What England has done across the centuries and in the world is recognized as immense, although there have often been conflicts with France. Britain's glorious participation in the victory that crowned the First World War—we French shall always admire it. As for the role England played in the most dramatic and decisive moment of the 2d World War, no one has the right to forget it. In truth, the destiny of the free world, and first of all ours and even that of the United States and Russia, depended in a large measure on the resolution, the solidity, and the courage of the English people, as Churchill was able to harness them. Even at the present moment no one can contest British capacity and worth.

"Moreover, I repeat, even if the Brussels negotiations were shortly not to succeed, nothing would prevent the conclusion between the Common Market and Great Britain of an agreement of association designed to safeguard exchanges, and nothing would prevent close relations between England and France from being maintained, nor the pursuit and development of their direct cooperation in all kinds of fields, notably the scientific, technical and industrial—as the 2 countries have just proved by deciding to build together the supersonic aircraft *Concorde*.

"Lastly, it is very possible that Britain's own evolution, and the evolution of the universe, might bring the English towards the continent, whatever delays this achievement might demand. For my part, that is what I readily believe, and that is why, in my opinion, it will in any case have been a great honor for the British prime minister, my friend Harold Macmillan, and for his government, to have discerned that goal in good time, to have had enough political courage to have proclaimed it, and to have led their country the first steps along the path which one day, perhaps, will lead it to moor alongside the continent."

At his press conference, de Gaulle rejected Anglo-U.S. defense proposals formulated by Pres. John F. Kennedy and Prime Min. Macmillan at a meeting held Dec. 18-21, 1962 in Nassau. These proposals were part of an agreement under which the U.S. offered to help Britain build a Polaris submarine force to replace its nuclear-armed Vulcan bomber fleet, condemned to obsolescence by the U.S.' cancellation of the Skybolt air-to-ground missile. De Gaulle said:

"Then... America and Britain concluded an agreement, and we were asked to subscribe to it ourselves.... It is a question of constituting a so-called multilateral atomic force in which Britain would turn over the weapons it has... and... the Americans would place a few of their own. This multilateral force is assigned to the defense of Europe and is under the American NATO command.... As for the bulk of American nuclear weapons, it remains outside the multilateral force and under the direct orders of the President.... France has taken note of the... agreement.... No one will be surprised that we cannot subscribe to it."

De Gaulle's statements were made after U.S. State Undersecy. George Ball had conferred with French Foreign Min. Maurice Courve de Murville Jan. 10 on "certain aspects of the Nassau agreement." Ball, in Paris Jan. 9-13, was joined by British permanent Representative-to-NATO Sir Evelyn Shuckburgh Jan. 11 in addressing the NATO Permanent Council on the proposed multilateral NATO nuclear force. (Ball continued on to Bonn Jan. 13 for talks with West German Chancellor Konrad Adenauer.)

French Stand Criticized

De Gaulle's apparent repudiation of the negotiations for British membership in the EEC was assailed in early January by representatives of Britain and of the 5 other EEC nations. The attacks on the French position were disclosed in Brussels, where Britain and the EEC countries formally resumed their negotiations Jan. 14 for the first time since Dec. 20, 1962. Edward Heath, Lord Privy Seal and Britain's chief representative in the negotiations, declared Jan. 14 that he already had told de Gaulle that Britain would not accept "association" as a substitute for full membership in the Common Market. Heath had declared earlier that the basic barrier to a settlement of terms for Britain's entry into the EEC was political rather than economic; he had also implied that it was French rather than European.

A British Foreign Office spokesman said Jan. 15: "Pres. de Gaulle was clearly referring to the Nassau agreement entirely from the French point of view. We ourselves regard the Nassau agreement as a constructive contribution to the indivisible defense of the Western Alliance, and we would hope that other members of the Alliance would so regard it. The NATO nuclear force is under discussion between all the NATO Allies, and we would hope that France herself would one day have second thoughts."

De Gaulle's views were also disavowed by the Belgian, West German, Italian and Netherlands representatives to the Brussels talks. Luxembourg made no statement but was known to have associated itself with the criticism of the other 4. Belgian Foreign Min. Paul-Henri Spaak said at a news conference Jan. 15 that Belgium had been embarrassed by the de Gaulle statement and had rejected it. "For us," he said, "... it is difficult to admit that Great Britain should not be an integral part of Europe." Spaak also said that "as far as the Belgian government is concerned, the approach of Great Britain as put forward at [the] Brussels negotiations is altogether different from the picture of it which the President of the French Republic has given." Spaak told the Belgian Senate Jan. 24 that "if the negotiations with England are suspended, it will be the end of the Common Market, because it will be impossible to carry on or open negotiations with other countries." Spaak also said: "The French president says that we must keep Britain out of Europe.... In 1914 or 1940 we would not have dared to say that Britain was not a part of Europe." The Belgian Senate the same date unanimously approved a motion "hoping that the effort of the Belgian government and of the Executive Commission of the Common Market will result in the accession of Great Britain."

The Italian EEC delegation called for pursuit of the negotiations with "firmness," while Budget Min. Ugo La Malfa stated Jan. 15 that "Italy and the other countries of the Common Market cannot be treated like colonies." Italian Premier Amintore Fanfani told the Chamber of Deputies Jan. 26 that he had warned French and West German leaders against signing the Franco-German pact and against any action that might lead to the exclusion of Britain from Europe. He strongly committed the Italian government to continuing the fight for British admission, and he denounced the Franco-German pact as a threat to other European nations and to the goals of the EEC.

Dutch Foreign Min. Joseph M. A. H. Luns emphasized Jan. 14 that de Gaulle spoke only for France. He said: "We are negotiating with Great Britain for her adherence to the Community as a full member."

The West German delegation said Britain's full membership was essential for both political and economic reasons.

The Brussels conferees were said to have given Heath a warm response when he arrived at the meeting Jan. 15. The conferees, who had resumed their talks Jan. 14 under the chairmanship of Belgian Deputy Foreign Min. Henri Fayat, had agreed at their initial session to begin codification of the compromises reached in past negotiations. They resumed discussion Jan. 15 of British proposals for transitional arrangements for the alignment of Britain's agricultural economy with the farm system adopted by the 6 EEC states.

(The resumption of the Brussels negotiations had been preceded by a series of meetings among several of the foreign ministers of the nations concerned. West German Foreign Min. Gerhard Schroeder had visited Britain Jan. 7-8 for 2 days of talks with Prime Min. Macmillan and had pledged every effort to produce a "positive conclusion" to the Brussels talks. Italian Foreign Min. Attilo Piccioni conferred with Schroeder and West German Chancellor Adenauer in Bonn Jan. 11-13 and was reported to have reached agreement with Schroeder on joint Italian-German action to resolve the British-EEC farm problem. Netherlands Foreign Min. Luns went to Brussels Jan. 13 to meet with Heath and Spaak; his position was bound by a resolution in which the Dutch Parliament's lower house called on the government to do "everything in its power" to bring Britain into the EEC. Heath visited Paris Jan. 11-13 to confer with de Gaulle and Foreign Min. Maurice Couve de Murville, but these talks brought no progress. Macmillan had said Jan. 10 that Britain was determined to negotiate its entry into the Common Market but that it could not permit the Brussels talks to "drag on" indefinitely. Macmillan, in a TV interview marking the completion of his 6th year in office, spoke optimistically of expanding British economic opportunities, which, he said, inevitably would follow British membership in the EEC.)

The EEC meetings ended Jan. 18. A statement, issued the same date and approved by the ministers of all 6 EEC nations and Heath, said: "The French delegation has requested that the negotiations with Great Britain should be suspended. The 5 other delegations of the EEC and the British delegation have opposed this. Discussion of this question will be continued in the course of the next session of the conference which has been set for Jan. 28, 1963, in Brussels."

Vice Chancellor Ludwig Erhard, West German delegate to the Brussels talks, said Jan. 15: "For many centuries there were good relations between [Britain and Germany], . . . but, alas, during the past 50 years they were overshadowed by 2 World Wars. It would be foolish to pass that over in silence and believe that everything has been forgotten. But to forgive and forget, and to understand, is only possible if there is a genuine readiness to help one another to cooperate. That is the way we see things, and I believe that is also the British attitude." Erhard said Jan. 20 that "for political and economic reasons, the entry of Britain into the EEC is necessary, urgent, and even very urgent." In a press statement in Paris Jan. 23 he added that "the negotiations with Britain must proceed. No one should retard or obstruct them. They are a test of the will of the European peoples to determine their fate in common."

Erhard and West German Chancellor Adenauer were then in Paris for the conclusion of a Franco-German reconciliation treaty. At a press conference Jan. 23, Adenauer was asked if he had discussed Britain's EEC application with de Gaulle. He replied: "Yes, I talked about it with Gen. de Gaulle, as did my cabinet colleagues. This development does not leave anyone unconcerned. Where consultation is applicable, as provided for in the treaty, we have the right to be consulted.... We talked in complete friendship and frankness. But in delicate matters it is best to show calmness and patience. The more wind is created, the higher the flames. The ministers of the 6 are going to discuss this question. I cannot anticipate the result of their labors."

De Gaulle was also subjected to domestic criticism. Jean Monnet, widely acknowledged leader of the "united Europe" philosophy,had said Jan. 16: "Whatever Gen. de Gaulle may say, I think that the negotiations for England's entry into the EEC could be rapidly concluded"; it is "necessary for world peace that England should unite with the Community and that a relationship as equal partners should be established between a united Europe, including England, and the United States."

The Paris newspaper *Le Monde* reported Jan. 18 that de Gaulle had told a group of National Assembly deputies that Britain would be admitted to the EEC but not in the near future. He was quoted as saying: "Either the English will sign or they will leave Brussels and think it over. One day they will come into the Common Market, but no doubt I will no longer be here." Replying to a deputy who insisted that the Brussels talks had been near agreement, he reportedly said that Britain had been "multiplying the exceptions [to the EEC treaty] at every turn. There is a treaty and it ought to be respected."

De Gaulle's Jan. 14 European policy declaration was reaffirmed by the French government Jan. 24. Addressing the National Assembly, Foreign Min. Couve de Murville again warned that Britain was not prepared for the vast changes necessary to make its industrial, financial and agricultural sectors mesh with those of the other European countries. He asserted that Britain had shown in the Brussels negotiations that it was not prepared to accept the EEC treaty in its entirety and that its demands for special concessions in fact amounted to violations of the European community's rules and procedures. He warned that if Britain and the 6 other European Free Trade Association nations were permitted easy entry into the EEC, each with the special concession it would require, the current European community would become "extracontinental" and would inalterably change its basic aims and functions. He reiterated that France could not accept this.

Couve de Murville repeated de Gaulle's pledge that Britain would be welcomed into the EEC when it succeeded in transforming itself to match more closely the European system. He said: "From the moment...that Great Britain asked not, as is generally believed, to adhere to the Treaty of Rome under the terms of Article 237, but to study with us the conditions under which she could envisage participation in the Common Market, we very clearly defined our position on this basis.... If Great Britain accepts all the provisions of the Treaty of Rome, nothing could prevent her from entering the Common Market; but the burden of proof lies upon her and not upon us." He reiterated that,in the interim, France was ready to offer Britain a close association short of membership in the EEC.

Franco-German Treaty

A treaty pledging cooperation and consultation between France and West Germany in foreign policy, defense and cultural affairs was signed in Paris Jan. 22 by Pres. de Gaulle and Chancellor Adenauer. The pact was hailed by both as an act symbolizing the end of 400 years of rivalry and war between the French and German peoples and the creation of a new European unity based on Franco-German cooperation.

Signed at a time when de Gaulle had virtually destroyed Britain's immediate chances of entering the Common Market, the pact was viewed as a major step in de Gaulle's plan for French leadership of a European community freed from dependence on the U.S.

The Franco-German treaty was concluded at the end of a 2-day Paris meeting held by de Gaulle and Adenauer with the participation of French Premier Georges Pompidou, Foreign Mins. Maurice Couve de Murville and Gerhard Schroeder, Defense Mins. Pierre Messmer and Kai-Uwe von Hassel, and other ministers. It was accompanied by a joint declaration in which de Gaulle and Adenauer proclaimed their belief that the treaty sealed "the reconciliation of the German people and the French people, ending a centuries-old rivalry," and was a "historic event which profoundly transforms the relations between the 2 peoples." The "reinforcement of cooperation between the 2 countries," they declared, "constitutes an indispensable stage on the way to a united Europe which is the aim of the 2 peoples."

The pact, entitled a "Reconciliation Treaty," contained these provisions for French-West German consultation and cooperation:

Organization—The French and West German heads of state or government were to meet at least twice yearly to determine general policy. Execution of the program as a whole was to be the responsibility of the 2 foreign ministers, who were to meet at least 4 times yearly. Monthly meetings to assess current problems were to be held by foreign ministry officials made responsible for political, economic and cultural affairs. Defense ministers were to meet at least 4 times yearly, and the 2 countries' chiefs of staff were to consult every 2 months.

Foreign affairs—"The 2 governments will consult before any decision on all important questions of foreign policy . . . with a view to reaching as far as possible an analogous position." These consultations would bear primarily on "problems relating to the European Communities and to European political cooperation," "East-West relations, both on the political and economic plans," and on NATO, the Council of Europe, WEU, OECD, and UN. The 2 countries especially would seek to coordinate their programs of aid to less-developed countries.

Defense—"In the field of strategy and tactics . . . the 2 countries will endeavor to bring their doctrines closer together." "Exchanges of personnel between the armies will be increased." These exchanges would include instructors and students of the 2 countries' general staff colleges and "the temporary detachment of entire units." "With regard to armaments, the 2 governments will endeavor to organize work in common from the stage of drawing up appropriate armament plans and of the preparation of plans for financing them." Joint operational research institutes would be created.

Culture—The 2 countries would: (1) stimulate the teaching of each others' language at every level of schooling; (2) coordinate courses of study, examinations and university degrees; (3) develop contacts and information exchanges between French and West German research and scientific institutes; (4) organize collective exchanges of youth, student, artisan and workers' groups.

In a brief statement to witnesses at the ceremonial signing of the treaty, de Gaulle said: "There is not a man in the world who does not grasp the capital importance of this act, not only because it turns the page after so long and so bloody a history of battles and struggles, but also because it opens wide the gates of a new future for France, for Germany, for Europe, and, consequently, for the whole world."

(The treaty became effective July 2 after ratification by the French and West German parliaments.)

Macmillan's January Speech

Prime Min. Harold Macmillan delivered a major policy speech Jan. 21 at the Conservative Party meeting in Liverpool. In his address he summarized the British position on the EEC negotiations and presented his recommendations for domestic policy, especially regarding unemployment, in the light of the EEC rejection of Britain's application for membership.

Speaking about the EEC negotiations, Macmillan rejected de Gaulle's stated objections to British membership in the EEC. Macmillan suggested that France had not negotiated in good faith and that de Gaulle had not been wholly honest when they discussed the talks at their last meeting, in Dec. 1962. He asserted that de Gaulle's Jan. 14 declaration had been a "setback" to the talks but not a "fatal setback" in view of the worldwide demand for a successful conclusion of the negotiations. Saying that he wished "to put the record straight," Macmillan declared that if France did not want Britain in the EEC, this should have been made clear at the start of the negotiations. "Indeed, at my meeting with him, . . . Gen. Gen. de Gaulle himself reminded me that the length of the negotiations was inevitable in view of their complicated character," he disclosed.

Macmillan said:

"Immediately after the war, when Europe lay in ruins, it was natural that the U.S.A. should take the lead. It was natural, too, that the mere size and strength of America should give her an important place in the Alliance—not a dominating place but carrying the influence that her population, size and economic strength naturally command. Happily, in recent years, Europe has recovered. We and our friends on the continent are all persuaded that Europe has a particular role, a distinctive influence to bring to bear as well as definite interests in the world.

"Just as the French have themselves retained special links with their former overseas territories, so we in Britain believe that we too can be loyal Europeans without disloyalty to our great Commonwealth tradition and duty. We believe that the future of the free world lies in emphasizing unity and not in exaggerating differences. The movement for European unity was founded immediately after the war, with the help of many distinguished European figures, by the greatest English patriot of his or any other time, Sir Winston Churchill. It was supported in Britain by leading Labor figures likes Mr. Ernest Bevin. It fitted the mood of Europe. It blossomed and developed. All these years Europe has been working by various institutions towards a solution of the problem of unity in diversity.

"A few years ago this movement took its most advanced shape so far, in the successful efforts of 6 European countries to bring about, through the Treaty of Rome, the European Economic Community. Its principle and its method have both been based on partnership, not on domination. It was in this spirit that, with the assent of Parliament, the British government 18 months ago decided to open negotiations for our entry into the European Community. When, after long months of negotiation, this last round started a week ago, it was recognized on all sides that the few outstanding problems were capable of solution.

"This was the general view—and for good reasons. We had made it abundantly clear that we accepted the Treaty of Rome and aligned ourselves with the political implications as well as the economic content of the treaty. In particular, we had accepted a common agricultural policy and the common tariff. We have reached agreed solutions over a very large part of the field; we still believe that, given the will, the remaining difficulties can be surmounted.*

"What has happened has been a setback. I trust and pray not a fatal setback. It would be wrong at this moment not to pay tribute to the overwhelming demand that has been shown throughout Europe and the free world for the constructive settlement. And while recrimination is useless, it is, nevertheless, right that the truth should be known and that the record should be kept straight.

"When we made our application . . . this was accepted by all the 6, including, of course, the French. No point was made . . . that our joining would alter the whole balance of the community. Our size and our worldwide trading connections were not held against us as a sort of reproach. The channel was not regarded as an unbridgeable chasm. . . . I cannot believe that any of the 6 countries which accepted our application in principle can now reject it, not on any economic grounds, not because the negotiations have failed, but because in principle they prefer the community without Britain. . . .

"Unemployment is a subject on which we all naturally feel so strongly that it is difficult to get the balance and perspective right. To hear some people talk one would think that we were back in the dark days of the 30s, or at any rate on the way back to them. That sort of talk is, of course, nonsense. At the same time I am sure that no one wants to underestimate the national waste of unemployment or its distressing consequences for the families affected. No one wants to hold back in any way any possible effort to maintain full employment and to spread it to all areas. We wish to see the United Kingdom united not only in loyalty but also in prosperity.

"Among the reasons why employment in Britain as a whole has become less buoyant of late, one of the most important is the slow-down in the growth of world production and trade which has affected our exports. Another is the fall in private industrial investment. That has been due to uncertainty—uncertainty about world trade; about the buoyancy of the United States economy; and uncertainty about the Common Market. And then, let's face it, unemployment can be traced to uncertainty about the outcome of the next general election. Let us not be mealy-mouthed. When the only alternative government is a party wedded to widespread nationalization, high taxation, and inflationary policies generally, the prospect of an election is bound to cause a certain hesitation in the investment and development plans of those responsible for industry. Nor do people find the possibility of a minority government with the Liberals holding the balance of power—or, the balance of impotence—any more attractive."

Governmental policy recommendations followed shortly. A government bill for a 17% increase in pensions, social assistance and unemployment compensation was introduced in the House of Commons Jan. 23 by

---

* The leaders of Britain's National Farmers Union, however, voted unanimously at a London meeting Jan. 21 to adopt a resolution rejecting the EEC's agricultural system as unacceptable to British farmers. It also rejected the Macmillan government's proposals for special arrangements to cushion the shock to British farmers during a transitional period ending in 1969.

Pensions & National Insurance Min. Niall MacPherson. The plan was aimed partly at stimulating lagging industries in such high-unemployment areas as Scotland, Northern Ireland, northeast England and Merseyside. (The Labor Ministry reported Jan. 24 that unemployment the previous week had totaled 814,632, the highest figure since the winter of 1946-7. The jobless total between Dec. 10, 1962 and Jan. 14, 1963 had risen by 248,474. Of these 248,474 workers, 104,113 were entirely unemployed and the remainder temporarily out of work, the ministry reported.) The government said the plan would cost £227 million ($636.6 million) a year at first. Example of increased unemployment benefits: a single man's basic weekly unemployment pay would rise by 10 shillings ($1.40), from 57 shillings 6 pence ($8.05). Similar increases were proposed for retirement pensions, family allowances, widows' pensions, industrial injury benefits and war pensions. Employes' contributions to the national insurance system would be increased by 1 shilling 1 penny (15¢) a week at the minimum rate.

Brussels Negotiations End

The 6 EEC nations informed Britain Jan. 29 that they were unable to continue their Brussels negotiations on the British application for admission to the Common Market. The European nations' decision was reached at the end of a 2-day meeting that had been called in the hope that settlement could be reached despite de Gaulle's opposition to Britain's entry to the EEC.

The collapse of the Brussels negotiations was a direct outgrowth of the open declaration of opposition to Britain's entry made by de Gaulle at his Paris press conference Jan. 14. The de Gaulle declaration, which had been denounced by Britain, the U.S. and most European countries, was acted on by France Jan. 17, when it submitted to the Brussels negotiations its demand that the talks be suspended. The other 5 EEC states attempted to avert an immediate break-off of the talks but succeeded only in delaying the French veto despite a West German effort to mitigate the harshness of the French position. The French government's Jan. 17th demand was submitted by Foreign Min. Couve de Murville.

Speaking at a specially summoned meeting of the foreign ministers of the 6 EEC nations, Couve de Murville charged that the talks had been dragging on without progress for more than a year and that no further purpose could be served by continuing them. He reportedly asserted that the negotiations had wasted the time of officials who had more important matters to attend to. The French demand contained the suggestion, made by de Gaulle at his Jan. 14 press conference, that, instead of full membership, Britain be offered a form of association with the EEC.

The French demand was rejected in its entirety by the other 5 EEC states, which united Jan. 18 to force Couve de Murville to accept a postponement until Jan. 28 of a final decision on the fate of the talks. It was reported that Dutch Foreign Min. Luns had warned Couve de Murville that his government might not be able to assure ratification of the special ties negotiated between the EEC and 18 African nations, most of them former French colonies, unless the British negotiations were continued. Couve de Murville agreed to attend the Jan. 28 meeting but only on condition that it would be devoted to discussion of the French request.

A formal statement issued after the meeting said: "The French delegation has requested that the negotiations with Great Britain be suspended. The 5 other ... delegations and Great Britain opposed this proposal. The discussion of this question will be pursued during the next session ... Jan. 28. ..."

Officials of the 5 EEC nations opposed to the French stand told newsmen Jan. 18 that they had forced the French to accept the postponement in the hope that West German Chancellor Adenauer would be able to persuade de Gaulle to alter his policy during Adenauer's visit to Paris Jan. 20-23 to conclude the French-West German treaty of reconciliation.

In what was regarded as a gesture of opposition to the French position, the 5 EEC states met with British representatives in Luxembourg Jan. 22 to hold, without France, a planned session of the British negotiations for admission to the ECSC. France had withdrawn its representatives from all technical negotiations related to the British-EEC talks after the Jan. 18 Brussels meeting.

The Bonn government's attempt to mitigate de Gaulle's position was begun by Adenauer during his visit to Paris Jan. 20-23. Adenauer reportedly informed de Gaulle that his government favored continued discussion of the British application and feared that the network of Western economic and military institutions would be harmed if France persisted in its demand for immediate suspension of the Brussels talks. Adenauer failed to persuade de Gaulle to reverse his avowed opposition to Britain's joining the EEC, but he was said to have advanced the proposal, initially made by Italy, that the EEC Executive Commission make an inventory of the progress of the British-EEC negotiations and propose specific solutions for those problems remaining outstanding.

Many observers expressed doubt, however, that Adenauer had used his full political weight to persuade de Gaulle to reverse his position. They noted that despite Adenauer's professed support for the British application, he had signed the Franco-German treaty and had returned to Bonn without a specific commitment from de Gaulle on the fate of the Brussels talks. This assessment was hinted at by U.S. State Secy. Dean Rusk Jan. 27, when he said in a TV interview that the Franco-German pact and the Brussels crisis might eventually force West Germany to choose between a close relationship with France and one with the U.S.

On his return to Bonn Jan. 23, Adenauer refused to act on demands by most West German political leaders that he take strong action to prevent suspension of the Brussels talks. Instead, he summoned a news conference to hail the signing of the French-German treaty and to caution against any precipitate action that might further aggravate the "touchy question" of the Brussels talks. Adenauer's position was clarified Jan. 24 when he appeared before the Bundestag's Foreign Affairs Committee and asserted that he had won a promise of French acceptance for the proposed EEC Commission study of the British negotiations. Under what was described as strong pressure from the Bundestag members, he affirmed that the formal position of the Bonn government was one of support for the British application.

The Bonn government formally announced Jan. 25 that Foreign Min. Schroeder would present the proposal for an EEC Commission study at the Brussels talks when they were resumed Jan. 28. The announcement reaffirmed West Germany's support for British admission to the Common Market, and it revealed that Vice Chancellor Erhard, an opponent of de Gaulle's European policies, would join the Bonn delegation at the Jan. 28 Brussels meeting.

It was reported from Bonn Jan. 25 that the Bonn action had been provoked by Foreign Min. Schroeder, who was described as dissatisfied with Adenauer's position during his meeting with de Gaulle. Schroeder reportedly intervened with cabinet members and CDU leaders to urge them to pressure Adenauer into more direct support for Britain. Bonn sources also reported Jan. 25 that Adenauer had written U.S. Pres. Kennedy to reassure him that the French-Germany treaty would not become the basis for an alliance against U.S. interests or the U.S.' continued presence in Europe. He was said to have informed Mr. Kennedy that it had proved impossible to dissuade de Gaulle from his opposition to Britain's entry into EEC.

American opposition to de Gaulle's European policies—particularly his rejection of British membership in EEC—was made clear by Pres. Kennedy at his news conference Jan. 24. The President's statement, made after de Gaulle's Jan. 14 declaration of European policy but before the final French veto in Brussels, rejected the French thesis that the U.S. sought Britain's entry into the Common Market so that it could serve as the U.S.' agent in Europe and assure the European Community's continued dependence on America. The statement reiterated the U.S.' past service to European unification and stressed that Pres. Kennedy's proposals for an "Atlantic partnership" of America and Europe called for a relationship of equals. Mr. Kennedy, who did not mention de Gaulle by name, said:

●"We have strongly supported Britain's admission to the Common Market ... because it helps ... build a united Europe which, working in equal partnership with the United States, will provide security for Europe and the United States, and together, Europe and the United States, we can concern ourselves with the pressing problems which affect so much of the world ... Latin America, Africa, and Asia."

●"In Latin America alone we face critical problems in this decade. If Latin America is unable to trade with Europe and with the Common Market, we face very, very grave economic problems which we cannot solve alone.... But there are problems throughout the globe which occupy our attention. The United States does not have the resources to meet them alone. We hope Europe and the United States together can do it on the basis of equality. That is why we supported the admission of Britain to the Common Market."

●"What kind of a Europe do they want? Do they want one looking out? Or looking in? What do they see as the balance of forces in the world today? Europe is relatively secure. The day may come when Europe will not need the United States and its guarantees. I don't think that day has come yet, but it may come and we would welcome it."

●"We have no desire to stay in Europe except to participate in the defense of Europe. Once Europe ... feels itself secure, then the United States has 400,000 troops there, and we would of course want to bring them home. We do not desire to influence or dominate. What we do desire ... is to see Europe and the United States together engaged in the struggle of ... the world. We cannot possibly survive if Europe and the United States are rich and prosperous and isolated."

Mr. Kennedy made his statement in reply to a reporter's question on what trade policy the U.S. would adopt if Britain were denied entry to the EEC. He stressed that the U.S.' policy would remain the same: "We don't plan to associate ourselves with the Community. We plan to negotiate with the Community in order to provide for the admission of American goods as we have planned to negotiate with other countries which are not members of the Common Market." (The *N.Y. Times* [Western edition] reported Jan. 23 that Mr. Kennedy, at an expanded meeting of the National Security Council Jan. 22, had emphasized the need to ascertain the specifically American interest in each foreign policy problem and then, insofar as possible, to formulate policy to serve this interest best. The meeting, described by the White House as a "start-of-the-year review," was attended by 50 leading Administration officials.)

The President's news conference statement was more moderate than comments on de Gaulle's policy made by leading Congress members and other Administration officials:

State Undersecy. George W. Ball, speaking Jan. 23 at a New York meeting honoring European planner Jean Monnet, obviously referred to de Gaulle when he lauded Monnet for never being "tempted into the unhappy error—induced by a nostalgic longing for a world that never was—of seeking to recapture the past." Ball said Monnet "has not sought to unfurl ancient banners, reinstate old forms, revive the vanished symbols that beglamored the centuries gone by. Instead he has pursued the more relevant purpose of bending men's efforts toward a nobler future."

Sen. Jacob K. Javits (R., N.Y.) Jan. 22 denounced de Gaulle's stand and called for U.S. negotiations with Britain and the Commonwealth nations to strengthen the British negotiating position with the EEC. Comparing U.S. trade patterns with those of the EEC and of Britain and the Commonwealth, Javits concluded that "the basis for an effective [U.S.-British-Commonwealth] partnership exists."

Sen. J. William Fulbright (D., Ark.), chairman of the Senate Foreign Relations Committee, declared Jan. 24 that de Gaulle had endangered the Western alliance by following "the romantic illusions of a Napoleon." He charged that de Gaulle's "imperious disruption" of the Brussels talks even had led to the suggestion of a U.S. withdrawal from Europe. He added: "The great lesson of 2 world wars and the postwar struggle with communism is that no free nation can hope to realize its own national ambitions in utter disregard of friends and allies. But Gen. de Gaulle apparently does not think so." Fulbright's assessment of what de Gaulle did think: "He appears to have persuaded himself that if he remains intransigent and uncooperative on matters that vitally affect France's partners, America will reward him with gifts of nuclear weapons, Britain will depart obligingly from the European scene, and the Common Market countries will submit tamely to French leadership. I am reminded of the saying of an old Arkansas farmer: 'It's better to be ignorant than to know what ain't so.'"

The formal breaking-off of the Brussels negotiations took place when Lord Privy Seal Edward Heath, Britain's chief European negotiator, was summoned by the representatives of the 6 EEC powers and told that, in view of France's opposition to continuing the talks, they had been unable to agree on a procedure for further meetings. The representatives of the 5 other EEC states told Heath that their governments had wanted to press for a successful conclusion of the negotiations (and were certain that an agreement was possible) but had been prevented from doing so by France.

Belgian Deputy Foreign Min. Henri Fayat, chairman of the final Brussels session, told Heath that he regretted the negotiators' failure. "I am convinced," he added, "that this regret will be echoed throughout the free world as with anxiety and fear people consider the unhappy consequences which will follow from what has happened." Vice Chancellor Ludwig Erhard, West German representative, declared: "This is a black day in the history of the free world." Dutch Foreign Min. Joseph M. A. H. Luns said that the decision had "shattered" the other 5 nations' confidence in France and could threaten the EEC itself.

Heath, in a statement issued following the adjournment of the talks Jan. 29, said: "We entered these negotiations 16 months ago in good faith and have endeavored strenuously to reach a successful conclusion. 5 countries and the commission have said publicly that all remaining problems in the negotiations were capable of solution. I share that view. The 5 governments and ourselves all wished to continue negotiations and bring them to a successful conclusion. The high hopes of so many have thus been thwarted for political reasons and the will of one man. The end of the negotiations is a blow to the cause of that wider European unity for which we have been striving."

The French position was presented Jan. 29 by a French Foreign Ministry spokesman: "Whatever may have been said or written, [France] did not exercise a veto against Great Britain's entry into the Common Market. She stated—and the experience of the past months seems conclusive in this respect—that England, as a result of her situation and traditions, was not at present in a position to accept certain of the essential clauses of the Treaty of Rome. She deduced from this that, rather than continue down a dead-end, it was better to adjourn—I say adjourn and not break because, as has been said and repeated by the leading persons of responsibility in French politics, England has only to accept the clauses of the Treaty of Rome for her accession to pose no further questions."

The final Brussels meeting had been convened Jan. 28 to study a West German proposal that the EEC Executive Commission, headed by Walter Hallstein of West Germany, review the negotiations to date and recommend specific solutions for the major problems encountered—alignment of Britain's agriculture with the new EEC farm system, the problem of the Commonwealth and less-developed nations' traditional trade with Britain. The plan, submitted by West German Foreign Min. Gerhard Schroeder, called for the commission to report to the conference in detail within 2-3 weeks and for the 7 participants to agree in advance to immediately resume negotiations based on the report. The West German compromise had been formulated as part of Chancellor Adenauer's last-minute effort to prevent a rupture of the talks.

The attempted compromise collapsed when French Foreign Min. Maurice Couve de Murville, apparently acting to prevent any prolongation of the negotiations, raised a series of procedural objections to the proposed commission's work. He particularly objected to the suggestion that the commission study only the specific problems posed by Britain's application and that its report be directed to the 7 conferring powers rather than to the 6 EEC nations. He demanded that the report be kept an EEC matter and be devoted to an examination of the broader problems posed by the admission of new members to the 6-nation bloc.

The final confrontation between the British and the French viewpoints took place at the Jan. 29 meeting. Couve de Murville declared that there were 2 unsolved problems raised by Britain's application: (1) "the problem of the position Britain will have in Europe or in relation to Europe"; (2) "the problem of the European Economic Community's relations with the underdeveloped countries and with the other principal industrial countries of the world." He added that it was clear to France that "Great Britain is not yet in a position to accept the disciplines of the [EEC] treaty and particularly those of the agricultural policy." Heath, who realized that the talks were at an end, replied that Britain had given concrete evidence of its readiness to accept the provisions of the EEC treaty. He pointed out that Britain had accepted the 6 nations' common farm policies and had asked only that it be permitted to cushion the

impact of the transition to the EEC farm system by special arrangements for British farming for a period ending in 1969. As for French
charges that Britain had delayed specific agreements required on its
tariff levels, Heath noted that the Brussels negotiators already had
reached complete accord on the British tariffs to be applied to all but 26
items on the list of 2,500 studied. Heath said that the basic French contention was that Britain was not European enough to fulfill the requirements of EEC membership. He observed that many millions of Europeans knew how closely Britain had been involved in Europe in the past
and were grateful for it. He added that the French were breaking off
the negotiations for political reasons, not because they were close to
failure, but because they very nearly had succeeded.

Reports from Brussels said that the French had blocked further
discussion of a compromise settlement by invoking the EEC treaty's rule
of unanimity on all basic decisions affecting the treaty. The French delegation reportedly insisted that the talks be ended despite the united
opposition of the other 5 EEC nations and the last-minute intervention
of the U.S. The U.S. action was in the form of a message delivered to
Erhard and the West German delegation Jan. 29 by U.S. Amb.-to-EEC
John Tuthill. The message was said to have expressed the U.S.' anxiety
about the consequences to the Western alliance of a breakdown in the
Brussels talks.

Following the meeting, Heath conferred with the representatives
of the 5 EEC states favoring Britain's membership. The 6 countries
agreed to maintain contact on the problem, but they rejected suggestions that they continue to negotiate without France.

Heath gave the following report Jan. 30 to the House of Commons:

"... The 6 met at about 7:15 p.m. on Jan. 28 and again at noon and in the early afternoon of Jan. 29. The ministers of Belgium, the Federal Republic of Germany, Italy, Luxembourg, and the Netherlands did all they could, during these meetings, to persuade the French
delegation to agree on a basis for continuing the negotiations. As the House knows, their
efforts were of no avail. I was, of course, kept fully informed throughout their discussions.
At about 4:30 yesterday afternoon, the full conference of the 7 met to consider the situation.
I was accompanied at this meeting by ... the Commonwealth secretary [Duncan Sandys] and
the Minister of Agriculture, Fisheries & Food [Christopher Soames]. The chairman of the
conference, M. Fayat, opened the meeting by reading a statement, of which the following is a
translation:

"'Following the decision taken by the 7 governments on Jan. 18 last, the 6 have
resumed their discussions on the proposal of the French delegation to break off the negotiations between the member-states of the EEC and the U.K. The 5 other delegations of the
EEC and the British delegation opposed this proposal at the time it was made. In the discussions held by the 6 yesterday and today various compromise proposals have been examined.
It has finally become apparent that the Belgian, the German, the Italian, the Luxembourg
and the Netherlands delegations agree to accept the following text...:

"'The European Commission is requested to draw up, during the next 3 weeks, a report
on the present state of the negotiations for accession between Great Britain and the 6 states
of the EEC; in this report the commission will set out the results already obtained and the
questions still in suspense and will give its opinion on the latter. This report will be transmitted to each of the 7 delegations comprising the conference. The work of the conference
will be resumed not later than 10 days after the submission of this report.... The French
delegation has refused to accept this text because of a different view which they will explain
in the course of this meeting.'

"After hearing this statement, ministers representing Belgium, the Netherlands, Germany, France, Italy and Luxembourg then each spoke in turn. With the exception of the French foreign minister, each declared that it was his government's wish to continue the negotiations and his government's conviction that the outstanding problems could be resolved. Each one expressed deep regret at the situation which had arisen and anxiety as to its consequences. Prof. [Walter] Hallstein . . . also spoke. He said that the European Commission would seek to reduce to the minimum the harmful effects of these developments, both within the EEC and in its relations with other countries.

"M. Couve de Murville stated his government's reasons for having proposed a suspension of the negotiations. He argued that they had made no progress since October, that Britain had not been able to accept the disciplines of the Rome Treaty, notably the common agricultural policy, and that the entry of new members to a club which was not yet complete raised serious questions, notably for the founder-members.

"I then said that, had the 6 countries been able to agree on the draft terms of reference for a report by the European Commission which had been proposed by the 5 delegations, we should have been able to accept them, because they would have shown that the negotiations were being resumed in good faith. I recalled the reasons for our application to enter into negotiations with the Community. I completely repudiated the arguments advanced by the French delegation for advocating the suspension of negotiations; I said that we would not turn our backs on the continent because of these events but would continue to work with all our friends in Europe for its future strength and unity.

"The chairman of the conference then said that, in the circumstances, he was forced to record the fact, with great regret, that the member-states of the EEC were prevented from continuing the negotiations. He was convinced that this regret would be echoed throughout the world. M. Fayat then declared the meeting closed. . . ."

Duncan Sandys told Parliament Jan. 30 that the failure of the negotiations was the fault of one "misguided man [de Gaulle], who seemed to think that France is Europe and he is France."

Aftermath of Brussels Failure

British Prime Min. Macmillan declared Jan. 30 that the French veto of British admission to the Common Market had been dictated by de Gaulle's apparent scheme for French domination of Western Europe. Addressing a TV audience that covered not only Britain but the 6 Common Market countries, Macmillan blamed de Gaulle for "brutally" causing the collapse of the British-European negotiations and for jeopardizing the West's postwar steps toward unity. He added that the failure of the talks in Brussels had been "bad for us, bad for Europe, bad for the whole free world," but that it did not mean Britain would turn its back on Europe or shirk its NATO responsibilities.

Macmillan distinguished pointedly between France under de Gaulle and the other nations of Europe. In an obvious allusion to de Gaulle's allegedly autocratic methods of rule, he said: Twice in his lifetime Britain had been forced to intervene in "frightful internecine wars" caused by European dictatorships; "these great conflicts have generally been brought about by the attempts of one nation, or sometimes of one man, to dominate the whole of Europe, to create a kind of sham united Europe, not by agreements, nor by partnership or cooperation, but by power"; "I fear . . . that France, or at least the present [de Gaulle] government, . . [is] looking backwards"; "they seem to think one nation can dominate Europe or—equally wrong—that Europe can rule alone without friends and without allies."

Britain's attempt to negotiate admission to the Common Market had been motivated at least in part by a desire to prevent such events from recurring, Macmillan said. "We want to stop this happening again. We want to heal the divisions of Europe by real unity, and we want to see this freely united Europe use her strength and prosperity for the benefit of the whole world." This had been one of the primary aims of the Marshal Plan, the Atlantic alliance and the other postwar efforts to unify the West, Macmillan said. "What folly it is for anyone now to try to put all this at risk."

Macmillan reaffirmed Britain's adherence to its ties, not only with Europe, but with the U.S. and the Commonwealth. "Of course," he said, "we must cooperate with the rest of the world, with the Commonwealth and with the United States..., in an equal and honorable partnership, and that is why we in Britain are determined to stand by the Atlantic Alliance." Macmillan said Britain's future trade plans were dependent on a new round of talks with the Commonwealth, the U.S. and the 6 other nations of the British-led European Free Trade Association. He rejected the idea of a Commonwealth Market as unworkable. Macmillan concluded with an appeal to the British people—"all of us"—for unity and for hard work in solving Britain's trade difficulties. Britain must be prepared to "rely on our own determination, our own vigor, our own resources," he said. "It is the kind of situation in which we have always done best in the past and so it will be again."

The French position remained unchanged. The veto of Britain's admission to the Common Market was reaffirmed Jan. 30 by the French cabinet at a meeting attended by de Gaulle. The cabinet, which heard reports on the Brussels veto from de Gaulle and Foreign Min. Couve de Murville, issued a statement in which it "fully indorsed the foreign minister's attitude at Brussels and particularly the European position adopted by France, which helped to maintain the [EEC's] Treaty of Rome, come what may." Information Min. Alain Peyrefitte, reading the statement to newsmen, declared that "the Common Market carries on better than ever" as a result of the French action. He added that "the present situation does not exclude possible future developments; it leaves the way open for a true admission of Britain into a true Common Market when Britain is ready for this."

Britain's negotiations for admission to the ECSC and Euratom were suspended Jan. 30, following the collapse of Britain's negotiations with the EEC. A statement by the Euratom Executive Commission said that the Brussels developments prevented "pursuit for the time being" of the British application to Euratom. The statement added: "It has been clear that, since the 3 European communities together form a single grouping with common institutions, there could only be membership of the 3 communities together." The ECSC's announcement, issued in Bonn, said only that a planned Feb. 5 ministerial meeting on Britain's membership bid had been postponed.

The break in negotiations in Brussels provoked a political crisis in West Germany, where the French-German Treaty of Cooperation was before Parliament for ratification. Bonn's "European" faction, led by Vice Chancellor Ludwig Erhard, accused Chancellor Adenauer of having permitted de Gaulle to wreck the Brussels negotiations. Spurred by Erhard's continued fight for designation as Adenauer's successor, many of the more militant of Bonn's "Europeans" indicated that they would support the French-German treaty only if Adenauer gave assurances that he would force a reopening of the negotiations for British membership in EEC. Adenauer gave the sought-for assurances but without committing himself to a specific timetable for action; the promised renewal of negotiations never materialized.

The West German government's first formal expression of support for renewed negotiations was given Jan. 30, after Adenauer had met with his cabinet to discuss the results of the Brussels break. A government statement said: "The Federal government is convinced that the present situation must be constructively overcome. With this aim it will work for the restoration of unity... among the Common Market partners and to facilitate the entry of Britain into the community." Fixing the blame for the break on France, the statement declared that the EEC nations "were unable to agree on... continuing the negotiations with Great Britain, despite the intensive efforts of 5 of the 6." Bonn press spokesman Karl Guenther von Hase said after reading the statement that "the goal remains quite clearly Britain's membership in the... market." (Alfred Mueller-Armack, Economics Ministry state secretary who had served as Bonn's permanent representative during the lengthy negotiations with Britain, resigned his post Feb. 2.)

The U.S. Jan. 30 formally expressed its disappointment at the collapse of the Brussels negotiations. It did so in a special statement issued by the State Department with the approval of State Secy. Dean Rusk. The statement, the first official U.S. reaction to the break, was said to reflect Kennedy Administration reluctance to worsen the current Western rift by a public attack on de Gaulle and his foreign policy. The statement, reaffirming the U.S.' fundamental belief in the strength of the West's alliances, said: "The United States considers the breakdown in the negotiations... as most unfortunate. We do not believe, however, that the present difficulty can do more than delay the movement toward a strong and united Europe working in effective partnership with the United States for the solution of mutual problems. For our part, we will continue to pursue policies which derive from the hard realities of the situation.... These policies include the strengthening of NATO, the creation of a multilateral defense force, and the liberalization of trade. Most Europeans recognize with us that the defense of the free world is indivisible, that the Atlantic Community is economically interdependent and that we and Europe share joint responsibilities in the rest of the world." (White House press secretary Pierre Salinger confirmed to newsmen Feb. 1 that Pres. Kennedy and Prime Min. Macmillan had been in communication during the British-Common Market crisis.)

Dutch Foreign Min. Joseph M. A. H. Luns told the Netherlands Parliament Jan. 31 that France's veto of Britain had been "shocking" but that it had only succeeded in delaying, not in preventing, Britain's membership in Europe. Luns asserted that Britain was an "essential part of continental Europe" and that it should be kept informed of all major Common Market decisions. Luns denounced the "authoritarian character" of the French government and charged de Gaulle with trying to impose his will "not only in France, but in other countries." (It was reported from Brussels Feb. 1 that the Netherlands had informed the 5 other EEC nations that it would boycott all Common Market ministerial meetings scheduled for February as a protest against the Brussels failure.)

Vice Pres. Sicco Mansholt of the EEC Executive Commission warned at a Brussels press conference Feb. 1 that "no progress can be made, or will be made, before this political breach [caused by France's action] has been repaired and agreement had been restored." "The touchstone of this agreement," he asserted, "is acceptance in principle to allow Britain to join the Community on the basis of the Rome Treaty, which Britain is ready to accept."

Prime Min. Macmillan visited Rome Feb. 1-3 for talks with Italian Premier Amintore Fanfani on proposals for a new attempt to bring Britain into the Common Market. They were said to have reached agreement that a new British membership might be made through the Western European Union. Macmillan, accompanied by Heath, began his talks with Fanfani and Foreign Min. Attilio Piccioni immediately after their arrival in Rome. The talks continued for 2 days, with interruptions for visits by Macmillan to Pope John XXIII Feb. 2 and Italian Pres. Antonio Segni Feb. 3. A final communique issued by Macmillan and Fanfani Feb. 3 expressed Macmillan's "gratitude for the strong and friendly support consistently given [to Britain] by the Italian government during the Brussels negotiations." It said that "the 2 prime ministers were as one in deploring the breakdown in these negotiations and in resolving that this setback must not do lasting damage to the cause of European unity." It pledged them to "extend and strengthen the close consultation which already exists [between Britain and Italy] in the political and economic fields." It affirmed "their determination to maintain the existing collaboration with the United States...and welcomed the opportunity to establish a NATO multilateral nuclear force." At a Rome news conference before his return to London Feb. 3, Macmillan warned that Europe would be acting from "folly" and "ingratitude" if it tried to turn itself into "a small inward-looking group" of states.

Criticism of French Stand Continues

The French opposition to British participation in European institutions was denounced by most of the European leaders known to consider themselves "European" citizens.

Jean Monnet, 73, architect of France's postwar recovery and of the European unity movement that led to the ECSC and EEC, had denounced his country's position Jan. 16. Monnet declared that "despite what Gen. de Gaulle had said, the negotiations for Britain's entry into the Common Market can be quickly concluded" and were essential to the future of Europe and of the Western alliance. "Americans and Europeans must realize," he said, "that neither one nor the other is defending a particular country, but that the ensemble is defending a civilization." Monnet, in a statement issued Feb. 3, after the Brussels talks had failed, termed the French action "very serious because the mutual confidence essential to any common accord has been shaken."

(Monnet had expressed these sentiments in an address delivered to Freedom House in New York Jan. 23 as he accepted the organization's annual Freedom Award. Asserting that British participation in the European community was "essential" if Europe was to assume the role of a co-equal with the U.S., he called on Britons and Europeans to abandon their ancient distrust of each other's interests. "I still hope and believe," he said, "... that the negotiations on Britain's entry into Europe will succeed." He said that the proposed alliance of the U.S. and Europe was "natural and inevitable" but required a new understanding of both entities' needs. "You, in the United States," he said, "must realize that the claims of Europe to share common responsibility and authority for decisions on defense, including the nuclear weapons, is natural since any decision involves the very existence of the European peoples. On the other hand, I think the Europeans must understand that the nuclear terror is indivisible and that they too must shoulder an adequate share of the common defense.")

Belgian Foreign Min. Paul-Henri Spaak asserted Feb. 4, in an interview in the Brussels Socialist newspaper Le Peuple, that de Gaulle's Jan. 14 press conference had threatened the West's entire postwar policies. He demanded that action be taken to assure Britain's participation in Europe.

France's position was defended by Amb.-to-U.S. Herve Alphand Feb. 4 in an address at an ambassadors' forum in Chambersburg, Pa. Alphand described de Gaulle's European policy as follows: "Through a Europe economically and politically united—a Europe to which one day we hope Great Britain will belong by accepting its rules—and through a close cooperation between this Europe and America, we believe we can facilitate the realization of a modus vivendi between East and West which has always been one of the bases of French policy." Alphand said France would be able to facilitate an East-West accord only if "the threat from the East" ceased; its current policy remained to "preserve the alliance with America and safeguard the future of European co-operation."

Premier Georges Pompidou confirmed Feb. 5, in an address to Paris newsmen, that the British-U.S. Nassau agreement on the creation of a NATO nuclear force had been a key element in de Gaulle's decision to veto Britain's EEC application. By the Nassau pact, he said, "Britain has shown that she is tied first of all to the United States, which is not in Europe." Pompidou declared that "the door of the Common Market is not closed to Britain" but that Britain's entry was not feasible until it had accepted completely the conditions and disciplines of the EEC Rome Treaty.

Meeting with French deputies at a Presidential reception in Paris Feb. 5, de Gaulle declared that Britain had acted as a U.S. pawn in its application to join the EEC. He said: "Making use of England, America is seeking, in fact, to establish a vast liberal exchange deal with the Irish, the Icelanders, *et al.* The Americans can no longer sell anything—or else they are selling for practically nothing—to the Africans, the South Americans, even to the Arabs. So they are forced to sell to Europe, which is in a position to pay."

Paris dispatches reported Feb. 13 that French officials had been ordered to cease public statements on the Common Market question. It was reported that this was a preliminary to resumption of French contacts with the other EEC states on alternative proposals for British association with the Common Market. French official sources told Paris newsmen Feb. 14 that France was willing to begin discussion of such proposals.

European Parliament Meets

Pres. Walter Hallstein of the EEC Executive Commission declared Feb. 5, in an address before the 6-nation European Parliament in Strasbourg, that the French action had caused a "crisis of confidence" in Europe's institutions. Hallstein asserted that Britain's entry into Europe had only been "deferred" and that "Europe will never turn her back on England," despite the French veto. He denounced the way in which France had broken the negotiations as "not in harmony with the duties imposed by the Community." He added this indorsement of the U.S.' position in the current rift: "In agreement with American policy, Europe seeks to replace the system harnessing one giant with a number of comparative dwarfs by a true parternship of America and Europe."

The European Parliament debated the failure of the Brussels talks Feb. 5-6. Despite repeated denunciations of the French veto by deputies from each of the Parliament's 3 major blocs—Socialists, Christian Democrats and Liberals—the Parliament refused, in a 38-38 tie vote Feb. 6, to adopt a Socialist motion protesting the method of the French action. 2 other motions relating to the problem, one setting up a commission to investigate the current state of the British negotiations, the other indorsing the aims of a United States of Europe and of a larger Atlantic partnership, were adopted by the 142-member body, the advisory legislative organ of the EEC, ECSC and Euratom groupings.

German & U.S. Support for Britain Continues

West German Vice Chancellor Ludwig Erhard challenged Chancellor Konrad Adenauer's policies and the French-German treaty Feb. 5 in a newspaper interview in which he announced his candidacy for the chancellorship. Erhard's statement, published by Munich's *Suddeutsche Zeitung,* said: If summoned by Parliament to succeed Adenauer, he would accept the "call." "The whole German people wants... this reconciliation and understanding with Britain as the starting point of a unified Europe. And this is not the end of it. It extends... even to the Atlantic Alliance." The French action in Brussels had been an insult to German democracy; de Gaulle "knew full well how the whole German people... felt" about Britain's entry to the EEC.

Adenauer's reply to his critics was delivered Feb. 6 in a state-of-the-union address to the West German Bundestag. He said: The break in British-EEC negotiations was temporary; all Common Market nations, "especially we Germans," would work to revive the talks as quickly as possible. West Germany associated itself fully with Britain in its hopes for EEC membership and with the U.S. in its plans for strengthening NATO and making it a cornerstone of an Atlantic partnership. But the French-German alliance was a historic necessity.

The Adenauer statement was attacked in the Bundestag Feb. 7 by Socialist leaders Erich Ollenhauer and Fritz Erler, who asked the chancellor (in Ollenhauer's words) "whether the German government is really resolved to go the limit in working for Britain's acceptance" in the EEC. Adenauer answered that West Germany had made clear to France its position in favor of British membership and would press for a quick reopening of the matter. He said that at his Jan. 23 Paris meeting with de Gaulle, the French leader had "promised me that the first subject of joint consultation after the [French-German] treaty goes into effect will be British entry into the European Economic Community." Adenauer appealed for an end to German dissension on the matter; he said Bonn's unity was essential if the negotiations were to be reopened successfully. He added: "I want the British to believe my word" that the talks would be resumed.

Ex-Foreign Min. Heinrich von Brentano, leader of Adenauer's Christian Democratic Union in the Bundestag, declared in the Feb. 7 debate that "our determination... to pursue the policy of European integration was not weakened but strengthened by the recent event in Brussels." Foreign Min. Gerhard Schroeder asserted that Bonn would press bilateral talks with Britain to examine the possibility of some form of associate British membership in the EEC.

The West German Bundesrat (upper house) Feb. 8 unanimously approved a resolution calling on the Adenauer government to "do everything possible to ... bring about the resumption of negotiations with Britain." The resolution, an unusual action for the Bundesrat, declared that Britain's application had been in "the spirit of the Common Market treaty, which contains an invitation to all other European peoples to become members."

Despite Adenauer's professions of support for Britain's admission to the Common Market, reports persisted that he was not personally a partisan of the British application and that he had done little to dissuade de Gaulle from rupturing negotiations. Defense Min. Kai-Uwe von Hassel was reported to have said at a CDU meeting in Kiel Jan. 26 that Adenauer was "politically concerned that if [Britain and] all the others come in, the whole of Europe might become a structure in which socialism, whose attitude is basically neutralist, is suddenly dominant." Von Hassel was forced Feb. 10 to issue a statement charging that his remarks had been misinterpreted. Bonn spokesmen insisted Feb. 11 that West Germany had done everything possible to win EEC membership for Britain and the other EFTA nations.

U.S. support for Britain's eventual admission to the Common Market was reaffirmed by Pres. Kennedy Feb. 7 at his first news conference since the suspension of the British-EEC negotiations. Mr. Kennedy stressed that the entire U.S. program of postwar aid for Europe had been intended, at least in part, to create a united Europe that would include Britain and would be able to share equally with the U.S. the responsibilities of Western leadership. The President, responding to newsmen's questions, said: "We are concerned at the failure of the British to secure admission to the Common Market. We have supported the unification of Europe, economically and militarily.... We put over $50 billion worth of assistance in rebuilding Europe [after World War II]. We supported strongly the Common Market, Euratom and the other efforts to provide for a more unified Europe ... to accept greater responsibility and greater burdens, as well as to take advantage of greater opportunities.... We felt Britain would be an effective part of that Europe. And it ... still is our hope that a powerful Europe, joined with the power of the North American continent, would provide a source of strength in this decade which would permit the balance of power to be maintained with us."

Mr. Kennedy expressed the view that "it is possible there may be some reconsiderations of the British application" for EEC membership. He said that until the final outcome of the British bid was certain he would not ask for Congressional action to restore his authority to negotiate sweeping tariff cuts with the Common Market. (Mr. Kennedy previously had requested such authority—and had been granted it in the 1962 Trade Expansion Act—as essential to maintain U.S. exports to a Common Market that would include Britain.)

New British-EEC Talks Studied

It was reported from London and European capitals Feb. 8-14 that the EEC countries that had supported Britain against France's veto of its Common Market application were examining proposals for a renewal of efforts to negotiate ties between Britain and the European group. British terms for negotiating an "association" with the 6 EEC countries were laid down Feb. 12 by Edward Heath, Lord Privy Seal and chief British representative at the defunct Brussels talks. Addressing the House of Commons, Heath indicated that Britain might entertain proposals for an associate tie with the EEC despite its previous refusals to consider anything short of full membership. He made it clear, however, that "if there is to be an alternative arrangement, whatever it may be, it must come from the whole Community [of Common Market states]... [and] it cannot involve another long negotiation." He declared that if new and meaningful negotiations were to be attempted, the EEC nations would have to demonstrate their good faith and "the will to succeed must be there as apparently it was not there" in the past Brussels talks.

Belgian and Dutch trade officials conferred with British representatives in Brussels Feb. 14, reportedly to submit a proposal for association between Britain and the EEC as a step toward eventual extension of the 6-nation customs union to include Britain. The Belgian-Dutch proposals had been formulated as a Benelux response to France's veto of full British membership in the EEC. They were discussed by Lord Home, British foreign secretary, and Belgian Foreign Min. Paul-Henri Spaak at a Brussels meeting Feb. 8 and presumably won Home's approval as a basis for further negotiations. Although the Belgian and Dutch governments refused to reveal the substance of the proposal before it was discussed fully with the other EEC states and Britain, it was reported to call for (1) a transitional arrangement for British association with the EEC, primarily with respect to free internal trade and common external tariffs for manufactured and industrial goods; (2) a clear understanding that the transitional arrangement would lead to full British membership in the Common Market within a specified period. (It was reported from Brussels Feb. 8 that Spaak and Home, in addition to the above proposals, had discussed plans for a British-EEC treaty that would provide for regular ministerial-level political consultation through the framework of the Western European Union organization.)

West German press reports that the Bonn government was studying a 4-stage proposal for British entry to the EEC and the creation of an Atlantic union with the U.S. were denied Feb. 15 by Heinrich von Brentano, parliamentary leader of the governing CDU. The proposal had been reported in detail the previous day after von Brentano had conferred with Economics Min. Ludwig Erhard and Pres. Walter Hallstein of the EEC Executive Commission. Despite von Brentano's disavowal,

Bonn dispatches said again Feb. 15 that the proposal was under discussion and that it consisted of these 4 major points: (1) rapid British association with the EEC; (2) full British membership in the Common Market by 1966; (3) creation of a European political union; (4) conclusion of a U.S.-West European treaty along the lines of Pres. Kennedy's proposals for Atlantic partnership.

British Debate EEC Negotiations

The breakdown of the Brussels negotiations was debated Feb. 11-12 in the House of Commons. The debate was opened by Prime Min. Macmillan, who outlined Britain's proposed economic and trade policies in the light of the Brussels failure. Macmillan began his address with a renewed denunciation of de Gaulle for his personal action barring Britain from the EEC. He declared: "If the European vision has been obscured, it has not been through some minor obstruction. It was brought to an end by a dramatic, if somewhat brutal, stroke of policy." He asserted that the talks had been broken off not because they were nearing failure but because they posed the threat of success. "That the French government in their hearts had long feared success, I do not doubt," he said. "It is inevitable that people are beginning to wonder whether these [French actions] are not indications of a policy which, if it was pursued, would bring the whole of the Western alliance into great jeopardy, if not collapse."

Making it clear that Britain did not envisage a rapid resumption of the European negotiations, Macmillan said that his government's trade and economic policies would be as follows: "We propose a conference of Commonwealth [trade] ministers. We shall work for close cooperation with the Commonwealth, the United States, and the European Free Trade Association. We shall work for world commodity agreements. And at home we shall work for an expanding economy without inflation based upon an incomes policy." He pledged that, despite the French rebuff, Britain would work to expand its trade with EEC countries "by all practical means within our power." He said Britain's major effort to achieve world tariff cuts and commodity agreements would be made at the "Kennedy round" of tariff-cutting talks to be held by the General Agreement on Tariffs & Trade (GATT) in 1964.

The Macmillan government's position during and following the Brussels negotiations was assailed Feb. 12 by George Brown, deputy Labor Party leader in Parliament. Brown declared that under Macmillan's leadership the British government had been "humiliated time after time in a fashion which leaders of this country have not had to tolerate for a thousand years." He added that "their only reply was to stop Princess Margaret going to raise funds for the British hospital in Paris." (Buckingham Palace had announced Feb. 7 that a planned Paris visit Mar. 9-10 of the princess and her husband, the Earl of Snowden, had been cancelled on the advice of the Macmillan government. The reason given was that Margaret's position as a counselor of state required her presence in Britain during a tour Queen Elizabeth was making in New Zealand. The action was denounced by British newspapers and political leaders on the ground that it clearly was political and had involved the royal family in the controversy with France. Macmillan, defending his decision in Parliament Feb. 12, asserted that it had been taken in response to French policy toward Britain but also in view of political overtones that the princess' visit inevitably would have been given in Paris. Margaret was to have attended a Paris film benefit for the British hospital there and was to have been de Gaulle's guest at an Elysee Palace luncheon.)

Addressing the British Chamber of Commerce at a meeting in Brussels, the Earl of Home, British foreign secretary, declared that the Brussels negotiations had collapsed because "2 visions of Europe came into head-on collision." Explaining the nature of these contending views, he added: "The one was of Europe so ordered that it would be a 3d force between Russia and the United States, a Europe protected, exclusive, narcissus-like in its self-glory. The other was of a Europe of people, democratic, politically mature nations in complete partnership, doing their duty by the whole world outside. Britain and Belgium have stated with absolute clarity which vision of Europe is their choice."

EEC & EFTA Hold Meetings

The 7 member states of the British-led European Free Trade Association conferred in Geneva Feb. 18-19 on coordinated policies in the wake of the EEC's rejection of Britain's application. It was reported that the 7 had agreed to postpone all further negotiations for EEC ties until the final disposition of the British application and until France had given proof that it would enter such negotiations in good faith. Lord Privy Seal Edward Heath reportedly informed the conferees Feb. 18 that Britain did not believe the EEC negotiations would be resumed in the immediate future. Austrian Foreign Min. Bruno Kreisky was reported to have said at the meeting Feb. 18 that Austria, whose foreign trade was principally with the EEC nations, would be forced to pursue its approach for association with the EEC unless EFTA states could produce a feasible alternative.

The EFTA Ministerial Council announced in a communique Feb. 19 that the 7 states had agreed on measures to eliminate industrial tariffs among the 7 by 1966, one year before the EEC's scheduled attainment of the same goal. The communique said, however, that the 7 had agreed not to take any actions that would make the eventual integration of Europe into one trading bloc more difficult. Although the planned tariff abolition did not apply to farm products, it was made conditional on member states' prior acceptance of EFTA measures affecting agricultural trade (particularly those affecting the entry of Danish butter into the British market and the problem of Norwegian fisheries).

The EFTA Ministerial Council met May 9-11 in Lisbon and discussed accelerated intra-EFTA tariff cuts. The Council met again in Stockholm Sept. 11-12 and repeated the EFTA's desire to achieve a single European market, taking "every opportunity to cooperate with the EEC and its members in matters of mutual concern."

The first Common Market meeting to take place after the veto of Britain's application was held in Brussels Feb. 19-20 on the question of EEC agricultural regulations. No decisions were taken at the meeting. Netherlands representatives, who had been expected to boycott the meeting, participated but made it clear that they would block any actions predicated on Britain's long-term exclusion from the association. Dutch spokesmen had confirmed Feb. 18 that the Belgian and Netherlands governments were consulting on plans to reopen the British application through the Western European Union, whose membership consisted of Britain and the 6 EEC states. They warned that nearly all recent Common Market decisions had been based on Britain's membership in the bloc and that these decisions would have to be reviewed.

The Netherlands and Italy acted on this warning at the next Common Market meeting, held in Brussels Feb. 25-26. They refused, on the ground that each country faced imminent elections, to sign a convention providing for the association with the Common Market of 18 newly independent African states, nearly all of them former French colonies that had retained close political and economic ties with France. A program of $800 million in EEC aid for the 18 countries was delayed indefinitely by the Italian-Netherlands action, and the convention and aid agreements were not signed until July 20. (The African-Common Market convention of association had been negotiated and initialed in 1962. The 18 African countries: Central African Republic, Cameroun, Chad, Congo Republic [Leopoldville], Congo Republic [Brazzaville], Ivory Coast, Dahomey, Madagascar, Mali, Niger, Senegal, Togo, Burundi, Rwanda, Somalia, Gabon, Upper Volta, Mauritania.) The Feb. 25-26 meeting had been called at the foreign ministers' level, but Netherlands Foreign Min. Joseph M. A. H. Luns and Italian Foreign Min. Attilio Piccioni boycotted the session and were represented by deputies.

(Frankfurt's *Allgemeine Zeitung* reported Mar. 5 that Adenauer had rebuked Erhard for attending the latest Brussels meeting without his permission. Adenauer was said to have written Erhard that his Brussels trip had been a waste in view of Britain's decision to postpone all further EEC negotiations. Erhard reportedly replied in a letter that his trip to Brussels had been within his competence as a minister and that it was France, not Britain, that had canceled the January talks.)

EEC Report on Britain's Application

The EEC Executive Commission made public in Brussels Mar. 4 its formal report on the unsuccessful January negotiations. The report, requested by the European Parliament (the Common Market's deliberative body) over French objections, implied that the negotiations eventually might have succeeded if France had not forced their suspension.

Although the report refrained from stating clearly whether a total settlement would have been possible within the framework of the January talks, it suggested specific solutions that might have been found for the major problems then remaining—Britain's ties with its fellow Commonwealth nations, the meshing of the British and European agricultural systems, and internal and external tariff levels. The report said that many of these questions had been made more difficult by the fact that the 6 EEC countries themselves had reached no agreement on them. Commenting on "the real difficulties in the negotiations," the report concluded that "the question was not only one of reconciling British systems and commitments with the letter of the Treaty of Rome; it was rather one of reconciling them with a community in the full surge of development." The document outlined steps that might be taken "should some British government wish to align its policies... with the Common Market preparatory to applying for membership."

Walter Hallstein, president of the Executive Commission, told newsmen in Washington Mar. 4 that "everybody" in the Common Market, including the French, agreed that Britain would eventually join the EEC. Hallstein, who conferred that day with Pres. Kennedy and with State Secy. Rusk, said that he had urged the U.S. to shape its European policy on the assumption that the talks would be renewed and would succeed. In an address at Columbia University in New York Mar. 2, Hallstein had urged that the Brussels "interruption" not be permitted to delay progress toward a partnership of America and Europe.

The EEC report was debated in the European Parliament Mar. 27-29. The Parliament then unanimously passed a resolution expressing the desire that Britain (and other EFTA countries) join the EEC, provided that the integration policies of the EEC or the rules of the Treaty of Rome were not endangered.

(The *N.Y. Times* had reported from London Mar. 14 that the Belgian and Netherlands governments had abandoned proposals for a customs union in industrial goods between Britain and the 6 Common Market states. According to the *Times*, the plan had been communicated to Britain but had been dropped after the British replied that they saw little hope that France would accept even this limited form of association.)

British Policy

Britain's intention to continue seeking a role in a united Europe was made clear by Foreign Secy. Lord Home Mar. 20 in an address at a Paris meeting of the North Atlantic Council. Appealing for an end to disruptive influences within the Atlantic Alliance, Home said that Britain, rebuffed in its attempt to join the Common Market, would seek the "closest partnership" in NATO with the 6 EEC countries and their allies. He declared that Britain was ready, as proof of its good will, to cooperate fully in plans to give European nations a share in the West's nuclear defense. He urged all NATO states to abandon "autarchial and introverted" policies that might, he warned, destroy the alliance.

The NATO Council session was attended neither by French Foreign Min. Couve de Murville nor West German Foreign Min. Schroeder despite the fact that Lord Home had given advance notice that he would deliver a major address at the meeting. Couve de Murville reportedly ignored Home's Paris visit, omitting even the courtesy invitation common in such cases. The meeting, one of the Council's regular weekly sessions, was attended, however, by the foreign ministers of all other EEC countries—Italy, Belgium, the Netherlands and Luxembourg.

An attempt to bring together Lord Home and the 6 EEC foreign ministers within the framework of the Western European Union (WEU) was reported Mar. 23 to have foundered due to French opposition. Although the meeting was said to have been called by Schroeder, in his capacity as WEU Council president for March, the *N.Y. Times* reported from Bonn Mar. 29 that Schroeder had sided with France in insisting that the question of the British-EEC negotiations be kept off the agenda. Schroeder was said to have been rebuked by several of the WEU countries, especially Italy and the Netherlands; except for France, all WEU members, including Britain, had agreed to the meeting on Schroeder's promise that the agenda would be open for discussion of any matter of general interest. Before the other ministers could reply to the French-German demand, Couve de Murville informed Schroeder that France considered the ministers' meeting premature and would not attend even if the agenda was restricted.

The London *Times* reported Mar. 25 that the French action in blocking the proposed WEU meeting had been expected by the Macmillan government. Couve de Murville was said to have informed British Amb.-to-France Sir Pierson Dixon in Paris Mar. 21 that France did not believe a 7-nation discussion of its differences with Britain would be fruitful, but that it was prepared to resume talks bilaterally at a future date.

The question of the effect a Labor Party election victory would have on Britain's policy toward Europe was discussed by Harold Wilson, newly elected Laborite leader, in a major address Apr. 1 before the National Press Club in Washington. Wilson asserted that a Socialist government would seek to renew the EEC negotiations if conditions were favorable. Wilson stressed that "constructive alternatives" to rapid British EEC membership existed: (1) "urgent action" to make a success of the planned "Kennedy round" of tariff reduction talks in 1964 and thus expand world trade; (2) "a medium for the creation of international credit through the established machinery of the International Monetary Fund" to finance the potential growth in world trade. Wilson warned that a growing shortage of international liquidity (he noted that world trade had quadrupled since 1939, but world monetary resources barely had doubled) could wreck the planned attempt to expand trade by cutting or eliminating tariff barriers.

The budget for fiscal 1964, presented to Parliament Apr. 3 by Chancellor of the Exchequer Reginald Maudling, provided for a £ 269 million ($753.2 million) tax cut. The budget, described as geared to the theme of "expansion without inflation," estimated revenues at £ 7.434 billion and expenditures at £ 8.121 billion. A £ 687 billion ($1.924 billion) deficit was anticipated. The tax cuts would affect mainly the lower-income bracket. The new rates were to provide total tax exemptions for 3,750,000 unmarried persons with annual incomes of £ 250 ($700) or less.

The Board of Trade May 10 announced special tariff assurances to Australia and New Zealand for butter and butter products. Similar assurances were made to Ireland June 14. These assurances were made in keeping with continued Commonwealth nations' concern over the status of their exports (to Britain) as EFTA tariff schedules changed. This was illustrated when Britain, suffering a butter shortage, authorized the import of approximately 12,000 tons of butter, mainly from Denmark. New Zealand Prime Min. Keith J. Holyoake said Aug. 13: "The [New Zealand] government has made a firm protest at the action taken by the British government. There is a clear difference of opinion between us and the British government as to the consequences which these additional quantities will have on the price of butter. We hold firmly to our assessment of the position, and we will watch the trend of the market closely. If our assessment should prove correct, the [New Zealand] government will make the strongest possible representations for emergency action by the British government to meet the situation." (The EFTA Ministerial Council had met in Lisbon May 9-11 and had agreed to accelerate scheduled tariff cuts. All tariffs on industrial products were rescheduled to be eliminated by Dec. 31, 1966.)

EEC Policy Debated

The 6 EEC foreign ministers met in Brussels again Apr. 1-2 but failed to make any progress on the major reason for their meeting: negotiation of an agreement to extend to their agricultural trade those Common Market pricing and selling practices already in effect for industrial trade. They discussed proposals for a limited resumption of contact with Britain and for launching preliminary discussions of the world tariff-cutting conference to be held in 1964, but France refused to give its assent clearly on either matter. The Apr. 1-2 meeting was taken as proof that the Common Market had come to a halt as a result of the divisions created by the veto of British membership.

Jean Monnet, a founder of the movement for European unity and leader of the nongovernmental Action Committee for a United States of Europe, warned Apr. 7 that the French action against Britain had caused a "crisis of confidence" in Europe. Monnet urged Europe's leaders to act decisively to prevent this atmosphere from crippling the Common Market and other institutions. He called for swift action to (1) negotiate a Common Market policy for agriculture and finance; (2) use the planned U.S.-EEC tariff reduction negotiations to renew negotiations with Britain. Monnet's views were made known in an interview published in Milan's *Corriere della Sera.*

Vice Pres. Sicco Mansholt of the EEC Executive Commission said in Washington Apr. 9 that the French-German Treaty of Cooperation and the policies it engendered were a menace to "the mutual confidence" of the Common Market nations. Mansholt, in the U.S. for talks with Pres. Kennedy, spoke at a National Press Club luncheon attended by representatives of every EEC country except France. He charged that the French-German treaty made sense only if it was recognized that de Gaulle regarded "the renaissance of Europe as being possible only under the leadership of one nation [France]."

The next 2 Common Market meetings—a session held at the deputy minister level in Brussels Apr. 22-23 and a meeting at the foreign minister level May 8-9—were marked by a clash between France and West Germany over a West German plan to generate further progress toward EEC goals by setting a timetable for action on the agricultural and tariff-reduction problems. The Bonn plan was designed to renew limited contacts with Britain and to prepare a coordinated EEC policy for the 1964 tariff-cutting negotiations. France opposed the timetable on the ground that it would delay action on a common market in agriculture until after the world tariff talks opened; France wanted the farm problem settled to its advantage before the talks, at which the EEC might be forced to grant the U.S. concessions on farm imports. Despite French objections, the West German proposal, known as the EEC " action program," was adopted.

A formal proposal for a renewal of contact between Britain and the 6 Common Market states was vetoed by France May 31 at an EEC foreign ministers' meeting in Brussels. The 5 other representatives, who had jointly sponsored the proposal, professed shock and anger at the French action. Luxembourg Foreign Min. Eugene Schaus, EEC Council president at the May 31 meeting, warned that there was "not much sense in going on with the action program until the British problem is solved." The proposal, advanced by the 5 other EEC nations under West German leadership, had called for regular and permanent contacts to be established between the British mission in Brussels and the 6 nations' permanent Brussels representatives to the EEC Council. French Foreign Min. Couve de Murville was reported to have refused to consider any plan that would have permitted a renewal of contact between Britain and the EEC rather than bilaterally, with each of the 6 governments, as favored by France.

British-EEC Contacts

A new attempt was made by Britain June 5 to revive its consultations with the Common Market nations. Speaking at a Paris meeting of the WEU (Western European Union) Assembly, Edward Heath, British Lord Privy Seal and Britain's chief negotiator during the talks with the EEC, proposed that the WEU Council of Ministers meet to consider the political, economic and strategic problems faced by the 7 WEU nations. Heath, noting that the WEU ministers had not met for 14 months, declared that such a meeting would be "admirably suited" for discussion of all the questions that had gone untreated since the British-EEC break. Michel Habib-Deloncle, French delegate to the WEU Assembly, replied that France would accept such a meeting only if it were clear that it was not to be used for polemics and was limited to WEU matters of a military or political nature. The Assembly voted by 51-8 (France opposed) with 8 abstentions June 6 to approve a motion urging the establishment of a liaison commission to study economic relations between Britain and the 6 EEC states and to resume diplomatic contacts that might later be extended to the 6 other members of the EFTA. (The Assembly was an advisory body whose recommendations were passed on by the WEU Council.)

The EEC foreign ministers, meeting July 10-11 in Brussels, announced their agreement on resuming periodic contacts with Britain within the framework of the WEU. The agreement, made public July 11, provided for quarterly meetings among the 7 countries in each of their capitals in rotation. Despite previous French objections, it was agreed that the talks, to take place as meetings of the WEU Council of Ministers, were to extend to economic as well as political and defense questions. The plan adopted by the EEC ministers, a compromise submitted by Italy, would permit the EEC Executive Commission to participate in the meetings whenever economic questions were on the agenda. (West Germany had proposed that the EEC commission be a regular participant in the meetings; France had demanded that the WEU talks be kept separate from the EEC commission and from the periodic Common Market ministerial sessions. The 3 Benelux countries had urged that the WEU meetings be held monthly, but this idea was dropped, apparently as part of the price for France's acquiescence in the plan.)

Brussels informants attributed the sudden reversal of France's position to a warning that the other 5 EEC countries would block an agreement on Common Market farm policy unless France agreed to accept at least limited contacts with Britain. The French were said to have agreed reluctantly, rather than face total isolation within the trade group and risk a farm settlement that did not give France's surplus-ridden farmers new European markets. Another factor in France's agreement to the proposal was the announcement July 11 that the EEC ministers had agreed to the signing July 20 of the Common Market's convention of association with 18 African countries, most of them former French colonies. De Gaulle, at a Paris press conference July 29, confirmed that France had accepted a resumption of contacts with Britain through the WEU only on the condition that the 5 other EEC countries agree to settle the Common Market agricultural question by the end of 1963.

Franco-German Treaty Ratified, Talks Held

The Franco-German Treaty of Jan. 22 came into effect officially July 2 after ratification by the French and German parliamentary bodies. The German Bundesrat approved the treaty May 16 after Chancellor Adenauer, West Berlin Mayor (Chief Burgomaster) Willy Brandt and EEC Commission Pres. Hallstein all spoke in favor of it. The Bundestag approved the treaty May 16. The French National Assembly approved the treaty June 12 after debate between Foreign Min. Maurice Couve de Murville and Socialist Guy Mollet. Premier Georges Pompidou also spoke in favor of it. The Senate approved the treaty June 18.

The first meeting of French and German officials under the conditions of the treaty was held July 4-5 in Bonn. The French delegation consisted of Pres. de Gaulle, Pompidou, Couve de Murville, Finance Min. Valery Giscard d'Estaing, Armed Forces Min. Pierre Messmer, Agriculture Min. Edgard Pisani, Education Min. Christian Fouchet and State Secy. for Youth & Sport Maurice Herzog. Chancellor Adenauer, Foreign Min. Schroeder, Vice Chancellor (and Economics Min.) Erhard, Finance Min. Rolf Dahlgrun, Food, Agriculture & Forestry Min. Werner Schwarz, Defense Min. Kai-Uwe von Hassel, Family Affairs & Youth Min. Bruno Heck and Kurt Georg Kiesinger, premier of Baden-Wuerttemburg and Federal commissioner for cultural cooperation (under the treaty) represented West Germany.

The question of Europe's progress toward economic and political unity and of Britain's association with it was taken up by de Gaulle and Adenauer July 4-5. The 2 leaders were said to have discussed several of the proposals for a renewal of British-EEC contacts. Adenauer was reported to have brought up, without result, a Bonn plan for the joining of the 6 nations' existing institutions—the Common Market, Euratom and the European Coal & Steel Community—in one supranational agency. They agreed that steps would be taken to study the European farm problem and reach a solution to it within the current timetable, early in 1964. It became clear within a few days that the 2 men had agreed on a formula for renewed contact between Britain and the EEC nations.

A joint communique issued July 5 stated in part: "Economic questions, especially with regard to the Common Market, gave rise to extensive exchanges of views, with particular reference to agriculture and the negotiations which will take place within GATT in May 1964. Both governments agreed that the decisions reached [at the EEC ministerial meeting] on May 9 in Brussels concerning the working program of the EEC in the months to come will permit considerable progress in the various spheres envisaged within a short time.... As regards the development of a joint agricultural policy, both governments regard the putting into effect of regulations for beef, dairy products, and rice during the first quarter of 1964 as an essential objective. Because of the complexity of the difficult questions raised by the definition of a European price policy for foodstuffs, and notably cereals, the 2 governments will propose within the framework of the EEC a working scheme for researches and studies aimed at... arriving at fair solutions. . . . Trade negotiations within the framework of GATT appear to offer a propitious opportunity for liberating international exchanges and facilitating relations between regional economic groups. The 2 governments have therefore expressed their intention to continue to orient their actions within the EEC with the aim of assuring the success of these negotiations. Both governments jointly aim at the participation of all interested governments, fair reciprocity of the benefits granted by one side to the other, reduction of tariffs as well as of existing disparities, and the maintenance of a reduced but unified common external tariff for the EEC."

Erhard Succeeds Adenauer

Konrad Adenauer, 87, formally tendered his resignation as West German chancellor to the Bundestag (lower house) Oct. 15. Economics Min. Ludwig Erhard, 66, succeeded him as chancellor Oct. 16.

In a farewell Bundestag speech, Adenauer said he was "proud of what the German people have achieved" during his 14 years in office. He said: "We have entered the alliance of free nations." But "we have not achieved everything. We have not yet achieved reunification. The chances for reunification are good if we proceed cautiously.... Whenever you call upon me, I shall speak, but only when necessary."

Erhard was elected chancellor by a 279-180 Bundestag vote, 36 votes more than the required majority. Of the 24 deputies who abstained, all but one (a Social Democrat) were members of Erhard's governing Christian Democratic Union. (The CDU abstainers re-

portedly were from farm areas opposed to Erhard's free-trade policies.) One vote was invalid.

Erhard visited Paris Nov. 21-22 for his first regular consultation
with French Pres. de Gaulle under the Franco-German treaty. In a brief
statement made on his arrival, Erhard, whose talks with de Gaulle were
held in private, said it was his "credo" that "cooperation between our 2
peoples is essential if we wish to make of Europe something other than a
vague geographic notion. Only then will we be able to throw all our
weight into the balance, in view of a close Atlantic partnership." His re-
mark was taken to mean that Bonn felt that its new alliance with France
could become an essential part of the Atlantic partnership advanced by
the late U.S. Pres. Kennedy and heretofore rejected by de Gaulle.

Erhard's remarks appeared to carry special significance in the light
of a French offer to place France's nuclear force at the disposal of an
eventually united Europe. This offer had been submitted to the
European Assembly in Strasbourg Sept. 23 but had failed to win the
support of a single other European nation. The proposal, as made by
French Deputy Foreign Min. Michel Habib-Deloncle: "Tomorrow,
when Europe will have strengthened her political institutions, it will be
necessary to outline how the nuclear effort undertaken by France can be
used by all the European nations for common defense. . . . If Great Britain conceives of her future as being inside the European community, it
can find in this field an opportunity for a positive contribution—taking
into account the necessary choice entailed in such a decision." Habib-
Deloncle reaffirmed France's ties to NATO, but he noted that "the
functioning of the Atlantic Alliance, the division of responsibilities within it, cannot be the same . . . now that the countries of Europe are again
erect and have the desire . . . to assume full charge of their defense." The
Assembly's response was indicated, indirectly, in its rejection by 68-4
vote of French motions dealing with current East-West negotiations
and Common Market policies.

Erhard also conferred with the new U.S. President, Lyndon B.
Johnson, while in Washington Nov. 26 for the funeral of the late John
F. Kennedy. The 2-day talks produced a communique that said:

"The chancellor stated, and the President agreed, that efforts to achieve such unity
must always respect the traditionally open trading relationship Europe has enjoyed with the
United States and the rest of the free world. The President and the chancellor agreed that
the forthcoming trade negotiations should be guided by the double objective of enlarged
international trade and increasing economic integration in Europe. They agreed that agricultural as well as industrial products must be included and that the negotiation should proceed without delay. Finally, the President and the chancellor reaffirmed their commitment
not simply to close German-American cooperation, but to the wider interest of both countries
in the growing partnership of free nations—of the Atlantic and of the world."

Macmillan Resigns, Home New Prime Minister

Harold Macmillan, 69, announced Oct. 10 that he would retire as British prime minister and Conservative Party leader for reasons of health. Macmillan's decision was made public after he had undergone successful surgery that day for removal of a diseased prostate gland.

Macmillan's announcement was made in a letter to the Conservative Party's annual conference, which had opened in Blackpool Oct. 9. The letter, received Oct. 8 and read by Foreign Secy. Lord Home as president of the conference, said: "It is now clear that ... it will not be possible for me to carry out the physical burden of leading the party at the next general election. If the operation, which I am to undergo tomorrow, proves successful, it is clear that I will need a considerable period of convalescence. I would not be able to face ... a prolonged electoral campaign. Nor could I hope to fulfill the tasks of prime minister, and I have so informed the queen. In these circumstances I hope that it will soon be possible for the customary processes of consultation [to] be carried out within the party about its future leadership. ..."

The remainder of the party conference, which ended Oct. 12, was devoted largely to behind-the-scenes maneuvers on behalf of prospective successors to Macmillan.

One of the favorites mentioned for the post, Science Min. Lord Hailsham, 56, announced that "I'm available" and said at a party rally Oct. 10 that he would renounce his peerage and run for a seat in the House of Commons. Legislation passed by Parliament the previous session permitted such quick renunciation of a peerage. As a member of the House of Lords and not of Commons, Hailsham would have been barred by tradition from becoming prime minister. (Hailsham had served in Commons as Quintin Hogg until 1950, when he inherited his father's title.)

Lord Home announced on a TV program Oct. 11 that he, too, was available for Macmillan's post. 2 other prospective candidates were Deputy Prime Min. R. A. Butler, 60, and Chancellor of the Exchequer Reginald Maudling, 46.

Macmillan submitted to Queen Elizabeth Oct. 18 his resignation as prime minister. The queen visited Macmillan at the London hospital, where he was recovering, and she approved Macmillan's recommendation that Foreign Secy. Lord (Sir) Alec Douglas-Home succeed him as prime minister and as First Lord of the Treasury. Home accepted the appointment Oct. 19 after he had put down a revolt of members of his Conservative Party who had opposed his leadership.

The challenge to Home had been led by these 3 contenders for the posts of party leader and prime minister: Deputy Prime Min. Richard Austen Butler; Science Min. Lord Hailsham; Chancellor of the Exchequer Reginald Maudling. These 3, along with party co-chairman Iain MacLeod and Board of Trade Pres. Frederick J. Erroll, had met in the home of Health Min. Enoch Powell Oct. 17 to plan a "stop Home" movement. The conferees, who represented the party's progressive faction, called on Martin Redmayne, chief party whip in Commons, and advised him to inform Macmillan that Hailsham and Maudling would support Butler for prime minister; Butler was regarded as having the greatest backing according to party and public polls conducted the previous week. Butler telephoned Macmillan Oct. 19, but his call was not accepted.

(Butler had been given credit for the election campaign in 1951 that brought the Conservatives back into power. As Lord Privy Seal in 1957, Butler had been regarded as the most likely successor to Anthony Eden but lost out to Macmillan.)

Home finally persuaded his 3 major rivals to end their resistance to his leadership and to join his cabinet. The first break in the opposition occurred when Butler, after talks with Home, agreed to serve in his government. Hailsham's and Maudling's acquiescence followed. Powell and MacLeod, however, refused to join.

In an Oct. 19 TV address announcing his acceptance of the post of prime minister, Home said: "... my task is to serve the whole nation.... No one need expect any stunts from me—merely plain straight talking."

Home announced the completion of his cabinet Oct. 20. The new cabinet: Prime Minister & First Lord of the Treasury—Home; Foreign —Butler; Lord President of the Council and Science—Hailsham; Lord Chancellor—Lord Dilhorne; Home Secretary—Henry Brooke; Commonwealth & Colonial Secretary—Duncan Sandys; Secretary of State for Industry, Trade & Regional Development and President of the Board of Trade—Heath; Defense—Peter Thorneycroft; Lord Privy Seal and Leader of House of Commons—Lloyd; Chancellor of the Duchy of Lancaster—John Hare; Agriculture, Fisheries & Food—Christopher Soames; Transport—Ernest Marples; Chief Secretary to the Treasury and Paymaster General—John Boyd-Carpenter; Secretary of State for Scotland—Michael Noble; Education—Sir Edward Boyle; Labor—Sir Joseph Godber; Housing & Local Government and Minister for Welsh Affairs—Sir Keith Joseph; Health—Barber; Power—Erroll; Public Building & Works—Geoffrey Rippon; Ministers Without Portfolio—Lord Carrington and William Deedes.

MacLeod and Lord Poole formally resigned as the Conservative Party's co-chairmen Oct. 21. Lord Aldington's resignation as the party's special adviser also was announced. Hare formally assumed chairmanship of the party. (Aldington, like MacLeod, had supported Butler in the struggle for Macmillan's job; Poole had backed Hailsham.)

The appointment of these new ministers was announced Oct. 21: Maurice Macmillan, 42, son of the ex-prime minister, as the Treasury's economic secretary; James Ramsden, 35, as war minister.

George Brown, deputy Labor Party leader, asserted Oct. 18 that Home's selection was a poor one. He said "no party can ever have portrayed such a total lack of confidence in each other as to have to resort to such a drama in order to find the lowest common denominator."

Liberal Party leader Jo Grimond called Home an amateur whose selection had "no democratic endorsement."

British newspapers, particularly those that supported the Conservatives, also expressed opposition to Home's appointment.

Home announced Oct. 22 that he had rescheduled the reopening of Parliament from Oct. 29 to Nov. 12 to permit him to run in a by-election for a House of Commons seat in Kinross, Scotland Nov. 7. Tradition required a prime minister to be a member of Commons.

Labor Party leader Harold Wilson met with Home Oct. 22 and said later that he had told him there was "no case whatsoever for postponing the recall of Parliament to suit the convenience of one individual who, though he is a prime minister, is not a member of the House of Commons."

British-EEC Talks Resume

A meeting of the 7 WEU foreign ministers took place in The Hague Oct. 25-26. The major subject before the meeting—that of renewal of British-EEC discussions on trade and other related matters—was emphasized in the final communique, issued Oct. 26. The ministers said they had "examined the question of economic cooperation between the United Kingdom and the European Common Market." They "noted with satisfaction the progress already made and...expressed their determination to cooperate closely in order to facilitate new progress."

Reports from The Hague said that the session had been marked by an unusual cordiality between R. A. Butler, Britain's newly appointed foreign secretary, and Couve de Murville. This was attributed in part to Butler's repeated assertion of Britain's readiness to commit itself to Europe. Arriving in The Hague Oct. 23, Butler had said: "I wish to make it clear that Britain, politically and physically, is very much a part of Europe." It was reported that the conferees had agreed that British trade specialists were to meet with EEC experts in Brussels within a week to begin preliminary discussions of the positions to be taken by each group in the 1964 trade expansion negotiations. The next British-EEC ministerial contact was to take place at a WEU Council meeting in London in Jan. 1964.

The Hague negotiations were followed by a meeting Oct. 29-30 of the Anglo-French Economic Committee, a bilateral trade relations body that had been dormant for more than 2 years. The meeting, held in London, was attended only by specialists.

Foreign Secy. Butler visited Bonn Dec. 9-10 and conferred with Chancellor Erhard, Pres. Heinrich Lubke and Foreign Min. Schroeder. A joint communique following the Butler-Schroeder meeting said in part: "The progress of European unification was discussed in detail. Both sides emphasized the value of the regular contacts established during 1963 between the members of the EEC and Britain within the framework of Western European Union." It was "agreed that both governments would seek to ensure that the course pursued by Great Britain and her EFTA partners on the one hand and by the EEC countries on the other hand would remain closely aligned."

In spite of the implied promise of the renewed British-EEC contacts, de Gaulle, in a New Year's statement broadcast to the French people, made it clear that his opposition in principle to British membership had not changed. Citing what he said was France's major effort "to help build the Common Market and, in so doing, clear the path leading to a United Europe," de Gaulle asserted that these goals had become possible because France had refused to allow the EEC "either to disintegrate as a result of the admission of a new member which could not conform to the rules" or to be "annexed to a system existing on the other side of the Atlantic." France's European policies, he said, had been based on the reconciliation with Germany and on the determination "to see that the European Economic Community was truly a community and truly European." De Gaulle said that one of France's major tasks was "the union of Europe, including as soon as possible the regular and organized cooperation of Germany, Italy, the Netherlands, Belgium, Luxembourg and France in the domains of politics, defense and culture, as will be the case of economics."

(Ending a 2-day meeting in Paris Dec. 14, the 17-nation ministerial committee of the Council of Europe had issued a communique in which it declared full support for the Atlantic partnership proposals advanced by the late Pres. Kennedy. The communique said that the committee had discussed the questions of "close and systematic cooperation between Europe and North America" and the "political aspects of European economic integration" and, in this context, "emphasized . . . the significance of the declaration of interdependence made by Pres. Kennedy in 1962 and of his proposal for a partnership between Europe and America on a basis of complete equality.")

EEC Farm & Tariff Accords

The European Common Market nations reached a series of agreements Dec. 9-23 on the creation of a Europe-wide market in basic foodstuffs and the fixing of a unified policy on world tariff reductions. The tariff question was to come up in 1964, first at a UN World Trade Conference, and then at the "Kennedy round" of tariff reduction negotiations to be held by the 40 GATT nations.

The farm accords provided for the extension of EEC practices, already applied to industrial and manufactured goods, to 3 of Europe's most basic agricultural categories: rice and cereals, milk and dairy products, beef and veal. The agreements were negotiated under a Dec. 31 deadline imposed by France; de Gaulle had warned that the Common Market might "disappear" unless its advantages were applied to agriculture by the end of 1963. The accords generally represented a victory for France, the largest agricultural producer and exporter of the 6; they represented a major concession on the part of West Germany, which had sought to retain some measure of protection for its relatively high-cost agriculture.

The tariff-cutting policies agreed on were not officially disclosed, but it was known that West Germany, a supporter of a liberal trade policy, had made agreement on the matter a precondition to an accord on farm policies.

The crucial December meetings had been opened in Brussels Dec. 9 by the 6 nations' agriculture ministers. They were disrupted almost immediately by French Agriculture Min. Edgar Pisani, who walked out Dec. 10 after rejecting other participants' demands that the talks be extended into January and warning that France intended to hold them to the Dec. 31 deadline set by de Gaulle. The ministers met again Dec. 11 and 12 but made no progress. The West German cabinet, in a statement Dec. 11 on the talks, made it clear that no farm accord was possible without an agreement on liberal tariff policies. West German agriculture Min. Werner Schwarz, apparently on orders from Bonn, boycotted the Dec. 12 meeting. The agriculture ministers resumed their meetings Dec. 16-17 but were said to have agreed only on minor regulations regarding a common market in beef. (West Germany, a beef-importing nation, sought a low EEC tariff against imports from nations outside the group; France and Italy, beef-exporting nations, sought a non-member tariff that would keep external beef 10% more expensive and assure them the West German market.)

The Brussels talks were transferred to the foreign ministers' level Dec. 18 and the farm question was set aside temporarily for a decision on the policy to be followed by the Common Market in the 1964 tariff negotiations. The foreign ministers reached agreement Dec. 19 on a liberal policy toward tariffs on manufactured and semi-finished goods; in cases where application of the 50% across-the-board reduction advocated by the U.S. left a substantial "disparity" between American and EEC tariffs on the same item, the higher tariff was to be subject to a cut of more than 50%. The ministers turned Dec. 20 to the question of a joint policy on reduction of world tariffs on agricultural products; they agreed Dec. 21 to support efforts to end agricultural protectionism, with a detailed policy to be formulated at a later date.

The foreign ministers again took up the European farm problem Dec. 21. They announced Dec. 23 that they had reached a compromise agreement satisfying French demands for a common market in farm products that would pave the way to uniform pricing and free movement of basic foodstuffs among the 6 countries. The agreement: (1) ordered steps toward the gradual establishment of a common market in milk and dairy products, with Luxembourg and West Germany given until 1966-7 to end their current system of direct subsidies to dairy farmers in favor of the EEC system of variable agricultural levies and price supports; (2) provided for gradual creation of a common market in rice and cereals, with a common price pattern for cereals to be set by Apr. 15, 1964; (3) established a "target price" system, based on variable duties on imports of beef from non-member countries and price supports by EEC governments when needed, to create a common market in beef.

In the final phase of the Brussels negotiations, the foreign ministers were joined by the agriculture, finance and economics ministers of the 6 countries. The talks, stalemated Dec. 21, had been pressed to a rapid conclusion after West Germany, defying the French year-end ultimatum, had warned that it would recall its ministers to celebrate Christmas at home even if no agreement had been reached. The French demand for a farm agreement by Dec. 31 had been made by de Gaulle at a Paris press conference July 29. Citing the repeated failure of the 6 EEC nations to come to agreement on the matter, de Gaulle said: "What would the very words 'European Economic Community' mean if Europe did not for the most part assure its food supplies from its own agricultural products...?" Acknowledging that the founding Treaty of Rome had dealt primarily with the question of industry, treating agriculture as a secondary issue, de Gaulle declared that the farm problem would have to be settled by Dec. 31. By that date, he warned, "it will be necessary...that the Common Market be standing on its feet, complete and assured, or that it disappear."

Little progress on the farm question had taken place at EEC meetings held in September and October. The first sign of a break in the stalemate appeared Nov. 5, with the presentation to the EEC Council of a plan for setting Europe-wide grain and cereal prices by July 1, 1964, 5 years earlier than originally planned. The proposal, the work of Vice Pres. Sicco L. Mansholt of the EEC Executive Commission, provided for a uniform "target price" for wheat, rye, corn, barley and rice in all 6 countries. The target price would result in substantial increases in prices received by farmers in France, Belgium and the Netherlands. Luxembourg and West German farmers would suffer losses averaging 10%-15% of current prices, but they would receive subsidies to make up part of the difference. The Mansholt plan was discussed at a Brussels meeting of EEC agriculture ministers Nov. 12-13, but, principally due to West German opposition, final action on the farm matter was deferred until the trade bloc's December meetings. (The compromise farm program adopted by the EEC Dec. 23 contained elements of the Mansholt plan, among them the requirement that a Europe-wide grain price be set in 1964.)

The path to the December agreement apparently was opened by de Gaulle and Erhard at a Paris meeting held Nov. 21-22 under the French-West German cooperation treaty. Although no detailed farm accord was produced at the meeting, it was clear that the 2 leaders had agreed on the basic pattern that led to the December accords: French acceptance of the West German demand for a liberal EEC tariff policy in the 1964 world trade talks; West German acceptance of a Europe-wide farm price system that would assure France continental outlets for its agricultural surpluses.

The 6 EEC nations had reduced their tariffs on imports from non-members by 30% July 1. This was the second such step taken by EEC members in their effort to align their individual tariffs on non-members and brought about a total cut of 60% between former individual nation tariff levels and the agreed-upon common external tariff.

1964

British financial difficulties and EEC political arguments were major areas of concern during 1964. Britain's Conservative Party was ousted by the Labor Party under Harold Wilson in the October general elections. Labor inherited growing financial problems and was forced into tighter economic policies, including a 15% tariff surcharge and international loans of $4 billion to prevent devaluation of the pound. Within the EEC, the differences between the philosophies of West German Chancellor Ludwig Erhard and French Pres. Charles de Gaulle remained unresolved as Erhard pushed for a greater EEC political integration that de Gaulle opposed. Further EEC progress was achieved as an agricultural policy agreement was reached in December. Worldwide tariff cuts and freer trade policies were sought as the "Kennedy Round" of tariff negotiations opened in Geneva.

GREAT BRITAIN

Labor Wins Election, Wilson Heads Government

In general elections held Oct. 15, the 13-year reign of the Conservative Party ended as the Labor Party won a narrow victory.
(James) Harold Wilson was designated the new prime minister to replace Sir Alec Douglas-Home, who had held office only since Oct. 1963,
when he replaced the ailing Harold Macmillan.

Home Apr. 9 had announced his government's decision to hold
general elections in October rather than in June, the previously considered month. The Conservative regime's 5-year term expired Nov. 5.
The choice of October was assailed by Labor Party leader Wilson, who
charged that Home's "refusal to face the electors until the last possible
moment shows that whatever else has motivated him it has not been the
national interest." Asserting that "vital national decisions have already
been deferred for far too long pending the election of a government with
authority," Wilson said the prime minister's refusal to hold earlier
elections was based on "fear of certain defeat for his party." Home Sept.
15 officially designated Oct. 15 for the House of Commons elections,
and Parliament was dissolved Sept. 25.

The Labor Party had made wide gains in county council elections
held throughout Britain Apr. 9. The party scored a major victory by
winning 64 seats in the Greater London Council; the Conservatives won
34. In the 390 Town Council elections in England and Wales, May 7,
Labor gained 254 seats. The Conservatives lost 132 seats, the Liberals
59 and the independents 64. The Communists gained one seat. The Conservative Party won 3 seats and the Labor Party one in May 14 by-
elections.

Following the narrow Labor victory in the Oct. 15 parliamentary
elections, Wilson, 48, assumed office as prime minister Oct. 16 and became the youngest man to hold the post in the 20th Century. The
Laborites attained a majority of only 4 seats in the 630-member House
of Commons. New standings of the parties in Commons (previously-held
seats in parentheses): Labor—317 (258); Conservatives—304 (366);
Liberals—9 (6). Popular vote: Labor—12,205,576 (44.1% of the total);
Conservatives—12,002,407 (43.4%); Liberals—3,093,316 (11.2%);
others—348,914 (1.3%).

Ignoring the narrowness of his victory, Wilson said in a TV address Oct. 16 that his party had received a mandate to undertake "many
changes" in government. "We intend to fulfill that mandate," he said.
Liberal Party leader Jo Grimond said Oct. 19 that "in the short run" his
party would "support the Labor government in any steps to meet
present economic difficulties." But he pledged that in the long run the
Liberals would "build up an effective radical, non-Socialist alternative to
the Tories."

During the campaign, Wilson had called for nationalizing the entire steel industry (part of it was already government-owned), reimposing rent controls and discouraging private real estate speculation. Wilson had opposed British possession of an independent nuclear deterrent and had pledged to renegotiate the Nassau pact, under which the U.S. had agreed to sell Polaris missiles to the British for use by a small fleet of British submarines. Contending that Britain's nuclear force was not independent, Wilson had declared in a speech in Manchester Oct. 12: "We are not going to stay in the nuclear arms race on the basis of a deterrent hired from America and fired under water." The Laborites had argued for abandonment of Britain's national control of nuclear weapons in exchange for some type of joint U.S.-British control of atomic arms.

Home had argued in the campaign that the adoption of Labor's nuclear stand "would hand over the right to decide our future to another country." In a TV address Oct. 13, Home said British control of nuclear weapons was the country's only defense against "blackmail or attack."

(The Laborite victory margin was believed to have been reduced by a crippling wildcat strike on the London subways Oct. 12-13. 3,500 guards and motormen employed by the London Transport system walked off their jobs in protest against the introduction of new train schedules, which they claimed would result in transfers and loss of jobs. The new schedules, designed to provide more regular service, had been agreed to the previous week by union leaders in a meeting with London Transport negotiators. The agreement also gave employes efficiency bonuses of $1.40-$2.50 a week and other fringe benefits. The striking guards and motormen began to return to their jobs Oct. 13 after Wilson assailed the walkout as an "intolerable" inconvenience to subway riders. Wilson said the Conservatives' wage policies were responsible for labor unrest in the subways and in other municipal services.)

Announcing his first cabinet appointments Oct. 16, Wilson disclosed that Patrick Gordon Walker, 57, would be foreign secretary. Gordon Walker, who had been a Commonwealth relations secretary in Prime Min. Clement Attlee's cabinet, had been defeated Oct. 15 for reelection to Parliament from the Birmingham constituency of Smethwick, a seat he had held since 1945. He lost to Conservative Peter Griffith, accused of having based his campaign on an appeal to racial prejudice in an area that had many immigrants from India, Pakistan and the West Indies. To meet the cabinet requirement of Parliamentary membership, Gordon Walker was to run in a by-election in a safe Laborite district.

Other cabinet appointees: George Brown, 50, the Labor Party's deputy leader, became first secretary of state and minister for economic affairs (a post that, in effect, made him deputy prime minister). Herbert Bowden, 59, Laborite chief whip in Parliament since 1955, became lord president of the Council and leader of the House of Commons.

(Leonard) James Callaghan, 52, ranked 3d in the party's leadership, became chancellor of the exchequer. Denis Winston Healey, 47, became defense minister. Lord Gardiner, 64, became lord chancellor. Edward Short was named parliamentary chief whip, a non-cabinet post that permitted him to attend cabinet meetings.

Wilson completed his cabinet Oct. 17, and he simultaneously created 2 new ministries—the Ministry of Technology and the secretary of state for Wales. Frank Cousins, 60, secretary general of the Transport & General Workers Union, was appointed to head the Technology Ministry. James Griffiths, 74, became secretary of state for Wales.

The remaining Oct. 17 cabinet appointees:

Overseas Development Minister—Mrs. Barbara Castle, 53, ex-Labor Party chairman (1958-9). *Home Secretary*—Sir Frank Soskice, 62. *Commonwealth Relations Secretary*—Arthur George Bottomley, 57, ex-mayor of Walthamstow, foreign trade mission expert, Wilson's assistant on the Board of Trade 1947-51. *Colonial Affairs Secretary*—Anthony Greenwood, 53, Labor Party chairman. *Secretary of State for Scotland*—William Ross. *Education & Science Minister*—Michael Stewart, 58, justice of the peace in East London. *Lord Privy Seal and Leader of the House of Lords*—the Earl of Longford (Frank Pakenham), 58, civil aviation minister 1948-51, First Lord of the Admiralty May-Oct. 1951. *President of the Board of Trade*—Douglas Patrick Thomas Jay, 57, professional economist who had served as Prime Min. Clement Attlee's personal assistant. *Chancellor of the Duchy of Lancaster*—Douglas Houghton, 66, ex-income tax inspector, proponent of reform of country's tax structure. *Agriculture Minister*—Fred Peart, 50, ex-chairman of the Labor Party's atomic energy committee. *Housing & Local Government Minister*—Richard H. S. Crossman, 56. *Labor Minister*—Raymond Jones Gunter, 57, party adviser on trade union affairs. *Power Minister*—Fred Lee, 58, ex-parliamentary secretary for the Labor Ministry in last Laborite government, Fuel & Power Minister in Hugh Gaitskell's 1959 shadow cabinet and Aviation Minister in Wilson's shadow cabinet. *Transport Minister*—Thomas Fraser, Miners' Union official in 1943, parliamentary private secretary to the Board of Trade president in the World War II coalition government, joint parliamentary secretary of state in the Scottish office 1945-51.

Ministerial appointments announced Oct. 19: *Parliamentary secretary to the Technology Ministry*—novelist Sir Charles Percy Snow. *Postmaster General*—Anthony Wedgwood Benn, 39. *Land & Natural Resources Minister* (a new post)—Frederick Willey, 54, ex-junior minister in the postwar Labor government. *State Minister for Home Affairs*—Alice Bacon. *Minister Without Portfolio*—Eric Fletcher, 61. *Deputy State Secretary for Defense and Army Defense Minister*—Frederick Mulley, 46. *Economic Secretary to the Treasury*—Anthony Crosland, 46. *State Minister for the Education & Science Department*—Lord Bowden, 54. *Defense Minister for the Royal Air Force*—Lord Shackleton, 53. *Defense Minister for the Royal Navy*—Christopher Mayhew, 49. *Parliamentary secretary for the Housing & Local Government Minister*—Robert Mellish, 51. *State Minister for Commonwealth Relations*—Cledwyn Hughes, 48.

Wilson's appointment of 23 new ministers Oct. 23 brought to 101 the number of officials he had designated since assuming office. Prof. Patrick Maynard Stuart Blackett, Nobel Prize physicist, was appointed deputy chairman of the Ministry of Technology's Council of Technology. Technology Min. Cousins, who also was Council chairman, resigned Oct. 28 as general secretary of the Transport & General Workers.

(Foreign Secy. Gordon Walker conferred with Pres. Johnson and other U.S. officials in Washington Oct. 26-27 to pave the way for a scheduled December meeting of the President with Prime Min. Wilson.

The Johnson-Wilson talks were to deal with the reorganization of NATO and possible renegotiation of the 1962 U.S.-British Nassau agreement, which provided for purchase of U.S. Polaris missiles for British submarines. Gordon Walker said at a news conference that Britain had asked for "adequate time" to set forth its position on the proposed NATO multilateral nuclear naval force [MLF]. He said his government could not reach a final decision by the end of the year, the time the Johnson Administration hoped the MLF treaty would be signed.)

Labor's Parliamentary majority increased Oct. 27 from 4 seats to 5 as Conservative Sir Harry Hylton-Foster was reelected Speaker of the House of Commons. Under parliamentary procedure, the Speaker could vote only to break a tie, and his ballot could not bring down a government.

Steel Nationalization Planned

A plan to renationalize the steel industry and to undertake other major reforms was proposed by the Labor government at the state opening of the new Parliament Nov. 3. The legislative program drawn up by Prime Min. Wilson was outlined in the speech from the Throne, read by Queen Elizabeth II in the House of Lords. *Major points of the legislative program:* Steel shareholders affected by the proposed nationalization program would be compensated by the government; retirement pensions and sickness, unemployment and widows' benefits would be increased; the 2-shilling (28¢) charge for National Health Service medicine prescriptions would be eliminated; companies would be required to divulge their financial contributions to political parties; rent control would be restored; monopolies and business mergers would be dealt with more stringently; the government would press for the abolition of capital punishment.

In opening House of Commons debate on the program, Conservative Party leader Sir Alec Douglas-Home vowed that "we shall do everything we can" to prevent steel nationalization. Home also criticized Wilson for appointing an unusually large number of government ministers (more than 100). The former prime minister indicated that this violated legislation restricting the number of cabinet ministers to 27 and other ministers to 70. Asserting that he would seek to remove these legislative restrictions, Wilson declared that "we cannot . . . afford to perpetuate a principle which restricts the appointments of men best fitted for the jobs and yet allow full freedom of appointment from an aristocratic caste."

(Home had carried out a major reorganization of his Conservative Party. He accepted the resignations of Lord Poole and Dame Barbara Brooke as vice chairmen of the party's Central Office Oct. 22. Poole was replaced by Sir Michael Fraser, director of the party's Research Department. Mrs. Brooke, wife of ex-Home Secy. Henry Brooke, was succeeded by Susan Walker, deputy chief organization officer. Home Oct. 28 announced a shake-up of the front bench (renamed the consultative committee) of the Conservative Opposition in the new Parliament. He appointed to the committee ex-party co-chairman Iain MacLeod, 50, and ex-Health Min. Enoch Powell. Both men, who had served in ex-Prime Min. Harold Macmillan's government, had refused to join Home's cabinet when Home became prime minister in Oct. 1963. Other committee members were ex-Board of Trade Pres. Edward Heath, 48, and ex-House of Commons leader Selwyn Lloyd, 60. These 3 were dropped from the consultative committee: Henry Brooke, ex-Power Min. Frederick Hall and ex-Min. Without Portfolio William Deedes.)

Wilson's new Labor government survived its first tests in the House of Commons by defeating Conservative no-confidence motions Nov. 9 and 10. The Nov. 9 motion, stating that the government's proposed renationalization of the steel industry was "irrelevant" and "damaging" to the economy, was rejected by 307-301 vote; Commons' 9 Liberals lined up with 291 Conservatives against Labor. Conservative Iain Macleod, attacking the steel measure in debate, asserted that nationalization would be an act by "small and foolish men" to apply a "19th century solution to a 20th century problem." Power Min. Fred Lee contended that nationalization would create more effective steel industry competition and efficiency. He complained that steel imports were high and that no increase in steel exports was anticipated in 6 years. Lee rejected a Liberal compromise that would have merely stipulated government acquisition of majority shareholdings in major steel firms. Under the government plan, 10 to 12 of the largest steel companies would be nationalized, their operations would be conducted by a central agency similar to the coal and rail boards and the government would compensate the shareholders. The Conservatives' 2d no-confidence motion, attacking the government's entire legislative program, was defeated Nov. 10 by 315-294 vote; the Liberals this time voted with Labor.

The Budget

Some 6 months before his party's election defeat and ouster from power, Conservative Party Chancellor of the Exchequer Reginald Maudling had presented to the House of Commons Apr. 14 a fiscal 1965 (12 months ending in Mar. 1965) budget providing for a 6.6% increase in spending and a 10% increase in cigarette and alcoholic beverage taxes. The tax increases went into effect Apr. 15. Income taxes were unaffected. Expenditures were estimated at £7.388 billion ($20.786 billion), including £1.999 billion ($5.597 billion), an 8.8% increase, for defense. Other major increases were for grants to local authorities and provisions for higher education and road building. Agricultural support and grants to the nationalized railways were reduced. Anticipated total revenues were £7.352 billion ($20.586 billion), a 9.6% increase. The anticipated deficit of £894 million ($2.503 billion) was 30.9% higher than in fiscal 1964 and was the highest deficit in Britain's peacetime history. In an effort to encourage savings, the government raised the limit on holdings of 2 government savings bond issues and introduced a 5-year 5% bond in place of defense bonds.

Maudling called the budget's theme continued expansion without inflation. He said, in part:

"The task this year is to ensure that this expansion continues at a rate that can be sustained without inflation. We have been eating into the reserve of capacity and, in the process, we have achieved the rate of growth to which I have just referred. Before 1964 is out, this reserve will have been brought fully into use and we must therefore aim, in the course of this year, to set the economy on the rate of expansion which can be maintained through the regular growth of productive capacity. As the progress report of the National Economic Development Council said: 'Output cannot continue to increase indefinitely at the present high rate since this depends to a considerable extent on the bringing into use of under-employed resources and is more than the average rate required to achieve the growth programme during the rest of the period to 1966.' In other words the purpose of this budget is to achieve a smooth transition from the recent exceptionally rapid rate of growth to the long-term growth rate of 4%. This then is to be my main theme. But before I turn to it I want to repeat the procedure I adopted last year, by dealing first with a number of incidental matters including certain tax changes which must be dealt with now, but which are extraneous to the main economic argument. . . .

"The past year has seen great economic progress. Production has risen by about 5% overall, and by about 8% in manufacturing industry. The expansion has been broadly based, extending from consumer goods to steel, where the latest figures show an increase of 20% over a year ago. Production, investment, and exports are all now reaching record levels. The number of people wholly unemployed has fallen since last April from 570,000 to 415,000, that is by more than 150,000; and, as an even more significant indication of the way things are moving, notified vacancies for adults have risen from 138,000 to 202,000 in the same period. Prices remained relatively stable, with the retail price index rising by less than 2% in a year when import prices rose by over 5% and prices in the European Economic Community rose by about 6%. Exports rose during 1963 by 10% and imports by 13% by value. In 1963 we had a current account surplus of £120 million, but by the early months of this year we had begun to show some deficit. In so far as this arises from increased imports it is neither surprising nor undesirable. I have foreshadowed on many occasions that this would happen. It is the inevitable result of economic expansion, particularly of stockbuilding, and it is reasonable to remember that imports of raw material and semi-manufactures precede the production on which future exports will be based. . . .

"In the coming year all the major components of demand should be increasing or, in simpler language, the demand for British goods should continue to rise vigorously, with all that this means for employment and prosperity. To begin with exports, there is no doubt that the opportunity is there for another substantial increase this year. The U. S. economy should be expanding well under the influence of their tax cut. A good rate of growth is likely to continue in most of Western Europe, and, with higher commodity prices, demand from the primary producers, who are so important to our exports, should again be higher. . . .

"To sum up, the purpose of this budget is to maintain expansion without inflation. Expansion now is heartening and vigorous. The possibilities are great and the prospects exciting. To realize them we must avoid the danger of pushing ahead just that marginal amount too fast. . . ."

An emergency deflationary budget submitted to Commons by Labor Party Chancellor of the Exchequer James Callaghan Nov. 11 provided for tax increases and other government measures to reduce over-all purchasing power. After debate, Commons then approved by 312-286 vote a rise in the "standard" income tax (paid by 7 million of the country's 21 million taxpayers) from the current rate of 38.75% to 41.25%, effective Apr. 6, 1965. A provision raising the tax on gasoline and motor oil (effective immediately) to 6 pence (7¢) an imperial gallon (this increased the cost of regular-grade gasoline to about 75¢ a gallon) was approved by 303-293 vote. The budget also provided for increased widows' and war pensions, higher benefits for the needy and elimination of National Health Insurance prescription charges. The new taxes were expected to provide the Treasury with almost 3 times as much revenue as it would have to pay out for the increased welfare funds. Callaghan said the government was forced to take the emergency measures because of economic difficulties it had inherited from its Conservative predecessors. In denying this contention, ex-Prime Min. Sir Alec Douglas-Home asserted that the economy was "basically strong" and that the new budget was designed "to raise revenue for social purposes and raise it by increased taxation." Prime Min. Wilson replied that the economy was stagnant.

Surcharge Imposed on Imports

The optimism expressed by Conservative Party Chancellor of the Exchequer Maudling Apr. 14 was not substantiated by subsequent developments. The successor government, therefore, announced action to reverse the unfavorable foreign trade balance, to maintain economic growth and to halt inflation.

The imposition of a temporary 15% surcharge on imports, tax incentives for exports and other measures to protect the British pound and bolster the country's economy were announced in a Labor government White Paper issued Oct. 26. This tariff surcharge effectively doubled the British tariff level and wiped out every reduction that Britain had made as a member of EFTA. Explaining the new program, Prime Min. Wilson said in a nationwide TV address that the measures were aimed at effecting a basic change in the approach to the British economy, whose condition he called "extremely serious." The government predicted a £700-£800 million ($1.96-$2.24 billion) balance-of-payment deficit for 1964—the largest in British history. Britain's growing excess of imports over exports represented a potential drain on reserves that threatened the pound.

The White Paper said in part:

"H. M. government have now completed their first review of the financial and economic state of the nation. The general character of the problems is clear. The government's task has been to gauge their extent and urgency, so as to judge the direction and strength of the action required. . . .

"First, the government took stock of the international financial situation. They have satisfied themselves that, with the facilities available, the strength of sterling can and will be maintained. But the underlying economic situation remains profoundly unsatisfactory. The policies on which the government have decided are directed therefore both at the short-term and the longer-term economic problems.

"The government have examined the balance-of-payments prospect for the rest of this year.... It is expected that, when the accounts for 1964 as a whole are available, they will show a deficit on the balance of payments, taking current and long-term capital account together, which is most unlikely to be below £700 million and may well reach £800 million. In 1965, if there were no change in policy, the estimate is that, although there should be a considerable improvement, the deficit would still be at an unacceptable level. All this calls for immediate but strictly temporary action; drastic at first, but less so as both the immediate measures and the longer-term policies begin to take hold. Whilst there is ample support for sterling in the facilities available to us, we cannot rely on them alone or indefinitely, nor are the government willing to do so. We must no longer be in the position that every time we seek to increase our national production we are forced almost immediately into deficit. The object of the action is to arrest the tendency of imports to rise and get exports on an upward trend. So far as imports are concerned a sharp distinction must be drawn between the increase in raw material imports required to service an expansion in production and the disturbing increase in manufactured goods, most of which this country should be perfectly capable of producing on a competitive basis. This calls for a wholly new approach to the problem of balance-of-payments difficulties both on the import side and on the side of exports.

"The government further examined the domestic economic situation. Apart from special problems of individual areas and a limited number of industries there is no undue pressure on resources calling for action. Moreover, the government reject any policy based on a return to 'stop-go' economics.

"An attack must be made on the problem of increasing prices. Not only do they inflict hardship on those least able to bear it, but continually rising prices undermine our competitive power....

"The government have had in mind as well the hopes and aspirations of the friends of this country throughout the world. They have earnestly considered the interests of the nations of the Commonwealth, both new and old, their partners in the European Free Trade Association and the wider community of peace-loving and freely trading nations, together with the many organizations in which the business of international cooperation is carried on. They have been, and are, in continuous communication with the government of the U.S.A. and are now in touch with the international organizations concerned on the international aspects of their present program."

Exempted from the 15% surcharge on imports were foodstuffs, including animal feed, basic raw materials for industry and unmanufactured tobacco. The industrial nations most affected by the British actions were the 6 Common Market members; 57% of their exports to Britain were subject to the surcharge. In contrast, 36% of Britain's imports from the 6 other EFTA member nations would be affected; 48% of the US exports to Britain, 13% of the Commonwealth's exports to Britain and 13% of all other imports would be affected as well.

The plan to encourage exports called for the elimination of some of the indirect taxes that entered into the cost of production. These tax rebates were expected to average 1.5% of the value of exported goods. Other economic measures announced in the White Paper called for: persuading labor and management to increase productivity and to agree to relate all forms of income to production gains; facilitating job changes for workers to meet the needs of technological progress; more rapid development of the country's unused areas; strict studies of all government expenditures to ease the balance-of-payment deficit and release resources for more productive uses by eliminating spending on items with low economic priority; inauguration of social programs but with strict delineation of their aims and costs; consultation with the International Monetary Fund on the $1 billion IMF credit already approved.

Chancellor of the Exchequer Callaghan defended his government's stand in a speech in London Nov. 3. In part, he said:

"Between 1963 and 1964 our external position has suffered deterioration at great speed and on a vast scale.... It is a discouraging experience on the first day on which you become chancellor of the exchequer to learn that the figures published that day reveal a yawning gap between imports and exports for the previous month of £111 million; that the crude trade gap for the previous quarter is £292 million; and that the prospective total balance-of-payments deficit for the year might be as large as £800 million. This government cannot accept the position that a worthwhile expansion in production and any approach to a reasonable rate of growth will always land us in a large external deficit. Moreover, the methods of slowing down industrial activity that we commonly call 'stop and go' are clearly inappropriate at a time when official estimates show that industrial production has been stationary since the beginning of the year. We therefore devised new methods for dealing with the short-term situation. . . . The principal short-term measure is, of course, the 15% additional charge on imports, mainly of manufactured goods. The advantage of this method over the more conventional quantitative restrictions is that the burden can be spread over a wider field and will, therefore, bear less heavily at any given point; it is quicker in operation and more flexible; it creates less barriers and therefore a smaller disturbance to established trade; it leaves a wider area of choice to the consumer. . . . I must make it clear that we have no protectionist purpose whatever in putting on the charge. We aim to reduce it steadily as soon as our position shows an unmistakable improvement. We shall watch the consequences of the charge and be ready once we have had experience of its effects to amend, to reduce and then to remove it as soon as we are confident that we are well and truly set on the road to a permanent improvement in our external position.

"Now ... about our measures for encouraging exports. What we have tried to do here is to examine the burdens which fall unnecessarily on our exporters, and to remove some of them. We are not giving a subsidy to exporters but removing a tax burden from them. It is a substantial encouragement, and its purpose is to stimulate Britain's industrialists and merchants to sell more abroad; to use the rebates to finance a more aggressive salesmanship, more efficient overseas facilities [and] keener price competition with their overseas rivals. These rebates will fail unless our exporters take full advantage of them to sell more abroad. I hope that exporters will not be diverted into the gap that will be created in the home market as a result of our import measures."

International Reaction

EFTA Secy. Gen. Frank Edward Figgures held Oct. 28 that the British steps were "in contravention of the Stockholm Treaty." The EFTA Consultative Committee met in Strasbourg Nov. 9 and issued a communique regretting "both the manner in which the British import surcharge was imposed and also the effects which this surcharge would have on the industrial exports of Britain's EFTA partners." The committee said it was "unanimous in asking for the earliest possible relaxation and removal of the UK import surcharge."

The EFTA Ministerial Council met in Geneva Nov. 19-20. Its final communique said in part:

"The application of the 15% charge on imports into the United Kingdom was inconsistent with the UK's obligation under the convention and the association agreement. It was generally urged on British ministers that a firm date in a few months' time should be fixed for removing or reducing the charge. It was also urged that the charge should be reduced to 10% in a matter of weeks, that imports should be exempted from the charge in all cases where there was bona fide evidence that contracts were concluded before Oct. 27, 1964, and that the charge should not be applied to goods subject to quantitative restrictions (import quota or other) in the United Kingdom. British ministers, while not claiming that the surcharge came within the terms of the convention and the association agreement, pointed out that Article 19 provided for the use of quantitative restrictions on imports to correct a serious balance-of-payments deficit. Although such measures would have brought the United Kingdom within the terms of the Stockholm Convention, they would, in the British view, have been more damaging to EFTA and to the development of EFTA trade in the UK market. British ministers affirmed that the charge was a temporary measure and that the British government was firmly resolved in the interests of the United Kingdom, as well as of their EFTA partners, to reduce it and to abolish it at the earliest possible moment. The Council of Ministers . . . instructed the working party, which had examined the British economic situation, to reconvene in December with a view to prepare a new report on the recent developments and steps planned by the British government to restore the equilibrium of the balance of payments. It was understood that legal rights of all parties to the agreement remained unprejudiced."

Britain Nov. 19 offered 3 minor concessions to EFTA nations in an attempt to compensate for its new 15% tariff surcharge. Douglas Jay, president of the British Board of Trade, and British Foreign Secy. Gordon Walker assured the EFTA ministerial council in Geneva that the surcharge was merely a temporary defense measure on behalf of sterling and would be lifted as soon as confidence in sterling was restored. The concessions: Britain would welcome the establishment of a permanent committee to consult on members' economic policies; Britain would consult first with the EFTA members when Britain was ready to lift the surcharge; Britain would consider exempting exporters from the surcharge on orders that were negotiated at a fixed price before the surcharge went into effect Oct. 26.

Britain was informed by the 6 other EFTA countries Dec. 17 that its 15% surcharge had nullified the tariff concessions enjoyed by EFTA states and checked the trade zone's progress. The 6 nations' statement, issued in Geneva, demanded "early relaxation and removal of the . . . surcharge, opening the way to further progress in the free-trade area." A Swiss government statement made public Dec. 24 estimated that 88% of Switzerland's exports to Britain were affected by the surcharge and warned similarly that the tax had negated the advantages to Switzerland of EFTA membership.

The GATT Council, meeting in Geneva Dec. 18, ruled that Britain's imposition of the surcharge had violated its free-trade obligations under the GATT treaty and that the tax should be removed as quickly as possible. The GATT Council expressed understanding of the reasons for Britain's action, but its ruling left member states free to apply for authorization to retaliate against imports from Britain in 1965.

The EEC Commission said Oct. 29: "The commission has followed, with sympathetic interest . . . , the development of the economic situation in the United Kingdom It is aware of the difficulties facing those directing British economic policy. Countries trading with Britain, including the EEC, are seriously affected by the measures taken by the British government, and the commission has asked itself whether measures increasing protection are in fact appropriate. It feels that they are not. The commission finds it regrettable that the British government made no prior approach to the countries with which it has trade relations and which are fellow-members of several international organizations. The commission feels it to be essential that these measures should not cause difficulties, in particular by their duration, for the current GATT negotiations. It therefore considers that they should be rapidly withdrawn, and will take part in the consultations which the contracting parties will be having in Geneva on this subject."

The OECD Ministerial Council, meeting Dec. 2-3 in Paris, said: "The large deficit of the UK . . . gives reason for concern. It calls for economic policies designed to bring about a lasting improvement in the UK's external financial position. The situation will be kept under close examination in the organization [OECD]. Ministers noted the series of measures which had already been decided upon. They further noted the temporary character and non-discriminatory form of the import surcharge, and that the UK government was firmly resolved to reduce it in a nondiscriminatory manner and abolish it at the earliest possible moment. The ministers noted with satisfaction that the organization will undertake a special study of the balance-of-payments adjustment process and play an active role in the multilateral surveillance of means to finance imbalances, as requested by the 10 countries parties to the General Arrangements to Borrow."

French Foreign Min. Valery Giscard d'Estaing had noted Oct. 26 that it was "especially desirable that these corrective measures should have a temporary character." Several other immediate reactions were voiced Oct. 26: A West German Economics Ministry spokesman called the British action "deplorable" and regretted that London had not consulted Bonn beforehand. Swedish Commerce Min. Gunnar Lange said his country's exports to Britain totaled $500 million annually, and the British surcharge "may affect this very seriously." Lange said the import restriction was "contrary to the European Free Trade Association's rules and may be dealt with accordingly." Danish Foreign Min. Per Haekkerup sympathized with the reasons for the British move but said it violated the spirit of the EFTA treaty.

US Treasury Secy. C. Douglas Dillon said Oct. 26: "The new British government has acted promptly and effectively to maintain the strength and stability of the pound sterling. Its temporary measures strike at the inflated imports which have been the principal source of immediate pressure on the pound. Its longer-run measures affecting productivity, incomes and prices can provide the improvement that is needed in the competitive position of the UK in world markets. It is gratifying that the action taken is non-discriminatory in form and avoids any damaging repercussions upon the functioning of the international monetary system. The import charges will, for a time, have a moderately adverse effect upon our trade as well as upon that of other countries, but there is no painless corrective, either for the UK or for the rest of the world. The United States welcomes the British determination to reduce and remove these import charges at the earliest opportunity."

French Information Min. Alain Peyrefitte said Oct. 28: "We do not know much about the British government's intentions. We will wait for the practical measures which may be taken before examining ourselves for the practical measures which France might take or might propose to her Common Market partners. It is also important to know whether the British measures will be of a transitory or lasting character and if they will discriminate against us."

Bank Rate Raised

The Wilson government raised the bank interest rate Nov. 23 from 5% to 7% in an additional effort to bring in foreign money, protect the value of the pound and halt inflationary speculation in sterling. The bank rate, the Bank of England's charge for money lent to Treasury bill dealers, provided the standards for lending rates throughout England. The rise meant that the cost of borrowing automatically increased and that commercial banks probably would charge 8% to 9% for loans instead of the previous 6% to 7%.

The U.S. Federal Reserve Board (FRB) reacted later Nov. 23 by raising its discount rate, which was similar to the British bank rate, from 3.5% to 4% to prevent an outflow of money abroad in search of the higher yield. FRB Chairman William McChesney Martin said Nov. 23 that "if it hadn't been for the British action, the Federal Reserve Board wouldn't have increased the discount rate at this time." The FRB and the U.S. Federal Deposit Insurance Corp. Nov. 23 also raised commercial banks' interest ceilings: (1) Ceilings on interest rates on savings deposits of less than one year were raised from 3.5% to 4% (deposits held for more than a year remained at 4%). (2) Ceilings on interest rates on time deposits and certificates with maturities of less than 90 days were raised from 1% to 4% and those held for longer maturities from 4% to 4.5%.

The British cabinet had made its decision Nov. 22 after the selling of sterling in the foreign exchange market had reached crisis proportions and the value of the pound in the foreign exchange market had dropped to $2.7825 Nov. 20 (a Friday). The higher bank rate was intended to change the international interest-rate structure to encourage holdings in British treasury bills and other British investments. British exports had not risen as quickly as imports, and there had been capital outflows. Thus Britain was in the dangerous financial position of having to cover an estimated 1964 deficit in its international payments of as high as £800 million ($2.24 billion) despite the fact that Britain's gold and currency reserves were only slightly higher than this figure.

Chancellor of the Exchequer Callaghan told the House of Commons Nov. 23 that the bank rate was being raised "to place beyond any doubt the government's determination to maintain sterling at its present parity, and thus to bring to an end the outflow of funds which has been taking place." He said the action would reinforce earlier government measures aimed at restoring confidence in sterling. Callaghan stressed at a news conference later Nov. 23 that Britain had a heavy responsibility to the world to maintain the parity of sterling, and "this we intend to do."

An increase in the bank rate had been widely anticipated in London financial circles, although an increase of only 1% had been anticipated by most informed observers, according to the *Wall Street Journal.* The *Journal* Nov. 25 reported doubt among London bankers that this step would achieve the desired results. The increase was termed "at best a stop-gap solution to [Britain's] financial woes." The increase, while serving to stem the outflow of capital from Britain, would also serve to hinder domestic British economic growth by raising the cost of borrowed capital.

Reginald Maudling, who had been chancellor of the exchequer in the former Conservative government, told the House of Commons Nov. 23 that the speculative movements against sterling had been caused by the recent measures of the Labor government, including "inept" handling of import surcharges.

The British bank rate had been raised to 7% between July 25, 1961 and Oct. 5, 1961, later dropped to 4%, then raised to 5% Feb. 27, 1964 in an attempt to discourage borrowing and stabilize the economy.

International Aid for the Pound; Reserves Fall

The IMF (International Monetary Fund) Nov. 20 approved a stand-by loan arrangement for Britain of $1 billion (£357 million) effective through Aug. 8, 1965. Britain drew the entire amount Dec. 2 to repay earlier credits extended by European, U.S. and Canadian central banks. The $1 billion had been raised by the IMF under its General Arrangements to Borrow, drawing on Fund holdings, borrowings and gold sales for Fund members' currencies. IMF Managing Director Pierre-Paul Schweitzer had said Nov. 12 that Britain's 15% tariff surcharge was the "least bad way" to deal with balance of payments difficulties and that "all the steps connected with the balance-of-payments problem are in the right direction."

The central banks of 11 nations pledged $3 billion (£1.017 billion) in credit to Britain Nov. 25 in an effort to bolster the pound and maintain it at its official foreign exchange value of $2.80. The U.S. pledged $1 billion. The 10 nations pledging the remaining $2 billion were Austria, Belgium, Canada, France, West Germany, Italy, Japan, the Netherlands, Sweden and Switzerland. The object was to instill confidence in the pound by making the $3 billion available in various currencies (not necessarily to be used) to the Bank of England so that it could buy pounds and thus maintain the market price if there was no other demand for pounds at that price. It was hoped that the operation would discourage large-scale foreign selling of pounds. The *Wall Street Journal* Nov. 26 termed the 11-nation action "the largest rescue operation ever mounted to protect a currency."

Alfred Hayes, president of the N.Y. Federal Reserve Bank, and Charles A. Coombs, vice president in charge of the bank's foreign exchange operations, had obtained support for this plan from the central banks of the 10 other nations in negotiations Nov. 24-25. U.S. Federal Reserve and Treasury officials had expressed fears that if the value of sterling continued to drop on the world market, confidence in the dollar (the other major trading currency in the western world) might be undermined. The U.S. initiated the emergency action after the Nov. 23 rise in the Bank of England's interest rate apparently had failed to stabilize the pound. The pound's price had risen from its Nov. 20 low of $2.7825 to $2.7875 Nov. 23, immediately after the rate increase, but it dropped to $2.78625 at the close of trading Nov. 24 under pressure of a wave of foreign speculation in sterling. The international rescue plan implemented Nov. 25 had the desired salutary effect, and the pound closed at $2.790625 Nov. 26 as sterling began to show strength in key European money-trading centers.

The Bank of England, announcing the $3 billion credit, said: "The Bank of England have made arrangements under which $3 billion are made available for the support of sterling. The central banks of Austria, Belgium, Canada, France, [West] Germany, Italy, Japan, the Netherlands, Sweden, Switzerland and the United States are taking part, as is also the Bank for International Settlements. Included in the total is a loan from the Export-Import Bank of the United States. The credits newly made available are separate from the existing central bank credits which have been drawn on over recent months and which will mature shortly. These latter credits will be repaid after the forthcoming drawing by the United Kingdom from the IMF has been completed."

Chancellor of the Exchequer Callaghan reported these aid provisions in Parliament Nov. 26. He said, in part:

"The House will recall that, in my [Nov. 23] statement,I said that the Bank of England were in close touch with other central banks with the object of maintaining co-operation. Yesterday evening the Bank announced the result of these endeavours.... $3 billion ... has been placed at their disposal by 11 central banks to defend sterling. This massive support ... demonstrates the vital importance of the strength of sterling not only to ourselves but to the monetary and trading systems of the world. These credits are separate from the assistance already received, which will be repaid from the drawing of $1 billion, which we intend to make next week from the International Monetary Fund. This concerted action of the monetary authorities of the Western world will demonstrate to those who have been influenced by rumors about the future of sterling that their fears are groundless. A stable currency is the product of a strong economy. The value of these credits is that they give time to press forward with the government's longer-term plans to strengthen the economy. The government intend that we should be seen to be paying our way overseas as well as at home. Firstly, therefore, priority is being given to increasing our exports through measures that are being urgently worked out as well as those already announced. Secondly, a strict review is taking place of the whole range of government expenditure, including overseas defence commitments, in order to secure a reduction in the burden on our balance of payments. Thirdly, we intend that resources of skilled manpower and of capacity should be released in order to put them behind the export effort."

Reginald Maudling, former chancellor of the exchequer under the Conservative government, said: "The government will have a brief opportunity to repair the damage done in the past 10 days."

British gold and dollar reserves fell substantially in late 1964. A decline of £31 million to an £876 million level (the lowest since July 1961) in October was surpassed by a loss of £39 million in November to an £837 million level, the lowest since Dec. 1957. This £837 million figure included short-run credits extended by European and North American central banks and repaid in December from the $1 billion IMF credit.

Maudling had predicted the possibility of reserve losses in his Apr. 14 budget message, when he said:

"We have very large first- and 2d-line reserves and other borrowing facilities which can be mobilized to deal with a position of temporary imbalance or with movements of short-term funds. In addition to the gold and dollar reserves, there is the government's dollar portfolio which has averaged around $1 billion in value. Short-term assistance from other central banks is available, as we saw a year ago, and we have the $500 million swap agreement with the United States. Our stand-by arrangement with the IMF enables us to draw quickly $1 billion from that source, and our total drawing rights amount to nearly $2.5 billion. These are strong defences. I hope, moreover, that the work of the Group of 10 ... and the coming meeting of the IMF this autumn will further strengthen the international liquidity system, with benefit to the position of sterling along with the other major currencies. We cannot, however, be confident that the worsening in our overall balance will be temporary unless we keep control of our own costs, and particularly of our export prices. It is manifest from the figures that I have given and from the studies published ... that the key to all our success is a vigorous increase of exports, and that this depends upon keeping our costs competitive."

Britain's gold and convertible currency reserves dropped during 1964 by £122 million ($341,600,000), or by more than double the rate of the decrease in 1963. Britain's total reserves were £827 million at the end of 1964.

BRITAIN & THE EUROPEAN COMMUNITY

While there were no significant contacts between the European Economic Community and Great Britain regarding British membership in the EEC during 1964, there was a movement throughout Europe and the rest of the world towards generally freer trade and reduced restrictions.

The 'Kennedy Round' Tariff Negotiations

A new round of world tariff-cutting negotiations—the "Kennedy Round"—was opened in Geneva Nov. 16 by delegations representing 17 of the world's major industrial nations. The negotiations, convened under the auspices of the General Agreement on Tariffs & Trade (GATT), were considered the most important of GATT's 6 tariff-cutting conferences since its inception in 1948. Although the negotiations were primarily in the hands of the 17 largest industrial powers affiliated with GATT, 73 states participated. The negotiations were known as the "Kennedy Round" in tribute to the late Pres. John F. Kennedy, whose proposals for trade liberalization, embodied in the U.S. Trade Expansion Act of 1962, were the inspiration for the negotiations. In the 5 previous rounds of GATT tariff-cutting negotiations, participating countries had agreed to reduce some 60,000 tariff rates on specific goods or classifications of goods. The "Dillon Round," held in 1961-2, had produced more than 4,000 tariff concessions averaging 20% of existing charges on the goods covered. These negotiations, involving bargaining between pairs of countries on specific tariff items, were complex and time-consuming. The GATT countries had agreed in 1961 to attempt to try tariff-cutting negotiations on the principle of a massive "across-the-board" reduction to be applied by all participating nations.

The Kennedy Round negotiations were aimed at producing reciprocal tariff cuts of 50% on the greatest possible number of industrial products involved in world trade. The negotiations were intended to produce a 50% across-the-board tariff reduction agreement, rather than the product-by-product reductions sought in previous world tariff negotiations. Under the ground rules formulated for the Kennedy Round meeting, the exemption lists prepared by participants were to be deposited with a special GATT trade negotiating committee, which would make them public early in 1965, when the negotiations were expected to have reached the stage of bargaining over tariff cuts on specific products. The U.S. was reported to have submitted a list of products comprising only 10% of its dutiable industrial imports. Britain's list was reported to be smaller than the U.S.'; Switzerland and several Scandinavian countries were said to have submitted "blank" lists, signifying willingness to negotiate reductions on all industrial products. GATT member states, among them the 6 Common Market nations, had agreed earlier in 1964 that only imports deemed to affect defense or other overriding national interests would be exempted from the tariff-cutting negotiations.

The U.S. Trade Expansion Act, the major incentive for the new series of talks, greatly increased the previously limited power of the U.S. President to negotiate tariff concessions. The President was empowered to: (1) negotiate tariff reductions of up to 50%, effective in stages over a 5-year period; (2) reduce or abolish tariffs or import restrictions on agricultural products if such action would aid U.S. exports of farm products; (3) reduce or abolish tariffs or restrictions on imports of tropical products not produced in great quantities in the U.S., provided that the EEC nations accepted similar liberalization.

A 43-nation GATT trade negotiations committee had been created in 1963 to prepare for the tariff-cutting talks. The committee drafted a set of guidelines that were submitted at a preliminary meeting of Kennedy Round participants in Geneva May 4-6. The preliminary Geneva meeting had adopted without vote May 6 a statement embodying the major recommendations of the GATT committee, although it did not include committee-recommended guidelines on liberalizing agricultural trade and making an across-the-board reduction of disproportionate tariffs charged by different countries on the same goods. The statement of principle, worked out by delegations representing the U.S., Britain and the 6 EEC nations, contained these major points:

●Participants accepted the "working hypothesis" that a 50% across-the-board tariff reduction was to be sought.

●They would submit by Sept. 10 (the date later was put off to Nov. 16) lists of specific goods that, for reasons of over-riding national interest, they wished exempted from tariff reduction.

●They would make genuine efforts to solve the 3 remaining major problems—reduction of disproportionate industrial tariffs, elimination of non-tariff restrictions and arrangements for world trade in agricultural products.

The statement was issued in the names of the 43 member nations of the GATT trade negotiation committee. It was welcomed May 6 "with considerable satisfaction" by ex-State Secy. Christian A. Herter, U.S. special representative for trade negotiations and head of the U.S. delegation to the Kennedy Round talks. Herter had read at the opening session of the Geneva meeting May 4 a message in which Pres. Johnson pledged that "we shall spare no effort" to make the negotiations successful.

The 6 Common Market states reached agreement in Brussels Nov. 15 on a unified negotiating position for the Kennedy Round talks due to be convened in Geneva the following day. The agreement was made possible by France's announcement Nov. 11 that it had dropped demands for settlement of the European grain-price question as a precondition for Common Market participation in the Kennedy Round negotiations. The French reversal was announced in Brussels Nov. 11 by Foreign Min. Maurice Couve de Murville at a meeting of the EEC Council of Ministers. Couve de Murville reportedly stressed that France did not believe the Kennedy Round negotiations could be successful unless the Common Market states first settled their differences on agricultural matters. But, he reportedly said, France would not therefore delay negotiations on industrial tariffs, the primary concern of the Kennedy Round negotiations. The Nov. 11 Brussels meeting had been called in a final attempt to agree on a list of products that the Common Market nations wished to have exempted from the Geneva tariff-cutting negotiations. Each major industrial state or group of states participating in the Kennedy Round negotiations had agreed to submit such a list to the officers of GATT, under whose auspices the negotiations were held. An initial list of suggested Common Market exemptions had been prepared by the EEC Executive Commission, but France, Italy and Belgium had each submitted additional lists of products that they wanted included in the unified exemption list. The Executive Commission list was said to have sought exemptions for goods constituting 12% of all Common Market dutiable imports.

It was feared that the addition of the full lists submitted by France, Italy and Belgium would increase the product exemptions sought by the Common Market as a whole to 40% of the total of the 6 nations' current dutiable imports. But the 4 days of negotiations held in Brussels reduced the unified exemption list to products constituting 20% of the 6 nations' imports from outside nations.

The Kennedy Round's substantive negotiations began in Geneva Nov. 16 when the 17 principal industrial powers submitted lists of products they wished exempted from the negotiations. The lists, in sealed envelopes, were deposited with Eric Wyndham-White, GATT executive secretary. The nations submitting lists were the U.S., Canada, Japan, the 6 EEC countries, Britain and the 6 other members of European Free Trade Association and Czechoslovakia, the only Communist nation to hold full membership in GATT. The exemption lists were circulated among participating nations Nov. 17. The list submitted by Britain was the shortest presented by a major power despite Britain's preferential trade arrangements with Commonwealth nations and the 6 other members of EFTA. British officials said that the products listed constituted only 4.7% of Britain's imports. The U.S. list was kept secret for fear of adverse domestic reaction when the items it contained became known; however, the list was reported to comprise products that made up only 7% of U.S. imports currently subject to tariffs. The joint list submitted by the 6 EEC nations was reported to apply to products constituting 19% of the EEC's total dutiable imports; the largest category of products on the Common Market list was machinery, ranging from tools to heavy industrial equipment. The longest list was Japan's. Delegations to the conference began discussion

Dec. 9 of the procedures to be used in evaluating and approving exemption lists.

The lists covered 3 categories of exemptions: (1) Products for which total exemption from the tariff-cutting negotiations was sought. (2) Products for which a partial exemption or a special tariff adjustment was claimed. (3) Products for which conditional exemptions were sought, depending on the concessions offered by other countries on the same or related items.

Speaking at the opening session of the 51st National Foreign Trade Convention in New York Nov. 16, State Secy. Dean Rusk warned that it was essential that the Kennedy Round negotiations succeed. Rusk declared that it was up to the major industrial powers to prove they were ready to "abandon" the protectionism they had created for themselves at the expense of other nations. Rusk said that if the negotiations failed, the industrial nations would be guilty of "a break of faith with the emerging nations of the world." He said: "If we and other industrial countries prove to be so short-sighted as to restrict our markets to each other, we would do more than hurt ourselves. We would also lessen the export possibilities and hence the development prospects of the poorer nations of the world."

EEC Political Integration

Subtle but steady pressures were exerted by the West German government of Chancellor Ludwig Erhard throughout 1964 for further political integration of the EEC. Countervailing pressures, however, emanated from France and Pres. Charles de Gaulle.

Erhard proposed Jan. 9 that the leaders of the 6 European Common Market nations meet to deal with the "political malaise" arising from their differences over the admission of Britain to the EEC and the political organization of Western Europe. Erhard's assertion that a "malaise" existed was directed at de Gaulle, who had opposed all efforts to organize in Western Europe more than a loose confederation based on periodic consultation among European governments. Addressing the West German Bundestag, Erhard prefaced his remarks with a reaffirmation of his commitment to the French-West German treaty of reconciliation. "There would be no Europe, ... no European integration and no Atlantic partnership without this basis," he said. Equally, there was no contradiction in West Germany's close association with both France and the U.S., he declared. "We need American protection, but we are not an American protectorate." Erhard reported that de Gaulle had given his assent to the idea of a European summit conference during their meeting in Paris in Nov. 1963. Erhard said de Gaulle had made it clear he would not agree to such a meeting being used to launch a new drive for European political union. But, Erhard disclosed, de Gaulle had indicated that he would support any attempt to restore solidarity among the Common Market nations.

Bonn officials said Jan. 10 that Erhard intended to press other European leaders to accept a merger of the existing 6-nation economic institutions: the EEC, ECSC and Euratom. It was suggested that such a merger would constitute a strong first step toward eventual political union without instigating a divisive debate on political integration.

London informants reported Jan. 14 that the British government had informed all EEC nations except France of its desire to take part in any negotiations toward European political unity. Britain reportedly asked that it be represented, not in the European summit meeting proposed by Erhard, but in any political negotiations that might result from such a meeting. (Belgian Foreign Min. Paul-Henri Spaak called Jan. 14 for a new attempt to negotiate European unity but expressed doubt that a United States of Europe would evolve from the negotiations. Spaak, addressing the Council of Europe in Strasbourg, added that in view of the French position, he was skeptical that Britain could be brought into the Common Market.)

Support for the Erhard position was expressed by Italian Pres. Antonio Segni who visited the U.S. with Foreign Min. Guiseppe Saragat for talks with Pres. Johnson and State Secy. Dean Rusk. In an address Jan. 15 at a joint session of Congress, Segni made clear Italy's commitment to a Europe linked with the U.S. in an "indissoluble" Atlantic partnership. He declared that Italy sought an "open" Europe that "include[d] all the peoples that . . . have been the actors in the drama of the Western world, from Great Britain to the ultimate border [with Eastern Europe]." Meeting with newsmen later Jan. 15, Saragat made it clear that Segni's remarks referred to Italy's opposition to de Gaulle's European policies. He said that Italy's primary European aim remained the incorporation of Britain and Scandinavia into every continental institution in which Italy participated.

British-West German policy consultations held in London Jan. 15-16 by Chancellor Erhard and Britain's then-Prime Min. Alec Douglas-Home resulted in no major changes of policy but gave Erhard an opportunity to declare again his support for British participation in Europe. Speaking at a luncheon given in his honor Jan. 15 by the Lord Mayor of London, Erhard asserted that the new Europe must include Britain and must "play its role in world politics" as a member of the Atlantic community. Rejecting de Gaulle's concept of a European entity standing between America and Russia, Erhard said that "to speak of the European mainland [alone] in the political sense can be only political reminiscence, not . . . reality." "There cannot be the slightest doubt about Germany's attitude," he declared. "The Atlantic community is indispensable if . . . we are to stand the test."

Erhard and Home, assisted by Foreign Min. Schroeder and then-Foreign Secy. R. A. Butler, conferred Jan. 15 and 16 and concluded their talks with a joint communique in which they expressed agreement that the "unity of Europe on a broad basis remains their common objective." The communique pledged West Germany's support for continued Western-Soviet negotiations to reduce tensions and made clear Britain's view that a just solution of the Berlin and German problems was of "cardinal importance" for any genuine East-West settlement.

France's total opposition to any formula for European unity involving supranational institutions was made clear by de Gaulle at his press conference in Paris Jan. 31. De Gaulle stressed that France would not participate in any European program that would limit the sovereignty of the nations associated in it. He reiterated that the only form of European political association acceptable to France was a confederation in which each member state would remain fully independent while coordinating its policies with those of other member states. Asked for his views on the political future of the EEC, de Gaulle said that the 6 nations thus far had accomplished the objectives fixed by the treaties establishing the EEC but that in the attainment of these objectives they had "seen clearly that the executive power...belongs to the governments alone." He conceded that the EEC Executive Commission had formulated the settlements ultimately adopted by the member governments, but he insisted that in each case "the [6] governments nonetheless found themselves obliged to take decisive steps and assume their responsibilities."

De Gaulle declared: "We know ... the project for the political union of the 6 has not yet materialized, and we also know the reasons why, the opponents formulating 3 conditions which are, in our opinion, unattainable...." "No European union, they say, unless through integration under supranational leadership. No European union if England does not belong to it. No European union without its being incorporated in an Atlantic community. Yet it is clear that not one of the peoples of Europe would allow their destiny to be handed over to an assembly composed mainly of foreigners. In any case this is true for France. It is also clear that England... would accept it less than anyone else. Finally, it is clear that to merge the policy of Europe in a multilateral Atlantic policy would be tantamount to Europe's having no policy itself and, in that case, we do not see why it would want to federate." The future of the EEC required a "practical cooperation project"; France would be ready to give such a project "careful consideration" when and if it appeared.

De Gaulle's views were assailed Feb. 1 in Belgium and the Netherlands. Brussels spokesmen declared that Belgium "will firmly oppose any political organization of Europe that is not based on the Atlantic partnership." Dutch Foreign Min. Joseph M. A. H. Luns said that there had been "no change" in his government's demand that a European political union include Britain, have close ties with the U.S. and NATO and be governed by supranational institutions incorporating the EEC, ECSC and Euratom.

Italian Pres. Segni visited Paris Feb. 19-22 to discuss the European political question. A joint communique issued by Segni and de Gaulle Feb. 21 said that they had agreed on the "necessity" for progress toward European political unity but had encountered "differences of concept" in their discussion. Foreign Min. Saragat, who accompanied Segni, stressed Feb. 20 in an address to the French Diplomatic Press Association that Italy sought a European community whose members would "progressively transfer some of their sovereignty to joint institutions whose actions would be submitted to the control of an elected assembly." This community, he said, should be open to "all European democratic states" ready to accept the commitments of the EEC's Rome treaties. French and Italian spokesmen confirmed Feb. 21 that de Gaulle and the Italian leaders had failed to find any common ground in their discussions. They were said to have agreed only that functions of the 3 European communities should be consolidated by their merger into one institution.

Ending a tour of Common Market countries, Chancellor Erhard announced in Brussels Apr. 24 that he had given up plans for the convening of a summit conference of leaders of the 6 governments. He said that his recent visits to Paris, Rome, The Hague and London had convinced him that fundamental differences divided the EEC countries on the question of political integration. Commenting on his own and Italian calls for a summit meeting, he said: "I think that at this moment a new summit conference would be unlikely because... the member countries don't agree... that there should be such a conference."

West Germany's intention to initiate new proposals on European political unity were approved by de Gaulle in Bonn July 4 at the end of a meeting with Erhard July 3-4. The meeting, one of the regular semi-annual conferences under the French-West German treaty, produced an agreed-on statement July 4 that "discussions on the political cooperation of Europe will be further intensified... with the objective of bringing into being a united Europe and a common European policy.... To this purpose, proposals will be made from the German side." The statement was taken as evidence that de Gaulle had abandoned his plan to create a French-West German committee to prepare proposals on European unity for submission to the 4 other EEC states. Although the statement made no mention of the French proposal, de Gaulle was known to have communicated it to the Bonn government before the meeting and to have taken it up with Erhard on his arrival in Bonn July 3. Bonn dispatches reported that Erhard had rejected the de Gaulle plan because he felt that the EEC states—particularly Belgium, the Netherlands and Luxembourg—would regard it as an attempt to establish a legal French-West German hegemony over the 6-nation community. It was apparent, further, that the French plan was based on de Gaulle's proposal of a confederation of sovereign continental European states, a concept unacceptable to the smaller EEC nations and opposed by Erhard.

A French government statement issued July 7, after de Gaulle had reported to his cabinet on the results of his Bonn talks, confirmed that Erhard had rejected his European proposals. Read to Paris newsmen by French Information Min. Alain Peyrefitte, the statement said that "the French delegation [to Bonn] found that . . . [West German leaders] do not yet seem altogether ready to practice the common policy we desire and consider necessary."

Erhard's refusal to accept the French proposals was attacked publicly July 9 by ex-Chancellor Konrad Adenauer and ex-Defense Min. Franz-Josef Strauss, leaders of the "Gaullist" faction of Erhard's Christian Democratic Party. Their attacks were based on reports that de Gaulle, toasting French-West German cooperation during his Bonn visit, had appealed for a "complete union" of France and West Germany. Adenauer, in an interview for the Hamburg newspaper *Bild Zeitung,* said that France and West Germany, with a combined population of 100 million and enormous industrial resources, were in a position to force progress toward European unity. In an interview for the *Bayern Kurier,* Strauss called on the Christian Democratic Party to order Erhard to open talks on an immediate union with France or any other EEC nation willing to join with it.

Erhard returned to Bonn July 10 from a visit to Denmark and summoned Adenauer to a personal meeting in his office. A government statement issued after their meeting said that Erhard had "confirmed" his European policy and that "a German-French union alone could never be the ultimate aim" of this policy. Addressing the annual congress in Munich of the Christian Social Union—the Christian Democrats' Bavarian affiliate, led by Strauss—Erhard declared July 12 that he alone was responsible for foreign policy. "I cannot surrender it and I will not," he declared.

France's position of opposition to supranational European unity was reiterated by de Gaulle at his July 23 press conference. He asserted that France's opponents had invoked "contradictory" arguments in their rejection of the French plan for confederal cooperation among sovereign European states. He said that the plan had been rejected because it did not conform to its opponents' "conception" of a Europe that included Britain and was subordinated to "a commission of experts" and "a parliament cut off from national realities." De Gaulle added that "we have seen many people . . . advocate for Europe not an independent policy, which in reality they do not visualize, but an organization unsuited to have one, linked with . . . an Atlantic system, . . . and consequently subordinate to what the United States calls its leadership." De Gaulle conceded that France's differences with its neighbors had stalemated the discussions on European political unity. He said that even France and West Germany, bound by a treaty of cooperation, had not been able to elaborate a common European policy because "Bonn has not believed . . . that this [European political] policy should be European and independent." In the absence of any other acceptable proposal, de Gaulle said, France would wait patiently for the West German initiative foreseen in the statement issued in Bonn July 4 after his meeting with Erhard. The French president said, regarding Franco-German relations:

"France took the initiative in proposing to her 5 Rome Treaty partners a start in organizing their cooperation. Thus we should have begun to live together; and in time, from this beginning, habit and evolution would have strengthened the ties little by little. It is known that the [West] German government gave its agreement to this project in principle. It is known that a meeting of the 6 states in Paris [in Feb. 1961] and another in Bonn [in July 1961] seemed to be on the way to achieving it, but that Rome refused to convoke the meeting which would have been decisive, and that her objections, together with those of The Hague and Brussels, were strong enough to stop everything. Finally, it is known that the opponents [of the project] invoked 2 arguments, which were moreover contradictory. First argument—'the French plan, which would preserve national sovereignties, does not meet our concept of a Europe having a commission of experts as an executive, and a parliament divorced from national realities as the legislative arm.' 2d argument—'although Britain does not agree to relinquish her sovereignty, we shall not enter any European political organization to which she does not belong.'

"Since the French plan for European organization was not adopted by Italy and the Benelux countries; since integration could not end in anything other than an American protectorate; and finally, since Great Britain had shown, during the interminable Brussels negotiations, that she was not in a position to accept the joint economic rules, and, by the Nassau agreement, that her defense force, notably in the nuclear field, could not be European for want of being independent of the United States—it appeared to the German Federal government and the French government that bilateral cooperation between them could be of some value. It was then—on the German government's proposal—that the Treaty of Jan. 22, 1963, was concluded.... However, although the Franco-German Treaty has in several fields made possible results in matters of detail, and has led the 2 governments and their administrative services to develop contacts which... we consider can be useful,... it must be stated that up to the present it has not led to a line of common policy.

"Certainly there cannot be opposition, properly called, between Bonn and Paris. But whether it is a question of effective solidarity between France and Germany for their defense; or the new structure to be given to the Atlantic Alliance; or the attitude to take and the policy to pursue towards the East, above all Moscow's satellites; or, in corollary, the question of the frontiers and nationalities of Central and Eastern Europe; or the recognition of China and the diplomatic and economic activities which could be open to Europe in relation to that great people; or peace in Asia, notably Indo-China and Indonesia; or aid to the developing countries of Africa, Asia and Latin America; or the establishment of the Common Market in agriculture and hence the future of the Community of the 6—one cannot say that Germany and France have yet agreed together on formulating a policy, and one cannot deny that this results from the fact that up to the present Bonn does not agree that this policy should be European and independent. If this state of affairs were to last, in the long run it would risk producing doubt among the French people, concern among the Germans, and, among their 4 Rome Treaty partners, a strengthened inclination to remain where they stand, perhaps pending a splitting-up.

"Across the world, nevertheless, the force of circumstances is at work. In proposing and seeking the building up of a Europe with its own policy, France is convinced she is serving the cause of world equilibrium, peace and progress. Moreover, she is now sufficiently solid and sure of herself to be able to be patient, unless there are great external changes which would throw everything into question and might as a result lead her to change her outlook. In addition, during the meeting which has just taken place between the Bonn and Paris governments, Chancellor Erhard foreshadowed a forthcoming German initiative. While waiting for the sky to clear, France is pursuing by her own efforts what can and must be a European and independent policy...."

The West German government Nov. 6 published a plan for the resumption of negotiations on West European political unification. The Bonn program, submitted Nov. 4 to the 5 other EEC member states, called for accelerated implementation of the Common Market at the same time that a committee of experts would draft a treaty for eventual political union. The German proposal was intended primarily to achieve a renewal of the European unity discussions halted by de Gaulle's opposition to any supranational political institutions that would diminish the sovereignty of the individual West European governments. It came at a time when France and West Germany were at loggerheads over terms for creating a Europe-wide agricultural market within the EEC. A Bonn Foreign Ministry statement said that the proposal aimed at providing, "in the first section, for cooperation in the spheres of foreign policy, defense and culture, and, in the 2d section, for further development of European unity in the fields of economic and social policy." It gave this summary of the plan of action proposed by West Germany:

"In the first phase, the governments should prepare for a closer union and lay down the conditions for the entry of other European states.... Consultations should be taken up between governments with the aim of reaching as far as possible corresponding positions in all important questions.... An advisory committee, whose members would be nominated by the governments and should only serve the common interest, would assist the governments. The European Parliament should be included in the political cooperation from the beginning. The proposed cooperation should serve to strengthen the Atlantic Alliance."

In the 2d phase, there should be a speedup in completion of the Common Market customs union and external tariff system to provide the basis for the subsequent political integration of Western Europe. The EEC should implement "an additional 10% cut from Jan. 1, 1965 on internal tariffs in the industrial and agricultural sectors" and "the removal of the remaining 20% in the industrial sector on Jan. 1, 1967." Tax differences among the 6 EEC states would be eliminated during this period, as would be the remaining obstacles to development of a common agricultural market.

"In the further development of the communities, a common course in the field of current policy, a conformity of national budget policies, and finally the amalgamation of the 3 community treaties [EEC, ECSC and Euratom] to one single community encompassing the total economy of the member states appears necessary. At this point in time the European Parliament should be given real parliamentary authority."

The Bonn proposals were received coolly by most of the other Common Market nations. French officials said in Paris Nov. 6 that the plan could not be discussed before a settlement had been reached on a common farm market and on the fate of the U.S.-proposed NATO nuclear fleet. EEC officials in Brussels said Nov. 6 that no discussion of the proposal was likely until 1965. British officials said Nov. 6 that the plan was unreal in that it could not force an alteration of de Gaulle's opposition to any European political integration.

It was reported from Rome Nov. 28 that Italian Foreign Min. Saragat had transmitted to ambassadors of the 5 other EEC nations new proposals to break the deadlock in negotiations on European integration. The Italian proposal would require the 6 nations to commit themselves only to the basic principle of a "democratic and federated Europe" and to agree to regular consultations. It provided for at least

one annual meeting at the head-of-state or government level and for 4
ministerial meetings a year. The meetings were to be set up by a
commission appointed by the 6 governments and assisted by a secretariat. They would be devoted primarily to elaboration of European
political institutions. Under the Italian plan, the 6 governments would
attempt to write a treaty for European political integration within 3
years. The plan combined France's demands for regular consultation
among the 6 governments with the demands of other EEC states for an
agreement in principle on a federated Europe.

The British representative to the EEC, Sir Con O'Neill, warned
Dec. 17 that the basis for the Western political and military alliance
would be undermined unless the Common Market states abandoned
policies of exclusion and worked toward political unity with Britain and
the rest of Western Europe. O'Neill, addressing the American and Common Market Club in Brussels, conceded that it would not be "realistic"
to expect Britain to join the EEC under current conditions. But he
stressed that "Britain wants to participate... in any political decisions
affecting European unity." He cited as an example current talks among
the 6 EEC nations on a proposed European patent convention. He
warned that unless the talks were broadened to include other European
nations, the convention might not be honored outside EEC frontiers.

During most of 1964, Britain and the EEC nations had continued
talks within the Western European Union on proposals for economic
and political cooperation. The WEU contacts had been set up by the 7
countries following the collapse in 1963 of Britain's negotiations for
membership in the Common Market. As in the past, the French delegation rejected every major British proposal submitted to the WEU for
cooperation among the 7 or for British participation in the EEC states'
discussions of proposals for their eventual political association. Reflecting growing pessimism about the possibility of an eventual extension of
the Common Market to include Britain and other European nations,
Netherlands Foreign Min. Joseph M. A. H. Luns was reported to have
informed British Foreign Secy. Patrick Gordon Walker in London Oct.
20 that the Netherlands could not continue its support of Britain's inclusion in European political negotiations unless Britain's new Labor
government made clear its intentions toward association with Europe.

EEC Agricultural Agreement

A major threat to the future of the European Economic
Community was resolved conditionally Dec. 1 with West Germany's
agreement to reduce its grain prices to uniform levels required under
Common Market plans for completion of a Europe-wide agricultural
system. The system ultimately would lead to integration of the agricultural economies of the 6 EEC states. The West German decision was
taken in the wake of a French threat to withdraw from the Common

Market unless the farm program was fully implemented. French grain prices were substantially lower than those of West Germany, and the Bonn government, facing general elections in 1965, was reported to fear the political reaction if it deprived German farmers of grain subsidies and forced them to compete against large French exports of cheap surplus wheat.

The grain-price compromise proposed by Bonn was submitted to the Common Market Ministerial Council in Brussels by West German Agriculture Min. Werner Schwarz. The Bonn plan suggested that the basic European price for wheat be set at $110 a ton and that this price be made effective July 1, 1967, subject to revision if inflation or other economic factors made a change necessary by that date. It proposed that the Common Market revise its current plans for the use of customs levies on imported farm produce, earmarked generally for export rebates to EEC members producing agricultural surpluses. It urged that the Common Market raise from $140 million to $175 million its planned annual compensation of West German farmers for losses they were expected to suffer when the uniform European grain price went into effect. Bonn demanded that any agreement reached on the basis of its proposal be made permanent and not be subject to revision by majority vote. Major policy decisions currently required unanimous approval of the EEC Ministerial Council; however, decision by a simple majority was to be instituted by the Council Jan. 1, 1966.

(A Europe-wide grain price was one of the key points of the Mansholt Plan for the creation of a European Common Market in agriculture. Drawn up in 1963 by Sicco L. Mansholt of the Netherlands, EEC commissioner for agriculture, the plan was intended to create a unified 6-nation farm market by 1970. The first of the major agricultural regulations, among them the uniform grain price, were to be applied in 1967, but a 3-year transitional period was allowed to permit member states to cushion the economic shock to their agricultural sectors. The Mansholt Plan suggested that the European grain price be fixed at $106.25 a ton; West Germany's current wheat price was $118 a ton.)

West Germany's decision to cut its grain prices to the suggested European level constituted a reversal of its past position on the matter. Chancellor Ludwig Erhard had declared in the Bundestag Mar. 19 that "the federal government will not accept a reduction in cereal prices for 1964-1965" and would not commit itself on any future reduction. EEC ministers had discussed the problem at a Brussels meeting Apr. 14 but were prevented by West German intransigence from reaching a settlement. The 6 nations were criticized June 4 by Walter Hallstein, president of the EEC Executive Commission, for failure to make progress on the grain-price question. Hallstein, in a letter sent to the EEC governments and made public the same day, expressed "grave concern" that a further postponement of the decision would jeopardize the Kennedy

Round of tariff negotiations scheduled to begin in December. Reflecting Bonn's refusal to negotiate on grain prices, the 5 other EEC states July 17 rejected a West German request for further delay in the application of uniform policies on dairy products, rice and beef. The 5 informed the West German representative at a Brussels meeting that they considered the dairy-rice-beef agreement to be effective on the basis of commitments accepted by the Bonn delegate the previous day. The dairy-beef-rice regulations, originally approved by the EEC Ministerial Council in Dec. 1963, were to become fully effective Sept. 1 (rice) and Nov. 1 (dairy products and beef). West Germany's agreement to begin substantive negotiations on a reduction of its grain prices was announced Nov. 10, after France had issued its threat to quit the EEC unless a grain settlement was reached by the end of the year. Meeting with the EEC Council of Ministers in Brussels, West German Foreign Min. Gerhard Schroeder declared that Bonn was "prepared to reach an agreement now on common grain prices." 3 weeks of negotiations were necessary to produce the West German compromise announced Dec. 1.

France's warning that it would withdraw from the Common Market unless West Germany permitted completion of a European agricultural market had been delivered in Paris Oct. 21. A statement issued after a cabinet meeting presided over by Pres. de Gaulle declared that the government had "stressed once again that France will cease to participate in the European Economic Community if the agricultural market is not organized." The statement, read to newsmen by Information Min. Alain Peyrefitte, said that without a grain-price agreement there would be "no possibility of negotiating usefully with the United States" in the Kennedy Round talks. Peyrefitte said: France was "categoric" in its insistence that creation of a common agricultural market was "the touch-stone of European development"; France's unyielding position had been made necessary by West Germany's refusal to negotiate at a Brussels meeting Oct. 20 of EEC agriculture ministers; French Agriculture Min. Edgard Pisani had reported to the cabinet that the Brussels deadlock, unless broken, would pose "very grave difficulties" in settling the grain-price question and carrying out the Mansholt Plan for a uniform European farm system.

The French position was in effect supported Oct. 22 by the European Parliament, the advisory legislative body for the European communities. The Parliament, meeting in Strasbourg, voted, 139-3, to adopt a resolution demanding that the EEC governments fix a uniform grain price by Dec. 15.

(Brussels legal experts, however, noted Oct. 22 that the Rome Treaties founding the Common Market committed signatories to remain EEC members on pain of judgment by an international tribunal empowered to impose economic sanctions on violators of the treaties. The treaties did not require the completion of a common agricultural market before Dec. 31, 1969, and it was not believed that France could legally base a withdrawal from the EEC on Bonn's failure to accept European agricultural regulations before that date. Despite the wording of the treaty, Belgian Foreign Min. Paul-Henri Spaak declared Oct. 29, following a Paris meeting with de Gaulle, that "the fundamental French position is correct" and the 6 nations should be compelled to "hold to the promises made.")

The EEC Ministerial Council agreed in Brussels Dec. 15 on uniform "target" prices for wholesale grain purchases throughout the EEC's 6 member states. The grain price agreement ended a year-long deadlock that had brought the French threat to withdraw unless the matter was settled to France's satisfaction. The Brussels agreement was hailed Dec. 15 by EEC Vice Pres. Mansholt as the "most important" decision ever taken by the 6 governments. It was clear, Mansholt said, that "the big decisions on farm policy will be taken in Brussels from now on," rather than in the 6 capitals. Most Brussels observers agreed with Mansholt that the grain-price decision had been crucial to the future development of an effective Common Market and that its adoption virtually assured the EEC's future.

The grain agreement was worked out at a Council meeting begun in Brussels Dec. 12. Although West Germany initially expressed reservations at the price levels proposed, Bonn's representatives Dec. 12 reaffirmed their government's commitment to negotiate uniform grain prices. They did so despite last-minute opposition expressed by West German Agriculture Min. Schwarz, who raced to Brussels from Bonn by car earlier that day in a vain attempt to dissuade his government's delegation from making the grain-price concessions demanded by France. Italy's opposition to the agreement was overcome Dec. 15 by special concessions granted it by the other 5 EEC states.

Major provisions of the grain-price agreement: (1) "Target" wholesale prices on grain products throughout the 6-nation group were fixed at $106.25 a metric ton for soft wheat, $125 a metric ton for hard (durum) wheat, $91.25 for barley, $93.75 for rye and $90.63 for feed corn. (2) The target prices, to be used for computing tariffs and price supports on grain products, were to take effect July 1, 1967. (3) During a 3-year period beginning in 1967, the EEC Agricultural Fund would pay West Germany $280 million and Italy $131 million to reimburse them for compensation to be paid their farmers for losses expected as a result of the uniform grain price. (4) The following price concessions were granted to Italy and West Germany in return for their acceptance of the plan: Italy would be permitted to keep its feed-corn price $7.50 to $15.63 a ton lower than the European price for 5 years after July 1, 1967; Italy was permitted to set a target price for hard wheat $20 higher than the European target price; West Germany was permitted to keep rye and barley prices at a level $2.50 above the uniform European price.

(According to the Dec. 15 *Wall St. Journal,* the uniform European grain prices could pose a serious threat to the U.S. grain exports to the EEC area, currently amounting to $400 million a year. Although the grain prices set by the EEC were 30% to 50% higher than the prices charged by U.S. traders for the same products, they were expected to stimulate a large increase in French grain production, reducing Common Market purchases of U.S. grain. At the same time, EEC tariffs on imported grain would remain at a uniformly high level unless some reduction was achieved by the Kennedy Round tariff talks in Geneva.)

De Gaulle, in a statement issued in Paris Dec. 16 following a cabinet meeting, declared that the grain-price agreement was a "capital" step that created "all sorts of possibilities in the way of European construction." In his statement, de Gaulle expressed gratitude to the EEC Executive Commission for its key role in arranging the grain-price accord, but he repeated his contention that the basic responsibility for such decisions remained with the 6 sovereign EEC nations.

West German Chancellor Erhard's cabinet also discussed and approved the grain-price pact Dec. 16. A Bonn government spokesman said that the cabinet viewed the decision as a significant step toward European unity.

France informed the other EEC nations Dec. 17 that it expected the 6-nation Common Market in agriculture to be completed in 1965. The French representative in Brussels submitted timetables for completion of the required farm regulations: (1) Setting of uniform European meat prices, Feb. 15, 1965. (2) Final marketing regulations for fruit and vegetables, Apr. 28, 1965. (3) Revision of agricultural-financial regulations, May 1, 1965. (4) Final sugar regulations, June 1, 1965. (5) Creation of a Common Market for rice and setting of uniform milk and dairy prices, July 1, 1965.

Other EEC Developments

The chief executives of the 3 European "pools"—the Common Market, Euratom and ECSC—were reelected to new 2-year terms Jan. 10 at a Brussels meeting of EEC ministers. The officials' new terms were made subject to review if action was taken on proposals for a merger of the 3 institutions. Those reelected: Pres. Walter Hallstein of the EEC Executive Commission, Pres. Pierre Chatenet of the Euratom Executive Commission and Pres. Dino Delbo of the ECSC High Authority. Also reelected were EEC Executive Commission Vice Presidents Sicco Mansholt (agricultural affairs) and Robert Marjolin (financial affairs).

Tariffs on imports of fresh eggs from outside countries were raised by 35% Jan. 20. The increase meant that the egg levy imposed by West Germany, the EEC's major importer of fresh eggs, was raised from 9¢ to 12¢ a pound.

The EEC Executive Commission *Bulletin* reported Mar. 12 that the 6 nations' collective deficit in trade with non-member countries had grown from $1.4 billion in 1962 to $2.8 billion in 1963. $2.5 billion of the total was due to the EEC's trade deficit with the U.S. Of the 6 nations, only West Germany showed a high trade surplus, recording a 28% increase in exports and a 15% increase in imports in 1963.

A 14-point anti-inflation program was adopted Apr. 14 by the EEC Ministerial Council. The program was a watered-down version of an inflation control plan drawn up by Executive Commission Vice Pres. Robert Marjolin. The council declined to accept Marjolin's suggestion that the program be accepted in the names of the 6 governments. The plan instead was adopted as a series of recommendations for possible action by the 6 states. Among its major provisions: (1) stabilization of EEC prices and production costs by the end of 1964 as an "overriding" objective; (2) limitation of budgetary increases by the 6 states and their local government bodies to 5% annually; (3) increased tariffs to cut the deficits of nationalized industries, and the raising of taxes to reduce consumer spending; (4) strict enforcement of antitrust laws to increase competition within the Common Market.

The foundation of a common energy policy covering coal, oil, gas, and nuclear and water power was adopted Apr. 22 by the EEC Ministerial Council. The plan, considered only the first step toward a common energy policy, fixed the general principles to be followed in elaborating such a policy and urged agreement on policies to be followed in dealing with the need for curtailment of French, West German and Belgian coal production. The principles fixed by the agreement: low energy prices; freedom of consumer choice; assured supplies of energy for consumers; safeguards for regions supplying specific types of energy.

The Common Market and Israel May 6 signed a trade agreement providing cuts averaging 20% in EEC tariffs on 20 Israeli products, among them fruit and fruit juices, wearing apparel and certain chemical and aluminum products. The Israeli agreement, effective July 1, was the 2d purely commercial accord to be negotiated by the EEC; the first such pact had been signed with Iran in 1963. Israel, whose imports from the EEC averaged $150 million annually, pledged under the agreement to increase its purchases from the 6 nations. Israeli exports to the 6 nations were reported to total only $75 million annually, and the Israeli negotiators were said to have been disappointed at the terms of the final agreement.

A preliminary agreement for the establishment of a unified Common Market airline system was reached in Brussels June 10 by representatives of the 6 nations and their airlines. The projected air union was to include Air France, Lufthansa, Alitalia, KLM, Sabena and Luxair. It would form the basic structure for an eventual integration of the 6 nations' airlines into a single EEC air system. One of its first objectives would be to set up a common pool of aircraft and personnel to coordinate passenger and freight traffic. The 6 airlines were to form a joint executive committee to plan integration of their schedules and operations.

The EEC Ministerial Council announced June 11 that it had authorized the European Coal & Steel Community's High Authority to enter negotiations with other major steel-producing nations on modifying the 50% steel tariff reduction to be sought in the Kennedy Round talks. Common Market steel tariffs currently were at 9%, but the Council agreed that a reduction to 7.5% would be acceptable. In the event that none of the other steel-producing powers agreed with the EEC proposal, Common Market spokesmen said that ECSC steel tariffs might be doubled to nullify the 50% cut sought by other nations. (The ECSC High Authority had announced Jan. 10 that it had ordered an increase in members' tariffs on steel [from 6% to 9% average] and pig iron [to $7 per ton], effective in mid-February. The tariff rise was imposed after Italy and the Netherlands had refused to raise their tariffs voluntarily. The increase in tariffs was attributed to a 50% rise in foreign steel imports into the ECSC area during 1963. ECSC steel prices had declined from 9% to 40% for various steel products during the past year. ECSC steel capacity was 90 million tons annually; production averaged 80 million tons, exports 14 million tons and foreign steel imports 5 million tons.)

An EEC Executive Commission report published Aug. 17 said that cost-of-living indexes in the 6 nations had risen sharply in 1963. The increases reported: Belgium 2.1%, Luxembourg 2.9%, West Germany 3.1%, the Netherlands 4.2%, France 4.8% and Italy 7.5%. (The U.S. consumer price index increase in 1963: 1.3%.)

The first anti-trust ruling under the Common Market treaty was handed down Sept. 21 by the EEC Executive Commission. Although the ruling did not identify the industry or the firms involved, it was clear that it had been issued to nullify an agreement involving more than a dozen companies in 2 or more Common Market countries. The commission ordered the firms to end the agreement or face heavy fines. The companies' agreement reportedly had violated EEC regulations against restriction of competition.

A plan to accelerate the Common Market's planned uniform external tariff barrier and its internal customs union was presented to the 6 member states in Brussels Oct. 2 by EEC Executive Commission Pres. Walter Hallstein. The program, labeled "Initiative 1964," called for: (1) Replacement of the 6 states' existing tariffs on imports from the rest of the world by a single external EEC tariff Jan. 1, 1966, a year earlier than planned. (2) The abolition of all internal tariffs among the 6 member states by Jan. 1, 1967, thus completing the customs union that was the key objective of the original Common Market proposal. Hallstein, outlining the new program to the Ministerial Council, said he was convinced that "the customs union would promote the economic integration of Europe, which, in its turn, would make it more urgent to intensify moves toward political unification" of the 6 countries.

The revised timetable for the application of Common Market regulations provided for a 3-stage reduction in internal customs duties on industrial goods. A 15% reduction in duties on industrial products was effective Jan. 1, 1965 and a similar cut Jan. 1, 1966; all remaining customs charges on industrial products traded among the 6 nations were to be abolished Jan. 1, 1967. Duties on agricultural products traded within the Common Market were to be eliminated by Jan. 1, 1968. (Tariffs on manufactured goods traded among the 6 nations already had been reduced by 60% since the first stage of the Common Market treaties became effective in 1958.) The program further provided for the abolition of all indirect obstacles to trade among the 6 states, particularly through the elimination of controls over goods passing frontiers, the progressive introduction of a monetary union among the 6 nations and the advancement of measures for Common Market-wide social legislation and social welfare measures.

Proposals for the opening of negotiations on the granting of associate Common Market status to Austria were submitted to the EEC Ministerial Council Oct. 12 but were not acted on. The proposal was the outgrowth of exploratory talks under way between Austrian officials and the Common Market Executive Commission since April 1963. The Executive Commission had been reported June 4 to have submitted a report to the EEC Ministerial Council on the principles under which Austrian association with the Common Market would be possible. Austria earlier had indicated that it hoped for a close economic association with the Common Market but preferred to remain outside the community's legal institutions. The Executive Commission was said to have informed Austria that associate status involved commitments to Common Market policies in tariffs, agriculture and other major categories. It was assumed that under any form of association with the EEC, Austria would have to abandon its membership in the EFTA.

The Common Market Ministerial Council announced Oct. 13 that it had agreed to negotiate with Kenya, Uganda and Tanzania to provide the 3 former British colonies with preferential trade arrangements similar in kind to those already granted to 18 newly independent French-speaking African nations.

An agreement granting Turkey a formal association with the Common Market was initialed in Brussels Dec. 1 by Turkish Foreign Min. Feridun Cemal Erkin and representatives of the 6 EEC countries. The Turkish association pact set up a 3-stage program intended to create a full customs union between Turkey and the Common Market within 20 years. During the first 5-year stage, Turkey was to be granted quotas for tariff-free export to the EEC of agricultural items, including dried grapes and figs and tobacco, and the EEC's European Investment Bank was to grant Turkey $175 million in loans for economic development. The customs union was to be implemented progressively during the 12-year 2d stage; at the same time, Turkey's economy was to be "harmonized" with that of the Common Market in matters of commercial law, taxes and fiscal policy. The association agreement was intended to form the basis for full Turkish membership in the EEC at the end of the 20-year period.

EFTA Trade Gains

The European Free Trade Association, in an annual report published Sept. 27, declared that its 4 years of operations ended June 30 had demonstrated the success of the 8-nation trade zone. The EFTA was made up of 7 full members—Austria, Britain, Denmark, Norway, Portugal, Sweden, and Switzerland—and one associate member, Finland. The report said that "the combined gross national product of the EFTA countries rose by 3.7% in real [constant price level] terms in 1963, or double the increase of the previous year." It attributed the rise primarily to a revival of the British economy, producer of more than 50% of total EFTA output. EFTA countries' combined imports from outside countries during the fiscal year ended June 30 reached $27.584 billion, an increase of 6.8% over 1963 and 32.3% over 1959, the last year before the trade zone became effective. EFTA nations' exports to outside countries in the year ended June 30 reached $23.294 billion, an increase of 8.2% for the year and 30.6% over 1959.

Noting that EFTA nations had reduced tariffs on each others' products to 40% of the levels existing in 1960, the report said that progressive elimination of remaining restrictions would mean that by the end of 1966 the 8 nations "will have become a single market of 100 million people, almost completely free of tariffs and other restrictions on industrial goods" traded among them. In a presumed reference to the organization of the EFTA as a counterbalance to the 6-nation European Common Market, the report said that it would continue to work toward the "long-term objective of a single market embracing all of Western Europe." It made clear that the EFTA would "seek all possible means of liberalizing world trade" in the Kennedy Round tariff negotiations.

The EFTA Ministerial Council met in Edinburgh July 9-10 and in Geneva Nov. 19-20. Both meetings concentrated on Kennedy Round developments; the latter also involved discussions of the British 15% tariff surcharge.

EFTA instituted a 10% cut in industrial goods tariffs effective Dec. 31. This brought the level of EFTA internal tariffs on industrial goods down to 30% of the level existing among EFTA states when the association was formed in 1960. EFTA planned to abolish its internal industrial tariffs entirely by late 1966, the same timetable contemplated by the rival EEC. EFTA originally had planned to eliminate internal tariffs on industrial products by the end of 1969, but it had emulated the Common Market in speeding up its program by 3 years.

British Review Concorde Project

The desire of Britain's Labor government to "re-examine urgently the Concorde project" disturbed French authorities connected with the project. British Aviation Min. Roy Jenkins visited Paris Oct. 29-30 to confer with French officials. While no communique was issued, it was reported that the British government was concerned about the level of expenditures involved, estimated at about £140 million, compared with the original £75 to £85 million estimate. French Premier Georges Pompidou said Nov. 5, regarding the Concorde:

"The position of the British government consists in practice of delaying and in fact of abandoning the Concorde project. We have not yet exactly determined our reaction to the British government's attitude. More generally, I can only say that, whatever discussions may have taken place in the past on the economic viability of the project, we can only regret an attitude which, on the one hand, puts an end to an important, significant and symbolic piece of Franco-British cooperation and, on the other, in one of the most important industrial fields..., seems to indicate a certain 'contracting-out' of Europe in favour of the United States. If it should be shown clearly that this abandonment was not unconnected with the American attitude itself—the British decision having been immediately followed by a U.S. statement to the effect that the Americans were ready to accelerate their own project—it would indicate a 'resignation from Europe' [*demission Europeenne*] which we should regard as most serious.

"What can we do?... In the immediate future it seems difficult, if not impossible, for France to go ahead alone in carrying out such a vast and costly project. In view of the difficulties which will inevitably be encountered by our industry because up to now it has not been able to produce jet engines powerful enough for the *Concorde,* it would be very difficult for it to make a start on such an important aircraft destined to carry so many passengers.... As for the possibility of other competition, we shall see. In any case, we shall do our utmost to maintain an aeronautical industry in France and to safeguard everything in the way of research so as not to be outdistanced in the race for technical progress. We shall therefore try to spare our industry and our workers as far as possible from the results of the Labor government's decision."

1965

During 1965 Britain and the EEC concentrated largely on internal issues. Britain achieved a degree of success in the battle to stabilize the pound and reverse serious balance-of-payments deficits, thus averting an immediate devaluation of the pound; but this success was at the cost of domestic austerity. A White Paper on steel nationalization was approved by the House of Commons. EEC suffered a serious setback in June when France withdrew from active participation in a dispute over agricultural policies. France was also at odds with its Common Market partners over the issue of European political integration.

GREAT BRITAIN

Domestic Austerity

A balanced budget designed to promote greater confidence in the pound was submitted to the British House of Commons Apr. 6 by Chancellor of the Exchequer James Callaghan. The proposals, for the fiscal year beginning Apr. 8 (fiscal 1965-6), called for a program of austerity. Callaghan estimated the fiscal year's revenues at £8.862 billion ($25.273 billion) and expenditures at £8.482 billion ($23.75 billion). In fiscal 1964-5, expenditures had been budgeted at £7.792 billion ($20.6 billion) and revenues at £7.88 billion. A major saving disclosed in the budget was the cancellation of the TSR-2 (tactical-strike-reconnaissance jet) project, an item that would have cost almost $100 million.

Callaghan told Parliament: "Our country has suffered from a weak balance of payments for many years. In the past decade we have preserved solvency only by periodic bouts of deflation which immediately reduce imports but also sap the confidence of management and labor at home and weaken our industrial position." "The task is not to secure the underemployment of our resources but their re-deployment. . . . The measures I have announced indicate the sacrifices the British people will have to make so that we can get our economy right and pay our debts to foreign creditors. I want to encourage industry to be more dynamic and productive. I want to reform the tax system and to get a proper return for heavy expenditure and to be fair."

The budget revealed decisions: (1) To decrease British consumption at home by £250 million ($700 million) annually by setting up a series of new excise levies that would produce more than £217 million ($608 million) yearly in new revenues. (The House of Commons immediately approved the new tax measures on a temporary basis to allow them to go into effect Apr. 8. The taxes were on cigarettes, liquor, and auto licenses.) (2) To discourage long-term foreign investments by reducing tax advantages. (3) To levy a new tax of 30% on long-term capital gains (the first such tax in Britain) and to require that assets be held for at least one year to qualify for this rate. (4) To raise the basic income tax rate from 38.75% to 41.25% (although this raise was announced in Nov. 1964, it went into effect Apr. 8). (5) To start a new corporate tax system (of up to 40%) in the next fiscal year. (6) To disallow all entertainment expenses (except those involving foreign buyers) as regular business deductions.

Among statistics on which budget policy was based: (a) Britain's gross national product in 1964 totaled £28.691 billion ($80,334,100,000), up 7.5% over 1963 (or up only 5.5% if calculated at "constant prices"). (b) In 1964 British consumers spent £21.038 billion ($58,906,400,000), up 6.5% (up 3.5% in terms of 1958 prices). (c) Britain's balance of international payments (current account) showed a deficit of £374 million in 1964 compared with a surplus of £96 million in 1963. The balance of current and long-term capital transactions showed a £745 million deficit, compared with 1963's deficit of £78 million.

The British government Feb. 22 reduced the surcharge on industrial imports from 15% to 10%, effective Apr. 27. Chancellor of the Exchequer James Callaghan explained: "We have decided that enough progress is being made to enable us to reduce the charge after it has been in operation for 6 months." The government had imposed the surcharge Oct. 26, 1964 to strengthen the pound and help end the balance-of-payments deficit. The House of Commons Nov. 29 adopted by 279-276 vote (Conservatives and Liberals opposed) a motion authorizing the government to extend until Nov. 1966 its 10% surcharge on imports. Callaghan told the House that a reduction in the surcharge "would hamper our recovery and delay the improvement in our balance of payments."

The bank rate was increased to 6% June 3.

Callaghan announced in the House of Commons July 27 new measures to cut down the rate of spending and thus protect the value of the pound. Callaghan said that the nation's economic situation made the government unable "to fulfill the social programs" it had promised. Among measures he proposed: (1) A call on all local authorities to postpone as far as possible the building of schools, roads and other projects; (2) a reduction of the maximum period for repayment of goods bought on installment plans from 36 months to 30; (3) a reduction in the number of home mortgages issued by government bodies; (4) the reduction of defense expenditures by £100 million ($280 million) for fiscal 1966-7 and by £310 million ($1.12 billion) by fiscal 1969-70; (5) a reduction of the cost of short-term credit; (6) a reduction from £50,000 ($140,000) to £25,000 ($70,000) of the contract value required for government credit guarantee of exports.

The House of Commons approved the Labor government's controversial finance bill by 291-285 vote July 15 on the bill's 3d (final) reading. The measure imposed a tax on long-term capital gains and a single tax on corporation earnings.

Economic Affairs Min. George Brown announced Sept. 3 that the Labor government would introduce legislation to impose delays on wage and price increases in key sectors of the economy. The anti-inflation plan would give statutory power to the National Prices & Incomes Board to consider proposed wage and price increases affecting important economic areas to be designated by the government. Management and labor would be required to give advance notice of such increases, which would be frozen while the board collected information and called witnesses. The board's findings would be advisory. The 32-member General Council of Britain's Trades Union Congress (TUC) voted Sept. 3 to urge union cooperation with the plan. But the council Sept. 4 approved a plan under which it would advise unions itself whether proposed wage increases should be pursued in the national interest. Acting General Secy. Harold Nicholas of the Transport & General Workers Union said Sept. 5 that union leaders opposed the government plan as "quite unnecessary" and "interference with the normal negotiating rights of the unions." The TUC voted at its annual meeting in Brighton Sept. 8 to support the General Council's voluntary plan.

Prime Min. Harold Wilson defended his government's "unpopular" anti-inflation stand at a Labor Party meeting in Bristol Sept. 4, but 10 local party members Sept. 4 issued a leaflet expressing disillusionment with the government's policies. In his speech, Wilson proposed the creation of factory production committees to block such production hindrances as "overmanning, restrictive work rules, inefficient layout, outdated equipment and poor handling of materials." (U.S. Treasury Secy. Henry H. Fowler said Sept. 3 that Labor's stand against inflation "strengthens my confidence in both the short- and long-term outlook for the British economy.")

A 490-page White Paper entitled the "National Plan," published by the government Sept. 16, detailed a program under which Britain's economic production in 1970 would exceed 1964 output by 25%. The plan was prepared by the Department of Economic Affairs after consultation with industry and unions. The National Plan envisaged an £8 billion ($22.4 billion) increase in the national product. £1.5 billion of this increase would be added to industrial investment and £500 million used to offset the balance-of-payments deficit. The remaining £6 billion ($16.8 billion) would be divided between personal spending and "social developments." The proposed output increase would require a yearly economic real (stable price) growth rate of 3.8% and a productivity increase per worker (because of the slow growth of the British labor force) of 3.4%, some 20% higher than had been achieved in recent years.

As further means of reversing Britain's balance-of-payments deficit, the plan set a target of a 5.25% average annual increase in exports, and it proposed restrictions on foreign aid and defense spending abroad. Imports, which grew 5% annually in the decade 1954-64, were seen growing at a rate of 4% annually through 1970. Export growth in 1954-64 was only 3% annually. The plan also called for a 7% annual increase in manufacturing investment.

A major objective of the National Plan was to improve the regional and social balance in the use of the country's resources. The White Paper pointed to the need for large-scale labor movements because of increased labor requirements in engineering, construction, public administration and education. It estimated that a 200,000-man labor shortage would remain after transfers of 600,000 from shrinking industries and a growth in the labor force of 400,000. The plan called on labor unions to give up make-work and feather-bedding practices.

The White Paper reaffirmed the government's February decision to limit the growth of public spending to 4.25% yearly. It announced plans to limit defense spending to £2 billion ($5.6 billion) by 1969-70, as opposed to earlier plans for increasing such outlays to £2.4 billion ($6.72 billion). The National Plan proposed no compulsory controls. It was described as "an attempt at democratic planning."

British output rose by approximately 2.5% during 1965. The rate of growth slowed appreciably during the last quarter, however, despite a rise in exports during the entire 2d half of the year.

Steel Nationalization

The House of Commons had approved by 310-306 vote May 6 a government White Paper as "a basis for legislation" to nationalize 85%-90% of the steel industry. The full labor vote was mustered for the crucial proposal, and all 10 Liberal members of Parliament joined the Conservatives in voting against it. The White Paper, issued Apr. 30, proposed that nationalization be effected by vesting in a "National Steel Corporation" (NSC) all shares and securities (with minor exceptions) of 14 major companies. 210 other companies with annual production work of £200 million ($560 million)—10%-15% of the total national output—would remain in private hands. Compensation to holders of securities of nationalized properties would be based on stock exchange values. The price of each share would be calculated on the basis of either (a) the average price during the period Oct. 1959-Oct. 1964 or (b) the average price during the period May-Oct. 1964. Either formula would mean a price nearly 30% above the current market price. The cost of such compensation was estimated Apr. 30 at £550 million ($1.54 billion) by Treasury Financial Secy. Jack Diamond.

The White Paper listed these objectives of the steel nationalization plan: (1) to insure the best use of the industry in accordance with the national interest; (2) to expand the export market and render it more competitive; (3) to achieve central planning of investment programs.

At least 2 votes—and possibly the margin of victory—were won for the government at the end of the debate prior to the balloting. Economic Affairs Min. George Brown said: "In my view nothing short of 100% [government] ownership will do. . . . [But]if the industry and its friends in the Tory party will come to us and say they are prepared for the government to assume control, we would of course listen to what they had to say." Woodrow L. Wyatt, a Labor MP who opposed 100% government ownership but agreed to "complete [government] control," had planned to abstain in the vote. After Brown's apparent concession, Wyatt and his "rebel" colleague Desmond Donnelly backed the White Paper.

Iain MacLeod, the Conservative floor leader, had pledged during the debate that "if the industry is nationalized. we will de-nationalize it."

Brown repeated in a May 7 statement: "If the industry can produce proposals by which complete public control can be achieved with the government taking over less than 100% of the shareholdings, then the government is prepared to listen to them." 3 leftwing Labor MPs, Ian Mikardo, Michael Foot and Tom Driberg, criticized Brown May 7 for the concession. But the chief spokesman for the Iron & Steel Federation, E. T. Judge, said his group was "interested in discussions" if the government was prepared to listen.

Political Developments & Challenges

The House of Commons Feb. 2 had given Prime Min. Harold Wilson a 306-289 vote of confidence after he had presented plans to abandon 2 types of military aircraft scheduled for production (the P-1154 vertical take-off fighter and the HS-681 transport) and to take other measures aimed at bolstering Britain's economy. He delayed a final decision on the controversial TSR-2 attack-bomber. Wilson said it cost far too much to develop expensive modern planes, of which Britain needed a relatively small number. A solution, he suggested, would be cooperative development projects with the U.S., France or other allies. Wilson said the government would introduce legislation to restrict corporate mergers and would propose harsher laws against monopoly and price fixing. He announced the naming of a royal commission, headed by Lord Donovan, 66, a judge, to look into Britain's labor-management relations law with a view toward "accelerating the social and economic advance of the nation."

The Defense Ministry had announced Jan. 26 that it would have to scrap all its Valiant bombers. The planes had been in service for 9 years, and their structure was said to have been drastically weakened by metal fatigue.

Wilson won a narrow 306-301 vote of confidence in Commons Feb. 9 after Aviation Min. Roy Jenkins had declared: "Whether we like it or not, the all-British plane is out.... We are at the end of the road in the production of complicated weapons systems for an exclusively British market." In the debate, ex-Conservative Defense Min. Peter Thorneycroft suggested that the U.S. might be "dumping" F-111s in Britain in a move to kill off the British aircraft industry.

Ex-Prime Min. Sir Alec Douglas-Home, leader of the opposition Conservative Party, named the following shadow cabinet Feb. 16: Ex-Chancellor of the Exchequer Reginald Mauldling, foreign secretary, succeeding R. A. Butler, who had retired from politics to take a life peerage (as Baron Butler of Saffron Walden of Halstead); (shadow) Economy Min. Edward Heath to the additional post of treasury and home affairs; Iain MacLeod, retained as steel minister; Peter Thorneycroft as home secretary, replacing Sir Edward Boyle, who became education and science minister; Christopher Soames, a son-in-law of the late Sir Winston Churchill, defense; Quintin Hogg, special duties; Anthony Barber, trade, replacing Edward du Cann, who had been appointed a party chairman; Sir Martin Redmayne to replace Soames as agriculture minister; Sir Peter Rawlinson to replace Redmayne as communications minister.

Conservatives retained a Commons seat in a by-election May 7 in the Hall Green, Birmingham constituency. Reginald E. Eyre was elected to the seat previously held for 15 years by Conservative MP Aubrey Jones, who had resigned to head the National Incomes & Prices Board.

The Conservative Party gained 562 seats and lost 10 in British municipal elections May 13. The Labor Party lost at least 419 seats and gained only 45. Liberal candidates lost 213 and gained 39. Independent groups lost 73, gained 70. The Communists lost one and made no gains.

Sir Alec Douglas-Home, 62, resigned July 22 as Conservative leader. He was succeeded in the leadership July 28 by Edward Heath, 49, former Lord Privy Seal, who had led Britain's unsuccessful negotiations in 1962-3 for admission to the European Common Market. Heath, economics minister in the Conservative shadow cabinet, was elected to the leadership unanimously by Conservative MPs July 28 after his 2 opponents—Reginald Maudling, 48, and ex-Health Min. Enoch Powell, 53—quit the race before the 2d ballot. Both candidates withdrew for the sake of party unity. (First ballot results: Heath 150 votes, Maudling 133, Powell 15.) Heath was the first Conservative leader to win his post by election; previous Tory leaders had been chosen by their predecessors. Home said in his resignation announcement July 22 that he had decided to quit because "a considerable number of people felt another leader might be better able to win a general election." (Home, who had relinquished his title of Earl of Home in 1963 in order to become prime minister, said that he did not want to resume his title.)

In his first act as leader of the opposition, Edward Heath introduced in the House of Commons Aug. 2 a motion to censure the Labor government for its handling of the nation's economy. The motion was defeated by 303-290 vote with the 10 Liberal Party members abstaining.

(In a by-election July 22 in the Hove constituency, the Conservatives retained a seat vacated by Anthony Marlowe because of ill health. Standings of the parties: Labor 316 seats, Conservatives 303, Liberals 10.)

The Pound Is Stabilized

The "rescue" of the pound undertaken in 1964 by the International Monetary Fund (IMF) and 11 Western European and North American nations restored stability at least temporarily and made it unnecessary to devalue the pound during 1965. Pressures driving the market value of the pound below $2.80 had disappeared, and "the spot [market] rate [remained]...clearly above par for about 2 months," the IMF reported Dec. 3. The British bank rate was reduced from its 7% high to 6% in early June.

The finance ministers of the 6 EEC nations had agreed in Cannes, France May 4 to a program for bolstering the British pound. Under the program, Britain would borrow in late May about $900 million from the IMF and about $500 million from the General Agreement to Borrow, a pool financed from the Group of 10 (Belgium, Britain, Canada, France, Germany, Italy, Japan, Sweden, the Netherlands and the U.S.), although managed by the IMF. This loan, drawn May 12, raised total British borrowing from the IMF (including the "pool") to $2.4 billion. The price of the pound and London stock market prices rose after the Bank of England announcement at 2 p.m. The price of the pound, which had been $2.7919 in the morning, rose to $2.7938 after the announcement, and closed at $2.7941. When the London market opened Monday, Sept. 13, the pound was quoted at $2.7969. The New York rate rose from $2.7944 Friday, Sept. 10, to $2.7970 Monday, Sept. 13.

The Bank of England disclosed Dec. 4 in its quarterly report that it had also drawn its entire $750 million credit with the U.S. Federal Reserve Bank plus an additional $140 million from the U.S. Treasury during June-August to strengthen the pound in international money markets. The bank and the U.S. Treasury said the $140 million had been repaid. The bank said it had made repayments in October and November to the Federal Reserve Bank, but it did not disclose the amounts. The reciprocal borrowing agreement between the Federal Reserve and the Bank of England had been increased in Nov. 1964 to $750 million and had been followed by an IMF/10-nation agreement in Dec. 1964 to support the pound. The EEC agreement was essential since the 6 EEC members (West Germany, France, Italy, Belgium, the Netherlands and Luxembourg) were to contribute much of the IMF money for Britain.

Britain planned to use about half of the expected $1.4 billion total as an emergency reserve to guarantee the stability of the pound at its $2.80 international exchange rate. The other half was to be used to repay the $700 million that Britain had borrowed thus far from the central banks of 11 nations that Nov. 25, 1964 had pledged as much as $3 billion in credit to bolster the pound.

The Bank of England Sept. 10 announced a new 10-nation agreement to support the pound. Details of the accord were not disclosed. The countries involved were the U.S., Austria, Belgium, Canada, West Germany, Holland, Italy, Japan, Sweden and Switzerland. The Bank for International Settlements (BIS) also participated, but France, which had joined a similar agreement in Nov. 1964, did not take part in the current arrangement. The 10-nation deal had been negotiated Sept. 3-4 at the BIS in Basle, Switzerland at a meeting of central bank presidents; Pres. Alfred Hayes of the Federal Reserve Bank of New York represented the U.S.

British Chancellor of the Exchequer James Callaghan said at a press conference in London Sept. 10 that "the importance of the [undisclosed] measures is that they should scare off speculators and others who have been banking on pound devaluation." "This is a movement from strength and not from weakness," Callaghan declared. "This distinguishes it from other operations we have had to embark on during the last 12 months."

U.S. Treasury Secy. Henry H. Fowler, in London on the last stop of a European trip, told newsmen Sept. 10: "The new initiative should be looked upon as a further development of cooperation between monetary authorities of the free world. It is desired to strengthen sterling, on which the monetary system rests."

The pound rose Nov. 2 to a 2 1/2-year high of $2.8047 on the London exchange. The pound Sept. 29 had risen above parity ($2.80) for the first time since May 1964. The Sept. 29 closing: $2.8003.

Balance of Payments & Reserves

Britain's balance of payments improved as the deficit dropped from the £763 million ($2.136 billion) current and long-term deficit of 1964 to a figure of £357 million ($1 billion) for 1965. Much of the improvement was explained by the rising foreign capital investment in Britain, attracted by the high interest rates pegged to the 6% bank rate. Foreign investment in Britain by the end of 1965 amounted to $25 billion, $10 billion of which was in portfolio investment and $15 billion in long-term projects. While this capital inflow (net of £3 million for the 2d quarter vs. a net loss of £89 million during the first quarter) strengthened reserves, it also imposed long-term repayment obligations on the productivity of the British economy.

The gold and convertible currency reserve position improved steadily during the year. By the end of October it had reached a level of £1.026 billion ($2.873 billion), the highest level since May 1963, and the total at the end of the year was £1.073 billion ($3 billion). These increases reflected both the inflow of foreign capital investment and loans from the IMF and other sources.

Britain's gold and convertible currency reserves rose in December by $16,800,000 to a total of $3,004,400,000. This was the first time British reserves had topped $3 billion since mid-1961.

Domestic inflationary pressures threatened to endanger the reserve and balance of payments positions. Both wage rates and prices rose despite the government's Feb. 11 announcement of plans to establish price and wage review boards to offset inflation. A White Paper warned that "other [anti-inflation] methods" would have to be used if voluntary compliance failed.

COMMON MARKET

France, the Agricultural Issue & Unity

The EEC Council of Ministers met in Brussels June 28-30 to discuss measures for financing the EEC's agricultural program after July 1. (Temporary regulations covering the financing of the EEC's interim agricultural program expired at midnight June 30.) At 2 a.m. July 1 French Foreign Min. Maurice Couve de Murville, presiding as chairman of the Council, adjourned the meeting unilaterally and announced that no agreement had been reached. The meeting's failure left the EEC without an agricultural finance program. The French government, which had demanded a settlement of the agricultural finance problem by the June 30 deadline, began an immediate boycott of the Common Market institutions, bringing to a halt action on all EEC political and economic matters currently under discussion.

The French boycott created the most serious problem faced by the EEC in its 8-year history, and involved basic issues beyond the agricultural problem level. The dispute centered on the question of economic cooperation vs. integration, and the disputants were EEC Executive Commission Pres. Walter Hallstein and 5 of the EEC members vs. France and French Pres. Charles de Gaulle. The rejection of Britain's application for EEC membership in 1963 had widened the gulf between these 2 factions, and the agricultural policy question—a simple issue of the length of an interim farm subsidy arrangement—brought this clash to the stage where a solution became vital.

The EEC Council of Ministers Dec. 15, 1964 had reached an agreement setting common agricultural (cereal) prices effective July 1, 1967. France, the major EEC wheat producer, feared lower prices and lost export markets (especially in other EEC countries). The "Mansholt plan" (proposed by Dr. Sicco Mansholt of the Netherlands and adopted Nov. 4, 1963) called for a reduction of grain prices in West Germany, Luxembourg and (for some grains) Italy, which would depress farm income, and an increase in (most) grain prices in France, the Netherlands and (for some grains) Italy, which would raise farm income but also raise overall prices in an inflationary manner. German, Luxembourg and Italian farmers would be compensated for lost income from an EEC fund. France objected on the ground that this would be an interference in the EEC's goal of a free economic community.

West German Chancellor Ludwig Erhard and de Gaulle had conferred Jan. 19-20 at de Gaulle's Chateau of Rambouillet, southwest of Paris, on such problems as political unification of Western Europe, German reunification and West Germany's role in Western nuclear defense. French Foreign Min. Couve de Murville and West German Foreign

Min. Gerhard Schroeder had met simultaneously in Paris—both separately and with Erhard and de Gaulle. The West German embassy in Paris said in a statement Jan. 20, after the discussions had concluded, that the 2 leaders had agreed that "the moment has come to proceed to a new study of the problems of political cooperation in Europe." The other governments of the European Common Market—Italy, Belgium, the Netherlands and Luxembourg—were to be asked to join France and West Germany in discussions "at various levels on a political treaty." Erhard and de Gaulle were said to "hope in the most sincere manner to find among their partners a conception corresponding to that which animates themselves." It had been reported Jan. 8 that de Gaulle had written Erhard of his fervent hope that the Dec. 15, 1964 European Common Market grain price agreement would give added impetus to West European unity. Erhard said late Jan. 20, just before flying back to Bonn, that the talks had been "crowned with success. . . . Positive results were achieved in numerous very important fields. . . . After this meeting I can say that on both sides—Gen. de Gaulle and myself—our opinion agreed."

At his press conference Feb. 4, de Gaulle said, with respect to European unity, that "the 6 nations which, let us hope, are in the process of establishing the economic community of Western Europe, must succeed in organizing themselves in the political domain as well as in that of defense, in order to make a new equilibrium possible on our continent. Europe, the mother of modern civilization, must establish herself from the Atlantic to the Urals in harmony and cooperation."

The EEC's 6 farm ministers agreed Feb. 24 on a list of common 1965-6 farm prices for beef, veal and milk. A common protective system for fruit and vegetable growers also was adopted. French Farm Min. Edgard Pisani explained that the ministers had agreed in Brussels on special compensatory levies from non-member countries equal to the difference between a community reference price and prices at which fruit and vegetables went into the community. The tax calculation was to be based on transport costs, and the reference price on the average of the EEC market prices for the previous 3 years (excluding abnormal years). West German Agriculture State Secy. Rudolph Huettebrauker had objected Feb. 22 to Pisani's suggestion that a common system of prices for beef products be set by Apr. 1. But agreement was reached Feb. 24 on a common farm price plan.

Italian Foreign Min. Amintore Fanfani was reported Mar. 18 to have suggested that the foreign ministers of the 6 EEC countries hold a political unity meeting in Venice in May. French Foreign Min. Couve de Murville conferred with Fanfani in Rome Mar. 27-29 and reportedly agreed in principle that a unity meeting would be desirable but rejected a spring date on the ground that there was insufficient evidence of agreement among the EEC nations on goals and means for achieving European political unity.

De Gaulle insisted Mar. 31 that talks on political "cooperation" among the EEC nations could take place only if there were a favorable outcome to EEC negotiations on common prices for farm products. A government statement following a French cabinet meeting called "co-operation" talks "necessary." It said a conference of the chiefs of state of the 6 nations would be "opportune" as soon as the Brussels discussions currently being conducted, "especially on the subject of agriculture," had been favorably decided. It indicated that a meeting of foreign ministers would be a wise measure as a preliminary to a top-level conference.

Couve de Murville, moving to block a grant of some supranational powers to the European Parliament, offered June 15 to pay for the anti-supranationality action by accepting an expensive 2-1/2-year delay in French plans for a common European market in farm products. Couve de Murville made his proposal in Brussels at a meeting of the EEC Council of Ministers. Negotiations for establishing the EEC farm market had been under way in the EEC Council in Brussels since Apr. 1, when the EEC Executive Commission, headed by Walter Hallstein, submitted proposals for fundamental changes in the financing of EEC's agricultural program. It was planned that the proposals would go into effect July 1 to finance EEC farm policy through June 30, 1967. Under the original regulations for financing a common EEC agricultural policy, adopted in 1962 and due to expire June 30, the 6 member states had been collecting import levies separately and then paying national assessments into a fund established by the EEC to finance its farm program. Under the commission's new proposals, import levies would be paid directly to the EEC fund, and budgetary control of the fund would be assumed by the European Parliament, which until 1965 had had a purely consultative role. To avoid this additional step toward supranationality, Couve de Murville proposed to the EEC Council June 15 that complete control of agriculture in the 6 nations be delayed from July 1, 1967, the date previously backed by France, until the end of 1969, the date scheduled by the Rome treaty, under which the EEC had been founded. His proposal actually was that current EEC agricultural financing arrangements be continued through 1969.

It was estimated that this French blow against supranationality might cost France's farm economy $1 billion during the 2-1/2 years that the common farm market would be delayed; France, as the lowest-cost producer of the EEC, stood to gain the most by early free farm trade within the EEC. The French action was criticized by Hallstein, who told the European Parliament in Strasbourg June 17 that Europe needed to speak with a single voice but not one of a nation "imposing its hegemony."

The June 15 French proposal called for the adoption of an agricultural finance plan covering the rest of the EEC's "transitional" period, from July 1, 1965 through Dec. 31, 1969, the date established by the EEC's founding Treaty of Rome for final elimination of all agricultural and industrial customs duties among member states and completion of the EEC's uniform external tariff system.

Under the French plan, the EEC's farm finance program during the rest of the transitional period would be based on a continuation of the temporary program adopted Jan. 14, 1962 to cover the period to June 30, 1965. The temporary program had established the European Agricultural Guidance & Guarantee Fund (EAGGF) to finance these major EEC farm programs: (1) EEC purchase of surplus farm products; (2) export subsidies for sales of EEC farm products to non-EEC countries at world prices. (World agricultural prices generally were lower than farm prices within the 6-nation community.) During the period covered by the temporary regulations, the fund had covered a progressively larger proportion of the above costs—1/6 in the year July 1, 1962 to June 30, 1963, 1/3 in 1963-4 and 1/2 in the year ending June 30, 1965. The remaining portion of these costs was paid by each EEC state directly to its own agricultural producers. The fund, during the 1962-5 period, was supported by direct yearly contributions from EEC members. The amount each member paid was determined by 2 factors: (1) 80% of the total was obtained by flat percentage rates set for each EEC member (28% for France, 28% for Germany and 28% for Italy). (2) The remaining 20% paid into the fund was divided among the 6 in proportion to each one's share of net EEC agricultural imports from outside sources.

The temporary regulations also included a system of import "levies," tariff-like payments imposed on agricultural imports from non-EEC nations. The levy on each imported product was equivalent to the difference between the world price of the product and its (generally higher) price on the internal market of the importing EEC nation. The regulations stipulated that levies be paid into the national treasuries of the 6 through June 30, 1965. After Jan. 1, 1970, according to the 1962 agreement, agricultural levies would be paid directly into the common EEC fund.

Under France's June 15 proposal for extending the temporary regulations to cover the 4-1/2 years remaining before the application of the final EEC farm program (Jan. 1, 1970), the fund would continue to assume additional sixths of the cost of the EEC's farm programs each year and would cover 100% of the costs by July 1, 1967. (By 1967-8, according to an estimate by the EEC Commission, the fund's expenditures would reach $1.3 billion.) According to the French plan, agricultural levies on imports from non-EEC sources would increasingly replace national contributions as the fund's principal source of income until 1970, when levies would replace the flat percentages entirely. (France, as the EEC's major agricultural producer and exporter, was the principal beneficiary of the temporary regulations. Under its proposal for extending the 1962 EEC agreement through 1969, France would increasingly benefit from the reduction of national contributions and the rise of levies as the fund's source of support. France's net receipts from the fund had been $13.8 million in 1962-3, $28 million in 1963-4 and $60.5 million in the year ending July 1, 1965, far greater than the receipts of any other EEC state.

Opposition to the French proposal was led by Italian Foreign Min. Fanfani. Fanfani proposed to the council June 30 that the EEC fund export subsidies be suspended for a year beginning July 1. He also requested a 2-year standstill on the progressive replacement of national contributions to the fund by levies. Italy, he said, would not agree to agricultural regulations lasting more than 2 years. Dutch Foreign Min. Joseph M. A. H. Luns supported the Italian demand for a finance plan to cover no more than a 2-year period. (Italy had hoped to benefit from the temporary finance plan adopted in 1962 by receiving more in export subsidies than it would pay to the EEC fund. But since 1962 Italian farm imports from non-EEC sources had increased, while its exports of olive oil, fruits and vegetables were not yet eligible for EEC subsidies. Italy's net payments into the fund had risen from $9.6 million in 1962-3 to $57.2 million in 1964-5.)

The council also had before it a series of EEC Executive Commission proposals that covered not only the question of agricultural finance but went beyond it and were intended to advance the supranational aspects of the EEC. The commission, in response to a council request for an interim agricultural finance program covering the mid-1965 to 1969 period, had submitted such a plan Apr. 1. Its proposal called for advancing the date on which the EEC would assume full control over the 6 nations' agricultural policy from Jan. 1, 1970 to July 1, 1967. On that date the EEC fund would cover all costs of the EEC's agricultural program, all levies on farm imports would go directly to the fund, and the levies would completely replace national contributions as the fund's source of financing. (The commission had submitted to the council Oct. 2, 1964 a proposal, entitled "Initiative 1964," calling for a speed-up in all phases of the Common Market system. Under this proposal, the date for removal of all agricultural and industrial customs among the members as well as the establishment of the uniform external tariff was to be advanced from Jan. 1, 1970 to July 1, 1967. This proposal was still before the council at its June 30 meeting. The commission's Apr. 1 proposal for agricultural finance was geared to "Initiative 1964" in that the EEC would assume full control over the 6 nations' agricultural policies on the same day [July 1, 1967] that the customs union among them was complete.) The commission linked its Apr. 1 proposal to its program for increasing the supranational aspects of the EEC. It suggested that, beginning July 1, 1967, a percentage of all custom duties on industrial imports from non-EEC nations should be paid directly to the EEC treasury. By 1972, the commission proposed, 100% of these customs should go directly to the EEC. These customs duties, added to the agricultural levies, would give the EEC a source of financing that would make it independent of the annual contributions of member states. The commission also proposed Apr. 1 that the EEC Parliamentary Assembly be given powers to control the Common Market's financing activities.

The EEC commission's proposal to advance by 2-1/2 years the establishment of the community's permanent agricultural finance program offered financial advantages to France that were estimated by observers to amount to $1 billion in the 2-1/2-year period starting July 1, 1967. But Foreign Min. Couve de Murville opposed the commission's plan at the June 15 meeting of the EEC Council, the session at which he presented France's counter-proposals for extending the temporary agricultural regulations through the rest of the transitional period. In the French view, the supranational aspects of the commission's plan were unacceptable. Couve de Murville explained the French position before the French National Assembly June 16: "In our view,...[the EEC Parliamentary] Assembly should...remain within the limits of the role which is given to it by the Treaty of Rome, that is to say, a consultative role which...can also be important and useful." (As for the commission's proposal that members' customs collections be paid to the community after July 1, 1967, Couve de Murville said that the plan, "which would now allocate to the community receipts which would far exceed its annual expenditures..., is an entirely abnormal decision in whose favor no serious reason has been brought forth." The commission had estimated community expenditures for 1967 at $1.237 billion and receipts from levies and customs duties at $2.3 billion. According to the commission's Apr. 1 proposal, the EEC Council would decide, on the basis of commission proposals, to what purposes this surplus would be put.)

The commission's proposals to strengthen the supranational character of the EEC were backed at the June 28-30 Brussels meeting of the council by Italian Foreign Min. Fanfani, West German Foreign Min. Schroeder and Netherlands Foreign Min. Luns. (The Dutch Parliament Feb. 2 had unanimously adopted a resolution calling for control of the EEC's budget by the Parliamentary Assembly. The West German Bundestag June 30 had approved a motion urging added powers for the Parliamentary Assembly.) The 3 ministers, together with EEC Commission Pres. Hallstein, opposed Couve de Murville's demand for an agreement on agricultural financing arrangements by midnight June 30. The 3 and Hallstein contended that an agreement could be reached but that more time was needed. Luxembourg Premier Pierre Werner attempted to compromise the opposing positions. Only Belgian Foreign Min. Paul-Henri Spaak supported the French view that an

agricultural finance program was required by June 30; the supranational issues, he said, could be discussed later. Couve de Murville
adjourned the meeting early July 1 after it became clear that the 2
groups had not been able to resolve their differences within the time
limit demanded by France.

De Gaulle had visited Bonn June 11-12 for discussions with West
German Chancellor Erhard. Their talks ended in disagreement over
France's insistence on a June 30 deadline, later abandoned in Brussels,
for concluding an accord on establishing a common farm market. De
Gaulle made the agricultural agreement a condition for a 6-nation
heads-of-state meeting, desired by Erhard, to discuss European political
integration. At the de Gaulle-Erhard meeting, one of the semi-annual
consultations under the French-West German Treaty of Cooperation,
West German press chief Karl Gunther von Hase announced June 12
that de Gaulle and Erhard had agreed to recommend to the other 4 EEC
members that the proposed EEC heads-of-state meeting be held before
the end of 1965. Shortly after this announcement, French Premier
Georges Pompidou declared that such a meeting was no more than a
"possibility not to be excluded." Until Pompidou's statement, it had
appeared that the meeting had been more fruitful than had been
expected. In discussions with West German Finance Min. Rolf
Dahlgrun and Economics Min. Kurt Schmuecker, French Finance Min.
Valery Giscard d'Estaing was reported to have indicated France's
willingness to make concessions in trade, taxation and industrial policies
in return for the early uniform agricultural regulations desired by
France. West German Defense Min. Kai-Uwe von Hassel and French
Defense Min. Pierre Messmer conferred about increasing meetings on
tactics and strategy by French and German military institutes and the
joint development of computers for use on French and German
warships.

The French government June 14 eased its opposition to a heads-of-
government meeting by announcing that it would attend "if the time is
right."

The French cabinet met in Paris July 1, with de Gaulle presiding,
to discuss the failure of the Brussels meeting. After the session, Information Min. Alain Peyrefitte read a cabinet statement saying the government had "decided for its part to draw the political, economic and
judicial consequences of the situation now created." Explaining the
cabinet's decision, Peyrefitte said: "Everything is at a standstill. No new
meetings are presently scheduled in Brussels." Peyrefitte added that
France was considering whether or not to seek a return to the EEC
internal tariff levels of 1961, an action that would raise them from the
current 40% to 70% of the levels in force in 1957, before the EEC's
Rome Treaties went into effect.

Pompidou said July 2, in a speech in Vannes, France, that "whatever may be the future of the Common Market, whatever may be the problems presented to French farmers,... the farmer will not meet the cost of possible failures by our partners to meet their obligations." Peyrefitte announced in Paris July 7 that France had granted its farmers new subsidies.

Paris announced July 6 that its permanent representative at the EEC headquarters in Brussels, Jean-Marc Boegner, had been "invited" to return to Paris and that "for the moment" France no longer would take part in the EEC Council meetings. The announcement was part of a statement issued July 6 in Brussels by the secretariat of the EEC Council after a meeting between Christian Calmes, secretary general to the council and Maurice Ulrich, Boegner's deputy. According to the statement, Ulrich was to remain in Brussels to run the French mission, but he was not to attend meetings of the 6 permanent representatives to the EEC. Since all EEC Council decisions required unanimous approval of the 6 during the Common Market's 2d stage, ending Dec. 31, 1965, Brussels observers expressed the view that a French boycott of the EEC meetings would "freeze" the further economic and political integration of the EEC nations. (Boegner also served as France's representative to Euratom and the ECSC High Authority, based in Luxembourg.)

It was announced in Paris July 8 that French Industry Min. Michel Maurice-Bokanowski would not attend a meeting July 13 of the ECSC and that Finance Min. Valery Giscard d'Estaing would not attend a meeting of the 6 EEC finance ministers, scheduled to begin July 19 in Stresa, Italy, to discuss EEC monetary policy. French representatives announced in Brussels July 6 that they would not take part in discussions on EEC regulations on fruits and vegetables. Other French officials boycotted EEC meetings held July 5 on the negotiation of a treaty linking Tunisia with the community and July 6 on the preparation of the EEC position in the Kennedy Round GATT tariff reduction talks scheduled to resume in Geneva Sept. 16. A technical meeting of EEC agricultural ministers, scheduled for July 12, was cancelled after a July 2 Brussels meeting at which Boegner apparently informed the 5 other EEC envoys that France would not take part.

Pres. Hallstein of the EEC Executive Commission told newsmen in Brussels July 1 that the commission would review the proposals on agricultural financing and other matters it had placed before the council. "The clock," he said, "should be stopped" at midnight June 30 and discussions should be resumed. Hallstein expressed hope that the next scheduled meeting of the council (July 26) would be held, but, he said, "I don't think there's a real chance of it."

Speaking in Duesseldorf July 8, Hallstein told a businessmen's group that a threat to the existence of the Common Market would be "the greatest destructive act in the history of Europe... since the days of Hitler." Ex-Chancellor Konrad Adenauer of West Germany told the same audience that the EEC deadlock was "an internal affair of the affected institutions and not a big political event."

The West German Bundestag's Foreign Affairs Committee July 2 gave unanimous approval to the position taken in Brussels by the German delegation at the EEC Council meeting. It did so after hearing a report from Foreign Min. Gerhard Schroeder, who had led the Bonn group in Brussels. Schroeder, speaking at a Christian Democratic Union meeting July 10 in Cologne, said it would be a "dangerous anachronism" if EEC members lapsed back into nationalistic policies. The Common Market, he said, would survive its current crisis in spite of France's "disappointing" action. Karl Gunther von Hase, West German government spokesman, had said in Bonn July 2 that Bonn hoped France "would take up an attitude hindering to crises and favorable to the EEC" before the July 26 EEC Council meeting.

Italian Pres. Giuseppe Saragat, in West Germany for a state visit, said in Bonn July 7: "We are convinced that the European nations, while keeping their individual tradition, must fuse into an economic and political unity."

The EEC Council of Ministers met July 26-27 in Brussels to discuss revised proposals on agricultural finance submitted by the EEC Executive Commission. The new proposals were designed primarily to satisfy France, which boycotted the council's July 26-27 meeting. (The French boycott had been announced July 6 after the council had failed at its June 30 meeting to adopt France's agricultural finance plan.) The revised proposals, made public July 27, had been submitted by the commission to the 6 EEC states July 22. French Premier Pompidou criticized the commission sharply July 27 in a French TV interview in which he made no mention of the commission's new proposals. The proposals, presented at the council's July 26 session by EEC Executive Commission Pres. Hallstein, included 2 major concessions to France: (a) The commission dropped its earlier plans under which the EEC would have had an independent revenue from industrial duties and agricultural levies beginning July 1, 1967 and control over the EEC's budget would be vested in the EEC Parliamentary Assembly. (b) The commission accepted the French proposal, made at the June 15 and June 30 council meetings, for the adoption of an agricultural finance plan to run from July 1, 1965 through Dec. 31, 1969. The commission also made concessions designed to meet Italian opposition, expressed at the June 30 council meeting, to an agricultural finance plan covering more than a 2-year period. The commission's new plan recommended that progress toward full EEC payment of agricultural export subsidies should be slowed if the EEC did not adopt, by Nov. 1, 1965, market regulations covering fruits, vegetables, fats and oils—all of which were large Italian export items not yet eligible for subsidies from the EEC agricultural fund.

Pompidou, in his TV interview July 27, reiterated France's position that the 6 governments had agreed in 1962 to the adoption, by June 30, 1965, of an agricultural finance plan covering the period July 1, 1965-Dec. 31, 1969. The Common Market had "placed..: French [industry]...in direct competition...with the powerful German industry", he said. "This could be tolerated only if it was compensated for by an agricultural common market, providing our agriculture with large outlets at remunerative prices, and thus enabling the state, largely released from the need for supporting our agriculture, to lighten the burdens borne by industry." In a direct criticism of the role of the EEC commission, he declared that France "cannot leave to a commission which has no political calling the task of determining the living standard of the French people and...the destiny of our agriculture and our industry."

Vice Chrmn. Sicco L. Mansholt of the EEC Executive Commission told newsmen after the July 26 council meeting that the EEC would be unable to meet the Sept. 16 deadline for agricultural proposals in the Kennedy Round tariff-cutting negotiations. (France had boycotted a July 12 Geneva meeting of underdeveloped and industrial countries [among them the EEC bloc] for preliminary talks on farm tariff cuts.) It was disclosed at the July 27 session of the council that France would continue to participate in EEC decisions on a number of minor matters. Antonio Venturini, the Italian representative, announced that France would review proposals the other 5 had agreed on for an increase in Dutch resin quotas, insurance against civil liability at the EEC atomic research center at Karlsruhe, West Germany and a budget for the EEC's Economic & Social Committee.

De Gaulle indicated at the Elysee Palace in Paris Sept. 9 that France would quit NATO by 1970. He also announced that France would end its boycott of EEC ministerial meetings only if France's EEC partners agreed to include an agricultural finance program within the framework of the EEC. Speaking at his 12th press conference since 1959, de Gaulle said France would continue to follow an independent foreign policy and would oppose further integration within the EEC or NATO. After 1969, he declared, France would no longer accept " 'integration'...provided for by NATO." (The 1949 NATO treaty provided that any member could withdraw after 1969 on one year's notice.) De Gaulle also discussed France's relations with Eastern Europe and the USSR, German reunification, the Vietnamese war, the UN dispute over peacekeeping assessments and international monetary reform, and he outlined the economic objectives of France's 5th Plan. De Gaulle said.

"What happened in Brussels on June 30 with regard to the agricultural financial regulation has brought to light not only the persistent reserves of most of our partners toward the inclusion of agriculture in the Common Market but also certain basic errors or ambiguities that appear in the treaties on the economic union of the 6. That is why, sooner or later, the crisis was inevitable . . . .

"I must add that in the light of this event, we more clearly measured the situation in which our country would risk finding itself if one provision or another initially provided for by the Rome Treaty were actually applied. Thus, in the terms of the text, the decisions of the Council of Ministers of the 6 would, beginning on Jan. 1, 1966, be taken by majority vote; in other words, France would be prepared to see her hand forced in any economic matter—therefore social and often even political—and, in particular, what would have seemed gained in the agricultural area could be, despite her, placed at stake again at any moment. In addition, from that time on, the proposals made by the Brussels commission would have to be adopted or not, as is, by the Council of Ministers, without the states being able to change anything, unless, miraculously, they were unanimous in drafting an amendment. Now, we know that the members of the commission, in the past appointed by agreement among the governments, are from now on in no way responsible [to the governments] and that, even at the end of their mandate, the unanimous consent of the 6 will be required to replace them, which, in fact, makes them irremovable. We see where we could be led by such a disposal of ourselves and of our constitution, which stipulates that 'French sovereignty belongs to the French people, which shall exercise it through its representatives and by means of referendum,' and makes no provision for any kind of exception. . . .

". . . The 3 treaties which respectively set up the ECSC [European Coal & Steel Community], Euratom and the Common Market were concluded before France's recovery in 1958. They therefore made allowance primarily for what the others requested. . . . The Treaty of Rome . . . fully governed the conditions for the industrial community that was the prime concern of our neighbors but in no way governed those for the agricultural common market, in which we were the most interested. . . . Each of the 3 treaties instituted . . . an executive in the form of a commission independent from the states . . . and . . . a legislature in the form of an Assembly bringing together the various parliaments, yet without their electors' [voters] having given them any mandate that was not national. This claim held by a technocracy, for the most part foreign, destined to infringe upon France's democracy in settling problems that dictate the very existence of our country, obviously could not suit our purposes once we were determined to take our destiny into our own hands.

"Who can ignore that the idea of grouping the states of Western Europe together from the economic and, I might add, political standpoints has long been ours? . . . That is why, for 7 years, we have very actively helped to build [the EEC]. . . . But, what we wanted yesterday and what we want today is a community that is fair and reasonable. Fair: that means that agricultural products . . . should be included . . . concurrently with industrial goods. Reasonable: that means that nothing which is important at present in the organization, and later in the operation of the 6, should be decided . . . except by the responsible public authorities in the 6 states, that is, the governments controlled by the parliaments.

"Now we know . . . there is a different concept of a European federation in which . . . the countries would lose their national personalities. . . . We know that France is opposing this project, which contradicts all reality, with a plan for organized cooperation among the states, evolving, doubtless, toward a confederation. This plan alone . . . could one day make possible the adherence of countries such as Britain or Spain, which, like ours, could in no way accept the loss of their sovereignty. It alone would make the future entente of all of Europe conceivable. . . .

". . . in Brussels on June 30, our delegation came up against a refusal with regard to final drafting of a financial regulation in accordance with the commitments made. . . . The commission [the EEC Executive Commission] . . . had formulated on the subject of this regulation conditions intended to give itself its own budget, . . . as much as $4 billion, . . . that would have made it literally a major independent financial power. It is true that, according to the authors [the Executive Commission] of this draft, this enormous budget . . . would be subject to examination by the European Assembly. But the intervention of this body, . . . essentially consultative . . , would only aggravate the usurpatory character of what was demanded. . . . [The] combination . . . of the supra-national demands of the Brussels' commission [and] . . . the support that several delegations declared themselves ready to give . . . forced us to bring the negotiations to a close.

". . . In the light of this event, we . . . measured the situation in which our country would risk finding itself if one provision . . . [of] the Rome Treaty were actually applied. Thus, in . . . the text, the decisions of the Council of Ministers of the 6 would, beginning Jan. 1, 1966, be taken by majority vote; in other words, France would . . . see her hand forced in any economic matter. . . . We see where we could be led by such a disposal of ourselves and of our constitution, which stipulates that 'French sovereignty belongs to the French people,' . . . and makes no provision for any kind of exception. . . .

". . . [France] is ready to participate in all exchanges of views. . . . If necessary, she envisages resuming the Brussels negotiations, once the inclusion of agriculture into the Common Market is truly adopted. . . ."

Foreign Min. Couve de Murville acted as spokesman for the de Gaulle position before the National Assembly Oct. 20. After de Gaulle's Sept. 9 press conference, the remaining 5 EEC members had begun to realize the significance of the French withdrawal. Couve de Murville reinforced this realization when, discussing economic over political European integration, he said: "That was the reason why, as early as 1960, France sought to organize among the members of this community a form of political cooperation capable of broad development. Finally, this was the scope of the Jan. 1963 French-German Treaty of Cooperation. . . . Political Europe is still pending. Only time, which always brings experience and consequently lessons, will make it possible to determine whether it is a matter of a mere delay. In the meantime, and doubtless to a large extent because the political aspect did not follow, economic Europe is now experiencing a crisis. I repeat, because the political aspect did not follow."

Information Min. Alain Peyrefitte said Oct. 21: "Gen. de Gaulle, M. Pompidou and the government have, once again, made it clear that France would cease to play an active part in the EEC if the common agricultural market were not organized as it had been agreed it should be organized. The resolution passed by the Council of Ministers [cabinet] was couched in the most categorical terms so that the common agricultural market would be recognized as the touchstone of European integration and indeed a *sine qua non* for such an aim. This should be regarded as a categorical reassertion of an attitude that France has always taken but as to the firmness of which some of our partners have entertained doubts."

Couve de Murville told the National Assembly Oct. 25: "The matter was very simple, but of major importance to France, for, without a financial regulation, the common agricultural policy no longer has any meaning, inasmuch as this policy is based on the establishment of European prices. In particular, it was an inevitable consequence of the decisions of Dec. 1964 on grain prices which were to stimulate the production of wheat and barley in France and consequently bring about growing surpluses which would have to be sold at world rates on foreign markets."

Ministers of 5 EEC nations Oct. 26 urged the 6th nation, France, to attend a special meeting of the EEC Council of Ministers to work out a solution to the impasse resulting from the French boycott of council meetings. The decision to invite France to return was taken at a regular session of the EEC council, held in Brussels Oct. 25-26. In their Oct. 26 communique, the 5 nations "solemnly reaffirmed the necessity to pursue the execution...[of the Common Market] with a view to realize...the fusion of their national economies." The communique said: The 5 nations were "convinced that the negotiations interrupted June 30[by the French boycott]must be begun again as rapidly as possible," and they invited France to attend an "extraordinary session of the Council of Ministers in Brussels"; this special meeting would not include the EEC Executive Commission (the Hallstein Commission); only the ministers of the 6 governments would attend; the purpose of the "extraordinary session" would be to "examine the general situation of the community"; the session should be held "as soon as possible."

The exclusion of the EEC Executive Commission from the proposed "extraordinary session" of the council had originally been proposed Sept. 27 by Belgian Foreign Min. Paul-Henri Spaak in a Brussels speech. The commission had been criticized by de Gaulle at his Sept. 9 press conference for its alleged supranational demands. French Premier Pompidou had said in an Oct. 14 radio-TV speech that France was "prepared to entertain...proposals made...by the governments of the other 5 countries." Maurice Couve de Murville, in a speech to the French National Assembly Oct. 20, indicated that the commission had caused the impasse by proposing "measures of a political character, the object of which was to transform profoundly the character of the community...by making itself a veritable political authority, less and less controlled by governments."

(At their Oct. 25-26 meeting the ministers of the 5 nations adopted the EEC Executive Commission's compromise plan on agricultural finance, first presented at the July 26 meeting of the 5 by Hallstein.

(At the annual session of the 142-member EEC Parliamentary Assembly, held in Strasbourg Sept. 24-Oct. 22, the Assembly Oct. 22 adopted a resolution calling on the 6 EEC governments to begin negotiations in Brussels as soon as possible. The resolution was adopted unanimously, but French delegates from the Union for the New Republic [Gaullist] party walked out of the Assembly before the vote was taken. The resolution had originally been proposed by a French delegate from the Popular Republican [MRP] party. The Assembly Sept. 24 had elected Victor Leemans, leader of the Belgian Social Christian Party in the Belgian Senate, as president for a renewable term of one year.)

Couve de Murville, before the French National Assembly Nov. 3, reiterated the French stand. Discussing the lag of EEC agricultural progress behind progress in the industrial sector, he said: "Should one file a suit for default and throw the whole of the community's future into the balance? All that I can say is that we shall see in Brussels how the talks progress not only as regards cereals but also dairy produce,

meat, the financial regulation and the regulations for products that still
have to be drawn up. In the meanwhile, it is advisable for France to act
in full cognizance of the risk of a break-up which the conduct of certain
partners forces us to regard as a possibility." After conferring with
British negotiator Edward Heath, Couve de Murville said Nov. 24:
"Gen. de Gaulle declared that 'there are a number of signs pointing to
the fact that former obstacles to a rapprochement between the United
Kingdom and continental Europe have now been removed. The problem
appears to be gradually maturing in a positive sense. This development,
should it become more clearly evident, would be favorably viewed by
France.' " De Gaulle told his cabinet the same day that "conditions
which, in the past, obstructed Britain's rapprochement with Europe are
in the process of weakening" and that France would view further
progress in this direction with "sympathy"; de Gaulle's remarks were
made public by Information Min. Peyrefitte.

The EEC Executive Commission Nov. 15 had published a report
on trends in agricultural trade of the 6 in 1958-64. According to the
report, France had benefitted more, proportionally, than any other
member state from the application of EEC regulations on agricultural
trade. French exports of products covered by the regulations to the
other 5 EEC nations had risen from $77,100,000 in 1958 to $426,900,000
in 1964. The Netherlands, largest exporter of products covered by the
EEC regulations, increased its exports of these items from $302 million
in 1958 to $579 million in 1964. The report confirmed that the 6 were
buying a larger proportion of agricultural products from other EEC
members than from non-EEC nations. EEC nations' agricultural
imports from each other rose from $636 million in 1958 to $1.471 billion
in 1964; imports from non-EEC nations rose from $2 billion in 1958 to
$2.7 billion in 1964.

The French government announced Dec. 22 that it would accept a
proposal for a meeting with the other 5 member states of the EEC in
Jan. 1966 to discuss all aspects of the current deadlock over the EEC's
financing and common farm market programs. The announcement was
made after a meeting of the French cabinet at which de Gaulle presided.
The offer, originally made Oct. 26, had been renewed at EEC council
meetings Nov. 29-30 and Dec. 20. Although the council meetings were
boycotted by France, the French deputy representative to the EEC,
Maurice Ulrich, attended a luncheon with the 5 other envoys Dec. 20.
Italian Treasury Min. Emilio Colombo, currently president of the EEC
Council, had conferred Dec. 9 in Rome with Couve de Murville on the
EEC impasse, and French Information Min. Peyrefitte told reporters
Dec. 15 that Couve de Murville had informed the French cabinet that he
believed the 6 foreign ministers would be able to meet jointly "in the
near future."

De Gaulle, in his annual year-end TV address Dec. 31, restated his independent foreign policy. While "rival hegemonies place numerous countries in tension," he declared, "... we are engaged nowhere and we do what is necessary not to be involved ... in any war that would not be ours." France, he said, was "able to resume the organization of the Common Market ... but under conditions which are equitable and reasonable and with the hope that on such a basis, other neighbors will join."

Other EEC & Related Developments

The European Common Market put its new 10% tariff reduction into effect Jan. 1. The cut brought EEC internal tariffs on most industrial products down to 30% of the average tariffs in effect among the 6 states when the trade group had begun operations Jan. 1, 1958. Agricultural goods tariffs were at the 45%-to-50% level, depending on the particular product.

Pres. Walter Hallstein of the EEC Executive Commission declared in a Frankfurt radio broadcast Jan. 6 that the trade zone's success had assured the first phase of European unification and that "nothing can stop the European federation if we retain patience and firmness of will." He said that the EEC's Dec. 15, 1964 agreement on a unified grain price had been crucial to Europe's eventual integration. He reported that during the EEC's 7 years of existence trade among the member nations had risen by 166% and their combined gross national product by 38%. "These are brilliant figures to which other economies have nothing comparable to offer," Hallstein asserted.

The EEC Executive Commission Jan. 13 approved a plan to eliminate industrial tariffs among the 6 member nations by mid-1967. Tariffs would be reduced an additional 10% Jan. 1, 1966 and the final 20% July 1, 1967. The original timetable had called for the complete dismantling of the industrial tariffs by 1970. (The EEC apparently decided to accelerate the program to keep pace with its competitor, the EFTA, which had decided to aim for free internal industrial trade by 1967.)

Hallstein, in a speech at the University of Kiel Feb. 19, appealed for European unity. He warned that the continued existence of national and economic frontiers in Europe was a "costly and suicidal luxury." "It is an elementary fact that frontiers in Europe are a mistake," he declared. "It does not make economic sense to split up a large coherent economic center such as Europe." He cited the separate cases of the U.S. and USSR, which, because of their individual unity, were "infinitely better off in this respect." Hallstein called the free movement of goods the backbone of the EEC. "In short, to free trade, it is by no means enough simply to open the frontiers," he declared. "On the contrary, extensive action will have to be taken by the community, embracing vital parts of fiscal, budgetary, economic and monetary policy."

Hallstein conferred with Pres. Johnson at the White House Mar. 18. According to a joint communique afterwards, "Pres. Johnson assured Dr. Hallstein of the continued strong support of the United States for the goal of European unity"; the 2 leaders "agreed that continued progress toward European integration strengthens the free world as European partnership with the United States grows closer." Hallstein told newsmen in the White House lobby that Mr. Johnson had "happily confirmed" that the "fundamental orientation" of the U.S. toward Europe remained strong. Hallstein called this a "basic point for Europeans."

Cabinet ministers of West Germany, France, Italy, Belgium, the Netherlands and Luxembourg agreed in Brussels Mar. 2 on a merger of the executive bodies of the European Community's 3 groups —EEC, ECSC and Euratom— effective Jan. 1, 1966. The agreement was viewed as a major step toward economic integration of the 6 nations and toward possible eventual political unity of Western Europe. The merger agreement called for the transfer of 1,500 ECSC staff workers from Luxembourg to a new central headquarters in Brussels. Luxembourg was to remain an administrative center, with the staff members of the 3 blocs' banking and legal institutions transferring there. Luxembourg had been the headquarters for the ECSC since its formation in 1951. The executive commissions of the EEC and Euratom had been headquartered in Brussels since their formation in 1958. The merger on an executive level opened the way for an increasing transfer of national sovereignty to the new executive organization by the 6 nations of the European Community. The merger treaty was signed by cabinet members of EEC member nations Apr. 8 in Brussels. (Ratification by the national parliaments of the 6 member nations still was required.)

The EEC also agreed Mar. 2 to begin negotiations with Austria, an EFTA member, on a treaty of association.

A common tax plan was presented by Pieter Verloren van Themaat, director general of the Tax Division of the EEC Executive Commission, at a meeting in Cannes, France May 3 of the central bankers and finance ministers of the EEC nations. The goal was to achieve, eventually, the same basic consumer tax rate in all 6 nations. This was part of a plan to coordinate the fiscal structures of the 6 nations.

The Action Committee for the United States of Europe, meeting in West Berlin with Jean Monnet of France presiding, urged European powers May 9 to proceed with the task of setting up an "equal and lasting partnership" with the U.S. It stressed the need to expand the European community to include foreign and defense policy. The committee, made up of European political and labor leaders, met on the 15th anniversary of the late Robert Schuman's proposal to pool European coal and steel industries (the idea that resulted in the European Coal & Steel Community). West German Chancellor Ludwig Erhard, who attended the committee meeting, declared May 9: "Only through a close union can Europe become strong, and peace can be secured—only by a strong and self-confident Europe in trustful alliance with its Atlantic partners."

The EEC's 142-member Parliament in Strasbourg May 10 called for increased trade with Communist countries, particularly in Eastern Europe. The Parliament approved a resolution urging Eastern Europe to adopt a "more realistic attitude" toward the EEC and asking for "a greater understanding by the community [EEC] of the problems and preoccupations of the countries with state-controlled trade [in Eastern Europe]."

The Consultative Assembly of the 18-nation Council of Europe held its autumn session in Strasbourg Sept. 28-Oct. 1. The major subject of debate, trade between East and West Europe, had also been the principal topic of the annual joint session of the EEC Parliamentary Assembly and the Council of Europe's Consultative Assembly, held in Strasbourg Sept. 24-25.

Negotiations for cutting world tariffs in farm commodities opened in Geneva Sept. 16 within the framework of the 79-nation General Agreement on Tariffs & Trade (GATT). The EEC, which previously had participated in GATT tariff-cutting sessions, was absent from the current session as a result of France's boycott of the EEC. At the opening session, the U.S., Britain, Argentina, Austria, Canada, Denmark, Finland, New Zealand, Sweden and Switzerland presented offers to reduce tariffs on certain agricultural items; all other GATT members failed to meet GATT's Sept. 16 deadline for presenting offers. GATT Executive Gen. Eric Wyndham White told reporters Sept. 17 that the countries that had presented offers Sept. 16 had restricted their offers to items that "in general excluded agricultural products of interest to the countries of EEC." He added that these countries would add to their lists when the EEC re-entered the Kennedy Round negotiations. An EEC spokesman in Geneva said Sept. 16 that "for reasons beyond its control" the EEC could not submit its offers but hoped it would be able to do so later. (Pres. Johnson said in an Oct. 13 message to Congress, written to accompany the Administration's Annual Report on the Trade Agreements Program: "We must make every effort to assure the success of the current Geneva negotiations,... the Kennedy Round"; U.S. exports in 1964 had reached a "new high" of $25.6 billion, $6.9 billion more than imports, and farm exports in 1964 were at an "all time high" of $6.4 billion.)

The EEC Council of Ministers, meeting without France, agreed Nov. 29 to set the EEC's budget at $41,600,000 for 1966. Euratom's research budget was fixed at $102 million. (The budget agreements were sent to the French government for approval.)

France Reelects de Gaulle

Charles de Gaulle, 75, was reelected president of France Dec. 19 by defeating leftist candidate Francois Mitterand in a runoff election. According to complete election returns, including returns from France's overseas territories, de Gaulle received 13,085,407 votes, or 55.2% of the valid ballots. Mitterand received 10,623,247 (44.8%). 661,791 ballots (2.34% of those in metropolitan France) were marked blank and were void. 23,864,586 (84.5%) of France's registered voters cast ballots, compared with the record 24,002,093 (85%) in the original balloting Dec. 5.

The runoff had been made necessary because, in a stunning political upset, de Gaulle had failed to obtain an absolute majority of votes when the original election was held Dec. 5. The runoff was then scheduled between de Gaulle and his closest competitor, Mitterand, who had campaigned on an independent leftist program and had received the indorsement of France's large Communist Party.

De Gaulle's failure to obtain a majority on the first ballot apparently surprised observers of virtually all political viewpoints. In mid-October, an opinion poll by the French Institute of Public Opinion had indicated that he would win about 68% of the vote. In announcing his candidacy, de Gaulle, in a nationwide radio-TV address Nov. 4, had asked the voters to give him a "frank and massive indorsement." Such a vote "would assure the future of the new republic indefinitely," he declared. Without it, "no one can doubt that she [the 5th Republic] will soon crumble and that France—this time without any hope of recourse— will be reduced to confusion more disastrous than she has ever known."

During the official original campaign period (Nov. 19-Dec. 3) the 5 opposition candidates were permitted equal time (4 hours) with de Gaulle on the state controlled radio-TV system. (Not counted in the equal time were talks by Gaullist ministers before or after the campaign began. For example, Finance Min. Valery Giscard d'Estaing Nov. 18 gave a radio-TV address on the healthy state of the French economy. Supporters of the opposition candidates could not use the state radio-TV system; as a result, ex-Premier Pierre Mendes-France, who backed Mitterand, twice debated former Gaullist Premier Michel Debre, who backed de Gaulle, from a Luxembourg radio station which could be heard in France. The radio-TV addresses by the 5 opposition candidates were taped in advance and submitted to a 5-man government commission before being cleared for broadcast.) De Gaulle had originally planned to make a single radio-TV address Dec. 3, the final night of the campaign. He decided, however, to speak Nov. 30, when it became apparent that 2 candidates, Mitterand and Sen. Jean Lecanuet, former head of the Popular Republican (MRP) party, were making a favorable impression on TV and opinion polls showed de Gaulle's percentage dropping.

Lecanuet, 45, a relative unknown before the election, conducted a vigorous campaign and became known as a "Kennedy"-type candidate. In his Nov. 25 TV address he declared: "Don't worry general, France will continue!" Throughout the campaign he sharply criticized de Gaulle's Common Market and NATO policies and opposed France's independent nuclear force. Mitterand, 49, a member of the small Democratic & Socialist Union (UDSR) party and 11 times a minister during the 4th Republic, also criticized de Gaulle's foreign policy. In a Bordeaux address Dec. 1, he said "education" and domestic economic progress were more important than an independent atomic weapons program. In a reference to charges that he would be controlled by the Communists, he pledged Dec. 1 that he would be "dominated by no single party, however friendly." The French Communist Party had endorsed Mitterand Sept. 23 in a central committee statement issued by party chief Waldeck Rochet. The declaration referred to Mitterand as the "sole candidate of the left" and termed its union with Mitterand a "popular front." Although no common program had been agreed on, the party said it backed Mitterand because he opposed "personal power" and was "acceptable to all democrats." The party, said Rochet, "takes it for granted that the Common Market exists."

De Gaulle, in his Dec. 3 TV address, made what were reported as concessions to the critics of his foreign policy. He pledged to work for the "economic union" of the Common Market, and he avoided all references to the anti-American stand he had taken in the Nov. 30 speech when he had spoken of U.S. "domination" in NATO and termed the Vietnamese war "absurd."

During the official runoff campaign period Dec. 11-17, de Gaulle and Mitterand spoke on radio and TV under equal-time regulations. De Gaulle changed his TV style from that used during the campaign for the first ballot by permitting himself to be interviewed on TV by a reporter. In what was reported as his first public statement about the problem of choosing his successor, de Gaulle said Dec. 15: "Naturally, a day will come... when de Gaulle will pass away"; France would then have to select a man "faithful to the line it has pursued at my calling." But he described himself as "still, for the moment, a national necessity," and he warned that repudiating him in favor of a "regime of the parties would be an immense disaster." In his final TV appeal (Dec. 17), he said: "I am not saying that I am perfect or that I am younger than my age. I know, better than anyone that I will have to have successors and that the nation will choose them so that he will follow the same line. But I am in the process of working to assure progress.... This is why I am ready to assume again the highest duty."

Mitterand Dec. 13 said de Gaulle's foreign policy was "anti-American with the Russians; anti-Russian with the Americans; anti-British with the Germans; anti-German with the British; anti-Chinese with the Russians, and anti-Russian—I want to stop here." He declared

Dec. 17 that he offered the voters a "fundamental choice between authoritarianism and a republic of citizens." "Who can pretend," he said, "that France is nothing without him [de Gaulle]?"

All the candidates eliminated on the Dec. 5 ballot (Lecanuet, Jean Louis Tixier-Vignancour, Sen. Pierre Marcilhacy and Marcel Barbu) opposed de Gaulle. Lecanuet urged his supporters Dec. 16 not to vote for de Gaulle, but he did not indorse Mitterand.

Mitterand conceded his defeat Dec. 19 about an hour after the polls closed. He said: "We are faced with a dying regime, a reborn Left and a republic which will be rejuvenated some day. When we see how shaky Gaullism is with de Gaulle, what will it be without de Gaulle? I shall resume the struggle against Gaullism tomorrow."

De Gaulle returned to Paris from his country home Dec. 21 and released a statement saying he had received "a direct mandate from the whole French people" that had "decidedly confirmed" his regime "before the nation and the world."

Other Developments Involving EEC Members

The West German Bundesbank (central bank) estimated Nov. 11 that West Germany's 1965 balance of payments would have a $1.75 billion deficit. The Bundesbank cited "surplus domestic demand" and a loss of "competitive ability" by German producers "in the domestic market itself, with importers often able to offer more favorable prices," as the main reasons for the deficit. (In 1964 West Germany had a payments surplus of $250 million.)

Amintore Fanfani, 57, resigned as Italian foreign minister Dec. 28 following the publication Dec. 27 in the rightwing weekly *Il Borghese* of an alleged interview between Giorgio La Pira, a friend of Fanfani who had been involved in a peace-feeler trip to Hanoi, and Mrs. Gianna Preda, editor of *Il Borghese*. The meeting between La Pira and Mrs. Preda took place Dec. 20 at the Rome apartment of Fanfani during a party given by Mrs. Fanfani while Fanfani was in New York in his capacity as president of the UN General Assembly. The article in *Il Borghese* said La Pira had: (a) Favorably compared Fanfani to French Pres. de Gaulle, expressed admiration for deceased dictator Benito Mussolini and criticized Italian Premier Aldo Moro as "sad and soft." (b) Said that Fanfani, who had been premier 4 times, would be a good successor to Moro as premier and that a Fanfani cabinet would include both Communists and neo-Fascists. (c) Said that U.S. State Secy. Dean Rusk "doesn't know anything" and that Pres. Johnson would have to accept peace in Vietnam because "the aggressive spirit of America" was declining. La Pira told reporters Dec. 27, after the article appeared, that he had talked openly and in jest to a "lady unknown to me." Mrs. Preda said La Pira was a "liar." Fanfani, in his Dec. 28 letter of resignation to Moro, said "unjust and unfounded considerations and judgments by a friend [La Pira] and an improvident initiative by a member of my family [Mrs. Fanfani] are wrongly or rightly creating doubts about the foreign minister's conduct, damaging his work and causing harm to the government as a result." Fanfani said he did not share La Pira's alleged views. He said he wanted his resignation to be effective Jan. 6, 1966 so that he could appear Jan. 5 before the Chamber of Deputies' Foreign Affairs Commission to defend his role in the peace-feeler attempt. After appealing unsuccessfully to Fanfani to stay on as foreign minister, Moro accepted his resignation Dec. 29. Moro Dec. 30 assumed interim control of the Italian Foreign Ministry.

Le Monde (Paris) had reported Mar. 8, 1966 that France in 1965 had a balance-of-payments surplus of $1.1 billion, up from previous surpluses of $786 million in 1964 and $924 million in 1963. France disposed of the surplus by: (1) repaying a $178 million debt to the U.S.' Export-Import Bank and thereby reducing its total foreign debt to $454 million from a 1958 total of $3.093 billion; (2) increasing by $360 million its reserves held by the Bank of France; (3) lending the IMF $560 million in francs to aid nations with payments problems.

BRITAIN, THE EEC & EFTA

Britain & the EEC

Contacts continued between both Britain and the European Free Trade Association (EFTA) on the one hand and the EEC on the other during 1965, although no significant progress was made regarding possible British membership in the EEC. Tentative support for Britain was expressed by U.S. Pres. Johnson in his Jan. 4 State-of-the-Union address. Mr. Johnson said, regarding Western European unity: "In the Atlantic community we continue to pursue our goal of 20 years—a Europe growing in strength, unity and cooperation with America.... This European policy is not based on any abstract design. It is based on the realities of common interests and common values, common dangers and common expectations. These realities will continue to have their way—especially in our expanding trade and our common defense."

British Foreign Secy. Michael Stewart insisted in a talk at a British Chamber of Commerce dinner in Brussels Feb. 11 that the British-led EFTA should be included in any European unity plans. Stewart said: "It would not serve the cause of European and Atlantic unity if important decisions affecting the political future of Europe were taken by a restricted group.... We regret that the latest proposals for such talks envisage the participation of the 6 European Economic Community countries only.... If these economic divisions [between the EEC and EFTA] persist, they will in time inevitably lead to political divisions. There are already signs of this.... We recognize, of course, the contribution which economic unity can make to political unity. But in international politics, as in national economics, we see no merit in the closed shop or in restrictive practices."

British Prime Min. Harold Wilson told the House of Commons Feb. 16 that his government was maintaining a cautious position on the possibility of entering the EEC. He stressed the need to safeguard "British and Commonwealth interests" and advocated new economic "bridges" to the EEC. He called British entry into the EEC "a practical possibility." Wilson said: "The position of the British government is and remains that if a favorable opportunity were to arise for negotiating entry we would be prepared to negotiate if, and only if, the necessary conditions relating to essential British and Commonwealth interests could be fulfilled."

British Amb.-to-France Sir Patrick Reilly declared in Paris Mar. 8, in a speech to the Anglo-American Press Association, that Britain remained "convinced that a Europe capable of being an equal partner with the United States in a wider Atlantic framework can never emerge unless Britain herself plays her full and proper part in it." He called for progress in European political unity, tariff reduction and nuclear strategy. He stressed that Britain would press for negotiations that might lead to British entry into the EEC.

British Foreign Secy. Stewart Mar. 9 reaffirmed in a statement to representatives of the 6 EEC countries at the quarterly ministerial meeting of the Western European Union in Rome that Britain wanted to join a "common European market" if her "essential" Commonwealth and other special interests could be protected.

Prime Min. Wilson and French Pres. de Gaulle conferred in Paris Apr. 2-3. In a communique issued Apr. 3, a spirit of cooperation between the EEC and the EFTA was called for. The communique said: "The president and the prime minister agreed that a successful conclusion of the Geneva tariff negotiations [the Kennedy Round] would contribute to more fruitful relations between the EEC and EFTA countries.... The president and the prime minister agreed that their talks had been of great value and had provided a basis for the development of Anglo-French relations in a spirit of cordiality. They agreed that they and their governments would remain in close contact and that further ministerial talks would take place as appropriate."

Wilson had visited Bonn Mar. 6-9 for economic and political talks with West German Chancellor Ludwig Erhard. A policy statement at the Berlin City Hall Mar. 6 said that Britain and Bonn favored "strengthening the links" between the EEC and EFTA. At a news conference Mar. 9 Wilson called for "functional links" between EEC and

EFTA since British membership in the EEC was "not a practical proposition at the present time."

Wilson visited Rome Apr. 28-29 and conferred with Italian Premier Aldo Moro, Italian Pres. Giuseppe Saragat and other government officials. Indicating a hope that Western Europe's economic disunity could be ended, Wilson disclosed at a Rome news conference Apr. 29 that Britain had proposed meeting in Vienna May 24 with EFTA partners to adopt common policies on the EEC. He said there was "no question in the foreseeable future of Britain joining or seeking to join the Common Market."

EFTA Developments

The EFTA Ministerial Council met in Geneva Feb. 22 and concentrated its attention on the 15% British tariff surcharge. Britain announced at this meeting that the surcharge would be cut to 10% Apr. 26. The council met again in Vienna May 23-25 and suggested May 24 that EFTA and the EEC hold ministerial conferences. They warned of a "deepening division" between the 2 blocs and called for new efforts to alleviate the split. They proposed May 25 that the EFTA and EEC set up a common patents system. Should this plan fail, they suggested a patents system just for EFTA. The *Wall Street Journal* reported June 16, however, that internal divisions within the EEC mitigated against prompt EEC replies to the EFTA overtures.

The EFTA Council of Ministers called Oct. 29 for a "dialogue" to establish links between EFTA and the EEC. The decision was made at a regular session of the EFTA Council held Oct. 28-29 in Copenhagen. Danish Foreign Min. Per Haekkerup, current chairman of the EFTA Council, called in the ambassadors of the 6 EEC nations to Denmark Oct. 29 to hand them EFTA's statement urging a "dialogue." He told newsmen that the major subject of such a "dialogue" would be to "insure a successful conclusion of the negotiations under the Kennedy Round." Among the points covered in the Oct. 29 EFTA communique summarizing the council's 2-day talks: Britain's decision to maintain its 10% surcharge on imports for another year was "regretted" by the other 6 nations; discussion would be opened with Yugoslavia to improve "commercial relations" between EFTA and Belgrade. (The *N.Y. Times* reported Oct. 28 that Yugoslavia had addressed a request to Haekkerup for "arrangements" with EFTA.)

At a regular ministerial meeting of the 7-nation Western European Union (comprising Britain and the 6 EEC members), held Nov. 4-5 at The Hague, British Foreign Min. Michael Stewart proposed a "dialogue" between the EFTA and EEC. 5 of the Common Market representatives favored Stewart's proposal. France's delegate did not participate in the discussion of relations between the EFTA and EEC.

The EFTA Dec. 31 reduced tariffs among its members by 10%, bringing the trading bloc's customs rates down to 20% of the 1960 level. The final 20% reduction was scheduled to take place Dec. 31, 1966. The EFTA had announced Dec. 5 that overall exports of the 8 nations to the rest of the world had risen 8.7% in the first 9 months of 1965 compared to exports for the same period of 1964. Exports for the 1965 period were $20.3 billion, imports $25 billion. The trade deficit for the bloc was $370 million less than for the first 9 months of 1964.

Anglo-French Concorde Developments

Aviation Min. Roy Jenkins announced in Parliament Jan. 20 that Britain would honor its treaty obligations with France in the development of the supersonic Concorde aircraft, despite rising costs. Jenkins said: "We have now completed the review of the Concorde project which we set in hand in October [1964], and we have exchanged views with the French government. We had, and we still retain, some doubts about the financial and economic aspects of the project. We have, however, been much impressed by the confidence of our French partners, and the prime minister has informed the French prime minister that we stand by the treaty obligations into which the last government decided to enter. During the coming months we shall be discussing with our partners the detailed program of development and production. Now that the uncertainty over the future of this project has been removed, I am sure that all those concerned with it on both sides of the Channel will press forward with a real sense of purpose. In this they will have the full backing of H.M. government."

Jenkins announced Mar. 17 that the first prototype flight had been rescheduled from late 1967 to early 1968. (A total of 45 of the planes were ordered by airlines by July 15.)

(British Prime Min. Harold Wilson visited French Pres. de Gaulle in Paris Apr. 2-3 and then said at his Paris press conference Apr. 3 that the 2 leaders had agreed on Anglo-French cooperation in aircraft production and other technological areas.)

1966

During 1966 Britain found it necessary to institute severe wage and price controls in order to restrict increases in export prices and stimulate export sales. Increased exports were considered an absolute necessity to provide adequate foreign exchange (currency) to maintain the pound at its $2.80 parity. Devaluation, the only alternative, was a step the Wilson government wished to avoid at practically all costs. Within the EEC, an agreement was reached under which France was able to end its boycott of Common Market sessions. Domestically, the French economy showed increasing strength, as measured by rising gold and currency reserves. In West Germany, Kurt-Georg Kiesinger replaced Ludwig Erhard as chancellor despite controversy over Kiesinger's alleged Nazi background. Britain once again indicated that it would seek EEC membership, and Prime Min. Harold Wilson announced plans to visit EEC capitals in 1967 to seek support. Austria and Denmark also sought EEC membership, while Norway and Sweden, reportedly interested, remained undecided.

Austerity Tightened

During all of 1966 Prime Min. Harold Wilson faced the unpleasant task of tightening the domestic economy almost to the point of recession in an attempt to preserve the international value of the pound. By reducing domestic demand for goods and services, he hoped to relieve pressure on prices, keep Britain's exports competitive in world trade and bring in the necessary foreign capital to preserve the pound at $2.80. Failure to accomplish this would mean a loss of so much foreign exchange (currency) that the pound's value would have to be reduced.

Board of Trade Pres. Douglas Jay announced in the House of Commons Feb. 7 that new restrictions were being imposed on installment credit in an attempt to lessen the balance-of-payments deficit. The new rules, which would reduce domestic consumption and hence relieve pressure on export prices, shortened maximum repayment periods for autos and increased minimum down payments for furniture and household goods.

Further spending reductions were disclosed Feb. 22 by Defense Min. Denis Healey, who presented to the House of Commons the Labor government's defense budget for 1966-7 and a Defense Ministry White Paper that projected Britain's defense policy and spending into the 1970s. The White Paper fulfilled a Labor promise made in 1965 to cut back the nation's defense spending to £2 billion ($5.6 billion) by 1970. The White Paper outlined substantial reductions in Britain's overseas troop commitments and stated that the Royal Navy's aircraft carriers would be discontinued in the 1970s. The document's release led to the immediate resignation Feb. 22 of Adm. Sir David Luce as naval chief of staff and First Sea Lord. Navy Min. Christopher Mayhew's resignation had been announced Feb. 19 following the publication of an exchange of letters written Feb. 17 by Mayhew and Prime Min. Harold Wilson. (Joseph P. W. Mallalieu was appointed Feb. 19 to replace Mayhew, and Adm. Sir Varyl Begg was appointed Feb. 22 to replace Luce.)

Healey told Parliament that the 1966-7 defense budget would be approximately £2.172 billion, or 6.6% of gross national product (GNP). He said this was a decrease of £72 million from the 1965-6 figure of £2.12 billion, or 6.8% of GNP after allowing for price increases and certain pay raises. He said it was the first step toward bringing the defense budget down to £2 billion at 1964 prices and toward keeping defense spending within 6% of Britain's gross national product.

Reading from the White Paper, Healey outlined Labor's long-term defense policy: "In future,...[Britain] will not accept commitments overseas which might require her to undertake major operations without the cooperation of allies, nor shall we attempt to maintain defense facilities in any independent country against its wishes." The major decisions the government had made were: (1) To withdraw its 12,000 troops from Aden in 1968 when the Federation of South Arabia would be due for independence. (2) Not to build a new aircraft carrier to replace carriers that would become obsolete in the 1970s. (3) To buy from the U.S. 50 F111A swing-wing supersonic bombers. (4) To give the Royal Navy, with its Polaris missile submarines, full responsibility for the UK's contribution to NATO's nuclear forces after 1969-70; Britain would continue to maintain its 51,000-man "ground forces in Germany at about their existing level... provided, however, that some means is found for meeting the foreign exchange costs of these forces"; air support for these "conventional ground forces" would be strengthened "at the cost of some reduction in our nuclear strike aircraft based there." (5) To maintain the 55,000-man force currently serving in Malaysia and Singapore.

Healey summarized the White Paper's conclusions by saying Britain would be able "to make significant savings of money and foreign exchange in return for a comparatively small reduction of our military capacity."

(Ex-Navy Min. Mayhew told Parliament Feb. 22 that the White Paper's £2 billion figure for the 1970s was inadequate if Britain wanted to maintain a commitment in the Far East and too large if the Far East commitment was dropped.)

Chancellor of the Exchequer James Callaghan presented to the House of Commons May 3 a fiscal 1966-7 budget of £9.177 billion ($25.696 billion) that proposed measures to correct underemployment in manufacturing and to reduce the balance-of-payments deficit. Callaghan announced that income and sales taxes would not be increased but that a "selective employment tax," designed to increase labor costs in service industries and reduce them in manufacturing, would be imposed, effective Sept. 5. The payroll tax initially would be paid by all employers, but manufacturing firms would receive "premiums" equivalent to 30% more than their tax payment while service firms would receive nothing. It was hoped that the tax's net effect would be to transfer labor to manufacturing industries and to reduce purchasing power, thus increasing exports and reducing the demand for imports.

The budget was adopted by the House of Commons May 10, after a week of debate in which the employment tax came under sharp criticism from Conservative MPs.

Among other measures announced in the budget message: (1) A 40% corporate tax, effective retroactive to Apr. 6, replacing the 35% capital-gains tax. (2) A 2.5% tax on betting (announced Mar. 1), effective in October. (3) Dropping of the 10% surcharge on imports when current legislation expired in November. (4) A voluntary program to limit investment in 4 developed nations of the sterling area (Australia, New Zealand, South Africa and the Irish Republic). (5) Talks with Bonn on offsetting, through trade or other arrangements, the cost of maintaining British troops in West Germany. Callaghan announced that Britain would repay on schedule, and possibly "ahead of time," $1.1 billion in loans from the International Monetary Fund due in Nov. 1967. Budgeted expenditures represented a £721 million ($2.019 billion) increase over 1965-6; despite an estimated £386 million ($1.081 billion) increase in tax revenues, income was expected to fall £287 million ($803,600,000) below expenditures.

Labor government plans to reduce the balance-of-payments deficit and increase "the productivity and competitive power of British industry" had been outlined at the opening of the new Parliament Apr. 21 in the Speech from the Throne delivered by Queen Elizabeth II.

Speculation that the bank rate would be increased mounted in early June as pressure on the pound increased. The bank rate currently stood at 6%, unchanged since the reduction from 7% June 3, 1965. In the New York market June 6, the pound closed at an 18-month low of $2.7894. It had reached the lowest value since Nov. 1964, $2.789375, 9375, the same day in London before closing there at $2.7896875.

The expectation of an increased bank rate came true in July. In an effort to protect the pound against foreign exchange speculation and at the same time to reduce inflationary pressures in the economy, the Bank of England increased the bank rate Thursday, July 14, to 7%. In another credit-tightening move, the bank announced July 14 that London and Scottish banks would be required to double the size of their deposits held with the Bank of England—from 1% to 2% for London banks and from 0.5% to 1% for Scottish banks. A Bank of England statement said the measures were aimed at relieving "the pressure on the exchanges both by reinforcing...credit restraint at home and by counteracting higher interest rates and tight money abroad." The tightened regulations would impede the banks' ability to extend loans and thus limit consumer spending.

The action by the Bank of England, although designed to support the pound, was in keeping with similar steps taken by other European central banks and the U.S. Federal Reserve System. Discount rate changes by these institutions included:

	Date	New Rate	Previous Rate
West Germany	Aug. 13, 1965	4 %	3.5 %
U. S.	Dec. 6, 1965	4.5 %	4 %
Canada	Dec. 6, 1965	4.75%	4.25%
Canada	Mar. 14, 1966	5.25%	4.75%
Netherlands	May 2, 1966	5 %	4.5 %
West Germany	May 27, 1966	5 %	4 %
Belgium	June 2, 1966	5.25%	4.75%
Sweden	June 10, 1966	6 %	5.5 %
Switzerland	July 6, 1966	3.5 %	2.5 %
South Africa	July 8, 1966	6 %	5 %
Britain	July 14, 1966	7 %	6 %

Further pound-supporting steps were hinted at that weekend as Prime Min. Harold Wilson said: "When people see what we have to say, they will see we have worked out a prepared package, and not one of the old scratching-together-of-a-panic measures we sometimes had in the past."

The announcement of deflationary action came July 20, when Wilson presented a package of drastic measures designed, he estimated, to cut domestic spending by $1.4 billion and overseas spending by $420 million. His statement, made in the House of Commons, simultaneously called for a 12-month voluntary "standstill" on wages and prices. Explaining the reasons for the crisis, Wilson cited a crippling 45-day seamen's strike but conceded that "there were deeper and more fundamental causes." Among them, he mentioned the U.S.' efforts to control its payments deficits, high interest rates in most of the world's financial centers, and, above all, domestic inflation under which "incomes have been rising faster than productivity." "Action is needed" to correct the "payments balance" and "to check inflation," he declared. Among the measures announced by Wilson July 20:

Installment buying—Down-payments on a variety of consumer goods, including cars, furniture, radios, TV sets, refrigerators, were increased. In addition, the payment periods were reduced.

Taxes—Gasoline and liquor taxes were increased 10%. The surtax, a tax affecting high income brackets, was increased by 10%.

Communications—Overseas postal rates were increased, effective Oct. 3. Local phone-call rates from coin-operated phones were doubled. Down-payments on phone installations were increased from 3 months' rental to 12 months'.

Travel—Tourists visiting non-sterling area countries would be restricted to a $140 foreign exchange allowance after Nov. 1.

Government spending—Spending by the national and local governments would be cut £55 million in 1967-8. Investment by nationalized industries would be cut £95 million in the same period. Overseas spending by the government in 1967-8 would be cut £100 million. (Wilson said that savings would be possible in Malaysia, "given an end to confrontation [between Indonesia and Malaysia]." Defense Min. Healey told the House Aug. 3 that UK troops would be withdrawn from eastern Malaysia after the confrontation ended.)

These measures, Wilson said, would amount to a net saving of "£150 million [$420 million]" in overseas spending and a reduction in "demand on the domestic economy by more than £500 million [$1.4 billion]." Nevertheless, he said, "the whole operation stands or falls on the extent to which we can keep our costs and prices under control." He said that wages in Britain had increased £1.8 billion in 1965 but that production had increased only £600 million in the same year. Hence, Wilson said, the government was calling for voluntary wage and price controls. A voluntary "standstill" on wage increases was requested for a 6-month period and "severe restraint" for the next 6 months. In cases of pre-existing commitments to raise wages, Wilson called for a 6-month postponement. (Approximately 6 million Britons were due for wage increases under agreements scheduled for implementation in the 12 months beginning July 20.) Wilson called for a 12-month standstill on prices. Wilson said:

"Sterling has been under pressure for the past 2 1/2 weeks. After improvement in the early weeks of May we were blown off course by the 7-week seamen's strike, and when the bill for that strike was presented in terms of the gold and convertible currency figures in June, the foreign exchange markets reacted adversely. But there were deeper and more fundamental causes. Many have been at home, and of these I shall speak in a moment. Several have been overseas. For several weeks past there has been an increasing pressure on liquidity in the world's financial centers. Action taken by the U.S. authorities to strengthen the American balance of payments has led to an acute shortage of dollars and Euro-dollars in world trade, and this has led to a progressive rise in interest rates in most financial centers and to the selling of sterling to replenish dollar balances. Last Thursday action was taken by the Bank of England to raise its discount rate and to double its call on the clearing banks for special deposits. On that day I informed the House that I would shortly be announcing further measures to deal not only with the short-run pressure on sterling but also with the underlying economic situation.

"Action is needed for the purpose of making a direct impact on our payments balance, and particularly on certain parts of our overseas expenditure, which in recent years has been growing rapidly. Action is needed equally to deal with the problem of internal demand, public and private, and to redeploy resources, both manpower and capacity, according to national priorities, and check inflation.... What is needed is a shake-out which will release the nation's manpower, skilled and unskilled, and lead to a more purposive use of labor for the sake of increasing exports and giving effect to other national priorities. This redeployment can be achieved only by cuts in the present inflated level of demand, both in the private and public sectors. Not until we can get this redeployment through an attack on the problem of demand can we confidently expect growth in industrial production, which is needed to realize our economic and social policies. . . ."

Insisting on the voluntary nature of the proposed standstill, Wilson said: "It is not our intention to introduce elaborate statutory controls over incomes and prices. . . . Nevertheless, in order to insure that the selfish do not benefit at the expense of those who cooperate, it is our intention to strengthen the provisions of the Prices & Incomes Bill [published July 4] . . . [and] to speed its passage."

Economic Affairs Min. George Brown offered his resignation immediately after the disclosure of the emergency measures. Brown, who also was deputy prime minister, apparently disagreed with the deflationary nature of the measures. Later in the day, after a 2d meeting with Wilson and after receiving a number of requests from Labor MPs to remain in the cabinet, he announced that he would stay on and would support the emergency program.

Frank Cousins, general secretary of Britain's largest union, the 1.5 million-member Transport & General Workers' Union, denounced the emergency measures July 20 and said he would not cooperate with the proposed standstill on wages. Cousins had resigned July 3 as technology minister in protest over the government's Prices & Incomes Bill. In a July 3 letter to Wilson, he described the bill as "meaningless" and unfair to labor. The bill would grant statutory powers to the National Price & Incomes Board (NPIB) to impose "temporary standstills" on increases in wages, prices and dividends. In addition, companies and unions would be required under the bill to give NPIB advance notice of intentions to grant or demand wage increases and price rises. (NPIB had been set up in Mar. 1965. Britain's labor union federation, the Trades Union Congress [TUC] had voted in Sept. 1965 to approve proposals that

NPIB be given statutory powers. The Labor government's intention to establish a wages and prices policy had been announced in 1964.)

(Following Cousins' resignation, Wilson July 3 announced these appointments: Anthony Wedgewood Benn, former postmaster general, to replace Cousins as technology minister; Edward Short, former chief whip in Parliament, to become postmaster general; John Silkin, former deputy whip, as chief whip; George Lawson as deputy whip. Cousins retained his seat in Parliament.)

The TUC General Council July 27 approved by 20-12 vote the government's planned wage standstill, "in interests both of trade unionists and of the nation as a whole, in the current critical situation." Following the council's meeting, however, Cousins declared: "I don't have to change my mind because the TUC have had a meeting." The council had also rejected by 19-4 vote a proposal, formulated by Cousins, to call a special conference of all TUC unions to debate the government's economic policy. (Cousins was not a member of the General Council, although his union was the largest TUC affiliate.)

The Wilson government overcame a Conservative Party censure motion in Commons July 27 by a 325-246 vote. The motion centered on the proposed austerity program. The House of Commons had already defeated a Jan. 27 Conservative motion of censure against Labor's economic policy by 287-284 vote. The Conservative motion charged that Labor had failed "to curb the rapid rises in the cost of living."

The July 20 austerity recommendations were formalized July 29 in a White Paper entitled "Prices & Income Standstill." The severity of the situation was emphasized by the opening paragraphs of the paper: "...The country needs a breathing space of 12 months in which productivity can catch up with the excessive increases in incomes which have been taking place. The broad intention is to secure in the first 6 months (which can be regarded, for convenience, as the period to the end of Dec. 1966) a standstill in which increases in prices or in incomes will so far as possible be avoided altogether. The first half of 1967 will be regarded as a period of severe restraint in which some increases may be justified where there are particularly compelling reasons for them, but exceptional restraint will be needed by all who are concerned with determining prices and incomes. The introduction of a general standstill on prices and charges until the end of 1966, to be followed by a 6-month period of severe restraint, is intended to apply to prices of all goods and services, whether provided by private or public enterprise. All enterprises will be expected to make every effort to absorb increases in costs, whatever the circumstances in which these arise."

The government's intention to switch from voluntary controls, as announced July 20 by Wilson, to compulsory measures, as embodied in the July 29 White Paper, had been reported July 24 from London by the *N.Y. Times.* According to the *Times,* the major factor compelling the move was a persistent lack of confidence on the part of foreign financial leaders in the Labor government's willingness to protect the pound through strong anti-inflationary measures.

The Confederation of British Industry announced Aug. 3 that it would cooperate with the government's price-freeze plan. The British Medical Association announced Aug. 3 that it had instructed doctors to cooperate with the plan; Britain's doctors had been scheduled to receive pay increases.

Commons Aug. 10 voted final passage of the Prices & Incomes Bill. Incorporated in the legislation were amendments giving the government statutory power for a 12-month period to impose mandatory orders against wage or price increases. In addition, the government was em-powered to order a rollback of any price or wage increase during the 12-month period to its July 20, 1966 level. The new controls were the most stringent ever imposed in Britain; during both world wars, no statutory powers existed to impose a wage standstill. The vote on the bill Aug. 10 was a comparatively close 272-214. The Labor Party had a 95-seat plurality in Parliament, but 22 Labor MPs abstained in protest against the government's stiff austerity measures. 22 Laborites had abstained Aug. 3 in a vote on a Conservative motion to force floor debate of the wage-price freeze amendments. The motion was defeated 277-225.

Prime Min. Wilson, apparently acting to restore Labor Party unity, announced a major cabinet shift Aug. 10. In the most important change, Economic Affairs Min. George Brown was appointed foreign secretary, replacing Michael Stewart, who became economic affairs minister. Brown retained his positions as deputy prime minister and deputy Labor Party leader. Herbert Bowden replaced Arthur Bot-tomley as Commonwealth secretary, and Bottomley became overseas development minister. Housing Min. Richard Crossman replaced Bowden as Lord of the Council and leader of the House of Commons. Anthony Greenwood, former overseas development minister, became housing minister.

The wage-price freeze voted Aug. 10 closely paralleled Wilson's July 20 call for voluntary controls. It established an absolute wage-price freeze for the 6 months ending Dec. 31, 1966, to be followed by an addi-tional "6-month period of severe restraint." The only price rises to be permitted were those resulting from increases in import supply costs or increased taxation. The wage freeze, which also prohibited a reduction in working hours, permitted pay raises only on condition they were directly tied to increased production—for example, piece-work earnings and sales commissions. The wage freeze also postponed for 6 months wage increases for those 6 million Britons due to get raises under long-term agreements. Violations of the wage-price freeze would be subject to a $1,400 fine for individuals, and there was no limit to the sums that could be imposed on unions or corporations.

The TUC, at its Blackpool convention, indorsed the government's economic policy Sept. 7 by a narrow vote of 4,567,000-4,223,000. Wilson had told the TUC Sept. 5 that the freeze was essential so that Britain could "gain time" in its efforts to return to a "planned growth of incomes." He warned that, because of rising world interest rates and the growing scarcity of money, "one false, careless step... could push the world into conditions not unlike those of the early '30s." If that were to happen, he said, "we, as a nation more dependent than almost any other on overseas trade, could well be plunged into a depression... where the workless might be numbered not at 1-1/2 to 2% but at 1-1/2 to 2 million."

The Liberal Party Assembly Sept. 22 voted overwhelmingly to deplore the Labor Party program, citing "dangerous consequences of the freeze."

At its annual conference, held in Brighton Oct. 3-7, the Labor Party indorsed the government's economic policy Oct. 5 by a vote of 3,836,000 to 2,515,000. But the convention also adopted, by a vote of 3,289,000 to 3,137,000, a resolution introduced by ex-Technology Min. Frank Cousins that urged that some part-time work be provided to ease the effects of unemployment. (Cousins announced Nov. 5 that he would resign from Parliament to devote full time to his leadership of the Transport & General Workers' Union.)

Opposition to the Wilson policy was expressed by the CBI (Confederation of British Industry) Oct. 12. CBI Pres. A. J. Stephen Brown said in a letter to CBI members:

"All experience teaches us that governments which acquire strong powers find reason to use them and to use them more and more. If they are used first for the odd cases which break the wages freeze, there will soon be a call for them to be used more generally and to be used on prices. As the more difficult period of severe restraint begins there will be a strong temptation to use them as backing for bureaucratic decisions as to what wage or price increase satisfies the new criteria. If this happens we would find our voluntary bargaining machinery overthrown and the main wage bargaining fixed by Whitehall decisions with a new impetus to wage drift which could escape the controls. Industry would no longer be free to fix its prices, which would be the subject of decision by government departments after what could only be a cursory examination of the factors involved. Attempts to control wages and prices by law would lead to a situation in which only the letter of the law and not its spirit was observed. I believe that the general view of our members is that it is of the utmost importance that the responsibility for wage and price decisions should be retained by industry.... I therefore urge CBI members to continue to observe the standstill on the voluntary basis which we have consistently supported in the past and which still remains the principal feature of government policy."

The Conservative Party Conference Oct. 14 condemned the government's action as "utterly misconceived."

The House of Commons, by 307-239 vote Oct. 25, approved the implementation of the Prices & Incomes Act. Opposition came from a combination of Liberal and Conservative representatives, with at least 26 left-wing Laborites abstaining.

The government announced Nov. 22, in a White Paper entitled "Prices & Income Standstill; Period of Severe Restraint," that it would extend its freeze on wages and prices to July 1, 1967. The Prices & Incomes Act had specified an absolute wage-price freeze for the 6 months ending Dec. 31 and an additional "6-month period of severe restraint." But it also granted the government power for a 12-month period to impose mandatory orders against wage or price increases. The White Paper prohibited reductions in working hours, increases in vacation time or pay raises based on comparisons with workers' wages elsewhere. The only exceptions permitted were: (1) cost-of-living increases that had been provided for in union contracts (to be paid after 6 months); (2) wage increases that had been negotiated before the imposition of the freeze and then halted by it (to be paid after 6 months); (3) certain wage increases for low-paid workers with large families; (4) certain wage increases based on "productivity bargains," *i.e.,* assurance of lower consumer prices or higher quality of production.

The government had made the freeze mandatory Oct. 4 after several labor unions and business concerns had indicated that they would honor wage increases that had been negotiated prior to the adoption of the Prices & Incomes Act.

The Labor Ministry reported Dec. 22 that, as of Dec. 12, total unemployment stood at 564,083, or 21,515 above the Nov. 11 level and the highest figure since Apr. 1963, when 604,619 persons were jobless. The unemployed represented 2.4% of the work force, up from 2.3% in November. The ministry reported that, as of Dec. 7, there were 234,187 job vacancies, 18,883 below the Nov. 6 level.

Other Domestic Developments

Prime Min. Wilson's Labor Party won a landslide victory Jan. 27 in a by-election in North Hull to fill a House of Commons seat vacated by the death of a Labor MP. The victory, together with the death Jan. 27 of a Conservative MP, increased Labor's margin in the 630-seat House of Commons to 4 votes. (Party membership in Parliament: Labor 315 plus the non-voting house speaker, Conservative 302 plus the non-voting party chairman, Liberal 9 plus the non-voting party chairman. One seat, which had been held by the late Conservative MP Dame Edith Pitt, was vacant.)

The National Union of Seamen May 16 began a 45-day strike that idled 891 of the 2,500 ships of Britain's merchant fleet and 26,500 of the union's 62,500 members before the walkout was called off June 29 by 29-16 vote of the union's executive council. (Work on ships not docking in Britain during the strike was not affected.) The strike resulted in an estimated $75 million loss in British export and shipping revenues and cost the union about $1,400,000 in strike benefits. It was the first strike called by the union in 55 years, although there had been several unofficial seamen's strikes in 1960. In calling the strike, the union had demanded an immediate reduction in the work week from 56 hours to 40 with no loss in pay; the Shipping Federation, representing 350 firms, had offered a reduction to 40 hours in 3 stages ending in 1968. A 4-man court of inquiry appointed by the government May 26 submitted a report June 7 recommending a 2-stage reduction to a 40-hour week, ending in 1967, and a reduction in annual leave (representing holidays and work done on Sundays) from 51 days to 39. (The union had demanded 52 days of leave.) The recommendations were rejected by the union June 8. The final settlement, based on a 2d offer made by the shipowners June 28, called for 48 days of annual leave and for the workweek reduction recommended by the court of inquiry—an immediate reduction to 48 hours and a reduction to 40 hours in 1967. In accepting the offer, the union's executive committee voted to "adjourn strike action" for one year while the court of inquiry, headed by Lord Pearson of the House of Lords Court of Appeal, continued its study of employment in the shipping industry.

It was estimated that the settlement would increase the industry's labor costs by about 9.5%; the government's anti-inflation policy had attempted to set a 3.5% ceiling on wage increases.

A month-long state of emergency, giving the government special powers to cope with the maritime strike, had been declared in a proclamation by Queen Elizabeth May 23 and renewed in a 2d proclamation June 22; 35 emergency regulations were approved by the queen May 23 and ratified by Parliament May 26. The regulations empowered the government to impose controls on food prices and to clear congested ports to permit the docking of foreign ships. The only use the government made of its emergency powers came June 22, when Prime Min. Wilson announced the formation of emergency port committees at 16 major ports to try to prevent port congestion from halting the movement of essential goods.

Attempts by the seamen's union to enlist support from other unions during the strike were not successful. The union's executive council June 7 had urged a worldwide labor-union embargo against British ships and against foreign ships docking in British ports. At a June 9 meeting, the Inner Council of Britain's Trade Union Congress told William Hogarth, general secretary of the National Union of Seamen, that the congress would not advise other unions to support the strike and that the congress backed the recommendations of the court of inquiry. The International Transport Workers Federation June 11 refused to indorse the seamen's call for worldwide union action against British shipping.

Prime Min. Wilson had raised the issue of Communist influence in the seamen's union as a source of difficulty in settling the strike. In a report on the strike to the House of Commons, Wilson June 20 did not mention Communists explicitly but charged that "pressure" for a continuation of the strike was being brought "to bear on a select few on the executive council" by a "tightly knit group of politically motivated men who, as the last general election showed, utterly failed to secure acceptance of their views by the British electorate." (The Communist Party [CP] had run 57 candidates, none of whom was elected, in the Mar. 31 general elections.) Hogarth replied June 21 that "as far as I know, there is no political control over this strike." In a report to Commons June 28, Wilson named 8 Communists (3 of them seamen's union members) who, he said, were active in the strike and 2 members of the union's executive committee who, he said, were responsive to Communist pressure. The strike activities of CP members, he added, were not illegal but involved a "deliberate exploitation" of the seamen's "genuine grievances"; he accused the executive committee of a "lack of guts" in failing to resist such exploitation.

Balance of Trade & Payments

Prime Min. Wilson's austerity program achieved limited success during 1966 in stimulating British exports and reducing imports. The balance of trade (excess of exports over imports) for January was in deficit by $263.2 million. The deficit declined in February to $165.2 million but rose in March to $215.6 million. The April deficit was $196.8 million. The monthly deficit rose again in May to $226.8 million (while exports rose, imports rose more, despite the dock strike) and in June to $296.8 million, the worst trade deficit of the year. In June, exports fell significantly (from $1.178 billion in May to $996 million in June), while imports fell by about half that much (from $1.453 billion to $1.305 billion). The monthly trade deficit declined slightly to $294.0 million in July, then fell sharply in August to $187.6 million (reflecting the end of the dock strike July 2) and to $131.6 million in September (reflecting the tightened economic policies proclaimed by Wilson in late July). The October trade deficit was only $56 million and the balance of payments, reflecting capital movements as well as exports and imports, was in surplus ($81.2 million) for the first time in 1966. November was the peak month for Britain; there was a trade surplus ($106.4 million) for the first time since the end of World War II, largely because of the government's decision to lift the 10% tariff surcharge on non-food imports Dec. 1. The trade deficit reappeared in December—$190.4 million—and there was a $67.2 million deficit in the balance of payments as well.

For the year as a whole, the balance of trade improved somewhat; The 1966 deficit of $2.073 billion compared with a deficit of $2.473 billion in 1965. The 1966 balance-of-payments deficit was $403.2 million, a substantial improvement over 1965's $772.8 million deficit.

Reserves & the Pound

Britain's reserves of gold and dollars fell consistently each month from March through October. Reserves, at a 1966 high of $3,648,400,000 at the end of February, had fallen by $75.6 million in March, by $53.2 million in April, by $106.4 million in May, by $137.2 million in June and by $70 million in July (to $3.246 billion July 31). These massive losses in reserves were accompanied by widespread speculation against the pound in foreign exchange markets. The pound, which had been selling above $2.80 in January, fell July 12 to $2.7865625, the lowest rate since the Nov. 1964 financial crisis. The immediate cause of the financial crisis was the deterioration in Britain's balance of payments. (Britain's payments deficit had been $165.2 million in February, $215.6 million in March, $198 million in April, $226.8 million in May and $294 million in June. The fundamental reasons for the deficit were cited in the annual report of the Bank for International Settlements [BIS], published June 13 at the bank's Basel headquarters. The BIS attributed Britain's deficit to inflationary wage increases and heavy government expenditures, both of which had increased Britain's domestic demand and consequently its imports. An aggravating factor was the seamen's strike, which had cut exports.)

To protect the value of the pound, the Bank of England was forced in June and July to intervene heavily on foreign exchange markets, offering undisclosed amounts of its dollar and gold holdings to purchase the increased sterling offerings. (Agreements between Britain and the International Monetary Fund pegged the pound at an official rate of $2.80.) In addition to drawing on reserves to protect the pound, British financial authorities borrowed undisclosed sums of short-term foreign exchange (mainly dollars) in June and July from other leading financial nations. The UK had been forced to draw on its $750 million currency-swap account with the U.S. Federal Reserve System during June to protect the pound. (Under the arrangement, the U.S. and UK stood ready to furnish each other with $750 million in credit to protect their currencies against speculation. The Bank of England had announced June 13, following a June 11-12 meeting held in Basel by BIS and central bank officials from the U.S., Canada, Japan and leading West European financial nations, that the group had agreed to new sterling support arrangements to replace those agreed to in Sept. 1965 and expiring June 15. The new agreements were renewable every 3 months and included the BIS and the central banks of Austria, Canada, Belgium, West Germany, Italy, Japan, the Netherlands, Sweden and Switzerland. A separate bilateral agreement between the Bank of England and the Bank of France also was announced June 13; France had not joined in the 1965 agreement. The Bank of England's June 13 announcement said that the U.S.-UK $750 million currency-swap agreement, as well as U.S.-UK borrowing arrangements above $750 million, "continue alongside the new arrangement."

The market experienced what the Aug. 3 *Wall Street Journal* called "a massive run on the British pound" in July as British reserves continued to fall. The real loss of reserves actually far exceeded the $70 million reported for July, but the true loss was hidden by British drawings, estimated to be at least $150 million, from the $750 million credit available from the N.Y. Federal Reserve Bank. This pattern continued through August, as reserves fell an additional $53.2 million (again, disguised by drawings from the N.Y. Federal Reserve Bank). Britain's repayment of $39.2 million to West Germany and the European Payments Union (EPU) during August accounted for part of the reserve loss.

The N.Y. Federal Reserve Bank and the Bank of England announced Sept. 13 that mutual credit arrangements ("currency swaps") with 10 foreign central banks and BIS had been increased from $2.8 billion to $4.5 billion to provide "a broader margin of safety for the stability of the international monetary system." The sum earmarked for Britain was $1.35 billion, an increase of $600 million over the former line of credit, of which Britain had drawn $300 million as of Aug. 31.

Reserves seemed strengthened by the end of the year, however. The austerity efforts of the Wilson administration appeared to have the same effect as they did on exports and imports, and reserves actually rose in November by $64.4 million to a level of $3.282 billion (compared with $2.988 billion a year earlier). The pound seemed sufficiently strengthened for the Wilson government to announce in early December that it would not seek a renewal of the $250 million line of credit from the Export-Import Bank in Washington "in view of the improvement of the position of sterling."

THE EUROPEAN COMMUNITY

France & The EEC

France kept in step with its 5 European Economic Community partners by reducing its tariffs to the other EEC members by 10%, effective Jan. 1. An announcement of the French decision was made by Information Min. Alain Peyrefitte Jan. 5 after a meeting of the French cabinet. The scheduled 10% tariff reduction among the 6 Common Market nations brought duties down to 20% of the levels that had prevailed Jan. 1, 1958, the date they began their first round of reductions. Peyrefitte said that a decision on a further joint EEC move toward a projected common external EEC tariff to non-EEC nations would have to be postponed until the 6 had reached agreement.

Foreign ministers of the 6 EEC nations convened Jan. 17-18 for their first joint meeting since July 1, 1965, when France had begun its boycott of EEC meetings because of its opposition to growing supra-nationality within the EEC. As a concession to France, the meeting was held in Luxembourg, not at EEC headquarters in Brussels. In addition, the meeting took place without the presence of the EEC Executive (Hallstein) Commission, which had come under fire from French Pres. de Gaulle for its alleged supranational ambitions.

The major development of the 2-day meeting was the presentation by French Foreign Min. Maurice Couve de Murville Jan. 17 of France's conditions for resuming normal relations between Paris and the EEC. Couve de Murville detailed a 10-point program calling for changes in the "style" of the EEC Executive Commission. Among the major points were: (1) A provision requiring the commission to consult with the EEC states before adopting proposals of special importance to EEC member states. (2) A prohibition preventing the commission president from receiving the credentials of ambassadors to EEC headquarters from non-EEC nations. (3) Closer control over the EEC budget by member governments. (4) Creation of a joint public information office for the EEC Executive Commission and the EEC Council of Ministers with the council, EEC's supreme policy-making organ, retaining real control.

Couve de Murville insisted that the 6 nations subscribe to a "political agreement" not to invoke the majority voting provisions of the EEC's 1957 Rome Treaty. (According to the treaty, when the EEC entered its 3d stage Jan. 1, 1966, Council of Ministers decisions would be taken by a "qualified majority" vote: Germany, France and Italy would have 4 votes each, Belgium and the Netherlands 2 votes each, and Luxembourg one vote. 12 votes would be sufficient under the treaty for the Council of Ministers to make a decision.) Couve de Murville suggested that if any EEC member believed an issue before the council involved vital national interests, the member could so declare and thereby remove that issue from the provisions of "qualified majority" voting. Couve de Murville also pressed for quick ratification by the Netherlands, Italy, Belgium and Luxembourg of a treaty signed in 1965 by the 6 to merge the executive commissions of the EEC, the High Authority of the European Coal & Steel Community and Euratom. It was reported that France backed the quick merger of the 3 commissions as a first step toward ousting EEC Executive Commission Pres. Walter Hallstein. (Under the terms of the treaty merging the 3 commissions, the number of commissioners would be reduced from 23 to 14. France had ratified the treaty June 25, 1965.)

Couve de Murville established the following timetable for implementing his proposals: Before the end of January, France wanted agreement on the question of majority voting, agreement on the 10-point program reducing the powers of the EEC Executive Commission and agreement on a date for depositing ratifications of the treaty merging the 3 commissions. By Apr. 18, France wanted the new 14-member commission nominated. In addition, Couve de Murville stipulated that the 1966 budgets of EEC and Euratom be approved by Feb. 7, that the agricultural financial program be adopted by Mar. 31 and that the problem of adjusting members' tariffs to non-EEC nations, left pending since Dec. 31, 1965, be settled by Apr. 30.

The ministers took no action on Couve de Murville's proposals; they agreed to meet again in Luxembourg Jan. 28. In the interim they left discussion of the issues to their permanent ambassadors at EEC's headquarters in Brussels; but as a further concession to France, the ambassadors would continue to meet in Luxembourg. After the Jan. 18 meeting, Luxembourg Premier Pierre Werner, who had become president of the EEC Council of Ministers Jan. 1, said the 6 were close together on their wish to get the community working again. Dutch Foreign Min. Joseph M. A. H. Luns, who was reported to have presented the strongest opposition to Couve de Murville during the ministers' closed meeting, asked: "How can you have a timetable when the issues that divide France and the 5 are unresolved?"

Following a special meeting in Luxembourg Jan. 28-30 of ministers of the 6 EEC nations, it was announced that France had ended its 7-month boycott of EEC and would return to EEC headquarters in Brussels for regular meetings of the Council of Ministers. The dispute was resolved by a compromise agreement proposed Jan. 29 by foreign ministers Paul-Henri Spaak of Belgium and Joseph M. A. H. Luns. The plan, embodied in a Jan. 30 communique of the 6, provided for a "gentlemen's agreement" to disagree on the key issue of majority voting within the council. It made concessions to France on the question of the powers of the EEC's Executive Commission, but it preserved for the commission its key power to initiate EEC legislative proposals. The ministers' meeting ended at about 1 a.m. Jan. 30, and general satisfaction with the agreement was expressed by all participants. The Jan. 30 communique gave this explanation of the agreement on the majority voting issue: (1) "Where... very important interests... are at stake, the members of the Council [of Ministers] will endeavor, within a reasonable time, to reach solutions which can be adopted by all the members." (2) "With regard to the preceding paragraph [1], the French delegation considers that where very important decisions are at stake, the discussion must be considered until unanimous agreement is reached." (3) "The 6 delegations note that there is a divergence of views on what should be done in the event of failure to reach complete agreement." (4) "The 6 delegations nevertheless consider that this divergence does not prevent the community's [EEC's] work being resumed in accordance with normal procedure."

The plan did not change the EEC Executive Commission's power of initiation, but the communique said a way must be found to raise "the efficiency of supervision" of the commission-prepared EEC budget by the Council of Ministers. The commission was instructed to "take up appropriate contacts with the governments of member states" before it adopted "any particularly important proposal." The commission would be required to inform the Council of Ministers of its proposals before releasing them to the press. It was also stipulated that credentials of diplomatic missions to EEC headquarters from non-EEC nations would be presented jointly to the Council of Ministers and the president of the commission. At a press conference following the meeting, Belgium's Paul-Henri Spaak said Jan. 29: "One cannot say that all the difficulties have been overcome, by any means, but we have succeeded in what we had to do.... As for majority voting, we are obliged to recognize that we are not entirely in agreement. But what is essential is that we recognize that the disagreement which continues does not hinder France from coming back to Brussels, nor, therefore, the community from resuming its activities."

At his 13th press conference since resuming power, Pres. de Gaulle said Feb. 21, with regard to the significance of the Brussels agreement:

"This agreement between the 6 governments is of great and auspicious significance. Indeed, for the first time since the Common Market affair got under way, one openly departed from that sort of fiction in which the economic organization of Europe had to emanate from an authority other than that of the states, with their powers and their responsibilities. By the very fact that it was handled successfully between the foreign affairs ministers and outside of Brussels, it was explicitly recognized that to succeed in the economic sphere, political foundations and decisions were necessary, that those foundations and decisions sprung from the states, and from them alone and, lastly, that it behove each of the governments to evaluate whether the measures to be adopted in common would or would not be compatible with the vital interests of its country. Now, starting from there, it can be asked whether the economic negotiations that are going to resume will culminate in a satisfactory result. The political question had to be settled.

"Without disregarding what can be the value of the Brussels commission's studies and proposals, for a long time it was actually due to the interventions of the states and, as regards the common agricultural market, due to those of France, that European economic construction gradually overcame its difficulties. But the imminent application of the 'majority' rule and the correlative extension of the commission's powers threatened to replace this reasonable procedure by a permanent usurpation of sovereignty. As reason prevailed, one can think that the economic negotiations are going to be pursued in good conditions.

"But would that be the only goal of the European ambition? Must it be admitted that the 6 states of Western Europe, which have just agreed on the political conditions concerning their economies, should decidedly abstain from dealing between them with other questions that also eminently affect them? In short, under what evil spell will the 6 find it impossible to consider between them political subjects of common interest, in short, to organize their political contacts? It is known that France has long proposed doing so. It is known that, on their side, the German government, the Italian government and the Belgian foreign affairs minister subsequently advanced similar proposals. Doubtless, these projects differ somewhat one from another, but all agreed on one essential point, which is this: to bring the 6 governments to meet regularly to consider together political subjects of common interest. Since, following Luxembourg, the economic organization of the 6 has resumed its normal course, France believes that it is more than ever appropriate to put political meetings into practice.

"Obviously, the issue for the 6 is not to brandish once again absolute theories as to what should ideally be the future European edifice; not to impose a rigid framework conceived *a priori* for realities as complex and changing as those of the life of our continent and of its relations with the outside; not to assume the problem of the construction of Europe solved before even having begun to live together, politically speaking; in short, not to become lost again in the myths and abstractions that have always prevented the 6 from undertaking in common anything other than painful adjustment of their economic production and trade. No! What is imperative, on the contrary, is that they meet in order to work for the purpose of cooperating. In point of fact, at the time of the recent French-German conversations, which took place during Chancellor [Ludwig] Erhard's visit to Paris [Feb. 7-8], the 2 governments reached agreement on this point, and that appears to me to be one of the main results of their cordial meeting.

"The security of the 6, taking into account their reciprocal closeness, as well as their geographic and consequently their strategic location; their relations of all kinds with the peoples near them—England, Spain, Scandinavia, etc.—or with the United States, or with the countries of the East, or with China, or with Asia, the Orient, Africa and Latin America; their joint action in such fields as science, technology, culture and space, on which the future of mankind depends—this is what, in our view, the 6 should tackle. Just as motion is demonstrated by walking, so their solidarity will be demonstrated by cooperating.

"This solidarity—will it have to shut itself in a sort of political and economic citadel? On the contrary, the union of the 6, once achieved—and all the more if it comes to be supplemented then by new European memberships and associations—can and must be, toward the United States, a valid partner in all areas, I mean powerful and independent. The union of the 6 can and must also be one of the piers on which will gradually be built first the equilibrium, then the cooperation and then, perhaps one day, the union of all of Europe, which would enable our continent to settle its own problems peacefully, particularly that of Germany, including its reunification, and to attain, inasmuch as it is the main hearth of civilization, a material and human development worthy of its resources and its capacities. Already now, moreover, that union, if it is achieved, would be an active element of the first order for the progress, the understanding and the peace of all the world's peoples.

"And that is why, if one of the states that are in the process of building the European Economic Community with us believed that, in this spirit, it should in turn take the initiative to propose a political meeting of the 6 governments, France would reply to it positively and wholeheartedly."

West German Chancellor Erhard had met with de Gaulle and other top French officials in Paris Feb. 7-8. Joining in the talks were West German Foreign Min. Gerhard Schroeder, Defense Min. Kai-Uwe von Hassel and Economics Min. Kurt Schmuecker and French Premier Georges Pompidou, Foreign Min. Maurice Couve de Murville, Economics Min. Michel Debre and Agriculture Min. Edgar Faure. The meeting was the 6th of the semiannual heads-of-government consultations under the French-West German Treaty of Cooperation. Both delegations expressed satisfaction with the talks during the 2 days, but no communique was released. At a lunch in honor of Erhard Feb. 7 at the Elysee Palace, de Gaulle reportedly called for the peaceful reunification of Germany. Following a Feb. 9 meeting of the French cabinet, at which de Gaulle presided, State Information Secy. Yvon Bourges read a cabinet statement on the Erhard-de Gaulle meeting. It said: "The construction of Europe was a desire shared by both delegations" although "the methods of political construction [of Europe] have not been detailed." The French government was satisfied with "the results obtained at [the] Luxembourg" meeting of the EEC foreign ministers.

Agricultural Agreement

The EEC Council of Ministers May 11 adopted financial regulations for the community's common agricultural program and simultaneously set a firm date (July 1, 1968) for the completion of a customs union covering virtually all EEC industrial and farm products. The decisions were taken at the regularly scheduled May 9-10 meeting of the Council at EEC headquarters in Brussels. The May 10 meeting ran until 5 a.m. May 11 in an all-night bargaining session, at the conclusion of which Prime Min. Pierre Werner of Luxembourg, who presided, announced to reporters that "the text of the financial regulations has been adopted."

The agreement on agricultural finance marked a major breakthrough for EEC, which had been deadlocked on the issue since June 30, 1965, when the previous farm finance regulations (adopted in 1962) expired. The new agreement, which would operate retroactively from July 1, 1965 and continue through Dec. 31, 1969, would cover the remaining 4½ years of the farm program's transitional period, during which the program would still be partially financed by direct national assessments from the 6 EEC members. After Dec. 31, 1969, under the terms of the 1957 Treaty of Rome, the farm program would be completely self-supporting. A later agreement, reached in 1962, provided that the program's main source of income would be levies (*i.e.*, import duties) charged on farm imports coming from non-EEC nations.

The new agreement, which provided for gradually increasing coverage of the program's costs through the levies during the 4 1/2-year period (July 1, 1965 to Dec. 31, 1969), conformed essentially to the demands made by the French government in June 1965; it was similar to compromise proposals presented in July 1965 by the EEC Executive Commission. The Council's failure to reach such an agreement at its June 28-30, 1965 meeting had precipitated a 7-month boycott of Council meetings by France. *Details of the May 11 decisions:*

Industrial & agricultural customs union—The 6 agreed to establish by July 1, 1968 a customs union providing for free movement of all industrial and agricultural products within the community together with a common external tariff to non-EEC nations. Movement toward the industrial union would take place in 2 steps. From the EEC's current industrial tariff level, 80% below levels existing Jan. 1, 1957, the 6 would cut tariffs 5% July 1, 1967 and eliminate the remaining 15% July 1, 1968. Their common external tariff would go into effect July 1, 1968.

Advances toward completely free movement of farm products within the community would be completed in a series of steps under which agricultural products not yet subject to EEC's common agricultural policy (i.e., market organization and common prices) would become subject to EEC control on or before July 1, 1968. The Council agreed May 11 on a timetable that would bring olive oil, fruits and vegetables, grains, poultry, pork, eggs, sugar, fats and oils, rice, dairy products, beef and veal completely within EEC's common agricultural policy by July 1, 1968. This would bring all farm products of the 6, with the exception of wine, under EEC regulations by July 1, 1968. The Council instructed the EEC Executive Commission to propose by Mar. 1967 a system covering wine that could become effective by Oct. 31, 1969.

Agricultural finance—The 6 agreed that, beginning July 1, 1967, the EEC's European Agricultural Guidance & Guarantee Fund (EAGGF) would assume full financial responsibility for all expenses of the community's agricultural policy for those farm products for which the community had established a market organization; other products would be covered by the EAGGF when the EEC set up market organization for them. Since the 6 had also agreed May 11 that every farm product, with the exception of wine, would be covered by market organization by July 1, 1968, the EAGGF would, in effect, cover virtually all EEC agricultural policy expenses after July 1, 1968. (Expenses covered by the EAGGF included market interventions to maintain prices, subsidies for exports to non-EEC nations below EEC prices and modernization programs for EEC farmers.)

For the 2 years from July 1, 1965 (the date EEC's last agricultural finance arrangement expired) through June 30, 1967, the 6 agreed on a transitional finance plan: For 1965-6, the EAGGF would assume 6/10 of the expenses of the common agricultural policy, the remaining 4/10 being the responsibility of each nation. For 1966-7, the EAGGF's share of the payments would rise to 7/10. The 6 also agreed that the EAGGF's share could rise to 4/6 in 1965-6 and to 5/6 in 1966-7, provided that by July 1, 1966 the 6 had made certain decisions regarding the organization of markets and common prices. In the last year (1964-5) the previous finance plan was in force, the EAGGF had assumed half the expenses of the common agricultural policy.

For the 2 years 1965-6 and 1966-7, the 6 agreed that the EAGGF's financial resources should be contributed by the member states as follows: 1965-6—France 32.58%, West Germany 31.67%, Italy 18%, the Netherlands 9.58%, Belgium 7.95% and Luxembourg .22%; 1966-7—France 29.26%, West Germany 30.83%, Italy 22%, the Netherlands 9.74%, Belgium 7.95% and Luxembourg .22%.

From July 1, 1967 through Dec. 31, 1969, the 6 agreed that the EAGGF would be supported from 2 sources: variable levies on agricultural imports from non-EEC nations and straight payments by each EEC member to the EAGGF. 90% of the levies on agricultural imports would go to the EAGGF; it was estimated that this would cover about 45% of the EAGGF's expenditures. The remaining cost would be paid in direct national assessments divided among the 6 as follows: France 32%, West Germany 31.2%, Italy 20.3%, the Netherlands 8.2%, Belgium 8.1% and Luxembourg .2%. The purpose of the levy system was to encourage nations to import agricultural products from EEC nations by penalizing them financially for importing from outside the community. The EEC Executive Commission estimated that in 1967, West Germany, a large agricultural importer, would contribute about 31% (in levies plus direct payments) of the EAGGF's resources but would receive only 18% of the EAGGF's expenditures. France, a large agricultural exporter, would receive about 45% of the EAGGF's payments in 1967 and pay only 24% (in levies plus direct national assessment) into the EAGGF. It was estimated that the EAGGF would have annual resources of about $1.5 billion to $1.6 billion by 1967.

After Dec. 31, 1969, the EAGGF would cover all farm expenditures and would receive directly all levies from agricultural imports.

It was also decided at the meeting May 11 that the EAGGF would pay Italy $45 million for structural improvements in the fruit and vegetable and olive oil sectors for the 1965-6 season. Italy would receive a similar payment of $15 million for tobacco for the 1966-7 season. The purpose of the payments was to compensate Italy for the fact that these products were not yet subject to EEC market organization and hence not eligible for benefits from the EAGGF. Belgium would receive payments of $4 million yearly, starting with the 1965-6 season for marketing sugar.

The May 11 decisions set a ceiling limit of $285 million yearly on EAGGF payments for structural modernization.

Statements issued by the French and West German governments May 11 following cabinet meetings in Paris and Bonn indicated that both governments viewed the Council decisions as satisfactory. Information Secy. Yvon Bourges told reporters after the French cabinet meeting that de Gaulle had congratulated France's negotiators at Brussels. West German press officer Karl Gunther von Hase said in Bonn that the German cabinet viewed the Council's decisions as "important preconditions for the realization of a common economic policy." His government, he explained, had desired an earlier establishment of the EEC customs union (*i.e.*, before July 1, 1968), but the date agreed on was "certainly presentable." West Germany's negotiator at the May 9-11 Council meeting, Economics Min. Kurt Schmuecker, had pressed for a date in 1967 for the beginning of the complete customs union. He had also said at the all-night May 10-11 session that West Germany viewed its agreement to accept the agricultural finance agreement as part of a larger package that included a commitment by EEC to move ahead on tariff reductions in the Kennedy Round trade negotiations in Geneva. Kennedy Round negotiations under GATT had been blocked by the EEC's inability to present a common set of offers during France's 1965 boycott.

The Council had agreed at an earlier Brussels meeting held Apr. 4-5 to authorize the EEC Executive Commission to present by Apr. 15 the community's offers for tariff reduction in 3 categories of chemicals and in aluminum at the Kennedy Round negotiations. The authorization represented a compromise between France and the other 5 EEC members: France agreed to further EEC tariff negotiations within GATT in return for a firm commitment by the other 5 to agree by early May to the agricultural finance plan desired by France. (After the Apr. 5 meeting, Schmuecker told reporters: "We should have an agreement on the financial regulations for the common agricultural policy at our next meeting to be held May 4-5; and if we don't have enough time, it will be necessary to have another meeting May 9-10." At the May 4-5 meeting the Council authorized the commission to present a working paper on the agricultural finance problem for the May 9-10 meeting.)

The EEC Council reached final agreement July 24 on common prices for most farm commodities produced within the 6-nation economic bloc. The agreement, to take effect by July 1, 1968 (some prices to be established before that date and others on it), was announced at 5 a.m., at the conclusion of a July 21-24 Brussels meeting of EEC foreign and agricultural ministers. The farm-price agreement was the necessary complement to the EEC's May 11 finance agreement on the community's agricultural program of price supports, export subsidies and farm modernization. The May 11 agreement had stipulated: (1) that the farm program would be financed increasingly by levies charged on agricultural imports from non-EEC nations and (2) that the size of the levies would be determined by the difference between the import's price on the world market and the price (presumably higher) of the same product within the Common Market. Hence, uniform EEC farm prices were required to implement the levy system. The July 1, 1968 date for full implementation of the farm-price agreement corresponded to the deadline set at the May 11 meeting for attainment of the EEC's goal of completely free movement of industrial and agricultural products within the EEC as well as final establishment of the EEC's common external tariff to non-EEC nations.

The July 24 agreement enabled the Council of Ministers to agree July 27, at another Brussels meeting, on their remaining agricultural offers for presentation in GATT's Kennedy Round of tariff negotiations. The 6 had agreed at a June 14 meeting on their offers for certain industrial products and for grain. Their agreed common price for grain (hard and soft wheat) had been set in Dec. 1964.

The July 24 agreement, together with the earlier decision on grain prices, brought an estimated 86% of the EEC's farm production within the EEC's system of uniform prices. Among major products included in the July 24 agreement (effective price date in parenthesis): beef on the hoof (Nov. 1, 1967), milk (Apr. 1, 1968), sugar beets (July 1, 1968), rice (July 1, 1967), olive oil (Nov. 1, 1966) and fruits and vegetables (July 1, 1967). The uniform grain price, under the 1964 agreement, was set for July 1, 1967. Among major products not covered by EEC price agreements: fats and oils, wine and tobacco. The agreement on fruits and vegetables, the major obstacle at the July 23-24 marathon negotiating session, provided for a complicated system of market intervention by the EEC's European Agricultural Guidance & Guarantee Fund (EAGGF) when prices fell below a "crisis" level. The arrangement, demanded by Italy, the EEC's largest producer of fruits and vegetables, set a $60 million annual ceiling on the EAGGF's market intervention; it would be reviewed in 3 years. Decision as to what would constitute "crisis" price levels for fruits and vegetables was postponed July 24 for later Council meetings.

EEC Executive Commission Pres. Walter Hallstein July 24 hailed the farm-price agreement as an "unprecedented" case of nations joining in "a costly affair for pooling their farm interests." Hallstein said:

"The negotiations which were concluded a few minutes ago are perhaps the most significant single step which has so far been taken in building up the European Economic Community, because it is not merely a milestone in the existence of the community but the conclusion of one of the first great stages in its development: the completion of the community's agricultural policy. Without a common agricultural policy the community cannot become what it should properly stand for, that is, a living economic community of 6 nations, which is to provide the solid basis for the development of a political community.

"To underline the importance of this event I should first like to place it in relation to other achievements—and here I do not mean so much its connection with the crisis, although the decisions of July have of course played a substantial part in consolidating the community anew. I mean rather the fact that these decisions embrace an area made up of 4 separate spheres, whose importance reaches beyond domestic farm policy: agricultural financing, the common agricultural policy, agricultural offers for the Kennedy Round and, lastly, completion of the customs union.

"The first, agricultural financing, was finally settled some time ago. Here, too, there are certain internal links with other problems, links which have not been created artificially but arise out of the subject itself. The significance of a European system of agricultural financing cannot be overrated. It regulates on a permanent basis and by written agreement the transfer between member states of sums on a scale unprecedented in history. The completion of this European system of agricultural financing means that from now on European agricultural policy will receive financial support from public funds; what is more, from the public funds not of a single European state—nowadays this would not mean very much in view of the small size of European states—but from the financial resources of the 6 states as a whole.

"The 2d sphere is that of agricultural policy, which from the political [standpoint] is the most significant part of the achievement. It embraces the most difficult agricultural provisions conceivable that had to be decided upon under the common agricultural policy. The extraordinary problems connected with it have never before arisen in this form on the international plane. All this had led to a comprehensive system of agricultural market-organizations and prices, a system which was worked out in the first big package deals of 1961 and 1962 and in the decision of Dec. 1964 on cereal prices. The system has now been completed.

"Before today no other international economic grouping than the European Economic Community has succeeded in the history of agriculture, in merging completely the agricultural policies of several states.

"The 3d sphere concerns the agricultural offers to be made by the community at the Kennedy Round negotiations. All the essential preparatory work has been done and the final decisions will be taken next Tuesday. Here, too, we have a considerable achievement which belongs to the external branch of agricultural policy, to agricultural foreign policy.

"Under the 4th hearing, I include the decisions completing the customs union and furthering the development of the community in the spheres of fiscal, commercial, social, regional and competition policy. These are the things which, as I said, have an inherent connection with agricultural policy. Here, too, the main negotiations took place on May 11 of this year.

"I should like to conclude my remarks on the significance of the Council's decisions . . . with a comment which has become a cliche but still holds good: once again the community has demonstrated its unquenchable vitality."

French Foreign Min. Maurice Couve de Murville was reported to have said that the prices agreed on were too high but that France was satisfied that EEC agreement on the question had been achieved. West German Agriculture Min. Rudolf Hoecherl described the agreement as "bearable." In Washington, State Department press officer Robert J. McCloskey said July 25 that the U.S. hoped that the agreement meant that the EEC would quickly complete its offers in the Kennedy Round. Following a meeting of the French cabinet July 27, it was announced that de Gaulle had expressed satisfaction with the farm-price agreement.

EEC Executive Commission spokesmen conceded July 24 that the agreement was inflationary. One official said: The "agreed price list was higher in every case than the schedules suggested by the commission. So you can draw your own conclusions about their inflationary effects." Another official said that earlier estimates of funds available for the EEC's farm program from levies charged on imports from non-EEC nations ($1.6 billion annually) would have to be revised. "Since the ministers were so generous in establishing the price levels on various commodities, it appears that the estimate of the fund's size may be very conservative," he declared.

The 6-nation agreement July 27 on offers for presentation in the Kennedy Round included these major agricultural products: beef, fish, fruits and vegetables, dairy products, rice, sugar, beer, wine, whiskey and tobacco. The offers were not disclosed but were reported to include a system of quotas permitting agricultural imports into the EEC up to certain ceiling levels, a proposal to freeze existing national farm subsidy programs and the abolition of existing agreements guaranteeing certain nations exclusive access to certain markets. At the July 27 meeting the 6 also decided that the EAGGF's share of full responsibility for EEC's farm program would increase from its 1964-5 level of 50% at a rate of 10% per year through the end of 1969, at which time the EAGGF would cover all community farm expenditures. The rate at which the EAGGF's share of the program's expenditures would increase had been left open in the May 11 finance agreement pending decisions on uniform farm prices.

Tariff Negotiations & Other Developments

The EEC Council of Ministers agreed in Brussels June 14 on tariff reduction proposals to be presented at the Kennedy Round of world tariff negotiations, currently under way within the General Agreement on Tariffs & Trade (GATT) in Geneva. Negotiators sought progress towards world tariff reduction before July 1, 1967—the date the U.S.' authority to reduce tariffs would expire under the 1962 Trade Expansion Act. The Council authorized the EEC Executive Commission, which negotiated for the EEC in GATT, to make these proposals:

Grain—A world reference price should be established at a level equal to the current Canadian price plus an additional $2.50 to $3.50 a ton. All major wheat-producing countries would maintain their current levels of price support. Major producers would be assigned a given self-sufficiency level for grain production; production above this level would be considered surplus. The EEC would set for itself a self-sufficiency level at 90% of total consumption plus net commercial sales and an acceptable amount of stock. Surplus (above the self-sufficiency level) would be sold at low prices or given away to needy developing countries; each grain producer would be responsible for financing its donations to developing countries. The EEC's own surplus disposal would be financed by its European Agricultural Guidance & Guarantee Fund.

Aluminum—The EEC would maintain its current tariff of 9% but would offer an import quota of 100,000 tons a year at the reduced rate of 5% to non-EEC nations.

Paper pulp—The EEC would offer to reduce its tariff from the current 6% level to 3% and possibly to suspend it completely. (The Council simultaneously agreed to establish a 10-year program of assistance to paper pulp producers in the 6-nation community.)

Newsprint—The EEC would offer a duty-free quota on 420,000 tons a year but would maintain its current tariff of 7%.

In a separate decision, the Council instructed the commission to reject the U.S.' proposals on chemical products. The U.S. had reportedly proposed in GATT to abolish its current selling-price system under which an importer paid a duty based on the product's selling price in the U.S. rather than on its price in the country of origin.

The 6 EEC members Dec. 23 presented most of their agricultural tariff-reducing offers at the Kennedy Round negotiations in Geneva. Although the offers—involving tobacco, fruits, vegetables and poultry—were officially secret, EEC sources in Brussels said they included proposals to cut poultry tariffs by 5% and raw tobacco tariffs by 26% to 28%. The EEC had announced in October that it would make its final offers by Jan. 10, 1967. (Norway, Denmark, Sweden and Finland had agreed in Stockholm Nov. 21 to bargain jointly in the Kennedy Round negotiations. Nils Montan, 50, Swedish deputy undersecretary of state, was named chief negotiator for the 4 countries.)

At the Apr. 4-5 meeting, the EEC Ministerial Council had discussed the single executive commission, which, according to the terms of a 1965 treaty signed by the 6, would replace the current 3 separate commissions—the EEC Executive Commission, the High Authority of the European Coal & Steel Community and the Euratom Executive Commission. The ministers decided that the top 4 posts on the new commission (the president and the 3 vice presidents) would be divided as follows: one each for France, West Germany and Italy and one representing the 3 Benelux nations. The 4 officers would serve 2-year terms and could be elected for only one term. No agreement was reached on the composition of the new commission. West Germany had renominated EEC Executive Commission Pres. Hallstein to head the new commission, and the Netherlands had nominated EEC Executive Commission Vice Pres. Sicco Mansholt. At the May 4-5 Council meeting, the composition of the single commission was again discussed with no progress towards selecting the new commissioners. (The treaty merging the 3 commissions was approved by Belgium's lower house Jan. 27 and by its Senate Apr. 5. 3 EEC members—the Netherlands, Luxembourg and Italy—had yet to ratify the treaty.)

A treaty of association between Nigeria and the EEC was signed in Lagos July 16 by Netherlands Foreign Min. Joseph M. A. H. Luns, president of the EEC Council of Ministers, and the Nigerian army chief of staff, Brig. B. A. O. Ogundipe. Under the treaty, Nigeria was granted duty-free entry for its major exports—cocoa, coffee, peanuts and palm oil. The volume of exports, however, was limited to an annual level based on Nigeria's exports to EEC nations in the previous 3 years. EEC received duty-free entry for 26 products under the treaty; none of the 26 products threatened Britain's preferred trade position in Nigeria, and the 26 products accounted for only 4% of Nigerian imports. Dr. P. N. C. Okigbo, who had negotiated the agreement, pointed out that Nigeria had associated itself with the EEC without leaving the Commonwealth.

Common Market sources reported in Brussels Oct. 13 that during the first 6 months of 1966 EEC exports to the U.S. had risen to a $1.9 billion total—up 20% over January-June 1965—and that imports from the U.S. had totaled $3.033 billion (up 10%). West Germany was the only EEC member that did not have a deficit in its U.S. trade during the period; its exports to the U.S. exceeded imports by $539 million. Deficits of the other countries: Italy $558 million, France $448 million, the Netherlands $429 million, Belgium-Luxembourg $222 million.

The European Coal & Steel Community announced Nov. 23 that it would subsidize coking coal production in Europe to allow the EEC to compete more favorably with lower-priced U.S. and East European coal. (EEC prices ranged from $14 to $17 a metric ton, while U.S. prices were $11 to $12.) A committee established by the ECSC was to determine the size and distribution of the subsidy.

French International Finance & Reserves

U.S. Treasury Secy. Henry Fowler announced Sept. 16 that France had made a prepayment of $70.8 million on its remaining indebtedness to the U.S., reducing to about $300 million the amount it still owed the U.S. on post-World War II reconstruction loans. Of the $1.85 billion France had repaid to the U.S. since 1947, the Treasury said, $810 million had been in the form of prepayments.

France's gold and currency reserves at the end of July had stood at $5.967 billion and was exceeded only by the U.S.' All but an estimated $800 million of the reserves were in gold. France had converted approximately $1.5 billion in U.S. dollars into gold during the 18 months ended in July, but France's dollar holding in July increased by $146 million. By the end of 1966 France's reserves had mounted to $6.733 billion, including $5.238 billion in gold.

Kiesinger Becomes West German Chancellor

Kurt-Georg Kiesinger succeeded Ludwig Erhard as chancellor of West Germany Dec. 1. He was elected by the Bundestag (lower house of parliament) by 340-109 vote, with 23 abstentions. Kiesinger, 62, minister-president of Baden-Wuerttemberg, had been nominated by the Christian Democratic Union/Christian Social Union (CDU/CSU) Nov. 10.

The new government was formed by a "grand coalition" of the CDU/CSU and the Social Democratic Party (SPD). Willy Brandt, 52, SPD chairman and governing mayor of West Berlin, was named vice chancellor and foreign minister. This was the SPD's first return to power since 1930.

The formation of the new regime ended a government crisis that had developed Oct. 27 when the cabinet's 4 Free Democratic Party (FDP) ministers resigned from the cabinet. The resignations ended a CDU/CSU-FDP coalition that had ruled since 1962 and left Erhard with 6 seats short of a majority in the Bundestag. The FDP ministers who resigned—Vice Chancellor and FDP Chrmn. Erich Mende, Finance Min. Dr. Rolf Dahlgrun, Housing Min. Ewald Bucher and Economic Cooperation Min. Walter Scheel—had quit ostensibly because of Erhard's decision to raise taxes to eliminate an estimated 4 billion-DM ($1 billion) deficit in the 1967 budget. (The deficit resulted primarily from a West German commitment to buy U.S. arms to offset the cost of maintaining U.S. forces in West Germany.) The FDP had insisted that the deficit be met through reduced federal spending and a cut in government subsidies rather than by higher taxes.

Despite his loss of a majority, Erhard, 69, had insisted Oct. 30 that he was "not ready to capitulate." He refused Nov. 8 to submit to a vote of confidence, which the SPD had demanded in a resolution approved

Nov. 8 by 255-246 Bundestag vote. (Since the resolution did not concern legislation, the votes of the 22 West Berlin delegates, who had no vote on legislative matters, were counted.) Erhard said he would "refuse to take part in a show trial," since he considered himself "the guardian of good democratic order and keeper of the constitution." (Under the West German constitution, only the chancellor could call for a vote of confidence.)

The CDU executive committee Nov. 8 nominated Kiesinger and 3 others—CDU Bundestag floor leader Rainer Barzel, Bundestag Pres. Eugen Gerstenmaier and Foreign Min. Gerhard Schroeder—as candidates to succeed Erhard as chancellor. The CSU, led by ex-Defense Min. Franz Josef Strauss, endorsed Kiesinger Nov. 9; Gerstenmaier withdrew his candidacy the same day. Kiesinger won the nomination on the 3d ballot Nov. 10 when the CDU/CSU Bundestag delegates gave him 137 votes (a majority).

After Kiesinger's nomination, controversy developed over his 1933-45 membership in the National Socialist (Nazi) Party. According to Kiesinger's own admission, he had joined the Nazi Party in 1933 but went into "opposition" after Hitler purged the Storm Troopers and their leader, Capt. Ernst Roehm, in 1934. Kiesinger told reporters Nov. 10 that he had joined the party "in the hope that it would become a good thing" but insisted that "from 1934 onward I dissociated myself from the party and had nothing more to do with it." The East German news agency ADN charged Nov. 10 that Kiesinger had acted as a "liaison man between Nazi Foreign Min. [Joachim von] Ribbentrop and Propaganda Min. [Joseph] Goebbels" during World War II. Kiesinger denied the charge. As proof of his opposition to Nazi policies, Kiesinger referred Nov. 11 to a report by a senior official of the Nazi secret police. The report, dated Nov. 7, 1944 and attributed to an Obersturmbahn fuehrer (Lt. Col.) Klumm, quoted an informant to the effect that Kiesinger was one of the "important" officials in the Foreign Ministry's foreign information section "who systematically thwart every strong activation in anti-Jewish education." The report mentioned 7 specific cases in which Kiesinger had blocked anti-Jewish actions. Kiesinger Nov. 24 released the record of his exoneration by a West German de-Nazification court. The report said that, although Kiesinger had not resigned his Nazi Party membership, he had never held office.

It stated that he had opposed Nazi policies "to the full extent of his powers" by: (1) successfully aiding political victims of the Nazi regime, (2) refusing to join the Nazi lawyers' guild, (3) rejecting Nazi totalitarianism and supporting the concept of constitutionalism in his capacity as a private law tutor and (4) organizing an opposition group in 1944, after the attempt to assassinate Hitler had failed, in order to overthrow the Nazi regime.

After protracted negotiations Nov. 15-26 between the CDU/CSU, SPD and FDP, Kiesinger and Brandt announced Nov. 26 that they had agreed upon a "grand coalition" of their 2 parties. The CDU presidium, meeting under the chairmanship of Erhard, unanimously approved the coalition Nov. 28. The SPD executive committee indorsed the coalition by 73-19 vote Nov. 29. Although Brandt probably could have been assured of the chancellorship in an SPD-FDP coalition, he rejected FDP Chrmn. Mende's offer Nov. 26 because of the slight majority the coalition would have commanded in the Bundestag (251 seats as against 245 for the CDU/CSU). But by stating Nov. 26 that the SPD had entered into "a partnership [with the CDU/CSU] for a limited time," Brandt served notice that the SPD would seek to obtain a majority in the 1969 national elections.

Erhard submitted his resignation to West German Pres. Heinrich Luebke Nov. 30. In a farewell broadcast to the nation that evening, Erhard promised to give Kiesinger his loyal support and urged his countrymen to do likewise.

After 3 days of hard bargaining, Kiesinger and Brandt Nov. 30 announced agreement on the composition of the new coalition cabinet. The CDU/CSU was allotted 10 seats (7 and 3, respectively), the SPD 9. One seat—that of special affairs—was abolished in order to unify within the Defense Ministry all control over defense activities. Among the 10 newcomers to the cabinet was ex-Defense Min. Strauss, who was appointed finance minister. As CSU chairman and a prime backer of Kiesinger, Strauss had been assured an important position in the new government. (One of the major complications in the negotiations had been Strauss' insistence on receiving both the finance and the economy portfolios. He agreed at the last moment, Dec. 1, to accept the finance post.) Other major cabinet changes included the transfers of foreign Min. Schroeder to the Defense Ministry and of controversial Defense Min. Kai-Uwe von Hassel to the Refugees Ministry. The new cabinet was sworn in Dec. 1.

The SPD's Bundestag delegates earlier Dec. 1 had approved the cabinet by 126-53 vote, with 8 abstentions. This vote, together with the vote on Kiesinger's candidacy, indicated that a significant number of Social Democrats opposed the coalition. (Although the voting for Kiesinger was by secret ballot, it was apparent that 63 coalition delegates had voted against him since only 46 Free Democrats were present during the balloting.)

In a TV broadcast after his election Dec. 1, Kiesinger said his government would seek "to clarify and, as I hope, to promote" relations with France while maintaining good relations with the U.S. "We wish to have relations of trust with every nation," Kiesinger said, "including the East, the Soviet Union."

Britain, the EEC & EFTA

Britain Again Seeks EEC Membership

Prime Min. Harold Wilson announced in Parliament Nov. 10 that Britain would again seek membership in the European Economic Community. Britain's previous application had been vetoed by French Pres. de Gaulle in Jan. 1963.

Britain's interest in joining the EEC had been apparent well before Wilson's November speech. At the opening of a London ministerial meeting of the Western European Union (WEU) Mar. 15 then-British Foreign Secy. Michael Stewart had said that French policy seriously damaged NATO's machinery and thereby the fulfilment of the defense commitments undertaken under the Brussels Treaty. He emphasized Britain's determination to maintain the treaty and its organization. Jean de Broglie, the French representative at the meeting, said France's desire to reform NATO was as strong as its desire to maintain the North Atlantic Treaty. He said France desired Britain's adhesion to the EEC as long as "the necessary conditions" were met.

West German Chancellor Ludwig Erhard had visited London May 22-25 to confer with Prime Min. Wilson. Others participating in the talks were then-West German Foreign Min. Gerhard Schroeder and British Deputy Prime Min. George Brown, Foreign Secy. Stewart, Chancellor of the Exchequer James Callaghan and Defense Min. Denis Healey. In a communiqué on their talks, released May 25, Erhard and Wilson agreed that "decisions should be taken [at the June 7-8 North Atlantic Treaty ministerial meeting] which will enable both this reorganization [of NATO] to go forward and agreements to be reached with France on her continuing place in the alliance." The communique said: Both parties viewed the alliance as a means for achieving "a peaceful settlement of the outstanding problems of East-West relations." Both "recognized the importance of the role of the United States ... as well as that of their other allies in arranging such a settlement." Wilson "reaffirmed the willingness of Britain to join the European Economic Community, together with the other members of the EFTA who wished to do so, provided that ways could be found to safeguard essential British and Commonwealth interests." Erhard "emphasized anew that the German government had always supported British accession to the European Economic Community and that it would continue to do so." Both parties "reaffirmed" their intent to bring the Kennedy Round tariff negotiations to a "successful conclusion."

Chancellor of the Duchy of Lancaster George Thomson, responsible for British relations with other European countries, stated June 13 at a WEU meeting in Paris that "the political will to join the

EEC exists in Britain today.... The general debate on whether Britain should or should not join is finished." He stressed, however, that Commonwealth interests, while not as significant as they were in 1962-3, still presented special problems. This dialogue continued at WEU meetings in Brussels June 27-28 and in Paris Sept. 29-30.

193 members of the House of Commons and House of Lords, headed by Liberal peer Lord Gladwyn, signed a "Campaign for Europe" declaration June 28 calling for British entry into the EEC with the intention of transforming the EEC into a political community "within the framework of the Atlantic Alliance." The group included 71 Labor, 71 Conservative and 9 Liberal members of the House of Commons and 42 peers from the 3 parties. An opposing group of 80 Labor members of the House of Commons issued a statement declaring that Britain could enter the EEC only if safeguards were arranged for Commonwealth nations, members of EFTA and British agriculture. The group was headed by Emanuel Shinwell, the Labor Party's parliamentary chairman, Vice Chrmn. William Hamilton and Michael Foot, a left-wing member of the party.

West German Foreign Min. Schroeder said during a radio interview July 2 that his government had sent a note to the other 5 EEC nations calling for a "readiness plan" to prepare for negotiations on Britain's entry into the EEC. He said the other 5 members had "reacted positively" to the Bonn proposal.

French Premier Georges Pompidou, accompanied by Foreign Min. Maurice Couve de Murville, visited London July 6-8 for talks with Prime Min. Wilson and Foreign Min. Stewart on Britain's possible entry into the EEC. This was the highest-level Anglo-French meeting since Wilson had met de Gaulle in Paris in Apr. 1965. A communique on the Wilson-Pompidou talks, released in London July 8, said:

"The 2 prime ministers discussed the situation resulting from the membership of France and Britain in separate European economic groups. They reaffirmed that the successful outcome of the Geneva [Kennedy Round] tariff negotiations would mitigate the effects of this situation. Mr. Wilson reaffirmed the readiness of Britain to join the EEC provided her essential interests could be met. M. Pompidou recalled that nothing prevented the entry of Britain into the Common Market provided that she accepted the Treaty of Rome and the arrangements subsequently agreed. [The "arrangements subsequently agreed" referred to EEC decisions on economic integration reached after 1957—in particular, the common agricultural policy that protected EEC's farm-products market behind a high tariff wall. Britain, a heavy importer of food, currently had lower tariffs on farm products.] It was agreed that the 2 governments would remain in contact with each other ... for further discussion of these questions. The prime minister [Wilson] described the rigorous measures which Britain had taken to strengthen her economy and redress the balance of payments. The French prime minister expressed his government's interest in the success of these measures."

At a London press conference, Pompidou denied that France had ever vetoed Britain's entry into the EEC. He said: "Once the British government considers it possible and opportune to take part in this great European economic task and to take on its obligations and responsibilities, France ... will be only too pleased, and will strive to seek with her [EEC] partners the indispensable transitions." The 6 EEC members, however, had made "too many sacrifices for us to agree to go back to square one."

(British Defense Min. Healey had apologized in the House of Commons June 27 for remarks he had made June 25 about de Gaulle. Healey had said at a meeting organized by *Socialist Commentary,* a Laborite monthly: "No one trusts him [de Gaulle] in Europe." De Gaulle was "a bad ally in NATO and a bad partner in the Common Market. A bad ally and a bad partner cannot negotiate for the rest of the partnership." He told Parliament that he had been stressing the need for loyalty "to our alliances . . . [and] had occasion to illustrate my remarks with a reference to French policy. . . . I much regret that in doing so I used words which, on reflection, I think I should not have used. . . . I did not intend any personal discourtesy.")

Wilson informed the House of Commons Nov. 10 of his government's "clear intention and determination" to bring Britain into the EEC. Wilson said:

"In recent weeks the government have conducted a deep and searching review of the whole problem of Britain's relations with the EEC, including our membership of EFTA and of the Commonwealth. Every aspect of the Treaty of Rome itself, of decisions taken subsequent to its signature, and all the implications and consequences which might be expected to flow from British entry, have been examined in depth. In the light of this review, the government have decided that a new high-level approach must now be made to see whether the conditions exist—or do not exist—for fruitful negotiations, and the basis on which such negotiations could take place.

"It is vital that we maintain the closest relations with our EFTA colleagues. H.M. government therefore now propose to invite the heads of government of the EFTA countries to attend a conference in London in the next few weeks to discuss the problems involved in moves by EFTA countries to join the EEC. Following that conference the foreign secretary and I intend to engage in a series of discussions with each of the heads of government of the 6 for the purpose of establishing whether it appears likely that essential British and Commonwealth interests could be safeguarded if Britain were to accept the Treaty of Rome and join the EEC. In the light of these discussions the government will then take its decision whether or not to activate the arrangements for negotiating for entry, and what the appropriate time for such negotiations would be. Commonwealth governments, as well as EFTA governments, have been informed, and we shall maintain the closest degree of consultation with them throughout.

"The House will agree that— provided the right conditions for negotiations are established—it is vital that we should enter only when we have secured a healthy economy and a strong balance of payments, with the pound standing no less firm and high than it is today. I want the House, the country and our friends abroad to know that the government are approaching the discussions I have foreshadowed with the clear intention and determination to enter EEC if, as we hope, our essential British and Commonwealth interests can be safeguarded. We mean business."

Edward Heath, leader of the Conservative opposition, had urged Nov. 5 that Wilson declare "a firm program of action" for British entry into the EEC. Warning that "time is not on our side," Heath said: "By July 1, 1968 [when all internal tariffs within the EEC were to be abolished], the community will have crystallized. Nearly everything will have been settled." There were "just 20 months to go, and this Labor government has not even taken the first step."

Wilson urged Nov. 14 that a European technological community be established along lines similar to the European Coal & Steel Community and Euratom. Such a technological community, Wilson said, would allow Europe, "on a competitive basis, to become more self-reliant and neither dependent on imports nor dominated from outside but basing itself on the creation of competitive indigenous European industries." Speaking at the Lord Mayor's Guildhall banquet, Wilson said:

"Britain has much to give but also much to gain, provided our essential interests can be met, as those of the Common Market countries were met 9 years ago [during the Treaty of Rome negotiations]. To join EEC means joining the European Coal & Steel Community and Euratom, and few countries have more to contribute in the fields covered by these communities. In particular, Britain leads the world, barring none, in the peaceful application of atomic energy. I hope that we are not, at every stage in the debates within this country on the government's decision, going to be dominated by the failures of the past. Many of the anxieties that some of us expressed 3 or 4 years ago are much less real because of developments within the Common Market and within EFTA."

"I do not guarantee that this new venture will lead to success, but I believe the tide is right, the time is right and the winds are right to make the effort. I believe the will is there in our industry and in our commerce. . . . It is right for me tonight to proclaim that Britain, our partners in EFTA and so many of our Commonwealth countries who will be involved will feel that it is right to try. For there is no future for Britain in a 'little England' philosophy. There is no future, either, for anyone in a 'little Europe' philosophy. For we do not see this venture, any more than our friends in Europe do, as a self-sufficient rich man's club—the identification of EEC with the development of so many African territories is a manifestation of this, as is the aid the countries of EEC have given on a wider scale.

"Our loyalty to the Commonwealth, our responsibilities and concern for African development . . . similarly inspire our hopes of an outwardly responsible community."

Commons debated Wilson's proposal Nov. 16-17. George Brown, who had replaced Michael Stewart as foreign secretary, defended the Wilson stand. He said:

"Great Britain would bring more to the EEC than just an additional market of 54 million people, important as that is. The industrial and technological competence that we possess would go a long way to redress the imbalance at present existing between Europe and America. We would bring to the community a large sector of industry which, with tariff problems removed, would be a base strength against its international competitors. We would bring an outstandingly efficient agriculture and, perhaps more than anything, Great Britain would bring her world standing and her position at the center of the Commonwealth.

"We are far from being suitors. The proposal to enlarge the Common Market is as much in the interests of the 6 as it is in our interests. We do not pursue this policy just for our own economic interests or for the economic benefits we could bring to the EEC. From an en-larged community great political benefits would also flow. An enlarged community, which included Great Britain and others at present outside, could contribute an enormously in-creased influence to the wider problems affecting our continent, in the Atlantic Alliance and in the world at large. We could clearly play a much greater role from within the community in influencing these affairs than we can play from outside."

Ex-Prime Min. Sir Alec Douglas-Home stated his support during the debate: "The opposition and Parliament are convinced, and have been for some time, that it is right for Britain to seek entry in the highest interests of the nation, and it is in that belief that we ask the government to go ahead and to gain the confidence of the governments of Europe in their intention to enter into the community."

Wilson Nov. 30 delivered a major policy address that was viewed as an attempt to quiet French Pres. de Gaulle's qualms about possible British entry into the EEC. In his speech, Wilson warned against U.S. economic domination of Europe and said that Britain wanted to participate in the development of Europe as a "pillar of equal strength" with the U.S. Wilson declared: "However much we welcome new American investment here, as in other parts of Europe, there is no one on either side of the Channel who wants to see capital investment in Europe involve domination or, in the last resort, subjugation." "America enjoys the fruits of a market of nearly 200 million people. Our aim is that Britain should play her full part in a [European] market, industrial or agricultural, of nearly 300 million." "The freer trading world for which we are working" must free "the channels of East-West trade as well."

West German support for Britain's application was expressed by the new chancellor, Kurt-Georg Kiesinger, in a major policy address before the Bundestag Dec. 13. Kiesinger stressed that "the decisive role for Europe's future" depended on "a close and trusting relationship between Germany and France." Toward this end he pledged to honor the terms of the 1963 French-West German friendship treaty that, he indicated, had been largely abrogated under the administration of ex-Chancellor Ludwig Erhard. Kiesinger said: "The community of the 6 must stand open to all European states that identify themselves with its aims. We would especially welcome the participation of Britain and other European Free Trade Association countries."

U.S. Backs Wilson Policy

Pres. Johnson strongly supported the Wilson government in both its financial struggles and its application to the EEC. The U.S. Administration's position on Britain in the EEC was expressed by Asst. State Secy. Anthony M. Solomon Apr. 21 in testimony before the Senate Antitrust & Monopoly Subcommittee:

"Regional economic integration can have a politically unifying force of significance. Our attitude toward . . . regional groupings reflects both economic and political considerations. As to Europe, political considerations are dominant in our thinking. Over the past 15 years, the United States has supported the concept of a united Western Europe as an integral part of our Atlantic and NATO policies. We believe that a united Europe is necessary for an Atlantic partnership in which the United States and Europe share common responsibilities as equals. The European Common Market of the 6 is the core and principal expression of the European unity movement. . . . While it is too early to be certain, we believe that the idea of European integration which the Common Market symbolizes is too powerful to be abandoned. We have, of course, always recognized an element of trade discrimination inherent in the Common Market idea, but we have believed strongly that the political advantages of a united Europe, able to play a full and equal role in strengthening the free world and keeping it free, far outweighed the trade disadvantages to us. The European Free Trade Association does not have the same ambitious goals of economic integration and political unity as the European Economic Community. We would hope that it would be possible for members of the European Free Trade Association in the years ahead to accept the goals of political unity and the full integration of their economies into the European Economic Community.... The possibility of British entry into the Common Market has been revived, and, should negotiations be resumed, other nations... would almost surely follow.

"We believe that the internal trade liberalization that has taken place within the EFTA can facilitate the entry of these countries into the EEC in due course and end the artificial separation among partners in the Atlantic alliance. For our part, we do not favor discriminatory trade blocs within the Atlantic community that are purely commercial in purpose and have no broader political goal. We would be opposed, therefore, to a merger of the EEC and EFTA having only a commercial character. We do believe that the participation of the United Kingdom and other European states in a fully integrated Western Europe is essential."

Prime Min. Wilson conferred with Pres. Johnson in Washington July 29 and said: To overcome its financial crisis, Britain had "taken steps which have not been taken by any other government in the world. We are taking steps with regard to prices and wages which no other British government, even in wartime, had taken. I hope this will be now accepted as a sign of our determination."

Pres. Johnson, in a speech in New York Oct. 7, expressed further U.S. support for Britain's application to EEC: "Among our tasks is the vigorous pursuit of further unity in the West.... A united Western Europe can be our equal partner in helping to build a peaceful and just world order. A united Western Europe can move more confidently in peaceful initiatives towards the East. Unity can provide a framework within which a unified Germany can be a full partner without arousing fears. We look forward to the expansion and the further strengthening of the European community. Of course, we realize that the obstacles are great. But perseverance has already reaped larger rewards than many of us dared hope for only a few years ago. The outlines of the new Europe are clearly discernible. It is a stronger, an increasingly united, but open Europe, with Great Britain a part of it and with close ties to America."

Austria & Others in EFTA Seek EEC Membership

The EEC Council of Ministers Dec. 13 reopened talks on Austria's application for affiliation with the EEC, a topic discussed previously in 1965. Austria's geographic location relative to the EEC 6 made it especially sensitive to EEC external tariffs. Thus tariff negotiations were of special significance. Austria and the 6 EEC members agreed Dec. 17 on mutual tariff cuts for industrial products. The agreement, conditioned on the outcome of further negotiations to determine Austria's relationship with the EEC, provided that: (1) the 6 EEC members would reduce their tariffs by 15% the day a final agreement came into effect and by 45%, 10%, 10% and 20% in 4 successive annual cuts; (2) Austria would reduce its tariffs by 15% the first year and by 25%, 20%, 20% and 20% in 4 successive annual cuts.

French Foreign Min. Maurice Couve de Murville had warned the EEC Council of Ministers Dec. 6 that the council should proceed with caution on Austria's membership application. He cited recent Soviet statements to the effect that close Austrian association with the EEC would violate the terms of the 1955 Soviet-Austrian treaty, which prohibited Austrian economic or political union with West Germany. Couve de Murville said that, according to the Soviet view, Austrian association with the EEC should be limited to a commercial treaty. Strong objections to close Austrian ties with EEC were voiced by Soviet Pres. Nikolai V. Podgorny during a Nov. 14-21 state visit to Austria. During a 3-hour meeting with Austrian Pres. Franz Jonas Nov. 15, Podgorny asserted that the USSR could approve only "normal trade agreements" between Austria and the EEC. Elaborating in a radio-TV speech Nov. 20, Podgorny said: "Any arrangement between Austria and the Common Market, no matter what form it would take, would result not only in economic but also in specific political bonds.... This, in turn, would...lead away from the state treaty and the proven neutral course which is of great benefit to the Austrian people." During a visit to the United Austrian Iron & Steel Works Nov. 17, Podgorny warned that Austrian association with the EEC would jeopardize its relations with the Soviet Union.

Austria and Britain had indicated at a May 12-13 EFTA ministerial meeting in Bergen, Norway that they were each considering bilateral negotiations with the EEC on joining or associating with the Common Market.

The application of Denmark—and possible applications from Norway and Sweden—for EEC membership were discussed by Danish Premier Jens Otto Krag with the Council of Europe's Consultative Assembly in Strasbourg Sept. 27. Krag said: "There is an intensive debate in Denmark about the question how we can help to get European cooperation on the move again. In that respect the Nordic countries might, perhaps, be able to play a part.... I do not think that an isolated Danish entry into the Common Market would solve Denmark's problems. Nor would it be desirable from an overall European point of view.... We intend in the near future to discuss our views with Sweden during the visit by the Swedish premier to Denmark at the beginning of October. I think that the matter should be taken up among all the Nordic countries at the coming session of the Nordic Council next February. A Nordic initiative—if it should prove possible—may have an importance of its own, also as an appeal to the United Kingdom and France to re-establish the contacts that were broken off in Jan. 1963 and to resume the negotiations in which, among others, Denmark took part simultaneously."

The Consultative Assembly Sept. 28 adopted a motion favoring the resumption of negotiations by Britain and other EFTA nations for EEC membership. Norway and Sweden had announced Sept. 27 that their actions would depend on Britain's decision and that the Danish announcement had been, in effect, a surprise to them. Tyge Dahlgaard, Danish minister for European market relations, said Oct. 20 that "Denmark may consider joining the Common Market alone in about a year's time if neither Britain nor Norway and Sweden are approaching the 6, but for the time being it is out of the question for Denmark to join the EEC."

Ludwig Erhard, then chancellor of West Germany, had visited Norway Aug. 28-Sept. 1. The trip marked the first official visit to Norway of a West German chancellor. During his talks with Norwegian Premier Per Borten and other officials, Erhard stressed particularly the need for closer contacts between the EFTA and EEC, with the ultimate aim of establishing "mutually satisfactory solutions for trade problems."

EFTA Activities

The first 1966 meeting of the EFTA Council of Ministers was held May 12-13 in Bergen, Norway. In a communique dated May 13, the ministers expressed their "satisfaction" with the British decision, announced May 3 by Chancellor of the Exchequer James Callaghan in his budget message, to terminate the UK's 10% import surtax by Nov. 1966. The ministers restated their standing "invitation" to the EEC countries to discuss trade and economic expansion. They noted with "deep concern" the "slow rate of progress" in Kennedy Round of tariff negotiations.

Austrian Vice Chancellor Fritz Bock told the Council May 12 that his government would postpone a decision on joining with the other EFTA nations in eliminating final tariff restrictions within the EFTA. (EFTA tariffs were currently 80% below their 1960 levels.) Bock said Austria's decision would depend on the progress of its negotiations with the EEC. British Deputy Prime Min. George Brown told the Council May 12 that Britain would act "in closest coordination" with its Commonwealth and EFTA "partners" in its negotiations for EEC entry.

The Bergen communique said: "The EFTA Council directed their main attention to the problems of European integration and found themselves in agreement on the fundamental issues. It was recalled that EFTA was designed to promote economic unity in Europe. EFTA had already invited the EEC member countries to take part in a dialogue on the pursuit of policies leading to the mutual growth of trade and the expansion of their economies. This invitation still stands. The ministers remained convinced of the benefits which an integration of the European economies would confer on Europe itself and indeed the world as a whole. They pledged their governments to pursue, by all available means, the objective of such integration."

Austrian Foreign Min. Lujo Toncic-Sorinj announced Sept. 26 that Austria would cut its tariffs with the EFTA countries at the end of the year. He said that Austria had always believed that membership in both the EEC and EFTA was possible.

The EFTA had noted in its 6th annual report Sept. 11 that intra-EFTA trade had doubled since 1959. The annual rate of increase was nearly 12%, compared to 5.6% a year in the 6 years before 1959. EFTA's world exports in the first 6 months of 1966 totaled $14,537,200,000, an increase of 7.8% over the corresponding 1965 period, while imports totaled $17,751,500,000, an increase of 6.2%. Statistics given for January-June 1966 (percentage increase over the corresponding 1965 period in parenthesis):

● Intra-EFTA trade (measured by imports) $3,856,200,000 (9.5%). (Intra-EFTA trade for the full year 1965 totaled $7,187,400,000, up 10.8% over 1964.)

● Exports to the U.S. $1,449,500,000 (29%), imports $1.815 billion (13.3%). (The report noted that these trade results were strongly influenced by the U.S. dock strike in the first quarter of 1965. The trade deficit with the U.S. for 1965 totaled $740 million.)

● Exports to EEC countries $3.86 billion (8%); imports $5,491,500,000 (7%). (The trade deficit with the EEC for 1965 totaled a record $3 billion.)

● Exports to countries other than the EEC and U.S. $5,579,200,000 (2.6%); imports $6,588,400,000 (2.1%). (The EFTA trade deficit with these countries had risen from $1 billion for all of 1959 to $1.7 billion for 1965.)

The report stressed that the major concern of the EFTA ministers during the past year had been the objective of creating a single European market. It also reaffirmed the interest of the EFTA countries in a successful outcome of the Kennedy Round negotiations.

The EFTA Council met in Lisbon Oct. 27-28 and reviewed the progress reported Sept. 11. Discussion continued on EFTA participation in the Kennedy Round negotiations and on EFTA relations with the EEC. The communique issued at the conclusion of the meeting said: "In their belief that the most immediate prospects of expanding intra-European and world trade lie in a successful conclusion of the Kennedy Round, the ministers reaffirmed that the EFTA countries during the final and decisive phase of these negotiations would do everything in their power to secure the most extensive reductions in world trade barriers. They will continue to cooperate closely for this purpose. In the EFTA Council's discussion of economic integration in Europe, ministers reaffirmed their view that the single Western European market remains their ultimate goal. . . . It was the unanimous view that the EFTA countries could best contribute to the ending of the economic division of Europe by coordinated action as agreed at previous meetings." The ministers also agreed to consider establishing formal ties between EFTA and Yugoslavia at the next ministerial meeting. Yugoslavia had requested association with EFTA in 1965.

The EFTA held a special one-day conference in London Dec. 5 to study the developing discussions between EFTA members and the EEC.

At this meeting, British Prime Min. Wilson explained the objectives of his planned trips to EEC capitals with Foreign Secy. George Brown in early 1967. A communique issued at the close of the meeting supported the British plans. It said: Wilson would travel "with a view to determining whether the appropriate conditions exist in which it might be possible to activate the arrangements for a negotiation with the Community for British membership. The other ministers welcomed the British move as an important step along the road to determining the prospects for a solution to the question of European economic integration in which they could all participate in an appropriate manner.... All ministers emphasised the importance of developing the free market of nearly 100 million people which the European Free Trade Association will be by the end of the year. This market would be an important contribution to the European Economic Community. The 2 markets together would constitute a larger market in Europe consisting of nearly 300 million people, thereby creating a stronger basis for the economies of all participating states. At the same time it would make it possible for Europe to contribute more effectively to the developing world. The EFTA ministers welcomed the British ministers' intention . . . to stress the outstanding importance of a successful conclusion to the Kennedy Round of tariff negotiations in the GATT."

The 7 full EFTA members Dec. 30 eliminated all remaining tariffs on industrial goods traded within the group. The creation of an industrial free-trade area, which began in 1960 with a 20% cut in tariffs, occurred 3 years ahead of the original schedule. Finland, an associate member of EFTA, cut its industrial tariffs to EFTA members Dec. 30 to 10% of their original levels. Since it had begun the tariff-cutting process a year later than the 7 full members, Finland was given an additional year to abolish its tariffs completely. Special concessions were also made to Portugal, as the least economically developed of the EFTA nations, and for limited commodities, to Norway, Austria and Switzerland.

Anglo-French Concorde & Channel Tunnel Progress

During French Premier Georges Pompidou's visit to London July 7-8, he discussed with Prime Min. Wilson progress on both the supersonic Concorde and the proposed tunnel under the English Channel (referred to by supporters and some critics as the "Chunnel"). A communique issued July 8 said: "The prime ministers examined the situation of and prospects for Franco-British cooperation in the field of aeronautical construction. In particular they discussed the fulfilment of the *Concorde* program. They confirmed their intention of proceeding with this, while maintaining constant scrutiny of the financial aspects." "They noted with satisfaction that the mixed commission set up to study the technical, juridical, economic, and financial problems relating to the Channel Tunnel project was on the point of completing its work. It was agreed that the reports of the commission . . . would be discussed between the 2 governments with a view to finding a solution for the construction work on mutually acceptable terms. Subject to finding a satisfactory solution, the 2 governments have now taken the decision that the tunnel should be built."

1967

Harold Wilson's 3-year fight against devaluing the pound ended in failure during 1967. A 14.3% devaluation was ordered Nov. 18. Devaluation by 32 other countries followed within days. Britain's balance-of-payments deficit amounted to more than $1.3 billion in 1967. Britain's 2d application for EEC membership was vetoed by French Pres. de Gaulle for reasons similar to those used when France vetoed the first British application. The EEC adopted a 5-year economic plan designed as a framework for farm, trade, labor and regional policy. The executive bodies of the EEC, ECSC and Euratom were merged. Major worldwide tariff cuts were agreed on as the Kennedy Round reached a successful conclusion.

British Economy Before Devaluation

In the 10 months from January to the beginning of November, Prime Min. Harold Wilson continued his battle begun in 1965 to defend the pound by means of domestic austerity. Wilson had apparently won short-run battles in late 1965 and again in late 1966, and he continued to follow the same economic policy during 1967. But he lost this final battle.

The Trades Union Council (TUC) expressed doubt about the Wilson incomes policies of 1966. A TUC report issued Jan. 25 stressed that the incomes policies were long-run in nature while a flexible "relaxation of restraint" was called for in preference to legislating policies "on reluctant trade unionists."

The British bank rate was cut from 7% to 6.5% Jan. 26. The cut, according to the Bank of England, was justified "by lessening of pressures on the domestic economy and by the recent reduction of interest rates and in monetary pressures in other important financial centers." The finance and economic affairs ministers of the U.S., Britain, France, Italy and West Germany had met at Chequers, England Jan. 21-22 to discuss what British Chancellor of the Exchequer James Callaghan termed an "international disarmament in the present level of interest rates." A communique issued at the conclusion of the meeting Jan. 22 said: "The ministers welcomed recent steps by some of the countries represented to ease credit and monetary stringency, which in the past had played a useful part in moderating their domestic inflationary pressures. They agreed that in some countries some further easing would be helpful in the context of the development of their own economies and of the world economy as a whole. The monetary policies called for in the present situation should be adapted to the different conditions obtaining in their respective countries and should have regard to their effect on other countries. The ministers agreed that they would all make it their objective within the limits of their respective responsibilities to cooperate in such a way as to enable interest rates in their respective countries to be lower than they otherwise would be."

The Bank of England announced Mar. 14, following a Mar. 11-12 meeting in Basel of the Bank for International Settlements (BIS) and central bank officials of the U.S., Canada, Japan and leading European financial nations, that the group had agreed to extend for an additional year the sterling support arrangements due to expire June 15. Under the agreement, Britain could borrow up to the equivalent of $1 billion to counteract fluctuations in its external sterling balances. Those participating in the agreement were the BIS and the central banks of Austria, Belgium, Canada, Italy, Japan, the Netherlands, Sweden, Switzerland and West Germany. The participants had agreed to the sterling support arrangements in Dec. 1965 and had renewed them for one year in June 1966.

The Bank of England also announced Mar. 14 that its bilateral credit agreement with the Bank of France had been extended for another year and that the U.S.-UK $750 million currency-swap agreement, as well as the U.S.-UK borrowing arrangements above $750 million, remained in force. The Federal Reserve Bank of New York had announced Mar. 9 that Britain had repaid to the U.S. all it had borrowed in 1966 under the reciprocal foreign exchange agreements. While the FRB did not disclose the full amount of the repayment, it said that $510 million had been repaid since the first of the year. The *Wall Street Journal* reported Mar. 9 that the repayment had "exceeded $625 million."

The British bank rate was cut again Mar. 17 from 6.5% to 6%.

A White Paper on prices and income policy after June 30 was presented to Parliament Mar. 22. The paper called for a continuation of the current price and wage restraint, although it stressed greater voluntary cooperation from the TUC and CBI (Confederation of British Industry). Wage increases, under the proposal, would be justified only by productivity gains (although price cuts, given productivity gains, were still expected) or when wages were below the level of a reasonable standard of living.

Prime Min. Wilson's Parliamentary majority was reduced in by-elections held during the spring. The Conservative Party in a Mar. 9 election won 1 of 3 seats at stake; all had been held by Labor. The Conservative Party Mar. 17 retained a seat it already held, and it won 3 parliamentary by-elections Apr. 27 and Sept. 21, retaining one seat and capturing 2 others from Labor. As a result of the Conservative victories, Labor's parliamentary majority fell to 86 seats by September. The new composition of the House of Commons: Labor—356, Conservatives—255, Liberals—12, Welsh Nationalists—one, Independents—one, Republican Laborites—one. 3 seats remained vacant.

In county elections held throughout Britain Apr. 10-14, Labor won control of only 3 of the 59 county councils and lost control of 14; the Conservatives gained at least 197 seats while Labor lost at least 135. In elections to the 100-member Greater London Council Apr. 13, the Conservatives won a landslide victory after 33 years of Labor control. In borough elections held throughout England and Wales May 12, the Conservatives also made large gains at the expense of Labor.

Chancellor of the Exchequer James Callaghan presented the fiscal 1967-8 budget in Commons Apr. 11. The budget estimated government expenditures for the fiscal year commencing Apr. 1 (fiscal 1967-8) at £11.07 billion ($31 billion), government income at £11.7 billion ($32.8 billion). Although it called for no reduction of taxes, it provided for an 8.5% increase in government spending. It predicted an economic growth rate of about 3%. Callaghan warned in his budget message that he would be forced to hold back economic expansion if there was a "general scramble for substantially higher wages" during the new fiscal year. He pledged that the government would repay by Dec. 2 (the due date) the $818 million it owed the International Monetary Fund and $78 million it owed Switzerland for funds advanced the previous year to help stabilize the pound. He added that, "on present prospects," the government would be able to repay by 1970 (the due date) the remaining $1.4 billion it had drawn from the Fund. To do this, Callaghan said, "we must continue to earn a surplus in our balance of payments."

The defense plans for fiscal 1967-8 had been proposed by the government in a White Paper Feb. 16. Defense spending was estimated at £2.205 billion ($6.174 billion), or 6.5% of the gross national product, as compared to the fiscal 1966-7 expenditure of £2.172 billion ($6.081 billion), or 6.6% of the gross national product. The White Paper noted that, by Apr. 1, 1968, Britain planned to return 25,000 men and 6,000 service families from overseas bases. A motion approving the government's defense policy was accepted in Commons Feb. 28 by the relatively narrow vote of 270-231. The margin of 39 votes, compared with the Labor majority of 94, was an indication that a large number of Labor MPs had abstained in the voting. Prime Min. Wilson reportedly said at a closed-door Labor Party meeting Mar. 2 that he would not tolerate such flagrant violation of party discipline. He was quoted as saying: "No one elected to support this government, as you all were, is going to bring this government down. The Parliamentary party has its rights and so has the government—including the right to appeal to the country for a fresh mandate with supporters who can be counted upon to support it."

In its monthly report Apr. 6, the Treasury asserted that "business confidence appears to be recovering," with car sales and home construction up and the rise in unemployment slowing. The Treasury noted that Britain's balance of payments in 1966 had been aided by £224 million ($627.2 million) worth of direct foreign investment in British industry, as compared to £189 million ($529.2 million) in 1965. Gross national product in 1966 was £32.4 billion ($90.7 billion), up 4% from 1965, or 1.5% after taking into account price increases.

British Economic Affairs Min. Michael Stewart announced Apr. 17 that the government would modify but extend its freeze on wages and prices for an additional year (from July 1). The freeze had been instituted in Aug. 1966 in a program to curb inflation, increase exports and restore confidence in the pound. Stewart said the extension was necessary to insure that business and labor unions practicing voluntary restraints were not harmed. He said the government would activate Part II of the 1966 Prices & Incomes Act, which provided for (1) delays of up to 4 months before a pay or price rise could go into effect and (2) an automatic 3-month suspension of price or wage increases instituted after the 4-month delay period if the government referred them to the National Board for Prices & Incomes, which had the power to determine whether they were justified. Unlike the more stringent parts of the act that had been in force earlier, however, the new rules did not give the government power to order a reduction in prices or to prohibit retroactive payment of wages that had been suspended because of a wage raise.

The CBI supported the Wilson stand Apr. 30. CBI Pres. A.J. Stephen Brown, in a letter to members, characterized the government's policy as "substantially in line with industry's views."

Unemployment in Britain rose to 2.1% of the labor force in early April, up from 2.0% in March, the Labor Ministry reported March 21. This was the 7th rise in 10 months. The news prompted the Scottish TUC, meeting in Dunoon, Scotland, to demand by a 970-637 vote the repeal of the government's emergency legislation freezing wages and prices. This vote was taken after the TUC delegates had heard Chancellor of the Exchequer James Callaghan defend the Wilson government's policies. Callaghan had implied that such a repeal would be an example of the "stop-go" economics for which the Conservative administrations of Harold Macmillan and Sir Alec Douglas-Home had been criticized. (The executive committee of the British TUC Feb. 22 had unanimously opposed the government's proposed extension of the freeze.)

The TUC, at its 99th annual meeting in Brighton Sept. 1-8, adopted (Sept. 6) a resolution criticizing the government for utilizing "deflationary measures to manage the economy which involved the creation of a pool of unemployed." The vote was 4,883,000 to 3,502,000. The resolution rejected government intervention in collective bargaining and urged repeal of the 1966 Prices & Incomes Act, which provided for wage and price freezes.

Unemployment subsequently rose to 2.4% by late April, then fell to 2.3% by mid-May. The Labor Ministry reported May 18 that the number of jobless people had reached almost 541,000, the largest total for any April since 1963. This rate remained high during the summer, reaching 2.3% in mid-July and 2.4% in mid-August. The level in Aug. 1966 had been 1.4%.

Chancellor of the Exchequer Callaghan announced May 9 that Britain would prepay 6 months early $484.4 million of the December debt installment of $817.6 million still due to the IMF. A total of $1.078 billion had originally been due but $817.6 million had been prepaid in Apr. 1966. The money had been borrowed in Dec. 1964 to support the pound. Such repayments, Callaghan noted, would increase England's drawing rights with the IMF. The IMF announced May 26 that it had received from Britain an advance repayment actually totaling $405 million. The repayment allowed the IMF to repay the following amounts (in equivalent dollar terms) to the 8 countries that had contributed to the loan: Belgium—$30 million, Canada—$15 million, France—$100 million, Italy—$5 million, Japan—$20 million, the Netherlands—$40 million, Sweden—$15 million, West Germany—$180 million.

A bill empowering the government to delay wage and price increases up to 7 months was passed by 130-96 vote of the House of Commons on its 2d reading July 12 and then approved by the House of Lords. The measure, which became fully operative Aug. 11, had a life of only one year. An extension of the Prices & Incomes Act, the bill obliged companies and unions to inform the government 30 days in advance of any wage and price increase. The government then had the option of investigating the proposed rise for a period of 6 months.

The Prices & Incomes Board Dec. 19 rejected a blanket wage increase requested for more than 2 million industrial workers represented by the 31 unions of the Confederation of Shipbuilding & Engineering Unions. Employers had estimated that the cost of the requested increases would total about $3.4 billion a year. The board instead proposed modest increases for workers in lower-paid grades.

2d-quarter economic indicators showed a decline in British economic strength as compared with the first quarter, the IMF reported July 28. Exports fell 4% from the first-quarter level, retail sales declined, and industrial production leveled off. Imports rose an average of 2% over first-quarter levels and helped produce a balance of trade deficit (excess of exports over imports) of $280 million for the 2d quarter.

Prime Min. Wilson dropped Michael Stewart as economic affairs secretary Aug. 28 and appointed Peter Shore to replace him. Stewart was appointed first secretary in the Wilson cabinet. Other changes included the appointment of Anthony Crosland to replace Douglas Jay as president of the Board of Trade. Wilson actually assigned to himself the prime responsibility for economic affairs. Conservative leader Edward Heath characterized Wilson's acts as "the final throw of a desperately worried man at last forced to acknowledge the economic mess in which 3 years of Labor rule has landed the country." Heath portrayed Wilson as "a man convinced that by personally taking over economic portfolios himself, people will be kidded into believing all is well."

Installment buying curbs on consumer goods were reduced Aug. 30. For autos, down payments were cut from 30% to 25% and repayment terms extended from 30 months to 36. Similar changes were made for consumer appliances. The IMF reported Sept. 22 that these improved terms had helped stimulate auto sales and that bank credit had picked up.

Chancellor of the Exchequer James Callaghan asserted Oct. 3, in a speech at the Oct. 2-6 Labor Party conference, that the economic restraints imposed by the government to reduce Britain's balance-of-payments deficit were still essential. He said he could not guarantee radical improvement of the economy in the near future and held that "the figures that we've got so far don't justify any general wage increase in the next 12 months." Callaghan dismissed as "gimmicks" proposals to reduce the payments deficit through devaluation of the pound and imposition of import quotas. Prime Min. Wilson told the conferees Oct. 4 that there was no alternative to the deflationary policy he was pursuing if Britain wanted to end its balance-of-payments deficit. On the positive side, Wilson noted the increased spending of the Labor government in the social sphere and said this had "ended the slide to social inequality and public neglect."

The bank rate was raised twice within one month, from 5.5% to 6% Oct. 20 and to 6.5% Nov. 9. It had been cut May 4 (for the 3d time in 1967) from 6% to 5.5%. In a statement issued Nov. 9, the Bank of England said it had become necessary to raise its discount rate because "further pressures toward higher short-term rates in other international markets" had developed. The U.S. Treasury said Nov. 9 that the interest raise reflected changes in the "international pattern of interest rates" that had required "technical adjustment in Britain's money market rates to restore balanced conditions in the international money market."

As pressures on the pound mounted, Britain obtained some additional foreign financial support. The Treasury Oct. 10 accepted a loan of about $103 million from 3 Swiss banks: the Swiss Bank Corp. of Basel and the Swiss Credit Bank and the Union Bank of Switzerland, both of Zurich. The loan was in the form of 450 million Swiss francs, payable within 12 months at a rate of 5.5%. The Treasury confirmed Nov. 14 that it had obtained a $250 million loan from the BIS in Basel. About a dozen nations reportedly had contributed to the loan. This support, however, proved to be inadequate in terms of Britain's total needs.

DEVALUATION OF THE POUND

Britain Cuts Pound 14.3%

The battle to save the pound ended Nov. 18 when the Wilson government announced the decision to devalue the pound by 14.3%, from $2.80 to $2.40. The pound had been pegged at $2.80 since 1949. The devaluation was designed to make British exports cheaper in foreign markets, thus increasing sales and generating foreign exchange for England while making foreign imports more expensive and consequently reducing the sale of foreign products and stemming the outflow of foreign exchange from England. The net effect would be to increase Britain's reserves (gold and foreign currency).

The government also instituted other emergency economic measures designed to restore confidence in the pound and improve Britain's international financial position. Among the measures were a rise in the central bank rate to 8% and a cutback in defense and home spending.

The devaluation dealt a sharp blow to the Labor government of Prime Min. Wilson, who had based his economic policy on maintenance of the pound at $2.80. But speculation that the government would fall as a result of the devaluation was apparently disproved Nov. 22 when the House of Commons indorsed the devaluation by a 77-vote majority.

In order to protect the pound further, Britain obtained assurances of a $1.4 billion loan from the International Monetary Fund (IMF) and a $1.6 billion credit package from the world's major industrialized nations.

The devaluation was one result of the Labor government's inability to close the gap in Britain's balance-of-trade and balance-of-payments deficits, which had progressively widened in the preceding months. Other specific factors contributing to Britain's financial difficulties were a 9-week dock-workers' strike that tied up exports and the increased shipping costs incurred through the closure of the Suez Canal during and since the Arab-Israeli war in June.

Devaluation had become imminent during the latter part of the week of Nov. 12, when speculators began to trade heavily on the pound in the world's major money markets and forced the British Treasury to put up millions of its reserves to maintain the price of the pound. The government withheld announcing the devaluation until after it had conferred with representatives of the world's leading industrialized nations and had received assurances that they would not devalue their currencies, lest they nullify the expected benefits of the British devaluation and set in motion a world monetary crisis. Britain reportedly received assurances of international cooperation if it would not devalue the pound by more than 15%.

32 countries devalued their currencies after Britain did, but most were smaller countries heavily dependent on trade with Britain. Among other international developments following the devaluation were increases in the U.S. and Canadian bank rates and a 4-day run on gold that threatened the position of the dollar.

These emergency measures were announced by British Chancellor of the Exchequer James Callaghan Nov. 18 in conjunction with the devaluation of the pound: (a) Effective immediately, the Bank of England's discount rate was raised from 6.5% to 8%, the highest rate in 53 years. (b) Banks were ordered to limit advances to priority borrowers, particularly exporters. (c) Defense spending abroad would be reduced by more than £100 million ($240 million at the new rate) during the next year. (d) Other public expenditures, including nationalized industries capital expenditure, would be reduced by £100 million (e) Except in development areas, the extra amount received by manufacturers in the Selective Employment Tax premium would be withdrawn (this would save the government more than £100 million). (f) The export rebate, currently costing the government nearly £100 million annually, would be abolished as no longer necessary. (g) A strict watch would be placed on dividends, and the corporate profit tax would be raised to 41.5% from 40% (h) Effective midnight Nov. 18, installment purchase of autos in Britain would require a minimum deposit of 33.33% and a maximum repayment period of 27 months. (i) An application had been submitted to the IMF for an immediate stand-by loan of $1.4 billion (j) Arrangements had been made for a loan of about $1.6 billion from the central banks of the world's major industrialized nations, the majority of which were members of the Group of 10 (Belgium, Britain, Canada, France, Italy, Japan, the Netherlands, Sweden, the U.S., West Germany). (k) Banks and the stock exchange were ordered closed Nov. 20.

In his statement Callaghan said: "This change [in the par value of the pound] brings with it fresh opportunities—but at a heavy cost. The main opportunity is that our exporters should be able to sell more goods overseas.... But if we are to derive the full benefit from it we must reduce the growth of demand by consumers at home.... We need an improvement in our balance of payments of at least £500 million a year, and the government intend[s] to ensure that this is achieved.... The major disadvantage of the change in the exchange rate is that it will cause a rise in certain prices though...[not] all at once. It is essential that price increases should be confined to those unavoidable cases brought about by increased import costs. It is essential, equally, to ensure that these price increases do not result in large wage claims and settlements.... It is the government's firm intention to take, at the right time, the steps that will be needed in order to protect the most vulnerable sections of the community from hardship resulting from the change in the exchange rate."

In a televised address Nov. 19, Prime Min. Wilson presented a critique of the sterling crisis and outlined the hoped-for effects of the devaluation and other financial measures he had taken. Wilson cited the more-than $2 billion international-payments deficit he had inherited from his Conservative predecessors in 1964 and said this figure had been reduced to less than $560 million by 1966. But further improvement had been disrupted, he said, by (1) the "successive waves of speculation" on the pound, (2) the "heavy cost to our trade and payments of the war in the Middle East" and (3) the "temporary disruption of our exports by the dock strikes." (Wilson had noted in his annual speech at the Lord Mayor's banquet in London Nov. 13 that the closing of the Suez Canal during the Mideast war had imposed a "fine" on Britain so far of more than $280 million, a reflection of the increased shipping costs incurred through longer voyages.)

Given these circumstances, Wilson said, Britain was placed in the position of either borrowing or devaluing. The government had decided against the former, he explained, because of the unacceptable restrictions that would have been placed on the economy and the fact that borrowing would not have attacked the "root cause of the speculation."

Thus Britain had devalued and had gained thereby a chance to "break out from the straitjacket of these past years." Wilson urged the British people to "take with both hands the opportunity now presented to us." He warned against "excessive wage demands" but did not specifically mention a new wage freeze. Among Wilson's remarks:

"It would have been possible to ride out this present tide of foreign speculation against the pound by borrowing from central banks and governments abroad. . . . It would have been irresponsible to go on dealing with these successive waves of speculation by borrowing for short periods at a time, without attacking the root cause of the speculation. Failure to attack the root cause would have meant trying to borrow, this time, in conditions in which our creditors abroad might well insist on guarantees about this or that aspect of our national policies. . . . The government decided that we were not prepared to accept any solution which placed rigid limitations on the ability of our people and government to solve our problems by our own exertions; that we could not accept restrictions on our national growth, on industrial expansion, on our determination to achieve and maintain full employment.

"We are determined to break out from the straitjacket which has constricted us, under successive governments, for 15 years, a straitjacket which meant that every time we tried to solve our problems by expanding production, by mobilizing the efforts and skill of our people on the basis of full employment, the immediate result was a desperate trade and payment deficit. The deficit we inherited 3 years ago, over £800 million [$2.24 billion at the old rate], was itself the result of an attempt by our predecessors to fight their way our of this dilemma by an unrestrained boom. For 3 years we have fought . . . to overcome that deficit and to maintain the external value of sterling. . . . We had reduced that deficit last year to less than a quarter. Our exports had risen at about double the rate of the past few years, and we were all set to get into balance, indeed surplus, this year.

"But there was never enough margin to meet the change and chance of world events. Nor to guarantee the repayment of the vast borrowing we had incurred to pay for the deficit we found on taking office. . . . Time was needed to restructure and modernize our industries, to build up our trade . . . to cut down our overseas defense commitments too. That time was denied us. Whenever Britain ran into short-term difficulties, there were some who sold sterling in a panic, and there were others who gambled against us in the hope of a quick gain. And all this, even though our basic position was showing a steady improvement. Take the seamen's strike last year. There was a tidal wave of pressure on the pound and yet, grievous though that strike was, it did not prevent us over the year as a whole from reducing our deficit to less than £200 million against the £800 million deficit we took over 2 years earlier. . . .

"The problem is this: we, Britain, are a major trading country, and like any business firm our financial position depends on how much we sell to others. But because we are also an international bank, and because sterling is an international currency, it is subject to speculative attacks for short-run reasons which have nothing to do with Britain's trading position.

"Our decision to devalue attacks our problems at the root. . . .

"We shall now be able to sell more goods abroad on a competitive basis. . . .[But] the goods we buy from abroad will be dearer and so, for many goods, it will be cheaper to buy British. . . .

"Saving [on] imports, and still more the export drive, will mean that industrial production will go up. . . . This means more work—more jobs in the development areas, because we intend to be ruthless in diverting new enterprise to those areas. But all this will be at a cost— at any rate for a time.

"The needs of the export drive will mean that we have got to shift £500 million [$1.2 billion at the new rate] of our national output into exports and import-saving. . . . Imports will cost more, and this means higher prices over a period for some of our imports, including some of our basic foods. It is vital that price rises are limited to those cases where increased import costs make this unavoidable. . . . We shall keep a very tight watch on prices and we shall use the powers we have under the Prices & Incomes Act.

"It is just as vital that any prices that do go up are not used as an excuse for excessive wage demands. That would simply increase our export costs and this would cut into the benefit our export industries have now got. . .

"We will do everything in our power to create the climate in which an effective prices and incomes policy can be pursued by those whose job it is.... The government have decided to refer to the National Board for Prices & Incomes certain council rent increases....

"This devaluation has been a hard decision and some of its consequences will themselves be hard, for a time. But ... [we] must make a success of it. We must take with both hands the opportunity now presented to us. ... Any who fail through laziness or self-seeking, any who frustrate the work of others by unofficial strikes will imperil the right of all our people to work, the right to work not only for themselves but for the nation....

"This is a proud nation. ... We have the chance now to break out from the straitjacket of these past years. We're out on our own now. It means Britain first."

Among domestic reactions to the devaluation:

●Edward Heath, leader of the Conservative Party, declared Nov. 19: "In 3 years, the Socialist government has reduced Britain from a prosperous nation to an international pauper. Mr. Wilson himself bears the responsibility, for he has taken personal charge of the conduct of the economy." Heath Nov. 20 described the devaluation as a "defeat" for the Labor government. He expressed fear that the government would "fritter away" the expected benefits of devaluation through "an easy spending spree at home."

●Frank Cousins, leader of the Transport & General Workers Union. Britain's largest union, answered "of course" when asked Nov. 19 if his union would continue to press for higher wages. "Patriotism goes out the window when money is involved." Cousins said. Noting that some had been getting rich by speculating on the pound, Cousins asked: "Why should we be patriotic if other people are going to cash in on it?"

●The Trades Union Congress pledged Nov. 22 to support the government's economic policy by restricting demands for higher wages to factors other than those associated solely with the devaluation, such as price increases.

●After debating the devaluation Nov. 21-22, the House of Commons indorsed the government action Nov. 22 by 335-258 vote.

International Reaction

Pierre-Paul Schweitzer, managing director of the IMF, said Nov. 18 on behalf of the IMF:

"In concurring in the UK [devaluation] proposal, the Fund has indicated its agreement that the change is needed to deal with a fundamental disequilibrium reflected in the continued weakness in the balance of payments of the United Kingdom and, during the past few months, in heavy losses of reserves. Some of the causes of this weakness are temporary, but deficits in the current account have persisted despite determined and courageous efforts by the UK authorities to bring about a surplus. In connection with the change in the par value of the pound sterling, the Government of the United Kingdom has announced its intention to carry out a program comprising credit and fiscal measures and a strengthening of prices and incomes policy. This will make it possible for the United Kingdom to improve its balance of payments, rebuild gradually its reserves, and repay the large debts incurred in recent years, while allowing for adequate growth in the economy.

"The United Kingdom has stressed the importance of rebuilding confidence in sterling through the change in par value and the other measures which are being taken, and in this connection it has requested a new stand-by arrangement in the amount equivalent to $1.4 billion. The Fund is giving prompt attention to the request with the expectation of reaching a favorable decision in a few days.

"The par value of the pound sterling which became effective Nov. 18, 1967 is as follows, expressed in terms of gold and in terms of the U. S. dollar of the weight and fineness in effect on July 1, 1944: 2.13281 grams of fine gold per pound sterling; 14.5833 pounds sterling per troy ounce of fine gold; 0.416667 pound sterling per U. S. dollar; 240.000 U. S. cents per pound sterling."

Within the next few days, 32 countries announced plans to devalue their currencies, most of them by 14.3%, to match the British cut, while 46 others announced that they would not devalue. Those devaluing, effective dates, and the percentage changes if not 14.3%: Barbados (Nov. 21), Bermuda (Nov. 21), British Honduras (Nov. 21), Ceylon (20%, Nov. 22) Cyprus (Nov. 20), Denmark (7.9% Nov. 19-20), the east Caribbean dollar (Antigua, Dominica, Montserrat, St. Kitts-Nevis-Anguilla, St. Lucia and St. Vincent), Fiji (7% Nov. 19), Gambia (Nov. 20), Gibraltar, Guyana (Nov. 19), Hong Kong (10% Nov. 19-23), Iceland (24.6% Nov. 24), Ireland (Nov. 18), Israel (Nov. 19), Jamaica (Nov. 21), Macao (5% Nov. 27), Malawi (Nov. 20), Malaysia (Nov. 22-23), Malta (Nov. 20), Mauritius (Nov. 20), New Zealand (Nov. 21), Seychelles, Sierra Leone (Nov. 22), Southern Yemen, Spain (Nov. 19), Trinidad & Tobago (Nov. 22). Those not devaluing: Australia, Austria, Bahamas, Bahrein, Belgium, Brazil (Brazil devalued the cruzeiro 16% Dec. 29, citing domestic inflation of 64% over 23 months as the reason), Brunei, Canada, Chad, Congo (Brazzaville), Dahomey, Finland, France, Ghana, Greece, India, Iraq, Italy, Japan, Jordan, Kenya, Kuwait, Lebanon, Libya, Luxembourg, Morocco, Nepal, Netherlands, Nigeria, Norway, Pakistan, Portugal, Rhodesia, Saudi Arabia, South Africa, Singapore, Sweden, Switzerland, Tanzania, Turkey, Uganda, the UAR, the US, West Germany, Yugoslavia and Zambia. (Finland, however, had devalued the markka by 31.25% Oct. 12.)

Expressing his support of the British action, U.S. Pres. Johnson Nov. 18 indicated his determination to maintain the current value of the dollar. He reaffirmed "unequivocally" the U.S.' commitment "to buy and sell gold at the existing price of $35 an ounce." The President said: "The nations of the free world are united in their determination to keep the international monetary system strong. The U.S. will continue to meet its international monetary responsibilities." Noting that the British had "worked hard over a number of years to correct their trade deficit," Mr. Johnson said that it had become clear to both Britain and the IMF that a "fundamental imbalance" in Britain's international monetary position had required an "adjustment in the exchange rate." He expressed the belief that the new parity of the pound would allow Britain to "achieve the needed improvements in its ability to compete in world markets."

The U.S. Federal Reserve Board (FRB) Nov. 19 raised its discount rate from 4% to 4.5%, effective Nov. 20. A few hours later, the Bank of Canada announced a rise in its rate to 6% from 5%. In a statement issued Nov. 19, the FRB said it had raised its rate "to assure the continued orderly functioning of U.S. financial markets and to maintain the availability of reserves to the banking system on terms and conditions that will foster sustainable economic growth at home and a sound international position for the dollar." Emphasizing that there was sufficient credit available for member banks that might be faced with unusually large withdrawals, the FRB affirmed that "borrowing by member banks [from the FRB] for purposes of making adjustments to market pressures is an appropriate use of the discount mechanism."

Announcing the increase in the Canadian bank rate, Bank of Canada Gov. Louis Rasminsky said Nov. 19 that "it would continue to be the policy of the bank to facilitate the provision of adequate credit to meet the needs of sound economic expansion." The new bank rate was the highest since 1962.

In response to the rise in the FRB discount rate, major U.S. commercial banks raised their lending rates Nov. 20-21. The Continental Illinois National Bank & Trust Co., Chicago's largest bank, was the first to do so, announcing an increase in its prime (minimum) interest rate on business loans to 6% from 5.5% Nov. 20. Practically all of the U.S.' 20 largest banks quickly followed suit Nov. 21 and raised their rates on business loans an equal amount.

Support was forthcoming from the Common Market as well. The finance and economics ministers of the Common Market countries met in Paris Nov. 19. They then issued a communique describing the British devaluation as "courageous" and affirming the intention of the EEC "to contribute to the success" of the measure. In this light, they said, their countries would not devalue their currencies; thus, they would permit Britain to gain the benefits of its devaluation. This decision of the Common Market countries was "a measure of their determination to make a positive contribution to international monetary cooperation," the communique said. It warned, however, that the British devaluation would impose an "increased vigilance" on the Common Market since Britain would become a stronger competitor in world markets.

The EEC Council of Ministers met Nov. 20 to deliberate further on the British devaluation and to discuss its implications on Britain's bid for Common Market membership. A statement read at the opening of the meeting by Karl Schiller, West German economics minister, praised the British for handling the sterling crisis courageously and expressed the hope that the measures taken would lead to "lasting success." Citing the decision of the EEC nations to maintain the par values of their currencies and to contribute to new international support for the pound, Schiller said this demonstrated the "solidarity of the 6 and solidarity toward Britain and toward preparedness for intimate cooperation on financial policy." All the ministers except the French viewed the devaluation as improving Britain's chances for Common Market membership. French Foreign Min. Maurice Couve de Murville argued that devaluation was not the "fundamental point" and bore no relation to the membership bid. He asserted that the problems associated with improving the British economy were still "immense" and that "no immediate solution was possible." He declared that Britain would have to take all the "necessary measures" before negotiations on membership could begin. Accordingly, the ministers agreed to postpone any further discussions of the British bid until their Dec. 18-19 meeting.

At a news conference Nov. 19, French Finance & Economic Affairs Min. Michel Debre had described the British action as a "courageous and difficult" move, but he asserted that this had produced "no fundamental change" in France's opposition to British membership in the Common Market.

Tass, the Soviet news agency, asserted Nov. 19 that the devaluation of the pound "cannot serve as a magic remedy" for Britain's economic ills and that it would place a "heavy burden on the shoulders of the working people of Britain." Tass called the devaluation a "new attempt to safeguard the high profits of the monopolies at the expense of the workers."

Devaluation a Necessity

The *N.Y. Times* Nov. 19 characterized the devaluation as "the longest-running melodrama in the financial world—the perils of the pound." The step was widely described as unavoidable. The pound had fallen in October from its par of $2.80 to $2.7825, the lowest level permitted by IMF rules, and the British government was losing reserves rapidly in maintaining this level, as it was required to do. It was at this point that the bank rate was raised from 5.5% to 6% Oct. 20 in an attempt either to stem the outflow of capital from Britain or, better yet, to attract foreign capital to Britain in response to higher earnings. This method was tried once more Nov. 9 when the rate was raised again, this time to 6.5%. Short-run loans had provided temporary relief since 1964, when Prime Min. Wilson inherited an estimated $2 billion balance-of-payments deficit, but these were stop-gap measures rather than a solution.

Economic prospects had seemed to be improving for Britain. "Indications are increasing that expansion in the UK domestic economy is being resumed," the IMF had reported Oct. 27. Unemployment had leveled off, and wages and prices were being restrained. The trade deficit was serious, having risen sharply in September to £52 million ($145.6 million), due to increased imports (primarily oil) and reduced exports (with dock strikes in both London and Liverpool). Wilson, in his Lord Mayor's Guildhall speech in October, however, had dismissed the balance-of-trade figures as "meaningless" in the light of the dock strikes.

The devaluation had been anticipated. Prices on the London stock market fell significantly Friday, Nov. 17. Prices of gold shares had risen, however, as did silver bullion prices, the latter up 6.2% Nov. 17. Tourists and others at Paris' Le Bourget Airport had discovered Nov.

17 that British currency was not being accepted for purchases, as it always had been, and American diplomats in Paris could no longer pay their hotel bills with sterling.

The question was whether 14.3% would be enough. British exports would not fall 14.3% in price, as transportation costs, (foreign) sales and excise taxes and retailers' mark-ups would not change with the devaluation. Likewise, the devaluation by 32 other nations would nullify the impact of the British devaluation in these countries. The question of the adequacy of the devaluation could only be answered by forthcoming events.

Aid for the Pound

To protect the devalued pound from further speculation, Britain Nov. 18 sought and was promised new international credits amounting to about $3 billion. The finance and economics ministers of the 6 European Common Market countries announced in Paris Nov. 19 that their countries would make substantial contributions to the $1.4 billion standby loan arranged with the IMF. West German Finance Min. Franz Josef Strauss said his country's share would be $200 million. It was reported Nov. 19 that the U.S. had agreed to provide $500 million of the $1.6 billion loan that Britain had negotiated with the central banks of the major industrial nations; the West German and Italian contributions were $250 million each. French officials disclosed Nov. 20 that France would not contribute to the $1.6 billion loan, but it was reported Nov. 21 that these other countries had agreed to advance part of the loan: Canada, Japan, the Netherlands, Norway and Sweden. The loan would be in the form of short-term 3-month credits. The Bank of England announced Nov. 23 that the central bank credits "had been finalized in detail for a total amount in excess of $1.5 billion."

The British reserve problem was complicated by the repeated need to repay earlier debts. Britain Nov. 20 repaid to the IMF the equivalent of $249.84 million as the last payment on the $1 billion it had borrowed in Dec. 1964. The repayment was in the form of the following 11 currencies (expressed in U.S. dollar equivalents): Australian dollars—$10 million, Belgian francs—$17 million, Canadian dollars—$15 million, Danish kroner—$10 million, French francs—$45 million, Italian lire—$40 million, Japanese yen—$20 million, Netherlands guilders—$16 million, Norwegian kroner—$10 million, Swedish kroner—$15 million and West German marks—$51.84 million. In addition to the $1 billion Dec. 1964 drawing, Britain had drawn the equivalent of $1.4 billion from the IMF in May 1965 and $122.5 million in Mar. 1966.

The IMF Nov. 29 approved Britain's request for the 12-month standby credit of $1.4 billion. In a statement issued Nov. 29, the IMF said the new credit "will assist the United Kingdom authorities in establishing confidence in the new parity for sterling and will thus help to pre-

serve stability of the international monetary system." The IMF said the
devaluation of the pound and the other economic measures taken by
Britain would "lay the basis for a major improvement in...[Britain's]
balance-of-payments position." Following a meeting in Paris Nov.
29 of the Organization for Economic Cooperation & Development and the
Group-of-10 nations, it was announced that, if Britain were to draw the
full amount of the credit, the IMF would provide the funds by (1) borrowing $525 million from the central banks of the Group of 10, (2)
selling $400 million worth of its gold stock of about $3.8 billion and (3)
supplying the remainder through its current foreign-exchange holdings.

Roy Jenkins, who had succeeded James Callaghan as chancellor of
the exchequer Nov. 29, denied in the House of Commons Nov. 30 that
the IMF had attached "conditions" on the new credit. Jenkins' answer
was in response to questioning concerning a Nov. 23 "Letter of Intent"
in which Callaghan had described to IMF managing director Pierre-
Paul Schweitzer the post-devaluation measures Britain intended to take.
The letter, made public Nov. 30, was widely interpreted as an indication
that the IMF (particularly the Group of 10 members) had imposed
conditions for authorizing the credit. But Jenkins maintained that the
letter had merely outlined the measures that the government had submitted to the House of Commons Nov. 18. Among the major goals
described in the letter: (a) A balance-of-payments surplus whose annual
rate would be £200 million ($480 million) by the 2d half of 1968 and £500
million ($1.2 billion) in 1969. (b) A reduction in consumer demand by
£750-£800 million ($1.8-$1.92 billion) a year. (c) A reduction in private
borrowing in 1968 by about £100 million ($240 million) and a ceiling on
government borrowing of "not more than £1 billion" ($2.4 billion).

The letter disclosed that Britain would review the state of the
economy and balance-of-payments position in February, July and
November 1968 and that it would consult with the IMF on the results of
this review. If "present policies should turn out to be inadequate," the
letter said, the government was "firmly determined to take such further
measures as may be necessary to achieve" the economic goals cited in
the letter. If it were the opinion of the government or the IMF that the
policies were "not producing the desired improvement in the balance of
payments," the letter concluded, Britain would consult with the IMF
"during the period of the standby arrangement and as long thereafter as
Fund holdings of sterling exceed 125% of [the UK IMF] quota, to find
appropriate solutions."

In parliamentary debate Dec. 5, Jenkins called for severe wage
restraints and suggested that government spending, including defense
spending, would be cut further. He said: "We have lived too long under
successive governments within an economic straitjacket. The straitjacket arises out of the fact that we have been spending more than we
have been earning, at home and abroad." While admitting that Britain
faced a "hard prospect" in the immediate months ahead, Jenkins

asserted that the austerity measures described in the letter to the IMF were "the only way to avoid having people looking over our shoulders." Several left-wing Labor MPs challenged this view. Michael Foot, a prominent Labor backbencher, charged that the IMF letter was "ignominious" and that it represented an "elaborate, labyrinthine commitment" to "foreign bankers." The dissident Laborites then forced the issue to a vote. The vote was 231-17 in favor of the government. Conservatives and Liberals deliberately abstained to dramatize the split in the Labor Party. Of the 17 negative votes, 16 were Labor and one was Scottish National. 18 Laborites abstained.

Other Post-Devaluation Developments

Defense Min. Denis Healey had said Nov. 22 that the reduced defense spending called for in the new economic measures "must not involve any change in our political commitments, . . . in the broad structure of our forces . . ., nor any major increase in the rate" of reduction of overseas forces, as set forth in the July Defense Ministry White Paper. He said the planned savings of £100 million annually would come "almost entirely" from reductions in military "hardware." "We shall have to make a large range of . . . postponements in new equipment and building, and we shall have to run down our stocks," Healey said. He outlined these specific measures:

●The aircraft carrier *Victorious* would be phased out of service about a year earlier than planned. The ship was the oldest of 3 carriers that were to be retired from service by the mid-1970s.

●A $28 million order for the purchase from the U.S. of 15 Chinook CH47 helicopters would be cancelled, as would an order for 8 Buccaneer jet fighters.

●Plans for the construction of a British-U.S. military staging post on the Indian Ocean island of Aldabra would be abandoned. While Healey conceded that this decision would "reduce the flexibility of our deployment in the 1970s," he said Britain still had a "variety of routes to the Middle East and Far East on which to rely." The construction of an airstrip and supporting facilities on Aldabra, at a cost of about $48 million, had been planned to enable Britain to maintain a defense role east of the Suez once it had withdrawn its troops from Aden (currently under way) and from Singapore and Malaysia (planned for about 1975).

●The army would "suffer cuts on a wide range of equipment, involving some of its weapons, ammunition, vehicles and instruments."

Healey said it was not "inconceivable" that cancelled programs could be restored later. He admitted that the defense cutback would reduce "temporarily . . . the level at which we can meet our commitments overseas," particularly for "major operations outside Europe." But he said the reductions were "acceptable" in terms of Britain's economic position and the fact that "the risk of being involved in major operations outside Europe during the period when these cuts will take effect, say from the middle of next year to 2 years after that, is very much less than it was when 'confrontation' was still under way and we still had our forces in South Arabia." The cutback would reduce Britain's total defense spending in 1968 by about $240 million, to about $4.56 billion (new par value). Originally, the government had planned to reach this level of defense spending by 1970-1.

Roy Jenkins, 47, succeeded James Callaghan, 55, as British chancellor of the exchequer Nov. 29, and Callaghan took over Jenkins' functions as secretary of state for the Home Department, responsible for police and other internal affairs. In his letter of resignation, transmitted to Prime Min. Wilson Nov. 18 and made public Nov. 29, Callaghan said he had recommended the devaluation of the pound. "When I did so," he wrote, "I was very conscious that I was going back on pledges that I had given in good faith to a number of overseas countries about the value of their sterling holdings. No chancellor can escape this dilemma, but I do not think it right that I should continue in office." Callaghan had headed the Treasury since the Labor Party returned to power in Oct. 1964.

Reserves & Balance of Payments

Balance-of-trade and balance-of-payments figures issued monthly by the British Board of Trade provided an index of Britain's mounting financial difficulties. The release of the October figures, indicating the largest monthly deficits ever recorded by the Board of Trade, was widely viewed as one of the major factors prompting the heavy speculation on the pound during the latter part of the week of Nov. 12. These revised figures were reported (amounts in equivalent dollar terms computed in terms of the old $2.80 par value of the pound):

February: balance-of-trade deficit—$151.2 billion; balance-of-payments deficit—$2.8 million.

March: balance-of-trade deficit—$168.0 million; balance-of-payments deficit—$33.6 million.

April: balance-of-trade deficit—$280.0 million; balance-of-payments deficit—$114.5 million.

May: balance-of-trade deficit—$218.4 million; balance-of-payments deficit—$67.2 million.

June: balance-of-trade deficit—$249.2 million; balance-of-payments deficit—$126 million.

July: balance-of-trade deficit—$123.2 million; balance-of-payments surplus—$11.2 million.

August: balance-of-trade deficit—$235.2 million; balance-of-payments deficit—$58.8 million.

September: balance-of-trade deficit—$308 million; balance-of-payments deficit—$128.8 million.

October: balance-of-trade deficit—$464.8 million; balance-of-payments deficit—$299.6 million.

Recalculated at a pound value of $2.40, the October and November figures were:

October: balance-of-trade deficit—$398.4 million.

November: balance-of-trade deficit—$530.4 million.

(A wildcat dock-workers' strike in London, Liverpool and other British ports Sept. 18-Nov. 27 had contributed to Britain's balance-of-trade deficit by tying up about $240 million worth of exports. The strike had been called by a splinter group of the Transport & General Workers Union that feared layoffs on the docks as a result of the institution Sept. 18 of regular salaried employment for dock workers to replace the previous system of casual day-to-day labor. The Liverpool dock hands returned to work Oct. 30, the London hands Nov. 27.)

Exports in November totaled $816 million, as compared to the October total of $811.2 million, while imports in November climbed to $1.38 billion, from the October total of $1,245,600,000. The Board of Trade stressed that "it continues to be impossible to make any reliable assessment of current trade trends" since the November figures had been "severely affected" by the September-November dock workers' strike. The board also pointed out that the high November import figure had resulted in part from these factors: (1) the value of all imports received after devaluation of the pound had been determined at the new rate of exchange, and this raised the import figure by $36-$48 million; (2) British importers had increased their stocks in anticipation of the devaluation of the pound, and (3) the value of fuel imports "rose to the equivalent of $182.4 million from $117.6 million; not only did arrivals of oil increase in volume, but landed prices were sharply higher."

The Treasury reported Dec. 4 that British gold and foreign exchange reserves had increased by £53 million ($127.2 million) in November to a £1.223 billion ($2,935,200,000) total. But the Treasury noted that the November gain reflected the addition to the reserves of about $489.6 million representing the remainder of the government's portfolio of dollar securities. Without this addition, British reserves would have registered a loss of $362.4 million for November. But British gold and foreign exchange reserves fell by £100 million ($240 million) in December to a year-end total of £1.123 billion ($2,695,200,000). Most of the December decline reflected a payment to the U.S. and Canada of £92 million ($220.8 million) in interest and service charges on loans, a payment always made in the last month of the year.

Britain's balance-of-trade deficit amounted to the equivalent of $2,966,400,000 in 1967, compared with a 1966 deficit of $1.699 billion. The balance-of-payments deficit rose from $259,200,000 in 1966 to $1,353,600,000 in 1967. The trade deficit for December totaled $350.4 million on a seasonally adjusted basis, down $180 million from the November deficit. Exports in December rose to $1.068 billion, compared with the November total of $816 million, while imports in December climbed to $1,456,800,000 from the November total of $1.38 billion. Re-export of goods rose from $36.6 million in November to $38.4 million in December. On a seasonally-adjusted balance-of-payments basis, the British trade deficit dropped from $367.2 million in November to $168 million in December. The Board of Trade said that "part of the increase in December's import bill reflects the rise in prices ... following devaluation, and a little is attributable to arrivals delayed by the dock strikes in September." The board also noted that fuel import costs remained high because of the closure of the Suez Canal.

EUROPE, THE EEC & FREE TRADE AGREEMENTS

Common Market

The EEC Ministerial Council Feb. 9 adopted a plan for harmonizing the levying of turnover taxes in the 6 Common Market countries. The plan, to go into effect Jan. 1, 1970, called for instituting a "value added" tax at each stage in the production of an item, with each new tax replacing the preceding one and the final levy being passed on to the consumer in the form of a sales tax. The tax would apply to the production of all goods up to the wholesale level and to some services but not currently to agricultural products. The national treasuries of the 6 countries would continue to receive the tax revenues.

The Common Market's first 5-year economic plan had been adopted by the EEC Council Feb. 8. The plan, called the Medium-Term Economic Policy, was to cover the period 1966-70 and was to serve as the framework for all EEC agricultural, trade, labor and regional policy decisions. The plan: (a) Called for an annual growth rate of 4.3% in the 6 countries. Noting their chronic labor shortages, the plan said "the key to economic growth will have to be improvement in productivity." (EEC growth rate in 1966:4.5%.) (b) Called for an annual increase in productivity of 3.8%. Because of the "fragile economic balance" between supply and demand, the plan urged an increase in production in order to meet expected consumer demand. (c) Urged measures for the maintenance of price stability. (d) Called for the development of a program for scientific and technological advancement. (e) Cautioned against exorbitant tax increases so as not to depress industrial investment and private savings.

The plan called on each of the 6 EEC countries to develop "national budget previews" several years in advance of each fiscal year in order to safeguard against unnecessary government expenditures. EEC Executive Commission Vice Pres. Robert Marjolin, the author of the plan, described it as a "rolling program" that could be amended every 2 years. He noted: "We agreed last year on policies for industry and agriculture. This decision now gives us the 3d element we needed—economic policy."

The EEC Statistical Office Mar. 16 released figures indicating that trade between the countries of the Common Market and those of Eastern Europe had doubled during the period 1958-65. According to the figures, the EEC countries had exported goods worth $1.48 billion to Eastern Europe in 1965, compared with $698 million worth in 1958.

During the same period East European exports to the EEC rose from $698 million to $1.476 billion. (The figures also indicated that trade between Eastern Europe and Communist China had dropped off sharply during 1958-65. In 1958 East Europe exported goods worth $1.04 billion to China, compared to $284 million worth in 1965. During the same period Communist Chinese exports to East Europe fell from $1.17 billion to $312 million.)

The heads of government of the 6 Common Market states met in Rome May 29-30 to commemorate the 10th anniversary of the signing of the Treaty of Rome. It was the first time in 6 years that the EEC heads of government had met together. Among those attending the ceremonies: French Pres. de Gaulle, Premier Georges Pompidou and Foreign Min. Maurice Couve de Murville; West German Chancellor Kurt-Georg Kiesinger and Foreign Min. Willy Brandt; Belgian Premier Paul Vanden Boeynants and Foreign Min. Pierre Harmel; Netherlands Premier Petrus J. S. de Jong and Foreign Min. Joseph M. A. H. Luns; Luxembourg Premier Pierre Werner and Foreign Min. Pierre Gregoire; Italian Pres. Giuseppe Saragat, Premier Aldo Moro and Foreign Min. Amintore Fanfani.

Italian Pres. Saragat delivered the keynote address. He noted that the progress made by the EEC in the first 10 years of its existence had been "far better than even the most optimistic forecasts." He added, however, that "new problems await us, among them the question of the community's geographical and historical dimensions, and the accession of other countries." He expressed the hope that "negotiations will open soon with Great Britain, whose name is almost synonymous with political liberty." Saragat also reminded the audience of the "common destiny" that linked Europe "to the other great democracies of the Atlantic area and first of all to the United States of America." He added that he envisaged a united Europe that would "maintain with the United States its ties of friendship, of cooperation and of alliance" while at the same time applying "its own action to the direction of the affairs of the world."

A summit meeting of the 6 leaders and their foreign ministers was held May 30 in the Italian Foreign Ministry. According to news reports, the main topic of discussion was Britain's bid for membership in the EEC; all delegations except the French reportedly favored Britain's admission. A communique issued at the end of the meeting said: (a) At its meeting June 5-6, the EEC Council of Ministers would examine the membership applications that had been submitted by Britain, Ireland and Denmark May 11. (b) The Council would study means of bringing the 6 EEC members into closer political cooperation. (c) Another meeting of the EEC heads of state would be held, "probably" by the end of the year.

The Common Market nations reached agreement June 1 on remaining problems relating to pork, eggs, poultry and oil seed. The agreement cleared the way for the establishment of single markets for these products by July 1, in conformity with a timetable set in December 1964. Among the provisions of the agreement: (1) A guaranteed minimum price on pork was set at the equivalent of $62.75 per 100 kilograms. The support price represented a compromise between the higher amount that France had sought and the lower sum that West Germany and the Benelux countries had wanted. (Because of its large number of small producers, France's pork costs were generally higher than those in West Germany and the Benelux countries, where there was a greater concentration of large-scale pork producers.) France had sought to obtain a double-pricing system, under which small producers would receive higher prices than the large industrial producers. (2) In poultry and eggs, producers' associations were authorized to aid farmers in changing over to new systems of production but were barred from extending direct price support subsidies. (3) The import levy on oil seeds was reduced in order to aid Italy, which produced no seeds but imported large quantities for processing in refineries around Ravenna.

The EEC Council of Ministers agreed July 11 on terms for negotiating a preferential trade agreement between the Common Market and Spain. Under the terms of the proposed 6-year agreement, EEC would reduce by 60% its tariffs on imports from Spain, while Spain would reduce its tariffs on EEC goods by 40%. The agreement would be restricted primarily to industrial goods.

The EEC Council agreed July 11 to a one-year extension of the EEC-Israeli trade agreement (expired July 1), pending a decision on Israel's request for closer association with the Common Market. The EEC commission had recommended to the council June 10 that it consider one of 3 alternative approaches towards Israel's request: a new trade agreement, a system of trade preferences or associate membership.

EEC-ECSC-Euratom Merger

The long-awaited merger of the executive bodies of the 3 European communities took place July 1 with the formation of a single 14-member European Commission. The organs merged: the EEC Executive Commission, the High Authority of the European Coal & Steel Community (ECSC) and the Executive Commission of Euratom. The new commission was headed by Jean Rey, who had succeeded Walter Hallstein as president of the EEC Executive Commission June 5. The merger was viewed as a significant step toward the economic integration of the 6 nations comprising the communities—France, West Germany, Italy, Belgium, the Netherlands and Luxembourg—and toward the eventual prospect of a politically united Western Europe. The merger of the executive bodies was to be effective for a 3-year period, after which the treaties establishing the 3 communities would be amended to merge the EEC, ECSC and Euratom into a single European Community.

As a result of the merger, the headquarters of the ECSC was transferred from Luxembourg to Brussels, where the headquarters of the EEC and Euratom were located. The 14 new European commissioners replaced the 9 members of the ECSC High Authority, the 5 Euratom commissioners and the 9 EEC commissioners.

Members of the new commission, nominated June 27: *France*—Raymond Barre, 43; Henri Rochereau, 59; Jean-Francois Deniau, 38. *West Germany*—Fritz Hellwig, 54; Hans von der Groeben, 60, a vice president; Willy Haferkamp, 43. *Italy*—Lionello Levi-Sandri, 56, a vice president; Guido Colonna Di Paliano, 59, Eduardo Martino, 57. *Belgium*—Jean Rey (65 July 15), president; Albert Coppe, 55. *Netherlands*—Sicco Mansholt, 58, a vice president; Emanuel M. J. A. Sassen, 56. *Luxembourg*—Victor Bodson, 65.

The merger of the 3 executive bodies, approved by the EEC Council of Ministers in Mar. 1965, was to have gone into effect Jan. 1, 1966, but it had been delayed by a controversy between France and West Germany over the status of Walter Hallstein, then president of the EEC Commission. Germany had wanted Hallstein to become president of the merged executives, but France had opposed the nomination on the ground that Hallstein's supranational policies made him unsuitable for the post. As a compromise, French Pres. de Gaulle and West German Chancellor Kiesinger agreed during a meeting in Paris Jan. 13-14 to make Hallstein president of the new commission for an interim period of 6 months. However, it was reported May 6 that Hallstein had informed Bonn that he would not accept a temporary post on the new commission because he did not think fusion of the 3 bodies could be accomplished within 6 months.

Hallstein's letter said: "I ... hope you will understand if I request that no further action be taken to nominate me as first president of the single commission of the European communities.... There is a practical consideration. I believe I am correctly interpreting the intention of those member-governments putting forward my nomination as first president of the single commission if I attribute their attitude to the wish that I should pass on in a lasting form to the single commission the lesson learned in my 9-1/2 years as president of the EEC Commission. However, in view of the long-term nature of the work of the European Executive, there can be no question of fulfilling this wish between July 1 and Dec. 31, 1967, a period which will in fact be further considerably shortened by the summer and Christmas holidays. I have never considered the idea of being a member or vice president of the single commission. Nor do I do so today."

The impasse was resolved after France nominated as Hallstein's successor Jean Rey, the EEC's chief negotiator at the Kennedy Round tariff negotiations and a vice president of the EEC Executive Commission. The EEC Council of Ministers approved the nomination June 5. Rey's term of office was 2 years, beginning July 1.

Kiesinger & de Gaulle

West German Chancellor Kiesinger and French Pres. de Gaulle conferred in Bonn July 12-13. This was their 2d semi-annual meeting under the Franco-German friendship treaty of 1963. The meeting was held amid growing apprehension by the West Germans stemming from de Gaulle's failure to brief them on talks he had held with Soviet Premier Aleksei N. Kosygin. Among those participating in the de Gaulle-Kiesinger meetings were French Premier Georges Pompidou, French Foreign Min. Maurice Couve de Murville, West German Foreign Min. Willy Brandt, French Defense Min. Pierre Messmer and West German Defense Min. Gerhard Schroeder.

In a statement made after the talks, de Gaulle July 13 listed these conditions as essential for the preservation of French and German "national personalities": (1) Maintenance of the close Franco-German tie "to avoid the preponderance of America"; (2) maintenance of the European Common Market as an assurance against U.S. domination; (3) understanding and cooperation between Eastern and Western Europe "so that there shall exist something other than the system of the 2 blocs" (de Gaulle and the USSR favored a European security conference from which the U.S. would be barred; Bonn had been known to favor U.S. participation).

Kiesinger had said in Bonn Jan. 16, after he had conferred with de Gaulle in Paris Jan. 13-14: "As far as our relations with America are concerned, we have clearly stated that—contrary to France—we wish to remain within the system of an integrated military alliance and wish to have the presence of American troops in Europe for our security. We both agreed, however, that though Europeans must try to make an important contribution to the shaping of their own future, Europe continues to require for its protection the presence of the U.S. troops. As regards Great Britain, I referred to our policy statement and the proposals of maintaining an open door, but I added that we must now wait what the British themselves wished to do and that in any case it would be a matter for the 6 to come to a decision after considering such moves."

Major agreements reached by Kiesinger and de Gaulle July 12-13 called for: (a) the establishment of a joint commission to deal with the "political security" needs of the 2 countries; (b) the formation of a commission for economic, technical and industrial cooperation, with high-level representatives from both sides; (c) meetings in "special situations" at the highest level of the 2 governments; (d) a jointly sponsored study of the political and strategic circumstances in Europe in the 1970s.

De Gaulle declared after the talks July 13 that the U.S.' "enormous power" dominated the world scene and that this "automatically led" to the extension of U.S. "hegemony ... over others." But he called the U.S. "our natural friend and, for the time being and as long as the threat lasts, our ally."

French Unrest

Thousands of farmers demonstrated, sometimes violently, throughout France Oct. 2 and 12 in protest against the government's agricultural policies. The demonstrations were the first conducted at the national level since the farmer riots in 1963.

Demonstrations were staged Oct. 2 in response to a call by the National Farmers Union for a nationwide "action day" to press farmer demands, particularly for higher prices and greater government protection. While the majority of the demonstrations were orderly, violence broke out in more than a dozen cities and towns. In Quimper, Brittany, a crowd of 6,000 to 10,000 farmers clashed with police. The demonstrators burned the gatehouse of the prefecture, sacked the office of the Gaullist party and burned police vehicles before police dispersed them with tear gas. 179 policemen and more than 100 farmers were injured. Demonstrators and police also clashed at Redon, Pau and Dijon. In other parts of the country farmers barricaded roads and tore down telegraph poles.

Pres. de Gaulle met with his cabinet Oct. 3 to discuss the farmer unrest. In a statement issued after the meeting, de Gaulle noted that small farmers had experienced difficulties because of "unavoidable economic changes," but he asserted that these were changes that "the government has tried to direct and whose worst consequences it has tried to alleviate." He asserted that it would "undoubtedly be better if farmers' organizations associated themselves with these efforts instead of opposing them."

The leftist opposition (Communist Party and Federation of the Democratic & Socialist Left) introduced in the National Assembly Oct. 3 a censure motion attacking the government's social and economic policy. The motion charged in part that the government had to bear the "basic responsibility" for the "morass pushing the farmers to demonstrations and revolt." The motion was defeated Oct. 10 when it received only 207 of the 244 votes necessary for adoption. During the debate Oct. 10, Premier Georges Pompidou pledged new aid and credit to farmers and said the government would ask France's 5 Common Market partners to agree to certain increases in EEC meat prices.

Farmers demonstrated Oct. 12, but few incidents of violence were reported. The demonstrators barricaded major roads, harangued motorists and handed out leaflets. Paris express trains were halted for several hours near Limoges when farmers built a bonfire on the tracks. The

demonstrations were organized by leftist farm organizations and did not
have the official backing of the National Farmers Union.

In an effort to raise pork prices, the government announced Oct.
12 that it would ban all imports of pork from non-EEC countries.
(Major non-Common Market pork exporters to France were Poland and
Hungary.) The EEC commission met in emergency session Oct. 13 to
discuss the French action and agreed to permit France to maintain the
ban for one week while the commission sought a permanent solution.
France had sought unsuccessfully in earlier EEC agricultural negotiations to obtain a higher support price for pork.

The French Communist Party (PCF) registered the largest single
gains in elections held Sept. 24 and Oct. 1 to fill approximately half of
the seats of the general councils (assemblies) of the 99 departments in
metropolitan and overseas France. For the first time in the history of
the PCF, the Communists gained control of a general council—that of
the Paris suburb of Seine-Saint-Denis. In Seine-Saint-Denis, the PCF
won 25 of the 34 seats. In another Paris region department, Val-de-
Marne, the PCF won 13 of the council's 33 seats, while the Socialists,
with whom the PCF was allied, gained 4 seats. Both general councils
elected Communists as presidents Oct. 4.

Figures issued by the French Finance Ministry Dec. 2 indicated
that total French gold and foreign exchange reserves at the end of
November stood at $6.18 billion, up $334.4 million from October and
$437.3 million from the first of the year. Sources in Paris said that most
of the November gain had been in the form of dollars and had boosted
French holdings of U.S. currency to about $1 billion.

European Inflation

Inflation was a problem throughout Europe. The U.S. Commerce
Dept. calculated Oct. 27 that, on the basis of an index of 100 for the
1957-9 period for each country, the consumer price index in September
was 130 in Great Britain and in August was 143 in France and 123 in
West Germany. It had been 139 in Italy in June.

Several major Western countries lowered their central bank discount rates in 1967 in an effort to stimulate domestic economies that had
slowed down, compounding inflationary pressures. The action marked a
movement away from the tight-money policies that had been instituted
following the 1965-66 inflationary period. These changes were reported
(date in parentheses denotes date of effective change): *Austria*—from
4.25% to 3.75% (Oct. 26). *Belgium*—from 5.25% to 5% (Feb. 2), from
5% to 4.75% (Mar. 23), from 4.75% to 4.5% (May 11), from 4.5% to
4.25% (Sept. 14), from 4.25% to 4% (Oct. 26). *Netherlands*—from 5%
to 4.25% (Mar. 15). *Sweden*—from 6% to 5.5% (Feb. 3), from 5.5% to
5% (Mar. 9). *Switzerland*—from 3.5% to 3% (July 10). *U.S.*—from
4.5% to 4% (Apr. 7-11). *West Germany*—from 5% to 4.5% (Jan. 6),

from 4.5% to 4% (Feb. 17), from 4% to 3.5% (Apr. 14), from 3.5% to 3% (May 12). During the same period, the French, Italian and Japanese bank rates remained unchanged at 3.5%, 3.5%, and 5.48% respectively.

Kennedy Round Completed Successfully

53 nations participating in the Kennedy Round negotiations reached agreement May 15 on tariff reductions affecting about 60,000 items and more than $40 billion annually in world trade. Representatives of 46 of the nations signed the accords May 15. The accord marked the conclusion of talks held since 1964 under the auspices of the General Agreement on Tariffs & Trade (GATT). Although the initial objective of a 50% across-the-board cut in world tariffs was not realized, the accord represented the most significant international trade liberalization in history. Its major features included (1) a reduction of about 1/3 in world industrial tariffs over the 5-year period beginning Jan. 1, 1968; (2) liberalization of trade in agriculture; (3) a food-aid program for the less-developed countries.

The specific terms of the agreement were withheld pending final approval by the participating nations. Among the general provisions, reported May 15: (a) An average 33% to 35% reduction on world industrial tariffs. (b) A 2-stage 50% reduction on most chemical tariffs of major-producing nations. (c) The adjustment of world iron and steel tariffs to rates averaging about 6% as compared to the current averages of about 7% in the U.S. and 9% in the EEC countries; Britain consented to a 20% reduction on its iron and steel tariffs, which currently stood at 10% to 12%. (d) The reduction of duties on many items to "nuisance" levels of 5% or less. (e) The liberalization of trade in vegetables, fruits and other non-cereal products. (f) A minimum world wheat price of $1.73 per bushel for U.S. Hard Red Winter Ordinary Wheat f.o.b. Gulf ports (the reference grain), as compared to the current minimum price of $1.45 per bushel. (g) A food-aid program for the less-developed countries amounting to 4.5 million metric tons of grain annually. Of the total, the U.S. agreed to provide about 42%, the EEC about 23%, Canada 9% and Australia, Britain and Japan 5% each. (h) Reduction of barriers to trade in tropical produce, raw materials and manufactured items supplied by the less-developed countries. (i) An anti-dumping code to guard against discriminately low export prices and an agreement on action to be taken against certain other nontariff barriers to trade.

The agreement on chemical tariff reduction was to be implemented in 2 stages. In the first stage, the U.S., Japan and Switzerland would cut most of their tariffs by 50%, while the EEC would reduce its tariffs by 20%. In the 2d stage, the EEC would cut its tariffs an additional 30% once the U.S. had repealed its American Selling Price (ASP) system of evaluating certain import duties. (The ASP was a measure adopted by Congress in 1922, primarily to protect the developing American chemical industry. Under the measure, the U.S. adjusted the import duty on certain benzenoid [coal-tar] chemicals, rubber-soled footwear [mainly sneakers], certain varieties of canned clams and woolen knit gloves and mittens to force the price of the foreign product to the level of the price of the competitive American product. [Other import duties usually were fixed as a percentage of the wholesale price of the product in the country of origin.] Repeal of the ASP would require Congressional action.) Since the U.S. President's tariff-cutting authority expired June 30, final details of the agreement were to be elaborated by that date. Once incorporated into legal documents and signed by all participating nations, the agreement was to go into effect Jan. 1, 1968. Its provisions were to be implemented in stages over a 5-year period.

In a communique issued May 15, GATT Director Gen. Eric Wyndham White hailed the accord as "the most ambitious attempt ever made to achieve the liberalization of international trade." He noted that the results of the Kennedy Round were of a "far greater magnitude" than those achieved in previous trade negotiations and that, through the application of the most-favored-nation principle, all 86 members of GATT stood to benefit from the agreement. The communique noted, however, that "in a number of cases the action taken falls short of the expectations of the developing countries." The participants in the talks therefore agreed, it said, that "the immediate implementation" of tariff reductions for the developing countries would be of "great value in maximizing the benefits to them of these negotiations." They "declared their determination" to reach a final decision on this point by the time the accord was ready for signing.

The participants in the Kennedy Round negotiations included the U.S., Canada, Japan, the 6 Common Market countries, Britain and the 6 other members of the European Free Trade Association. Among other countries represented were 3 from the Communist bloc, 6 from Asia, 8 from Latin America and 9 from Africa. In addition to the 53 full members, 3 states—Lichtenstein, Monaco and San Marino—were represented through other countries.

The major stumbling-block to a final Kennedy Round agreement had stemmed from a deadlock between the U.S. and the Common Market countries over grains and chemicals. The agreement was reached in the final hours of negotiation May 15 after the U.S. and EEC had accepted compromise proposals on the grain and chemical packages. The U.S. had made its cuts in industrial tariffs contingent on EEC acceptance of a 3-part grain agreement that included (1) guaranteed access to 13% of the EEC grain market by the world's grain exporters, (2) a minimum export price for wheat of about $1.74 per bushel and (3) a food-aid program for the less-developed countries amounting to about 5 million tons of grain annually. The EEC in turn sought (1) to guarantee only 10% access to its grain market, (2) to obtain a minimum export price on secondary grains as well as on wheat and (3) to initiate a less substantial food-aid program. An agreement on grains was reached after the U.S. dropped its demand for guaranteed access to the EEC market in return for EEC acceptance of (1) a food-aid program amounting to 4.5 million tons of grain annually and (2) a minimum price ($1.73 per bushel) on wheat, but not on secondary grains.

In the chemical sector, the U.S. had offered to cut its tariffs by 50% in return for a similar cut by the EEC. The EEC negotiators insisted, however, that its reductions would be contingent on repeal by the U.S. of its ASP system. Since repeal of ASP would require Congressional action and since this could not be forthcoming before Presidential tariff-cutting authority expired June 30, the U.S. would not accede to the EEC demand. The EEC later altered its position by offering to reduce its tariffs unconditionally by 20% and by an additional 30% on repeal of ASP. The U.S. finally accepted this offer.

Pres. Johnson and foreign government spokesmen welcomed the successful conclusion of the negotiations May 16. Leaders of the U.S. chemical, steel and textile industries generally criticized the terms of the accord, while farm spokesmen indicated their support for it. Noting that the Kennedy Round negotiators had reached "general agreement" on major issues. Pres. Johnson asserted that "the way is now clear for the conclusion of a final agreement covering billions of dollars worth of trade among more than 50 countries."

British Board of Trade Pres. Douglas Jay said May 16 that, while the agreement opened up new opportunities for British exporters, it also would force many British industries to "look closely at their efficiency and margins" in light of the stiff competition that would result from the accord. The Confederation of British Industries May 16 welcomed the accord, which it said had "considerably exceeded expectations." Similar statements of support came from Japan, West Germany, Italy, Canada and Brazil May 16.

Canadian Prime Min. Lester B. Pearson had called May 15 for a new round of trade negotiations to deal with problems left unresolved by the Kennedy Round. Speaking at the opening session of the 21st biennial congress of the International Chamber of Commerce, Pearson particularly cited nontariff barriers to trade and the need for extending more favorable tariff treatment to the developing countries. At the conclusion of the congress May 19, the U.S. delegation proposed the establishment of a "world free trade association" to take care of "unfinished business" left over from the Kennedy Round.

A study prepared by the GATT secretariat and released June 30 gave these figures: The tariff reductions would affect 70% of the dutiable imports of Britain, Japan, Sweden, Switzerland, the U.S. and the 6 EEC members. 2/3 of these countries' tariff cuts would amount to 50% or more; 1/5 of the cuts would be between 25% and 50%. The greatest proportion of these countries' dutiable products affected by the agreement fell into these categories (percentage affected in parentheses):

chemicals (93%), pulp and paper (92%), machinery, transport equipment and precision instruments (91%), raw materials other than fuels and agricultural raw materials (83%), base metals other than iron and steel (81%), other manufactures (81%). Other categories affected: textiles and clothing (65%), iron and steel (63%), non-tropical agricultural products (49%), tropical agricultural products (39%), fuels (14%).

Under the Kennedy Round anti-dumping code: (1) the U.S. agreed to withhold dumping investigations unless there was "evidence of injury" to U.S. industry and then, if damage were proved, to limit the investigations to 90 days, during which time the amount of the penalty duty to be imposed would be ascertained and applied to bring the cost of the goods up to a "fair" level; (2) Canada agreed to adopt a requirement that damage must be proved before penalty duties could be applied; (3) the Common Market countries agreed to adopt uniform regulations. The new code was to go into effect July 1, 1968.

Figures released by the British Board of Trade June 30 indicated that Britain would cut by an average of 38% its tariffs on dutiable goods from countries outside the Commonwealth and European Free Trade Association. This figure included average reductions of 41% on U.S. goods and 37% on EEC goods. In return, the U.S. and Common Market agreed to cut their tariffs on British goods by an average of 40% and 36%, respectively.

Whereas most countries were to implement their tariff reductions in 5 equal installments beginning Jan. 1, 1968, the Common Market countries were cut their tariffs initially by 2/5 July 1, 1968 and then were to implement 3 additional reductions of 1/5 each Jan. 1, 1970, 1971 and 1972. This difference in timing was dictated by the EEC's planned implementation July 1, 1968 of the final stage of its common tariff schedule, at which time the Common Market would become a duty-free area with a common external tariff. Britain announced July 12 that it would implement its tariff reductions on the EEC timetable. The Board of Trade said that Norway, Sweden, Denmark and Finland also would follow this schedule.

Dr. Raul Prebisch, secretary general of the UN Conference on Trade & Development (UNCTAD), warned Sept. 6 that, unless there were "additional measures in the commercial field," the Kennedy Round accord would "contribute to a further decline in the relative share of developing countries in world trade." A "preliminary evaluation" of the Kennedy Round results, Prebisch said, showed that the "major reductions" in industrial tariffs, averaging 36%, would provide a "substantial impetus to the trade of developed countries" but that these cuts would have little effect on the developing countries, whose exports consisted for the most part of primary rather than industrial products. He noted that tariff reductions were substantially less on such products as foodstuffs, oils, fats, textile products, clothing, beverages and tobacco and that, in addition, these products encountered "high-tariff peaks" often "reinforced by severe non-tariff barriers."

Joseph A. Greenwald, U.S. Deputy Assistant State Secretary for international trade policy and economic defense, conceded Sept. 6 that "the major trading countries received concessions and benefits [in the Kennedy Round accord] outweighing those received by other countries." But he asserted that the benefits to the developing countries were not negligible. He noted that the developed countries had agreed to tariff cuts on 79% of the dutiable products that had been submitted by the developing countries and that the reductions had equaled or exceeded 50% on more than half of the items on the list. Greenwald said the U.S. had agreed to tariff reductions on dutiable goods from the developing countries accounting for $900 million worth of their exports in 1964.

Special concessions to the developing nations were proposed by delegates to GATT at GATT's annual meeting at the ministerial level in Geneva Nov. 22-24. A statement issued at the close of the meeting said the delegates had agreed to give "special attention" to the developing countries, "including the possibility of eliminating duties on products made by hand and other products of cottage industries and the possibility of eliminating or reducing duties on products of interest to developing countries." But it said "no new major initiatives could reasonably be expected in the near future" because time was needed to consolidate the gains made in the Kennedy Round. The delegates agreed to compile a list of non-tariff barriers to trade to be dealt with at future negotiations and to establish a committee to examine problems in agriculture. The ministers Nov. 24 elected Swiss Amb.-to-Britain Olivier Long, 52, to succeed Eric Wyndham White as director general of GATT, effective shortly after Jan. 1, 1968. White, 54, had affirmed his decision Nov. 7 not to seek a renewal of his position after its expiration Dec. 31. White had been director general of GATT since its formation in 1947. (Ireland Nov. 22 completed formalities for becoming a contracting [full] member of GATT. Ireland's accession increased the number of contracting parties in GATT to 75. 12 other countries held other forms of membership or association.)

Delegates to the 7th annual ministerial meeting of the 21-nation Organization for Economic Cooperation & Development, held in Paris Nov. 30-Dec. 1, agreed in principle Dec. 1 to a plan under which the developed nations would grant special tariff concessions to the developing nations. The other major topic of discussion at the meeting was the disequilibrium in the industrialized countries' international balance of payments, particularly the disparity between the U.S. deficit and the EEC surplus. The agreement on tariff concessions was in the form of guidelines to serve as the basic negotiating position for the developed countries at a UNCTAD meeting in Feb. 1968. Under the terms of the agreement, the developed countries would cut their tariffs for at least 10 years on manufactured and semi-manufactured goods produced by the developing countries without seeking reciprocal treatment on the goods they exported to the developing countries. The concessions would be "general" (*i.e.*, extended by all of the developed countries to all of the developing countries), would take the form of abolition of tariffs or "major reductions" in them and would be granted on an "equitable" basis.

BRITAIN, THE EEC & EFTA

France Vetoes Britain Again

Britain's 2d membership application to the EEC met the same fate as the first; French Pres. de Gaulle expressed his disapproval despite the support of the other 5 EEC members. Since unanimous approval was required for admission to the EEC, de Gaulle's expressed disapproval effectively prevented the issue from reaching the formal rejection level.

Support of Britain had been expressed early in the year by German Chancellor Kiesinger. Kiesinger, who had just returned from Paris and a conference with de Gaulle, was speaking in Bonn Jan. 16 when asked about the British application. To him, he said, it was "clear that there would be a serious controversy among the 6 if France wishes to resist such a request for any reason." Asked his opinion of de Gaulle's thoughts, Kiesinger replied: "I can neither confirm nor deny this on the basis of our talks, but I believe that he has still serious doubts about Britain's overall political attitude, *i.e.* the Commonwealth, America, etc...."

Soviet Premier Aleksei N. Kosygin, who visited London Feb. 6-13, said at a televised press conference Feb. 9; "The very name 'common market' is inexact. It cannot be called 'common' because it does not include many countries.... Exclusive markets will not do good for Europe. Therefore, such markets are needed which would enable cooperation of all European states on the basis of absolute equality."

Britain's chances for EEC membership were discussed informally by Western leaders who gathered in Bonn Apr. 25 for the funeral of ex-Chancellor Konrad Adenauer, who had died Apr. 19. Pres. Johnson and British Prime Min. Wilson each talked briefly with de Gaulle after a luncheon given by West German Pres. Luebke. Wilson reportedly told de Gaulle that the British government would soon announce its decision on whether to apply for EEC membership. De Gaulle conferred with Kiesinger; Johnson conferred later Apr. 25 with Wilson and Italian Premier Moro and Foreign Min. Fanfani. Wilson said afterwards that he had discussed Britain's Common Market "probes," general developments in Europe and the agenda for his visit to Washington in June. Johnson indicated that the major topics discussed with Moro and

Fanfani had been the proposed nuclear nonproliferation treaty and the Kennedy Round.

Britain formally reapplied May 11 for full membership in the EEC, the European Coal & Steel Community and Euratom. This decision had been announced by Prime Min. Wilson in the House of Commons May 2. After 3 days of debate May 8-10, Commons May 10 approved by 488-62 vote a motion supporting the government's decision. In his statement May 2, Wilson referred to the decision as one that could "well determine the future of Britain, of Europe and indeed of the world for decades to come." He cited the "long-term potential" to both Europe and Britain of a single market of nearly 300 million persons and the "enormous possibilities" that would be created by an integrated technology on a "truly continental scale." Above all, Wilson said, Britain's purpose in seeking membership in the European communities derived from its "recognition that Europe is now faced with the opportunity of a great move forward in political unity and that we can—and indeed we must—play our full part in it." Wilson said his government was prepared to accept the Treaty of Rome, "subject to the necessary adjustments consequent upon the accession of a new member and provided that we receive satisfaction on the points about which we see difficulty.... It is our hope that the negotiations will be followed through swiftly, and will relate to the small number of really important issues which have been identified...." Among the issues to be resolved, he said, were:

Agricultural policy—"We must be realistic and recognize that the [European Economic] Community's agricultural policy is an integral part of the community; we must come to terms with it. But ... [the implementation of] this policy would involve far-reaching changes in the structure of British agriculture..., [which] will require suitable arrangements, including an adequate transitional period.... The financial arrangements which have been devised to meet the requirements of the community's agricultural policy as it exists today would, if applied to Britain as they now stand, involve an inequitable sharing of the financial costs and impose on our balance of payments an additional burden which we should not in fairness be asked to carry."

Commonwealth interests—"There are also highly important Commonwealth interests, mainly in the field of agriculture.... These include in particular the special problems of New Zealand and of Commonwealth sugar-producing countries, whose needs are at present safeguarded by the Commonwealth Sugar Agreement."

Regional policies—"We should be able, as members of the community, to continue to take the necessary steps to ensure the industrial and social development of ... [the underdeveloped] areas of the country."

In reaction to Wilson's announcement, French Information Min. Georges Gorse said May 3 that Britain's bid was "a matter of great importance that requires exhaustive examination." "It is obvious," Gorse added, "that if there are problems, they result from reservations made by the British government, and from the changes it asks for in the Common Market's rules."

Among other reaction to Wilson's announcement: The European Trade Union Secretariat issued a statement in Brussels May 3 welcoming the British decision "with deep satisfaction." The Scottish National Party charged in a statement May 4 that Britain was in effect

destroying Scottish national identity by bringing Scotland into the EEC
without allowing it to decide the matter for itself. The EEC Legislative
Assembly voted unanimously May 10 to adopt a resolution welcoming
the British decision.

In an apparent effort to strengthen Britain's bargaining position
vis-a-vis the Common Market members, particularly France, Wilson
suggested in a TV interview May 8 that Britain might not purchase
U.S. Poseidon missiles to replace the Polaris missiles currently being
installed in several British submarines. "We are not going to throw into
these [EEC] negotiations another Nassau, a new era of dependence on
the Americans for nuclear weapons." Wilson declared. (The reference
was to the Dec. 1962 Nassau meeting between the late Pres. Kennedy
and then-Prime Min. Harold Macmillan, at which the U.S. agreed to
supply Britain with Polaris missiles. It was generally believed that the
Nassau agreement had been a factor in de Gaulle's Jan. 1963 veto of
Britain's application to the EEC.) British Chancellor of the Exchequer
James Callaghan announced May 9 that Britain would begin repaying
its international debts 6 months earlier than previously planned. He said
Britain would pay £145 million ($406 million) to the International
Monetary Fund and £28 million ($78.4 million) to Switzerland by May
25.

The 488-62 vote in Commons May 10 in support of the government
decision indicated that about 75 MPs had abstained. Of those voting
against the resolution, 34 were Labor Party members, 26 were Conservatives. In reprisal against the rebellious MPs, the party leadership May
11 expelled 7 of the rebels from their posts as parliamentary private sec-
retaries.

(Wilson and British Foreign Secy. George Brown had toured the 6
EEC capitals Jan. 16-Mar. 8 in exploratory talks aimed at determining
the prospects for British entry into the EEC. Wilson and Brown con-
ferred with Italian Premier Moro and Foreign Min. Fanfani in Rome
Jan. 16-17; with French Pres. de Gaulle, Premier Pompidou and Foreign
Min. Couve de Murville in Paris Jan. 24-25; with Belgian Premier Paul
van den Boeynants and Foreign Min. Pierre Harmel in Brussels Jan. 31-
Feb. 1; with West German Chancellor Kiesinger and Foreign Min.
Brandt in Bonn Feb. 15-16; with Netherlands Premier Jelle Zijlstra and
Foreign Min. Joseph M. A. H. Luns in The Hague Feb. 26-27; and with
Luxembourg Premier Pierre Werner and Foreign Min. Pierre Gregoire
in Luxembourg Mar. 8. In an address to the Assembly of the Council of
Europe in Strasbourg Jan. 23, Wilson had declared that "the fault will
not lie at Britain's door" if European unity were to fail. Wilson pressed
for full British membership in the European community, saying that it
would be "half-hearted and defeatist" to abandon full membership in
exchange for "loose association with something in which we ought to
be fully integrated.")

De Gaulle's rejection of the British bid was delivered at his semi-annual press conference in Paris May 16. His arguments were essentially the same as those he had raised in his Jan. 1963 rejection of Britain's original bid for EEC membership. De Gaulle prefaced his remarks by saying that he would make "no advance judgment about what negotiations could eventually—I say eventually—be." He said:

"The movement which seems at present to be leading England to link herself to Europe instead of keeping herself apart can only be satisfactory to France. This is why we note with sympathy the progress which appears to be revealed in this direction by the British government's declared aim and the step it has taken. For our part, there is no question of there being a veto, nor has there ever been one. It is simply a question of finding out whether a settlement is possible within the framework and under the conditions of the Common Market without bringing about destructive upheavals; or in what other situation, and in what other conditions, a settlement could be possible; or whether it would be desirable to preserve what has been built up until such time as it would appear conceivable to welcome an England which on her own part would have undergone a profound transformation. . . .

". . . The Common Market is a sort of prodigy. To introduce into it now new and massive elements . . . would obviously be to jeopardize the whole and the details and to raise the problem of an entirely different undertaking. . . . If the 6 have been able to build this famous edifice, it is because it concerned a group of continental countries, immediate neighbors to each other, doubtless offering differences of size, but complementary in their economic structure. Moreover, the 6 form through their territory a compact geographic and strategic unit. . . .

"Britain, who is not continental, who remains, because of the Commonwealth and because she is an island, committed far beyond the seas, who is tied to the U.S. by all kinds of special agreements, . . . declares she is ready to subscribe to the Rome Treaty, even though she is asking exceptional and prolonged delays and, as regards her, that basic changes be made in the treaty's implementation. At the same time, she acknowledges that . . . it will be necessary to surmount obstacles that . . . [are] formidable. This is true, for instance, of the agricultural regulations. . . . Britain nourishes herself, to a great extent, on foodstuffs bought inexpensively throughout the world and, particularly, in the Commonwealth. If she submits to the rules of the 6, then her balance of payments will be crushed by 'levies' and . . . she would then be forced to raise the price of her food to the price level adopted by the continental countries, consequently to increase the wages of her workers and, thereby, to sell her goods all the more at a higher price and with more difficulty. It is clear that she cannot do this. . . .

"Another essential difficulty arises from the fact that capital circulates freely within the 6 to help expansion, while capital which has entered England is prohibited from leaving in order to restrict the deficit on her balance of payments, which, despite meritorious efforts and a certain recent progress, still remains menacing. How to solve the problem? For England it would be an excessive risk to get rid of the lock-gates which block the movement of money to foreign countries, while for the Europeans it would be indefensible to allow into their organization a partner who in this respect would be isolated within such an exorbitant system.

"And how indeed can one not realize to what degree and why sterling's own position prevents the Common Market from incorporating England. The fact that the organization of the 6 has completely freed their mutual trade exchanges necessarily implies that their currencies have a relatively constant value and that, if one of them were shaken, the community would immediately ensure its restoration. But that is only possible because of the sound position of the mark, the lira, the guilder, the Belgian franc and the French franc. And so, while one does not despair of the pound holding its own, the fact is that it will be a long time before one is certain about this because, in its relationship to the currencies of the 6, the pound is in the special position of being what is called a reserve currency. This means that a large number of countries in the world, notably those of the Commonwealth, hold enormous sterling balances.

"No doubt one can attempt to distinguish the fate of the pound sterling as a national currency from the fate of the pound sterling as an international currency. It is also sometimes asserted that the community would not be responsible for what happened to the pound sterling once England and her currency joined the organization. But this is just a mental exercise. In fact, parity and monetary solidarity are essential conditions of the Common Market and could not possibly be extended to our neighbours across the Channel unless some day the pound sterling shows itself in a completely new position so that its future value appears assured, it too is freed from its character as a reserve currency and the mortgage of Britain's sterling balances within the sterling area disappears. But when and how will it be so?

"What is true as of now from the economic point of view would also eventually become true from the political point of view. The idea and the hope which led the Europeans to unite was no doubt the idea and the hope of forming a group which would be European in every respect; that is to say, one which would not only carry its full weight in trade and production, but would also be capable of dealing politically for itself and by itself vis-a-vis whomsoever it might be. Given England's special relationships, those of the British with America, the obligations as well as the advantages for them; given the existence of the Commonwealth and the privileged relationships its members have with England; and given that the British still bear, or think they must still bear, special obligations in various parts of the world, which distinguish them fundamentally from the Western nations, one can see how the policy of the 6, provided they have one, could be associated in certain cases, in many cases, with that of the British. But one cannot see at all how one policy and the other could be intermingled unless the British changed, notably in the field of defense, their entire outlook, or unless the continentals renounced for ever a Europe that would be European."

De Gaulle suggested 3 alternative approaches for Britain: (1) To permit Britain and some of its EFTA (European Free Trade Association) partners to join the EEC but accept the fact that this would entail building "an entirely new edifice, scrapping nearly all of that which has just been built." "What then would we end up with," de Gaulle asked, "if not, perhaps, the creation of a free-trade area of Western Europe, pending that of the Atlantic area, which would deprive our continent of any real personality?" (2) To grant associate membership to Britain and some EFTA countries, "which could, without creating an upheaval, multiply and facilitate the economic relations between the contracting parties." (3) To "wait until a certain internal and external evolution, of which Great Britain seems already to be showing signs, is eventually completed, . . . [until Britain] has itself accomplished first and for its part the necessary profound economic and political transformation so that it can join with the 6 continental countries." De Gaulle said: "I truly believe that this is the desire of many people who wish to see a Europe appear which would have its natural dimensions, and who have for England a deep admiration and a sincere friendship. If Britain one day reached this stage, with what joy would France then greet this historic transformation."

Prime Min. Wilson told the Confederation of British Industry May 17 that Britain would not take "no" for an answer to its application. He said that Britain was "determined not only to make these negotiations a success, but to carry them forward as quickly as lies in our power."

Belgian Foreign Min. Pierre Harmel said May 17 that the Belgian government would "do everything possible to activate the negotiations." Similar statements of support came from government officials in the Netherlands, Luxembourg and Italy May 17. West German government spokesman Conrad Ahlers said May 17 that British membership in the Common Market would depend on Britain's acceptance of the Rome Treaty and willingness to support the "further development" of the European community, particularly in terms of political unification. Ahlers said West Germany viewed its role as one of "mediator" between Britain and France.

At the Rome EEC conference May 27-29, Italian Pres. Giuseppe Saragat introduced the issue of the British application: "New problems await us, among which are those concerning the geographical and historical dimensions of the community with the accession of other countries—in the first place Great Britain, whose name is almost synonymous with political liberty. Let us express the wish that negotiations can open soon." It was decided at this meeting that the British (as well as Irish and Danish) applications should be examined in detail and reported on later.

The EEC Council of Ministers met in Brussels June 5 but failed to act on the application, despite this acknowledgement by Council Chairman Elslande June 7 to Prime Min. Wilson: "I have the honour to acknowledge receipt of the letter of May 10, 1967, in which your excellency informed me of the request by the United Kingdom of Great Britain & Northern Ireland to join the European Economic Community in accordance with the terms of Article 237 of the Treaty setting up the European Economic Community. I transmitted your letter on the same day to members of the Council, which decided to set in motion the procedure provided for in the above article. . . ." The Council met again in Brussels June 26-27 and July 9-10, at which time French Foreign Min. Couve de Murville expressed the French opposition to Britain's application. His position was opposed by the other 5 members.

The Assembly of the Western European Union (WEU), consisting of members of parliament of the 6 EEC countries and Britain, June 14 voted its "full support" for Britain's bid for EEC membership. The vote: 55-0, with 6 abstentions, all French. Labor M. P. Maurice Edelman, who had addressed the meeting, said of the vote: "This represents a substantial success for Britain's point of view in Europe. It was really a declaration of unanimous support. This is the first external organization to which Britain has put the question. My impression is that French resistance is crumbling because there is a movement of public opinion in France which is in favor of Britain coming in."

The Action Committee for the United States of Europe, meeting in Brussels June 15 under the chairmanship of Jean Monnet, declared itself "in favor of opening and rapidly bringing to a successful conclusion negotiations on the measures to be agreed in view of Great Britain's entry into the European Economic Community as it is today, with the same rights and the same obligations as the 6 countries that are already members." The committee, made up of European political leaders and trade unionists, also adopted a resolution declaring itself in favor of the entry of the other EFTA members willing to join EEC—"or, failing that, in favor of the establishment with them of appropriate forms of association or agreement."

Prime Min. Wilson conferred with de Gaulle for 5-1/2 hours June 19, and the 2 leaders met again briefly June 20 before Wilson returned to London; Wilson told the House of Commons June 20 that the talks had been devoted in large measure to the Mid-East crisis and the Vietnamese war. With respect to Britain's EEC bid, Wilson said that he did not want to give the impression that de Gaulle was "more enthusiastic about British entry than he has been at any other time. I think his greatest anxiety is still the change in the shape of the market if a number of new countries came in." But Wilson added that he had told the French president that "we do not intend to take 'no' for an answer." Wilson reportedly had reaffirmed the British position that associate membership in EEC was unacceptable, since it would entail adhering to the Common Market rules and policy without having a voice in influencing them.

Britain's efforts to obtain early negotiations on its EEC bid were pressed in June and July. Wilson conferred with de Gaulle in Paris June 19-20; Italian Premier Aldo Moro and Foreign Min. Amintore Fanfani conferred with Wilson and British Foreign Secy. George Brown in London June 27-28; and Brown, at a meeting of the Assembly of the Western European Union in The Hague July 4, outlined Britain's terms for entry into the EEC. At the latter meeting, Brown declared that Britain accepted, "without reserve, all the aims and objectives" of the EEC, ECSC and Euratom treaties. He added that Britain was prepared to contribute to the development of the communities "not only in the commercial and economic but also in the political and defense fields." While admitting that there would "of course be changes" if Britain were to join the EEC, Brown asserted that such changes were positive ones— "a larger community, a more powerful and more influential Europe." Among the conditions Britain would pose for membership, Brown said, were measures to aid British farmers in making the transition to the Common Market agricultural system and some form of compensation for the trade losses that would be suffered by such Commonwealth countries as New Zealand, as well as the developing countries in Africa and the Caribbean. Brown said: "We believe that Europe can emerge as a community expressing its own point of view and exercising influence in world affairs, not only in the commercial and economic, but also in the political and defense fields.... We shall play our full part in this process.... As a member we shall accept whatever responsibilities the evolving community may decide to assume, and we shall join as eagerly as other members in creating new opportunities for the expression of European unity.... Today the European spirit flows strongly in the movement towards a greater unity.... Surely it is in the interests of all our countries that Britain should make her full contribution to this unity.

With Britain as a member of the community Europe will be enabled to play a greater role in terms of power and influence...."

French Foreign Min. Couve de Murville July 10 rejected the idea of British membership. At a meeting of the EEC Council of Ministers in Brussels, Couve de Murville argued that Britain's membership would open the door to all the other countries in Europe, with the exception of Switzerland and Portugal, and that this would alter the basic character of the community. One of the consequences, he asserted, would be the transformation of the community into an Atlantic trading bloc; another would be an inevitable rise in Cold War tensions. West German Foreign Min. Willy Brandt rejected the French arguments, asserting that Britain's membership would not change the community and that there was nothing inherently wrong in the community assuming a greater Atlantic orientation. Other speakers who challenged Couve de Murville were Belgian Foreign Min. Pierre Harmel and Netherlands Foreign Min. Joseph M. A. H. Luns; all generally supported the West German arguments in favor of admitting Britain to full membership in the Common Market.

West German Chancellor Kiesinger visited the U.S. Aug. 13-20 in his first trip there as chancellor. In remarks before the National Press Club in Washington Aug. 16, Kiesinger said of the Common Market and Britain that "West Germany did not share the French hesitations about Britain's bid to enter the Common Market. While increased membership would surely pose new problems for the EEC, this was not a sufficient argument "to keep out one of the most important European countries, a power that really is now willing to join in the common endeavors to build up a united Europe...."

Within Britain, the TUC Sept. 7 remitted to its general council 2 resolutions on Britain's bid to enter the Common Market. One resolution supported the entry bid; the other urged the government to obtain prior guarantees on essential British and Commonwealth interests. Other influential domestic British groups also took positions favoring British membership in the EEC but insisting on guarantees of British and Commonwealth interests.

In a speech at the Labor Party Conference Oct. 5, Foreign Secy. Brown urged the delegates to indorse the Labor government's EEC application. He asserted that Britain's economic difficulties were likely "to get a lot tougher" if the British "just sit on these tiny islands and hope that all our troubles will go away." He said that Common Market membership would allow Britain to contribute its technological knowledge to a united Europe and obtain in return the market and production resources necessary for development of its own economy. Referring to the broader issue of East-West relations, Brown said: "As long as we maintain the economic division of Western Europe, we shall hinder the healing of the wide divisions with Eastern Europe.... We will not end political divisions by maintaining economic divisions.... Nobody is being asked to declare for unconditional membership of the European Economic Community. Nobody is being asked today to decide that tomorrow we shall be members of it. What we are asking you to do today is to decide that we shall negotiate to try to get in. In the course of these negotiations, we shall negotiate on...the essential interests of this nation."

The EEC commission Oct. 7 published a 103-page unanimous opinion proposing negotiations on the applications of Britain, Ireland, Denmark and Norway for EEC membership. The opinion said, in part:

"Those rules which are mainly determined by the supply position will not come up against a fundamentally changed situation once the community has been enlarged, even if some adjustment might be advisable for a few products. Adoption of the common agricultural policy and the price ratios now laid down for the 6 could produce changes in the pattern of production in the new member countries because of their different price ratios. Assessment of the possible consequences of any such changes could be profitably attempted only in cooperation with the countries concerned.

"In short, although extension of the community would affect the orders of magnitude of the basic data, it would be unlikely to change the situation fundamentally or, by itself, to make a revision of the common agricultural policy inevitable. Such changes as might be necessary could be introduced in the course of the future implementation and further development of this policy. However, certain natural, structural, or social difficulties which may exist in some border areas of the new member countries of the enlarged community will make it more urgent to complete the structural side of the common agricultural policy....

"On the basis of an experience repeated several times in the course of past years, it appears that a conflict has arisen much more sharply in Britain than elsewhere between, on the one hand, the achievement of a rate of growth corresponding to that reached over a period of several years by most industrial countries and, on the other, a balance of payments also examined on the basis of several years. Indeed, on several occasions, as soon as the British economy achieved a rate of growth comparable to that of other industrialized countries, the contributory factors of a payments crisis appeared. Numerous studies devoted to this problem in Britain and elsewhere appear to indicate that the difficulties involved are not merely of a temporary character, and therefore soluble on the basis of a more effective balance-of-payments policy. These difficulties involve essentially problems of a structural character connected either with shortcomings in the distribution of productive resources (inadequacy and bad orientation of investments, numerous obstacles to progress in productivity, distribution of labour, and taxation), or to economic, financial, and monetary burdens which this country inherited from its past, from the Second World War, and from its international position in the post-war era....

"In a general way, one can suggest that although the British economy has recently emerged from the state of tension in which it found itself during 1963-64, its fundamental position has hardly changed in relation to similar phases of its previous evolution....

"To sum up, the new membership applications are impelling the community to tackle at one and the same time the problems involved in its extension. Opinions differ as to the priority to be given to the one or the other of these objectives. The best way of overcoming the difficulty would be to try to attain them both simultaneously. But if this difficult operation is to be successfully concluded it is essential that extension should not hamper the pursuit of the normal activities of the communities and should not subsequently entail a weakening of their cohesion or their dynamism, especially where the establishment of economic union, the requisite measures of harmonization, and the functioning of the institutional machinery, are concerned.

"The commission is well aware that the cohesion and dynamism of the communities depend to a great extent on the convergence of national policies in the essential fields. If full advantage is to be taken of the opportunities which extension opens up for the community, it is apparent that member-states should within a reasonable period be in a position to make progress along the road to policical union.

"It follows from all the considerations set forth in this document that the commission is not at present in possession of all the information needed to give in final form the opinion requested by the Council.... Choices of considerable importance for any appraisal of the impact which the new members would have on the community are still to be made.... It is the commission's opinion that, in order to dispel the uncertainty which still attaches in particular to certain fundamental points, negotiations should be opened in the most appropriate forms with the states which have applied for membership, in order to examine in more detail... the problems brought out in this document and to see whether arrangements can be made under which the indispensable cohesion and dynamism will be maintained in an enlarged community."

Chancellor Kiesinger visited London Oct. 23-25 to confer with Wilson and Brown. In a statement at the London airport Oct. 25, Kiesinger said: "The Federal [West German] government considers that Great Britain should become a member of the European communities. It will carefully examine the objections to British membership which have been raised within the community of the 6. During the deliberations initiated among the 6, the Federal government will endeavor to help overcome the difficulties that have arisen and trusts that these deliberations will soon lead to the opening of negotiations with Great Britain."

Chancellor of the Exchequer James Callaghan Oct. 26 took issue with de Gaulle's stand on the position of the pound. In a speech in London, Callaghan said, in part:

"It is clear that sterling is a great world currency whose links extend to every continent. Many nations both inside and outside Europe use it for their own purposes and advantage, and it is therefore obvious that Britain's application to enter into the EEC does bring up the question of how best this great world currency can be fitted into the monetary and economic pattern of Europe. But is this a question that Europeans should approach timorously or fearfully? On the contrary. In my view the existence of this currency coupled with the expertise of the City of London presents Europe with new opportunities for financial and commercial expansion. With Britain in the Common Market, fuller use could be made of this instrument at the service of Europe, and, with constructive and imaginative statesmanship, we could prepare for a new stage in the evolution of the world monetary system.

"Let me glance at how far that evolution has come during the present century. There has been a marked development. We began with a situation in which gold and sterling were the 2 main assets held in the reserves of many countries. Then came a period in which the dollar was held to an increasing extent, until now it has far surpassed sterling as a reserve asset. But the use of gold and sterling has not been replaced by dollars—all 3 assets are now widely held.... The question now is whether Europe would wish to take advantage of Britain's application for entry to propel the evolution in a particular direction and so gain greater influence for the community as a whole. If so, we are ready to discuss such an evolution....

"First, it will be necessary to agree on the topics to be covered. The government has always made it clear that a primary objective of policy must be a strong balance of payments. Our policies are directed to that end, and we are confident that we shall be successful within the time-span that will in any case elapse before we can enter the Common Market. The other main question—that of the sterling balances—looms larger now during this period of reconstruction than it will do when we are seen to be in a strong balance-of-payments position. Nevertheless, let us look now at this question of sterling as a reserve currency.... I permit myself the observation that in the context of our application to join the Common Market the sterling balance question has been greatly exaggerated. It is not a problem that needs to be settled before we enter the Common Market. The new Special Drawing Rights scheme took 4 years to work out and even now it is not in its final form. Against that background is it likely that a further evolution of the monetary system affecting sterling will take place any more quickly?

"Nevertheless, if my view is not shared by some of our friends in Europe, we are prepared to take part in constructive discussions whenever they like, provided, of course, that such discussions are not intended to delay negotiations on entry into the EEC.

"It is clear from what I have said that the evolution of the monetary system cannot be settled by one nation in isolation. It needs painstaking examination at expert level and in a quiet atmosphere. But ... for such a discussion to be worth while there must be agreement on our objective, and that involves agreeing on the topics to be covered. Indeed, it is most important that we should do so if we and the EEC are to seize the opportunity which is now open to us to approach these problems in a constructive and European spirit.

"The question of a European common currency is another matter and would be a much longer-term one, since it could come about only if members of the community, including ourselves, had achieved a much greater degree of economic integration than at present. But our application to join the EEC does present an opportunity for bringing our thinking and, we hope, in due course our policies, much closer together."

At his semi-annual press conference, de Gaulle Nov. 27 again rejected Britain's bid for Common Market membership. He also denounced U.S. inroads into European industry and expressed hope that Britain's devaluation of the pound would facilitate the end of the current world monetary system (based on the U.S. dollar). The press conference, at the Elysee Palace, was attended by about 1,200 newsmen and the entire cabinet. Among de Gaulle's remarks:

Devaluation of the pound—"It is possible that the squalls currently being unleashed— without France having anything to do with it—and which have swept away the rate of the pound and which threaten that of the dollar, in the final analysis lead to reestablishing the international monetary system on the basis of immutability, impartiality and universality, which are the privileges of the gold."

UK & Common Market—"The idea of joining the British Isles to the Economic Community formed by the 6 continental states arouses wishes everywhere which are ideally very justified, but it is a matter of knowing whether and how this could actually be achieved without disrupting or destroying what already exists. Great Britain proposed the opening without delay of negotiations between itself and the 6 with a view to entering the Common Market. It did this with truly extraordinary insistence and haste, some of the reasons for which may have been made clear by the recent monetary events. At the same time, it declared it would accept all the regulations governing the community of the 6, which seemed a little contradictory with the request for negotiations, since why would one negotiate on clauses which one had fully accepted in advance? In fact, we were watching the 5th act of a play during which England has taken up very different and apparently inconsistent attitudes towards the Common Market. The first act was London's refusal to participate in the elaboration of the Treaty of Rome. On the other side of the Channel it was expected that this would lead to nothing. The 2d act demonstrated England's deep-seated hostility towards the building of Europe as soon as this began to be mapped out. I can still hear the notice which my friend [Harold] Macmillan, then prime minister, served on me in Paris in June 1958, comparing the Common Market with the [Napoleonic] continental blockade and threatening at least to declare a tariff war on it. The 3d act was negotiations carried out in Brussels by Mr. [Reginald] Maudling for a year and a half, negotiations aimed at bending the community to England's conditions. These were ended when France pointed out to its partners that it was not a question of doing that but precisely the opposite.

The 4th act, at the start of Mr. Wilson's government, was marked by London's disinterest in the Common Market, the maintenance around Britain of the 6 other European states forming the Free Trade Area, and a great effort to strengthen the internal links of the Commonwealth. "Now the 5th act is being perfromed. This time Britain has made its application and has embarked on all imaginable promises and pressures to get it adopted. This attitude is easily explained. The British people can no doubt see more and more clearly that the structures and customs of its activities, and even its national personality, are from now on put in jeopardy in the great movement which is sweeping the world—in face of the enormous power of the United States, the growing power of the Soviet Union, the renascent power of the continental nations, the new power of China, and the growing centrifugal movement apparent within the Commonwealth. After all, the serious economic, financial, monetary, and social difficulties with which Britain is grappling make her feel this day after day. From all this emerges a tendency to look for a framework, even a European one, which would help her to save and safeguard her own substance, allow her to play a leading role again, and relieve her of part of her burden.

"In principle, there is nothing in this which would not be salutary for her and, in a short time, satisfactory for Europe, on condition that the British people, like those whom it wishes to join, should want, and know how, to undergo wthe fundamental changes necessary for it to establish its own equilibrium. For it is a radical modification and transformation of Britain which is necessary for her to join the continentals. This is obvious from the political point of view. But today, to speak only of the economic sphere, the report addressed to the 6 governments on Sept. 29 by the Brussels commission demonstrates with the greatest clarity that the Common Market is incompatible with the economy, as it is, of England. The chronic deficit of the British economy's balance of payments demonstrates its permanent disequilibrium. In the realms of production, sources of supply, the practice of credit, working conditions, the economy includes fundamental factors which that country could not change without modifying its own character.

"The Common Market is also imcompatible with the way the British get their food, both from their own agricultural production, subsidized to the highest degree, and from the supplies bought cheaply all over the world and particularly in the Commonwealth. This rules out London ever really accepting the levies provided for in the financial arrangements, which would be crushing for it. The Common Market is incompatible also with the restrictions imposed by Britain on the outward movement of capital which, by contrast, circulates freely among the 6. The Common Market, finally, is incompatible with the state of sterling—as revealed again by the devaluation and by the loans which preceded and accompanied it. Moreover, in view of the pound's position as an international currency and the enormous external balances which weigh it down, the state of sterling would not allow it at present to become part of the solid, interdependent, and assured society in which the franc, the mark, the lira, the Belgian franc and the guilder are joined.

"In these conditions, what could be the result of what is called the entry of Britain into the Common Market? And if one wished, in spite of everything, to impose it, it would obviously mean the breaking up of a community which has been built and which functions according to rules which would not bear such a monumental exception. Moreover, this community would not bear the introduction among its principal members of a state which, precisely because of its currency, its economy, and its politics, is not at present a part of Europe as we have begun to build it.

"Since everyone knows the issues involved, if the 6 allowed Britain in and started negotiations to this effect, it would mean that they were giving their approval in advance to all the artifices, delays, and pretences which would conduce to covering up the destruction of an edifice built at a cost of so much effort and in the midst of so many hopes.

"It is true that while recognizing the impossibility of allowing the Britain of today into the Common Market as it exists, it is nevertheless possible to be in favour of sacrificing the Common Market for the sake of an agreement with Britain. Theoretically, in fact, the economic system which is practiced by the 6 is not necessarily the only one which Europe might practice. One can imagine, for example, a Free Trade Area covering the whole of the west of our continent. One can also imagine a sort of multilateral treaty of the kind which will come out of the Kennedy Round, settling between 10, 12, or 15 European states their reciprocal and respective quotas and tariffs. But in either case it would first be necessary to abolish the community and break up its institutions. And I tell you that France is certainly not asking for that. If, however, one or other of her partners proposed this, as is their right after all, France would examine it with the other signatories of the Treaty of Rome. But what France cannot do is to enter at present into any negotiations with Britain and its associate countries which would lead to the destruction of the European community to which it belongs.

"And then again, that would not be at all the road which could lead to the construction of a Europe, by itself and for itself, in such a way that it would not be dependent on an economic, monetary, and political system which was foreign to it. For Europe to be able to balance the immense power of the United States it must in no way weaken, but on the contrary strengthen, the links and rules of ths community.

"Certainly, those who have demonstrated by their actions, as I have, the exceptional esteem, attachment and respect which they bear for Britain keenly desire to see her choose and accomplish one day the immense effort which would transform her. France is certainly quite prepared, in order to make things easy for her, to enter into any arrangement which, under the name of association or any other name, would favor, as of now, commercial exchanges between the continentals on one hand and the British, Scandinavians and Irish on the other. We in Paris have certainly not been unaware of the psychological development which seems to be emerging among our friends across the Channel. Nor have we failed to recognize the merit of certain measures which they have already taken, and others which they are planning to take, for their internal equilibrium and external independence.

"In order that the British Isles can really make fast to the continent, there is still a very vast and deep mutation to be effected. Thus everything depends in fact not on negotiations, which for the 6 would be a step towards abandonment and would toll the knell of the community, but rather on the will and action of the great British people, which would make them into one of the pillars of European Europe."

Answering questions put to him in the House of Commons Nov. 28, Prime Min. Wilson said concerning de Gaulle's Nov. 27 statement: "There are no present alternatives" other than continued commitment to EEC membership for Britain. De Gaulle's arguments against Britain's membership were "wrong deductions based on a rather out-of-date approach to some of the modern problems of the world." Supporting Wilson's stand, Conservative Party leader Edward Heath Nov. 28 urged the government to "continue to work closely with Europe, ready for the day when any obstacles there may disappear."

Wilson Nov. 29 answered the questions that de Gaulle had raised about British admission. Among Wilson's answers and other statements:

"It was said, as proof of ...[British-EEC] incompatibility, that Britain's chronic balance-of-payments deficit proved the permanent disequilibrium of her economy.

"*Answer*—What was France's balance-of-payments disequilibrium in the 2 years after she signed the Treaty of Rome? Without going into the unprofitable question of what our balance of payments would have been this year but for the Middle East, have the French government not seen that the international staffs of the IMF and OECD strongly support the view that the decisions we have taken offer a firm prospect of transforming our balance of payments within 12 months?"

"We have made clear why association is out. In the first place, Britain cannot be asked to enter into what my predecessor, Mr. Macmillan, called 'country membership' and thereby accept obligations which would run through every aspect of Britain's economic and social life, and her international relationships, without having any voice in the formulation of future rules and future changes in those rules. But there is a 2d reason. France has always rejected any suggestion of Britain being linked with the 6 in an industrial free trade area, understandably because of the dependence of the French economy on her domestic agriculture. After all they have said about Britain's cheap food and its implication for our wage levels, and therefore our industrial competitiveness, it is inconceivable that negotiations for association would not involve even more complex, indeed perhaps interminable, discussions. Because, unlike an application for full membership, where we are negotiating fully within the Treaty of Rome and the subsequent decisions taken under that Treaty, here we should, all of us, be entering into uncharted seas, and with no rules to guide us.

"Our application is in. It remains in. Time is on our side in a narrow sense—as far as getting in is concerned. But in another sense...time is not on the side of Europe, including Britain in Europe. It is not on the side of those who want to take European action to stop the technological and industrial gap between Europe and America widening year by year, indeed month by month. It is not on the side of those of us whose concern about American domination of our national industries has been shown not by words but by deeds. Therefore this great debate will continue, not only in Britain, but throughout Europe."

Wilson was under fire from all sides during this period, and his government's stability was in doubt. De Gaulle's announcement had come just 9 days after the devaluation of the pound. The *Sunday Express* said: "What should Mr. Wilson do next? Just one thing. Quit. Never can one man have done so much harm to his own country in so short a time." The *News of the World* said: "The time has come to quote Cromwell's words, 'You have stayed too long. In the name of God, go!'"

De Gaulle was criticised as well. Netherlands Foreign Min. Joseph M. A. H. Luns, speaking for the Benelux nations, said Nov. 29: "Press conferences do not constitute a method of negotiating. There is a procedure for this in the Common Market, and this procedure must be followed." A West German government spokesman said Nov. 29: "Since the French government—judging by Gen. de Gaulle's statements—has no fundamental objections to British accession, but, on its part, too, regards such accession as necessary for European development; and since, on the other hand, Great Britain is standing by its application, as are the other countries that are willing to enter, the German government considers it still too early to express a final conclusion about the results of the discussions currently under way in Brussels. In this situation, it appears reasonable to the German government to continue its efforts, and to examine all imaginable possibilities of a solution."

France Dec. 19 successfully blocked the efforts of the 5 other EEC members to open negotiations with Britain on its bid for membership. This action came at the close of a 2-day meeting in Brussels of the EEC Council of Ministers. The 5 advocates of opening negotiations with Britain—Belgium, Italy, Luxembourg, the Netherlands and West Germany—did not bring the issue to a vote for fear of forcing France to a veto and thus damaging the unity of the EEC. Rather, after it became apparent that France would not alter its stand, the Council adopted a communique that said the application "remain[ed] on the agenda of the Council." West German Economics Min. Karl Schiller, current president of the Council, said afterwards that the "door has not been closed" to the British, Danish, Irish and Norwegian applications. But Netherlands Foreign Min. Luns said that it was a "black day" for Europe and that his government was "deeply disappointed and extremely worried about the heavy blow which Europe has received."

A statement issued by the British Foreign Office Dec. 19 said: "It is a matter of grave concern that the government of France has been unable to accept the unanimous view of its partners that negotiations for Britain's accession to the European communities should start at once. This can only delay the inevitable progress towards a united

Europe, including Britain, which is in the interest of Europe as a whole. There is no question of withdrawing Britain's application.... Given the support of the 5 governments and the overwhelming majority of opinion throughout Western Europe, European unity is bound to be achieved."

The EEC Council of Ministers had been meeting frequently during the fall. Meetings held Oct. 2-3, Oct. 23-24, Nov. 20 and Dec. 11 produced no definitive conclusions. The Dec. 18-19 meeting produced the following statement:

"Considering the objectives laid down in the preamble to the Treaty of Rome, and considering the tasks falling to the member-states pursuant to Article 5, which provides that they shall abstain from any measures which would jeopardize the attainment of the objectives of the Treaty, the Council of the European Communities, meeting at Brussels on Dec. 19, 1967, noted that no member-state has raised any fundamental objection to the enlargement of the communities. When noting this fact, the Council assumed that the new member-states would fully accept the Treaties and the decisions adopted by the community. One member-state, however, expressed the opinion that this enlargement would profoundly alter the nature of the communities and the methods of administering them.

"... All the member-states were of the opinion that the restoration of Great Britain's economic and monetary situation is of fundamental importance to the question of its accession. Several member-states, while fully in favor of re-establishing Great Britain's economic equilibrium, do not think that the British economy must necessarily be completely re-established at the moment of accession....

"... 5 member-states ... expressed their desire for the immediate opening of negotiations for the accession of Great Britain, Denmark, Ireland and Norway, so that these negotiations might be undertaken in parallel with the re-establishment of Great Britain's economic situation. One member-state considered that the re-establishment of the British economy must be completed before Great Britain's request can be reconsidered.... For this reason, there was no agreement in the Council at this stage on the next step to be taken. The President of the Council was instructed to inform the countries in question accordingly.

"... The requests for accession presented by the United Kingdom, Ireland, Denmark and Norway, and also the letter from the Swedish Government, remain on the Council's agenda."

Foreign Secy. George Brown Dec. 20 acknowledged the efforts of the EEC commission and of the 5 EEC governments. In an address in the House of Commons, Brown said:

"The prime minister said in the House some weeks ago that if, contrary to our hopes and the hopes of most people in Europe, a veto were to be imposed, we should still regard ourselves as committed to our main purpose in Europe. I reaffirm that today. We continue to believe that the long-term interests of this country and of Europe require that we should become members of the European communities.

"The communique which was issued after yesterday's meeting of the community Council of Ministers made clear that our application, as well as those of the other countries, remain on the agenda of the Council of Ministers. We in turn confirm that our application stands. We do not intend to withdraw it.

"We now propose to enter into consultations with those 5 members of the European community who supported the commission's view that negotiations should be started at an early stage. We shall of course also be in the closest touch with the members of EFTA and the Irish Republic. We are by no means the only country whose hopes of progress towards a genuine European unity have been temporarily disappointed.

"As regards the content of the consultations ... which will begin at once, we for our part want to see the links between us forged as strongly as possible. But we cannot expose ourselves to any further vetoes on the part of Pres. de Gaulle.

"As regards our relations with France, whilst we shall not indulge in any peevish or petty reaction to the present situation, it would be idle to pretend that what has happened is not a grave blow to our relationship. We think the attitude taken by the French government represents a false view of the future of our continent of Europe. We think it contains a deplorable number of mistaken ideas about the realities of the various questions at issue. We question its motivation.

"But I think it important to stress that this is not an Anglo-French affair. This is a European affair. We regret, of course, that Europe has been held back temporarily from achieving the unity which it now aspires to. But it is just because time and events in this technological age are running against Europe that we do not intend as a result of this temporary check to abandon all work along the road."

Other EFTA Nations Seek EEC Membership

Several of the nations associated with Britain in the European Free Trade Association announced that they would take parallel steps for membership in the Common Market. Sweden said May 2 that it would seek associate membership in the EEC, ECSC and Euratom, and it filed its application July 28. Ireland and Denmark applied for full membership in the 3 organizations May 11, as did Norway July 24. The Swedish cabinet July 7 had issued a statement affirming Sweden's desire "to participate on the broadest possible basis in an enlarged economic community, at the same time enabling us to maintain our policy of neutrality."

Consideration of Austria's bid for membership in the EEC and ECSC had been suspended indefinitely June 29 after Italy announced at an ECSC meeting that it would oppose any negotiation or preliminary contract with Austria until Austria could prove that its territory was not being used for organizing terrorist activities in Italy or serving as a refuge for terrorism. Italy subsequently announced that it would oppose Austria's bid for membership in the EEC on similar grounds. The Italian declaration referred to the terrorist activities by ethnic Germans in the Alto Adige (South Tyrol) section of Italy's northern Bolzano Province. The South Tyrol, once part of Austria, had been ceded to Italy at the end of World War I. Austrian Foreign Min. Lujo Toncic-Sorinj said July 8 that the Italian decision was "painful for Austria and painful for the cause of Europe." He declared that "progress toward European integration" was not furthered by "weighing down such matters with other problems." He charged that the aim of the terrorists in South Tyrol was to "smash all attempts at negotiation" between Austria and the EEC. During a visit to Moscow Mar. 14—21, Austrian Chancellor Josef Klaus had sought unsuccessfully to obtain Soviet support for his country's bid to join the Common Market. Klaus told Soviet officials Mar. 16 that Austrian participation "in the economic dynamism of Europe" was essential for the "maintenance of a free and independent Austria."

But, as it had in the past, the Soviet Union maintained that EEC membership would violate Austrian neutrality as specified in the 1955 treaty ending the 4-power occupation of the country. Klaus, accompanied by Foreign Min. Toncic-Sorinj, conferred with Soviet

Premier Aleksei N. Kosygin and Communist Party Gen. Secy. Leonid I. Brezhnev.

EFTA Developments

The EFTA Council and the Joint Council of EFTA and Finland convened jointly in Stockholm Mar. 2—3. A communique issued at the meeting Mar. 3 took note of the abolition in Dec. 1966 of all remaining tariffs on industrial goods within the group and said that "attention would now concentrate on other areas of economic cooperation such as non-tariff barriers and the enforcement of rules of fair competition." The ministers "reaffirmed their previous understanding that they would continue to keep each other informed of contacts with members of the EEC and remain in close consultation at all stages." The ministers "agreed on the pressing importance of the negotiations in the Kennedy Round...[and] appealed to all participants to do their utmost to reach agreement on a substantial worldwide reduction in tariffs and other barriers to trade."

The EFTA Council met at the ministerial level in London Apr. 28. In a communique issued at the conclusion of the meeting, the ministers endorsed Britain's bid for EEC membership. It said:

"The EFTA governments, desirous of bringing about a single European market in accordance with the purpose of the Stockholm Convention, recognized that, if the British government were to decide to seek a closer relationship with the EEC, that decision would open up new prospects for a solution of the question of European economic integration, in which they all intended to participate. In affirming their intention to work towards the goal of European economic integration, all the EFTA governments reiterated their strong interest in safeguarding, as an important part of an enlarged European community, the free market already established in EFTA by the successful dismantling of trade barriers within the Association. The change from the present division of Europe to a single market should be as smooth as possible. Were the UK or any other member of EFTA to apply for participation in the EEC, the process of negotiation and of ratifying any ensuing agreement could hardly be short. In addition, it would be the purpose of EFTA governments that sufficient transitional periods should be provided for in order to give—should it be necessary—a reasonable opportunity to their partners in the Free Trade Area to conclude negotiations, with a view to avoiding disruption in European trade patterns."

The EFTA Council met Oct. 25 in Lausanne. Intra-EFTA trade discussions were the dominant theme at this meeting. The EFTA announced Dec. 11 that Yugoslavia would be allowed to send observers to EFTA technical meetings. Finland announced that all internal EFTA tariffs would be removed by Dec. 31, thus aligning Finland with the other 7 in terms of free trade.

(Figures released early in 1968 disclosed that intra-EFTA trade rose by 9.7% in 1967, compared with 9.4% in 1966. EFTA exports to non-members rose by 2.4% in 1967, while imports rose by 5.3%; EFTA exports to the U.S. fell by 1.6%, while imports rose by 5.5%. Between 1959 and 1966, intra-EFTA trade had risen 11.2%—11.4% annually— while EFTA exports to non-members increased by 68% and imports from non-members rose by 71%.)

Finland Oct. 12 had devalued the markka by 31.25%, from a par value of 3.2 per U.S. dollar to 4.19997 per U.S. dollar. The government also placed a ceiling on certain key consumer prices to check any inflation that might develop as a result of the financial measure. Finland had requested and received approval from the International Monetary Fund to effect the devaluation, which was viewed in financial circles as aimed at narrowing Finland's trade deficit. (The value of Finnish imports in 1966 had totaled the equivalent of $1.7 billion, compared to total exports of $1.5 billion; in the first 6 months of 1967, Finland's trade deficit amounted to the equivalent of $122 million.)

1968

France and Britain concentrated on domestic affairs during 1968, and there were no significant developments in British-EEC relations. The Wilson government continued its policy of austerity in the aftermath of the Nov. 1967 devaluation of the pound. France, racked by student and worker activism, endured a loss of monetary reserves and faced the specter of devaluation for the first time in years. The de Gaulle government firmly denied the possibility of devaluation, and the franc was at least temporarily stabilized—but at the cost of stringent exchange convertibility controls. West Germany faced a possible revaluation of the mark, an upward rather than downward shift in the (gold) par value, as exports and reserves rose to embarrassingly high levels. Bonn acted as Britain's prime spokesman in EEC discussions but met with consistent French opposition. Kennedy Round and EEC tariff reductions were put into effect.

THE BRITISH ECONOMY

Domestic Developments

Prime Min. Harold Wilson announced in the House of Commons Jan. 16 a series of cutbacks in home and defense spending that were designed to "make devaluation work." The measures were the result of a review of public expenditures that had been announced by the government Dec. 18, 1967 as a follow-up to the devaluation of the pound. The purpose of the review, as described by Wilson Jan. 16, was "to achieve a progressive and massive shift of resources from home consumption, public and private, to the requirements of exports, import replacement and productive investments." Wilson stressed that the review had been conducted "on the basis that no spending program could be sacrosanct." Among the measures decided on in the review: (1) the complete withdrawal of all British forces from the Far East and the Persian Gulf, "apart from our remaining dependencies and certain other necessary exceptions," by the end of 1971 rather than by 1975 as originally planned; (2) the cancellation of an order for 50 F-111 jet fighters from the U.S.; (3) the postponement from 1971 to 1973 of a plan to make school attendance mandatory through age 16 instead of 15, as currently required; (4) the institution of a 30¢ charge on each prescription filled under the National Health Service program; (5) the extension of increases in welfare benefits to those "most in need" rather than to all without exception.

Wilson said the measures would supplement those that had been announced Nov. 18, 1967, when the pound was devalued. Excerpts from his statement:

Defense—"There is no military strength whether for Britain or for our alliances except on the basis of economic strength.... We therefore intend to make to the alliances of which we are members a contribution related to our economic capability while recognizing that our security lies fundamentally in Europe and must be based on the North Atlantic Alliance.... Defense must be related to the requirements of foreign policy, but it must not be asked...to undertake commitments beyond its capability.... It is not only at home that...we have been living beyond our means.... Our real influence and power for peace will be strengthened by realistic priorities." *Accordingly, the following decisions had been taken:*

●The withdrawal of British forces from Malaysia and Singapore would be accelerated and would be completed by the end of 1971. British forces would also be withdrawn from Bahrein and Sharjah on the Persian Gulf by the end of 1971. "The broad effect is that, apart from our remaining dependencies and certain other necessary exceptions, we shall by that date not be maintaining military bases outside Europe and the Mediterranean."

●Britain would "retain a general capability based in Europe (including the United Kingdom) which can be deployed overseas...,including support for United Nations operations."

●Britain would amend its troop commitments to the Southeast Asia Treaty Organization as its forces in the area were reduced.

●Britain would make an "early reduction" in the number of aircraft based on Cyprus but would maintain its membership in the Central Treaty Organization.

●The Aircraft Carrier Force would be phased out of service "as soon as" the troop withdrawal from the Far East and the Persian Gulf had been completed. There would also be reductions in the rate of new naval construction, e.g., in the nuclear-powered hunter/killer submarines.

●There would be a "considerable increase in the rate of rundown of the army and in the disbandment or amalgamation of major units." The Gurkha Brigade would continue to be reduced after 1969 and would be cut to a strength of 6,000 by 1971.

●The order for 50 F-111 jet fighters from the U.S. had been canceled. "Further study is being given to the consequences of this decision on the future equipment of the Royal Air Force.... The cancellation of the F-111 is estimated to yield total savings on the defense budget of about £400 million [$960 million] between now and 1977-78. This figure allows for likely cancellation charges. The saving in dollar expenditure over the period, again allowing for likely cancellation charges, will be well over $700 million. Because of the credit arrangements, these savings will mature over a period of years. We are discussing with the U.S. government future arrangements for offset orders and credit for the [F-4] Phantom and [C-130] Hercules aircraft. The reduction in our overseas commitments will make it possible to cut down the transport force."

(The cancellation would not affect the entire offset purchase agreement, which the U.S. had agreed Jan. 1 to increase from $725 million to $825 million. Under the agreement, the U.S. would have bought $425 million worth of military equipment from Britain and would have helped Britain obtain an additional $400 million by negotiating joint U.S.-UK arms sales to 3d countries. The offset agreement was aimed at helping Britain to meet the payment by the end of fiscal 1977 of a $2.875 billion order for the F-111s as well as for a number of F-4 Phantom jets and C-130 Hercules transports and spare parts for Polaris missiles bought from the U.S.)

●There would be no immediate reduction in defense spending because it would take time for the policy changes to become effective. In fiscal 1968-9 (Apr. 1, 1968 through Mar. 31, 1969), defense spending would actually increase because of cancellation payments and other transitional costs. But in 1969-70 the defense budget was expected to decrease by £110 million ($308 million), from a planned figure of £1.97 billion ($5.516 billion) at 1964 prices to one of about £1.86 billion ($5.208 billion) at 1964 prices. Still using 1964 prices (and £1= $2.80); by 1972-3 the budget was expected to be between £1.6 billion and £1.65 billion ($4.48 billion and $4.62 billion), a further decrease of £210 million, £260 million ($588 million to $728 million).

●Britain still faced the problem of the "heavy continuing cost in foreign exchange" of stationing its troops in West Germany as part of its North Atlantic Alliance commitment. Bilateral talks at the ministerial level would be held to examine ways to meet this problem once the current UK-West German offset agreement expired Mar. 31.

Domestic expenditure—Economies had been made in "almost every major area..., in the rising programs which we had before us," in an attempt to arrive at an over-all home spending program that was "coherent, credible and fair." *These decisions had been made:*

●There would be no general increase in national insurance and other social security benefits until at least the autumn of 1969.

●While family allowances would be increased by 7 shillings (80¢) in April, as planned, the government intended "to recover the full amount of the increase from taxpayers." The full benefit of the increase would "be confined to families most in need."

●The government had "no alternative to deferring from 1971 to 1973 the raising of the school-leaving age" requirement from 15 to 16. This would save the government an estimated £33 million ($79 million) in fiscal 1968-9 and £48 million ($115 million) in fiscal 1969-70, primarily through a cutback in school building.

●The government proposed to stop providing free milk in the secondary schools, effective from September.

●Capitation grants to direct-grant schools would be reduced, some new capital projects in the universities, colleges and elsewhere would be postponed during fiscal 1968-9 and, following the next review of students awards, the increase in September would cover only half the rise in the cost of living since the last review. These cutbacks were expected to yield savings of £39 million ($94 million) in fiscal 1968-9 and £58 million ($139 million) in fiscal 1969-70.

●After "most serious consideration and with the utmost reluctance," the government had decided to reintroduce a charge system for prescriptions filled under the National Health Service, at the rate of 2 shillings 6 pence (30¢) per item. The charge would become effective in the spring and would save an estimated £50 million ($120 million) in a full year. However, since exemptions for the elderly (over 65), children (up to 15), expectant and nursing mothers and the chronically sick would reduce the estimated saving to £25 million ($60 million), there would be a 6-pence (6¢) increase per week in employes' and employers' contributions to the National Health Service.

●The maximum charge for dental treatment, unchanged since 1952, would be raised from £1 ($2.40) to 30 shillings ($3.60). This would yield a further saving of £1.5 million ($3.6 million).

●The civil defense program would be placed on a "care and maintenance basis." The Civil Defense Corps, the Auxiliary Fire Service and the Territorial & Army Volunteer Reserve Category III would be disbanded.

●16,500 fewer new houses would be built in "both 1968 and 1969," but slum-clearance and priority-area programs would remain unaffected. Special emphasis would continue to be placed on the regeneration of the development areas. The savings were expected to be £27 million ($64.8 million) in fiscal 1968-9 and £55 million ($132 million) in 1969-70.

●Road-building and maintenance programs for fiscal 1967-8, estimated to cost £560 million ($1.324 billion), or a 52% increase over 1963-4, would be reduced to save £122 million ($292.8 million) over the next 2 years. Assistance to public passenger transportation would be limited to £10 million ($24 million) in fiscal 1968-9 and to £20 million ($48 million) in fiscal 1969-70.

●Savings in the Ministry of Technology's industrial program would be concentrated in the Atomic Energy Authority's nuclear research and development program and in the ministry's defense research. Savings were expected to amount to £28 million ($67 million) in the 2 years to fiscal 1969-70.

●Local authorities were ordered to restrict the rate of growth of their spending programs to about 3% above the amounts agreed on for fiscal 1968-9.

●"It should be possible to realize substantial savings in public expenditure...[in Northern Ireland], broadly comparable to those in Great Britain. Discussions with Northern Ireland ministers have already started."

●Government departments were notified that there would be no increase in the number of civil servants during fiscal 1968-9. This would save £15 million ($36 million).

Summary—The results of these changes "will be to reduce planned expenditure in 1968-9 by £300 million [$720 million] plus, of course, an additional £25 million [$80 million] income from the National Health Service contribution, and in 1969-70 by £416 million [$998 million], again plus the contribution. This implies an average annual rise in public expenditure in the period 1967-68 to 1969-70 of 2.8%."

Prices & incomes—"I must again emphasize the paramount importance of prices and incomes policy. The measures we have decided on and those which will be announced in succeeding months will be adequate if and only if the competitive advantages we have gained are not dissipated in increases in incomes over and above the very limited figures we the country can afford. It is this which must guide us."

The House of Commons Jan. 18, by 304-9 vote, indorsed the government's cutback in home and defense spending. The vote came at the end of 2 days of debate on the economy measures, which had been announced Jan. 16. 25 Laborites abstained in the voting in protest against the government's cuts in welfare spending. The Conservatives also abstained. The 9 MPs who opposed the motion were Liberals. In an earlier action Jan. 18, the House of Commons had defeated by 334-229 vote a Conservative motion opposing the government's decision to withdraw its main forces from the Persian Gulf and Far East by the end of 1971. The Labor rebels voted with the majority, as did 9 Liberal MPs.

In a speech to the House of Commons Jan. 18, Prime Min. Wilson announced that the government had set a new "ceiling" of 3.5% on wage increases for the fiscal year beginning in July. He warned that the government would seek new restraining legislation if the voluntary restraints currently in use failed to keep wages within the proposed guidelines.

In an effort to restore party discipline, Wilson Jan. 20 moved against the 25 Labor MPs who had abstained in the confidence vote; he suspended them from membership in the majority caucus. This meant that they could not attend Labor Party meetings or have a voice in government decision-making. Among those suspended: Michael Foot, a leading spokesman for the Labor leftwing, and Reginald Paget of the party's rightwing. The Labor Party liaison committee voted Jan. 22, however, to lift the ban pending a final decision by a caucus of Labor MPs. The committee also voted to have Labor MPs consider a new "code of conduct" that would impose stricter voting discipline on party members. (Lord Longford, lord privy seal and leader of the House of Lords, had resigned from the Labor cabinet Jan. 16 in protest against the government's decision to postpone for 2 years the plan to extend the school-leaving age from 15 to 16. Lord Shackleton, minister without portfolio outside the cabinet and deputy leader of the House of Lords, was appointed to succeed Longford.)

The British budget for fiscal 1968-9 (Apr. 1, 1968-Mar. 31, 1969), providing for an estimated £11.312 billion ($27.149 billion) in expenditures and £11.952 billion ($28.685 billion) in revenues, was presented in the House of Commons Mar. 19 by Chancellor of the Exchequer Roy Jenkins. Commons adopted the budget by 332-248 vote Mar. 25. Reporting on fiscal 1967-8, Jenkins said that revenues had totaled £11.177 billion (£84 million above the original estimate) and expenditures £10.878 billion (£519 million above the original estimate). Exchequer borrowing totaled £1.449 billion.

The 1968-9 budget, termed the harshest budget since World War II, (1) made increases of about £775 million ($1.86 billion) in taxes on goods and services, (2) imposed a £100 million surtax for fiscal 1968-9 only on investment incomes over £3,000, (3) proposed legislation to hold wage increases for one year to a maximum of 3.5% and (4) anticipated a 1% drop in the real standard of living. Jenkins admitted that the tax measures were severe but said they were necessary for Britain's economic revival. He expressed hope that, with the government spending cuts announced in January and the planned military withdrawal from east of Suez, the new budget would restore confidence in the pound and make "an important contribution to the stabilization of the international monetary situation." Jenkins announced that income, capital gains and corporation taxes would not be increased but that the added revenues would come largely from indirect taxes on goods and services. The government hoped that the new taxes would cut consumption by 2% a year, increase savings and achieve a £500 million ($1.2 billion) surplus in the balance of payments.

The budget also called for a 50% increase in the Selective Employment Tax (SET), from the current 25s. to 37s. 6d. a week for men, effective Sept. 2.

During debate in the House of Commons, the budget was criticized severely both within and outside the ruling Labor Party, especially for its wage and income curbs. Iain MacLeod, Conservative Party spokesman for economic affairs in the House of Commons, said Jenkins was guilty of "overkill" with his "brutal" budget.

The defense estimate for fiscal 1968-9 had been outlined in a government White Paper Feb. 22. Defense expenditures were estimated at £2.271 billion ($5.45 billion), or 6% of the gross national product (GNP), as compared with £2.205 billion, or 6.5% of the GNP, the previous fiscal year. The government also planned a reduction in Britain's overseas commitments of 35,000 servicemen, including 5,000 from West Germany.

The Bank of England lowered its lending rate from 8% to 7.5% Mar. 21. The rate had been at the 8% crisis level since the devaluation of the pound Nov. 18, 1967. A bank spokesman said the reduction was "appropriate" in terms of these developments: (1) the international monetary situation had become "calmer" following a Mar. 17 decision of the Gold Pool nations to establish a 2-tier pricing system for gold and (2) the "severe measures of fiscal policy" contained in the British budget announced Mar. 19 had "strengthened sterling."

The Bank of England lowered its bank rate from 7.5% to 7% Sept. 19. A bank spokesman said the reduction had been made possible by the $2 billion Basel agreement, the rise in exports in August and an improvement in the balance-of-payments situation.

The Conservative Party won all 4 seats contested in by-elections for the House of Commons Mar. 28. In one of the severest setbacks suffered in a by-election, the total vote polled by the Labor Party in the 4 districts dropped from 105,286 in the 1966 general election to 49,955. The Conservative vote rose from 94,439 to 102,516. Labor's losses were interpreted as reflecting growing disaffection over measures with which the Labor government had attempted to correct the country's economic and financial reverses. The losses reduced the Labor Party's majority in the 630-seat Parliament to 72. Party standings after Mar. 28: Labor—348 seats plus the non-voting house speaker; Conservative—257 plus the non-voting party chairman; Liberal—12 plus the non-voting party chairman; splinter parties—5 seats. 5 other seats, 3 of which had been held by the Labor Party, remained vacant.

A government bill providing reserve powers to curb increases in wages, prices and corporate dividends was approved by the House of Commons May 21 by 290-250 vote (35 abstentions). The measure, introduced Apr. 3, deferred pay and price rises for 12 months and required price cuts where recommended by the Prices & Incomes Board. Annual wage increases, price raises and dividend boosts, when permitted, were limited to 3.5%. The government powers were included in a new Prices & Income Act to take effect Aug. 11 and expire 18 months later unless renewed.

The British Labor Party, at its annual conference in Blackpool Sept. 30-Oct. 4, called for repeal of wage-and-price controls and turned down a demand for wholesale nationalization of industry. The wage-price resolution was approved at the Sept. 30 session by a vote of 5,098,000 to 1,124,000 (representing union membership). The resolution had been introduced by Frank Cousins, general secretary of the Transport & General Workers Union. By 3,282,000-2,921,000 vote the delegates also rejected a leftwing resolution demanding wholesale nationalization of industry. Prior to the balloting, Chancellor of the Exchequer Roy Jenkins had declared that the government would continue its policy of austere economy. He rejected demands for higher wages and said Britain must increase exports.

Prime Min. Wilson defended his economic policies in a speech at the Labor conference Oct. 1. He said: "To abandon the policies we believe to be right would be just as cowardly and in the long run destructive of this party as to have shirked bringing them in." The Laborite government had been forced to introduce unpopular measures to counteract the mistakes inherited from the previous (Conservative) government, he said. Among these, Wilson asserted, was "the role of world policeman with an intolerable weight of overseas military expenditure." In an address at the closing session Oct. 4, Wilson assailed conference votes against the government's economic policies. These included a vote earlier Oct. 4 to reject a resolution that would have placed the party on record as not opposing wage-and-price-control laws. Asserting that these votes were "a warning, not an instruction," Wilson said: "Everything we have achieved at so great a cost can be imperiled by ill-considered industrial action. This government will not readily forgive any action which endangers our own purpose."

The Trades Union Congress Sept. 5 urged repeal of the wage-control law approved by the House of Commons May 21. At its annual conference in Blackpool, the TUC's 1,000 delegates, representing more than 9 million trade unionists, voted 7,460,000 to 1,022,000 against wage restraint. The congress contended that the law hampered collective bargaining, economic expansion and improvements in industrial efficiency. Frank Cousins said the law was "a despicable weapon used in main against the lower paid."

In an attempt to curb the pressure of consumer demand in Britain and to improve the nation's trade balance, Chancellor of the Exchequer Roy Jenkins Nov. 22 announced the implementation of 3 restrictions, effective immediately. Sales taxes on most non-essential consumer goods (liquor, tobacco, gasoline) were raised through a "regulator" mechanism by an average of about 10%. Clearing banks were to bring their lending ceiling down to 98% of the Nov. 1967 level by Mar. 1969; this would mean a reduction by about £100 million in non-fixed-rate lending to the private sector. A system of import deposits, covering about 1/3 of British imports, would require importers of manufactured goods to deposit an amount equal to 50% of the value of their goods before their release from customs; the deposit was repayable in full after 6 months, and the system would be in effect for a year. The restrictions were expected to reduce domestic consumption by about .5% in 1969. Jenkins, who had just returned from Bonn, where international finance and the position of the pound had been discussed, said, in part:

"In a situation of speculative rumors of the kind we have just been through, it is inevitable that a great deal of the burden falls on reserve currencies. We suffered in the week before the conference, but, of course, there is no question of a movement in the sterling parity. This was not considered as a matter for discussion at the conference. However, there was a recognition of the need for effective action to neutralize the effect of speculative flows upon the reserves of different countries. The immediate difficulties in the exchange markets are . . . thus disposed of. . . . We have made considerable progress. On the basis of the 3-monthly moving average, the trade figures, including those for October, have shown an improvement in every month since May. The policies we have followed since devaluation are showing their results, especially in the performance of our exports. Nevertheless, . . . the speed of our movement into balance-of-payments surplus has been insufficient. Despite high exports our trade figures, while improving, have not done so as fast as necessary. One reason is the continuing high level of consumer spending. Another may be that there has been a rapid build-up of stocks.

"To accelerate our progress . . . we need to take further action to curtail demand, especially demand for imports. We must take action to get back into balance now without further delay, or without further drawings upon our limited reserves. I am taking action of 2 kinds—in the taxation field and in the field of credit. . . . The Treasury has today made an order, the effect of which is to put a surcharge of 10% on the duties on beer, wines, spirits, hydrocarbon oils, petrol substitutes, power methylated spirits, on the tobacco duty and on all the rates of purchase tax. . . .

"It is necessary for me to look to the banks for a further tightening of credit, particularly for the finance of consumer spending. I do not propose to inhibit finance for exports. . . . From now on, therefore, for the London clearing banks and Scottish banks the ceiling will exclude export credit at a fixed rate of 5.5% which is guaranteed by the Export Credits Guarantee Department, and fixed rate credit at the same rate for orders on domestic shipbuilders guaranteed by the Ministry of Technology. . . . The ceiling will continue to cover all other sterling lending by these banks to the private and overseas sector. The governor of the Bank of England is asking them to bring this lending by Mar. 1969 within a ceiling of 98% of the level of Nov. 1967. When allowance has been made for seasonal factors, I estimate that this revised ceiling will require these banks to reduce their non-fixed-rate lending to the private sector by about £100 million between now and next March. If, as we hope and expect, guaranteed credit at fixed rates for exports and shipbuilding increases by about the same amount over the period, there will be no increase in the credit granted to the private sector. . . .

"In addition, I propose a further measure of credit restriction designed to squeeze out excessive liquidity in the monetary system in a selective way which is, I believe, particularly appropriate in our current situation. Parliament will be asked immediately to enact legislation for a scheme of import deposits. This scheme will apply to imports of, broadly speaking, all goods other than basic foods, feedingstuffs, fuel and raw materials and certain categories of goods imported mainly from developing countries. It will cover goods amounting to just over 1/3 of our total imports—that is, goods valued at something under £3 billion. There will be provision for relief in certain cases, such as goods intended for export. Importers of goods covered by the scheme will be required to pay to the Customs a deposit of

50% of the value of those goods before the Customs will release them. The deposits will be repayable to the importer 180 days after the date of payment. The bill will continue in force for a year, but with provision for this period [and the deposit rate] to be reduced, but not increased. . . .

"These credit measures as a whole will involve a severe reduction in lending to the private sector. The banks are being asked to concentrate the reduction to the greatest extent possible upon finance for consumer spending. . . . The [import deposits] scheme is not one which can or should be kept in being for more than a limited period, but it will have powerful effects over the next few months when we most need its benefit. . . .

"The measures that I have just announced are undoubtedly hard. Taken together they will reduce the level of home demand by .5% in 1969, but we cannot escape the facts of our international financial position . . . . These measures are what is necessary for our over-riding objective of achieving and sustaining a sufficient balance-of-payments surplus. . . ."

International Finance

Britain's gold and foreign exchange reserves fell in 1968 by £114 million ($273.6 million), from $2.695 billion Jan. 1 to $2.442 billion Dec. 31, after rising and falling irregularly during the year. Reserves had risen in January and February by $74.4 million, then had fallen in March by $48 million. Reserves rose by $50.4 million in April but fell by $26.4 million in May and an additional $62.4 million in June. In July, reserves rose by $50.4 million. The Treasury speculated that the July increase would have been double if Britain had not made its scheduled monthly repayment of $21.6 million to the Bank for International Settlements for the $250 million loan granted in Nov. 1967. Britain also repaid the U.S. Export-Import Bank $2.8 million for credits advanced to help finance British purchases of U.S. military aircraft. Reserves fell by $68 million in August, rose by $49 million in September and fell by $12 million in October. Treasury officials, however, viewed the October figures as "extremely satisfactory," since they recorded only a small loss in a month in which Britain had made repayments of $124.8 million in debts to foreign banks.

Less optimism was expressed over November's figures, reported by the Treasury Dec. 4. Reserves fell in November by $196.8 million, the largest decline since Dec. 1967. The drop left total reserves at $2.4 billion, the lowest point since October 1967, one month before the pound's devaluation to $2.40. The November decrease was partly due to loss of reserves during the franc-mark crisis, when the pound fell to its effective floor. In addition, loan repayments of £54 million ($129.6 million) were made during the month. In December, reserves fell by an additional $87 million.

The British balance-of-payments deficit in 1968 amounted to £458 million ($1.1 billion), compared with £515 million ($1.24 billion) in 1967. The long-term capital outflow decreased from £116 million ($278 million) in 1967 to £39 million ($93.6 million) in 1968. The balance-of-trade deficit (excess of imports over exports) in 1968 amounted to £708 million ($1.7 billion), the largest gap since 1951.

The balance-of-trade and balance-of-payments deficits varied widely during the year, both being in deficit for every month. The most favorable trade deficit was $164 million in November, the least favorable, $381 million in May. The most favorable payments deficit was $38 million in November, the least favorable, $221 million in March. The month-by-month figures:

Month	Exports (including re-exports)	Imports (in billions)	Balance-of-trade deficit (in millions)	Balance-of-payments deficit (in millions)
January	$1.243	$1.490	$247	$ 84
February	1.235	1.596	363	175
March	1.214	1.579	365	221
April	1.209	1.562	353	209
May	1.199	1.580	381	206
June	1.221	1.459	238	120
July	1.224	1.596	372	194
August	1.289	1.665	376	65
September	1.340	1.560	220	70
October	1.246	1.600	354	158
November	1.396	1.560	164	38
December	1.311	1.550	239	123

Britain June 17 activated a $1.4 billion IMF drawing privilege that had been granted Nov. 29, 1967 following the devaluation of the pound. The credit was earmarked for repayment of short-term loans that had been advanced to Britain by various central banks. The IMF provided the funds by selling $365 million of its gold holdings, using $559 million of its holdings of 13 foreign currencies (including $250 million in U.S. currency) and borrowing $476 million from Belgium, Italy, the Netherlands, Sweden and West Germany under the General Arrangement to Borrow. The mix of the loan was altered from that originally envisaged because of France's financial difficulties. The drawing raised to about $2.9 billion the amount Britain would be required to repay the IMF by mid-1971. Britain May 7 had announced the following schedule for repayment of the $1.4 billion it had drawn from the IMF in May 1965: (1) 2 installments, each equivalent to $100 million, to be paid in Aug. 1968 and Nov. 1968; (2) 6 quarterly installments, each equivalent to $200 million, to be paid between Feb. 1969 and May 1970.

It was announced in London July 8 that Britain had received assurances of a $2 billion, medium-term (10-year) sterling support package from 12 central banks and the Bank for International Settlements. The announcement was made by Sir Leslie O'Brien, governor of the Bank of England, following a meeting of the BIS and the central banks in Basel July 7. The plan was concluded in Basel Sept. 9. Agreeing to provide the stand-by support, in addition to the BIS, were the central banks of Austria, Belgium, Canada, Denmark, Italy,

Japan, the Netherlands, Norway, Sweden, Switzerland, the U.S. and West Germany. France participated in the discussions but, because of its own financial difficulties, declined to participate in the credit arrangement. A Bank of England communique noted, however, that France had "expressed its sympathy with the steps being taken to deal with this problem." The new support, according to the communique, was designed to "provide new means for offsetting fluctuations in the sterling balances of sterling area countries," i.e., to bolster British reserves sufficiently to dissuade sterling area countries from making large withdrawals from their accounts with the Bank of England. O'Brien said the credit was "not a loan" or "an arrangement which could or will lead to any increase in our total of overseas indebtedness;" rather, the object of the support package was "to strengthen the position of sterling and thus of the international monetary system as a whole."

The agreement released Britain from the obligation to use its own decreasing reserves to pay for conversions out of sterling and allowed it instead to use its reserves to improve its balance-of-payments deficit. (Due to anxiety over the recent British devaluation and the future of the pound, the 66-member sterling bloc had been tempted to convert sterling holdings into other currencies. Their net sterling claims amounted to $5.6 billion, $4 billion of which was official holdings; but British reserves by mid-1968 had decreased to $2.7 billion, less than half the worth of the sterling held by sterling area countries.) The $2 billion credit guaranteed sterling bloc members against further devaluation of their holdings. It provided that if the pound was devalued in dollar value before 1971, the sterling value of bloc nations' balances would be written up and Britain's debt expanded by that amount. The agreement also provided that to the extent the $2 billion was used, London sterling deposits would be changed into dollar debts repayable within 10 years.

O'Brien Sept. 9 expressed optimism at the results of that day's Basel meeting, but he emphasized that the "credit does not solve all the pound's problems." "The arrangement merely changes one debt for another," he said. "We now have a dollar debt. We have been provided with cash dollars with which to meet the running down of sterling debts."

A major effect of the Basel plan would be the beginning of a gradual withdrawal of the pound sterling from its position as one of the world's 2 reserve currencies. (The other reserve currency was the dollar.) There was some fear, however, that the plan's guarantees for the pound would make sterling holders so confident about the safety of their holdings that they would fail to convert them or convert them too slowly to effectively lessen the role of sterling as a reserve. Under the arrangement, Britain was entitled to draw from the $2 billion credit for 3 years, with 10 years in which to repay. The plan stipulated that debts outstanding from a similar $1 billion credit, granted to Britain in 1966 and renewed in Mar. 1968, were to be settled and terminated by 1971.

EUROPE & THE EEC

European Community Activity

The EEC Executive Commission's 3d quarter economic review, issued Nov. 8, reported that the Common Market's trade balance "has of late shown a distinct tendency to deteriorate." The review said that the 2 main reasons for the deterioration were (1) an increased rate of consumer goods imports as a result of the market's expansion, and (2) a decrease in the growth of demand for EEC products by industrial countries. The review noted that the 6 governments' gold and foreign exchange reserves had decreased by $600 million during the 3d quarter, principally due to France's reserve losses and its trade deficit. The Common Market's trade surplus had decreased during the 2d quarter after having reached $473 million in the first quarter. An EEC report July 23 gave these reasons for the decline: (1) a decrease in exports to the U.S., (2) a decline in demand for European consumer goods in Britain and (3) economic expansion within the Common Market. (The U.S. Federal Reserve Board reported in its November *Bulletin* that real output—output changes adjusted for price changes—had grown within the EEC at an annual rate of 3% during the period 1966 to mid-1968, compared with a growth rate of 5% during 1962-5.)

The EEC Council of Ministers agreed Dec. 10 to reconvene the dormant Marechal committee on technological cooperation. The deadlock over technological discussions within the EEC was broken when France agreed to Britain's participation in the talks, thereby overcoming the Netherlands' refusal to enter such talks without Britain. By insisting, however, that all 6 EEC nations must first decide among themselves on discussions with other nations, France was able to block Dutch and Belgian plans for bilateral talks with other nations within the West European Union. The ministers instructed the Marechal committee to prepare a report on technological cooperation for the council meeting in Mar. 1969, at which time other European nations would be invited to submit recommendations.

Figures for 1968 EEC agricultural production reported Dec. 17: The total cereal harvest increased by 1.1 million tons in 1968 to 70.4 million tons, the highest level since World War II. Wheat production rose 900,000 tons to a postwar record of 32.2 million tons, indicating a higher yield per acre and a rise in land under cultivation. Barley production dropped by 700,000 tons to 15.3 million tons, but the harvest was 19% above the average annual production for the past 5 years. Rye and mixed wheat and rye crops production was 4.1 million tons, the same amount as in 1967. The maize harvest increased by 600,000 tons over 1967 to a postwar high of 9.4 million tons, reflecting a 29% increase above the 5-year annual production. Oats and mixed cereal production remained at the 5-year average of 8.4 million tons, and the grape harvest reached a record 635,000 tons. The sugar beet harvest increased 2 million tons above the 1967 output to 50.7 million tons.

The EEC's agriculture ministers had agreed May 29 to a unified price policy on dairy products. Action on the common policy was forced by France, which had warned that a lack of a dairy agreement might prevent it from carrying out the EEC industrial tariff reductions scheduled for July 1. The French stand was supported by dairy farmers in some other EEC countries. 5,000 farmers demonstrated in Brussels May 27 against any cuts in dairy prices. The agreement established a temporary ceiling of $630 million for Common Market dairy support payments in 1968. The official price of butter was set at $173.50 for 220 pounds in Italy and Holland, down from the $176.25 support price established in 1966. Belgian and Luxembourg farmers would receive an additional $2.75 for 220 pounds from the EEC's farm fund, while French farmers would get the $2.75 support subsidy from the French government. West Germany was allowed to drop its price of butter by $6 (to $167.50) per 220 pounds. The butter support prices were to be in effect for one year. In order to increase butter consumption, the ministers also agreed to adopt a new tax on margarine. The EEC currently had a reported 150,000 tons of surplus butter. (The introduction of a new EEC "value added" tax, approved by the EEC Feb. 9, 1967, had raised milk and bread prices in Paris Jan. 1 by nearly 10%.)

The EEC's chief farm expert, Dr. Sicco Mansholt of the Netherlands, proposed Dec. 13 that the number of Common Market farmers be reduced to 5 million by 1980. (The number of EEC farmers was expected to decrease from the 1960 level of 15 million to 10 million by 1970.) In support of his proposal, Mansholt asserted that 75% of EEC farms provided only 3/4 of a day's work for an average man, and 80% of EEC dairy farms had fewer than 10 cows. Under his plan, dairy farms would have a minimum of 40 cows and crop farms would have at least 200 acres. Mansholt also called for a sharp reduction in farm support prices from the current $2 billion annually to $750 million by 1980, 1/3 of the sum to be earmarked for dairy farms. Other Mansholt proposals included: (1) monetary inducements to encourage farmer migration to cities and the establishment of special industrial training programs for farmers; (2) payments to farmers who consolidated their holdings; (3) the conversion of 12.5 million acres of farm land into recreational or forest areas; (4) slaughtering of dairy cows to reduce large milk and butter surpluses. Mansholt did not estimate the cost of the program, but it was believed to total $3 to $4 billion annually. The Mansholt proposals evoked strong criticism from EEC farmers. The Flemish newspaper *Het Volk,* warning that the program could lead to price-fixing and control of agricultural production by a few persons, called Mansholt "a technocrat of the most dangerous sort."

The *Wall St. Journal* reported Dec. 16 that the U.S. intended to increase sharply import duties on West European agricultural and industrial products if the EEC imposed a proposed $60 per ton soybean tax. (The purported purpose of the tax was to make the price of European butter more competitive by forcing a rise in the price of margarine.) An EEC spokesman said that the new tax was not discriminatory and conformed to GATT agreements. He added that "I don't see how the U.S. could retaliate under GATT. They can't take illegal action just because they don't like what we do." But, according to a trade official in Washington, the U.S. was ready to take "retaliatory action." He said that the new tax was "a major trade problem because it involves U.S. exports to the Common Market countries valued at about $450 million this year and probably more than half a billion dollars next year." One of the measures the U.S. could take, he asserted, was to increase duties on imports of Common Market automobiles and "wipe them out of their current price brackets in our market." He added that the adoption of the new tax would "be equivalent to a tariff of 30%-50%," would greatly harm U.S. farm programs, and would adversely affect U.S. trade relations with the EEC.

The EEC Executive Commission, following an agreement by Common Market economic and finance ministers, had begun to prepare proposals for better economic and monetary cooperation, it was announced Dec. 13 and 16. The commission was reportedly seeking ways to divert capital from surplus to deficit countries and to change the monetary system in order to lower the frequency of crises. (There was also speculation that the EEC might create a capital reserve pool, based on member states' contributions, to be used in exchange markets.) Underscoring the importance of common economic and financial policy, an EEC official asserted that "The community can forge closer monetary links and go forward once again as a dynamic body, or each nation can continue doing more or less as it wants in the monetary field, and the community will eventually wither and die."

(EEC finance ministers had agreed Feb. 27 to a united policy to stabilize interest rates. Under the agreement, member nations would consult with one another before raising or lowering short-term bank rates. The adoption of the measure was viewed as an important step toward integrating Common Market economic policies.)

An 11th-hour effort by Euratom Dec. 21 saved the agency from extinction. France had sought to reduce Euratom's 1969 budget from $80 million to $20 million, but the other 5 nations rejected the cut. A compromise was reached as the 5 agreed to budgetary cuts but not to the extent France had wanted. The 5 also agreed to conduct their own research in order to maintain a large percentage of Euratom's programs.

French Turmoil

Pressures caused in France by domestic unrest and international financial reversals threatened to force the devaluation of the franc during 1968.

Total French gold and foreign exchange reserves had fallen by the equivalent of $74.3 million in Dec. 1967 to a year-end total of $6.108 billion. The decline was the first since April. Although over-all French reserves had increased by $363 million in 1967, the decline that began toward 1967's end continued into 1968. The Finance Ministry reported Mar. 1 that France's reserves had declined by the equivalent of $93.6 million since the beginning of the year—$55.1 million in January and $38.5 million in February. Total French reserves as of the end of February: $6,014,400,000. But French reserves then increased by the equivalent of $8.5 million in March and reached a total of $6,022,900,000 Mar. 31.

The economic and political structures of France were battered in May by student disorders that burst from the universities into the streets and by wildcat sit-in strikes that paralyzed the country's factories. The factory occupations came in the wake of a one-day general strike called May 13 to demonstrate solidarity with the students, who had taken control of the universities in an attack on the French political and educational systems. The student protests brought 10 days of bloody street clashes in Paris and other cities. But whereas the student rebels sought to remake French society, the workers generally wanted higher pay, a shorter work week, other economic improvements and, in some instances, a voice in management. The strikes halted nearly all of the nation's industrial production, commerce, communications and transportation and posed a major challenge to the 5th Republic and the rule of Pres. Charles de Gaulle. By May 20 probably more than 6 million workers—1/3 of France's labor force—had occupied factories and premises ranging from workshops to railroad yards and public service facilities throughout the country. Led in many cases by militant leftists who ran up red flags over the occupied factories, the strikes were considered to have raised the threat of social revolution.

The Gaullist government of Premier Georges Pompidou narrowly survived May 22 when a censure motion failed by a mere 11 votes. 2 days later de Gaulle asked the French people to give him a personal vote of confidence in a referendum to be held in June. Violent street fighting erupted again between students and police; the strike movement spread even further and began to include peasant demonstrations. There were worldwide rumors of de Gaulle's imminent resignation. Instead, he dissolved the National Assembly May 30 and called for new elections to be held at the end of June (the referendum was postponed).

Pompidou revised his cabinet May 31 amid signs of an emerging back-to-work trend among France's striking workers and civil servants, by then numbering some 10 million. The cabinet change appeared to most observers as a move by the Gaullist regime to remove men who had been compromised during the current disorders and an opportunity to bring in new men who might enjoy the confidence of the striking workers and students during negotiations to end the country's paralysis. Among nominations that caused surprise was the appointment of Rene Capitant to the Ministry of Justice portfolio vacated by Louis Joxe, who had been acting premier during the early phase of the student disturbances. Foreign Min. Maurice Couve de Murville and Finance Min. Michel Debre exchanged their portfolios in another surprise move. Education Min. Alain Peyrefitte had resigned earlier after mounting student protests.

Candidates supporting the de Gaulle regime won a landslide victory in a 2-round general election June 23 and 30. This was the first time in French republican history that any party had won an absolute majority of National Assembly seats. The opposition was reduced to little more than half the seats it had held in the outgoing assembly. The Gaullists polled less than a majority of the popular vote.

Gaullists won 358 of the assembly's 487 seats; the combined opposition won 128. (One seat in French Somalia remained to be filled after elections later in July.) Responding to Gaullist campaign attacks on the nationwide disorders and the alleged threat of Communist totalitarianism, the voters dealt a massive blow to the opposition leftist parties. French Communist Party (PCF) representation was reduced from 73 to 34, a loss of 39, despite repeated PFC attempts during the campaign to repudiate responsibility for the labor and student strife and despite the PFC posture during the campaign of standing for order and discipline. The other big loser was the non-Communist Federation of the Democratic & Socialist Left, headed by Francois Mitterrand, which won 57 seats, a loss of 61. The Unified Socialist Party (PSU) lost all 3 seats it had held in the previous assembly and remained without representation. Its leader, ex-Premier Pierre Mendes-France, was defeated by a bare 132 votes in Grenoble by a Gaullist, ex-Welfare Min. Jean-Mareel Jeanneney.

As in the 1967 election, de Gaulle had asked his ministers to stand as candidates, although in the 5th Republic ministers were not required to be National Assembly members. The only cabinet member defeated was Yvon Morandat, state secretary for social affairs; 21 cabinet members were elected, including Armed Forces Min. Pierre Messmer and Finance Min. Couve de Murville, both of whom had been narrowly defeated in 1967.

The government imposed a series of emergency trade and monetary controls to offset the threat of economic slowdown and to prevent the weakening of the franc in the wake of the strikes and social disorders. The impact of the strikes and the subsequent wage increases forced the government to dip into its gold and foreign exchange reserves, which had dropped by about $1.4 billion since May 1. *Among the government's actions and related developments:*

Money controls—The government May 31 imposed temporary but stiff control on the outflow of privately owned francs. The decree, issued to defend the franc, halted trading in francs in European currency exchanges but did not affect payments resulting from normal business transactions. The decree required government approval for most international transactions and payments involving gold, currency and securities. The Bank of France announced the same day that French tourists would be allowed to take only 1,000 francs ($200) per person out of the country for each journey. (Prior to the controls decree, the Bank of France had asked the Bank for International Settlements in Basel May 28 to buy, with French-owned dollars, French francs on the international currency markets.)

Bank rates up—The government announced July 3 that it had raised the basic interest rate from 3.5% to 5% in an effort to curb inflationary pressures on the franc and to help reverse the outflow of money. The announcement was made after the first cabinet meeting following the Gaullist victory at the polls June 23 and 30. The government also: (a) increased the interest rates for loans on stocks from 5% to 6.5%, (b) decided to raise $500 million in taxes and (c) approved a $1.5 billion supplementary budget for the current year. Reporting to the cabinet, Finance Min. Maurice Couve de Murville said that the $1.5 billion supplementary budget had been made necessary by the large-scale wage increases, benefits and strike indemnities resulting from the strike settlements and that the budget increase—partially offset by increased revenue—would raise the year's deficit from the envisaged $1.5 billion to $2 billion.

Reserves down—The Finance Ministry disclosed June 4 that France's gold and foreign exchange reserves had dropped by $306.6 million during May to a total of $5,720,500,000. A further decline of $203.6 million, reported July 5, brought reserves down to a total of $5.52 billion. The latter figure included $885 million drawn from the International Monetary Fund by June 17 to supplement France's gold and foreign exchange reserves. The IMF drawing, the first by France in a decade, was made in 2 installments—$745 million reported withdrawn June 4, $140 million by a transfer of drawing rights to 4 other countries June 17. The final drawing exhausted France's automatic drawing rights in the fund.

The U.S., Switzerland and France's 5 Common Market partners were reported July 10 to have agreed to "swap" their own currencies for $1.3 billion worth of francs; $600 million of the sum was from the U.S.

Financial sources in Washington, Paris and other capitals reported in late June and in July that France had sold $75-$100 million worth of gold to the U.S. and several hundred million dollars' worth to the central banks of other countries in June and early July in exchange for dollars and other foreign currencies. The price: $35 an ounce.

Trade curbs—The government June 26: (a) limited imports of automobiles, trucks, textiles, appliances and steel to no more than 7%-15% above 1967's imports, (b) reduced interest rates on government loans to exporters from 3% to 2% and (c) promised to subsidize exports not covered by the existing "economic insurance risk" program. The subsidy, designed to offset unforeseeable rises in the cost of production, was based on wages; it would amount to 6% in the period July-Oct. 1968 and 3% in Nov. 1968-Jan. 1969. (The government also indicated that it would take "necessary measures" against price increases beyond 3% in domestic markets. But it apparently did not intend to inhibit export price changes. Renault, Peugeot and Citroen, France's 3 major auto manufacturers, announced June 25 that they would raise the prices of their products by 3%.) In swift response, the U.S. announced June 26 that special duties would be levied on French goods. William M. Roth, Pres. Johnson's special representative for foreign trade negotiations, said: "Our laws and the General Agreement on Tariffs & Trade provide for the use of countervailing duties to offset export subsidies by others. They also provide redress if import quotas impair our trade."

The French Finance Ministry reported July 10 that France's foreign commerce (both imports and exports) had dropped by 30% from its normal level. The trade deficit fell from 550 million francs in April to 50 million in May (declines of 34% in imports and 24% in exports), but the ministry said the decline merely reflected the severe economic disruption of May and June.

Foreign Min. Michel Debre had announced June 14 that France was asking its EEC partners for special temporary exemption from earlier commitments to end all industrial trade barriers among member states July 1. Among the products included in the exemption were appliances and automobiles. The government also announced June 14 that it would trim its foreign aid program and that it would impose a ban on fruit and vegetable imports from countries outside the Common Market.

Pres. de Gaulle July 10 appointed Maurice Jacques Couve de Murville, 61, to replace Georges Pompidou, 57, as premier of France. 2 days later, Couve de Murville announced the formation of his cabinet, which consisted largely of members of Pompidou's cabinet. The dropping of Pompidou so soon after the spectacular Gaullist victory at the polls, for which Pompidou had been popularly assumed to deserve a large share of the credit, caused widespread bitterness in Gaullist circles and sparked speculation as to its motive. Generally 2 theories were advanced to explain it: (1) Pompidou had been long regarded as an heir apparent to de Gaulle; some observers believed that Pompidou's removal from the premiership was a prelude to his eventual elevation to the presidency when de Gaulle's term expired in 1972. (2) According to other observers, Pompidou had been dismissed because of policy disagreements between him and de Gaulle; as the chief architect of the landslide Gaullist victory, Pompidou had become a powerful political figure in his own right with considerable following.

Pompidou submitted his resignation to de Gaulle July 10, as required by the constitution. In his letter of reply of the same day, de Gaulle praised Pompidou as having been "exceptionally effective" during his 6-year tenure as premier. De Gaulle also lauded Pompidou for his success in handling "the grave crisis which the country traversed last May and June." A phrase in which de Gaulle held out the prospect of future mission for Pompidou was particularly regarded as significant. De Gaulle said in the letter: "Wherever you will be, be assured, my dear friend, that I will be anxious to keep particularly close relations with you. Finally, I wish that you keep yourself ready to accomplish any mission and assume any mandate that the nation may one day bestow upon you."

Couve de Murville, who had been foreign minister for 10 years—longer than any of his predecessors—and a finance minister in the previous government, was regarded a loyal Gaullist. Among key cabinet members, Michel Debre was kept as foreign minister, Andre Malraux as cultural affairs minister, Pierre Messmer as armed forces minister and Raymond Marcellin as interior minister. Among appointments causing the most surprise was the shifting of Francois-Xavier Ortoli, a friend of Pompidou's and education minister in the previous cabinet, to the finance ministry, and the naming of ex-Premier Edgar Faure to be the education minister. Both portfolios were regarded as crucial in the coming months as attempts were made to solve pressing problems emphasized by the May-June crisis. Other important appointments: Maurice Schumann was retained as social affairs minister and Rene

Capitant as justice minister. Schumann's responsibility was to implement the controversial new system of participation of workers in
management decision-making.

The EEC Executive Commission agreed July 23 to permit France
to impose import quotas on steel, textiles, automobiles and household
goods. (The French government had unilaterally imposed quotas June
26, and earlier had requested special exemptions from EEC agreements
to end industrial trade barriers.) The EEC authorization, intended to
soften the impact of "sudden and unexpected paralysis" of the French
economy following the student and worker disturbances, was to remain
in force until Dec. 31. Over-all, about 10% of France's total imports
were affected by the quota system; 70% of the affected imports came
from the 5 other EEC nations.

The Executive Commission of the European Coal & Steel Community had agreed July 6 to allow French import quotas on steel.
France received approval to limit steel imports to 7% above the 1967
level, thus holding these imports to 4.7 million metric tons (5.18 million
U.S. tons). As with the later decision, the commission did not extend the
quota system beyond Dec. 31, and it retained the right to annul the
arrangement if France's industrial position improved. France had
already imposed quota restrictions on steel from Sweden, Britain, Spain
and other nations. The quota system had little effect on U.S. steel
exports to France, which amounted to only $6 million in 1967. (This was
the first time in 10 years that an EEC country had been permitted to
impose import restrictions. The EEC agreed Dec. 9 that starting Jan. 1,
1969, no member could institute import quotas without the approval of
the entire Common Market. Because of West Germany's special problems in dealing with Communist countries, however, the new regulation
was not applied to Communist nations. The only exceptions were Cuba
and Yugoslavia.)

Reacting to the French implementation of temporary import
quotas and export subsidies June 26, the U.S. Treasury Department
Aug. 13 announced the imposition of "countervailing duties" of 2.5% on
most French imports. The counter-tariffs, to be added to the regular
U.S. import tariffs, were scheduled to go into effect Sept. 14 and end as
France abolished its temporary restrictions. (The French restrictions
were scheduled to be lifted in 2 stages—50% Oct. 31 and the remaining
50% Jan. 31, 1969.) U.S. officials emphasized that the measure was not
taken in "retaliation" but was a move required by the basic tariff law.
The French subsidy amounted to 6% of a product's labor cost.

The French government ended currency exchange controls Sept. 4.
The controls, which had been instituted May 31 to halt a run on French
monetary reserves, did not prevent French gold holdings from dropping
by 1/3—from $6.9 billion in May to $4.5 billion Aug. 30.

The Finance Ministry Nov. 12 raised the Bank of France lending rate from 5% to 6% (the rate had been raised from 3.5% to 5% July 3). Reserve requirements were tightened from 4.5% to 5.5% on demand deposits and from 2% to 2.5% on other deposits.

De Gaulle, in a radio broadcast Nov. 24, spelled out a program of domestic austerity designed to preserve the value of the franc. De Gaulle made clear his intention not to devalue the franc. Instead, he restricted the convertibility of the franc (into foreign currencies) and imposed import restrictions. (Premier Couve de Murville had announced Nov. 19 that the proposed deficit in the 1969 French budget would be cut 20%.) Among de Gaulle's remarks:

"The monetary crisis which France has gone through is the consequence of the moral, economic, and social shock which it suddenly underwent last May and June.... When, in the midst of world competition, a country—and I am speaking of ours—which was in a state of growing prosperity, and which had one of the strongest currencies in the world, has ceased working for weeks and weeks; when it has for a long period been deprived of trains, ships, public transport, mining products, postal communications, radio, petrol and electricity; and when to escape death by suffocation it has all at once had to impose enormous salary burdens on its economy, overstrain its budget with the weight of suddenly increased spending, exhaust its credit in support of subsidies hurriedly lavished on concerns which have become bankrupt—nothing can enable that country to find its equilibrium at once, even if it has been able to stop on the brink of the abyss.

"But, until it has recovered it, nothing can stop a good number of people, both here and abroad, withdrawing the confidence they had in the country and trying to put their own interests before the public interest. Naturally, it is the national currency which then risks having to pay the cost of this odious speculation. However, despite the foul blow which it suffered, our economy has recovered. Work has begun again everywhere. Expansion is developing once more. External trade is growing.... Furthermore, the richest states have just opened considerable credits to us which can still be increased and which supplement our own reserves.

"Finally, we can see the day coming when, as a result of an unhappy experience, the whole world will agree to establish an impartial and reasonable monetary system sheltering every country—so long as it merits it—from sudden and absurd speculative movements.

"In brief, we have ... all that is necessary to complete the recovery which has begun, and to take the lead once more. That is why, all things considered, I and the government have decided that we must complete our recovery without having recourse to devaluation."

The French Finance Ministry announced Dec. 5 that total reserves had fallen by $280 million in November. The decline, the largest since July, resulted mainly from the speculative flow of French francs into West German marks. The actual loss in reserves was believed to have been greater than that reported, since France had a $1.3 billion swap agreement on which it could draw to support the franc. The reserve level had stood at $4.265 billion Oct. 31 and then fell to a low of $3.868 billion Nov. 28. After de Gaulle's assurance that the franc would not be devalued, reserves rose to $3.985 billion by Nov. 30.

The French government took action to defend the franc Nov. 25 by putting into effect strict foreign exchange controls. Under the exchange controls, similar to those introduced following the May-June upheaval, currency transactions were essentially confined to authorized agencies and the free convertibility of the franc was halted. French nationals were required to deposit their foreign securities in authorized banks in

France; exporters were required to repatriate earnings from foreign transactions; and restrictions were placed on commercial payments overseas. In addition, foreign travel allowances were limited to 700 francs ($40) for French tourists and 2,000 francs, with a maximum of 200 francs per day, for businessmen; the regulations were to stay in effect 5 weeks for businessmen and until January 1969 for tourists. Only 500 francs ($100) could be converted into foreign currency.

The proposed austerity program was presented to the National Assembly Nov. 26 by Prime Min. Couve de Murville; it was approved by votes of 391-91 in the National Assembly Nov. 27 and of 157-87 in the Senate Nov. 28. The measures included a further cut in the 1969 budget deficit, from the originally planned 11.7 billion francs ($2.34 billion) to 6.35 billion francs ($1.27 billion). The military budget was slashed by $80 million, and the 1969 nuclear test program was cancelled. Couve de Murville also announced a cut of 60 million francs ($12 million) in the French contribution to the British-French *Concorde* supersonic jetliner project. To achieve the proposed cuts in the budget deficit, the government asked for abolition of the 4.25% payroll tax paid by employers. The resulting revenue loss would be offset by increasing the value added tax. This tax, borne largely by the consumer, was to be increased in 4 categories: from 6% to 7% for items such as foodstuffs, from 13% to 15% in the category including fuel and petroleum, from 16.66% to 19% on a large group of manufactured goods and from 20% to 25% on items such as autos and luxury goods. The bulk of the budget cuts affected subsidies to nationalized industries. As a result, effective Dec. 1, government-owned corporations raised rail freight rates by 6.2% and gas and electricity rates for industrial users by 4.8%.

Further price controls involving "contract programs" (under which an industry must obtain government permission to raise its prices) were announced by the Economics & Finance Ministry Nov. 29. The measures put a freeze on all prices in the service sector for industries that had not signed contract programs with the government (about 25% of France's industry). In addition, special taxes were imposed on companies in the professional sector that had contract programs but had not honored the restrictions involved. Further, if a company with a contract program made extra profit as a result of the abolition of the payroll tax and the increase of the value-added tax, that profit was to be passed on to the consumers. Enforcement measures announced Nov. 30 aimed at preventing prices from rising beyond the level reached after the cost of the value-added taxes had been calculated. (Several hundred new agents were hired to join tax inspectors, customs officers and police personnel in detecting unjustified price increases.)

The Finance Ministry reported Dec. 10 that in November the value of imports had exceeded the value of exports by one billion francs ($200 million). The trade deficit was almost 3 times higher than the October deficit of 319 million francs ($63.8 million). November imports totaled

6.65 billion·francs ($1.33 billion), while exports were only 5.65 billion francs ($1.13 billion). Financial sources attributed the deficit in large part to inflationary wage increases and consumer spending following the May-June upheaval.

The Franc, the Mark & the Speculators

The European monetary system was shaken in November by a crisis initiated by massive speculation against the French franc in favor of the West German mark. The crisis led to an emergency meeting of monetary powers in Bonn and the institution of French and West German measures to strengthen the international financial and trade situation without changing the parities of their currencies. Speculation also struck the British pound, forcing the Bank of England to intervene and the British government to order strict measures to control consumer demand and improve Britain's trade balance.

(The November Federal Reserve Board *Bulletin* documented West Germany's economic strength; it reported that West Germany's real output in 1968's first half had exceeded the January-June 1967 figure by 6% whereas domestic consumption was up only 3% in the same period. The result: export strength and rising reserves.)

Stimulated by rumors of an impending West German revaluation, the crisis had been built up by a persistent and increasing flight from the franc to the mark. Approximately $1.7 billion in francs were sold during the first 3 weeks of November, and France was forced to use its already depleted gold reserves to support the franc's parity. (French reserves had been decreasing since the May-June upheavals.) The Bank of France reported Nov. 28 that total French reserves had dropped by Nov. 21 to $3.819 billion, a decline of $3 billion since May. During the most intense period of speculation, Nov. 15, 18 and 19, the Bank of France had publicly reported a reserve loss of only $174.8 million, while the West German Bundesbank reported Nov. 27 a reserve gain of $2 billion for a similar period. The French official figures were lower than expected because of the expenditure of international credits in place of the French reserves. A Nov. 18 report asserted that France had lost $400 million in reserves in one 2-day period alone.

In attempts to shore up the franc, the Paris government Nov. 12 had announced a series of credit-tightening measures. They included the imposition of a 4% growth ceiling on short-term non-priority bank loans to the private sector for the remainder of the year. Finance Min. Francois-Xavier Ortoli said Nov. 12 that the restrictions had been made necessary by the depletion of reserves. De Gaulle followed this action Nov. 13 by asserting at a cabinet meeting that devaluation of the franc "would be the most absurd thing there could be."

The rumors that West Germany would revalue were denied at every stage of the new crisis. West German Finance Min. Franz-Josef Strauss asserted in the Bundestag Nov. 13 that "the Federal government has made no secret decision to revaluate the mark." Karl Blessing, president of the Bundesbank, echoed this Nov. 15 in stating: "We will not be forced to act either by foreign or domestic speculation on revaluation of the Deutschemark."

A regular meeting of 11 central bankers at the Bank for International Settlements in Basel, Switzerland Nov. 16-17 did nothing to resolve the crisis. Bundesbank Pres. Blessing told reporters after the meeting: "There will be no announcement. I shall not say anything. We are just going to risk a bad market tomorrow." Though the meeting was shrouded in secrecy, France was reportedly offered a $1 billion credit package to be financed mostly by West Germany. France, however, rejected the proposal, reportedly because of "strings" attached to it.

Premier Couve de Murville assured the French people Nov. 18 that France's allies had offered "all the help she might need or will need in the future, without any reservation." In an attempt to hold down fears of a devaluation of the franc and to prepare the public for austerity measures, he added that the National Assembly would be called on to make sharp cuts in the state budget and a "fundamental reform" of the French financial market.

The speculation in European foreign exchange markets continued and increased Nov. 18-19. The French government Nov. 19 ordered budget cuts of $400 million, and the action was approved by the National Assembly later that day.

The West German government announced Nov. 19 that it would seek "emergency" tax legislation in an attempt to resolve the crisis. The official statement said: "The Federal government will not revalue the mark. The government will, through immediate tax measures in the import and export sectors, ensure internal price stability. This will, at the same time, be an effective German contribution to the improvement of international payments balance." The West German tax measures included a reduction of 4% in border taxes on imports and a corresponding 4% increase in taxes on exports. The measures were to be in effect for 15 months. German officials speculated that they would have an effect on trade equivalent to that of a 4%-5% revaluation and would probably reduce Bonn's trade surplus by about 1/3. The Bundestag and the Bundesrat approved the package Nov. 28 and Nov. 29.

In a new attempt to halt the intense speculation, foreign exchange markets in the major European capitals were closed Nov. 20 and remained closed for the rest of that week. West German Finance Min. Karl Schiller, acting chairman of the IMF's Group of 10, called an emergency meeting of financial leaders in Bonn Nov. 20. The meeting focused on the desire of Paris and Bonn to maintain the parity of their currencies. Reports indicated that the French, supported by the U.S. and Britain, were in favor of a revaluation of the mark. The French felt that the "excessive" West German trade surplus showed that the mark was out of step with the other currencies and should be realigned. The Germans reportedly resented the pressure on them to devalue; they attributed their large trade surplus to their financial discipline. Bonn was opposed to revaluation because it would penalize industry, cut farm subsidies and pose the threat of unemployment; further, revaluation could create political repercussions, and 1969 was an election year in West Germany. The West German government Nov. 21 announced that minimum reserve requirements had been raised to 100% and German banks were to be subject to a licensing system for borrowing abroad and for accepting foreign deposits at home.

The Bonn meeting of Group of 10 and other key financial leaders was held Nov. 20-22 in secret. Reporters said that most of the discussion consisted of an extensive debate on devaluation of the franc and that the French delegation, though unwilling to change parity without a corresponding move by Germany, had finally decided on a small change in the franc's value. Almost everyone connected with the meeting was apparently convinced that the franc would be devalued. The conferees apparently agreed to leave the details and the announcement of devaluation to France. The conferees pledged $2 billion in short-term credits to help France reinforce its financial position. $600 million was to be provided by West Germany, $500 million by the U.S., $200 million by Italy, $100 million each by Belgium, Britain, Canada, the Netherlands, Switzerland and the Scandinavian countries as a unit, $50 million by Japan and $50 million by the Bank for International Settlements. The final communique, issued Nov. 22, said:

"... The participants agreed that international monetary stability is the joint responsibility of all countries in the international economic community. Both deficit and surplus countries expressed their willingness to contribute effectively to the stability of the international monetary system through appropriate and concerted economic policies. They agreed on measures to counter speculative capital movements." "After thorough discussion of the German measures, the ministers and governors agreed that ... [the German] measures would make a significant contribution to the stability of the monetary system and the adjustment process. In the light of these measures, they endorsed the decision by the federal government to maintain the parity of the D-mark. The French economic and finance minister explained the situation of the French currency, the measures already taken toward a restoration of internal and external equilibrium, and the problems still to be solved. It was decided to set up a new central bank credit facility for France in the amount of $2 billion. This is in addition to France's substantial drawing facilities in the IMF."

The Bonn meetings were held in an acrimonious political atmosphere. The West German press, citing official but unnamed government sources, claimed that British Prime Min. Wilson had threatened to reduce the number of British troops in Germany if Bonn did not revalue the mark; the threat allegedly was made by Wilson in an early morning meeting Nov. 20 with West German Amb.-to-Britain

Herbert Blankenhorn. Wilson, in response to charges in Parliament by Tory leader Edward Heath, claimed Nov. 26 that inaccurate information had been leaked by West German spokesmen. "It is not the practice for messages between heads of governments to be published," he said. The West German government Nov. 27 denied Wilson's charges that officials had leaked information to the press about the Wilson-Blankenhorn meeting. Reports during the conference indicated that tempers also had flared between the German and U.S. delegates. It was reported Nov. 29 that Treasury Secy. Henry H. Fowler had told Bonn Finance Min. Karl Schiller that the West German tax measures were inadequate and Bonn was not fulfilling its international responsibility. Schiller allegedly retorted: "If the lopping off of 1/3 of our export surplus is not a sacrifice, then it is obvious that we have quite different concepts of social values."

De Gaulle stunned the financial world Nov. 24 with an announcement that France would not devalue the franc. His brief statement, issued by the Presidential Palace at 7:45 p.m., said simply: "The president of the republic announces that after a meeting of the cabinet today, Nov. 24, the following decision has been taken: The present parity of the French franc is maintained."

De Gaulle's decision was given the endorsement of both Pres. Johnson and Treasury Secy. Henry Fowler. In a telegram dispatched Nov. 24, Mr. Johnson wished de Gaulle success in his austerity program and added that "we are ready to cooperate in any way we can to achieve your objective consistent with our national purpose." Fowler stated Nov. 24: "I do heartily approve, and, indeed, applaud Gen. de Gaulle's decision to maintain the parity of the franc." He emphasized that the dollar was not threatened by the crisis and that he saw no fundamental disequilibrium in the French economy.

When the European foreign exchange markets reopened Nov. 25, the franc and the pound both gained, while the mark fell in light-to-medium trading. It soon became evident, however, that de Gaulle's decision would not have a great effect on speculative trends.

A West German Bundesbank report Dec. 11 indicated that speculative funds that had moved into the country during the crisis were not moving out again as fast as officials had hoped. Of the approximately 10 billion Deutschemarks ($2.5 billion) in foreign currencies that had flowed in, only 3 billion DM ($750 million) had left the country since the Bonn meeting of the Group of 10 nations had ended Nov. 22. Total West German reserves, as of the first week in December, were 33 billion DM ($8.25 billion), compared with 26 billion DM ($6.5 billion) at the end of October.

Freer Trade

18 member-nations of GATT (General Agreement on Tariffs & Trade) July 1 carried out tariff reductions stipulated under the Kennedy Round agreement. For most of the 18, the reduction represented 40% of the total envisaged under the year-old agreement. The pact was intended to cut the Western world's tariffs by 35% over a 5-year period. The countries reducing tariffs under the agreement were: the Common Market nations (France, West Germany, Italy, Belgium, the Netherlands and Luxembourg), Britain, Japan, Norway, Sweden, Denmark, Finland, Spain, Brazil, India, Pakistan, Ceylon and Nigeria. The 6 Common Market nations simultaneously abolished all tariffs remaining among themselves and aligned their common external tariff with the Kennedy Round reductions.

France, though implementing the tariff cut as agreed, also imposed temporary import quotas and export subsidies to protect its weakened economy. The protectionist measures provided subsidies to exporters and limited imports of cars, steel, textiles and appliances.

A GATT meeting, called in Geneva July 1 in response to the French action, set up a 20-nation "working party" to study the measures. The group's first report, unanimously adopted by the organization July 19, criticized France for not consulting with GATT before acting and declared that the good of the international economic community should take precedence over individual nations' interests.

(The U.S., Canada, Australia, New Zealand, Austria and Switzerland had instituted similar 40% tariff cuts Jan. 1.)

The July 1 cuts followed a decision announced by 16 major trading nations May 1 to accelerate further tariff cuts as assistance to the U.S. in its balance-of-payments problem. The action of the 16, all GATT members, was designed to dampen protectionist pressures building up in Washington. It had been reported Feb. 5 that the U.S. had proposed the speed-up in the tariff-cutting schedule as a means of offsetting the damage dealt U.S. trade by the tax harmonization measures adopted by the EEC, which had the effect of raising border taxes. The 16 nations agreeing to the proposal were Canada, Japan, the members of EEC, and the members of the European Free Trade Association (EFTA)—Austria, Britain, Denmark, Finland (associate member), Norway, Portugal, Sweden and Switzerland. Under the terms of the proposal, announced by GATT director general Eric Wyndham White in Geneva May 1, the 16 nations would institute Jan. 1, 1969 a 20% tariff cut that they were not scheduled to make until Jan. 1, 1970. In addition, the U.S. would be permitted to postpone until Jan. 1, 1970 the 20% tariff cut it was scheduled to make Jan. 1, 1969.

Certain of the 16 nations, according to the statement, had been willing to institute Jan. 1, 1969 all of their remaining Kennedy Round tariff reductions—those scheduled for 1970, 1971 and 1972 (20% each year)—but general agreement could not be reached on this point. Britain and its EFTA partners had adopted such a position Mar. 14 during the early stages of the negotiations leading to the accord. But the EEC Executive Commission, largely at France's insistence, called Mar. 14 for "indirect acceleration" of the tariff cuts, *i.e.,* a unilateral slowdown in U.S. reductions while the other industrialized nations held to the original schedule. As a compromise proposal, Japan indicated Mar. 18 that, while it would not agree to institute all of its remaining tariff reductions Jan. 1, 1969, it would be willing to accelerate the reductions and to grant the U.S. a one-year reprieve on its obligations. The Japanese proposal, referred to as "asymmetrical acceleration," was supported by White Mar. 28 and by the EEC finance ministers (France included) Apr. 9. The May 1 accord conformed to the Japanese proposal.

At a meeting of the EEC Council of Ministers in Brussels Nov. 5, French Foreign Min. Michel Debre introduced a 9-point program for increased trade between the EEC and other European nations. The most important proposal suggested new European-wide tariff reductions. Under the plan, industrial tariffs would be reduced by 30% over a 4-year period. The reduction would be in addition to the cuts previously implemented under the Kennedy Round agreements. Another proposal advocated Europe-wide action to reduce restrictions on agricultural imports. Debre also proposed measures for increased EEC technical cooperation with Britain on "specific and practical projects" and suggested ways to strengthen internal EEC machinery. Debre emphasized, however, that his proposals for expanded EEC-European trade were not intended to open the Common Market to membership by any other nation. (France Sept. 27 had rejected a West German proposal that had linked similar tariff reductions with Britain's entry into the EEC.) West German Foreign Min. Willy Brandt said in Brussels Nov. 5 that the Bonn government hoped the French proposal would lead to a widening of EEC membership, but as a reported concession to France, he refrained from coupling tariff reductions directly to the membership issue. The Council of Ministers directed the EEC's Executive Commission and ambassadors to study the Debre proposals.

The U.S. was reported to have reacted sharply to Debre's tariff-reduction proposal. In addition to placing the U.S. and non-European trading nations at a disadvantage in European markets, trade officials in Washington said, the proposal "seems to amount to a preferential tariff system within Europe and appears to be a violation of international trading rules under GATT." (EEC Executive Commission Pres. Jean Rey and Dutch Foreign Min. Joseph M. A. H. Luns disapproved of the proposed tariff reduction for similar reasons.) The U.S., moreover, reportedly favored an arrangement for increased European economic unity only if it provided political benefits—*i.e.,* EEC membership for Britain.

Britain & the EEC

British Foreign Secy. George Brown visited Bonn Jan. 19 and conferred with West German Foreign Min. Willy Brandt about British-EEC cooperation, if not actual membership for Britain. Brown told the House of Commons Jan. 24 that Bonn wished "to explore the ground further with the French to see whether an interim arrangement about our relations with the community might still be agreed.... Between us there is complete identity of purpose." Brown also referred to a Brussels meeting Jan. 15 at which the foreign ministers of Belgium, Luxembourg and the Netherlands had dealt with the enlargement of the EEC. These Benelux recommendations were presented at the Jan. 30 WEU (Western European Union) meeting.

West German Chancellor Kurt Kiesinger and Foreign Min. Brandt met Feb. 1 with Italian Premier Aldo Moro and Foreign Min. Amintore Fanfani in Rome, where the 4 expressed support for the British and 3 other EFTA applications for membership in the EEC. Netherlands Foreign Min. Joseph M. A. H. Luns and Netherlands Premier Petrus J. S. de Jong visited London Feb. 19-20 and also expressed support for Britain's application.

Kiesinger and de Gaulle met in Paris Feb. 15-16 and issued a statement expressing a "wish" that the EEC eventually admit "other European countries, particularly those who have already applied for membership." The statement, made public Feb. 16, said:

"(1) The 2 governments affirm their determination to continue the work undertaken by them and their partners since the creation of the European Economic Community. They intend to make all efforts to complete and develop the Common Market: they reaffirm in particular their desire to achieve the fusion of the 3 existing communities.

"(2) In this spirit, they wish the communities to be enlarged to include other European countries, particularly those who have already applied for membership, once those countries are in a position either to enter effectively into these communities, or, as the case may be, to link themselves with them in another form. This applies particularly to Britain and means that the evolution already begun by this country should continue.

"(3) Until this enlargement becomes possible, the 2 governments are ready to envisage the conclusion by the community of arrangements with the applicant countries capable of developing exchanges of agricultural and industrial products between the 2 parties. Such arrangements, which would include progressive reductions of trade obstacles for industrial products, would be designed to facilitate the above-mentioned evolution and would in any case contribute to the development of relations between the European countries.

"(4) In stating their position regarding the development and the desired enlargement of the European Economic Community, the 2 governments aim at an essential objective of their policy, that of making a strong and united Europe play its proper role; in other words to be an organized, independent and active factor in world equilibrium and, as a result, in peace."

The EEC Council of Ministers met Feb. 29 and heard Brandt present the British case while French Foreign Min. Couve de Murville argued the opposing view. The Council met again Mar. 9; no agreements were reached. Participants at an Apr. 5 Council meeting discussed the possible alignment of British (and other EFTA) tariffs at the EEC level to facilitate possible membership, but no commitments were made. Foreign Secy. Michael Stewart presented the British case at the WEU Council meeting Apr. 26-27 in Paris.

Defense Min. Denis Healey, announcing a 40% increase in British defense spending May 10, made reference to greater British participation in European affairs. He said that the British contributions reflected the reorientation of Britain toward Europe and should aid closer cooperation between Britain and the EEC countries.

The WEU Council met July 9 and the EEC Ministerial Council July 30. At both meetings France was the only opponent in discussions of British-EEC relations. Foreign Min. Couve de Murville represented France at the EEC meeting, Herve Alphand at the WEU meeting.

The 3d French veto of British entry into the EEC was, in effect, cast Sept. 27 when France rejected a West German interim plan that could have led to UK membership. The West German proposal, advanced by West German Foreign Min. Brandt, would have cut industrial tariffs between Britain and the EEC by 30% over a period of 3 years and would have increased technological cooperation and regular ministerial contacts. The plan called for arrangements with Ireland, Norway and Denmark, countries that had also applied for membership. At a closed-door meeting in Brussels, French Foreign Min. Michel Debre told the EEC Council of Ministers that France could not accept preferential arrangements with Britain and would consider only tariff cuts that could be offered to all European countries. He added that such trade arrangements could in no way be considered a prelude to EEC membership by nations involved. Debre pointed out that France opposed any enlargement of the EEC. He held that Britain's weak economic situation still prevented its membership. Other Common Market members had accepted the West German plan as the minimum acceptable bridge to British membership.

The French rebuff to British membership coincided with de Gaulle's visit to Bonn Sept. 27-28 for talks with West German Chancellor Kurt-Georg Kiesinger. In Bonn Sept. 28 de Gaulle pledged that France would support West Germany in case current conflict within the Soviet bloc spread into West Europe. His pledge came in response to a series of Soviet warnings and threats to Germany following the Soviet-led invasion of Czechoslovakia. In return for his promise of French support, de Gaulle reportedly required the West German government to follow his plans for the future of the EEC. French sources said he warned Kiesinger that it was not the time to bring up "divisive" subjects, such as the matter of enlarging the European Community. Kiesinger, in his final statement Sept. 28, said it would be impossible for West Germany "to leave France out and work with the 5." De Gaulle agreed that "to enlarge . . . without France would result in nothing." "If the community is made without France, there will not be any community at all," he declared. (But in a speech to the Christian Democratic Party national committee Oct. 1, Kiesinger reportedly said he had not promised de Gaulle that Bonn would make no moves on the European community. West Germany reportedly had hinted earlier that it was considering enlarging the EEC's dealings with Britain—"if necessary without France.")

Belgian Foreign Min. Pierre Harmel Oct. 3 announced a proposal to revitalize the Western European Union (WEU) in order to expand Britain's role in Europe without facing a French veto.

At a meeting of the Western European Union in Rome Oct. 21-22, a move toward British entry into the EEC had been thwarted by France. Belgium's Pierre Harmel had proposed the establishment of an intergovernmental organization to study possible collaboration between Britain and EEC nations on political, defense, monetary, technological and youth problems. The proposal was supported by Britain and the EEC nations, but the French state secretary for foreign affairs, Jean de Lipkowski, while agreeing to the idea of a study group on collaboration, rejected proposals that would permit the study group to formulate policy by majority vote, and thereby bypass the French veto.

The West German plan to lower trade barriers between the EEC and nations seeking entry into the Common Market was publicly rebuffed by the U.S. Dec. 4. State Department spokesman Robert J. McCloskey said: "We have consistently supported European unification. We are opposed to preferential trading agreements between European communities and other countries not clearly linked to membership within a reasonable period of time." Britain maintained its opposition to any trade proposals that did not include EEC membership. One British source remarked that "the Germans contend this [the trade plan] is a transition step toward membership. If it is, why don't they come out and say it in their proposal?"

The EEC Council met twice more in 1968, Nov. 5 and Dec. 10, without making significant progress on membership for Britain.

EFTA Meetings

The EFTA Ministerial Council met in London May 9-10 and in Vienna Nov. 21-22. According to the communique on the London meeting, the EFTA nations had "reaffirmed their continuing determination to work for the wider integration of Europe, which has always been an objective of EFTA."

1969

The de Gaulle government fell in Apr. 1969 over a relatively unimportant issue; Georges Pompidou was subsequently elected president of France. Although he generally espoused de Gaulle's philosophies, Pompidou showed a more liberal attitude toward possible British-EEC association. The franc was devalued as France proved unable to hold out against falling reserves and domestic austerity. In West Germany, the mark was revalued after a new coalition government headed by Willy Brandt replaced the coalition cabinet of Kurt-Georg Kiesinger. Britain's economy stabilized, and Britain looked forward to the possibility of a substantial balance-of-payments surplus for the first time in years. Franco-British relations were strained severely in February over an alleged British leak of information connected with WEU meetings, but this strain did not appear to create an insurmountable barrier to British-EEC discussions in the Hague. These meetings, which opened in December, were to include the subject of British EEC membership, and they were under way as 1969 ended. The controversial Anglo-French *Concorde* airliner made its first test flight.

GREAT BRITAIN

"The British economy is currently in better balance than it has been in some time," the Chase Manhattan Bank reported in the Oct. 1969 issue of *World Business*. Industrial production was up 4% over the previous year, exports were up 17%, and the "chances are good" that Britain would achieve a $720 million balance-of-payments surplus by the end of the fiscal year in Mar. 1970, *World Business* said. This optimism was shared by others. The Organization for Economic Cooperation & Development (OECD) forecast a $1.2 billion balance-of-payments surplus for 1970. "With the considerable tightening of fiscal and monetary policies, the rise in domestic demand has been moderate, providing room in the economy for an intensified switch in resources to the balance of payments," the OECD said. "Moreover, the post-devaluation rise in labor costs has been kept within reasonable limits so that much of the competitive advantage resulting from pound devaluation has been maintained."

Domestic Developments

In an effort to strengthen a credit squeeze on commercial banks and bring imports and exports into better balance, the Bank of England Feb. 27 had increased its discount rate from 7% to 8%. This increase, which restored the rate of the Nov. 1967 crisis level, reflected recent increases in international interest rates. In a statement accompanying the announcement of the rise, the Bank of England criticized banks for extending private loans above the target set by the government; instead of declining, lending had increased. Officials said that the 8% rate was not a crisis action because conditions were different from those of 1967. (Commercial banks in Britain Sept. 17 raised their prime lending rate to 9%, effective Oct. 1, "to reduce the current pressure on bank lending.")

The British Central Statistical Office reported Apr. 9 that the nation's gross national product (GNP) had risen 3.5% in 1968 when measured in real terms (including allowance for price increases and averaging of various estimates). This growth took place largely in the 2d half of the year, when real GNP rose at an annual rate of 6.2%. GNP in 1968 amounted to £36.5 billion ($87.6 billion), or £660 ($1,584) per capita. Personal disposable income (after allowance for higher taxes and national insurance contributions) increased by about 6.5%.

Home Secy. James Callaghan was dismissed by Prime Min. Wilson from a newly-formed "inner cabinet" May 13 because of his opposition to a government labor reform bill aimed at curbing wildcat strikes. Callaghan retained his ministerial post.

Wilson had reformed the inner cabinet Apr. 29 to promote tighter ministerial discipline in the wake of mounting criticism of his policies from several cabinet members, including Callaghan. The inner cabinet was composed of 7 top ministers, all of whom remained unidentified, except for Callaghan. Wilson informed Callaghan of his dismissal from the inner cabinet as it was about to convene May 13.

The immediate opposition to Wilson centered on the labor reform bill, which ultimately was abandoned by Wilson June 18, but there was also discontent over his fiscal and other policies. Douglas Houghton, chairman of the Parliamentary Labor Party, had expressed opposition to the labor reform bill May 7. Speaking at a private party meeting, Houghton said: "Ministers must not fall into the error of believing that their determination and resolve to force things through the party and through the house is either desirable or possible."

Wilson had agreed May 12 to delay the first reading of the bill in the House of Commons until after June 5. Wilson made the decision after conferring with officials of the Trades Union Congress (TUC), scheduled to hold a special meeting on the bill June 5. The meeting was attended by Mrs. Barbara Castle, minister for employment and productivity and leading proponent of the legislation. A 40-member TUC delegation, led by Victor Feather, acting secretary general, sought unsuccessfully to have Wilson modify the measure by dropping plans for imposing penalties on wildcat strikers and to accept a milder approach proposed by the TUC. The TUC plan, detailed in a 30-page document, would give union leadership the authority to intervene in wildcat strikes and to impose binding solutions on interunion disputes.

Announcing his agreement to drop the labor-reform bill, Wilson said June 18 that he had done so on the promise of the TUC to use its self-policing powers, approved at a June 5 TUC emergency meeting, to prevent unauthorized walkouts and to impose binding arbitration to settle interunion disputes.

Labor Party candidates had been defeated in by-elections for 3 House of Commons seats Mar. 27. The Conservative Party retained 2 seats—in Brighton Pavilion and West-super-Mare—and won another seat held by a Laborite, in Walthamstow East in London. Labor's loss of Walthamstow was its 12th loss of a constituency since the 1966 general elections, and it reduced the party's parliamentary majority to 70.

The Labor Party suffered a severe setback in elections for local council seats in England and Wales May 8. The Conservative Party won 630 seats to dominate 32 more towns, while Laborites lost an equal number of seats. The Labor Party thus controlled only 25 of the 270 town councils in England and Wales.

Board of Trade Pres. Anthony Crosland announced July 22 that Britain, in response to textile industry demands, would impose tariffs on textile imports from such Commonwealth countries as Hong Kong, India and Pakistan starting Jan. 1, 1972. The Commonwealth's general import quota system, due to expire at the end of 1969, would be extended for one year and would then be replaced by a tariff as recommended by the industry, Crosland said. British textile sales had suffered as a result of Commonwealth imports, which constituted 53% of total domestic consumption.

The Labor Party held its annual conference in Brighton Sept. 29-Oct. 3. The meeting was dominated by discussion of a new government policy document, "Agenda for a Generation," of government-enforced wage curbs and of Britain's application for membership in the EEC. A resolution adopted Oct. 1 called on the government to (a) abandon support of the pound at a fixed rate, (b) impose new restrictions on the outflow of capital, and (c) lower interest rates. The resolution was approved after Chancellor of the Exchequer Roy Jenkins announced that during the past 4 months Britain's balance-of-payments surplus had run at an annual rate of nearly $1.2 billion.

A resolution adopted at the conference Oct. 2 urged the government in any future negotiations on joining the EEC "to insist on adequate safeguard for Britain's balance of payments, cost of living, national health and social security systems, and power of independent decision in economic planning and foreign policy." The statement asserted, however, that no definite British decision had been made to join the Common Market and that a decision would be made "only after the detailed results have been made known to the British public and have been subjected to the will of Parliament." In a speech on the opening day of the conference Sept. 29, Wilson had said Britain was ready to reopen negotiations on its bid to enter the EEC, "but we no longer face the challenge to Europe with cap in hand."

Agenda for a Generation was adopted Oct. 3 by a vote of 60%—40%, with most of the opposition coming from the country's 2 biggest labor organizations—the Transport & General Workers, led by Jack Jones, and the Amalgamated Engineering & Foundry Workers, headed by Hugh Scanlon. Scanlon and Jones voted against the document on the ground that it made vague reference to wage restraints opposed by the unions. It called for "ordered and progressive growth of incomes based on productivity and need." The Confederation of British Industry (CBI) also opposed Agenda for a Generation, contending that "most of the ideas contained in it seems irrelevant to our present economic condition." It particularly cited a proposed tax on wealth, which, it claimed, "would fall on capital and savings and would increase consumption rather than restrain it."

Wilson announced a change of lower-level cabinet positions Oct. 5 in an effort to "streamline" his government in preparation for national elections, possibly in 1970. The number of ministers was reduced from 23 to 21, and 2 new ministries were formed. George Thomson, Anthony Crosland and Anthony Wedgwood Benn, powerful figures in the Labor Party, were given top posts to help Wilson improve his position in the pre-election period. Thomson, a minister without portfolio, was appointed deputy foreign secretary with the title of chancellor of the Duchy of Lancaster. He was to specialize in European affairs and was expected to negotiate Britain's entry into the EEC. Crosland, president of the Board of Trade, was named secretary of state for local government and regional planning, one of the 2 new posts. This position gave him sweeping powers over housing, transport planning and regional planning, absorbing the Ministry of Housing & Local Government. Crosland also was given special responsibility for environmental pollution. In the new post of minister of technology, Benn assumed overall responsibility for Britain's industry as well as technology, absorbing the functions of the power minister, the industrial powers of the Board of Trade and many duties of the Department of Economic Affairs, which was abolished.

Power Min. Roy Mason replaced Crosland as president of the Board of Trade. Ex-Housing & Local Government Min. Anthony Greenwood continued to serve in the government but without cabinet status. Others dropped from the cabinet were Paymaster Gen. Judith Hart, who became minister of overseas development, and Transport Min. Richard Marsh, who was returning to Parliament. Peter Shore, whose Department of Economic Affairs was abolished, remained in the cabinet as a minister without portfolio.

Chancellor of the Exchequer Roy Jenkins announced Oct. 21 that the controversial import deposit scheme, introduced in Nov. 1968, would be extended for another year when it expired in November. But the rate would be reduced from 50% to 40%. Jenkins added that the overseas travel allowance would be maintained at the current level of £50 ($120) a year. The decision to extend import restrictions was met with disappointment by the EFTA Permanent Council Oct. 28. In addition, the GATT council decided Oct. 29 to have the International Monetary Fund undertake an investigation to see whether Britain was justified in retaining the scheme. A special GATT committee had decided Mar. 14 that the import-deposit plan was acceptable in light of Britain's uncertain financial situation. The committee noted that if British economic conditions improved, Britain was pledged to end the program before the 12 months were up. The IMF had advised previously that the measure was necessary if Britain was to achieve a "reasonable strenthening" of its financial reserves.

A government White Paper Dec. 11 proposed legislation that would limit annual salary increases to 2.5%-4.5%, beginning in 1970. Its purpose was to avoid a new inflationary "wages and prices explosion," according to Mrs. Barbara Castle, minister of employment and productivity, who submitted the proposals. The previous wage-raise ceiling had been 3.5%. The White Paper, entitled "Productivity, Prices & Incomes Policy after 1969," proposed to allow the government to retain power to defer price and pay boosts for up to 4 months. It recommended special raises for women and low-paid workers above the established limit. Industry was expected to absorb higher wage costs without increasing prices, and sharp rent rises would continue to be restricted. The Trades Union Congress denounced the proposals on the ground that they gave the government the continued right to interfere in collective bargaining.

International Finance

In a speech at Queens University in Kingston, Ontario June 2, IMF Managing Director Pierre-Paul Schweitzer called for a "less defensive attitude" to changes in exchange rates. Citing the strains of "a notorious series of currency crises" and the "less spectacular but more ominous... introduction in some cases of restrictions on currency transactions, the tinkering with border taxes, the reimposition of tightening of capital controls and a sluggish growth of aid," Schweitzer asserted that IMF founders did not "envisage that a country would have to be so much concerned about the public's changing views on the strength of its currency." He added that the current troubles of the international monetary system stemmed from "a reluctance to dampen down excessive aggregate demand until the inflationary process has caused substantial damage; and also in an unwillingness to make necessary adjustments in exchange rates, not simply for reasons of national prestige, but also because this is no easy option in terms of its effect on the real income of particular sectors of the community."

The IMF June 20 announced its approval of a long-awaited standby loan arrangement for Britain. The IMF acted after exacting a pledge that the British government would maintain a tight credit squeeze and work to attain a balance-of-payments surplus. Weeks of negotiations preceded the announcement of the loan, which authorized the purchase of foreign exchange up to the equivalent of $1 billion over a 12-month period. The arrangement was designed to help the British government make some $800 million in debt repayments due before May 1970 on a 1965 IMF loan. The plans included an immediate withdrawal of $500 million, with the remainder being withdrawn when needed after consultation with the fund.

The British pledges were made in a letter of intent from Chancellor of the Exchequer Roy Jenkins to IMF Managing Director Schweitzer. The letter, dated May 22 and published June 23, said that the government intended to "obtain a surplus of at least £300 million [$720 million] on the current and long-term capital account of the balance of payments" by the end of the current fiscal year, Mar. 31, 1970. Jenkins said that in 1969-70 "the central government accounts... are intended to be in surplus by at least £850 million [$2 billion] and the current estimate is of a surplus approaching £1 billion [$2.4 billion]." The government also promised to "watch closely the development of domestic credit expansion during the year" and pledged a "domestic credit expansion for the private and public sectors ... of not more than £400 million [$960 million], compared with some £1.225 billion [$2.9 billion] in 1968-9. It is the government's policy to ensure that the course ... of domestic credit expansion as a whole, and of the central government borrowing requirement within it, is consistent with the intended result for the year as a whole, and to take action as appropriate to this end."

Defending the letter of intent in Commons June 25, Jenkins asserted that there would be no recession in Britain and no change in government economic strategy. Answering accusations that the government had capitulated to the IMF, he maintained that there had been "no secret pact, no more stringent verbal undertakings, no verbal undertakings of any sort. With the exception of the estimated quarterly path, there is no intention, no undertaking, no commitment, which is not public." He added: "Even if the IMF did not exist, I would want to pursue the policies in the letter of intent." Ian MacLeod, Conservative Party shadow chancellor of the exchequer, charged that the letter of intent had been dictated by the IMF. He said that despite the danger signals evident in the British economy, he saw no cause for a more stringent squeeze, which he felt was implied in the letter of intent.

In the wake of the French devaluation of the franc, the British pound was buffeted on the currency markets. The pound fell in London markets to a low of $2.382 Aug. 12, and the Bank of England apparently abandoned its traditional support level of $2.3825. Despite the discouraging trade figures Aug. 13, the pound recovered to $2.3833, but at a substantial cost to Britain's reserves. The pound fell again Aug. 14 to $2.3813, its lowest level since devaluation in 1967, but selling was reported to be light, and intervention by the Bank of England prevented it from coming any closer to its absolute floor of $2.38. Pressures appeared to be lifting, and the pound recovered substantially Aug. 18. Officials emphasized that the day-to-day price of the pound was not as important as the extent of the selling and the amount of reserves the Bank of England was forced to expend.

Central bankers of the industrial nations, in Basel, Switzerland Sept. 7 for their regular monthly meeting at the Bank for International Settlements, renewed the short-term credits extended to Britain for the defense of the pound. (The credits had originally been accorded for only 3 months, although they had been extended almost automatically over the past few years.)

Britain drew $175 million from the IMF in December as the 3d drawing under the June $1 billion standby arrangement. A total of $850 million had thus far been drawn under this agreement; the remaining $150 million would be available in Mar. 1970, subject to British needs at that time. Following the December drawing, Britain owed a total of $2.65 billion to the IMF.

British gold and foreign currency reserves rose slowly during most of 1969, from a Jan. 1 level of $2.41 billion to $2.50 billion Nov. 30, despite large British repayment of international debts. At the same time, the balance of trade (calculated on a balance of payments basis) remained in deficit as exports (and re-exports) remained continually below the level of imports.

EUROPE & THE EEC

De Gaulle Quits, Pompidou Elected President

Charles de Gaulle, 78, resigned as president of France Apr. 28 after his government's proposals for Senate and regional reforms were rejected Apr. 27 in a national referendum. Georges Pompidou won a run-off election June 15 to succeed de Gaulle as president.

Before the presidential election, Alain Poher, 60, president of the Senate, was installed as interim president Apr. 28 (to serve pending the election of a permanent president no less than 20 days and no more than 35 days from the date of de Gaulle's resignation). Premier Maurice Couve de Murville and his cabinet remained as a caretaker government. One cabinet member, Justice Min. Rene Capitant, a leftwing Gaullist, refused to serve and resigned.

In his statement of resignation, issued from the Elysee Palace, de Gaulle said: "I cease to exercise my functions as president of the Republic. This decision takes effect today at noon." De Gaulle had issued a final appeal to the voters Apr. 25 for "a show of confidence" to permit him to serve out his 3d 7-year term, which was to end in 1972. "If I am solemnly disavowed by a majority of you, I will cease to exercise my functions immediately," he had said. De Gaulle had not been legally required to submit his reform plan to a public vote. He could have sent the bill to the National Assembly, and the Gaullist majority there would have assured its passage. But de Gaulle had decided to make the issue one of public confidence in his rule. Poher, who became interim president after de Gaulle's defeat, had been hostile to de Gaulle's reform program from the beginning and had expressed his opposition to it in a Senate speech Apr. 1. He gained national prominence Apr. 17 through a TV address in which he urged the electorate to cast a negative vote in the referendum. The results of the referendum: "No" votes—12,004,970 (52.40%); "yes" votes—10,905,453 (47.69%). Of the 29,394,456 registered voters, 5,832,452 abstained.

In Western Europe, the predominant initial reaction to de Gaulle's withdrawal from the political scene was one of hope that it would increase the chances of West European unity. Britain and Italy Apr. 28 issued a joint declaration in which they pledged to work for greater European unity. The statement was made during a state visit to London by Italian Pres. Giuseppe Saragat. A "joint declaration of policy," signed by Italian Foreign Min. Pietro Nenni and British Foreign Secy. Michael Stewart, said Italy and Britain "believe the common interests of the continent, its security and its prosperity, demand union." Alluding to France's objections, under de Gaulle, to enlargement of the EEC, the declaration said that expansion of the 6-member group would "not alter its nature but insure its fulfillment." After meeting with Prime Min. Wilson, Saragat said at a joint meeting of Parliament that Italy hoped for "full participation by your country in the establishment of the new Europe."

In what turned out to be only the first round in the presidential election, Pompidou won more than 44% of the vote June 1 and Poher got more than 23%. Communist Jacques Duclos ran a surprisingly close 3d with more than 21%. The remaining votes were shared by 4 other candidates. The totals: Pompidou 10,050,804 votes (44.46%); Poher 5,268,414 (23.31%); Duclos 4,811,037 (21.28%); Gaston Defferre 1,133,241 (5.01%); Michel Rocard 816,410 (3.61%); Louis Ducatel 268,481 (1.27%); Alain Krivine 239,078 (1.06%). Of 29,512,878 registered voters, 22,898,669 went to the polls. Invalid ballots totaled 293,200, and there were 6,614,209 abstentions. Since no candidate received a majority, a runoff was scheduled between the 2 leaders.

The French Communist Party's Central Committee urged its followers June 2 to abstain from voting in the runoff on the ground that Pompidou and Poher were both reactionaries and "stooges of capitalism." The Communist Party's action was regarded as virtually assuring Pompidou's election because it deprived Poher of needed leftist votes. It also reduced the number of votes required for a majority and thus further enhanced Pompidou's chances of victory.

Pompidou pledged May 16 that if elected, he would not "imitate the style of Gen. de Gaulle. I am a different man. I plan a policy of openness and dialogue.... The administration must become more flexible, more efficient, less meddlesome." Pompidou warned that if he lost the election France would face violent disorders, similar to the unrest in 1968. In an interview published in *Paris-Match* May 20, Poher advocated a reversal of de Gaulle's policies toward Europe, NATO and the Middle East. He indicated that he favored direct talks with Britain on membership in the EEC. Poher said he supported stronger French ties to NATO because France "cannot assure alone the effective protection of her borders." In a final TV appearance of all 7 candidates May 27, Poher charged that Pompidou, as premier under de Gaulle, had done the opposite of what he was currently promising the voters.

Pompidou was elected to a 7-year term as president of France June 15. He assumed office June 20 after the election results were certified by the Constitutional Council. Final results: Pompidou 11,060,080 votes (58.2%); Poher 7,942,915 (41.8%). Of 29,488,640 registered voters, 20,307,013 went to the polls and 9,181,672 abstained. Invalid ballots totaled 1,303,914. The Communist Party, which had called for abstentions, said June 17 that the abstentions were "the most important feature" of the election.

In a message sent to Pompidou June 15 from his vacation retreat in Ireland, de Gaulle said, "For all national and personal reasons, I address you my most cordial felicitations." A congratulatory message sent by U.S. Pres. Richard Nixon to Pompidou June 16 assured the president-elect and the French people of "the continued friendship and sympathetic interest of the American government and people." Mr. Nixon added: "I look forward to working with you, not only to develop closer relations between our countries but also to concert our efforts in the cause of peace and brotherhood of all peoples."

(Pompidou had said June 9 that if elected he would resign from the Gaullist party. Concluding a 3-day meeting in Montpellier, the National Council of the Gaullist party Nov. 30 pledged continued support of the policies of Pompidou and de Gaulle. The council said it supported the government's more flexible approach toward the problem of British entry into the EEC. It called for a "3d way" between communism and capitalism; this "3d way" would include government economic planning and the participation of employes both in the operation and the profits of the firms they worked for.)

In his first policy statement after becoming president, Pompidou June 25 pledged a more liberalized regime. Addressing a joint session of Parliament, Pompidou said: "It is not sufficient to restore this old and illustrious house which is France. It must be renovated and lit up with a new light." It was necessary to take measures to reform the universities and modernize the economy. France's goals were "to maintain our independence while respecting our alliances, reapproachment and cooperation with all peoples, and first of all in Europe." De Gaulle was "the greatest of Frenchmen," but Pompidou would operate differently. "I mean . . . to develop between the executive and Parliament as a whole effective and trusting relations."

Franc Is Devalued

The French government devalued the franc by 11.1% Aug. 8 in a move that caught other governments and the financial world completely by surprise. Although international monetary officials had long predicted a realignment of the franc's value, the timing of the French action was totally unexpected.

The devaluation was preceded by various French efforts to restore confidence in the franc. The Bank of France Jan. 20 had ordered curbs on the outflow of valuable foreign currencies. Under the new regulation, foreign currencies deposited in French banks by French residents or companies established in France could be lent only to other French residents; if such currency were lent to a foreign institution, the lending bank was required to deposit with the Bank of France an equal amount of that currency. The regulation, effective in 2 stages Feb. 25 and Mar. 25, affected all banks in France, including foreign banks and branches. The regulation was designed to halt the outflow from France of Euro-dollars, dollars deposited in European banks or held by European governments and businesses or foreign branches of American banks or businesses. In recent weeks, as credit was tightened in the U.S., Euro-dollar loans had increased substantially; U.S. banks wanted Eurodollars, on which there were no reserve requirements, in order to increase their lending ability in the domestic U.S. market where credit was tight. During the week ended Jan. 29, U.S. banks had borrowed a daily average of $6.17 billion in Eurodollars from European nations, including France. The French restriction, making Eurodollar loans less readily available, was expected to curb the inflow of funds into the U.S. and thus further tighten the domestic U.S. money market. (The U.S. Jan. 31 removed countervailing duties on imports from France. The duties had been imposed in response to export subsidies and import quotas that France had instituted in June 1968. The original 2.5% countervailing duty had been cut in half Nov. 1, 1968, when France had halved its subsidies.)

Monetary tensions tightened again in Europe in February and early March as French labor unrest and rumors of an imminent devaluation of the franc fed speculation on the gold and foreign currency markets. The free market price of gold hit record highs, and an increasingly weak French franc led to a faltering British pound as well. Fears of a major international financial crisis subsided when it became clear that a one-day general strike in France Mar. 10-11 had not led to a renewal of the May 1968 unrest and that the franc would not be de-valued at that time.

The free-market price of gold, which had been steady at about $42 an ounce, had begun a climb to record highs late in February. By Mar. 10 gold prices had reached a London peak of $43.82 and a Zurich peak of $43.75 to $44, the highest since the establishment of the 2-tier pricing system in Mar. 1968. Many of the buyers were thought to be French; demand had pushed prices up in the insulated Paris market, and francs were believed to have been smuggled out of France to buy cheaper gold in Zurich. The French gold market, which had reached a peak of $48.26 Mar. 10, had been consistently higher than the markets in Zurich and London. As the franc came under new pressure and fears of its de-valuation weakened the pound, the French and British central banks were forced into the market to support their currencies. In an effort to curb the smuggling of francs out of France, the Bank of France Mar. 7 ordered the Bank for International Settlements, acting as its agent, to reduce the price at which it would buy French banknotes from Swiss banks to about 9% below the official price in Swiss francs. The move penalized anyone attempting to convert French banknotes into Swiss francs or dollars to buy gold; Swiss banks would not exchange francs at a rate above that used by the BIS. It was reported by Mar. 18 that the Bank of France had decided to entirely stop buying French francs in Switzerland.

Central bankers of the major industrial nations expressed a belief that the franc would retain its value. Holding a regular meeting at the BIS in Basel, Switzerland, the bankers Mar. 9 decided that the situation required no special action if the French labor problem remained under control. Although much of the meeting centered on ways of implementing the recently negotiated program to deal with speculation crises, the bankers denied that the franc was seriously unstable and reportedly showed little concern about the rise in free-market gold prices. Jacques Brunet, governor of the Bank of France, reportedly told the bankers that French reserve losses in the previous week had remained under $100 million, compared with total French reserves of more than $4 billion and the availability of another $2 billion in swaps and credits. Reports from the BIS meeting also indicated that the French government had abandoned its traditional policy that the official price of gold should be increased.

The actual volume of trading on the bullion markets remained well below that of the gold crisis of Mar. 1968. At the height of the current speculation, the greatest daily turnover on the Zurich gold market reached about $11 million; sales had reached $50 million to $100 million per day during the 1968 crisis (South Africa, producer of about 80% of the free world's output, had stockpiled gold since 1968 to increase pressures for a higher official price or to obtain the right to sell gold to monetary authorities at the free market price; thus the supply of free-market gold was not sufficient to meet the recent demand.)

Following the French strike, gold prices fell Mar. 11—in Zurich from $43.80 an ounce to $43.02, in London from $43.82 to $42.95 and in Paris from $48.31 to $47.67; the French franc and British pound strengthened. The trend continued as fears of devaluation of the franc diminished.

Charles de Gaulle's resignation Apr. 28 led to renewed monetary speculation and a strong demand for gold Apr. 28, but intervention by the French, British and West German central banks kept the situation under control. European money markets had moved erratically since Apr. 22, due, at least in part, to uncertainty about the French referendum. The value of the French franc (and British pound) fell Apr. 28, while that of the West German mark rose. In addition, the free market price of gold in the Paris market rose to $49.06 an ounce, a record high.

Commodity and metal markets also rose sharply. Bankers in Frankfurt estimated that $200 million in foreign funds had come into West Germany Apr. 28. The New York Federal Reserve Bank intervened in the market to aid the pound. In an attempt to slow the flow of funds into West Germany, the Bundesbank, late Apr. 28, reinstituted a 100% reserve requirement on foreign funds retroactive to Apr. 15. Bundesbank President Karl Blessing said that central banks stood "firmly and united" behind the franc and indicated that any massive flood of speculative funds into Germany "would be swapped right back out."

The Bank of France June 13 increased its discount rate from 6% to 7% in response to rising international interest rates and domestic inflationary pressures. The new rate, highest in France since 1926, approached the record 7.5% imposed during a monetary crisis that year. In addition to lifting the discount rate, the bank also increased rates for short-term export credits from 4% to 5% and for advances on securities from 7.5% to 8.5%. French commercial banks followed the Bank of France and lifted their prime rate from 6.2% to 7.2% June 17.

Newly appointed Premier Jacques Chaban-Delmas vowed June 26 to maintain the exchange rate of the franc and to stem inflation and protect the purchasing power of the French worker. In a policy statement to the National Assembly, Chaban-Delmas emphasized that the government was opposed to devaluation as "dangerous" and "useless" domestically and as detrimental to cooperation in the EEC.

These statements and economic steps failed to achieve the desired goals.

The devaluation, which was announced following an unscheduled French cabinet meeting Friday evening, Aug. 8, after most of the world's financial markets were closed for the weekend, reduced the value of the franc from .18 grams of gold to .16 grams of gold, or from 20.255 U.S. cents to 18.004 U.S. cents. (Depending on the method used to calculate the devaluation, the percentage change was 12.5% or 11.1%.) The new parity officially went into effect Aug. 10, following approval that day by the International Monetary Fund. (Under IMF regulations, a country that devalues its currency by more than 10% forfeits IMF assistance if it does not seek the organization's approval of the action.)

In a nationwide radio-TV address Aug. 8, minutes after the announcement, Pres. Pompidou expressed his conviction that the devaluation was "unavoidable." Noting that the franc had been "traded on foreign markets at a sizable discount," he said: "To pretend to overcome this handicap would be to choose a policy of brutal deflation that would impose on the country intolerable sacrifices and massive unemployment and which, moreover, would jeopardize our investments—hence, our future." The government decision to act at that time was influenced by its desire "to act freely and not under the hold of outside pressures of a speculative crisis, as was the case in Nov. 1968 when Gen. Charles de Gaulle rightly refused to devalue." In order to frustrate speculation, "we have observed total secrecy and chosen for our decision a period that is usually devoted only to vacation." The devaluation was only a "starting point" toward restoring the French economy to health, and the government was preparing, "in the budgetary, financial and economic fields, a vigorous and rigorous overall action."

Finance Min. Valery Giscard d'Estaing, speaking after Pompidou, pointed out that the government's action was a "recognition of the franc's real value" as assessed by foreign currency buyers on the forward market, where the franc had been traded at a discount of 11% to 12%. "Had we not acted by the end of the year," he declared, "the real French reserves [reported central bank reserves minus short-term debts]... would have amounted to practically nothing. And at the end of the first half of 1970... they would have had a negative balance." In addition, he explained, the weakness of "our monetary situation... exposed us to the threats of international speculation." Giscard d'Estaing disclosed that the decision to devalue had been made July 16. "From the 16th until the day before yesterday," he said, "there were only 8 people who knew of this measure; all the preparations had been made in the evenings outside normal working hours and places."

Communist Party Political Bureau member Francois Billoux predicted Aug. 9 that devaluation would lower the purchasing power and standard of living for the majority of Frenchmen. He charged that the action "exposed the untrue promises made by Pompidou during the presidential campaign when he had already decided at that moment to devalue." Georges Seguy, secretary general of the Communist-dominated General Confederation of Labor (CGT), had denounced the devaluation Aug. 8 and pledged that the CGT would "use all the means of action within its power to defeat this new antisocial offensive and safeguard the interests of the workers." Andre Bergeron, secretary general of the Socialist-oriented union federation, Workers' Force (FO), expressed fear Aug. 8 that "once again those least able to afford it will be hit hardest." He added that only a few weeks ago the premier had told an FO delegation that the government had no intention of taking such a step. Laurent Lucas, associate secretary general of the non-Communist Democratic Confederation of French Workers (CFDT), Aug. 9 called the devaluation "an easy solution for capitalist interests," but predicted "grave consequences for the worker." Explaining that former devaluations had been followed by "speculation, higher prices, lower purchasing power and aggravation of the economic situation," he asserted that the current situation "can only reinforce our demand for guaranteed increases in the workers' purchasing power and priority action for the poorest sections of the population, large families and pensioners."

The French financial woes leading to deflation stemmed from the student-worker disruptions in May-June 1968. Reported reserves had fallen from more than $6 billion before May 1968 to $3.5 billion by the end of July 1969. Moreover, the reported reserves did not include reserve losses of more than $1 billion in short-term borrowings from foreign central banks. In addition, France's trade balance had worsened during 1969. The IMF's *International Financial Statistics* (Aug. 1969 issue) reported their 1969 reserve and trade figures for France: Monthly reserve totals—January $4.216 billion; February $4.126 billion; March $3.987 billion; April $3.775 billion; May $3.637 billion and June $3.611 billion. In July reserves had dropped by another $15.8 million to $3.59 billion. Monthly trade figures (in dollar equivalents)—January $1.14 billion in exports (f.o.b.) and $1.35 billion in imports (c.i.f.); February $1.164 billion exports, $1.3 billion imports; March $1.24 billion exports, $1.45 billion imports; April $1.31 billion exports, $1.54 billion imports; May $1.23 billion exports, $1.53 billion imports; June $1.34 billion exports, $1.53 billion imports.

In an effort to block a surge of price increases and inflation, the government ordered a freeze on prices Aug. 10. The decree, effective until Sept. 15, ordered virtually all industrial prices and wholesale and retail markups held at Aug. 8 levels. Although markups were frozen on 10 fruits and vegetables currently in season, the decree did not mention other farm prices, since action on these depended on the outcome of an emergency EEC meeting in Brussels Aug. 11-12. The Finance Ministry warned that firms refusing to obey the price-freeze order would be subject to sanctions and future price control. A ministry source noted that exceptions to the order would be allowed only if a firm could prove that it had been forced to pay more for imports because of the devaluation.

The government planned to draft a package of measures to support the devaluation and to have the measures ready for administrative and parliamentary action by Sept. 15. Premier Chaban-Delmas said Aug. 10 that the reforms would be severe and would probably provoke "much resistance." However, he added, without the reforms "France and Frenchmen would find themselves in one, 2 or 3 years in a situation similar to the one which just led us to a monetary adjustment." Conceding that "a crisis may arise" from the reforms, Chaban-Delmas stressed that it was "necessary to risk a crisis. That is better than renouncing a reform that is in the national interest."

The government Sept. 3 announced its promised austerity measures to protect the franc against inflationary pressures. The "economic recovery plan" was explained by Premier Chaban-Delmas and Finance Min. Giscard d'Estaing following its adoption by the cabinet. The purpose of the program was to reduce internal spending, encourage the export of domestic industrial goods, end the trade deficit and restore balance to the inflated economy. Under major goals announced by Giscard d'Estaing, the budget would be balanced by Jan. 1, 1970, internal supply and demand would be balanced by April 1, 1970 and foreign trade would be balanced by July 1, 1970. Among principal features of the austerity program:

●About $1 billion would be cut from the current 1969 budget, and these funds would be used to stimulate the economy in areas threatened by a business slump. An estimated $363-$541 million would be funneled from the 1970 budget for use as business credits when necessary. The budget would be balanced by limiting expenditure increases to 5.5%.
●Bank profits from current no-interest accounts would be subject to a .75% surtax.
●The special surtax on high-income brackets, imposed in 1968, would be extended.   Low wage-earners would pay less tax.
●The price freeze imposed at the time of devaluation Aug. 8 would be lifted Sept. 15, but a system of "surveillance" would be imposed. Giscard d'Estaing predicted that prices would not increase by more than 4% in 1970. Prices in the first half of 1969 had risen at an annual rate of 6%.
●Tax-deductible purchases of new machinery would be limited.
●Savings-bank interest rates would be increased from the current average of 3.5% to 5% to encourage savings.

In a previous move aimed at strengthening the franc, the government Aug. 28 had announced tighter consumer credits, to remain in effect until at least Jan. 31, 1970. Down payments on cars, for example, were increased from 30% to 50%, and the time required to pay the balance was reduced from 21 months to 15. Other goods, including furniture and appliances, required down payments of 40%, up 10%, with the balance to be paid in 15 months instead of 18.

The government had reported Aug. 21 that many retail shops had raised prices illegally since devaluation. The results of 618 Finance Ministry inspections made in one week showed that 150 merchants had raised their prices by amounts ranging from 20% to 100%. Most of the items affected were domestic grown foods such as fruits and vegetables.

Representatives of the 14 former French colonies, currently independent members of the franc zone, met in Paris Aug. 10 and decided to realign their currencies with the devalued franc. Their currencies were pegged to the franc; their reserves were on deposit with the Bank of France, and France was their chief market and source of imports and aid. The 14 countries: Mauritania, Senegal, Ivory Coast, Dahomey, Togo, Niger, Mali, Upper Volta, Congo (Brazzaville), the Central African Republic, Chad, Gabon, Cameroon and the Malagasy Republic.

International reaction to the French devaluation was marked by surprise. Several countries expressed resentment that France had not previously discussed the move with other governments. (EEC nations were committed to discuss important domestic economic measures with the other members.) The U.S. Treasury Department Aug. 8 issued a statement describing the devaluation as "an adjustment to economic developments in France during the past year." U.S. officials pointed out that the amount of the devaluation was the amount discussed during the Nov. 1968 monetary crisis and rejected at that time by deGaulle. In Britain, Treasury officials Aug. 8 expressed confidence that the French devaluation would not cause a devaluation of the pound. "There is no question of sterling following the franc," a spokesman said. Belgium confirmed Aug. 9 that the value of the Belgian franc would not be lowered, although Premier Gaston Eyskens conceded that the French action would hurt exports to France, one of Belgium's biggest customers. The Italian Treasury Ministry asserted Aug. 9 that the "parity of the lira to the dollar and its value in gold will remain unchanged." The West German government welcomed the devaluation and reportedly viewed it as a vindication of its own refusal to revalue the mark upward. Deputy government spokesman Conrad Ahlers said Aug. 8 that consultations within the EEC and international financial circles would show "if the French initiative is sufficient." He stressed that the French action would not in any way change the West German decision to retain the parity of the mark.

The French devaluation, however, did not diminish the conflict within West Germany about upward revaluation of the mark. Economics Min. Karl Schiller, a strong advocate of revaluation, asserted Aug. 9 that West German monetary decisions "are now more important than ever." He called the French devaluation "a courageous step" that opened opportunities to other nations to overcome the "stagnation" in international monetary policy. He stressed that a single action by France did not put world financial affairs in order. Finance Min. Franz Josef Strauss, an opponent of West German currency realignment, had said Aug. 8 that the French devaluation proved the correctness of the West German refusal to revalue the mark. "One of the chief disparities that might have existed in relation to the Deutschemark has now been eliminated," he observed.

Foreign Min. Willy Brandt Aug. 9 decried "self righteous, not to say, nationalistic reactions" to the French devaluation in what appeared to be a criticism of Strauss' comments. Brandt added that while the French decision was necessary, "one must learn that there are situations in which we Germans may not hide behind others when it is a question of our own responsibility." Chancellor Kurt-Georg Kiesinger Aug. 10 reasserted the government's pledge to maintain the mark's parity. "An upward mark revaluation, together with the devaluation of the franc," he said, "would now be a very dangerous dampening for our economy." But the Social Democratic Party (SPD), the party of Brandt and Schiller, announced Aug. 12 that it still considered revaluation of the mark a "necessity."

In an 18-hour emergency session in Brussels Aug. 11-12, the EEC Council of Ministers decided to exempt the French farm market from the organization's agricultural-pricing mechanism and thus suspend uniform support levels for Common Market farm prices. The agreement also provided that taxes would be levied on French agricultural exports, and subsidies would be paid on France's agricultural imports. The EEC action would help to protect France from the domestic disadvantages of devaluation, since French farm prices would not be increased; in addition, France's farm exports would not be cheaper for other nations. Under the agreement, France pledged to readjust its farm prices progressively so that by the end of the 1970-1 agricultural year, French farm prices would again be in line with those of the other EEC members.

If France had not been exempted from the agricultural price system, the devaluation would have meant that minimum support payments to French farmers would increase by 12.5%; such payments throughout the Common Market were based on the unit of account (a uniform price system in which one unit is equal to the gold equivalent of $1 U.S.), which was transferred into national currencies for payment. The cost of the higher payments to French farmers would have been passed on to the French consumer, creating an inflationary situation and eroding the benefits of the devaluation. In addition, if French prices increased, agricultural surpluses, already a problem within the EEC, would tend to grow even more. (The EEC support policies, which fixed prices well above world levels, had created excess production of grains, milk, butter, potatoes, tomatoes and other products in the member countries. The surpluses had already caused the EEC to question the joint price policies and to consider completely revising the EEC farm program.) The final agreement was blocked until the last moment by the Dutch, who felt France should apply domestic measures to counter inflation without affecting the common price mechanism. The Dutch also insisted that the exemption of France from the pricing system should be terminated by the beginning of 1970; but a compromise was finally reached whereby France would be phased back into the program over a period of 2 years and the Council of Ministers would assess the effects of the agreement before the end of 1969.

French Agriculture Min. Jacques Duhamel conceded Aug. 12 that the EEC had been forced to take a step backward in agreeing to isolate France from the common agricultural policies. He insisted, however, that the "principal concern of the French government was to prevent a rise in prices" and that the effort had been successful. He said the crisis demonstrated the necessity in the EEC for a common monetary policy if a common agricultural policy was to work.

The franc closed well above its new official value in European currency markets Aug. 11 in the first tests of the effects of the French devaluation. In London and New York, the British pound and Belgian franc came under heavy selling pressures and were supported by their central banks; forward trading in Belgian francs was suspended in London. The Danish krone and Italian lira also fell in European markets. The West German mark was under strong buying pressure, and at least one financial source estimated that up to $200 million had flowed into the Bundesbank (central bank) reserves. The U.S. dollar was generally unaffected by the market activity. Interest rates on Eurodollar loans increased.

The French devaluation and France's subsequent isolation from the EEC's common agricultural pricing mechanism aroused debate about the future membership of Britain in the EEC as well as about the policies of the organization itself. It was argued that since rules had been suspended for France, it would be easier to find a flexible path for British entrance.

Finance Min. Giscard d'Estaing said Aug. 28 that France had formally asked the International Monetary Fund for a standby agreement to provide $985 million—the maximum allowed France under its current quota. France's "automatic" IMF drawing entitlement had been exhausted in June, 1968. He added that another $1.6 billion in credits from "diverse sources" was available to France in its effort to defend the franc. The other $1.6 billion included a $1 billion standby credit or swap agreement, arranged with the N.Y. Federal Reserve Bank during the currency speculation crisis of Nov. 1968, drawn on substantially during 1969 but almost fully repaid. In addition, West Germany and other Common Market partners had offered credits up to $400 million, while the Bank of International Settlements in Basel, Switzerland had offered a credit of $200 million. The establishment of the credit facilities was designed to ward off possible speculation against the franc in future months, particularly after the West German elections in September. Giscard d'Estaing added that in the weeks since the franc's devaluation, $232 million in foreign reserves had flowed into France. The Finance Ministry announced Sept. 2 that official gold and foreign currency reserves had increased during the month of August by $187.6 million, bringing total reserves to $3.81 billion.

The Bank of France Oct. 8 announced an increase in its discount rate from 7% to 8%, the highest level in French history. The increase came in the wake of increasing pressure on the French franc in the foreign currency markets and was announced the day the government approved the 1970 budget. Pres. Pompidou told his cabinet Oct. 8: "All facts point up the formal and absolute determination of the government to insure balanced finances. The franc isn't threatened. The franc doesn't have to be defended. The measures that have been taken have been shaped so that the franc, won't even be challenged." French commercial banks raised their prime rates Oct. 13 from 7.6% to 8.75% for short and medium-term loans.

Brandt Becomes West German Chancellor

Although Chancellor Kurt-Georg Kiesinger's Christian Democratic Union (CDU) and its Bavarian wing, the Christian Socialist Union (CSU), outpolled Foreign Min. Willy Brandt's Social Democratic Party (SDP) by 46.1% to 42.7% in national elections for West Germany's Bundestag (lower house) Sept. 28, Brandt succeeded in putting together a coalition that ousted the Kiesinger government and put Brandt into office. Oct 21 as Chancellor.

Brandt's victory was preceded by months of political maneuvering. His SDP, meeting at a 3-day congress at Bad Godesberg April 16-18, adopted a platform for the Sept. 28 elections. The platform was supported by all but 10 of the party's 344-delegates. At the congress Brandt assailed the CSU and the CSU leader, Finance Min. Franz Josef Strauss. Brandt linked the CSU newspaper *Bayern-Kurier* with a neo-Nazi journal, calling them both "a double-voiced hate song." CDU officials charged Apr. 20 that the position taken by the SDP at its congress and its attacks against CSU leaders threatened the governing coalition of Christian Democrats and Social Democrats. Bruno Heck, secretary general of the CDU, deplored SDP's statement that it recognized East Germany's "existence as a state." A CSU spokesman asserted that, in calling for signing of the nuclear non-proliferation treaty, the SDP had stabbed Kiesinger in the back.

The rightwing National Democratic Party (NDP) approved an election platform at a congress held in Stuttgart May 10-11. Vowing to bring about a new "national consciousness of the Germans," the platform called for: amnesty for all crimes committed under the Nazis; a review of indemnity for Nazi victims; supervision of the press; encouragement of a high birth rate; opposition to West German approval of the treaty to ban the spread of nuclear weapons; a "drastic consolidation of the present 18 federal ministries"; the elimination of the remaining occupation rights of the World War II Allies; refusal to recognize East Germany or to accept post-war boundaries based on "robbed German land." Adolf von Thadden, the party leader and a former Nazi, declared: "The NDP wants neither to restore the 3d Reich, nor to remove democracy, nor to prepare a 3d world war."

The CDU won 42.6% of the votes and a slim victory in the Rhineland-Palatinate state, municipal and district council elections June 8. The SDP received 40.8%; the NDP and the German Communist Party, both competing for the first time in local elections, won 2.4% and .3% of the vote, respectively.

Ex-Justice Min. Gustav Heinemann was sworn in July 1 before a joint session of parliament as the Federal Republic's first Socialist president. Heinemann succeeded Pres. Heinrich Luebke. The new president's inaugural address included a plea for tolerance, mutual respect and more protection of individual freedoms as West Germany approached "the first truly free period of our history." The inauguration took place amid strong criticism of the president by Christian Democrats. *Political-Social Correspondence,* the CDU publication, accused Heinemann of sowing "political and constitutional unrest" because he had said he would oppose the chancellor on issues according to his conscience. The periodical also criticized the interest the president had expressed in conferring with radical left-wing student leaders. *Der Spiegel* had quoted Heinemann in an interview published June 30 as saying: "I would not sign a bill for reintroduction of the death penalty. I also would sign no bill through which the Federal army or government would acquire its own power over the use of atomic weapons." Heinemann declared that if he were constitutionally overruled on the nuclear issue, he would resign. But he said that, because the army was necessary to prevent the use of force by others, it was important to maintain Bonn's current defense efforts until a settlement between opposing European blocs could be made.

Kiesinger was quoted July 30 by the Ludwigshafen newspaper *5-Uhr-Blatt* as saying that the NDP "is not neo-Nazi." Kiesinger was said to have explained: "Granted, such elements are mixed into the leadership. However, the majority of the party's voters change over to the party from other parties out of dissatisfaction, because they await new initiatives from it." The government press office July 30 issued previous statements by Kiesinger aimed at showing that he opposed the NDP. He was quoted as having said at one time that the NDP "is simply a misfortune and must not, as far as is in our power, get into the next Bundestag."

Bundestag Pres. Kai-Uwe von Hassel was reported to have asserted July 28 that the NDP was not a neo-Nazi party and that most of its followers were "honorable people" seeking law and order. The SDP charged July 29 that von Hassel's remarks represented "a unique sleight of hand giving the neo-Nazis in West Germany a clean bill of health." Von Hassel replied July 29 that he had long opposed the NDP. But he said he was against a constitutional ban of the party, preferring to give the voters themselves an opportunity to reject it in the elections.

Following the Sept. 28 elections, in which Brandt's SDP trailed Kiesinger's CDU/CSU by 46.1% to 42.7%, Brandt announced his intention of seeking the chancellorship by withdrawing his party from its coalition with the CDU to form a new governing alliance with the Free Democratic Party (FDP), which had received 5.7% of the votes. (The NDP received only 4.3% of the vote, falling short of the 5% required to qualify for representation in the Bundestag.) Seats won by each party in the Bundestag (previously-held seats in parentheses): CDU 242 (245); SDP 224 (202); FDP 30 (49).

FDP leader Walter Scheel began coalition negotiations with Brandt Sept. 30 and the 2 parties reached agreement Oct. 3 on forming a coalition regime. Brandt and Scheel then formally informed Pres. Gustav Heinemann of their decision. A coalition program informally drawn up by Brandt and Scheel called for reducing the number of ministries to 15, recognition of the "territorial integrity" of West Germany's neighbors and of the "inviolability" of the neighboring frontiers, and reduction of the voting age from 21 to 18. The statement on territory in effect recognized the existence of 2 separate Germanys, East and West, and abandoned German claims to former territories occupied by Poland, Czechoslovakia and the Soviet Union since World War II. Kiesinger Oct. 6 abandoned efforts to stop Brandt from forming a new coalition.

The Bundestag Oct. 21 elected Brandt as the 4th chancellor of West Germany. As was the custom, Brandt was the only candidate, and he received 251 votes, 3 more than the required absolute majority. There were 235 votes cast against him, 5 abstentions and 4 invalid votes, and one deputy was absent because of illness. Following his election, Brandt went to the Federal chancellery in Bonn to take over formally from Kiesinger.

Kai-Uwe von Hassel had been reelected president of the Bundestag Oct. 20.

A new 14-member coalition cabinet headed by Brandt was sworn in Oct. 22. The cabinet, composed of 11 Social Democrats and three Free Democrats, with FDP leader Scheel serving as foreign minister, had 5 fewer ministers than the outgoing cabinet. The Ministries for Refugees, the Treasury, the Post Office, Family & Youth Affairs and matters relating to the Bundesrat, the upper house of parliament, were abolished and their functions absorbed by other ministries. The Interior Ministry took responsibility for Bundesrat questions and family and youth affairs. The Treasury function was to be divided between the Finance and Economics Ministries. Refugee problems were to come under the jurisdiction of the Labor Ministry and the Ministry of Intra-German Relations. The latter agency had formerly been called the Ministry for All-German Questions. Its redesignation was said to reflect the virtual acceptance of the division of Germany into 2 nations.

ExChancellor Kiesinger was reelected chairman of the CDU at a CDU conference in Mainz Nov. 18.

Value of Mark Is Raised

In its first major action, the new coalition government of West German Chancellor Willy Brandt increased the value of the Deutschemark by 9.29% Oct. 24, effective Oct. 26. It acted after a year of monetary dislocations had made a revaluation of the mark almost inevitable despite strong West German opposition to the move. The West German revaluation went into effect 2 1/2 months after France, in a step equally repugnant to many French political leaders, had devalued the franc.

Currency devaluation is a step usually taken when a nation's imports exceed its exports significantly and persistently and when, therefore, there is a net outflow of money (or gold) to pay for the excess of imports. The object of devaluation, the lowering of one country's currency in terms of others' (or in terms of gold), is to make exports cheaper and imports more expensive. Exports should thus rise and imports fall, and the devaluing country should then experience a net increase in the inflow of capital. Revaluation is the reverse of this process. When exports are significantly higher than imports, the availability of goods is restricted domestically, there is a net inflow of money in payment for the excess of exports and inflationary pressures are created. A currency may then be increased in value relative to others (or to gold). This should cause imports to rise (since they become cheaper) and exports to fall (since they become more expensive in terms of other nations' currencies); reserves should flow out of rather than into the revaluing nation. This was West Germany's problem in late 1968-early 1969. German revaluation, of course, was tied to the devaluation of other currencies *(e.g.,* the franc); West German revaluation or French devaluation would have the same effect on Franco-German trade and money flow. Taken together—the situation in 1969—they compound one another.

The West German Central Bank had reported Apr. 14 that the nation's gold reserves had risen by 1.2 billion marks ($300 million) in 1968 to 18.2 billion marks ($4.55 billion). Total monetary reserves had increased 7.1 billion marks ($1.175 billion) to 37.4 billion marks ($9.35 billion). Massive capital exports and a decline in goods exports, however, caused a deficit in the nation's balance of payments for January-February 1969 and a resultant fall in West German reserves during March. The payments deficit was 1.3 billion marks ($325 million) in January and 2.2 billion marks ($550 million) in February. As a result, gold holdings and foreign claims dropped by 1.4 billion marks ($350 million) in March to 30.3 billion marks ($7.575 billion). The Central Bank report noted that from Mar. 1968 to Mar. 1969, West Germany's long-term capital exports totaled 14 billion marks ($3.5 billion) or about 3 billion marks ($750 million) more than the previous year.

Finance Min. Franz Josef Strauss conceded Apr. 29 that the mark was undervalued, and he suggested an "8% to 10%" revaluation as part of a package of parity changes for major European currencies. "I am only against a unilateral action," Strauss asserted at a Foreign Press Association meeting in Bonn. In an interview with the German newspaper *Welt am Sonntag* May 4, Strauss added that the West German government was ready to participate in an international conference to discuss a multilateral parity realignment. He cautioned, however, that the conference must be carefully planned and not be held in a crisis atmosphere.

Rumors that the French and West German governments were engaged in currency negotiations fueled speculative fever Apr. 30. Prices of the franc and pound weakened on the currency markets while the mark strengthened. Banking sources estimated that as much as $500 million in foreign funds had poured into Germany since Apr. 28. Following a May Day holiday in most European currency markets, monetary chaos resumed May 2. Despite West German official statements that the "Federal government is not considering revaluation" and that Strauss' comments on revaluation had been erroneously interpreted, the franc and pound fell to their effective floors and the mark reached its ceiling; central banks intervened heavily, and the Bank of France tightened credit controls May 2 in an effort to slow the growth of consumer demand by making it more difficult to get installment credit. Currency speculation slowed May 5, but general uncertainty remained strong. The Bundesbank announced May 5 that West German gold and foreign currency reserves had increased by $675 million to $8.25 billion in April; the rise came after an encouraging $1.76 billion decrease in the first quarter of 1969.

Despite the April increase in reserves, the West German government May 9 decided against a revaluation of the mark. Instead, the government said, it planned alternative measures to check the speculation on the mark and to limit the country's growing export surplus. The decision, described as "final, unequivocal and for eternity," was announced after several hours of intense debate at an emergency cabinet meeting. Deputy government spokesman Conrad Ahlers explained that the decision ruled out any change in the mark's value, even as part of a package realignment of currencies.

Speculation in the currency markets had gained in intensity after Charles de Gaulle's resignation as president of France Apr. 28, and it reached a peak May 9 when more than $1 billion in foreign currencies poured into West Germany. The demand for marks was so intense that some smaller German banks were forced to suspend sales of marks, and many commercial banks limited their sales to 100-500 marks per customer. Almost every major currency, including the Japanese yen, was hit during the height of the crisis May 8-9. On a number of foreign currency markets the mark rose to points well above its official ceiling level (3.97 marks to $1 U.S.), while the British pound and French franc fell to their lower limits, forcing heavy intervention by the British and French central banks. The Dutch guilder and the Italian lira—both strong currencies—also fell almost to their official floors and were supported by the Netherlands and Italian central banks. The Swiss National Bank intervened in the currency market May 9, and early in the day the Danish central bank suspended dealings in the foreign exchange market. At times buying and selling was so chaotic that officials were unable to keep records of currency values. Estimates of the total amount of funds pouring into Germany since de Gaulle's resignation rose to $4-$5 billion.

Central bankers from 11 major Western monetary powers, meeting in Basel, Switzerland May 10-11 for their monthly session at the Bank for International Settlements (BIS), expressed optimism that the currency crisis could be contained. In a communique issued May 11, the bankers pledged "immediate [BIS-supported] action to begin the recycling of speculative flows in the foreign-exchange markets." In a message to the financial authorities attending the meeting, West German Chancellor Kiesinger stated that "the decision of the German government to maintain the present parity of the Deutschemark will not be altered."

The revaluation issue had split the West German coalition cabinet along party lines. Kiesinger of the Christian Democratic Union (CDU) and Finance Minister Strauss of the Christian Social Union (CSU) opposed revaluation, while Economics Min. Karl Schiller of the Socialist Democratic Party (SPD) favored it. The SPD presidium had voted May 7 to support a revaluation plan sponsored by Schiller. The plan, which entailed an upward revaluation of 6.25%, was formally presented to the cabinet May 9; included among its supporters was Bundesbank Pres. Karl Blessing. The CDU and CSU, forming a majority of the cabinet and holding 246 of the 496 parliament seats (excluding West Berlin), drew their main support from the big-business and small-farm sectors of the economy, both of which strongly opposed revaluation. Schiller and the SPD, however, feared that the continuing rise in exports was creating the danger of a serious inflation that could undo much of the economic progress achieved in the country.

SPD headquarters May 9 issued a statement expressing "regret" that the government had decided against revaluation, "the most effective solution for maintaining price stability." More than 60 West German professors and lecturers May 11 issued a statement attacking the government's decision not to revalue the mark. "The decision of May 9 will lead to a further disruption of the international monetary system through economic intervention and thus strengthen the trends towards world economic disintegration," the statement declared. The signatories of the statement included Wilhelm Bauer and Herbert Giersch, 2 of the 5 "wise men" who annually report to the government on the state of the economy.

The French government May 7 and 9 had delivered 2 protests to the West German government against the decision not to revalue the mark. According to French Information Min. Joel le Theule, the messages expressed "surprise at the public and often contradictory statements of responsible authorities in the German Federal Republic concerning an eventual revaluation of the Deutschemark, since these statements had brought on a new wave of speculation, ending in the present crisis." The French had tightened credit restrictions May 8 in a move that, they stressed, had been prepared 10 days earlier and had no direct connection with the currency crisis.

Denmark, especially hard hit by the speculation, raised its bank rate May 11 from 7% to a crisis level of 9%. This unprecedented action was in reaction to heavy losses of foreign exchange during the monetary crisis; it made the Danish bank rate the highest in Europe. The London *Financial Times* May 12 cited estimates that Denmark's foreign exchange reserves had fallen to 600 million kroner ($79.8 million) by May 8, from more than 3 billion kroner ($399 million) at the beginning of the year. It was estimated that more than 700 million kroner ($93.1 million) were lost during the first week of May; the heavy losses forced a halt in Denmark's foreign exchange dealings May 9. To boost its faltering position, Denmark May 9 obtained an emergency stand-by credit of 235 million marks ($58.8 million) from West Germany and was believed to have made considerable use of its U.S. Federal Reserve swap facilities, borrowing up to 800 million kroner ($106 million). In addition to increasing the bank rate, Denmark temporarily banned early repayment of foreign debts in an attempt to slow the outflow of foreign currency. (The Danes had raised their bank rate from 6% to 7% in March.)

As the currency markets opened May 12, funds began to flow out of West Germany in response to the decision against revaluation and to the recycling promise of central bankers in Basel. The outflow, however, was smaller than the inflow had been during the previous 2 weeks, and it slowed to a relative trickle May 13. (Otmar Emminger, a member of the Bundesbank Board of Governors, said June 17 that of $4.1 billion in speculative funds that had flowed into Germany during the crisis, $2.5 billion had moved out again and most of the rest had been "neutralized" by the central bank. Official estimates indicated that the total influx had included only about $150 million of French reserves and $500 million of British reserves. About 60% of the funds had come from the Eurodollar market, 40% from national reserves.) The mark fell below its ceiling of $.2519 U.S. May 12 and held at the same level May 13; it had risen to levels above $.256 in unofficial trading during the height of the crisis. Prices of the British pound and French franc rose. The slowdown in the exit of funds from West Germany May 13 was attributed to the publication of discouraging April trade figures for France and Britain as well as to the unwillingness of large holders to give up their marks while the West Germany government remained divided on the revaluation issue.

The West German cabinet's economic committee May 13 recommended "flanking measures" to support the decision against revaluation. The recommendations, adopted by the cabinet May 14, were aimed at curbing liquidity and cutting the influence of foreign trade and monetary pressures. Reports indicated that the measures were milder than had been expected, causing some fear that they might not prevent feared inflation. The economic committee agreed on 5 basic recommendations: (1) a freeze on excess federal and state tax revenues to shift up to $900 million into a "business cycle fluctuation fund"; (2) a budget cut of $500 million; (3) the purchase of $1.1 million worth of short-term West German Treasury notes in 1969 and of $500 million worth in 1970; (4) continuation of tax adjustments instituted during the Nov. 1968 currency crisis (a 4% reduction of taxes on imports and a 4% added tax on exports); (5) authorization for the Bundesbank to demand 100% minimum reserve requirements on foreign deposits. The measures would force a cut in government spending and temporarily halt tax income counted on by Federal and state governments for current costs.

Speaking in parliament June 19, Economics Min. Schiller announced a revision of 1969 economic forecasts due to an "unexpectedly big boom" in production since the start of the year. He estimated that exports would grow in 1969 by 9.5%, rather than by the 6.5% previously forecast, and that imports would increase by 15.5% rather than 12.5%. He predicted that the nation's gross national product would increase by 9%; the projected gain had been 7%.

The Bundesbank June 19 raised its discount rate from 4% to 5% in an effort to counter the dangers of "economic overheating." An earlier increase from 3% to 4% in April had failed to slow the economy. The Bundesbank July 17 increased reserve requirements, the minimum reserve rate for domestic and foreign currency holdings in commercial banks, 10%, effective Aug. 1. And on Sept. 11 the Bundesbank again raised its discount rate—from 5% to 6%. The new rate was the highest in 18 years. Karl Blessing, Bundesbank president, said the bank had felt "forced to act" since the "economy really needed strong measures to keep it from overheating." (The West German Lombard rate, which applies to rates charged commercial banks on Bundesbank loans, was also raised Sept. 11—from 6% to 7.5%.)

In the wake of the West German election, the new Brandt coalition government Sept. 29 temporarily freed the mark from its fixed exchange rate and allowed its value to fluctuate freely in foreign currency markets. The government took the action by ordering the Bundesbank to disregard its IMF obligation to sell marks when buying sent the price more than 1% above its official parity (3.98 marks to the U.S. dollar). Foreign exchange markets in West Germany, closed since Sept. 25 in an effort to stave off speculative buying of the mark, were ordered to reopen Sept. 30. In supplementary action, the government also asked the Bundesbank to make "far-reaching" use of its powers to restrict the inflow of foreign funds by increasing the minimum reserve rate for foreign holdings in West German commercial banks.

Finance ministers and central bank officials, in Washington for the annual IMF meeting, reportedly expressed approval of the West German action. Informing IMF delegates of Bonn's decision, IMF Managing Director Pierre Paul Schweitzer Sept. 29 said Bonn officials would "maintain close contact with the fund and resume the maintenance of the limits around par at the earliest opportunity." Noting that Bonn "technically" was not honoring its IMF obligations to support parity, he said he thought the action was the "wisest thing to do." Later in the day, IMF executive directors confirmed that they "recognized the exigencies of the situation." U.S. Treasury Secy. David M. Kennedy called the West German decision "understandable in the light of the present circumstances" and expressed the belief that it "will serve a constructive purpose in dampening potential speculative forces."

In foreign exchange markets Sept. 30, the mark increased in value by 4% to 5%. The British pound improved, while the French franc remained under pressure and was supported by the Bank of France. The Belgian central bank suspended official trading of marks Sept. 30. The central banks of Italy, Sweden and Finland, which had already suspended official dealings in marks, continued their suspensions.

The EEC commission met in emergency session in Brussels Sept. 29 and reportedly informed West Germany that it could not take such "autonomous measures" as setting a free-floating mark without first informing the EEC. The meeting was called to discuss the effect of the German decision on the Common Market's farm trade.

Bonn announced a 5.5% tax on all farm imports Sept. 30 in an attempt to protect West German farmers from a sudden increase in agricultural imports. Klaus von Dohnanyi, secretary of state for economic affairs, told the EEC commission Sept. 30, however, that the tax would be abolished when the mark returned to normal parity in several weeks. He stressed that the decision to allow the mark to fluctuate was not a prelude to its revaluation.

As the election campaign neared its climax, the Economics Ministry had ordered the closing of foreign exchange markets Sept. 25 and 26. (The Bundesbank announced Sept. 30 that its reserves had increased by $500 million in the 3 days before the markets were closed.) Chancellor Kiesinger Sept. 25 ordered an extension of the money market closure through Sept. 29, the day after the election, but Economics Min. Schiller refused to carry out the order. In separate statements Sept. 26, both major parties gave assurances that the mark, a key issue in the electoral campaign, would not be immediately revalued. The CDU stressed that it saw no reason to change the mark's value "for the present and for the foreseeable future," while the SDP referred only to the fact that "a decision over a parity change in the Deutschemark cannot be discussed in this situation." Currency markets had opened Sept. 29 but were abruptly ordered closed by Kiesinger following the inflow of an estimated $500 million in speculative funds during the first few hours of trade. The decision to free the mark from its parity restrictions was announced following an emergency cabinet meeting that day.

In directing Schiller to close the foreign exchange markets, Kiesinger had accused him of "heating up" the election campaign with the revaluation issue. Kiesinger said: "This propaganda systematically fostered by you and your party [in favor of revaluation] has given rise to fears that a wave of speculation would set in right before the election. This has now happened." The conflict had continued Sept. 25 as Schiller accused Kiesinger of "clumsy amateurism" in ordering an extension of the money market closure. "If the exchange markets remain closed Monday [Sept. 29]," he charged, "the impression must arise that something is going to happen Tuesday. This is the most drastic method yet of exciting and provoking speculation."

The EEC commission Oct. 5 formally called on West Germany to end the uncertainty over the mark and "return to a fixed exchange rate, whatever the level of parity that may appear preferable after the consultations provided for within the Community." An emergency EEC Council of Ministers meeting hammered out a compromise solution Oct.

6, following a pledge by Schiller that "the fixing of a new parity [for the mark] will be the first priority of the new West German government." Under the agreement, the Bonn government won EEC endorsement of a modified import tax plan that reduced the amount of the tax to 5% and that applied to fewer farm products than envisaged in the original proposal. In addition, the Germans pledged to automatically discontinue the tax when the mark was revalued. (In a related action Oct. 6, Common Market finance ministers agreed to work out a common community position on the issue of a more flexible exchange rate for national currencies.)

The value of the "floating" mark had slowly but steadily increased Oct. 1-7 to a point about 6% to 7% above its official parity. (The Bundesbank continued to intervene in the market from time to time in order to buy marks.) The British pound gained during the week, but the French franc fell steadily to a post-devaluation low Oct. 7 amid heavy intervention of the Bank of France.

In an effort to lessen the burden imposed on West German exporters by the rising value of the "floating" mark, the West German cabinet decided Oct. 8 to suspend until Dec. 1 the 4% surtax on exports and a similar rebate on imports introduced in Nov. 1968. The proposal was approved by the EEC Oct. 9. Schiller explained that the decision had been a "compromise" between the SDP and CDU forces in the cabinet. The Social Democrats had advocated a total abolition of the tax but had been outvoted by the Christian Democrats. Government spokesman Gunter Diehl said the "Christian Democrats do not want to share responsibility for revaluation."

The new Brandt government, taking its first major action, revalued the mark Oct. 24 to 27.3224 U.S. cents, an increase of 9.29% above the former parity of 25¢. The upward adjustment became effective Oct. 26. The IMF Oct. 24 announced its concurrence with the West German action. As the West German cabinet met in Bonn to finalize the decision on revaluation, West German economic officials in Luxembourg informed a specially convened session of the EEC's monetary committee about the mark's adjustment; France had been criticized for its failure to consult with the EEC when the franc was devalued in August.

Announcing the revaluation Oct. 24, Economics Min. Schiller called the increase a "courageous rate, but certainly not a foolhardy one." He said the 4% border tax adjustment, which had been suspended Oct. 8, would be eliminated. Schiller assured farmers, who stood to suffer most from revaluation, that action would be taken to compensate them for their losses. He added that the government was also prepared to aid export-oriented industries harmed by the revaluation. In a nationwide address Oct. 26, Brandt assured West Germans that they had "no need to worry" because of the revaluation. "No worker will lose his job," he said, and "no business enterprise will find its existence threatened."

Ex-Finance Min. Franz Josef Strauss, an opponent of revaluation, Oct. 24 called the action "a terrible disadvantage for the economy" that would have to be borne by the German taxpayer.

Since its detachment from its fixed parity, the mark (controlled by careful Bundesbank intervention) had risen from the official 25¢ to 27.02¢ by Oct. 24. The *N.Y. Times* had reported Oct. 23 that about $500 million in speculative funds had flowed out of West Germany during the mark's floating period. With the establishment of a new parity Oct. 26, one U.S. dollar bought 3.66 marks compared with 4 marks at the old parity. In addition, the mark's value rose from 0.222168 to 0.242806 grams of fine gold. In the money markets Oct. 27 and 28, more speculative funds began to move out of West Germany. Belgian, French, British, Japanese and Dutch currencies improved Oct. 27, although the Belgian franc weakened the following day after the government announced that the Belgian currency would not be revalued. The Bundesbank was reported to have lost $300 million-$350 million in foreign funds Oct. 27.

The long-awaited revaluation of the mark was greeted with relief in most financial and governmental circles. In Paris, French Finance Min. Valery Giscard d'Estaing Oct. 24 hailed the German action and said: "It is evident that the revaluation of the currency of our principal trading partner will have a favorable effect in re-establishing our foreign trade equilibrium." Giscard d'Estaing asserted that the "floating"-mark experiment had not proved "compatible with good functioning of international exchanges, particularly with the Common Market."

The U.S. Treasury expressed confidence Oct. 24 that the German revaluation "should resolve in a constructive manner the principal cause of uncertainty that has existed in the exchange market." British and Italian financial sources also welcomed the mark's upward adjustment. (Official dealings on the Italian money markets had been suspended in September in an effort to curb speculation.)

The revaluation raised questions about the status of currencies of Belgium, the Netherlands, Switzerland, Austria and Japan. However, Switzerland, the Netherlands and Austria announced Oct. 24 that they would not revalue their currencies. Belgium followed suit Oct. 28. (Austria announced Oct. 27 that it would cut import duties and import equalization taxes and would introduce tighter credit restrictions in an effort to counter the inflationary effects expected from the West German revaluation. About 41% of Austria's imports came from Germany.) Japanese financial sources expressed fear Oct. 25 that the mark's revaluation might increase pressure on Japan to revalue its yen, one of the world's strongest currencies.

The Bundesbank Nov. 6 reduced the minimum reserve requirement for member banks by an average of 10% and adjusted the reserve requirement on foreign accounts, lifted to 100% in April, to the domestic reserve rate. Both actions were retroactive to Nov. 1. Bundesbank Pres. Blessing explained that the 2 measures would increase bank liquidity by at least $546 million. (The cabinet Nov. 20 nominated Karl Klasen, 60, to succeed Blessing as Bundesbank president for 8 years.)

West Germany gained $1.09 billion in foreign currencies from the IMF in separate transactions Nov. 25 and Dec. 10. The drawings were to replenish West German reserves in response to the heavy outflow of funds following the mark's revaluation. The Nov. 25 step was a West German purchase of the equivalent of $540 million in 7 currencies held by the Fund. The purchase was within Germany's gold tranche position in the IMF and restored the Fund's holdings of the West German mark to 75% of Bonn's quota. The Dec. 10 transaction, providing a further $550 million from the organization, represented repayment of West Germany's past loans to the IMF under the 1962 General Arrangements to Borrow (GAB), an agreement under which the Group of 10 industrial nations pledged up to $6 billion in loans when needed to increase the IMF's supply of usable currencies. Of the $550 million repayment, $340 million came from the IMF itself, while the remaining $210 million was provided by 4 other GAB countries.

(The Bundesbank Dec. 4 increased the Lombard rate from 7.5% to 9%. The bank also reduced minimum reserve requirements by 10% for the month of December. The decisions were taken to curb the outflow of West German funds and to help ease the liquidity shortage.)

The EEC & European Agriculture

European Common Market agriculture ministers met in Brussels for a 14-hour session that ended in deadlock Mar. 26 with no agreements on new price levels for beef and dairy products. The EEC's main farm problem was a 300,000-ton butter surplus. EEC price supports had encouraged huge surpluses of dairy products, particularly butter, the stocks of which were increasing at an annual rate of 220,000 (short) tons.

The ministers met again Apr. 22 and May 13 and agreed to raise the price of corn and barley during the 1969-70 marketing year while maintaining the current price level for other cereals, rice, sugar and oil-seeds. Target prices (base prices determined in the EEC marketing center with the least adequate domestic supplies) for corn and barley were increased by $1 a metric ton.

At a meeting July 17, the ministers agreed in principle on the EEC commission's proposal to encourage farmers to slaughter dairy cattle in order to help reduce the EEC's large dairy surplus. There was no progress, however, on the controversial question of price supports for dairy products. At a subsequent meeting July 28-30, decisions were also delayed since Italy was then without a government.

In a further effort to reduce the increasing dairy surpluses, the ministers agreed Sept. 17 to establish subsidies for the slaughter of dairy cattle. Under the plan, to become effective after approval by the 6 members, farmers with 10 or fewer cows would receive a $200 subsidy for each slaughtered cow. Farmers owning more than 10 cows could receive the same subsidy on agreement to stop milk production and raise cows only for meat. The agreement would remain in effect until 500,000 cows had been removed from the dairy market. The cost of the subsidies would be borne by the 6 EEC members and the organization's farm fund.

The EEC commission ruled Oct. 1 that West Germany's imposition of a 5.5% tax on agricultural imports was illegal. Instead, the commission proposed that Bonn suspend all agricultural imports under the EEC's common price system until a fixed exchange rate was established for the mark. The tax had been imposed Sept. 30 in an effort to prevent a massive influx of cheap farm products following the government's decision to free the mark. The action conflicted with the Common Market's joint agricultural pricing policy, as had the French devaluation of the franc in August. Opposing the commission's refusal to authorize the import tax, the Bonn government announced Oct. 2 that it would request an urgent ruling by the European Court of Justice to suspend the commission's decision pending further hearings. Stressing the temporary nature of the tax, West German Agriculture Min. Hermann Hocherl maintained that the German solution was, in fact, "more community-minded and more in harmony with market principles" than was the commission's alternative proposal to ban all farm imports. The court, however, after a 7-hour session Oct. 5, rejected Bonn's request. It argued that a refusal by the commission to authorize a government action could not then be appealed to the court. The court also concluded that the commission had not violated EEC laws in refusing to authorize the agricultural import tax.

EEC agriculture and finance ministers agreed Oct. 28 on a compromise formula to protect West German farmers against the effects of the mark's revaluation. Under the plan, West Germany, whose farmers would automatically lose more than $400 million because of the mark's parity change, was to receive about $100 million from the EEC's joint farm fund the first year and $50 million the 2d. The rest of the compensation promised to German farmers would come from within West Germany—from a readjustment of agricultural taxes and from direct subsidies to farmers. In addition, the 5% agricultural import tax imposed in early October would be continued for 6 more weeks. The compromise was reached after 15 hours of intense debate, in which Economics Min. Schiller had threatened that West Germany might cause trouble in other Common Market agricultural areas if the EEC did not agree to help Bonn in compensating its farmers for losses (possibly more than $460 million a year) due to the revaluation. West

German Agriculture Min. Joseph Ertl had proposed that the German agricultural market be isolated from the EEC market as the French market had been in August. Other EEC members, particularly Italy and the Netherlands, argued that West Germany's economic circumstances showed no real need for EEC assistance in the matter. Schiller countered that the EEC had a responsibility to share the burden with West Germany.

The EEC Council of Ministers Nov. 12 reached final agreement on details of the program to compensate West German farmers for losses from the mark's revaluation. Under the plan, the Common Market agreed to provide $180 million from its farm fund (European Agricultural Guidance and Guarantee Fund, or EAGGF) over a period of 3 years beginning in 1971. West Germany was authorized to provide the rest over a 4-year schedule beginning Jan. 1, 1970. Until the Jan. 1 effective date of the agreement, West Germany was authorized to maintain its current system of border tax adjustments, originally scheduled to end in December. (Le Monde had reported Nov. 1 that the EEC farm fund had paid $1.313 billion in subsidies during 1967-8 and $2 billion in 1968-9 and would pay $2.5 billion in 1969-70.)

The EEC Executive Commission Nov. 20 proposed a plan to replace the current system of financing the Common Market's agricultural system. Under the proposal, prices of butter, soft wheat and sugar would be cut; this would result in reducing existing surpluses and forcing the farmers to suffer some of the financial consequences involved. The current system had maintained high agricultural prices through import levies and had artificially stimulated large surpluses. (Butter surpluses within EEC members currently stood at 350,000 tons and soft wheat surpluses at more than 8 million tons.)

The EEC Council of Ministers, at its Nov. 24-25 meeting, reached agreement on improved protection for fruit and vegetable producers. Under the agreement, concluded mainly at the insistence of the Italians, taxes would be placed on apples, pears and peaches if EEC prices fell too low. In addition, all imports of these products could be halted if the Commission decided the internal EEC market was seriously disturbed. Export subsidies were also set.

EEC agricultural ministers met in The Hague Dec. 1 and reached a general agreement on agricultural policies for the 1970s. Under the agreement, announced Dec. 22 although it had not yet been submitted to the 6 EEC member nations for ratification, a Common Market agricultural budget fund would be established and built up until 1975 by annual payments from agricultural levies and tariffs as well as possible assessments on member governments. These funds would be used to run the EEC's agricultural programs. By 1972, it was expected, $3.5 billion would be available in the fund. (Under the current common fund for financing agriculture, scheduled to expire Dec. 31, French agriculture received about $350 million a year, a sum approximately equal to the

West German contribution. Total Common Market spending on agriculture, estimated at $2.9 billion a year, was expected to rise to $3.5 billion annually by 1975.) The agreement did not include decisions on the problem of agricultural production control and surpluses.

The EEC & Monetary Policies

The impact of the French and German currency crises was felt in all EEC member nations and by the EEC as a body itself during 1969.

Finance ministers of the 6 EEC nations met Jan. 13-14 in the West German ski resort of Garmisch-Partenkirchen for a discussion of the organization's monetary policies. West German Finance Min. Franz Josef Strauss said at a news conference Jan. 13 that the delegates had discussed harmonizing tax rates within the Common Market and eliminating "nuisance" border taxes on goods bought by tourists. (The EEC had eliminated all internal tariffs July 1, 1968, but the border taxes, bringing taxes on imported products up to the level of taxes on similar domestic products, were still being levied.) Central bankers of the 6 countries joined the finance ministers Jan. 14 to explore methods to increase monetary cooperation among them. The meeting did not take up the controversial question of Europe's exchange rates and issued only a simple statement expressing satisfaction at the apparent calm of the international monetary atmosphere since the November 1968 currency crisis.

Central bankers of the major financial powers, meeting in Basel at a regular Bank for International Settlements session, agreed Feb. 9 on a program to prevent currency speculation from leading to devaluation. The plan was to be referred to the countries' political authorities for approval. Efforts to achieve some form of hot-money speculation curb stemmed from the Nov. 1968 franc/mark crisis. West German Economics Min. Karl Schiller indicated Feb. 14 that under the agreement, a deficit country "should have not only the occasion, but also some obligation, to go into the capital market of a stronger country." An earlier and more rigid plan, calling for automatic currency recycling, met opposition from West Germany and Switzerland, the 2 major creditor nations.

The Belgian Central Bank raised its discount rate from 4.5% to 5% Mar. 5, to 5.5% Apr. 10, to 6% May 29, to 7% July 30 and to 7.5% Sept. 18. The raises were viewed as attempts to combat inflation, to restrict Belgian activities in the Eurodollar market and to slow the outflow of capital from Belgium; rising interest rates in the U.S. and Europe had drawn an increasing amount of Belgian francs. The increase in the discount rate was the 2d within 3 months; Belgium had increased its rate from 3.75% to 4.5% in Dec. 1968. The central bank of Sweden, a non-EEC country, had raised its discount rate from 5% to 6% Feb. 28. The bank said that increased rates in other European nations and the U.S. since October [when the Swedish rate had been lowered] had "led to a situation where the Swedish rate was too low in relation to rates in other countries." The Belgian Central Bank announced Apr. 10 that it was placing restrictions on the flow of dollars out of the country by requiring commercial banks to reduce their holdings of foreign currencies before June 30. The restrictions made it difficult for Belgian banks to borrow or buy dollars and invest them in the Eurodollar market.

The Bank of Italy in March ordered commercial banks to repatriate about $800 million in net foreign credits by June 30. This action was taken to halt a growing flight of capital from Italy as a result of spiraling interest rates in international money markets. The Bank of Italy had been trying to encourage domestic economic expansion by maintaining the discount rate at 3.5%; but with net private capital outflows reaching $232 million in January and probably more in February and March, the supply of funds for Italian business investment was threatened. The Bank of Italy increased its discount rate on certain transactions from 3.5% to 5% July 1. The first increase in 10 years, it was designed to stem the flow of capital from Italy. The Bank of Italy raised its bank rate from 3.5% to 4%, effective Aug. 14, for banks not covered by the earlier increase to 5%. The announcement stated that the measure was necessary to maintain stable prices and because of the international monetary situation. It added that excessive credit had threatened to increase prices and damage Italy's economic program.

In response to the rising international interest rates and domestic inflationary pressures, the Dutch Central Bank raised its bank rate from 5% to 5.5% Apr. 8. At the same time, the Netherlands Parliament froze the prices of all goods and services at levels of Mar. 14. The Swiss Bankers Association announced Apr. 8 that Swiss commercial banks had raised their private discount rate from 3.75% to 4%. (The Swiss discount rate, fixed by the banks themselves, was independent of the national bank.)

The West German Bundesbank Apr. 17 raised its discount rate from 3% to 4% in an effort to slow inflationary pressures and decrease the flow of capital from the country. It was the first change since May 1967. The central bank also raised the Lombard rate from 4% to 5%. This is the rate German banks must pay when borrowing from the Bundesbank against securities. The 2 actions were effective Apr. 18. In March the government had announced cuts in federal spending, increases in tax prepayments, reductions in federal borrowing and steps to increase imports of certain foods and textiles.

The central bank of Austria raised its discount rate on loans within Austria to 4.75% from 3.75%, effective Sept. 11. The move was an attempt to slow the outflow of gold from Austria to nations with higher interest rates. Other Austrian banks were required by law to follow suit and charge the new rate on loans.

EEC finance ministers agreed in Mons, Belgium Apr. 21 to ask U.S. authorities to get American banks to cut down on their borrowing in the Eurodollar market. The European ministers did not agree on any formal demands to set before the U.S. but reportedly decided to increase pressure on U. S. officials to take some moderating action. Spiraling interest rates in the $20 billion Eurodollar market and throughout Europe were due in large part to tightened U.S. credit. Domestic restrictions intended to halt inflation had caused American banks to move into the relatively unrestricted Eurodollar market, causing interest rates to soar. Consequently, the Eurodollar interest rate for 3-month deposits had risen to more than 8.5% by mid-April, and the situation was reflected in soaring interest rates throughout Western Europe. Some banking circles were concerned that the trend had forced several countries to extend exchange controls to isolate their money markets from the Eurodollar market.

The U.S. Federal Reserve Board June 26 moved to apply reserve requirements to Eurodollars borrowed by its member banks and to "moderate the flow of Eurodollars between U.S. banks and their foreign branches and also between U.S. and foreign banks." The proposals, subject to amendment, were to go into effect in one month. Under the proposals: (1) U.S. banks borrowing Eurodollars from foreign branches would be required to hold in reserve 10% of these borrowings exceeding the average amount outstanding during the 4 weeks ended May 28; this reserve requirement would also apply to assets acquired by a branch from its U.S. offices. To reduce "potential inequities," Eurodollar transactions up to a minimum base of 3% of a bank's total deposits were exempt from the reserve requirement. (2) The plan imposed a 10% reserve requirement on foreign branch bank loans to U.S. residents when these loans exceeded the average amount outstanding in the 4 weeks ended May 28 or the actual amount outstanding June 25; member banks could chose which base period they preferred. Branches with less than $5 million in loans to U.S. residents "on any day of a relevant computation period" were exempt from the requirement. (3) The FRB imposed a 10% reserve requirement on borrowings by member banks from foreign banks. The proposals further stipulated that if a bank's Eurodollar borrowings fell below the May level, the "reserve-free base" would automatically be reduced to the level of the bank's current borrowings unless the board specifically waived the rule.

With the announcement of the proposed restrictions, interest rates on Eurodollar loans fell sharply June 27.

In announcing the proposals June 26, the FRB said they were "designed to remove a special advantage to member banks of using Eurodollars for adjustment to domestic credit restraint." Eurodollar borrowing had reached a record total of $13.38 billion in the week ended June 18, up $7 billion since the beginning of 1969 and averaging more than $1 billion a week in the first 3 weeks of June. The borrowing sent interest rates on 3-month Eurodollar loans soaring to as high as 13% and caused upward pressure on foreign interest rates. Some foreign central bankers specifically had asked Federal Reserve officials to modify the impact abroad of U.S. domestic financial restraints.

The EEC Executive Commission Feb. 13 had issued a 20-page proposal, the Barre plan, urging its members to increase their coordination in monetary affairs. Qualified approval of the plan was given by the EEC finance ministers at a meeting in Brussels July 17. The commission's proposal included a plan for members to place an unspecified portion of their gold and dollar reserves into a pool from which short-term drawings could be made by members with balance-of-payments problems. Each member would have automatic drawing rights for up to 3 months; drawing rights for longer periods would be permitted on condition that the borrowing nation accepted economic advice from the other 5 nations. Thus the plan, in requiring members to yield some of their economic sovereignty, would constitute an important step toward supranationality within the Common Market and toward the formation of a single EEC currency. France, usually opposed to plans leading to supranationality, was reported to be more sympathetic to the plan than were such other traditional supporters of supranationality as West Germany and the Netherlands. (Because of the weak position of the franc, it was thought that France would probably be among the first to benefit from the plan.) In preliminary consultations, West Germany, Italy and the Netherlands, the main EEC creditor nations, had expressed skepticism about a plan limited to the members of the EEC. As finally worked out by an EEC Committee of Central Bankers in conjunction with the BIS and announced Dec. 11 in Paris, a $2 billion stabilization fund would make $1 billion available automatically in short-run aid to any EEC nation. The 2d $1 billion would be available on the recommendation of EEC monetary authorities.

European Community & Freer Trade

The European Coal & Steel Community and 9 Japanese steel producers announced Jan. 14 that they had agreed to limit the growth of their steel exports to the U.S. to 5% in each of the next 3 years. Under the agreement, the 2 steelmaking blocs each would hold their 1969 exports to the U.S. at 5.7 million net tons (the 11.4 million-ton total would be equivalent to 82% of total U.S. imports of steel). State Secy. Dean Rusk, who announced the accord in Washington, said that total U.S. steel imports would amount to 14 million net tons in 1969, about 14.7 million tons in 1970, and about 15.4 million tons in 1971. (Sources in Washington said that before the agreement, 1969 U.S. steel imports had been estimated at 16 million net tons. U.S. steel imports in 1968 had amounted to 17.5 million net tons, about 16% of total consumption.) The foreign producers said that the restrictions had been accepted on the understanding that the U.S. would not impose import restrictions through duty increases, mandatory quotas, or other actions. (The London *Economist* reported Jan. 18 that the British Steel Corp. had refused to join the ECSC and Japan in restricting steel exports to the U.S. In 1968, Britain had exported less than one million tons of steel to the U.S.)

EEC ministers agreed Mar. 25 to reduce tariffs by 40% on citrus fruits from Israel, Spain and Turkey. They also adopted a 3-year work program designed to complete the integration tasks as outlined in the Treaty of Rome and approved a document that outlined the goals of harmonizing customs regulations and eliminating such administrative non-tariff barriers as unjustifiable safety and sanitary rules.

A U.S. mission headed by Commerce Secy. Maurice H. Stans visited 7 West European nations Apr. 11-26 "in pursuit of 'frank and friendly' discussions [on trade relations] with our traditional friends and trading partners of Western Europe." Stans conferred with government and trade leaders in Belgium, Holland, West Germany, Switzerland, Italy, France and Britain. Reporting on his trip in the May 5 issue of *International Commerce,* Stans emphasized that it was "a mission of exploration, not negotiation." He listed 5 principal subjects that had been discussed: (1) a reaffirmation of "the commitment of the Nixon Administration to the principle of freer trade throughout the world"; (2) trade barriers restricting U.S. exports to European nations; (3) the U.S. "concern about certain protectionist aspects of the Common Agricultural Policy of the European Community"; (4) assurance that "Pres. Nixon intends to take a strong initiative in preparing legislative proposals to submit to Congress to lead the United States toward freer trade in a number of ways"; (5) the current critical situation confronting the American textile industry due to increased imports in textiles of manmade fibers and wool. Specific proposals recommended that the U.S. and its trading partners call an "open table" conference on the reduction of non-tariff barriers to trade. Stans urged a multilateral solution to the textile problem under the auspices of the General Agreement on Tariffs & Trade.

The EEC Council of Ministers announced Sept. 11 that it would approve the suspension of duties on 4 types of steel products during the 4-month period starting Oct. 1. The Council had rejected an EEC commission proposal to reduce duties on all iron and steel products in accordance with Kennedy Round arrangements.

Japan and the Common Market signed an agreement on cotton textile trade Oct. 22. Under the accord, retroactive to Oct. 1, the EEC nations would drop their arbitrary controls on Japanese exports of cotton textiles, while Japan would submit its exports of cotton textiles to EEC markets to voluntary regulation.

18 industrial nations Nov. 14 proposed plans for extending tariff preferences for 10 years on manufactured and semi-manufactured goods from less developed nations. The nations, all 18 members of the Organization for Economic Cooperation & Development, submitted the plans in accordance with an agreement reached at the 2d session of UNCTAD (UN Conference on Trade & Development), held in New Delhi, India, in Mar. 1968. The proposals, submitted by OECD Secy. Gen. Emile van Lennep to UNCTAD Secy. Gen. Manuel Perez Guerrero, pointed out sharp differences between the U.S. and the EEC. Under the U.S. proposal, all developing nations were offered duty-free entry, with no quotas, on almost all manufactured and semi-manufactured products; exceptions included textiles, shoes and petroleum products. The U.S. plan contained an "escape clause" that would allow U.S. industries to demand import restrictions if they were hurt by a large increase in imports from developing nations. The U.S. offer included an "illustrative list," of agricultural products on which tariffs might be eliminated. The U.S. limited its offer to 10 years and extended it only to countries that eliminated such existing preferential arrangements as the EEC's accords with its African associated states and similar British arrangements with less developed Commonwealth nations. (Under the EEC proposal—a single plan submitted by the 6 members—a system of quotas retained the principle of special preferences for the 18 associated African states.)

Other EEC Developments

The EEC Executive Commission announced Jan. 16 that court proceedings would be instituted against France for its failure to adhere to a scheduled reduction of a special export subsidy. The subsidy, adopted in July 1968, was in the form of a low interest rate on government loans granted to exporters. Such credit subsidies had been declared illegal in the Common Market in the spring of 1968 and were abolished July 1, 1968, along with the market's last customs duties. France, however, had been given special dispensation in July to institute the subsidy because of its weakened economic situation following the May-June student-worker upheavals; under the agreement, the Bank of France was allowed to discount export loans at a rate 3 percentage points below the official French bank rate (5% at that time) but was to narrow the margin to 1.5 points by Oct. 31, 1968 and was to abolish the subsidy by Jan. 31, 1969.

In announcing the decision to take court action, the commission indicated that the French bank rate was 6%, but that export credit was still being extended at 3%. The commission had warned France Dec. 19, 1968 that if it did not adhere to the agreed reductions, legal action would be taken. This was the 3d time France had been brought before the EEC's 7 man Court of Justice in Luxembourg, which adjudicated the organization's internal disputes.

France was reported Mar. 6 to have filed suit in the European Court of Justice against the EEC commission. Challenging the commission's decision to take France to court, France asserted that its preferential subsidies were not an illegal aid to exports, and it demanded that the court annul the commission's decision that they be reduced. The French brought the issue to court under the Paris Treaty creating the European Coal & Steel Community; the Executive Commission had sued under the Rome Treaty, under which the EEC was founded. (The Rome Treaty stipulated that the commission could take a Common Market member to court if it failed to obey a directive; the Paris Treaty allowed the commission to immediately impose sanctions against a disobedient member unless that member challenged the commission's ruling in court.) In other court cases during 1969, the EEC Executive Commission filed suit in the EEC's Court of Justice against Italy and France for failure to adhere to community regulations. Among the actions: (a) The commission charged Italy Mar. 27 with imposing a higher tax on brandy imported from other EEC countries than on Italian brandy. (b) Italy was taken to court May 22 on charges of discriminatory border tax treatment of imported cotton yarn and other textile fibers. (c) The commission filed suit against France June 14 for failing to impose a levy on imported Tunisian olive oil as required under community regulations. (d) The commission accused Italy of failing to uphold community rules that required payment of subsidies to farmers exporting to developing countries.

In October, the commission brought suit against France in the European Court of Justice in a dispute over French regulation of foreign investment. The commission claimed that French legislation, introduced in 1967 and requiring government authorization of all major foreign investment in France, was a violation of EEC rules authorizing free flow of investment within the community. France had maintained that approval of investments by "community companies" would be automatic and had refused to modify its regulations. A large part of the dispute focused on the definition of a "company belonging to a community country." While most Common Market members reportedly stressed only the locale of the legal incorporation of a firm, France wanted to consider more detailed origins.

The EEC Council of Ministers Mar. 3 proposed the establishment of a central patent bureau to grant Europe-wide protection to inventions. It invited 7 other European nations to begin negotiations on a new patent convention in the fall. This action ended a 4-year EEC deadlock on the question; France had abandoned its opposition, which had been based on a demand for a convention limited to EEC members. An all-European convention would eliminate the need for inventors to apply to the patent office of each country. The council proposed that Americans be denied Europe-wide patents unless European patent seekers were given U.S. patent privileges equal to those accorded

Americans. The 7 European nations invited to join the EEC in negotiating a new patent convention: Britain, Denmark, Norway, Ireland, Austria, Switzerland and Sweden. Last-minute political objections blocked invitations to Greece, Spain and Portugal, although council sources explained that all interested European nations could participate in the conference.

The semiannual French-German "summit" meeting, held in Paris Mar. 13-14, was marked by an atmosphere of open disagreement between the 2 nations. Pres. de Gaulle was reported Mar. 14 to have set out for Chancellor Kiesinger 2 alternative routes for the future of Europe—maintenance of the current European Economic Community with 6 members, or formation of a larger and more loosely organized group that could include Britain, Scandinavia and, in de Gaulle's words, "the Turks and the Swiss." Such a proposal had been the subject of the recent British-French dispute over published reports of a meeting Feb. 4 between de Gaulle and UK Amb.-to-France Christopher Soames. Refering to the "Soames affair," de Gaulle was reported Mar. 14 to have repeated his assertion that Britain had misrepresented his views on an expanded European association.

Then-Foreign Min. Willy Brandt of West Germany assured his fellow EEC foreign ministers at a meeting in Brussels Mar. 25 that the Common Market "remains the cornerstone and most effective instrument for European unification." Indicating that his remarks were intended to show his country's attitude toward French proposals for replacing the EEC with a broader but looser association, Brandt emphasized that West Germany's commitment to EEC "should be understood everywhere."

The government of Tunisia Mar. 28 signed an association agreement with the EEC. Under the agreement, the EEC was to provide duty-free and quota-free entry to Tunisian industrial goods and was to grant preferences for certain agricultural commodities, including olive oil and citrus fruits. In return, Tunisia was to reduce customs tariffs currently applied to 40% of its imports from the EEC and to establish quotas for another 12% of its imports from the EEC. In order to protect new industry, however, Tunisia would be permitted to reduce or eliminate preferences accorded some imports from the EEC, but any such action would have to be accompanied by an equivalent increase in preferences to other imports from the EEC.

The EEC Executive Commission approved a new 5-year program for the organization's nuclear group, Euratom, the commission announced Apr. 29. The proposal, sent to the 6 Euratom members for approval, called for Euratom to concentrate on heavy water, high temperature and fast breeder nuclear reactors and not to limit itself to a single type of reactor at first. The plan would provide for increased standardization in technology among the 6 members and adoption of uniform safety measures and rules for fusion flow control. The report recommended more contacts between Euratom and industry and suggested that the organization do research for industry on a contractual basis. Another significant recommendation was to extend Euratom research into the non-nuclear field, particularly into areas of environmental damage and data processing. The 6 governments were committed to adopting a new Euratom plan by July 1. The organization had been almost stagnant during the past few years.

Premiers and foreign ministers of the 3 Benelux countries (Belgium, the Netherlands and Luxembourg, all EEC members) agreed Apr. 29 to abolish virtually all internal frontier controls in the area by Nov. 1, 1970. Excise taxes and methods of collection were to be harmonized, and the countries were to begin closer administrative and judicial coordination. The Benelux officials agreed to further coordinate their short- and medium-term economic policies and their social, transportation and tourism policies. They also agreed to further harmonize their national legislation, industrial and energy policies. The decisions constituted a definitive step in the creation of a single customs area of the 3 nations. The Benelux countries were 18 months behind their original target for full economic union set in the 1960 Benelux Treaty.

After almost 6 years of negotiation, Morocco Mar. 31 signed an accord of association with EEC. The accord, signed in Rabat, stipulated that almost 75% of Morocco's current exports to EEC nations would get preferential treatment. (Morocco was unable to include products such as tomatoes, wine and some processed foods in the accord, nor was it able to obtain as much financial aid and technical assistance as it had wanted; but Moroccan negotiators considered the accord a success, largely because it guaranteed a market for such important items as citrus fruits.) In return for preferential treatment of Moroccan products, the accord required Morocco to grant EEC members tariff and quota concessions for certain of their manufactured items. Morocco became the 4th associate EEC member; the first 3: Greece, Turkey and Tunisia.

EEC and 3 East African countries, formerly British colonies, reached agreement July 9 on the renewal of the Arusha Convention. The convention, associating the 6 EEC members with Kenya, Uganda and Tanzania, provided for the removal of duties on most of the products imported from the 3 African states. In addition, the annual coffee quota was raised and new annual quotas for pineapples and cloves were set. The East African nations in turn extended preferential tariffs to Common Market members on about 50 products. The original Arusha Convention, signed July 26, 1968, never came into force because France, West Germany, Luxembourg and Italy had not completed ratification by the expiration date, May 31, 1969.

The 2d Yaounde Convention, outlining the association of the EEC with 18 African nations, most of them former French colonies, was signed July 29 in Yaounde, Cameroon. The new agreement was to go into effect in 1970 following ratification by the parliaments of the EEC nations but was scheduled to expire Jan. 31, 1975 regardless of the date of ratification. (The former convention of association had expired May 31, but delegates negotiating the pact in Brussels had agreed May 29 on measures to continue the association until a new agreement was concluded.) Negotiations for Yaounde II, which had begun in Dec. 1968, were concluded June 28 in Luxembourg. Under the accord, the EEC pledged $918 million to the European Development Fund (EDF) for aid to the 18 African states—$748 million in grants and $170 million in loans. The total, a 23.29% increase over aid given under the previous convention, was less than the $1.5 billion requested by the Africans. The aid was supplemented by authorization for $100 million in loans from the European Investment Bank, although the Africans had requested unlimited drawing facilities from the bank. The EEC refused an African request to continue production aid through price supports but set aside a $75 million "disaster fund" to aid countries that suffered from natural disasters or excessive decreases in world prices for their main export commodities. The community also lowered its common external tariff for some tropical products (coffee from 9.6% to 7%, cocoa from 5.4% to 4%, palm oil from 9% to 6%).

Yaounde II specifically encouraged the associated states to intensify their regional efforts, even if such efforts were to harm free trade between EEC and the African states. Interstate organizations in Africa were authorized to take the initiative in submitting applications for funds. The convention also granted African firms that bid for EEC-financed projects a 15% advantage and required any project costing over $5 million to involve at least 2 EEC nations. The breakdown of aid contributions to the EDF (Yaounde I contribution in parantheses): West Germany—$298.5 million ($246.5 million); France—$298.5 million ($246.5 million); Italy—$140.6 million ($100 million); Belgium—$80 million ($69 million); the Netherlands—$80 million ($66 million), and Luxembourg—$2.4 million ($2 million).

Commenting on Yaounde II July 29, Cameroon Pres. Ahmadou Ahidjo asserted "with bitterness" that African exports to the Common Market, "far from being increased and diversified in any notable manner in the course of the first Yaounde Convention, had diminished in relative value, while other exporters succeeded in regularly improving their position with the European markets." Momar Ngeye, Senegalese delegate to the negotiating conference in Luxembourg, had said June 27, when the aid total was announced: "It's pitiful. The Europeans give us less than half of what they pay each year in aid to their own farmers." The 18 African nations in the convention: Burundi, Cameroon, Central African Republic, Chad, Congo (Brazzaville), Congo (Kinshasa), Dahomey,

Gabon, Ivory Coast, Malagasy Republic, Mali, Mauritania, Niger, Rwanda, Senegal, Somalia, Togo and Upper Volta.

During a 5-day visit to the U.S. Aug. 5-9, West German Chancellor Kiesinger had private talks with Secy. Gen. U Thant at the UN Aug. 6 and 2 days of talks with Pres. Nixon in Washington Aug. 7-8. Kiesinger expressed support for further moves to promote West European unification and broaden the EEC. He said neutral and non-neutral nations should work for political union, and he expressed hope that the new French government under Pres. Georges Pompidou would develop a more flexible policy toward the Common Market.

French Pres. Pompidou and Kiesinger, meeting in Bonn Sept. 8-9 for the semi-annual Franco-German summit talks, were reported to have agreed that the enlargement of the EEC should be negotiated only after the completion of the organization's "transitional phase." French government spokesman Leo Hamon and West German spokesman Gunter Diehl reported Sept. 9 that Pompidou and Kiesinger had agreed that a settlement on the financing of agricultural subsidies should be the EEC's first order of priority, after which the question of membership applications could be considered. Specifically, Pompidou and Kiesinger agreed to support a Common Market summit conference in which the matter of British membership presumably would be discussed. The 2 leaders also agreed to establish bilateral working committees to deal with problems of agricultural and industrial cooperation. France expressed readiness to resume participation in the Western European Union (WEU) on the condition that the body would not be used as a political "court of appeals" from the EEC. France had boycotted the WEU for several months.

The EEC Council of Ministers voted Sept. 15 to hold the EEC summit meeting at The Hague Nov. 17-18. In announcing the decision, Netherlands Foreign Min. Joseph Luns expressed the council's opinion that if both a pending EEC commission report on British membership and the summit meeting gave "rise to optimism, the 6 countries are agreed to pursue this enlargement as soon as possible." French Foreign Min. Maurice Schumann, however, stressed the French position that the problem of agricultural subsidies had to be solved first. He added: "The organization of the community's agricultural policy is a matter for the 6 only, since they and they alone are financing it." Following the council meeting, West German Foreign Min. Brandt said he did not "expect negotiations on British membership to start before next spring."

In response to Belgian and Italian proposals, the EEC commission Oct. 1 asked the Council of Ministers to postpone for one year the deadline for introducing the common value added tax (VAT). The commission proposed that by Jan. 1, 1971 the 6 members should set a timetable for harmonizing the rates of the VAT system. The EEC members had agreed in 1967 to adopt a common VAT system by the end of 1969, leaving each country to decide its own tax rates and exemptions. The

Commission's proposal requested the initiation of both phases at the same time. (Of the 6 members, France had a VAT before the establishment of the EEC; West Germany had adopted the system Jan. 1, 1968, and the Netherlands Jan. 1, 1969. Luxembourg planned to meet the 1970 deadline.) Italy had informed the commission July 14 that it could not meet the Jan. 1, 1970 deadline and requested a 2-year extension. Belgium applied for a one-year extension Sept. 12.

EEC cooperation with non-members expanded in October and November. France lifted its veto against the negotiation of an accord with Israel, allowing the EEC Council of Ministers to decide Oct. 17 that negotiations would be opened for a new 5-year agreement to replace the 1964 accord, which had expired in 1967. (The tariff concessions granted on the old accord had been maintained on an annual basis since 1967.) Common Market and Israeli officials began preliminary negotiations on the new accord Nov. 12-14. The Council also decided Oct. 17 to open exploratory talks toward a trade agreement with Egypt and Lebanon. Negotiations with Spain for a preferential trade accord began Oct. 27-30; a joint communique, published Oct. 30, stated that the talks had led to a convergence of views on "the majority of the essential points envisaged in the accord." The Council decided Nov. 10 to negotiate a trade accord with Japan and to reopen talks on a trade pact with Yugoslavia. The Austrian government announced Nov. 4 that it would request the reopening of talks with the EEC for a "special arrangement." Austria had opened talks for association with the EEC in 1961 but had faced opposition from the Soviet Union on the ground that such an arrangement would be incompatible with its neutrality status. The new negotiations would be aimed at obtaining a "preference agreement" that would not violate the nation's neutrality. Italy agreed Dec. 8 to drop its objection to talks with Austria.

Employes of the Common Market's administrative, judicial and scientific organizations staged a one-day strike Oct. 28 in protest against what they saw as a gradual weakening of the organization. About 1,000 Euratom civil servants and scientists picketed the Council of Ministers in Luxembourg in protest against the Council's failure to establish a viable research program for Euratom and against the impending prospect of hundreds of dismissals. About 4,000 workers were on strike at Brussels headquarters. The Brussels employes were upset by several members' proposals to rotate national civil servants in Common Market positions. (EEC finance ministers approved an average 3.3% pay increase Oct. 29, retroactive to Jan. 1, for the organization's 8,000 civil servants.

The Council of Ministers approved EEC's 1970 budget Oct. 29. The new budget, which totaled $211 million excluding the expenses of EAGGF (European Agricultural Guidance & Guarantee Fund), included $9.5 million for the European Parliament, $10.8 million for the Council of Ministers, $125 million for the Executive Commission and

$64 million for the social fund. The commission proposed that the powers of the European Parliament be strengthened and that it be given the power to overrule the Council on budgetary matters. The commission recommended a gradual extension of the parliament's powers from 1971 to 1973, during which time the Council could still overrule the commission and the Parliament concerning the budget, and a final stage beginning in 1974 when the European Parliament would be authorized to overrule the Council.

EEC foreign ministers agreed Dec. 8 that members planning trade agreements with Eastern European nations after Jan. 1, 1970 must seek approval of a majority of the Council of Ministers. This stipulation was to be binding for 3 years.

Britain, the EEC & EFTA

Britain & the EEC

Possible British membership in the EEC remained an open topic throughout 1969. The probability of Britain being accepted rose rapidly as discussions opened in December at The Hague with Georges Pompidou instead of Charles de Gaulle leading France.

Informal negotiations opened with the meeting of British Prime Min. Harold Wilson and then-West German Chancellor Kurt-Georg Kiesinger in Bonn Feb. 12-13. Their communique, dealing with British-EEC relations, said: "The security and prosperity of Europe demand unity, and only in unity can Europe exert her rightful and beneficial influence in the world. For both our countries a united Europe is inconceivable without Britain.... Both governments undertake to work for the realization of this aim. Together with other European governments, they will work out possibilities which may give a new impetus to the political unity of Europe. Both governments reaffirm that their security depends on the continuation and strengthening of the Atlantic Alliance. They are convinced that this Alliance is the only sure foundation for the *detente* and the European peace order to which both governments aspire." At a Bonn press conference, Wilson had said: "The continuing frustration over British entry can and must inevitably be damaging to the cohesion, development and dynamism of the Common Market itself. The Common Market must be a dynamic organization; it has got to advance or it will decline."

The Action Committee for a United States of Europe, made up of political and labor organizations from Britain and the 6 EEC nations, met in London Mar. 11 and adopted a declaration asserting the necessity "without delay to find solutions to the problems of British entry into the Common Market." The committee, also known as the Monnet Committee (it had been founded in 1955 by French economist Jean Monnet), set as its immediate goal the establishment of a dialogue between the 6 and Britain and the demonstration that the obstacles to Britain's entry could be solved. The committee said it would work out solutions to 4 main obstacles—monetary, institutional, agricultural and technological problems—to Britain's admission and would present proposals to the governments concerned. Guido Carli, governor of the Bank of Italy, was to work on solutions to the monetary problems; Walter Hallstein, ex-president of the EEC Executive Commission, on institutional problems; Edgard Pisani, ex-French agricultural minister, on agricultural issues, and Lord Plowden, former head of the UK Atomic Energy Authority, the problems of technological development. (The Action Committee called on the EEC July 16 to complete its economic integration and urged the 6 members and Britain to "indicate their willingness to commit themselves as soon as possible to the achievement of political unity." The committee recommended that the EEC should reach agreement on "essentials," admit Britain and then deal with other issues, since Britain's problems "would then be common problems and no longer separate problems external to the 6.")

British deputy Labor Party leader George Brown Mar. 6 urged the convening of "another Messina conference" to begin negotiations for a European political community. The new organization, which would operate alongside the EEC, would encompass foreign policy and defense, monetary policy, arms production and possibly technology. Its membership would include the EEC members, Britain and other European nations. The proposed community would be governed by a council of ministers (which, "in the first stages," would take orders from national governments), a parliament with real political power and a democratically controlled executive commission, Brown said. He emphasized that there would be no national veto. Brown explained that the plan would alleviate the current divisions that had made Europe "virtually impotent in the face of great dangers that threatened us all." By creating a strong and united Europe, he said, the proposed community could "build a constructive policy of detente with Russia and eastern Europe and make real progress towards dealing with the German problem."

The resignation of French Pres. Charles de Gaulle renewed British hopes of opening negotiations for EEC membership. Speaking in London May 5 at the 20th anniversary of the 18-member Council of Europe, British Prime Min. Harold Wilson said: "Our determination to join the communities did not weaken in the face of the delay in opening negotiations on our applications. . ., and it certainly will not weaken now." Wilson's position was supported by West German Foreign Min. Willy Brandt, who said at a press conference following the Council's anniversary celebration: "I not only hope, but I think there is a good chance that before the end of the year we will have entered into a period of serious negotiations." Brandt clarified this position May 6 by noting that "we must first of all know who is to be the next president of France." The 6 EEC foreign ministers agreed in Luxembourg May 12 that the issue of British entry should be postponed until after the elections in France and West Germany. Continuing de Gaulle's policies, French Foreign Min. Michel Debre criticized Common Market members for failing to consider the consequences of expanding the organization. He urged that the 6 first settle vital problems among themselves before taking up the issue of other members. Brandt indicated that the 6 were split along these lines: Italy, Belgium, Luxembourg and the Netherlands favored consideration of British membership as the first order of business; France favored completion of the EEC's internal arrangements first, and West Germany wanted to undertake simultaneous negotiations in both areas. "I think it is agreed we cannot do anything before the end of the year," he said.

The changing French position was hinted at by Georges Pompidou in his first formal policy statement of the French election campaign. Pompidou told the Central Committee of the Gaullist party May 9 that if he were elected, he would change de Gaulle's policies on foreign and domestic affairs. Pompidou said he would "favor the enlargement of Europe when the circumstances are fulfilled as far as our potential partners are concerned, in order to lead this Europe to a political consciousness permitting it to assume the position it deserves." This pledge was renewed by Pompidou July 10 when, at his first press conference after becoming president; he said that France had "no objection in principle" to British membership in the EEC. He insisted, however, that the 6 members must "agree among themselves on the conditions of that membership and the consequences that this membership could have on the future and the very nature of the community." In particular, Pompidou said that the integration of the 6 nations' agricultural systems had to be complete before negotiations could be started with Britain. (British Prime Min. Wilson said in the House of Commons July 8 that he did not believe Britain should immediately take the initiative for entry into the Common Market.)

French Premier Jacques Chaban-Delmas had said June 26 that de Gaulle's policy of "independence" would be continued, but, he insisted, "in a spirit of rapprochement [and] fidelity to the Atlantic alliance and our friendship with the U.S." He pledged that France would "go as fast and as far as our partners" in building a united Europe. In apparent contradiction of de Gaulle's stand that British entry into the EEC would change the nature of the alliance, Chaban-Delmas said that Britain's admission "must strengthen what has already been achieved, not weaken it."

The EEC Council of Ministers agreed July 22 to a French proposal that the 6 heads of state meet before the end of 1969 to discuss British membership. Submitting the proposal, French Foreign Min. Maurice Schumann said: "It is by no means inevitable that the entry of Great Britain and other new members should lead to the weakening of the community." But Schumann indicated that France still stressed the importance of completing Common Market economic integration before Jan. 1, 1970 as well as strengthening the agreements already in existence. The Council, however, decided that the Executive Commission and the permanent representatives should immediately begin plans for British entry negotiations. (West German Foreign Min. Brandt had proposed June 5 that the 6 EEC members and Britain hold a summit meeting before 1970. Brandt, speaking at a quarterly meeting of foreign ministers of the Western European Union, suggested that the summit conferees discuss enlarging the Common Market. France, whose government had been boycotting WEU meetings, did not attend the meeting, which was held in The Hague June 5-6.)

In a TV interview Aug. 22, West German Chancellor Kurt-Georg Kiesinger expressed hope that a European summit conference dealing with British entry in EEC would be held soon. He stressed that the Common Market must "act now, or else Europe will lose its last chance." He added: "We should continue to develop the Common Market, to orient it towards monetary unity. That which we are missing is a common European policy."

Kiesinger Aug. 25 asserted that it was "absolutely necessary" to advance toward a political unification of Europe without waiting for the effects of economic unification. Quoted in the West German newspaper *Die Welt*, Kiesinger declared: "I think that a Franco-German consensus is necessary in order to give new impetus to European policy. As far as Great Britain is concerned, I have always placed great hope in the policies and energy of that country."

French Agriculture Min. Jacques Duhamel said Aug. 21 that the "delay accorded to France for realignment of its agricultural prices to the European level should be put to profit for in-depth examinations of measures which can be taken, first to control production, next to better orient production to need." Duhamel also expressed his opinion that if West Germany revalued the mark, the Common Market would not be able to evade the necessity of revising the unit-of-account system on which agricultural exchanges were based.

French Foreign Min. Maurice Schumann, speaking at the UN General Assembly Sept. 24, asserted that "it is not only conceivable but eminently desirable" that applications for full and associate membership in the EEC succeed. He also said: "This community, which is free to determine its future, may enter into ever closer contact with the countries of Eastern Europe."

The EEC Executive Commission urged the Council of Ministers Oct. 2 to simultaneously consider problems of strengthening and enlarging the community. In a revised version of its 1967 report on British membership, the commission stressed that the entrance of Britain and the other countries that had applied for membership—Ireland, Denmark and Norway—must not hold back the process of a continually strengthening community. "Only a strong community will constitute an appropriate structure for receiving the applicant countries," the report stated. "These applications can only see their request for entry in this context." Recommending that negotiations "should be opened as soon as possible," the report maintained that the applicants "will have not only to express their agreement on the principle of accepting the achievements of the community... but equally... on the principle of its strengthening. Finally, it will be necessary for them to put into operation policies which are convergent with those being carried out in the community with a view to strengthening it."

The Hague Conference

EEC leaders committed themselves Dec. 2 to opening negotiations during 1970 on British membership. In a communique issued following a 2-day summit meeting of EEC heads of state and foreign ministers in The Hague, Netherlands, the 6 "reaffirmed their agreement on the principle of the enlargement of the community" and agreed that the necessary preparatory work should be "undertaken as soon as practically and conveniently possible." The communique, promising that the talks "would take place in a most positive spirit," echoed a point French Pres. Pompidou had stressed in an address earlier that day. The agreement to begin preparatory talks followed more than 18 hours of intensive debate, which had included a private meeting between Pompidou and West German Chancellor Brandt. Although the final communique declined to specify a date for the opening of formal negotiations with Britain, French Foreign Min. Schumann and other EEC spokesmen said at a press conference that preliminary talks should take no longer than 6 months; serious negotiations on new memberships could therefore begin by July 1970.

The agreement also involved compromise by France's EEC partners, who agreed to the French demand that the community "pass from the transitional period to the final stage of the European Community and accordingly lay down a definitive financial arrangement for the common agricultural policy by the end of 1969." The communique added, however, that "acceptance of a financial arrangement for the final stage does not exclude its amendment by unanimous vote." Among other major points outlined in the communique: The 6 EEC members agreed that "a plan in stages should be worked out during 1970 with a view to the creation of an economic and monetary union." They stressed that "development of monetary cooperation should depend on the harmonization of economic policies." In addition, the governments "agreed to arrange for the investigation of the possibility of setting up a European reserve fund in which a joint economic and monetary policy would have to result." The summit leaders also pledged themselves to achieve further "progress in the matter of political unification."

British Foreign Secy. Michael Stewart Dec. 3 called the result of the EEC talks "encouraging." "It indicates that the whole tide for unity in Europe is flowing strongly and that there is a feeling that to get that result you have got to have Britain there as well as the others," he said. "That is what Britain wants, and that, it is now clear, is what Europe wants too." West German Chancellor Brandt hailed the agreement Dec. 3 in a speech to the Bundestag. "Our thanks are due first of all to the French president, Georges Pompidou," he said. "Without him and his courageous stance we would have been wrecked. The course and result of the conference were a grand proof of German-French friendship. The French president and the German chancellor were agreed that our Europe must prepare itself to take on the challenge of the 1970s."

More than 1,000 young demonstrators had protested Dec. 1 against the slowness of governments in achieving European unity. The youths marched through The Hague shouting "United Europe now," and staged a sit-down demonstration outside the hall where the summit meeting was to take place. At least 37 organizations, grouped under the title of Young Federalists, had planned the protests. Most of the demonstrators, representing Federalist European Clubs, favored direct election of the European Parliament, British entry into the EEC and strengthened economic cooperation among Common Market members.

Meeting in Brussels Dec. 8 for their first session after The Hague summit conference, EEC foreign ministers set up a working committee of permanent representatives to draw up a common negotiating position with EEC applicants and present them to the ministers in Feb. 1970. 6 points to be studied were: (1) financing of farm policy within an enlarged EEC; (2) Britain's Commonwealth trade associations; (3) effects of increased membership on the European Coal & Steel Community and Euratom; (4) duration of a transitional period preceding full EEC membership; (5) effects of an enlarged community on existing EEC institutes; (6) negotiation procedures with potential EEC members Britain, Ireland, Norway and Denmark. The ministers also instructed the working group to consider Britain's balance-of-payments position.

Britain, France & the WEU

Accusing Britain of attempting to use the Western European Union as a back-door entrance to the EEC, France had announced Feb. 17 that it was ceasing all participation in WEU activities for an indefinite period. (WEU members: Britain, France, Italy, West Germany, Belgium, the Netherlands and Luxembourg.) The French action came on the eve of a regular fortnightly meeting at the organization's headquarters in London Feb. 18 and 3 days before a scheduled Paris session of the WEU Assembly (a biannual meeting of the 7 members' parliamentary representatives). The Feb. 18 meeting was held as scheduled, although France did not attend.

The French decision to abstain from WEU activities was regarded as significant, not because it would paralyze the WEU, which was only a consultative organ, but because it would increase tensions within the more important EEC. The WEU, established in 1955 to foster coordination and cooperation in defense, political, social, legal and cultural affairs, had gained in stature in recent years because it was the only European forum linking Britain to the 6 Common Market nations. Britain had been trying to turn the WEU into a meaningful organ for discussion of common European policies. The immediate crisis stemmed from the WEU's regular quarterly ministerial meeting, held in Luxembourg Feb. 6-7. At that time Britain had called for a meeting Feb. 14 in London to discuss the Middle East crisis. The proposal was accepted by all members except France, whose delegate, State Secy. for Foreign Affairs Jean de Lipkowski, emphatically rejected it. France contended that under the Brussels Treaty, which established WEU, all decisions had to be unanimous; it warned WEU Secy. Maurice Iweins d'Eeckhoutte to refuse to convene the London meeting. Britain, however, asserted that the unanimity rule did not apply to procedural matters such as the calling of a meeting. The meeting, attended by all WEU members but France, was held as a regular session despite French threats to "draw the consequences and . . . leave the WEU." In a statement issued Feb. 14, the French government explained: "France holds that the British, who are always inclined to align themselves with the position of the United States, are not yet ready to adhere to a [European] community whose vocation is independence."

Concluding a 2-day meeting in Bonn, Prime Min. Wilson and Chancellor Kiesinger Feb. 13 issued a joint declaration emphasizing British-West German solidarity for the goal of European unity and security. The statement said: "The security and prosperity of Europe demand unity; and only in unity can Europe exert her rightful and beneficial influence in the world. For both our countries a united Europe is inconceivable without Britain." Stressing the importance of British membership in EEC, the declaration pledged Britain and West Germany to "work out together with other European governments the means by which a new impetus can be given to the political unity of Europe." The statement continued: "The 2 governments reaffirm that their security depends on the continuation and strengthening of the Atlantic Alliance . . . the only sure foundation for the detente to which they aspire and the establishment of a peaceful system in Europe."

The French stand was stated officially in a Feb. 14 communique from the Quai d'Orsay. It said:

"The British have just endangered the very future of WEU and henceforth it will be very difficult to re-animate this organization. For, after all, France cannot agree to continue her participation in conditions becoming more and more disagreeable to her when the statutory rules are being deliberately broken.

"WEU is in fact based on the principle of unanimity. Paragraph 4 of Article VIII of the agreement forming its charter is, moreover, quite specific in this respect. Since France refused to agree to the holding of a meeting of the WEU Permanent Council in London on the Middle East question—a meeting she considered useless—no meeting without her participation can be considered to be a WEU meeting.... This implies that the consultations initiated by the British should not have taken place at the WEU Secretariat, and that the secretary general of this organization should have refrained from taking part in it. The latter had been advised of the French position and invited not to lend his presence to the meeting. He hesitated for a long time but was not in the end successful in withstanding the pressure exerted on him. By this action Paris considers that he has exceeded his powers and that he should suffer the consequences of the violation of the WEU statute permitted by him."

This "represents one more step in the escalation, in which the British and their supporters are indulging, to move round the French refusal to discuss between the 7 the British membership of the Common Market and of Europe generally. According to the terms of the Treaty of Rome, this membership must first be examined by the 6. In any case, France considers that the British, who always tend to align themselves on American positions, are not yet ready to become members of a European community whose way must be that of independence.

"Ever since France opposed British membership in 1962, efforts to change her opposition have not ceased. In 1963, however, an agreement was made between the 6 and Britain to make use of WEU and within its framework to hold at ministerial level quarterly discussions on the economic and political situation in Europe. These consultations took place more or less correctly until 1968. As from that date, however, the majority of France's partners, irritated by the maintenance of her opposition to Britain's membership and encouraged by the latter, have lent themselves to various maneuvers aimed at forcing the hand of the French government....

"What the UK government in fact wished was to call afterwards a WEU meeting on this same question at the level of the permanent representatives. It is therefore very clear now that this was a deliberate maneuver on the part of London to oblige France to accept compulsory political discussions between the 7 which would be the first step towards British entry into a European community. France considers that such a maneuver is bound to fail.. In any case, she could not accept this degradation of WEU from which she would withdraw if in the future the principle of unamimity ... were not respected. What happened on Feb. 14 will not happen twice, or else a crisis will occur which could not be attributed to France."

French State Secy. for Information Joel le Theule said Feb. 19: "In so far as our partners are not determined to apply the rules we will not attend. If they wish this organization to resume its normal functioning, they can inform us of their intention to return to the rules."

The WEU Assembly met as scheduled Feb. 20-21 in Paris, with French delegates participating in spite of the French boycott. French delegates to the Assembly had announced Feb. 18 that they would participate "to enlighten the debates without dramatizing anything and [to] dissipate the misunderstandings." (The regularly scheduled WEU council meeting had been held Feb. 18 in London without the participation of France.) Despite their participation, the French delegates were not able to prevent the adoption Feb. 21 of a resolution endorsing Britain's drive for closer political consultations within the WEU. Only 6

Gaullist delegates voted against the resolution, while 4 French opposition delegates joined delegates from Britain, West Germany, Italy, the Netherlands, Belgium and Luxembourg in overwhelmingly approving it.

The WEU Permanent Council met at its London headquarters Feb. 26 with all members except France in attendance. West Germany earlier had recommended that the council meet Mar. 5, the regular date for the bimonthly meeting; Germany apparently hoped that the French could be persuaded to attend the later session. France stated Feb. 24 that it would attend neither the Feb. 26, the Mar. 5 meeting, nor any other meeting until the council agreed to its condition that meetings be called unanimously. The London *Times* reported Feb. 27 that the WEU Council had established a committee to advise on matters of procedure during the absence of France. Normally decisions were taken unanimously, but members reportedly appeared to agree that decisions could be taken legally without France as long as France continued to boycott the council.

Italian Foreign Min. Pietro Nenni, opposing the French position, told the Italian Senate Feb. 26: "What sense is there in talking as Paris is doing about a European Europe if one applies vetoes in the EEC and in the WEU? A European Europe has need of all democratic countries like Great Britain, France and the Northern countries, as it will also have need one day of the Central and Eastern countries. Nothing can go ahead if European unity is not brought about by the creation of a truly supranational community. Because of this we refuse the right of veto. We cannot accept that the refusal of one government halts a move first towards concord and then towards unity."

British Foreign Secy. Michael Stewart Mar. 12 announced the appointment of Lord Chalfont, minister of state in the Foreign & Commonwealth Office, as Britain's permanent representative to the WEU Council to succeed retiring Viscount Hood. London officials pointed out that Chalfont had greater authority to make decisions than the senior civil servants who had held the post previously. It was emphasized that he would lead intensified efforts within WEU to strengthen Britain's ties to EEC members.

The French position apparently did not soften as Pompidou replaced de Gaulle. In his July 10 press conference, Pompidou said that France did not oppose WEU meetings provided "they become again what they were, what they should be with respect to the [Brussels] treaty. This is not the case nor has it been the case lately."

In the face of French resistance, advocates of admitting Britain to the Common Market continued their efforts on Britain's behalf. The Committee of Presidents of the WEU Assembly unanimously called on EEC governments Nov. 6 to open "in the immediate future negotiations concerning the entrance of Great Britain in the EEC."

The 'Soames Affair'

The European rift developed into a diplomatic crisis Feb. 21 with the publication in London of far-reaching proposals for a future European organization, allegedly outlined by French Pres. de Gaulle at a meeting Feb. 4 with British Amb.-to-France Christopher Soames. French government sources disputed British accounts of the meeting, and a diplomatic controversy ensued.

According to the British report, published by the London *Times* Feb. 22, de Gaulle told Soames that British membership in the European communities would inevitably change the nature of the organization. De Gaulle reportedly suggested that the current Common Market be supplanted by a larger form of free-trade association governed by a 4-power inner council composed of France, Britain, West Germany and Italy. He said that such an organization should be based on a totally independent Europe; Europe as it presently stood, he argued, was too closely tied to America. De Gaulle explained that once an independent Europe was achieved, there would no longer be a need for NATO, which he termed an American-dominated organization. The reports asserted that de Gaulle told Soames, in the London *Times'* words, "that he would be quite prepared to discuss with Britain what should take the place of the Common Market, and would like, as a first stage, political discussions between Britain and France."

French official sources immediately denied the accuracy of the London reports. A statement issued in Paris Feb. 21 through Agence France-Presse (AFP) declared that the reports were sensationalized and that at his meeting with Soames, de Gaulle had expressed no views different from those "which had been publicly and constantly defined by himself in the course of the past few years." A 2d statement issued through AFP less than an hour later termed the concept of a 4-power directorate "so strongly contrary to all that the French government has always expressed on the necessary independence of each nation that it doesn't even merit a denial." (A *Washington Post* report published Feb. 25 said that British officials had admitted erring in using the word "directorate" in describing the inner council suggested by de Gaulle.) AFP said: "French official sources deny...that the president of the Republic has in the course of a recent talk with the U.K. ambassador expressed orientations different from those he has publicly and constantly defined in recent years. They indicate that today, as yesterday, France, which remains attached to the good functioning of the European Economic Community, notes that any enlargement of this by new admissions, and especially that of Britain, would lead to a complete change of the community and, in practice, to its disappearance. It would then be possible to replace the community by a different system. It is recalled that Europe can only take shape on the political plane if the nations composing it agree on a European policy of independence."

British officials Feb. 21 affirmed the accuracy of their report of the meeting, a record of which, they said, had been approved by the British embassy in Paris and by de Gaulle's office as well. They said the decision to make public the details of the meeting was made after inaccurate accounts had appeared in 2 French newspapers early Feb. 21.

At a meeting with French Foreign Min. Michel Debre Feb. 12, Soames was reported to have termed de Gaulle's Feb. 4 views "significant." He was said to have emphasized that Britain thought it necessary to inform its WEU allies of the talks "because their vital interests and security were involved." Soames also reportedly made it clear that Britain rejected de Gaulle's position on NATO and "maintained its position on seeking entry to the EEC." On these assumptions, however, Britain was prepared to begin discussions with France, assuming that the UK's "partners in the alliances were kept informed." The British reports Feb. 21 added that Britain, in the London *Times'* words, disagreed "fundamentally with Gen. de Gaulle's thinking . . . on the European relationship with the United States and on the need for a 4-power directorate in Europe."

Controversy over the "Soames affair" deepened Feb. 22. The French repeated their accusations that Britain had dramatized and distorted de Gaulle's proposals, and the British strongly denied the charges. At the same time, officials at the French Foreign Ministry denied that they had ever endorsed Soames' record of the meeting, as the British had asserted. The French, however, did not publish their own account of the Soames-de Gaulle meeting. They held that de Gaulle had expressed a broad philosophical viewpoint about the consequences of enlarging the Common Market. Foreign Min. Debre, in a TV-radio interview Feb. 22, accused Britain of leaking to other West European governments the contents of what France had viewed as a confidential meeting. UK Foreign Secy. Michael Stewart admitted the same day that Britain had informed its allies in the WEU of the general's proposals. "If Gen. de Gaulle believes that there is another better way to European unity," he said, "he must convince not only us but these 5 other nations that there is indeed a better way. . . . We must therefore tell these countries—who are our friends and allies—about what was proposed by the French. This we did; if we had failed to do so we should have been less than straightforward." (The French boycott of the WEU apparently was begun after the British had revealed the details of the meetings to the other 5 members.)

Speaking in Parliament Feb. 24, Stewart emphasized that the British were still "ready at any time to talk to the French government, provided they understand where we stand on the essentials of security and European unity." He admitted that Prime Min. Wilson Feb. 12 had told West German Chancellor Kiesinger of the Soames-de Gaulle meeting before France had been informed of Britain's intentions to do so, but he added that "it would have been entirely improper to have allowed these conversations [during Wilson's trip to Germany]...to conclude without Dr. Kiesinger being made aware of what had happened." He added: "It was, of course, understood between the French government and ourselves that these conversations were confidential from the public at large, but we never entered into, nor would we have thought it right to enter into, any undertaking to conceal [them] from our allies and partners in Europe."

(According to the British embassy in Paris, Britain Feb. 24 sent a note to France offering to begin talks on de Gaulle's proposals on the condition that the other Common Market nations would be kept informed of their progress.)

In an apparent effort to lower tension over the controversy within the EEC, France Feb. 24 assured its 5 Common Market partners that its new differences with Britain had not lessened France's willingness to work within the existing framework of the EEC. Meeting with ambassadors of the 5 nations in Paris, Debre was reported to have said that since British entry into the organization would inevitably change its basic orientation, France had suggested a larger, loosely organized grouping to replace it.

The confusion over the French decision to boycott WEU activities was heightened by 2 developments: West Germany's attempt to take an independent position on the question and the WEU Assembly's adoption of a resolution endorsing Britain's efforts to encourage consultation within the WEU. Bonn lent support to the French stand Feb. 18 in an official statement that said unscheduled WEU Council meetings could be called without the agreement of all members only "under exceptional circumstances." "Apart from this exception," the statement said, "the council can be convened outside the normal term of meetings only by unanimous vote." The West German government thus took issue with the British contention that the Feb. 14 council meeting, which had been the public cause of the WEU crisis, was a routine session. In clarifying the Bonn position Feb. 19, however, Conrad Ahlers, deputy chief government spokesman, asserted that while West Germany supported the unanimity requirement in principle, it had been established in practice that routine meetings could be called without unanimous consent; unanimity was necessary only for quarterly ministerial sessions, "not for the routine [bimonthly] meetings of permanent representatives." But, he added, a regular council meeting could be considered "routine" only when the council's agenda was "normal," and in cases where the agenda was other than "normal," preliminary consultations were necessary.

British newspapers Feb. 24, cited Bonn as the source of the first public "leak" of accounts of Soames' meeting with de Gaulle Feb. 4. The *Washington Post* reported Feb. 25 that, contrary to the French accusation that Britain had leaked the information, the story had actually appeared in Bonn sometime Feb. 20. An evening newspaper in Paris was also reported by the *Post* to have carried an account of the meeting

Feb. 20; and French informants said that leaks of the meeting were reported to have come from the French Foreign Ministry a full day before the British account.

Soames Mar. 1 delivered a note in Paris replying to a Feb. 24 French Foreign Ministry protest over Soames' account of his talk with de Gaulle. According to the London *Times* Mar. 3, the British note neither accepted nor rejected the assertions made in the French protest, but reaffirmed the British government stand outlined earlier. That position stressed the point that French Foreign Min. Debre had seen Soames' account of the meeting and had told the British ambassador Feb. 8 that it was correct. The French Foreign Ministry, for its part, had issued a detailed chronology of the incident Feb. 24. The French statement, while it confirmed the British version of the dates concerned, asserted that Debre had "denied" Soames' version of the de Gaulle discussion. (Soames and Debre had met alone Feb. 8, and there was no official record of their conversation.) The French position was repeated Feb. 26 when the minister of information said: "In no form whatever was approval given by any French authority to the version drawn up by the staff of Mr. Soames of his conversation with Gen. de Gaulle."

French officials were reported Feb. 26 to have said that the controversy had hurt chances for Anglo-French discussions in the near future. Debre voiced this opinion Feb. 27 when he commented: "Instead of looking at the detail, at what was accessory, ... it would have been better to have looked at the essential, at what was 9/10 of the whole affair—the offer to open direct conversations." "The general opened the portals wide," he said. "An opportunity has been missed."

Soames, speaking before the French Diplomatic Press Association Mar. 12, said: "I deeply regret that our relations should be in their present state.... One can only recall that interests never lie, and that it is certainly true in present circumstances that it is in the interests of France, of Britain and of Europe that the relations between our 2 countries should improve. Time and patience are equally necessary. What is important is that the process should not be disturbed accidentally or by incomprehension."

The British House of Commons Feb. 25 had concluded an emergency debate with a 270-33 vote against a motion criticizing the Labor government's handling of the Soames affair. In the course of the debate, ex-Conservative Prime Min. Sir Alec Douglas-Home reproved the government for underestimating "the resources of diplomacy" by revealing the content of the meeting too soon. He suggested that Britain should have informed France first that it felt compelled to tell its allies of de Gaulle's new proposals for Europe and should have asked de Gaulle to explain them to the other 5 EEC members. Or, he continued, Britain could have informed its 5 partners that France had interesting ideas on the future of Europe without disclosing the details. Foreign Secy. Stewart rejected Douglas-Home's arguments, although he admitted that disclosures of diplomatic exchanges were not the usual practice. He asserted that if Britain had not told its allies of the proposals, it would have appeared to be seeking entry into the Common Market and to be secretly discussing the liquidation of the organization at the same time. He said that any alternative action was inferior to what the government had done. (Stewart also declared Feb. 25 that information on the meeting had been given to other nations Feb. 12. West Germany had been informed at 4:30 p.m., the U.S. at 11:30 p.m. [British time] and other allies during the evening and up until 2 a.m. Feb. 13. France had been informed of Britain's intentions at 8 p.m. Feb. 12, he said.)

EFTA Developments

The European Free Trade Association (EFTA) reported Jan. 14 that trade between the association's 8 members in 1965 had amounted to $830 million more than it would have if EFTA had not been formed. The study, entitled "The Effects of EFTA on the Economies of Member States," said that the combined balance-of-trade deficits for the EFTA countries in 1965 would have been $457 million greater if EFTA had not existed; in terms of imports, however, only $373 million of the $830 million overall increase could be attributed to expansion of trade within the organization. The study was limited to the years 1960-5 because of statistical complications involved in including subsequent years. (By 1965 the EFTA had cut tariffs on industrial goods by 70%; it had eliminated them in 1966) The study was part of a larger EFTA program to examine the effects of the split of Western Europe into 2 trade blocs—the EFTA and EEC.

The *EFTA Reporter* said Mar. 21 that EFTA members' exports to the world had increased by 8% to $33,175,500,000 in 1968, while imports had risen 6% to $39,623,600,000. The EFTA trade deficit had fallen $300 million to $6,448,100,000. Trade among the 8 EFTA members rose in 1968 to a level 145% higher than in 1959, the year before the EFTA was formed. Over the same period, total imports and exports rose 88% and 83%, respectively. Intra-EFTA exports increased in 1968 by 5.9% to $8,638,500,000, while intra-Scandinavian trade arose 5.7% to $2.591 billion (30% of intra-EFTA exports). (1968 was the first year in which intra-Scandinavian trade did not grow faster than intra-EFTA trade.) EFTA exports to the U.S. increased by 20% to $3,613,200,000 in 1968, while imports from the U.S. increased by 12% to $4,129,100,000. The area's imports from the EEC countries increased by 6% to $12,120,700,000 in 1968, and exports to EEC nations increased by 10% to $8,286,700,000. Trade with Eastern Europe grew slowly, with exports increasing by 6% to $1,658,700,000 and imports by 5% to $1,826,500,000.

The value of total imports and exports of each EFTA country in 1968 (in millions of U.S. dollars) and the percentage of change from 1967:

	Imports	Exports
Austria	$ 2,497.0 + 8.1%	$ 1,988.5 + 10.0%
Britain	18,958.5 + 7.0%	15,346.3 + 6.8%
Denmark	3,212.4 + 2.5%	2,581.7 + 4.3%
Finland	1,592.5 − 5.8%	1,635.7 + 7.1%
Norway	2,705.5 − 1.3%	1,937.6 + 11.6%
Portugal	1,039.2 + 2.5%	732.1 + 6.9%
Sweden	5,121.6 + 8.9%	4,937.2 + 9.0%
Switzerland	4,496.9 + 9.4%	4,016.4 + 14.6%

The EFTA Ministerial Council, closing a 2-day meeting in Geneva Nov. 7, reaffirmed its "readiness and desire to take part in early negotiations with a view to arriving at comprehensive solutions of the questions of European integration in which all members of the EFTA would have the possibility of participating." The organization also stressed its "strong interest in safeguarding as an important part of an enlarged European community the free market already established in EFTA." The Ministerial Council had formally approved the membership of Iceland Nov. 6.

Nordic Economic Cooperation

The governments of Denmark, Finland, Norway and Sweden, all EFTA members, released plans Jan. 15 for the economic integration of the 4 countries into a Nordic Economic Union (Nordek). The plans stressed that the union was meant as a step toward overall European integration, rather than toward a 3d trade bloc. In March the Nordic Council indorsed a unanimous recommendation of its economic committee that members continue work on the creation of the Nordic Economic Union. The Nordic Council, a consultative body of ministers and parliamentary members from Denmark, Finland, Iceland, Norway and Sweden, had been a major influence in the movement towards closer Nordic integration and the premiers of the 4 countries had been meeting at regular intervals to discuss the proposed Nordek.

Denmark, Sweden, Norway and Finland agreed July 17 on a draft Nordek treaty. The draft treaty, concluded at a week-long meeting of 50 experts in Copenhagen, called for the establishment of a customs union by 1972. It envisaged broad economic cooperation between the 4 Nordic countries, liberalization of the movements of capital and coordination of policy in the areas of trade, shipping, industry, labor, social welfare, education and aid to developing nations. The agreement specified that Nordek would be essentially an economic union and would not influence foreign or defense policies of the members.

Concorde Flies!

The controversial Anglo-French supersonic Concorde airliner made its first test flight Mar. 2 in Toulouse, France, one year behind schedule and 2 months after the maiden flight of the Soviet Union's supersonic TU-144. Climbing to 10,000 feet for a 28-minute flight at speeds below 250 m.p.h., the Concorde was piloted by France's Andre Turcat. The droop-nosed plane, designed to carry up to 140 passengers at a cruising speed of over 1,450 m.p.h. (twice the speed of sound), had been built jointly by the British Aircraft Corp. and France's Sud Aviation. According to their estimates, the plane could be in regular service by late 1973, 3 to 6 years ahead of supersonic airliner currently planned by the U.S. The Concorde so far had cost more than $725 million, well above the $420 million originally budgeted in 1962. Official estimates indicated that total costs would probably be close to $1.37 billion.